HISTORY
OF THE
AMERICAN ECONOMY
SIXTH EDITION

HISTORY
OF THE
AMERICAN ECONOMY
SIXTH EDITION

GARY M. WALTON
University of California, Davis

HUGH ROCKOFF
Rutgers, The State University of New Jersey

HARCOURT BRACE JOVANOVICH, PUBLISHERS
San Diego   New York   Chicago   Austin   Washington, D.C.
London   Sydney   Tokyo   Toronto

Dedication
To the memory of Ross M. Robertson

PHOTO CREDITS

PREFACE

The appearance of the Sixth Edition of *History of the American Economy* attests to the continued brisk advance of research in the field of economic history. Indeed, new evidence and revised interpretations of our economic past have been the most compelling reasons for offering this new edition. Each chapter has been substantially revised and many are entirely new. Besides adding some pedagogical features to this edition, we have also given greater emphasis to the modern period.

To realize our primary purpose, the teaching of American economic history, we have retained the presentation of material in chronological order, albeit not rigidly. And this edition also retains the four-part structure that users have found so useful. Part 1, "The Colonial Era, 1607–1776," has been shortened, but the critical issues and legacies of that era have been highlighted to stimulate appreciation and understanding of this colorful period. Part 2, "The Revolutionary, Early National, and Antebellum Eras, 1776–1860," and Part 3, "The Reunification Era, 1860–1920," each begin with a chapter on the impact of war and its aftermath. The other chapters in these sections follow a parallel sequence of discussion topics—land, agriculture, and natural resources; transportation; product markets and structural change; conditions of labor; and money, banking, and economic fluctuations. Each of these sections closes with a chapter on an issue of special importance to the period: (1) the causes of the American Revolution; (2) slavery; and (3) domestic markets and foreign trade. The most dramatic change from the fifth edition is in Part 4, "The Modern Era, 1920 to the Present." This section now encompasses eleven chapters, most of them new, and all of them expanded and updated.

Each section explicitly emphasizes and illustrates the five grand themes that provide the foundation of the textbook: (1) economic growth, (2) markets and the role of government, (3) the quest for security, (4) competitiveness and international rankings, and (5) demographic forces. These themes reflect the research interests of scholars, past and present, who have contributed to the revision of the historical record. We have purposely stressed these themes to excite the readers' interest in economic history. And we firmly believe that presenting specific policy issues in their web of economic, political, and demographic forces provides convincing evidence of the relevance of economic history to contemporary events and to our personal lives.

The Sixth Edition retains a strong emphasis on the importance of institutions and the influence, both positive and negative, of government policies. It gives special emphasis to particular issues of government intervention and regulation of business practices and markets, especially in the past hundred years. The textbook provides evidence on the distributions of income prevailing in each of the four major periods. This should encourage students to draw their own conclusions on matters of economic justice and to appreciate that economic change produces both winners and losers, at least relatively. Similarly, key legacies from the past, such as slavery and the failures of Reconstruction, are highlighted to add focus to the circumstances and issues we face today.

Finally, this Sixth Edition incorporates two new pedagogical features that add perspective to the fascinating story of the American economy. A list of historical and economic perspectives now precedes each of the four parts of the textbook, providing a brief summary of key characteristics and vital events that gave special historical distinction to each unfolding era. Furthermore, each chapter now ends with a reference list of articles and books. Each list is at once the basis of much of the scholarship underlying the chapter and a source of suggested additional readings.

This and earlier editions have been sustained and supported by many individuals whose influence has surely filtered through or directly benefited this one. We remain especially indebted to Hugh G. J. Aitken, Paul Uselding, and Stewart Lee, who offered critical comments and advice on the entire fourth edition, and similarly to George Green, Gavin Wright, and Richard Winkelman for their suggestions and criticism of drafts of the fifth edition. We are grateful for the continued advice and encouragement of Lee Alston, Terry Anderson, Fred Bateman, Diane Betts, Stuart Bruchey, Susan Carter, Philip Coelho, Paul A. David, Lance Davis, Richard A. Easterlin, Barry Eichengreen, Stanley L. Engerman, Albert Fishlow, Robert W. Fogel, Robert Gallman, Claudia Goldin, Robert Higgs, J. R. T. Hughes, Gary Libecap, James Mak, Russell Menard, Lloyd Mercer, Donald N. McCloskey, Douglass C. North, Edwin Perkins, Jack Purdum, Roger Ransom, Joseph D. Reid, Jr., Don Schaefer, Mark Schmitz, R. L. Sexton, James Shepherd, Austin Spencer, Jeffery Williamson, and Mary Yeager.

Gary Walton is especially grateful to the Institute of Governmental Affairs, University of California at Davis, and Director Alan Olmstead for supporting this project and to his colleagues, Peter Lindert, Morton Rothstein, and Elias Tuma, for their special encouragement and advice. Gary also expresses sincere thanks to long-time friend Richard Sutch for valuable tutoring.

Hugh Rockoff is especially grateful to his colleagues at Rutgers who stood willing and able to answer all manner of questions. His fellow economics historian, Eugene White, patiently shared his extensive knowledge of the 1920s and 1930s. Hugh owes his largest debt to his wife, Hope Corman, who provided instruction in the subtleties of labor economics and unflagging encouragement for the whole project. To all of them Hugh expresses his deepfelt thanks.

Our greatest personal and professional debt remains to Ross M. Robertson to whom we dedicate this edition.

Gary Walton
Hugh Rockoff

CONTENTS

HISTORY
OF THE
AMERICAN ECONOMY
SIXTH EDITION

CHAPTER 1

Economic History

A STUDY WITH A PURPOSE

Demographers inform us that in the United States one-year-olds today will live long lives, one-fifth reaching the age of 100. What will life be like in 100 years from now; in 50?

One hundred years ago, citizens of Great Britain enjoyed the highest standards of living in the world and the British Empire was the leading world power. In 1892, the dominant European powers upgraded the rank of their diplomats in Washington, D.C., from ministers to ambassadors, thereby elevating the United States to first-division status among nations. In 1950 the United States was the most powerful nation in the world and Americans enjoyed standards of living higher, by far, than any other people. Today people in Sweden and Switzerland have higher average incomes than Americans, and the British earn incomes that are among the lowest in Europe.

Such swings in international power, status, and relative well-being are sobering reminders that the present is forever changing and slipping into the past. Are the changes that each of us will see and experience in our lifetimes inevitable or can destinies be steered? How did we get to where we are today?

It is unfortunate that history is often presented in forms that seem irrelevant to our everyday lives. Memorizing long lists of dates and places, kings and nobles, generals and wars, presidents and legislative acts too often misdirects our attention to what happened to whom and when rather than the more useful focus on how and why events happened. One of the special virtues of the study of economic history is its focus on how and why. It provides us with a deeper understanding of how we developed as a nation, how different segments of the population have faired, what principle policies or compelling forces brought about differential progress, or regress, among regions and people. In short, the study of economic history holds great promise and enrichment for us. Not only does it enrich our intellectual development, and provide essential perspective on contemporary affairs,

1

but it also offers practical analytical guidance on matters of policy. The study of economic history is best suited for those who care about the next one to one thousand years and who want to make the future better than the past.

Such a claim is not just empty rhetoric. Surely one of the major reasons students major in economics or American history is ultimately to enhance the operation and performance of the American economy. Certainly instructors hope their students will be better informed citizens and more productive businesspeople, politicians, and professionals. "If this is so," as Gavin Wright recently properly chastised his economic colleagues, "if the whole operation has something to do with improving the performance of the U.S. Economy, then it is perfectly scandalous that the majority of economic students complete their studies with no knowledge whatsoever about how the United States became the leading economy in the world, as of the first half of the twentieth century. What sort of doctor would diagnosis and prescribe without taking a medical history."[1]

Too often students are victims of economic textbooks that convey no information on the rise and development of the U.S. economy. Rather textbooks convey the status quo of American preeminence as if it just happened, that there was no puzzle to it, as if growth was more or less an automatic year-by-year self-sustained process. Authors of such textbooks need and eye-opening sabbatical in England, or perhaps Greece.

Economic history is a longitudinal study, but not so long and slow as, say, geology in which only imperceptible changes occur in one's lifetime. In contrast, the pace of modern economic change is fast and accelerating in many dimensions. Within living memory, nations have risen from insignificance to world prominence, while others have fallen from first-position powers to stagnation. Whole new systems of international economic trade and payments have been developed. New institutions, regulations, and laws have swiftly emerged, which sometimes expand and sometimes constrain our range of economic choices. The role of government in the economy is vastly different than it was just 60 or 70 years ago; undoubtedly it will be strikingly different 50 years from now. The study of economic history stresses the role of institutional change and how certain groups brought about economic change and why. One important topic, for example, is how late nineteenth-century midwestern farmers enacted their Granger laws that ultimately led to the formation of the Interstate Commerce Commission, which influences our lives daily but silently. Another vital topic is the legacy of slavery and the policies and circumstances that have sustained poverty improportionately among American blacks. Another is the rise and impact of labor unions and their stagnation and decline in the United States in recent years. Tariffs and protectionism are another, and on goes the list.

---

[1] Gavin Wright, "History and the Future of Economics," in *Economic History and the Modern Economics,* ed. William Parker (New York: Basil Blackwell, 1986), p. 81.

Consider the following questions: Should we have free trade or raise tariffs? Who wins and who loses? Are mergers of firms in the public interest? Can the Great Depression reoccur? Are U.S. firms more poorly managed and organized than Japanese firms? Are we losing our status as the leader in technology and innovation? If we are, how are we losing it? How did we get it? Should incomes be more equally distributed? What makes them so unequal? Do past patterns of immigration and assimilation have any relevance for Hispanic, Asian, and other immigrants today? What is the basis for our rights to own and use property and to assure contracts? Should government bail out poorly managed banks, savings and loan institutions, and other businesses or should they be allowed to fail?

The study of history, then, is more than an activity to amuse or sharpen our wits; it is a vast body of information essential to a wide spectrum of public policy decisions. This is especially true of economic history because of its quantitative features and its theoretical basis to the organization of historical facts. In combination, these enhance our ability to test (refute or support) particular propositions on policy recommendations. Consider, for instance, a recommendation for mandatory wage and price controls as a means to combat inflation. Figure 1-1 traces a decade of inflation and reveals our experience with wage and price controls during the Nixon years.

As shown in Figure 1-1, Nixon's controls were imposed in August 1971, when the inflation rate was 4.5 percent. The precontrol rate of inflation was 6 percent in early 1970 and was actually falling at the time controls were imposed. The rate of inflation continued to drift down and remained around 3 percent throughout 1972, started to rise in 1973, and by the time the controls were completely lifted in early 1974 the rate was 10 percent and rising.

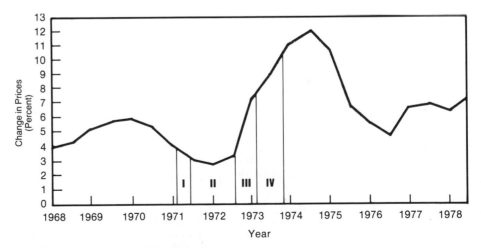

FIGURE 1-1   Inflation and Nixon's Price Controls

Source: U.S. Department of Commerce Statistical Abstract, 1978, p. 483.

On the face of it, controls did little to stop inflation. But what explains this dismal record? Were controls themselves to blame, or were there other factors at work? Only a careful study of the period can identify the role of controls in the acceleration of inflation. A contrast between Nixon's price controls and those during the Korean War (which were not followed by a price explosion) suggests two important things to look at—monetary and fiscal policies.

Price controls, moreover, disrupted the smooth functioning of the economic system. For example, to circumvent the Nixon controls, the lumber industry regularly exported lumber from the United States to Canada, then reimported it for sale at higher prices. As it became more profitable to sell fertilizers and chemical pesticides abroad rather than at home, agricultural production suffered for want of these essential inputs. These and many other similar disruptions to production made the growth rate of goods and services less and therefore the inflation worse than it would have been otherwise. We cannot explore this issue in depth here. Our point is simply that to evaluate policy proposals we must inevitably turn to the historical record.[2]

The use of wage and price controls during the Second World War provides another example adding to our understanding of their effectiveness. One important lesson this episode teaches is about the need to supplement quantitative studies with historical research. An economist cannot naively assume that price statistics always tell the truth. During the war, controls were evaded in numerous ways that were only partly reflected in the official numbers despite valiant efforts by the Bureau of Labor Statistics. One form of evasion was quality deterioration. Fat was added to hamburger, candy bars were made smaller and inferior ingredients were substituted, coarser fabrics were used in making clothes, maintenance on rental properties was reduced, and so on. Sometimes whole lines of low markup, low-quality merchandise were eliminated forcing even poor consumers to trade-up to high markup, high-quality lines. And, of course, black markets developed, like illegal markets in drugs today. It is the job of the economic historian to try to assess the overall effect of these activities.[3]

Many students ask the following question: granted that economic history is important to the professional economist or economic policymaker, is there any practical reason for studying it if I have other long-term goals? The answer is yes. The skills that are developed in studying economic history— critical analysis of the economic record, drawing conclusions from it based on economic theory, and writing up the results in clear English—are val-

---

[2] An attempt to compare and contrast American experiences with wage and price controls is presented in Hugh Rockoff, *Drastic Measures: A History of Wage and Price Controls in the United States* (New York: Cambridge Univ. Press, 1984).

[3] For one exploration of this issue see Hugh Rockoff, "Indirect Price Increases and Real Wages in World War II," *Explorations in Economic History* 15 (1978): 407–20.

uable skills in many lines of everyday work. The lawyer who reviews banking statutes to determine the intent of the law, the investment banker who studies past stock market crashes to find clues on how to respond to a recent crash, the owner-operator of a small business who thinks about what happened to other small businesses that were sold to larger firms—all are taking on the role of economic historian. It will help them if they can do it well.

Besides the importance of historical study for its vital role in deliberating private and public policy recommendations, knowledge of history has other merits. For one thing, history can be fun—especially as we get older and try to recapture parts of our lives in nostalgic reminiscence. For another, good history, especially in an appealing literary form, both entertains as well as enriches our self-consciousness. A sense of history is really a sense of participation in high drama—a sense of having a part in the great flow of events that link us with those of earlier times and with those yet to be born.

THE MERGING OF ECONOMICS AND HISTORY

The marriage of history and economics is not contrived or forced; the two disciplines are based on the common use of *both* theory and empirical information. This similarity is not always fully appreciated, but like any organized body of knowledge, both economics and history summarize events and reality. Without such aid, the human mind cannot comprehend the complexity of our economic system. We cannot simply look at the interrelationships among economic variables and make sense out of them. It is equally apparent that history must be selective—that any attempt to record the whole of the past would be an exercise in futility. Economists and historians make their respective subjects manageable by the prudent selection of relevant information and by disregarding irrelevant information. Which data and information are relevant is largely, indeed some would claim solely, determined by theoretical considerations. Oftentimes the theoretical underpinnings of a story or argument are implicit, but whenever cause and effect are implied, theory is being used. Economics enhances history by making explicit the use of theory, and history serves as the essential testing ground for economic theory. Together they stand stronger than either one alone. Still it is useful to understand and appreciate their separate domains and differences of scope, style, and approach.

History

We use the word *history* almost every day, usually without being aware of the ambiguity of the term. It has come to have a double meaning. When we speak of history, we may refer (1) to the narrative of past events or (2) to the events themselves. When we say, "Oh, that's past history," we are referring to events. When we say, "History proves that power corrupts," we are referring to the record. The familiar saying "Mankind makes history; historians make histories" emphasizes history's dual meaning.

We could begin with the simple remark that history is the narrative statement of happenings in the past. But such an assertion does not take us very far simply because it fails to stress the burdensome obligation of the historian, who must select from the whole of the known past the material to include in the narrative. Another definition—perhaps one that is too pretentious and formal for most purposes but one that points out the problem of fact selection—is "History is man's formal record of actual human phenomena as consecutively manifested in the past insofar as they have been ascertained to be general, important, enduring, and true, with the legitimate deductions drawn for the pleasure and education of mankind." Note the key words *general, important, enduring, true.* Obviously, history will rarely be concerned with the lives of everyday people. Rather, it will be concentrated around events that concern the community as a whole—events that have a high degree of importance in this sense. But who judges the importance of these events? The fact selectors, of course, who in the process impose their own value judgments on the reader.

So the historian, like the economist, is confronted with a jumble of facts that must be collected and molded into an intelligible, significant narrative. We can better understand the difficulty of the task when we realize that the historical event has happened in the unalterable past and can never be observed again. It can only be reconstructed from remaining evidence, chiefly in the form of documents of one kind or another, and much of the evidence is fragmentary and unreliable. But whatever difficulties historians encounter, they must collect and organize the facts, interpret them in the light of modern interests, and present them in usable form.

It has been said that there are three phrases of historical procedure. With caution, so that we do not jump to any conclusions about separating the historian's work into neat compartments, we may still find it useful to consider these steps.

1. *Reconstruction of the historical facts—"the science of history."* Historical facts can be reconstructed by people who do not write history at all—basic researchers who search through attics and cellars, courthouses, and business records and who publish their material in the form of collected letters, papers, memoirs, and journals. But no one has a monopoly on fact collection, and many historians who write at highly generalized levels enlist the aid of scholars in sociology, political science, and anthropology who often contribute to our knowledge of historical events.

2. *Writing the historical narrative—"the art of history."* Because the facts must be assembled to form a significant written record, the historian must make a literary effort. Sometimes this effort is so successful that the result is a high art form. Historians from Herodotus to Freeman have become famous

as a result of their literary abilities as well as their substantive contributions. Macaulay is still assigned in English literature classes, and contemporary readers even today are moved by Gibbon. For some time, the nineteenth-century emphasis on literary quality in historical works may have disappeared, but in recent years, first-class historians have revived it. The monograph of a young scholar, whose aim is to exhaust a subject of limited range, can afford perhaps to be both technical and unexciting. But general histories, including popularizations, that do not cast their spell will be quickly usurped by a TV program or the latest bestseller.

3. *Interpretation of history—"the philosophy of history."* After the facts have been gathered and the historical narrative has been written, the record should be explained in terms of the general principles that govern human conduct. Older historians sought to explain the flow of events by some grand central motivation; they exhibited an essentially *monistic* philosophy in opposition to the *pluralistic* philosophy of modern writers. The most common and best-known monistic theme was that history centered around political activity—around governments and the major phenomena of governments, such as wars, legislative acts, and changes in rulers. College students can hardly escape another monistic approach—the "great man" interpretation of Thomas Carlyle, who held that a few highly gifted people constituted the determining force in human affairs.[4] Alternatively, in the nineteenth century, the economic or materialistic view of Karl Marx emphasized the economic determinants of the cultural, social, and political values of life.[5] There have been many other attempts to find a single wellspring of human motivation centered on psychology, spirituality, science or technology, the "creative mind," and geography. Gradually, however, modern historians have come to believe that the vast sweep of history cannot be explained in terms of one aspect of human activity and have adapted the pluralistic view that in a physical environment more and more shaped and dominated by people, the human race progresses or retrogresses for a variety of reasons.

But if historical writing is only the result of a drastic sifting of evidence, can we ever be sure that the history we are reading is absolutely true? To this question, we must answer that we can never be certain. From a tangled web of facts, the historian must select some and discard others. Foremost historical scholars used to contend that this selection could be made on an "objective" basis. But one historian's objectivity is another historian's bias. No individual historian, however honorable or gifted, can write outside the

---

[4] For some examples of men and women who made a difference, written elegantly with charm and style, see Jonathan R. T. Hughes, *The Vital Few,* 2nd ed. (New York and London: Oxford Univ. Press, 1986).

[5] The strong tradition and more recent contributions of the "Marxist school" are outlined in Jon S. Cohen, "The Achievements of Economic History: The Marxist School," *Journal of Economic History* 38 (1978): 29–57.

context of his or her own experience and philosophy. We must include in our narrative those facts that we think are important in explaining changes and that in our opinion are worth explaining. Whether we like it or not, history involves implicit theorizing.

Does this argument lead us to conclude that progress in historical knowledge is impossible? Of course not! History is constantly moving toward greater clarification—toward a deeper, fuller knowledge of what has happened and how and why it has occurred. This progress is possible because a succession of historians, dedicated to the job of seeking new insights into and more logical explanations for events, endlessly rewrite history. It is this compulsion to take another look, to ask one more question, to perceive something a little more clearly, that makes history in the sense of the narrative a changing and vital subject.

Economics

Economics is the study of how scarce resources are allocated among alternative competing uses to satisfy unlimited individual and social wants. The scarcity of a nation's resources, its people (human capital including knowledge and skills), its natural endowments (land, water, minerals) and its stock of produced goods (physical capital), and the levels of utilized technology—all set limits on total output. Because of the conflict between scarcity and wide-ranging, unlimited wants, economic choices must be made. Producing more wine imposes costs, such as producing less bread perhaps, as land and labor must be shifted from wheat to grapes.

Any economic system must address the following questions:

1. How much and what kind of productive (factor) services should be provided? Specifically, how many clerks, managers, doctors, teachers, and other types of workers are required to manufacture goods and furnish services?

2. Which enterprises should obtain the different productive services?

3. How much of the total output of the economy should be relegated to households for immediate use (consumption), and how much should be added to the stock of real capital (tools, machinery, and so on) that will be needed for future productive effort?

4. How should consumer goods be distributed (rationed) among consumers, and how should additions to the stock of capital be parceled out among various enterprises?

Although many variations exist, there are two basic alternatives to respond to these questions and direct the allocation process. One is centrally controlled allocation. Although Mr. Gorbachev's *perestroika* promises somewhat greater decentralization of decision making, the Soviet Union remains a good example of a centrally planned economy. There a political commissariat decides what part of the country's productive services is to be devoted to providing consumer goods and services, what part is to be used to make capital goods, what part is to be allocated for space hardware, and so on. More detailed decisions are then made by lesser officials in the hierarchy and may or may not parallel the wishes of consumers. Although prices may be assigned to goods and services, they are mainly for the purpose of keeping accounts and informing planners.

The other alternative is a decentralized enterprise economy, like that of the United States, in which the allocation of resources is largely accomplished by means of the price system. On the one hand, households sell their services or the use of their property in markets where resources are bought and sold, thereby earning *incomes*. On the other hand, households are confronted with a battery of *prices* in the consumer market. The relationship between incomes and prices determines the levels of living both for individual households and for society. In the growing, progressing American economy, choices are continually being registered in the consumer market and telegraphed by price and quantity changes to the business sector, which responds to shifting consumer demands by changing its requirements for productive services.

It would be a mistake, however, to suppose that the price system performs its functions simply by sending impulses from consumers to business. The business sector is constantly introducing new products and innovating low-cost ways of making old ones, with resulting changes in consumer outlays. Moreover, through advertising, the business community constantly strives to sway consumer preferences among goods and services and also between making consumption expenditures and saving.

Indeed, because the choices registered by both business managers and consumers are often made *simultaneously*, it is hard to say which decisions are causes and which are effects. The important point is that through the pricing mechanism, consumer and producer choices are translated into ultimate decisions about how resources should be allocated. Because prices are so vitally important, their study and observation is the chief preoccupation of businesspeople and economists.

In action, the American economic system is one of the most fascinating and complex mechanisms ever devised by Western civilization. Even in its most trivial manifestations, the system ordinarily provides goods and services from all parts of the world, as if by magic, exactly when and where they are needed. The everyday items that we all take for granted—our morning coffee and our evening newspaper, our ride to work and our television program at home, a telephone call to a friend or a business letter to an office in New York—require the cooperative efforts of hundreds or thousands of people and the equipment with which they work. And when we wish to describe the system in all its intricate detail, the task seems formidable to the point of impossibility.

At this point, economists must resort to theory; that is, they must abstractly summarize the reality of the world about them to see the fundamental forces at work, most often in the conceptual form of supply and demand forces. In effect, they must construct models. Insofar as they abstract from reality to discover principles, economists are theorists.

But what do economists theorize about? First, they examine the workings of the principal mechanism used to allocate resources—the *pricing* system, which (1) establishes the order of priority in which producers obtain resources and (2) rations goods among consumers. For a long time, the central inquiry of economic theory was to discover how the prices and quantities of goods were determined. This inquiry led to the discovery of the laws of supply and demand. Since the 1930s and even earlier, another problem—periods of widespread unemployment of resources—has increasingly occupied the attention of economists, and a body of theory has developed to explain how unfulfilled wants can exist side by side with idle workers and ideal equipment. Another problem of economic stabilization has been one of unyielding inflation, although a theory of unemployment presumably provides prescriptions for containing intractable price rises. To the classical theory of price, then, economists appended the theory of income and employment—an analysis that complements the theory of price determination by showing how unemployment and/or inflation can exist.

The broad subject of economic theory has been subdivided into a number of specialties. Some economists specialize in the theory of the firm, with its recent emphasis on problems of strategy and conflict. Others devote their full time to the study of monetary theory or to the perfection of social accounting systems. Still others investigate the principles by which international trade is regulated and the intricate theory of the determination of international exchange rates. But in whatever way economists specialize or break down the job of analysis, the fact remains that there are two basic theoretical questions in economics: (1) How are resources allocated? and (2) What forces determine the level of a nation's income?

Whenever a subject has a body of theory, it also has a body of applied knowledge. Thus, we often speak of "applied" economics. As Kenneth Boulding puts it

> Any subject such as economics which is "empirical," in the sense that it is interested in the interpretation of actual human experience, must have two parts: the construction of logical frameworks (the "pure" subject) and the interpretation of reality by fitting the logical framework to the complex of empirical data (the "applied" subject).[6]

Thus, there is a part of economics that deals with more "practical" matters. The applied economist, like the theorist, can specialize in many areas. An economic statistician compiles, organizes, and interprets current quantitative information. An economic historian is concerned largely with the per-

---

[6]Kenneth E. Boulding, "Samuelson's Foundations: The Role of Mathematics in Economics," *Journal of Political Economy* 56 (June 1948): 190.

ception of *change* in economic phenomena. A practicing economic consultant furnishes executives who formulate policies with business forecasts to guide in their decision making.

Economists are fond of saying that economics is not an exact science.[7] But neither is it guesswork. By and large, economists rely on an almost universally accepted theoretical apparatus.[8] Social goals are subject to debate among economists just as they are among other occupational groups. But once they are furnished with a consensus about objectives—about ends—economists can offer—within tolerable limits of error—policy prescriptions calculated to achieve those objectives. In a word, economics is a way of thinking about the "unrelated confusion" of prices, production, and incomes that makes these phenomena intelligible and sufficiently well ordered to permit scientific prediction.

Like any scientist working in an applied field, the economist must ultimately answer the question, what *action* should be taken? To return to our earlier discussion, for example, is a policy of wage and price controls the best alternative to end inflation? Here an appeal must be made both to theory and to the lessons of experience. Advisers to government officials and other decision makers cannot reason through real-world problems without some means of eliminating the least relevant facts—without applying the principles of the theoretical economist. But any adviser with good sense must inevitably return to a reading of the record. We must turn finally to economic history to check faults by reasoning and to illuminate paths of action.

ECONOMIC HISTORY AND THE ROLES OF THE ECONOMIC HISTORIAN

Economic history then draws on each of the two great disciplines we have just examined. In their studies economic historians are committed to four primary objectives.

1. *The traditional assignment of the economic historian is to explain changes in the institutions that are most closely connected with the business of making a living.* In its simplest form, this work defines and describes markets, traces the behavior of sellers and buyers, and quantifies the outcome of their bargaining in statistical series that illustrate changes in prices and production

---

[7]Economics, once a branch of "moral philosophy," had little claim to scientific status until the publication of Adam Smith's *Wealth of Nations* in 1776. For another century and a half, while economists were developing their theoretical propositions and giving them mathematical formulation, economics was on its way to becoming scientific. But only in the last generation or so have economists been able to attempt to empirically verify these propositions.

[8]We commonly hear the expression *That's all right in theory, but it won't work in practice.* But this statement is nonsensical. If a theory is not right in practice, then the theory is wrong; that is, it fails to predict.

over time. But this mundane labor leads to a more exciting inquiry—the question of why the present economic system, rather than some other system, is an outgrowth of the past.

Perhaps the most fundamental question underlying this traditional realm of inquiry is which activities should be left to free choice and market forces and which should be partially constrained or entirely controlled by government. In the 1970s, the clamor over excessive government interference and wasteful regulation of business, the tax revolt, President Reagan's 1980 and 1984 mandates to halt inflation and the growth of government in our lives, and many other similar issues are varying aspects of that fundamental question. By no means is substantial government involvement a new phenomenon. The "government habit," to use Jonathon R. T. Hughes' insightful phrase,[9] was being well developed deep into the colonial period of American history. And debate among scholars, laymen, and politicians continues on the relative merits of market vis-à-vis government directives in determining production and distribution. And so often the debate leads to the past! Was the Great Depression of the 1930s a failure of capitalism (markets) or was it a failure of government? Which institution or sets of institutions broke down? Why has government grown so significantly since the 1930s? Is a correction in this growth path needed today? Which things should government leave to free choice and to markets? These and many other such questions are repeatedly addressed by economic historians, and one of the most promising areas of current research in economic history is the development of a theory of institutional change.[10]

2. Certainly the most fashionable subject in economics in recent decades has been the study of economic growth. The question of growth has always attracted economists, and economic historians have considered the problem central to their own efforts.

But in examining the problem of growth, economic history can make special contributions that cannot yet be obtained from theory alone. Economic growth can occur within varying social and political contexts. The forces that accelerated or retarded change are more likely to be discerned in their entirety by the historian, and even the fortuitous events that played so important a part in the growth of the Western economies may be overlooked by those whose experience is largely contemporary. It would be difficult indeed to overlook the effects of the Second World War on such economic determinants of the postwar American economy as the rate of capital formation, the rate of saving, and the level of output. But how likely is it that theorists today will reflect on some of the economic great chance happenings of the past that helped in large part to promote the economic

---

[9]J. R. T. Hughes, *The Government Habit* (New York: Basic Books, 1977).
[10]Lance E. Davis and Douglass C. North, *Institutional Change and American Economic Growth* (Cambridge: Cambridge Univ. Press, 1971), esp. pp. 3–79.

growth of the United States by forcing it to gather its momentum in the mid-nineteenth century?

Will they, for example, stop to think that the United States was founded after Europe had already made the change from medieval to modern times? When the American colonies were formed, many of the medieval rigidities that plague the underdeveloped countries today no longer existed in Europe and scarcely any of them were ever transplanted to the colonies. So the abundance of land not only enabled colonial Americans to feed themselves without creating huge drafts on their foreign exchange, but also made it largely unnecessary for them to throw off the shackles of feudalistic restrictions on land tenure. Or will the theorist who casts up the "fundamental equations" of growth stop to think that the United States was nurtured and sustained in its critical early years by the Napoleonic Wars, which stimulated the carrying trade of the young country, created foreign exchange to pay for capital imports, and swelled the mercantile fortunes that later sought investment outlets in one of the first American growth industries—cotton textiles?

More positively, economic history has lately progressed toward a unified, coherent historical narrative of the growth process. But now we are getting ahead of our story.

3. *Economic history and its kindred subject, business history, serve to test the propositions of economic theory.*[11] Our observations about the procedures of economic theorizing caution against expecting too much of history as a testing ground for theorems, because it is impossible to isolate only the relevant historical variables. Yet a careful and judicious observation of repeated phenomena helps us to verify or refute propositions we have reached through abstract reasoning. It is in this context that economic history can offer us its most valuable insights. One of the key propositions of economics, for example, is that competition operating through the price mechanism (Adam Smith's "invisible hand") is the most efficient way of allocating resources. We can test this theory by examining past periods of price controls when governments rather than markets determined prices.

A generation and more ago, economic historians were unwilling to pass judgment on the cherished notions of the then-contemporary theory. Today's historians, however, are not bashful about holding theorems up to the white light of recorded experience. In so doing, many are not only testing theory—they are writing a new kind of history and bringing to their generalizations a wealth of statistically reliable data. Thus, economic history that

---

[11] At the moment, a digression on the nature of business history would carry us far afield. Let's tentatively assume that business history is simply a specialty that focuses on the behavior of the firm and its management and lies within the larger field of economic history. We will have the opportunity to expand on this point in later chapters, particularly when we consider the role of the entrepreneur in economic organizations and the managerial revolution of the late nineteenth century.

once was expressed in such terms as "largely" and "mostly" now often contain such assertions as "60 percent" or "90 percent." The "new" economic history launched nearly a quarter of a century ago emphasizes the use of theory and statistical analysis not only to ascertain precisely documentable facts, but also to establish the outer limits of probability and thereby provide a basis for historical judgment.[12]

4. *Like all other historians, the specialists in economic history must at last confront their noblest task—the interpretation of the records they have forged.* Recognizing that most people are unable to separate the economic system from the social whole, economic historians must nonetheless assess the performance of that system in a world of conflicting ideologies. And, finally, we must give the best account we can of the mainsprings of the process of development, because more than half the peoples of the world require and wait for this special advice.

Scholars should never be apologists for any social organization, nor can we honorably defend the demonstrable failings of the system to which we bear allegiance. By the same token, a scrupulously fair examination of a country's economic development may be the most effective testimony to the justice and worth of its total social organization.

In the pages that follow, the history of the American economy is written once again. There would be no excuse for just another recounting of the same old facts and figures, updated by a few years that all too rapidly recede into the past. There is a solid reason, though, for recasting the record to further relieve it of its mythological overburden and to bear witness to the strengths and shortcomings of a democracy that operates within the discipline of markets constrained by laws and institutions.[13]

SELECTED REFERENCES AND SUGGESTED READINGS

Boulding, Kenneth E. "Samuelson's Foundations: The Role of Mathematics in Economics." *Journal of Political Economy* 56 (1948): 190.

Cohen, Jon S. "The Achievements of Economic History: The Marxist School." *Journal of Economic History* 38 (1978): 29–57.

Davis, Lance E., and Douglass C. North, *Institutional Change and American Economic Growth.* Cambridge: Cambridge Univ. Press, 1971, esp. pp. 3–79.

Hughes, Jonathan R. T. *The Government Habit.* New York: Basic Books, 1977.

———. *The Vital Few,* 2nd ed. New York and London: Oxford Univ. Press, 1986.

[12] The new economic history is also known as the Cliometrics School. See Donald N. McCloskey, "The Achievements of the Cliometrics School," *Journal of Economic History* 38 (1978): 13–28.

[13] For further insight into the relationship between economics and history provided by two outstanding economic historians, see Donald N. McCloskey, "Does the Past Have Useful Economics?" *Journal of Economic Literature* 14 (1976): 434–61; and Douglass C. North, "Structure and Performance: The Task of Economic History," *Journal of Economic Literature* 16 (1978): 963–78.

McCloskey, Donald N. "Does the Past Have Useful Economics?" *Journal of Economic Literature* 14 (1976): 434–61.

———. "The Achievements of the Cliometrics School." *Journal of Economic History* 38 (1978): 13–28.

North, Douglass C. "Structure and Performance: The Task of Economic History." *Journal of Economic Literature* 16 (1978): 963–78.

Rockoff, Hugh. "Indirect Price Increases and Real Wages in World War II." *Explorations in Economic History* 15 (1978): 407–20.

———. *Drastic Measures: A History of Wage and Price Controls in the United States.* New York: Cambridge Univ. Press, 1984.

Smith, Adam. *Wealth of Nations,* 1776.

Wright, Gavin. "History and the Future of Economics." In *Economic History and the Modern Economics,* ed. William Parker. New York: Basil Blackwell, 1986.

PART 1

THE COLONIAL ERA

1607–1776

1. The American colonial period was a time when poverty was the norm throughout the world and wars among nations were frequent. The earliest settlements in North America were costly in terms of great human suffering and capital losses.

2. The nation-states of Western Europe that emerged from the long, relatively stagnant period of feudalism rose to prominence in wealth and power relative to earlier leading centers in the Mediterranean and the Orient.

3. Spain, Portugal, Holland, England, and France each built international empires, and England and France especially further advanced their relative economic and military strength by successfully applying mercantilist policies. Great Britain ultimately dominated the colonization of North America and was the first nation to launch the industrial revolution, beginning in the second half of the eighteenth century.

4. Innovations in trade and commerce, the spread of practical learning, new and expanding settlements that added land and adapted it to best-uses, and falling risks in trade and frontier life raised living standards in the New World. By the time of the American Revolution, the material standards of living in the colonies were among the highest in the world and comparable to those in England. However, the distribution of wealth and human rights among the sexes, races, and among free citizens was vastly unequal.

5. Americans sustained their long English heritage even after independence, but their strong economic rise ultimately placed them in a position of rivalry with the mother country. The years 1763–76 saw confrontation, growing distrust, and ultimately rebellion.

CHAPTER 2

Founding the Colonies

For the pleasing entertainment of the Polite part of Mankind, I have printed the most Beautiful Poems of Mr. Stephen Duck, the famous Wiltshire Poet," announced "Fry, Stationer, Bookseller, Paper-Maker, and Rag Merchant, late of the City of London and now located in Boston." The advertisement, which appeared in the Boston *Gazette,* May 1–8, 1732, was not an introductory offer, for the notice continued, "It is a full demonstration to me that the People of New England have a fine taste for Good Sense and Polite Learning, having already sold 1,200 of these Poems."

No doubt Fry was anxious to please and entertain the "Polite part of Mankind," possibly at a profit. But his advertisement contained another, somewhat plainer matter that may have interested him more. It was "the common Method of the most curious merchants of Boston, to Procure their (account) Books from London," and Fry, for business reasons, took exception to the practice. He addressed the notice to all Gentlemen, Merchants, and Tradesmen. "This," he declared, "is to acquaint those Gentlemen, that I, said Fry, will sell all sorts of Accompt-Books, done after the most accurate manner, for 20 percent cheaper than they can have them from London."

That prepared "accompt" books "done after the most accurate manner" were offered for sale at such an early date should have occasioned no more surprise than that the polite part of New England was entertained by the poems of Mr. Stephen Duck of Wiltshire. *For in the beginning, the American colonies were only a small part of a greatly expanded Europe—a western frontier, so to speak.* The culture of the colonists, including double-entry bookkeeping and poetic preferences, was in many respects the culture of their former associates on the other side of the Atlantic. These ties were primarily to Great Britain. For in the race for empire among the European nation-states, it was ultimately Britain that prevailed in the quest for North America.

EUROPEAN ROOTS AND EXPANDING EMPIRES

Before focusing on this early British heritage, it is important to emphasize that shortly before America's discovery, the center of European wealth and commerce rested in the Mediterranean. That economic concentration was based primarily on long-distance trade between Asia and Europe. Because of the locational advantage and superior commercial skills and knowledge they provided, the Italian city-states of Milan, Florence, Genoa, and Venice dominated most of the Old World's trading for centuries. Critical to its prosperity was the maintenance of open routes to the East, because Europe had always been dependent on Asia for luxury goods and other products seemingly essential to medieval Europeans.

Of course, in an age before refrigeration, spices were used with almost unbelievable liberality by medieval cooks, whose fashion it was to conceal the taste of tainted meat and to embellish the flavor of monotonous food with pepper, cloves, ginger, nutmeg, and cinnamon. Where wild honey was the only local sweetener, sugar from North Africa and the Levant was greatly valued. And although drugs in those times were by no means infallible

Commercial splendor: Venice (rendered here by Caneletto) was almost as much an Eastern as a Western city, and for hundreds of years, its commercial and naval power was a great sustaining force of Western civilization.

(some of them probably were worse than taking nothing at all), some relief from European ailments came from Asian drugs.

As long as trade routes remained predominantly overland, Europe could export only a few products that sold for a high value relative to their weight and bulk: woolen textiles and certain metals and minerals, like arsenic, quicksilver, and copper. Not until sea transportation opened the possibility of further exportation from Europe to the East, could the balance of trade—the value of commodity exports compared to the value of commodity imports—become more even. But this did not happen for centuries, and gold and silver continuously drained eastward, because the balance of trade remained unfavorable to Europe.

Recognizing the inexorable difficulties of transporting a sufficient variety of exports over land routes, we can see why the discovery of an all-sea route to the East was inevitable, as soon as a country emerged that was powerful enough to engineer it. But in that early period of material awakening in Europe, it was not the powerful city-states that initiated the quest. Nor was Spain more than a latecomer in ocean discoveries; in many respects, it was somewhat of a historical accident that Christopher Columbus—a Genoese sailor in the employ of Spain—made the most vital of the landfalls.

Exploration and Expansion: Portugal and Spain

Curiously enough, tiny, seafaring Portugal was the great Atlantic pioneer. By the time Columbus embarked, Portugal could claim more than seven decades of ocean discoveries. Under the vigorous and imaginative leadership of Prince Henry the Navigator, whose Naval Arsenal at Sagres was a fifteenth-century Cape Canaveral, Portugal—from 1415 to 1460—sent one expedition after another down the western coast of Africa.

The great sea explorations from Europe took place within a little less than 35 years. In 1488, Bartolomeu Dias of Portugal rounded the Cape of Good Hope and would have reached India if his mutinous crew had not forced him to return home. In September 1522, the *Vittoria*—last of Ferdinand Magellan's fleet of five ships—put in at Seville; in a spectacular achievement, 18 Europeans had circumnavigated the globe. Between these two dates, there were two other voyages of no less importance. Columbus, certain that it was no more than 2,500 miles from the Canary Islands to Japan, persuaded the Spanish sovereigns Ferdinand and Isabella to finance his first trip. On October 12, 1492, his lookout sighted the little island of San Salvador in the Bahamas. Only a few years later, Vasco da Gama, sailing for the Portuguese, reached Calicut in India via the Cape of Good Hope, returning home in 1499. Thus, the sea-lanes opened with Portugal dominant in the East, and Spain supreme in the West. By the early sixteenth century, the wealth and commerce of Europe had shifted to the western Atlantic. The Mediterranean leaders did not decline absolutely; instead, they were simply overtaken and passed by. In an international context this

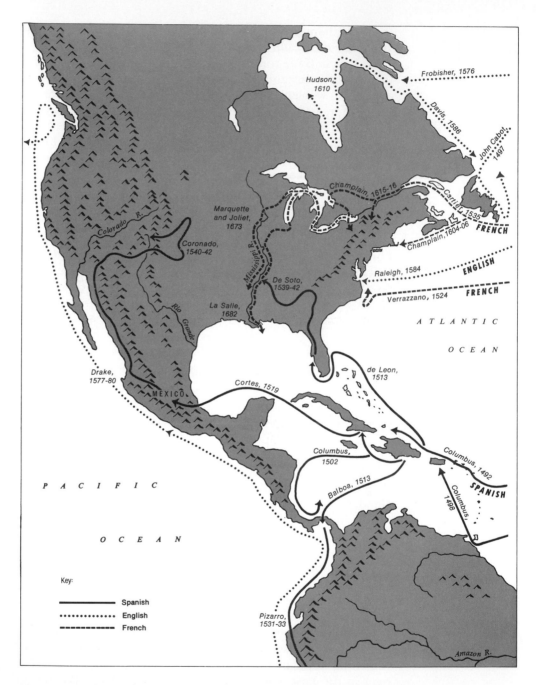

MAP 2-1   Exploration: Spain and Portugal came first; then France, Holland, and England. All of these nations explored vast amounts of territory in North America, giving rise to new economic opportunities, but England's explorations gave rise to the most extensive permanent settlements in the New World.

was a critical first phase in the relative rise and eventual supremacy of key western nation-states.

After Spain's conquest of Mexico by Hernando Cortés in 1521, American silver and gold flowed into Spain in ever-increasing quantities. When the Spanish king Philip II made good his claim to the throne of Portugal in 1580, Spanish prestige reached its zenith. Two great empires, strong in the Orient and unchallenged in the Americas, were now joined. When we reflect that no other country had as yet established a single permanent settlement in the New World, it seems astonishing that the decline of Spanish power was so imminent.

Although Spain was a colonizer, Spanish attempts to settle in the Americas lacked a solid foundation. Spain was remarkably poor in natural resources in the sixteenth century, and the main interest of both the conquistadors and the rulers at home was treasure from America's mines—especially silver. To be sure, attempts were made to extend agriculture and to establish manufacturing operations in the New World, but the Spaniards remained a ruling caste—dominating the natives who did the work and holding them in political and economic bondage. The Spanish were more like occupying rulers than permanent settlers.

When toward the end of the century, Spain became involved in war with the English and began to dissipate its energies in a futile attempt to bring the Low Countries (Holland and Belgium) under complete subjection, Spain lost the advantage of being the first nation to expand through explorations in America. Even more harmful to Spain than the wars, however, was the decline in gold and silver imports that began after 1600 with the exhaustion of better-grade ores.

Exploration and Expansion: Holland, France, and England

As Spanish power declined, Dutch power ascended. At first a nation of fishermen, Holland began to extend its trade routes to Scandinavia and the Baltic in the sixteenth century. Dutch exploration then turned southward, and by 1600, Holland had sent several expeditions to the East. The Dutch East India Company, established in 1602, quickly nudged the Portuguese aside in the Spice Islands. By 1650, Holland was the chief shipping, trading, and financial nation in Europe. Dutch preeminence, however, hardly lasted a century. Like Spain, Holland possessed a weak resource base at home, and its far-ranging sea captains and traders placed too much emphasis on the establishment of trading posts and too little on colonization. In the East Indies, the Dutch East India Company's ruthless exploitation of the natives resulted in fantastic profits, which for nearly two centuries bolstered Holland as a great entrepôt and money market. Amsterdam particularly became a great trade and financial center. But the East Indian empire did not provide the strength needed in a world where, as Herbert Heaton has remarked, "coal and iron were more important than spices and herrings."

THE DUTCH TRADE FOR FURS ~ 1640

Initially, the Dutch were active fur traders as well as shippers in earlier America.

Yet the Netherlands fell from eminence not so much because it regressed but because it was overtaken by two other countries with greater resources.

As it turned out, France and England became the chief competitors in the centuries-long race for supremacy. From 1608, when Samuel de Champlain established Québec, France successfully undertook explorations in America westward to the Great Lakes area and had pushed southward down the Mississippi Valley to Louisiana by the end of the century. And in the Orient, France, though a latecomer, competed successfully with the English for a time after the establishment of the French East India Company in 1664. In less than a century, however, the English defeated the French in India, as they would one day do in America. The English triumphed in both India and America because they had established the most extensive permanent settlements. It is not without significance that at the beginning of the French and Indian War in 1756, there were some 60,000 French settlers in Canada compared with 2 million in the English North American colonies.

For our purposes here, the most important feature of the expansion of Europe was the steady and persistent growth of settlements in the British colonies of North America. Why were the English such successful colonizers?

To be sure, the English, like the French and the Dutch, coveted the colonial wealth of the Spanish and the Portuguese, and English sailors and traders acted for a time as if their struggling outposts in the wilderness of

North America were merely temporary. They traded in Latin America, while privateers like Francis Drake and Thomas Cavendish plundered Spanish galleons for their treasures as they sailed the Main. English venturers, probing the East for profitable outposts, gained successive footholds in India as the seventeenth century progressed. Yet, unlike the leaders of some western European countries, Englishmen like Richard Hakluyt advocated permanent colonization and settlement in the New World, perceiving that true colonies would eventually become important markets for manufactured products from the mother country. Toward the end of the sixteenth century, this consideration became especially important to England. During the 1500s, its foreign trade had passed largely from the hands of foreigners into those of English merchants. Especially lucrative had been the growing exports of English woolens, paid for by England's best customer, Spain, with gold and silver from Mexico and Peru. But Spain became an enemy, largely due to English privateering, and the resultant need for new English markets was pressing.

It was not enough, however, for merchants and heads of states to reap the advantages of the thriving colonies: Commoners had to be persuaded of the benefits to themselves and their families of emigrating to the New World. The greatest motivations to emigrate were a desire to own land—still the European symbol of status and economic security—and to strive for a higher level of living than could be attained at home by any but the best-paid artisans. These economic motivations were often accompanied by a religious motivation. Unlike the Spanish, the English did not come to these shores to convert "the heathen"; the New England settlers in particular emigrated so that they could worship as they chose, provided those around them were of similar persuasion. In their zeal, most colonists became actual participants in the productive process, rather than supervisors of others. And once a cadre of able leaders arrived, the future settlement of the frontier was assured, because the British fortuitously colonized that part of the New World favored by location and special advantages in climate and natural resources to complement the Old.

FIRST BRITISH SETTLEMENTS IN NORTH AMERICA

Perilous Beginnings

Two half brothers, Sir Humphrey Gilbert and Sir Walter Raleigh, were the first Englishmen to undertake serious ventures in America. Gilbert, one of the more earnest seekers of the Northwest Passage, went to Newfoundland in 1578 and again in 1583, but due to many difficulties, he failed to colonize the territory either time. Sir Humphrey lost his life on the return voyage to England after the second attempt. Raleigh, like Gilbert, was granted the right to settle in "Virginia" and to have control of the land within a radius of 200 leagues from any colony that he might successfully establish. Raleigh actually brought two groups of colonists to the new continent. The first landed on the island of Roanoke off the coast of what is now North Carolina and stayed less than a year; anything but enthusiastic about their new home, these first colonists returned to England with Sir Francis Drake in the summer of 1586. Undaunted, Raleigh solicited the financial aid of a group of wealthy Londoners and, in the following year, sent a second contingent of 150 people under the leadership of Governor John White. Raleigh had given explicit instructions that this colony was to be planted somewhere on the Chesapeake Bay, but Governor White disregarded the order and landed at Roanoke. White went back to England for supplies; when he returned after much delay in 1590, the settlers had vanished. Not a single member of the famed "lost colony" was ever found.

After a long war between England and Spain from 1588 to 1603, England renewed attempts to colonize North America. In 1606, two charters were granted—one to a group of Londoners; the other, to merchants of the western port towns, of which Plymouth was the most important. The London Company was given the right to settle the southern part of the English territory in America; the Plymouth Company was given jurisdiction over the northern part.

So two widely separated colonies were established in 1607: one at Sagadahoc, near the mouth of the Kennebec River, in Maine; the other in modern Virginia.[1] Those who survived the winter in the northern colony gave up and went home, and the colony established at Jamestown won the hard-earned honor of being the first permanent English settlement in America.

Hard indeed! When the London Company landed three tiny vessels at the mouth of the Chesapeake Bay in 1607, 105 people disembarked to found the Jamestown Colony. Easily distracted by futile "get rich quick" schemes, they actually sent shiploads of mica and yellow ore back to England in 1607 and 1608. Before the news reached their ears that their treasure was worthless "fool's gold," disease, starvation, and misadventure had taken a heavy toll; 67 of the original 105 Jamestown settlers died in the first year.

The few remaining survivors (one who was convicted of cannibalism) were joined in 1609 by 800 new arrivals, sent over by the reorganized and renamed Virginia Company. By the following spring, frontier hardships had cut their number from 838 to 60. That summer, those who remained were found fleeing down river to return home to England by new settlers with fresh supplies who encouraged them to reconsider. This was Virginia's "starving time," to use Charles Andrews's vivid label.

Inadequately supplied and untutored in the art of colonization, the earliest frontier pioneers routinely suffered and died. In 1623, a royal inves-

---

[1]At this time, the name *Virginia* referred to all the territory claimed by the English on the North American continent. Early charters indicate that the area lay between the thirty-fourth and the forty-fifth parallels, roughly between the southern portion of the Carolinas and the northernmost boundary of New York.

tigation of the Virginia experience was launched in the wake of an Indian attack that took the lives of 500 settlers. The investigation reported that of the 6,000 who had migrated to Virginia since 1607, 4,000 had died. The life expectancy of these hardy settlers upon arriving was two years.

The heavy human costs of first settlement were accompanied by substantial capital losses. Without exception, the earliest colonial ventures were unprofitable. Indeed, they were financial disasters. Neither the principle nor the interest on the Virginia Company's accumulated investments of more than £200,000 were ever repaid.[2] The investments in New England were less disappointing, but overall, English capitalists were heavy losers in their quest to tame the frontier.

EARLY REFORMS

Nevertheless, the lessons of these first settlements proved useful in later ventures, and colonization continued with only intermittent lapses throughout the seventeenth and eighteenth centuries. Because North America rendered no early discoveries of gold or silver mines or ancient populations prepared to exchange exotic wares, trading-post establishments characteristic of the European outposts in South America and the Orient proved inadequate. North America's frontier demanded a more permanent form of settlement. For this to result without continuous company or Crown subsidization, the discovery of "cash crops" or other items that could be produced in the colonies and exchanged commercially was essential. Consequently, the production of tobacco, rice, and the expansion of many other economic activities we will discuss in Chapter 3 proved vital in giving deep roots and permanent features to British settlement in North America. In addition, substantial organizational changes were made to increase production efficiency. The joint-stock company arrangement, which facilitated the raising of capital and which had served the British well in other areas of the world, faltered when forced to conform to the conditions in North America. Modeled after such great eastern trading companies as the East India Company, new companies—including the London Company, the New Plymouth Company, the Massachusetts Bay Company, and others—must receive credit for establishing the first British settlements in the New World. But their success was limited merely to securing a colonial foothold. With the exceptions of the Hudson Bay Company (founded in 1670 and still in operation today) and the unique Georgia experiment in the late colonial period, the joint-stock company (with absentee direction from England) survived less than two decades in British North America.

The ordeals of the Jamestown experience forcefully accent the difficulties encountered and the adjustments required by the early settlers. The

[2]A very rough approximation of this amount would be $20,000,000 in today's values.

colony originally operated as a collective unit, in which both production methods and consumption were shared. But collectivity encouraged individuals to work less and resulted in much discontent. Unmarried men complained of working without recompense for other men's wives and children. Stronger, more able workers were embittered when they did not receive greater amounts of food and supplies than others who could or would not work as hard. In addition, common ownership stifled incentives to care for and improve lands and to make innovations in production.

In addition, absentee direction from England created problems, because successful production required local managerial direction. Futilely insistent demands from England for quick profits sidetracked productive effort and added to the settlers' discouragement.

Jamestown residents gained greater control over local matters in 1609 and again in 1612 when various institutional reforms were undertaken. Planter memberships were created, so that company shares became based on labor input as well as capital contributions. To generate more flexible leadership and local autonomy in that hostile environment, a deputy governor was stationed in Virginia. Steadily thereafter, centralized direction from England became less and less frequent.

Similarly, private landholdings swiftly replaced common ownership arrangements, and attitudes and work incentives improved as the full return for individual effort became a reality, superseding output sharing arrangements. In 1614, private landholdings of three acres were allowed. A second and more significant step toward private property came in 1618 with the establishment of the *headright* system. Under this system, any settler who paid his own way to Virginia was given 50 acres and another 50 acres for anyone else whose transportation he paid. In 1623—only 16 years after the first Jamestown settlers had arrived—all landholdings were converted to private ownership. The royal investigation of that year also ushered in the dissolutions of the corporate form of the colony. In 1625, Virginia was converted to a Crown colony.

Many of the difficulties experienced in early Jamestown were also felt elsewhere in the colonies. But the Puritan settlements of New England, first at Plymouth (the Plymouth Company, 1620) then at Boston (the Massachusetts Bay Company, 1630), avoided some common problems faced by most settlers. For instance, because the Massachusetts Bay Company actually carried its own charter to the New World, it avoided costly direction and absentee control from England. Moreover, although considerable amounts of New England land were commonly owned, collective production and shared consumption were less forcefully imposed. Stronger social and cultural cohesion and more homogeneous religious beliefs contributed to the greater relative success of communal arrangements there. Furthermore, town corporations prolonged the use of common landholdings. Nevertheless, private landholdings steadily replaced land held in common, and by 1650, privately owned family farms were predominant in New England.

Another noteworthy colony established by a joint-stock venture was New York, first settled by the Dutch West India Company (1620), but taken in a bloodless confrontation in 1664 by the British. Maryland and Pennsylvania were initiated through proprietary grants, respectively to Lord Baltimore in 1634 and to William Penn in 1681. The former's desire was to create a haven for Roman Catholics, profitably if possible, and the latter's was the same for Quakers and other persecuted religious groups. Rhode Island's settlement was also religiously motivated due to Roger Williams' banishment from Puritan Massachusetts in 1644. These, the Carolinas, and the last mainland colony to be settled, Georgia (1733), benefited from the many hardships and lessons provided by the earlier settlements. Despite each colony's organizational form, the Crown assured all settlers except slaves the rights due English citizens. The British empire in North America extended from French Canada to Spanish Florida and through to the sugar plantation islands of the Caribbean.

Bringing in Settlers

Despite the magnetic lure of cheap available land, favorable climate and comparative freedom, the Atlantic Ocean posed a great barrier to settlement in North America. In the early seventeenth century, the Atlantic passage was £9 to £10 per person. Throughout most of the later colonial period, the peacetime costs of passage were £5 to £6, nearly a half year's earnings. Consequently, in the seventeenth century, a majority of European newcomers did not pay their own way to America. They came in voluntary bondage as indentured servants.

The *indenture contract* was a device that enabled people to pay for their passage to America by selling their labor to someone in the New World for a specified period of time. These contracts were written in a variety of forms, but law and custom made them similar. Generally speaking, prospective immigrants would sign articles of indenture binding them to a period of service that varied from three to seven years, although four years was probably the most common term. Typically, an indenturer signed with a shipowner or a recruiting agent in England. As soon as the servant was delivered alive at an American port, the contract was sold to a planter or merchant. These contracts typically sold for £10 to £11 in the eighteenth century, nearly double the cost of passage. Indentured servants, thus bound, performed any work their "employers" demanded in exchange for room, board, and certain "freedom dues" of money or land that were received at the end of the period of indenture. This provided an active trade in human talent, and the indentured system should be viewed as an investment in migration as well as in job training (or apprenticeship).

The indentured servants were drawn from a wide spectrum of European society, from the ranks of farmers and unskilled workers, artisans, domestic servants, and others. Most came without specialized skills, but except for the few who were illegally kidnapped, they came to America voluntarily. This is perfectly understandable, because the likelihood of rising to the status of landowner was very low in Britain or on the Continent.

Whether the life of a servant was hard or easy depended primarily on the temperament of the taskmaster; the courts usually protected indentured servants from extreme cruelty, but the law could also be applied quickly to apprehend and return servants who ran away. The usual punishment for runaways was an extension of the contract period. Of course, the indentures' work conditions also depended on location and duration of service. Generally, the less healthful living areas such as the islands of the Caribbean offered shorter contractual periods of work than did the mainland colonies. And the more skilled and literate workers also obtained shorter contracts, as a rule. Overall it was a highly competitive labor market system steeped in rational conduct.

Recent work by David Galenson, Robert Heavener, and Farley Grubb reveal much of the intricacies of this market in bonded labor. For example, immigrants from continental Europe, mainly Germans, usually came as redemptioners, immigrants brought over on credit provided by ship captains. They were allowed a short period of time to repay the captain after arrival either by borrowing from a relative or a friend or by self contracting for their services. Because they usually arrived with no ready contacts and typically could not speak English, their contract period was generally longer, often six to seven years. In addition, German immigrants usually came over in families whereas English migrants were typically single and more likely to enter into indentured servitude. The longer period of service for German redemptioners also was in part a consequence of their preference to be very selective in choosing their master-employer, a right indentured servants did not have. Migrating in family groups encouraged this preference, and most Germans mainly settled in Pennsylvania.

As the decades passed, the percentage of European immigrants arriving as indentures or redemptioners declined. The costs of passage slowly fell over time, and the earnings of workers in Europe rose. In addition, the indentured period for women was originally shorter than for men, due to their greater scarcity in the colonies, but by the turn of the eighteenth century, the periods of service were comparable for both sexes. Overall, perhaps as many as one-half of European immigrants came as bonded servants, destined primarily for the colonies north of Virginia.

The counterpoint to white servitude—slavery—did not become an important source of labor until after 1650, although slaves were imported in increasing numbers after 1620. By 1700, slavery had become a firmly established institution from Maryland southward. Slaveholding was not unknown in New England and the Middle colonies, but it never firmly took hold there for several reasons.

Rarely was a slave in the South unable to work due to the rigors of bad weather, whereas working outdoors in the North could be impossible for days at a time. Also important was the fact that tobacco, then rice, and finally indigo were the staple crops of the South. Because they required much unskilled labor that could be performed under limited supervision in work groups, these cash crops were especially suited to cultivation by slaves. As in the huge sugar plantations of the Caribbean islands, large-scale farm units made slavery particularly profitable, and the size of farms became much larger in the South than in the Middle or New England colonies. The crops, especially rice and indigo, and the slave system itself generated *economies of scale* and fostered larger production units of team labor under supervision. Economies of scale occur when output expands relative to inputs (land, labor, and capital) as the production unit gets larger. Also *primogeniture,* a form of inheritance in which the land is transferred to the oldest son, prevailed in the Southern colonies. In the Middle and New England colonies, a more equal division was typically followed with the oldest son receiving only a double portion. Over time primogeniture perpetuated and built larger estates, comparatively. Also, the purchase of imported slaves in the South triggered the headright to land of 50 acres per slave purchased, reinforcing the growth in the size of farm units there. Finally, the mere momentum of the growth of slavery in the South was accompanied by moral and institutional adaptations to sustain it.

Unlike the indentured whites, African slaves were not protected in the colonies as British subjects. Terms of service were for life, and children of female slaves were born slaves regardless of who fathered the child. Only by self-purchase or benevolence could a slave become free. In 1774, there were nearly 500,000 blacks in the colonies, 18,000 of whom were free.

As we have emphasized, those coming to America on their own resources received 50 acres of land from headright land grants in most colonies. However, not only land but relatively high wages as well attracted workers to the colonies. Especially in the seaports, craftsmen and artisans of all sorts, merchants and seamen, even scholars gave vibrance to the commercial life on western Atlantic shores. Finally prisoners too, perhaps as many as 30,000, avoided the death sentence or indefinite imprisonment in England by voluntarily transporting themselves to the New World. After 1718 it was customary for convicts to serve 7 years of indenture for minor crimes and 14 years for major ones.

DEMOGRAPHIC CHANGE

Underpopulation Despite High Rate of Population Growth

One major fact of American economic life—underpopulation and labor scarcity—persisted throughout the entire colonial period. Another extremely important aspect of British colonization and a crucial factor in securing and maintaining Britain's hold on the North American frontier was the extremely high rate of population growth in the colonies. What generated the characteristic of apparent underpopulation was the vast amount of available land, which "thinned" the population spatially and established high population densities in only a few major port towns. This occurred despite the exceptionally high rate of growth, which was so high—the population approximately doubled every 25 years—that Thomas Malthus worrisomely referred to it as "a rapidity of increase, probably without parallel in history." Malthus and others pointed to the American colonies as a prime example of virtually unchecked population growth. Wouldn't such a rate of increase, which was twice the population growth rate in Europe, ultimately lead to famine, pestilence, and doom? Wasn't it an obvious truism that the aggregate supply of land—essential to food production—was fixed in amount?

Yes, but these European polemics were far from the minds of the colonists. Indeed, Benjamin Franklin wrote an essay in 1751 extolling the virtues of rapid population increases in the colonies. Overpopulation never resulted in the colonies, despite the various methods that were used to encourage or force (in the case of African captives) population relocation to the New World. Nor did the high natural rate of population increase create population pressures in the colonies; population growth was generally viewed as a sign of progress and a means of reducing the uncertainties, risks, and hazards of a sparsely populated frontier region.

Population Growth in British North America

The broad trends of population growth from both migration and natural causes are illustrated by region in Figure 2-1. Note that there is a remarkable similarity in the timing, rise, and levels of the total populations in New England and the upper South. The latecomers—the Middle colonies and the lower South—displayed somewhat higher growth rates, which allowed them to catch up somewhat. The rate of population expansion was quite steady for the colonies as a whole, slightly over 3 percent per year.

The period of greatest absolute migration occurred in the eighteenth century—particularly after 1720, when between 100,000 and 125,000 Scotch-Irish and about 100,000 Germans arrived in North America. Most immigrants in the seventeenth century were British, and there was another strong surge of British migration between 1768 and 1775. Perhaps as many as 300,000 white immigrants came to the New World between 1700 and 1775, and a similar number of blacks came as well. Plenty of highly fertile land and a favorable climate attracted Europeans and provided motives for securing African slaves. Nevertheless, migration was the dominant source of population growth in only the first decades of settlement in each region.

In New England immigration virtually halted in the late 1640s and natural causes were the source of population growth after 1650. For areas settled later, such as Pennsylvania, the forces of migration remained dominant later, but natural forces swiftly took over even there. Even the enslaved black population grew swiftly and predominantly from natural sources after

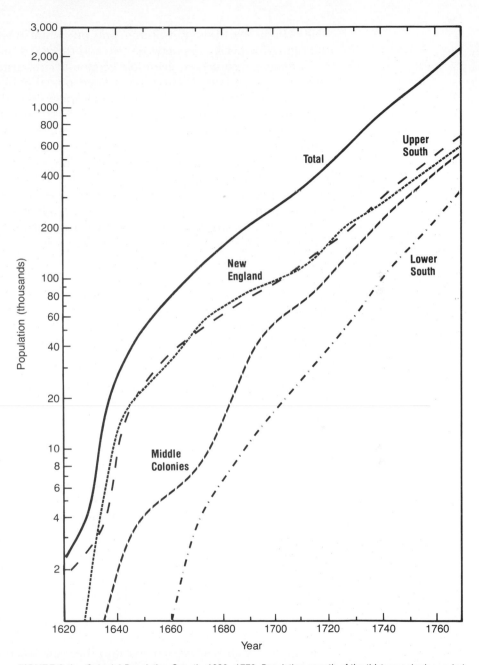

FIGURE 2-1   Colonial Population Growth, 1620–1770: Population growth of the thirteen colonies varied
among regions, but was very similar in New England and the upper South. Overall, the
rate of expansion was steady after 1650. Note: New England—Maine, Massachusetts,
Connecticut, Vermont, Rhode Island, New Hampshire; Middle Colonies—New York, Pennsylvania, New Jersey, Delaware; Upper South—Virginia, Maryland; Lower South—North
Carolina, South Carolina, and Georgia.

Source: U.S. Bureau of the Census, *Historical Statistics of the United States, Colonial Times to 1957* (Washington, D.C.: GPO,
1960), p. 756.

1700. On the eve of the Revolution, only one white in ten was foreign born; the figure for blacks was between two and three in ten.

Commercial successes, favorable economic circumstances, and the high value of labor powered a high rate of reproduction in the colonies. White birth rates in North America per 1,000 women ranged between 45 and 50 per year, compared to near 30 in Europe or 12 per 1,000 in the United States today. The colonial population was exceptionally young. By the 1770s, 57 percent were under the age of 21. Moreover, a higher percentage of its population was of childbearing age. Typically, colonial women tended to marry rather early—between the ages of 20 and 23, which was a couple of years younger than the average European. The cheapness of land encouraged early marriage in the colonies, and generally, it was easier for colonists than for Europeans to strike out on their own, acquire land, and set up a household. Childbearing was a major cause of death for women, and many men remarried to sustain their families. The average European married man produced four or five children, but earlier marriages and higher proportions of mothers in their childbearing years resulted in an average colonial family of about seven to eight children. Greater emphasis on rural economic activity also encouraged higher birthrates in the colonies. Children were more costly to raise in urban areas, and their labor contribution tended to be less there.

Also of great significance was the fact that once the first few years of starvation had passed, the colonies experienced rather low mortality rates. The annual death rate in Europe was about 40 per 1,000 people; in the colonies, it was 20–25 per 1,000.

The lower age structure of the colonial population accounts in part for this, but the exceptionally low rate of child mortality was an even more impressive statistic. On the average, white mothers in the colonies were better fed and housed than mothers in Europe. Consequently, colonial babies were healthier. The harsh winters of North America and the inferior medical technology of the frontier were more than offset by plentiful food supplies, fuel, and housing. And because the population was predominantly rural, epidemics were rare in the colonies.

Once past infancy, white colonial males typically lived to be 60 or more. Due to the hazards of childbirth, however, the comparable age for early colonial women was normally slightly over 40.[3]

The Racial Profile

Six percent of all slaves imported into the New World came to areas that became the United States. As shown in Figure 2-2, migration was the initiating force of population growth of blacks. By the eighteenth century,

---

[3]Although perhaps atypical, evidence presented by Philip Graven, "Family Structure in Seventeenth Century Andover Massachusetts," *William and Mary Quarterly* (April 1966), pp. 234–56, shows women also living into their sixties in that area.

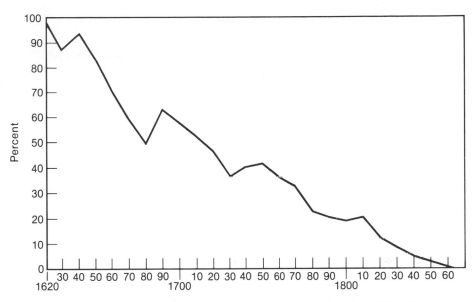

FIGURE 2-2   Foreign-born Blacks as a Percentage of the U.S. Black Population, 1620–1860

Source: Robert W. Fogel and Stanley L. Engerman, *Time on the Cross,* 1 (Boston: Little, Brown, 1974) p. 23.

however, natural forces dominated the growth of the black population. By mid-century the birth rate of blacks, similar to that of whites, was near the biological maximum. Death rates were also similar to that of whites in North America. Because the natural rate of increase was comparable for both races—which resulted in a doubling of the population nearly every 20–25 years—and because the actual number of imported slaves practically equaled the number of white immigrants, the proportion of the total population that was black increased significantly after 1700. In 1670, only about 4 percent of the total population was black. This proportion had increased to almost 20 percent 100 years later. In 1774, the black population was near one-half million.

Of course, regional differences were great, and over 90 percent of the slaves resided in southern regions. As Figure 2-3 indicates, however, relatively small proportions of the total population of the mainland colonies were composed of blacks, compared to the Caribbean islands. In New England the proportion of blacks was in the neighborhood of 2 percent; in the Middle colonies, 5 percent. In Maryland in the late colonial years, blacks comprised 32 percent of the total population; in Virginia, 42 percent. The more limited commercial development in North Carolina, due to inadequate harbors, generated a black population proportion of only 35 percent. In contrast, South Carolina contained the largest concentration of blacks— 60 percent. This especially high proportion in South Carolina resulted from the special advantages of slave labor and economies of scale in rice and indigo production. Consequently, the social profile of South Carolina suggested by its high concentration of enslaved blacks was similar to the profiles

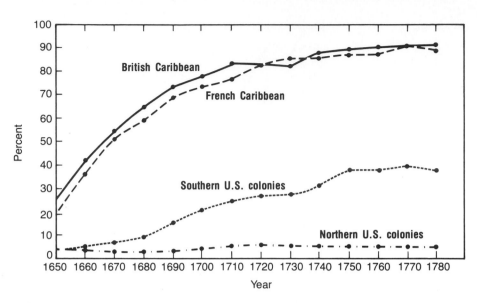

FIGURE 2-3   Blacks as a Percentage of the Total Population, 1650–1780: The population profile was much different on the North American continent than in the islands of the Caribbean. Only in South Carolina did the black population outnumber the resident white population.

Source: Robert W. Fogel and Stanley L. Engerman, *Time on the Cross,* 1 (Boston: Little, Brown, 1974), p. 21.

of the British and French West Indies sugar islands. Although Virginia's population profile did approach this proportion, South Carolina's profile of a majority of slaves controlled by a minority of plantation owners was unique among the mainland colonies. In contrast to their Caribbean counterparts, blacks typically remained a minority race on the mainland of North America.

Finally, the pattern of change for the native American population was in sharp contrast to that of whites and blacks. At the time Jamestown was founded, it was likely that as many as 300,000 Indians lived within 150 miles of the Atlantic seaboard. By the mid-eighteenth century the impact of battle, and especially the devastation of such communicable diseases as smallpox and measles, against which the natives had developed no immunity, reduced the population to nearly 50,000. This depopulation aspect was unique among North Americans, whatever skin color.

Spatial Distribution of the Population

The period from the founding of Jamestown to the first inauguration of President Washington is about equal to the span of time from our beginnings as a nation under the Constitution to the present. It took 50 years to secure a firm hold on the new continent, and at the end of the first century of colonial history, settlement of the eastern seaboard was far from complete. By 1660, Virginia, Maryland, and Massachusetts were established commonwealths, but the first settlers in Georgia did not move there for almost another 75 years. In 1640, perhaps 25,000 white people inhabited the English colonies on the mainland; by 1660, there were 80,000 colonists, and by 1690, 200,000. After 1690, population growth remained spectacular. From over one-third of a million people in 1710, the white colonial population had increased to about 2.18 million on the eve of the Revolution.

Map 2-2 shows the extent of settlement as of 1660, 1700, and 1760. Before 1660, there was nothing to speak of south of Norfolk, and at the turn of the century a wilderness still separated Charleston and its environs from the major inhabited area in upper North Carolina. By 1760, the land-hungry rich and poor had spread over nearly all of the coastal plain and into the Piedmont areas. As early as 1726, Germans and Scotch-Irish had begun moving into the Shenandoah Valley, and down this and the other great valleys in ever-increasing numbers, settlers sought the cheap land to the west. Through gaps in the mountains some turned east into the Piedmont area of Virginia and the Carolinas; only a few years later pioneers began to trickle to the west, particularly through the Cumberland Gap into Kentucky and Tennessee.

Imperial Rivalries in North America

The rivalry of empires persisted for a long time and the growth of population and the colonization of new territory were not restricted to the eastern coast of North America. During the sixteenth century, Spain had occupied northern Mexico and Florida, and while English settlement was taking place, the Spanish were moving northward into Texas, southern Arizona, and southern California. As we have already mentioned, in the seventeenth century, France established bases in the Lesser Antilles and in Canada, and from Canada, French explorers and traders pushed into the Mississippi Valley and on to the Gulf of Mexico. The three rival states were bound to clash in America, even if they had not been enemies in other parts of the world. To the general historian, we must leave the descriptions of these bitter rivalries and of the resulting complex, if small-scale, wars. Following intermittent conflict between the French and the English in the northeast and along most of the western frontier, the French and Indian War resulted in the temporary downfall of the French in North America. By the Treaty of 1763, only Spain and England were left in possession of the North American continent. Spain took all the territory west of the Mississippi, and England secured everything to the east, with the exception of certain fishing rights and small islands retained by the French off Newfoundland. According to this agreement, England acquired all of Florida, thereby settling perennial disputes with Spain that had long disturbed the colonies of South Carolina and Georgia. It is difficult to remember that Spain, not France, harassed the pioneers who moved out of the original thirteen colonies and into the old Southwest. Not until 1800, did France again own the Territory of Louisiana and its vital port of New Orleans, and that control did not last long.

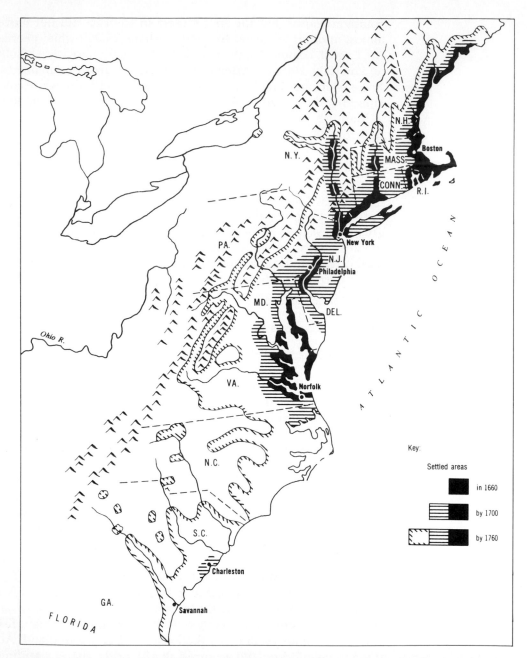

MAP 2-2   Settlement: Easily accessible coastal regions and river valleys provided the first sites for settlements, but settlers soon moved into the Piedmont areas, the great valleys of the Appalachians, and the inviting country of the mountains.

SELECTED REFERENCES AND SUGGESTED READINGS

Alston, Lee J., and Morton O. Shapiro. "Inheritance Laws Across the Colonies: Causes and Consequences." *Journal of Economic History* 44 (1984):277–87.

Anderson, Terry, and Robert P. Thomas. "The Growth of Population and Labor Force in the 17th-Century Chesapeake." *Explorations in Economic History* 15 (1978): 290–312.

———. "White Population, Labor Force, and Extensive Growth of the New England Economy in the Seventeenth Century." *Journal of Economic History* 33 (1973):634–67.

Andrews, Charles M. *The Colonial Period of American History.* New Haven: Yale Univ. Press, 1934.

Bancroft, George. *History of the United States of America from the Discovery of the Continent.* 6 vols. Boston: Little, Brown, 1879.

Boorstin, Daniel. *The Americans: The Colonial Experience.* New York: Vintage Books, 1958.

Bruce, Philip A. *Economic History of Virginia in the Seventeenth Century.* 2 vols. New York: Macmillan, 1896.

Bruchey, Stuart. *The Roots of American Economic Growth 1607–1861: An Essay in Social Causation.* London: Hutchinson Univ. Library, 1965.

Curtin, Philip. *The Atlantic Slave Trade: A Census.* Madison: Univ. of Wisconsin Press, 1969.

Earle, Carville. *The Evolution of a Tidewater Settlement System: All Hallow's Parish, 1650–1783.* Chicago: Univ. of Chicago Press, 1975.

Fogel, Robert, and Stanley Engerman. *Time on the Cross: The Economics of American Negro Slavery.* Boston: Little, Brown, 1974. Ch. 1.

Franklin, Benjamin. "Observations Concerning the Increase of Mankind." Philadelphia, 1751. In *The Papers of Ben Franklin,* ed., Leonard Laberee. New Haven: Yale Univ. Press, 1961.

Galenson, David W. "British Servants and the Colonial Indenture System in the Eighteenth Century." *Journal of Southern History* 44 (1978):41–66.

———. "Immigration and the Colonial Labor System: An Analysis of the Length of Indenture." *Explorations in Economic History* 14 (1977):361–77.

———. "The Market Evaluation of Human Capital: The Case of Indentured Servitude." *Journal of Political Economy* 89 (1981):446–67.

———. "The Rise and Fall of Indentured Servitude in the Americas: An Economic Analysis." *Journal of Economic History* 44 (1984):1–26.

———. *White Servitude in Colonial America.* Cambridge: Cambridge Univ. Press, 1981.

Gemery, Henry. "Emigration from the British Isles to the New World, 1630–1700." In *Research in Economic History,* ed., Paul Uselding. New York: Johnson, 1980, 5:179–232.

Grubb, Farley. "Colonial Labor Markets and the Length of Indenture: Further Evidence." *Explorations in Economic History* 24 (1987):101–106.

———. "Immigrant Servant Labor: Their Occupational and Geographic Distribution in the Late Eighteenth-Century Mid-Atlantic Economy." *Social Science History* 9 (1985):249–75.

———. "The Incidence of Servitude in Trans-Atlantic Migration, 1771–1804." *Explorations in Economic History* 22 (1985):316–39.

———. "The Market for Indentured Immigrants: Evidence on the Efficiency of Forward-Labor Contracting in Philadelphia, 1745–1773." *Journal of Economic History* 45 (1985):855–68.

———. "Redemption Immigration to Pennsylvania: Evidence on Contract Choice and Profitability." *Journal of Economic History* 46 (1986):407–18.

Heavener, Robert. "Indentured Servitude: The Philadelphia Market, 1771–1773." *Journal of Economic History* 38 (1978):701–13.

Higgs, Robert, and Louis Stettler. "Colonial New England Demography: A Sampling Approach." *William and Mary Quarterly* 27, no. 2 (1970):282–94.

Hughes, Jonathan R .T. "William Penn and the Holy Experiment." *The Vital Few: American Economic History and Its Protagonists.* New York: Oxford Univ. Press, 1973 (reprint), Ch. 2.

Kulikoff, Allan. "A 'Prolifick' People: Black Population Growth in the Chesapeake Colonies, 1700–1790." *Southern Studies* (1977):391–428.

Lemon, James. *The Best Poor Man's Country: A Geographical Study of Early Southeastern Pennsylvania.* Baltimore: Johns Hopkins Univ. Press, 1972.

Menard, Russell. "From Servants to Slaves: The Transformation of the Chesapeake Labor System." *Southern Studies* (1977):355–90.

Morgan, Edmund S. *American Slavery, American Freedom: The Ordeal of Colonial Virginia.* New York: W. W. Norton, 1975.

———. "The First American Boom: Virginia 1618 to 1630." *William and Mary Quarterly* 28 (1971).

———. *The Puritan Family: Religion and Domestic Relations in Seventeenth-Century New England.* New York: Harper & Row, 1966.

Morison, Samuel E. *The Oxford History of the American People.* New York: Oxford Univ. Press, 1964.

Morris, Richard. *Government and Labor in Early America.* New York: Columbia Univ. Press, 1946.

Nash, Gary. *Red, White, and Black: The Peoples of Early America.* Englewood Cliffs, N.J.: Prentice-Hall, 1974.

North, Douglass C. and R. P. Thomas. *The Rise of the Western World.* New York: Cambridge Univ. Press, 1973.

Perkins, Edwin J. *The Economy of Colonial America,* 2nd ed. New York: Columbia Univ. Press, 1988. Ch. 1.

Potter, Jim. "The Growth of Population in America, 1700–1860." In *Population in History: Essays in Historical Demography,* ed. D. V. Glass and B. E. C. Eaversley. Chicago: Aldine, 1960.

Powell, Sumner C. *Puritan Village: The Formation of a New England Town.* Middletown, Conn.: Wesleyan Univ. Press, 1963.

Rink, Oliver. *Holland on the Hudson: An Economic and Social History of New York.* Ithaca, N.Y.: Cornell Univ. Press, 1986.

Rosenberg, Nathan, and L. E. Birdzell, Jr. *How the West Grew Rich.* New York: Basic Books, 1986. Ch. 3.

Smith, Abbot E. *Colonists in Bondage: White Servitude and Convict Labor in America, 1607–1776.* Chapel Hill: Univ. of North Carolina Press, 1947.

Smith, Billy G. "Death and Life in a Colonial Immigrant City: A Demographic Analysis of Philadelphia." *Journal of Economic History* 38 (1977):863–89.

Smith, Daniel S. "The Demographic History of Colonial New England." *Journal of Economic History* 32 (1972):165–83.

———. "The Estimates of Early American Historical Demographers: Two Steps Forward, One Step Back, What Steps in the Future." *Historical Methods* (1979): 24–38.

Thomas, Robert P., and Richard Bean. "The Adoption of Slave Labor in British America." In *The Uncommon Market: Essays in the Economic History of the Atlantic Slave Trade,* ed., H. Genery and J. Hogendorn. New York: Academic Press, 1978.

Ver Steeg, Clarence. *The Formative Years, 1607–1763.* New York: Hill & Wang, 1964.

Walton, Gary M., and James F. Shepherd. *The Economic Rise of Early America.* Cambridge: Cambridge Univ. Press, 1979. Ch. 2.

Weeden, William B. *Economic and Social History of New England, 1620–1789.* 2 vols. Boston: Houghton Mifflin, 1890.

Wells, Robert V. *The Population of the British Colonies in America before 1776: A Survey of Census Data.* Princeton: Princeton Univ. Press, 1975.

CHAPTER 3

Colonial Economic Activities

ECONOMIC OPPORTUNITIES AND RESTRAINTS

It is merely a coincidence that in 1732, when Mr. Fry was selling his accounting books and poetry books in Boston, plans for the last British colony to
be settled in North America were being made. The colonization of Georgia
provides a vivid example of good intentions pitted against the economic
realities of opportunities and restraints.

Like Pennsylvania and Massachusetts, Georgia was founded to assist those
who had been beset with troubles in the Old World. Together with a group
of associates, Dr. Thomas Bray, an Anglican clergyman noted for his good
works, was persuaded by General James Edward Oglethorpe to attempt a
project for the relief of people condemned to prison for debt. This particular social evil of eighteenth-century England cried out to be remedied,
because debtors could spend years in horrible prisons of the time without
hope of escape except through organized charitable institutions. As long as
individuals were incarcerated, they were unable to earn any money to pay
their debts, and even if they were eventually released, years of imprisonment could make them unfit for work. It was Oglethorpe's idea to encourage
debtors to come to America, where they might become responsible and
even substantial citizens.

In addition to their wish to aid the "urban wretches" of England, Bray,
Oglethorpe, and their associates had another primary motivation, namely,
to secure a military buffer zone between the prosperous northern English
settlements and Spanish Florida. Besides their moral repugnance to slavery,
they believed that an all-white population was needed for security reasons.
It was doubtful that slaves could be depended on to fight, and with slavery,
rebellion was always a possibility. Therefore slavery was prohibited in Georgia—initially.

In 1732, King George II obligingly granted Dr. Bray and his associates
the land between the Savannah and the Altamaha rivers; the original tract
included considerably less territory than the modern state of Georgia. By
royal charter, a corporation was created that was to be governed by a group

of trustees; after 21 years, the territory was to revert to the Crown. Financed by both private and public funds, the venture had an auspicious beginning. Oglethorpe himself led the first contingent of several hundred immigrants—mostly debtors—to the new country, where a 50-acre farm awaited each colonist. Substantially larger grants were available to free settlers with families, and determined efforts were made, both on the Continent and in the British Isles, to secure colonists.

Unfortunately, the ideals and hopes of the trustees clashed with economic reality. Although "the Georgia experiment" was a modest success as a philanthropic enterprise, its economic development was to prove disappointing for many decades. The climate in the low coastal country—where the fertile land lay—was unhealthy and generated higher death rates than in areas farther north. As the scholarly work of Ralph Gray and Betty Wood has shown, since slavery was prohibited by the trustees, it was impossible to introduce the rice and indigo plantations in Georgia that were so profitable in South Carolina, and the 50-acre tracts given the charity immigrants were too small to achieve economies of scale and competitive levels of efficiency for commercial production.

Unable to secure the desired buffer state by attracting a sufficient number of whites without continuous subsidy and given the attractive potential profits of slave-operated plantation enterprises, the trustees eventually bowed to economic forces. By mid-century slavery was legalized and slaves were pouring into Georgia, which was converted to a Crown colony in 1751. By 1770, 45 percent of the population there was black.

This particular example of social-economic engineering reveals a wider truth: colonial economic freedoms were severely restrained—not merely by man-made laws or ordinances, but by the conditions of nature and the economic setting as well. Colonial production capabilities were determined and limited by the available factors of production—land and natural resources, capital, and labor—by the technology of the period, and by other influences such as economic organization and frontier hazards. The most distinctive characteristic of production in the colonies throughout the entire colonial period is that land and natural resources were plentiful, but labor and capital were exceedingly scarce, both absolutely and relatively. This relationship among the factors of production explains many institutional arrangements and patterns of regional development in the colonies.

Land and Natural Resource Abundance, Labor Shortage

Throughout the history of the British colonies, most people depended on the land for a livelihood. From New Hampshire to Georgia, agriculture was the chief occupation, and what industrial and commercial activity there was revolved almost entirely around materials extracted from the land, the forests, and the ocean. Where soil and climate were unfavorable to the cultivation of commercial crops, it was often possible to turn to fishing or trapping and to the production of ships, ship timbers, and naval stores. Land was seemingly limitless in extent and therefore not highly priced, but almost every colonist wanted to be a landholder. When we remember that ownership of land signified wealth and position to the European, this is not hard to understand. The ever-present desire for land explains why for the first century and a half of our history, many immigrants who might have been successful artisans or laborers in someone else's employ tended instead to turn to agriculture, thereby aggravating the persistent scarcity of labor in the New World. A shortage of workers with highly developed skills was most notable, because artisans and trained craftsmen in great demand in Europe were too content at home to be tempted even by substantially higher wages into a life of hardship at the very bounds of civilization. But all types of labor were generally scarce, because the high ratio of land to labor assured independent farmers fairly comfortable material standards of living once many of the early frontier hazards had been overcome.

Capital Shortages

Items of physical capital for production were in limited supply in the aggregate, especially during the first century of settlement. Particular forms of capital goods that could be obtained from natural resources with simple tools were in apparent abundance. For instance, so much wood was available that it was fairly easy to build houses, barns, and workshops. Wagons and carriages were largely made of wood, as were farm implements, wheels, gears, and shafts. Shipyards and shipways were also constructed from timber, and ships were built in quantity from an early date.

Alternatively, metal products were especially scarce, and mills and other industrial facilities remained few and small. Work on roads and harbors lagged far behind European standards until the end of the colonial period. Capital formation was a primary challenge to the colonists, and the colonies always needed much more capital than was ever available to them. English political leaders promoted legislation that hindered the export of tools and machinery from the home country. Moreover, English or colonials who had money to invest often preferred the safer investment in British firms, which were just beginning to thrive. But, as we shall see in Chapter 5, after all these considerations the fact remains that residents of the developing American colonies lived better lives in the eighteenth century than most other people, even in the most advanced nations of the time.

THE DOMINANCE OF AGRICULTURE

Generally, high ratios of land and other natural resources to labor generated exceptionally high levels of output per worker in the colonies. As late as the end of the eighteenth century, approximately 90 percent of the American people earned a major portion of their living by farming compared to about 3 percent today.

Most production in the New World was for the colonists' own consumption, but sizable proportions of colonial goods and services were produced for commercial exchange. In time, each region became increasingly specialized in the production of particular goods and services. Areas of specialization were largely determined by particular soil types, the climate, and the natural resource bounties of the forests and ocean.

The Southern Colonies

In terms of value of output, southern agriculture was dominant throughout the colonial period and well into the nineteenth century. The southern colonies present us with a good example of the comparative advantage that fertile new land can offer. Almost at the outset, settlers in the South grew tobacco that was both cheaper to produce and, before long, of better quality than the tobacco grown in most other parts of the world. Later the South began to produce two other staples—rice and indigo—and just after the Revolutionary War, a third—cotton. For nearly two and a half centuries, the southern economy was to revolve around a few export staples, because the soil and climate of the region provided the South with a pronounced advantage in the cultivation of crops that were in great demand in the populous industrializing areas of Europe.

Throughout the entire colonial period the southern colonies were especially important to the English. Unlike the commodities of the other colonies, very little that the South exported competed with British production, either in the Isles or in the rest of the Empire. Not that the lands and climate of Maryland, Virginia, the Carolinas, and Georgia were ideal in all respects. There was always the hope to produce more than ever materialized. For example, it was known that grapes would grow well in the South, and every effort was made to encourage the production of wines then being imported from France and Spain. But the quality of American wines was so poor that serious attempts to compete with established wine-producing areas were abandoned. Similarly, it was hoped that silk and hemp—two much-needed fibers—could be produced in quantity, and bounties and premiums were offered for their production; but again, quality was inferior, and high wage rates resulted in a high-cost product.

Tobacco   Tobacco, as we have noted, was exported from Virginia to England within a decade after the settlement of Jamestown. The weed had been known in Europe for over a century; sailors on the first voyages of exploration had brought back samples and descriptions of the ways in which natives had used it. Despite much opposition on moral grounds, smoking had increased in popularity during the sixteenth century; thus, even though James I viewed it "so vile and stinking a custom," it was a relief to the English to find a source of supply so that tobacco importation from the Spanish would be unnecessary. Tobacco needed a long growing season and fertile soil. Furthermore, it could be cultivated in small areas, on only partly cleared fields, and with the most rudimentary implements. All this suited the primitive Virginia community. But there were two additional advantages to tobacco production in the colonies. As successive plantings exhausted the original fertility of a particular plot, new land was readily available, and ships could move up the rivers of the Virginia coast to load their cargoes at the plantation docks. One marked disadvantage that lingered for most of the seventeenth century was that the colonists had much to learn about the proper curing, handling, and shipping of tobacco, and for many years the American product was inferior to tobacco produced in Spain. Nevertheless, colonial tobacco was protected in the English market, and the fact that it was cheaper led to steady increases in its portion of the tobacco market. The culture of tobacco spread northward around the Chesapeake Bay and moved up the many river valleys. By the end of the seventeenth century, there was some production in North Carolina.

During the early years of the seventeenth century, Spanish tobacco sold in England for an average retail price of about 40 shillings per pound. When Virginia tobacco was first marketed, it commanded 4–8 shillings per pound, and until 1627 the consensus was that a price of around 3 shillings per pound could be maintained. At that price, the production of tobacco was so profitable that colonists could scarcely be persuaded to grow anything else, and a mining-camp spirit pervaded the Virginia colony.[1]

All too soon, however, the tobacco growers of Virginia encountered the problem of volatile prices that forever besets agricultural producers. By 1630, Governor Harvey complained that tobacco was fetching less than a penny a pound. And although prices in the following years had their ups as well as their downs, colonists resorted to all kinds of devices, including burning half of one year's crop, to raise their incomes.[2] An especially difficult period ensued with the increased immigration to the colonies between the outbreak of the Civil War and the Restoration, and only the intervention of the weather in 1667, by reducing output to nearly zero, rescued the growers from desperately low prices.

Then, as now, restrictions on production led to disappointing and frustrating results. Planters who were limited to a specific number of plants per farm responded by moving more rapidly to new and fertile fields. If Virginia tried to limit the number of pounds of tobacco exported, it was unlikely that Maryland and North Carolina would cooperate. Marketing of tobacco by consignment to merchants resulted in uncertainties about the prices to be received, and in any case, individual planters correctly knew that they

---

[1] Lewis C. Gray, *History of Agriculture in the Southern United States to 1860,* I (Washington, D.C.: Carnegie Institution of Washington, 1933), pp. 259–60. Also see Russell Menard, "A Note on Chesapeake Tobacco Prices 1618–1660, " *Virginia Magazine of History and Biography* (1976):401–10.
[2] It should be emphasized that crop destruction would have raised incomes only if the price elasticity of demand was *inelastic*; that is, if the percentage increase in price due to the lower quantity supplied was greater than the percentage reduction in the quantity marketed.

could increase their own incomes by increasing their outputs. Overall, the absence of effective coercion and cooperation doomed the restrictive policies.

During the latter part of the seventeenth century and the first half of the eighteenth, there were years of relative prosperity to be sure, but the days in which tobacco was a profitable crop for every producer were gone. It slowly became apparent that the competition would be won by large plantations and that if the small planters were to succeed at all, they would have to specialize in high-quality tobacco or in the production of food. From the work of David Klingaman we have learned that in the eighteenth century substantial areas around the Chesapeake turned to the production of wheat, especially in Maryland.

Since slaves could be worked in large numbers very effectively in tobacco cultivation, large plantations were more efficient, and better able to continue production despite extremely low prices. In the colonial period, slaves ordinarily produced large surpluses of tobacco in comparison to the costs of their purchase and upkeep. To achieve the best results, however, a plantation owner had to have enough slaves to assure the economical use of a white manager. A plantation with less than ten slaves intermittently prospered, but only larger units earned substantial returns above cost, provided they were properly managed and contained sufficient acreage to avoid soil exhaustion. Thus, the wealthy or those who were able to secure adequate credit from English and Scottish merchants attained more efficient scales of tobacco production and, in so doing, became even wealthier and improved their credit standing further. In short, bigness fostered bigness, and wealth led to wealth. We should not conclude that slaves were held only by the largest plantation owners, however; the crude statistics available today indicate that in pre-Revolutionary times, as later, large numbers of planters owned less than ten slaves. Nonetheless, there was persistent pressure in the tobacco colonies to develop large-sized farms favored by lower per unit costs.

Rice   About 1695, the second of the great southern staples was introduced. Early Virginia colonists had experimented with rice production and South Carolina had tried to cultivate the staple in the first two years after settlement, but success awaited the introduction of new varieties of the grain.[3] By the early 1700s, rice was an established crop in the area around Charleston, although problems of irrigation still remained. It is possible to grow rice without intermittent flooding and draining, but the quality of the grain suffers. Rice was first cultivated in the inland swamps that could be flooded periodically from the rivers, but the flooding was dependent on uncertain stream flows. Besides, such a growing method could not be used on the extremely flat land that lay along the coast itself. Before long, a system of flooding was devised that enabled producers to utilize the force of tide

---

[3] Gray, p. 278.

flows. Dikes were built along the lower reaches of the rivers, and as the tide pushed back the fresh water, it could be let through gates into irrigation ditches crossing the fields.

Proper flooding remained unpredictable because no salt water could be let in and proper drainage demanded painstaking engineering. But the heavy investment of capital was worthwhile, because proper engineering permitted the two major floodings to occur at precisely the right time and the water could be removed just as accurately. Much labor was needed, and slaves were imported at a great rate during the eighteenth century for this purpose. The "task" system of working slaves, which gave each slave a particular piece of ground to cultivate, was emphasized. The work was backbreaking and was carried out in hot, mosquito-infested swamps; although contemporary opinion held that the African was better able to withstand the ravages of disease and the effects of overexertion than the white man, the mortality rate among blacks in this region was high. Despite production difficulties, rice output steadily increased until the end of the colonial period—its culture finally extending from below Savannah up into North Carolina.

Indigo   To the profits from rice were added those of another staple—indigo. Though earlier attempts had failed, the indigo plant was first successfully introduced in 1743 by a young woman, Eliza Lucas, who had come from the West Indies to live on a plantation near Charleston. Indigo almost certainly could not have been grown in the colonies without special permission or assistance, because its culture was demanding and the preparation of the dye required real skill. As a supplement to rice, however, it was an ideal crop, both because the plant could be grown on high ground where rice would not grow and because the peak work loads in processing indigo came at a time when the slaves were not busy in the rice fields. Indigo production, fostered by a British subsidy of sixpence a pound, added considerably to the profits of plantation owners, thereby attracting resources to the area.

In emphasizing the importance of tobacco, rice, and indigo, we are in some danger of overlooking the production of other commodities in the southern colonies. Throughout the South, there was a substantial output of hay and animal products and of Indian corn, wheat, and other grains. These items, like a wide variety of fruits and vegetables, were grown mostly to make the agricultural units as self-sufficient as possible. Yet upland farmers, especially in the Carolinas and Virginia, grew livestock for commercial sale, and exported meat, either on the hoof or in cured form, in quantity to other colonies.

The Middle Colonies

The land between the Potomac and the Hudson rivers was on the whole fertile and readily tillable and therefore enjoyed a comparative advantage in the production of grains and other foodstuffs. As the seventeenth century elapsed, two distinct types of agricultural operations developed there.

Colonial agriculture depended heavily on such cash crops as indigo—shown above being processed in South Carolina from fresh-cut sheaves to final drying—and rice, shown below, in a plantation setting.

A RICE FIELD

To the west, on the cutting edge of the frontier, succeeding generations continued to encounter many of the difficulties that had beset the first settlers. The trees in the forests—an ever-present obstacle—had to be felled, usually after they had been girdled and allowed to die. The felled trees were burned and their stumps were removed to allow for the use of horse-drawn plows. The soil was worked with tools that did not differ much from the implements used by medieval Europeans. A living had literally to be wrested from the earth. But in time, a stable and reasonably advanced agriculture began to develop to the east of the frontier. The Dutch in New York and the Germans in Pennsylvania, who brought skills and farming methods from areas with soils similar to those in this region, were encouraged from the first to cultivate crops for sale in the small but growing cities of New York, Philadelphia, and Baltimore. Gradually, a commercial agriculture developed. Wheat became the important staple, and although there was a considerable output of corn, rye, oats, and barley, the economy of the region was based on the great bread grain. During the latter part of the seventeenth century, a sufficient quantity of wheat and flour was produced to permit the export of these products, particularly to the West Indies.

The kind of agricultural unit that evolved in the Middle colonies later became typical of the great food belts of the midwestern United States. Individual farms, which were considerably smaller in acreage than the average plantation to the south, could be operated by the farmer and his family with little hired help. Slaveholding was rare, because wheat production was labor-intensive only during planting and harvest periods and because there were no apparent economies of large scale as in the southern plantation staples of tobacco or rice. It was normally preferable to acquire an indentured servant as a hand; the original outlay was not great, and the productivity of even a young and inexperienced servant was soon sufficient to return the owner's investment.

New England

Vital as the agriculture of New England was to the people of the area, it constituted a relatively unimportant part of commercial output for sale. Generally, poor soils, uneven terrain, and a severe climate led to typical "subsistence" farming, or the growth of only those crops that were necessary for family maintenance. Because it could be produced almost anywhere and because its yield even on poor land was satisfactory, Indian corn was the chief crop. Wheat and the other cereal grains, along with the hardier vegetables, were grown for family use. Due partly to climate and partly to the protection from wild predators that natural barriers furnished, the Narragansett region, including the large islands off its coast, became a cattle- and sheep-raising center. By the eve of the Revolution, however, New England was a net importer of food and fiber. Its destiny lay in another kind of economic endeavor; and from a very early date, many New Englanders combined farming with other work, thereby living better lives than they would have if they had been confined to the resources of their own farms. Homecraft employments of all varieties were common features of rural life, but especially in New England.

THE EXTRACTIVE INDUSTRIES

Although most colonial Americans made their living agriculturally, many earned their livelihood indirectly from the land in what we will call *extractive* pursuits. From the forest came the furs and wild animal skins, lumber, and naval stores. From the coastal waters came fish and that strange mammal, the whale. From the ground came minerals, but only in small quantities during the early colonial years. From the various industries that were built around these products arose an output second in value only to that of agriculture.

Furs, Forests, and Ores

The original thirteen colonies were a second-rate source of furs during most of the period before the Revolution, because the finest furs along the seaboard were processed quickly and the most lucrative catches were made long before the frontier moved into the interior. It was the French, not the English, who were the principle furriers in North America. Nonetheless, farmers trapped furs as a sideline to obtain cash, although they caught primarily muskrats and raccoons, whose pelts were less desirable then, as now.

The forest itself, more than its denizens, became an economically significant object of exploitation. As Map 3-1 illustrates, the colonials lived in an age of wood. Wood, rather than minerals and metals, was their chief fuel and their basic construction material. Almost without exception, the agricultural population engaged in some form of lumbering. Pioneers had to fell trees to clear ground, and wood was used to build houses, barns, furniture, and sometimes fences. Frequently, the timber was burned and the ashes were scattered, but enterprising farmers eventually discovered that they could use simple equipment to produce potash and the more highly refined pearlash. These chemicals, which were needed to manufacture glass, soap, and other products, provided much-needed cash to households throughout the colonies.

Along the fall line of the northern and Middle colonies, small sawmills sprang up in the earliest settlements. Using stream water as both a source of power and a means of transportation, sawmill operators tended to locate in areas that boasted the best combination of virgin timber and accessible rivers. The commercial manufacture of basic wood shapes—boards, planks, cooperage materials, and so forth—began in Main and New Hampshire

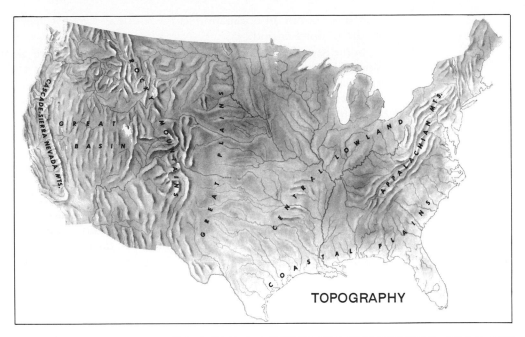

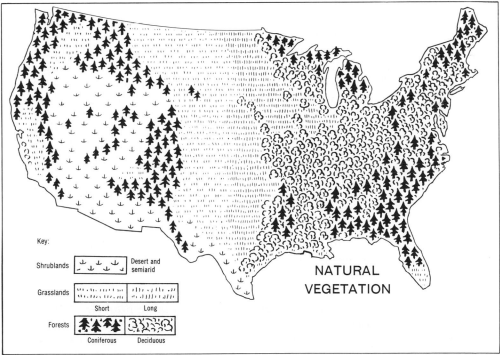

MAP 3-1   Natural Gifts: The channels of commerce and the stores of raw materials decreed by topography and natural vegetation established the initial pattern from which later economic development was to emerge.

and was a common occupation as far south as North Carolina by the end of the colonial period.

Some sawmills were totally devoted to the manufacture of materials for shipbuilding and ship repair. White pine was unmatched as a building material for the masts and yards of sailing ships, and white and red oak provided ship timbers of the same high quality. The pine trees that grew abundantly throughout the colonies furnished the raw material for the manufacture of so-called naval stores of pitch, tar, and resin. In the days of wooden vessels, naval stores were indispensable in the shipyard and were used mostly for protecting surfaces and caulking seams. These materials were in great demand in both the domestic and British shipbuilding industries. Considerable skilled labor was required to produce naval stores, and only in North Carolina, where slaves were trained to perform the required tasks, could these materials be produced profitably without British subsidy. Even so, English shipwrights complained that American pitch and tar were inferior to European products—a complaint never voiced against the incomparable American ship timbers.

The only mineral obtained by the colonials in any significant quantity was iron. A little copper and lead were found and negligible amounts of coal were mined, but in the young economy, iron was the chief metal and charcoal was the industrial fuel. For the moment, we will confine our attention to the processing of primary shapes—the "blooms" and "pigs" that were later worked into usable finished forms. This distinction may seem artificial, because at many of the ironworks established in these early years, the finishing processes were carried out—then, as now—by the same artisans who reduced the ore. But it is convenient, nevertheless, for us to consider the reduction of iron as one of the extractive industries and the finishing of iron as a manufacturing industry.

The methods used in the colonial iron industry did not differ greatly from those developed in the late Middle Ages, although by the time of the Revolution, furnace sizes had increased greatly. In the seventeenth century, the chief source of iron was bog ore, a sediment taken from swamps and ponds. When this sediment was treated with charcoal in a bloomery or forge until the charcoal absorbed the oxygen in the ore, an incandescent sponge of metal resulted. The glowing ball of iron was removed from the forge and in a white-hot condition was hammered to remove the slag and leave a substantial piece of wrought iron. The productive output of the bloomeries was small.

Rich rock ores were discovered as the population moved inward, and during the eighteenth century, a large number of furnaces were built for the reduction of these ores. Pig iron could then be produced in quantity. A mixture of rock ore, charcoal, and oyster shells or limestone was placed in a square or conical furnace and then ignited. Under a draft of air from bellows worked by water power, the iron ore was reduced to a spongy metal, which as it settled to the bottom of the furnace, alloyed itself with large amounts of carbon thereby becoming what we call cast iron. Poured into molds called "pigs" or "sows," the resulting metal could be either remelted and cast into final form later or further refined and reworked in a mill or blacksmith shop.

The discussion of these rudimentary processes provides us with an important background that will help us understand the later development in the American iron and steel industry. It is also worth noting that due to the simple processing required as well as to an abundance of charcoal, the colonial iron industry was able to compete with that of the British Isles in the sale of bars and pigs. There is agreement that the number of forges and furnaces in the colonies just before the Revolution probably exceeded the number in England and Wales combined, and the annual output of wrought and cast iron by then was in the neighborhood of 30,000 tons, or about one-seventh of the world's output. But the colonies remained heavy net importers of finished iron products.

Sea Products

Although restricted primarily to the northern colonies, the occupations of fishing and whaling were of major importance in the development of the entire early colonial economy. The sea provided New Englanders with a commodity for which there was a ready market and also furnished a stimulus for shipbuilding. When Jacques Cartier sailed up the St. Lawrence River in 1534, fisherman from many European countries were already at work near the mouth of the river and had probably been making the hazardous journey across the North Atlantic for a long time. Originally, these pioneers had operated a "wet fishery"—that is, the catch was partly cleaned, salted down, and returned to the home country for drying. The quality of the product was much better, however, if a "shore fishery" could be established to dry fish at a nearby land base, and during the sixteenth century, fishermen from Spain, Portugal, France, and England attached themselves temporarily to the northern coastal country.

When a permanent settlement was at last made not far from the banks that extended from Long Island to Newfoundland, the settlers there naturally turned to deep-sea fishing. There were many splendid harbors to house small fishing vessels and plenty of timber with which to build them. But more importantly, there was a great market for the magnificent cod. The large, fat, hard-to-cure cod were consumed at home. The best cod were exported to Catholic Europe; the poorer grades were sent to the West Indies, where they were fed to slaves. Gloucester, Salem, Boston, and Marblehead became the chief home ports for the great fishing fleets.

In colonial times, whale oil was highly prized as both an illuminant and a lubricant, ambergris, as a base for perfumes, and whalebone, as a material for stays. Whaling was therefore a profitable and vigorous, if small, industry. Before 1700, whalers operated near the New England coast, but their take

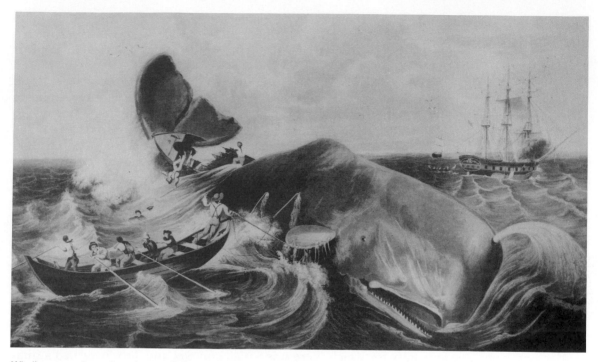

Whaling was a hazardous but profitable industry in early America.

was small. During the eighteenth century, however, whalers ranged far and wide, and by 1775, more than 300 vessels of all sizes sailed from the Massachusetts ports, of which Nantucket was the great whaling center.

THE MANUFACTURING INDUSTRIES

It is convenient for us to distinguish between the colonial extractive and manufacturing industries, even though these activities overlapped in actual practice. Included under the heading of manufacturing are the processes by which the crude or primary materials produced by the extractive industries became finished products. We should also realize that the word "industry" is ordinarily used rather loosely to describe any colonial activity, because the "firms" that comprised an industry were frequently heterogenous units that could range from a household to a fairly large shop or mill. Nevertheless, the output of each of the major categories of commodities *tended* to be produced by only one of the three major types of colonial organizations: households, craft shops, or mills and yards.

Once again, we must remind ourselves of the proportions in which the factors of production were available to business enterprises. Land was abundant. Capital goods and labor were scarce, but capital was relatively less important to a manufacturing organization than it was to be after the Industrial Revolution. On the other hand, labor was relatively more important; the skills of artisans—not tools or equipment—were the crucial agents in the more complicated production processes. Because of labor's importance and short supply, wage rates in the colonies were much higher than in the home country.

Except for a relatively few gifted traders, most people of the time found the greatest hope of ultimate reward in farming and land speculation. Because they were attached to the land, early Americans united in only a few urban settlements as their population grew, and in the rural areas—where most people lived—large quantities of goods were made in the home for home use. In the villages and towns, craftsmen tended to make those products that were in domestic demand but that required greater skill and somewhat more expensive tools to produce than the ordinary householder could provide. Finally, from mills and plants of varying sizes, came an increasing flow of goods for home trade and an even greater flow for export.

Household Manufacture

The first concerns of the colonial household were the manufacture of food and clothing. Finer items were imported, but household manufacture actually created a marketable surplus of some commodities. Animal products that we take for granted today resulted from serious efforts on the part of all members of the family at the first signs of winter. Cured or pickled meats, leather, and lard were essentials that only the well-to-do could afford to buy. Wheat, rye, or Indian corn grown on the farm was ground into flour at the local gristmill, but the women of the family made plentiful weekly rations of bread and hardtack. Jellies and jams were made with enough sweetening from honey, molasses, or maple syrup to preserve them for indefinite periods in open crocks. And we can be sure that the men of the family were rarely teetotalers. Beer, rum, and whiskey were easiest to make, but wines, mead, and an assortment of brandies and cordials were specialties of some households.

Making clothing—from preparing the raw fiber to sewing the finished garment—kept the women and children busy. There was nothing fine or beautiful about the resulting products, but they covered the body. Knit goods such as stockings, mittens, and sweaters were the major items of homemade apparel. Linsey-woolsey (made of flax and wool) and jeans (a combination of wool and cotton) were the standard textiles of the North and of the pioneer West. Equally indestructible, although perhaps a little easier on the skin, was fustian, a blend of cotton and flax used mostly in the South. Dress goods and fine suitings had to be imported from England, and even for the city dweller, the purchase of such luxuries was usually a rare and exciting occasion.

Early Americans who had special talents produced everything from nails and kitchen utensils to exquisite cabinets. Everywhere the men of the family participated in the construction of their own homes, although exacting woodwork and any necessary masonry might be done by a specialist. These specialists of widely varying abilities could be found both in cities and at country crossroads.

The Craft Shop

Much earlier than might be supposed, artisans began to ply their trades. Some of them were true craftsmen—experts in the European tradition. What distinguished workshop crafts from household manufactures was the specialization of the former. Household production was for family needs and presumably required neither the full time nor the complete attention of any member of the household. The craftsman might work at home, but the home was a craft shop if a craftsman earned his living at a trade.

The distinction between the specialized craftsman and the household worker was not always clear in colonial America. Skilled slaves on southern plantations might devote all their time to manufacture; this made them artisans, even though their output was considered a part of the household. On the other hand, the itinerant jack-of-all-trades, who moved from village to village selling reasonably expert services, was certainly not a craftsman in the European sense. Due to the scarcity of skilled labor, individual workers often performed functions more varied than they would have undertaken in their native country; a colonial tanner, for example, might also be a currier and a shoemaker. Furthermore, due to small local markets and the consequent geographic dispersal of nearly all types of production, few workers in the same trade were united in any particular locality. For this reason, there were not many guilds or associations of craftsmen in the same trade. As early as 1648, however, there were enough shoemakers in Boston to enable the General Court to incorporate them as a guild, and by 1718, tailors and cordwainers were so numerous in Philadelphia that they too applied for incorporation.[4]

Urban centers exhibited a great variety of skills at a rather early date. In 1697, for example, 51 manufacturing handicrafts, in addition to the building trades, were represented in Philadelphia. As one authority puts it:

> that a bare enumeration of the trades that we know were plied in the colonies indicates that varied and widely diffused handicraft manufactures then existed, in the aggregate contributing largely to colonial production, but chiefly important for the leaven of knowledge, skill, and habit which they supplied for subsequent industrial development.[5]

---

[4]Carl Bridenbaugh, *Cities in the Wilderness* (New York: Knopf, 1955), pp. 43 and 191.
[5]Victor S. Clark, *History of Manufactures in the United States, 1607–1860* (Washington, D.C.: Carnegie Institution of Washington, 1916), p. 164. Also see Thomas Doerflinger, "Commercial Specialization in Philadelphia's Merchant Community, 1750–1791," *Business History Review* (1983):20–49.

Mills and Yards

In our discussion of the extractive industries, we observed that somewhat more complex organizations were required even for rudimentary manufacture than were required in the household or the craft shop. For want of a more precise term, we will follow common usage and speak of the mill industries. To colonials, a mill was ". . . either a contrivance for grinding or any machinery operated by animal power, wind, or water."[6] Thus, mills turned out the basic wood shapes and the wrought-iron bars and iron pigs. Although the finished wooden and iron articles were frequently made by skilled artisans or even household members, they were also produced in mills and furnaces. Again, the "reproductive" manufacturing might be done in connection with the primary manufacture or in a totally different location. For example, furnaces for remelting iron and refining forges for making bar iron were usually attached to smelting furnaces, whereas slitting mills and plating forges were ordinarily independent establishments.

Until perhaps the middle of the eighteenth century, most of the mills were crude affairs, run by water power that was furnished by the small streams found all along the middle and north Atlantic coast. Dam sites suitable for large power development were not in general use until after the Revolution, because operations were conducted on a small scale and owners had the means to construct dams and canals of only minimum size. Throughout most of this period, primitive mechanisms were used; the cranks of sawmills and gristmills were almost always made of iron, but the wheels themselves and the cogs of the mill wheel were made of wood, preferably hickory. So little was understood about power transmission at this time that a separate water wheel was built to power each article of machinery. Shortly before the Revolution, improvements were made in the application of power to milling processes, and the mills along the Delaware River and the Chesapeake Bay were probably the finest in the world at that time.[7] In 1770, a fair-sized gristmill would grind 100 bushels a day; the largest mills, with several pairs of stones, might convert 75,000 bushels of grain into flour annually. The highest development of this kind of manufacture was represented by the establishment of Oliver Evans, who invented devices that enabled him to achieve a continuous process of manufacture from raw material to final product. In his mill, which began operations in 1782, grain was

> elevated mechanically to the top of the mill or warehouse, cleaned during gravity transmission to the hoppers, ground, conveyed by screw transmission and a second series of elevators to the top of the building again, cooled, bolted, and barreled during its second descent, without the intervention of any manual operation.[8]

[6]Clark, p. 174.
[7]Clark, p. 179.
[8]Clark, p. 179.

Employing only six men, mostly to close barrels, the Evans mill produced 100,000 bushels of grain annually.

We can only suggest the variety of the mill industries. Tanneries with bark mills were found in the North and the South. Paper-making establishments, common in Pennsylvania and not unusual in New England, were called mills because machinery was required to grind the linen rags into pulp. Textiles were essentially household products, but in Massachusetts, eastern New York, and Pennsylvania, a substantial number of mills were constructed to perform the more complicated processes of weaving and finishing. The rum distilleries of New England provided a major product for both foreign and domestic trade, and breweries everywhere ministered to convivial needs. The gristmill, like the sawmill, was found everywhere in the colonies, but the largest ones eventually developed in Pennsylvania, Delaware, and New Jersey.

Shipbuilding

Although large-scale manufacturing was not characteristic of colonial economic activity, one important exception—shipbuilding and the busy shipyards in the colonies—deserves special emphasis. As early as 1631, little more than a decade after the Pilgrims landed at Plymouth, a 30-ton sloop was completed in Boston. During the seventeenth century, shipyards sprang up all along the New England coast, with Boston and Newport leading the way. New York was a strong competitor until the Navigation Act of 1651 (to be discussed in Chapter 4) dealt its Dutch-dominated industry a crippling blow from which it did not recover until after 1720. By this time, Philadelphia boasted a dozen large shipyards along the banks of the Delaware River, and of the five major towns, only Charleston relied on ships produced by others. In the first half of the eighteenth century, the output of colonial shipyards reached its peak.

By 1700, the New England fleet exceeded 2,000, exclusive of fishing vessels. American industry not only furnished the vessels for a large domestic merchant fleet, it also sold a considerable number of ships abroad, chiefly to the English. An uncontradicted estimate attributes nearly one-third of the ships in the British Merchant Marine in 1775 to American manufacture.[9]

Many of the ships constructed were small. But whether they were building a square-rigged, three-masted vessel of several hundred tons or a fishing boat of ten tons, Americans had a marked and persistent advantage. The basis for success in colonial shipbuilding was the proximity of raw materials, mainly lumber. Although labor and capital costs were lower in England, the high costs of transport of bulky materials from the Baltic—or the colonies—

---

[9]Jacob Price, "A Note of the Value of Colonial Exports of Shipping," *Journal of Economic History,* 36(1976): 704–24.

Largely due to their ready supplies of first-class timber and naval stores, colonial shipbuilders enjoyed an early comparative advantage in shipbuilding.

made shipbuilding more expensive in England. Higher wages in the colonies encouraged sufficient numbers of shipwrights and artisans to migrate from Holland and England, where they built colonial vessels with low-cost materials at about two-thirds of British costs. Consequently, shipbuilding in the colonies was exceptional, for most manufacturers did not generate raw material cost savings enough to offset the much higher labor costs in the colonies. However, in this case, the high costs of transport of the bulky raw materials assured the comparative advantage of production in favor of the colonies. In addition, the Navigation Acts, discussed in Chapter 4, equally encouraged shipbuilding in both the colonies and in England.[10] There was an important distinction between England and North America in the first century of manufacturing development, however. In England raw materials were typically imported or brought to the craftsman, but, in contrast, in the New World workers located near raw materials.

---

[10]During the early colonial period, the Navigation Acts effectively subsidized both English and colonial shipbuilders. The American advantage became clear, however, soon after the beginning of the eighteenth century. See J.B. Condliffe, *The Commerce of Nations* (New York: W. W. Norton, 1950), p. 101.

The Merchant Marine

Finally, as the sizable New England fleet suggests, shipping services and other distribution services associated with the transportation, handling, and merchandising of goods were important commercial activities in the colonies. The merchant marines in New England and the Middle colonies, which employed thousands of men, were as efficient as the Dutch and English merchants in many trades throughout the world. Indeed, by the end of the colonial period, the colonies could boast of a sizable commercial sector, and as a source of foreign exchange earnings, the sale of shipping services was second only to tobacco exports. Overseas trade and these commercial activities were so important to the colonial economy that they will be given special emphasis in Chapter 4.

OCCUPATIONAL GROUPS

Although the colonies established a rich diversity of economic activities, from a functional occupational standpoint, daily life was fairly stable. Occupational roles changed little over the years in settled areas, and from today's perspective, occupational opportunities remained narrow and rigid. Most people expected the future to replicate the past and most young people followed the employment footsteps of their parents.

The male population generally fit into one of several employment categories, the most predominant being the family farmers. Other significant categories or classes were slave, indentured servant, unskilled laborer, and seaman. Upper middle classes included artisans, merchants and, landowning farmers, but the richest occupational groups included merchants in New England and the Middle colonies and large land-holding planters in the South. As Edwin Perkins and Alice Jones inform us, the very very wealthy were classified as esquires, gentlemen, or officials.

Most women participated in work to complement that of the male head of the household. Women's duties were dominated by child care, domestic service, livestock tending, and household production. Family farm life in particular, the most typical lifestyle of the period, had women and children engaged in handicraft production within the home. During harvest times, they usually turned to outdoor work to help the men. In seventeenth-century Maryland for instance, Louis G. Carr and Lorna Welsh have shown that wives routinely spent the spring and summer months in the tobacco fields. In the Middle colonies, according to Joan Jensen, women helped routinely in the easier tasks of spreading hay to dry, digging for potatoes, gathering flax, and picking fruit. Most out-of-the-house work for women, especially younger women, however, was in other people's homes. Such domestic service for extra income was common for women under the age of 25.

Children began helping their parents at about the age of 7 or 8; by the age of 12 they were usually important apprentice-type workers in the home or in the fields. For young men, however, though still limited, their range of occupational opportunities vastly exceeded those for young women. Young women faced a future, in colonial times, mostly of childrearing and homemaking.

SELECTED REFERENCES AND SUGGESTED READINGS

Adams, Donald. "Prices and Wages in Maryland 1750–1850." *The Journal of Economic History* 46 (1986):625–45.

Bailyn, Bernard. *The New England Merchants in the Seventeenth Century.* Cambridge: Harvard Univ. Press, 1955.

Bridenbaugh, Carl. *The Colonial Craftsman.* New York: New York Univ. Press, 1950.

Bridenbaugh, Carl. *Cities in the Wilderness: The First Century of Urban Life in America 1625–1742.* New York: Oxford Univ. Press, 1971.

Bruchey, Stuart. *The Colonial Merchant: Sources and Readings.* New York: Harcourt, Brace & World, 1966.

Carr, Lars G. and Lorna Walsh. "The Planting Wife: the Experience of White Women in Seventeenth Century Maryland." *William and Mary Quarterly* 34 (1977): 542–71.

Clark, Victor S. *History of Manufacturers in the United States 1607–1860.* Washington, D.C.: Carnegie Institution of Washington, 1916.

Coon, David. "Eliza Lucas Pinckney and the Reintroduction of Indigo Culture in South Carolina." *Journal of Southern History* (1976):61–76.

Carroll, Charles. *The Timber Economy of Puritan New England.* Providence: Brown Univ. Press, 1973.

Doerflinger, Thomas. "Commercial Specialization in Philadelphia's Merchant Community 1750–1791." *Business History Review* 57 (1983):20–49.

Goldenberg, Joseph. *Shipbuilding in Colonial America.* Charlottesville, VA.: Univ. Press of Virginia, 1976.

Gray, Lewis C. *History of Agriculture in the Southern United States to 1860.* Washington, D.C.: Carnegie Institute, 1933.

Gray, Ralph, and Betty Wood. "The Transition from Indentured Servant to Involuntary Servitude in Colonial Georgia." *Explorations in Economic History* 13 (Oct. 1976):353–70.

Greenberg, Michael. "William Byrd II and the World of the Market." *Southern Studies* (1977):429–56.

Hedges, James. *The Browns of Providence Plantation: The Colonial Years.* Cambridge: Harvard Univ. Press, 1952.

Henretta, James. "Economic Development and Social Structure in Colonial Boston." *William and Mary Quarterly* 22 (1965).

Jensen, Joan. *Loosening the Bonds: Mid-Atlantic Farm Women 1750–1850.* New Haven: Yale Univ. Press, 1986.

Klingaman, David. "The Significance of Grain in the Development of the Tobacco Colonies." *Journal of Economic History* (1969):267–78.

McCusker, J. J., and R. R. Menard. *The Economy of British America, 1607–1789.* Chapel Hill: Univ. of North Carolina Press, 1985. Part II and Ch. 14 and 15.

McManis, Douglas. *Colonial New England: A Historical Geography.* New York: Oxford Univ. Press, 1975.

Norton, Thomas. *The Fur Trade in Colonial New York, 1686–1766.* Madison: Univ. of Wisconsin Press, 1974.

Paskoff, Paul. *Industrial Evolution: Organization, Structure, and Growth of the Pennsylvania Iron Industry, 1750–1860.* Baltimore: Johns Hopkins Univ. Press, 1983.

Perkins, E. J. *The Economy of Colonial America*. 2nd ed. New York: Columbia Univ. Press, 1988. Section 1.

Price, Jacob. "A Note on the Colonial Exports of Shipping." *Journal of Economic History* 36 (1976):704–24.

Schweitzer, Mary. *Custom and Contract: Household Government, and the Economy in Colonial Pennsylvania*. New York: Columbia Univ. Press, 1987.

Shammas, Carol. "The Female Social Structure of Philadelphia in 1775." *Pennsylvania Magazine of History and Biography* (1983):69–38.

Stackpole, Edward. *The Sea-Hunters: The New England Whalemen during Two Centuries, 1635–1835*. Philadelphia: Lippincott, 1953.

Vickers, Daniel. "The First Whalemen of Nantucket." *William and Mary Quarterly* 40 (1983):560–83.

CHAPTER 4

The Economic Relations of the Colonies

ENGLISH MERCANTILISM AND THE COLONIES

In the broader period that falls approximately between 1500 and 1800, the countries of western Europe that became nation-states were invariably influenced by a set of ideas and beliefs known as the *mercantile system* or *mercantilism*. Mercantilist doctrine was not created by a particular group of thinkers, nor was it ever set forth in systematic fashion by a "school" of economists. In fact, although there had been a massive outpouring of economic literature during this period, mostly in the form of pamphlets and small books, the first "classical economist," Adam Smith, gained attention by attacking mercantilist beliefs. Nevertheless, the ideas of mercantilism were important because they were held by practical businesspeople and heads of state who—at different times in different countries—had strongly influenced public policy.

More than anything else, the mercantilists wanted to achieve power and wealth for the state. It was possible to reach these ends, they felt, by making their own country as self-sufficient as possible and by doing whatever they could to weaken the power of competing states. This prompted a type of cold war using economic means. Spain's experience in the sixteenth century had led most observers to conclude that an inflow of gold and silver was a potent help in attaining needed goods and services and in prosecuting wars.

To generate an inflow of gold or silver through trade, the value of exports should exceed the value of imports. The gold or silver paid for the differences between exports and imports. With such additions to amounts of money, called specie, domestic trade would be more brisk and tax revenues higher. It was further viewed that great power could be fully realized by the state only if political and economic *unity* became a fact. In a day when

63

productivity depended so greatly on the skill and knowledge of the individual worker, it was of primary importance to keep artisans at home. If all the materials necessary to domestic industry were not available, they could best be obtained by establishing colonies or friendly foreign trading posts from which they could be imported. A strong merchant marine could carry foreign goods, thereby helping to secure favorable trade balances, and merchant ships could be converted for war if the need arose. Nor was the attention of mercantilist leaders directed exclusively toward relations between the home country and the rest of the world. For one thing, a self-sufficient economy implied a strong and vigorous agriculture. For another, the high rate of industrial production necessitated not only the protection of old industries and the encouragement of new ones, but also the enforcement of regulations that would provide the poor and indigent with some kind of productive activity.

Mercantilists believed that these means of achieving national power could be made effective by the passage and strict enforcement of legislation directed toward regulating economic life. England had begun to pass such laws by the end of the fifteenth century, but its mercantilist efforts did not fully flower until after the British, together with the Dutch, had successfully turned back Spanish power. Indeed, it was largely a consequence of England's desire to surpass Holland—a nation that had reached the zenith of its power during the first half of the seventeenth century—that British legislation was passed marking the beginning of an organized and consistent effort to regulate colonial trade.

Adherence to mercantilist principles was, of course, implicit in the colonizing activity that began in the late 1500s. For that matter, after the first successful settlement in the New World, no one would have argued seriously that the colonies should not be regulated to benefit the Empire. Almost as soon as Virginia tobacco began to be shipped in commercial quantities to England, King James I levied a tax on it while agreeing to prohibit the growth of competing tobacco in England. Gradually, more and more restrictions were placed on cargoes shipped from the colonies in foreign vessels, and by the 1630s, foreigners were legally excluded from American trade. Furthermore, it had become well established by 1650 that certain products were to be taken to England either to be sold there or to be transshipped to other European countries. On the whole, there seems to have been little objection to such rules and little feeling among the colonials that they were unjust.

The Early Navigation Acts

During the English Civil War, which began in 1642 and ended in 1649, the British had too many troubles of their own to pay much attention to regulating trade with the colonies. In this period, Americans had slipped into the habit of shipping their goods directly to continental ports, and the Dutch made great inroads into the carrying trade. In 1651, Parliament passed the first of the so-called Navigation Acts, directed primarily at prohibiting the shipping of American products in Dutch vessels. Not until after the Restoration, however, was England in a position to enforce a strict commercial policy, and it is for this reason that we usually think of the Navigation Acts of 1660 and 1663 as the first really effective ones.

The first Navigation Acts were modified from time to time by literally hundreds of policy changes. Although we will devote some attention to a few crucial changes in policy, at this point it is sufficient to note the three primary categories of trade restriction:

1. All trade of the colonies was to be carried in vessels that were English-built and -owned, commanded by an English captain, and manned by a crew three-quarters of whom were English sailors. "English" was defined as "only his Majesty's subjects of England, Ireland, and the Plantations." Of great importance to colonists was the fact that colonists and colonial ships were both considered "English" under Navigation Acts.

2. All foreign merchants were excluded from dealing directly in the commerce of the English colonies. They could engage in colonial trade only through England and merchants resident there.

3. Certain commodities produced in the colonies could be exported only to England (or Wales, Berwick-on-Tweed, or other English colonies—essentially any destination within the Empire). These "enumerated" goods included sugar, tobacco, cotton, indigo, ginger, and various dyewoods (fustic, logwood, and braziletto). The list was later amended and lengthened, and Scotland was added as a legal destination after 1707.

It is important to keep these three categories of restrictions firmly in mind. Although they were the cause of occasional protests on the part of the colonists, they probably did little harm. Largely due to widespread evasion by smuggling, these restrictions caused practically no disruption of established trade patterns during the remaining decades of the seventeenth century. When, in 1696, a system of admiralty courts was established to enforce the Navigation Acts, their impact became somewhat more pronounced. Indeed, from the beginning of the eighteenth century, most spheres of colonial commercial activity were regulated.

OVERSEAS COMMERCE

The most important characteristic of colonial commerce was the predominance of the South as the producer of great staples. These staples—tobacco, rice, and indigo—in addition to naval stores, were the most desirable imports to the English under the mercantile system. If we look at the trade statistics at the beginning of the eighteenth century or just before the Revolution,

TABLE 4-1   The Percentage Share of Each Colonial Region's Commodity Trade to Each Overseas Area, 1768–72 (imports in parentheses)

	GREAT BRITAIN AND IRELAND		SOUTHERN EUROPE		WEST INDIES		AFRICA	
New England	18	(66)	14	(2)	64	(32)	4	(0)
Middle Colonies	23	(76)	33	(3)	44	(21)	0	(0)
Upper South	83	(89)	9	(1)	8	(10)	0	(0)
Lower South[a]	72	(86)	9	(1)	19	(13)	0	(0)
Total	56	(80)	18	(2)	26	(18)	1	(0)

[a]The Carolinas and Georgia.

Source: James F. Shepherd and Gary M. Walton, *Shipping, Maritime Trade and the Economic Development of Colonial North America* (Cambridge: Cambridge Univ. Press, 1972), pp. 160–61.

we are struck by the overwhelming importance of southern exports to England compared with the exports of other colonies. In the first decade of the eighteenth century, southern exports to England were roughly four times greater than those of New England, New York, and Pennsylvania. Half a century later, during the 1760s, the proportion was still approximately the same, although by this time the Carolinas were exporting many more goods than they had earlier. Southern imports from England, on the other hand, were only slightly greater than British imports to the northern colonies in the first decade of the century. During the 1760s, imports to New England, New York, and Pennsylvania exceeded imports to the South by some £300,000 sterling.

A statistical description of trade in the late colonial period will provide us with a useful summary of the relative importance of the various trading partners of the colonies. As shown in Table 4-1 and as we just emphasized, Great Britain was the main overseas region to receive colonial exports (56 percent of the total) and to supply colonial imports (80 percent of the total).[1] Nevertheless, the West Indies and southern Europe were important trading partners, especially as markets for American exports.

Another feature of colonial trade that is revealed by the statistics in Table 4-1 is the sharp difference among the regions' ties to various overseas markets. Commerce in the southern regions was overwhelmingly dominated by the English trades. Alternatively, trade in the Middle colonies was more evenly balanced among Great Britain, southern Europe, and the West Indies. New England's most important trading partner was the West Indies. Colonial imports in each region arrived predominantly by way of Great Britain. Few products were imported from southern Europe, and it is also worth noting that commodity trade with Africa was insignificant in terms of both exports and imports.

---

[1]Recall that due to reshipment allowed by the Navigation Acts not all of these amounts were actually consumed or produced in the British isles.

TABLE 4-2 Values and Balances of Commodity Trade Between England and the American Colonies (annual averages by decade in thousands of pounds sterling)

	IMPORTS	—	EXPORTS	—	DEFICIT
1721–30	£ 509		£ 442		£ 67
1731–40	698		559		139
1741–50	923		599		324
1751–60	1,704		808		809
1761–70	1,942		1,203		739

Source: Shepherd and Walton, p.42

TRADE DEFICITS WITH ENGLAND

The variety of measures implemented by the Crown to regulate trade and to generate favorable trade balances for the Empire overshadowed similar attempts at trade regulation by the colonials. Nevertheless, the continual drain of specie from colonial shores and the pervasive unstable conditions of various colonial currencies were matters of grave concern in the colonies. Because European manufactured goods were in great demand in the New World, colonists faced chronic deficits, especially in their trade with England. Table 4-2 shows the size and trend of these deficits over much of the eighteenth century. As we will soon see, most of these deficits were incurred by New England and the Middle colonies, but even the Southern colonies frequently faced deficits in their commodity trade with England.

Benjamin Franklin's reply to a Parliamentary committee in 1760 explaining Pennsylvania's payment of its trade deficit with England was

> The balance is paid by our produce carried to the West Indies, and sold in our own islands, or to the French, Spaniards, Danes, and Dutch; by the same carried to other colonies in North America, as to New England, Nova Scotia, Newfoundland, Carolina, and Georgia; by the same carried to different parts of Europe, as Spain, Portugal and Italy: In all which places we receive either money, bills of exchange, or commodities that suit for remittance to Britain; which, together with all the profits of the industry of our merchants and mariners arising in those circuitous voyages and the freights made by their ships, center finally in Britain to discharge the balance and pay for British manufactures continually used in the province or sold to foreigners by our traders.[2]

As emphasized by the esteemed Franklin, colonial trade deficits to Britain could be paid by surpluses earned in trades to other overseas areas as well as by earnings from shipping and other mercantile services. Of course,

---

[2]Harold U. Faulkner, *American Economic History,* 8th ed. (New York: Harper & Row, 1960), p. 81.

other sources of foreign exchange, such as expenditures by the British defense forces stationed in the colonies, also affected the inflow of sterling. To determine the relative importance of these and other sources of exchange earnings (and losses), we need to assess the various components of the colonies' overall balance of payments. But more was at stake than the mere question of how the trade deficits with Great Britain were paid. The problem of chronic money shortages was vital to the colonists. Were colonial trade deficits with Britain offset by surpluses in other trades or by other exchange earnings? Or did overall trade cause a persistent *net drain* of specie from the colonies? Alternatively, were the trade deficits financed by capital inflows to the colonies and by growing colonial indebtedness to British creditors? Was indebtedness to Britain increasing, and thereby providing a possible motivation for colonial revolt? At one time, historians placed great credence in such propositions, special advocates being Charles A. Beard and Louis M. Hacker. Were capital inflows sizeable, and did they contribute significantly to the economic development of the colonies? Could these inflows be construed as "foreign aid," signifying extensive British subsidization of colonial development? Although tedious and somewhat complex, a study of the colonial balance of payments will shed much light on these important issues.

A BALANCE OF PAYMENTS FOR THE THIRTEEN COLONIES

Surviving information on the myriad of exchanges for the years 1768–1772 gives us a reasonably clear picture of the colonies' balance of payments in the late colonial period. A breakdown of the colonies' commodity trade balances with the major overseas areas during this period is provided in Table 4-3. These data confirm the findings presented in Table 4-2,

TABLE 4-3   Average Annual Commodity Trade Balances of the Thirteen American Colonies, 1768–72 (in thousands of pounds sterling)

	GREAT BRITAIN AND IRELAND	SOUTHERN EUROPE	WEST INDIES	AFRICA	ALL TRADES
New England	− 609	+ 48	− 36	+ 19	− 577
Middle Colonies	− 786	+ 153	− 10	+ 1	− 643
Upper South	− 50	+ 90	− 9	0	+ 30
Lower South	− 23	+ 48	+ 44	0	+ 69
Total	− 1,468	+ 339	− 11	+ 20	− 1,121

Notes: (1) A plus sign denotes a surplus (exports exceed imports); a minus sign, a deficit (imports exceed exports).
(2) Values are expressed in prices in the mainland colonies; thus, import values include the costs of transportation, commissions, and other handling costs. Export values are also expressed in colonial prices and therefore do not include these distribution costs.
Source: Shepherd and Walton, p. 115.

indicating that sizable deficits were incurred in the English trade, especially by New England and the Middle colonies. Somewhat surprisingly, even the colonies' commodity trade to the West Indies was slightly unfavorable (except for the trade of the lower South). However, trades to southern Europe generated significant surpluses (augmented slightly by the African trades) that were sufficient to raise the southern colonial regions to a surplus position in their overall commodity exchanges.

Although commodity exchanges made up the lion's share of total colonial exchanges, the colonies did have other sources of foreign exchange earnings (and losses) as well. Table 4-4 begins with colonial commodity exchanges indicating the £1,120 aggregate deficit in that category.

The most important source of foreign exchange earnings to offset that average deficit was the sale of colonial shipping services. Shipping earnings totaled approximately £600,000 per year in the late colonial period. In addition, colonial merchants earned more than £200,000 annually through insurance charges and commissions. Together, these "invisible" earnings offset more than 60 percent of the overall colonial commodity trade deficit. Almost 80 percent of these invisible earnings reverted to residents of New

TABLE 4-4   Balance of Payments for the Thirteen Colonies, 1768–72 (in thousands of pounds sterling)

	DEBITS	CREDITS
Commodities		
Export earnings		2,800
Imports	3,920	
Trade deficit	1,120	
Ship sales to foreigners		140
Invisible earnings		
Shipping cargoes		600
Merchant commissions, insurance, etc.		220
Payments for human beings		
Indentured servants	80	
Slaves	200	
British collections and expenditures		
Taxes and duties	40	
Military and civil expenditures[a]		440–460
Payments deficit financed by specie flows and/or increased indebtedness		20–40

[a]Gwyn's estimates of total expenditures for military and civil purposes for 1768–72 are £365, but Thomas' study suggests higher arms payments by nearly £100,000 yearly, 1768–72. Neither account for savings by men stationed in the colonies who returned some of their earnings home; thus the £440–460 range. £460 assumes no savings sent home.

Sources: Data compiled from Gary M. Walton and James F. Shepherd, *The Economic Rise of Early America* (Cambridge: Cambridge Univ. Press, 1979), table 9, p. 101; Julian Gwyn, "British Government Spending and the North American Colonies, 1740–1775," in *The Atlantic Empire before the American Revolution*, ed. Peter Marshall and Glyn Williams (London: Frank Cass, 1980), pp. 74–84, fn. 7; also in *Journal of Imperial and Commonwealth History* (1980): 74–87, fn. 7; and Peter D.G. Thomas, "The Cost of the British Army in North America, 1763–1775," *William and Mary Quarterly* (1988): 510–16.

England and the Middle colonies. Thus, the mercantile activities of New Englanders and middle colonists, especially in the West Indian trade, enabled the colonies to import large quantities of manufactured goods from Great Britain. When all thirteen colonies are considered together, invisible earnings exceeded earnings from tobacco exports—the single most important colonial staple export.

Another aspect of seafaring, the sale of ships, also became a persistent credit item in the colonies' balance of payments. As Jacob Price has shown, colonial ship sales averaged at least £140,000 annually from 1763 to 1775, primarily to England. Again, the lion's share of these earnings went to New England shipbuilders, but the Middle colonies also received a portion of the profits from ship sales. Taken together, ship sales and "invisible" earnings reduced the colonies' negative balance of payments to only £160,000.

In contrast to these earning sources, funds for the trade of human beings were continually lost to foreign markets. An average of approximately £80,000 sterling was spent annually for the 5,000–10,000 indentured servants who arrived annually during the late colonial period. Most of these servants were sent to Pennsylvania and the Chesapeake Bay area. A more sizable amount was the nearly £200,000 spent each year to purchase approximately 5,000 slaves. Over 90 percent of these slaves were sent to the Southern colonies, especially to the lower South in the later colonial period.

Finally, expenditures made by the British government in the colonies on defense, civil administration, and justice notably offset the remaining deficits in the colonists' current account of trade. Table 4-4 does not indicate the total amount of these costs to Great Britain. Instead, it shows how much British currency was used to purchase goods and services in the colonies and how much was paid to men stationed there. The net inflow for these expenditures averaged between £440,000 and £460,000, in 1768–72, reducing the net deficit in the colonial balance of payments for these years to £40,000 per year at least, and probably less.

Money, Debt, and Capital

The estimated remaining annual colonial deficit of £20,000 to £40,000 was paid either by an outflow of specie or by growing indebtedness to Britain. Temporary net outflows of specie undoubtedly did occur, thereby straining trade and prices in the colonies. Certainly contemporary complaints of money scarcity, especially specie, indicate that this often happened. But no significant part of this normal deficit could have been paid persistently with precious metals. The colonists could not sustain a permanent net outflow of specie because gold and silver mines were not developed in colonial North America. Typically, then, the outflow of specie to England was matched by an inflow from various sources of colonial exchange earnings. Nevertheless, the erratic pattern of specie movement and the issuance of paper money of uncertain value caused monetary disturbances as reflected in price movements and alterations in rates of exchange among the currencies. But most colonists preferred to spend rather than to accumulate a stock of specie. After all, limited specie was simply another manifestation of a capital-scarce economy. To the colonists, it was more desirable to receive additional imports—especially manufactures—than to maintain a growing stock of specie.

The final remaining colonial deficits were normally financed on short-term credit, and American merchants usually purchased goods from England on one-year credit. This was so customary, in fact, that British merchants included a normal 5 percent interest charge in their prices and granted a rebate to accounts that were paid before the year ended. And in Virginia, Scottish firms generally established representatives in stores to sell or trade British wares for tobacco and other products. Short-term credit was a normal part of day-to-day colonial exchanges in these instances.

The growth of short-term credit reflected the expanding Atlantic trades and represented a modest amount of increasing colonial indebtedness to Britain. Sizable claims against southern planters by British merchants after the Revolution[3] have encouraged some historians to argue that the relationship between London merchants and southern planters was disastrous at that time and even to argue that increasing colonial indebtedness to Britain provided impetus for the Revolution. But was this, in fact, so?

By adding the "invisible" earnings and ship sales to the regional commodity trade deficits (and surpluses), we obtain these rough averages of the regional deficits (−) and surpluses (+) in the colonies.[4]

New England	− £ 50,000
Middle Colonies	− 350,000
Southern Colonies	+ 240,000

Clearly, the major deficit regions were north of the Chesapeake Bay area—primarily in the Middle colonies. The southern regions were favored with more than a sufficient surplus in their current accounts of trade to pay for their purchases of slaves and indentured servants.

---

[3]Of the approximately £5,000,000 claimed by British merchants in 1791, more than £2,300,000 was owed by Virginia; nearly £570,000, by Maryland; £690,000, by South Carolina; £380,000, by North Carolina, and £250,000, by Georgia. However, nearly one-half of these amounts represented accumulated interest on deficits that had been in effect since 1776. Moreover, Aubrey Land argues that these claims were exaggerated by as much as 800 percent, and in fact, the Americans honored only one-eight of such claims. See Aubrey C. Land, "Economic Behavior in a Planting Society: The Eighteenth Century Chesapeake," *Journal of Southern History* 32 (1967):482−83.

[4]The regional division of shipping earnings and other "invisibles" is derived from Shepherd and Walton, Chapter 7. Because the ownership of vessels is not given separately for the upper South and the lower South, we have combined these two regions here, but undoubtedly the upper South earned the greater portion of the combined £240,000 surplus. All ship sales have been credited to the northern regions; £100,000 to New England and £40,000 to the Middle colonies.

A fair number of planters availed themselves of greater credit from abroad, according to separate studies by Breen, and Price, and Kulikoff. Nevertheless, it appears there was no growing indebtedness on average in the South at this time, and British expenditures for military and administrative purposes eliminated the negative New England balance and reduced most of the Middle colonies' balances as well.[5]

Nevertheless, England's claims were real enough, although they may have been exaggerated. But remember that British merchants and their colonial representatives normally extended credit to southern planters and accepted their potential harvests as collateral. Usually, of course, the harvests came in, and the colonists' outstanding debts were paid. But with the outbreak of the Revolution, this picture changed radically. Colonial credit normally extended throughout the year was still outstanding at the end of the year, because agents or partners of British firms had retreated home before the crops were harvested and the debts were paid. But the mere existence of these debts did not indicate growing indebtedness—nor did it provide motivation for colonial revolt.

The capital inflows that did occur were rarely channeled directly into long-term investments in the colonies, and British merchants held few claims on such investments. Nevertheless, it is important to realize that because commercial short-term credit was furnished by the British, colonial savings were freed for other uses: to make long-term investments in land improvement, roads, and such physical capital as ships, warehouses, and public buildings. For the purposes of colonial development, British short-term credit represented a helping hand, and its form was much less important than its amount.

However, with the highly important exception of military and civil defense, the colonies apparently were not subsidized by Britain to any great extent. For the most part, the formation of capital in the New World was dependent on the steady accretion of savings and investment from the pockets of the colonists themselves. It is impossible to determine precisely how much was annually saved and invested in the late colonial period. According to our estimates, which will be elaborated in Chapter 5, incomes probably averaged at least £12 sterling per person in the colonies. Since more than 2 million people were living in the colonies on the eve of the Revolution, if we assume a savings rate of not less than 8 percent (£1 out of £12), total capital accumulation per year would have exceeded 2 million pounds at that time. Thus,

---

[5] Further alteration of the regional deficits and surpluses would have resulted from coastal trade among the regions. Surprisingly, however, the major regions in the thirteen colonies appear to have earned surpluses in coastal trade. Florida, the Bahamas, and the Bermuda Islands and the Northern colonies of Newfoundland, Nova Scotia, and Quebec, were the deficit areas in coastal trade. See James F. Shepherd and Samuel H. Williamson, "The Coastal Trade of the British North American Colonies, 1768–1772," *Journal of Economic History* 32 (1972):803.

the capital inflow from Britain probably contributed for 1 or 2 percent of capital formation in the colonies.

The sizable estimates of British military expenditures in North America, in 1763–1775, by Peter Thomas, and for civil and military expenditures for the longer period 1740–1775 by Julian Gwyn, support these general conclusions of small net deficits in the colonies' balance of payments throughout much of the late colonial period. Only the substantial British expenditures for military and administrative purposes reveal a form of British subsidization or colonial dependency in the decades just prior to the Revolution.

COMMUNICATION, SHIPPING, AND TRADE

As Table 4-5 shows, the leading population centers in the colonies were ports, particularly those safe harbors with productive accessible hinterlands. Linkages among these important centers were mostly by sea. At first, Americans settled near reasonably safe harbors or along navigable streams, for the obvious reason that these places were readily accessible. Before 1700, roads were little more than paths, and land travel was both difficult and dangerous. Even well into the eighteenth century, the wise traveler followed

TABLE 4-5   Top Twenty Colonial Ports and Urban Centers

TOWN/CITY	POPULATION
Philadelphia	40,000
New York City	25,000
Boston	16,000
Charleston	12,000
Newport	11,000
Providence	9,000
New Haven	8,300
Norwich	7,000
Norfolk	6,200
Baltimore	6,000
New London	5,400
Salem	5,300
Lancaster	5–6,000
Hartford	4,900
Middletown	4,700
Portsmouth	4,600
Marblehead	4,400
Albany	4,000
Annapolis	3,700
Savannah	3,200

Source: Carl Bridenbaugh. *Cities in the Wilderness* and *Cities in Revolt* (New York: Oxford Univ. Press, 1971).

a coastal route by ship whenever possible. Benjamin Franklin, for example, transferred his residence from Boston to Philadelphia by sea.

Two factors continued to make sea travel preferable to land travel between the colonies: the excessive cost of land transportation, and the bulky nature of the commodities produced in the colonial period. But as the population increased, people moved away from the waterways and into the interior, and land travel became increasingly necessary. Nearby communities—as soon as they could afford the considerable expense—became linked to one another by roads.

Both travel and communications were slow. A postal system emerged in the late seventeenth century, but at the time of the Revolution, it took about three weeks for news of any importance to spread to the chief settlements throughout the colonies. Those who lived on the frontier often waited much longer to learn of major events and were almost completely isolated from reports on such mundane matters as the state of trade markets. But the postal facilities in America were not much worse than those of the Old World. Even in the highly developed economies of western Europe, communication was still slow and uncertain. Bluff-bowed sailing ships typically took six weeks to cross the Atlantic. The colonial economy was shaped in part by the difficulties of overland travel and the slowness of communication in the New World, but these hindrances were common to all peoples of the eighteenth-century world.

Advantages of location and communcation went far in determining shipping and trade patterns. For example, British ships almost completely dominated the trades of the southern colonial regions, while New England shippers dominated the New England-West Indies trade route. Although there were exceptions of tramping among ports and triangular patterns, shippers mostly followed simple out-and-back shuttle patterns and specialized in particular routes and ports.

The evolution of these patterns of shipping and trade dominance was determined primarily by three critical factors: the high risks of maritime trade, the problems of acquiring and responding to information about markets, and the persistence of high labor costs.

In marketing their goods, New England merchants typically consigned them either to ship captains or to selling agents, called *factors,* who were stationed in overseas markets. Since these methods necessitated placing a high degree of trust in a third party, it is not surprising that colonial merchants favored colonial ship captains. After all, greater familiarity and more frequent contact between merchant and agent lowered the risks of trade.

Due to the rudimentary forms of communication and transportation in existence at the time, geographical closeness to a market was an important advantage. For example, British shippers and merchants in the tobacco trade could acquire information about changing market conditions in the Chesapeake Bay area and in Europe more easily than New England shippers could. However, in trades to the West Indies, colonial shippers and

New Amsterdam in the seventeenth century was a small but promising port city. Surrounded by relatively unproductive land, the town nevertheless combined a superb harbor with unexcelled access to the hinterland. It became New York in 1664.

merchants were nearer to their market and could respond more quickly to fluctuations in it. Because being close to a market reduced the cost of obtaining market information and allowed merchants to respond with more timely cargo arrivals, this also reduced the risks of trade.

Finally, the efficient use of labor time was always an important factor. It was general practice in colonial times for crews to be paid while a vessel was docked in foreign ports, and crews were normally discharged only at the end of the voyage in the home port. This meant that British crews in the tobacco trade were paid for the time they spent at sea and in southern colonial ports, but not for their port time in England. Therefore, New England shippers were at a disadvantage on this trade route, because they paid wages both in British ports and in the Chesapeake Bay. Alternatively, colonial shippers faced lower labor costs on trade routes between their home ports and the Caribbean.

These same considerations played a large role in determining the routes of trade. Although the desire to keep vessels as fully loaded as possible encouraged "tramping" from port to port to take advantage of differences in demand and cargo availability, such a practice often incurred offsetting large costs. For example, a New England ship captain in the West Indies trade, acting on behalf of his merchant, would attempt to locate the best markets for the commodities he carried. This might require several voyages among the islands before agreeing on prices, the medium of exchange, and even the question of settling past debts. Transactions were often complex even when the merchants and captains were acquainted with one another. Of course, in unfamiliar markets, poor communications, credit limitations, and other vexatious details compounded the difficulties. For all these

reasons, arrivals at strange ports often resulted in delays and costly extensions of port times; therefore, captains usually maintained regular runs
between a limited number of familiar destinations. The practice of dis-
charging crews only in their home ports further supported the growth of
shuttle trade routes, because they increased the percentage of total port
time that was home port (wage free) time.

For similar reasons colonials dominated the great volume of coastwise
commerce. Early in the seventeenth century, the Dutch of New Amsterdam
had anticipated the profit potential in distributing European products along
the coast in exchange for tobacco, furs, grain, and fish, which were then
sent to Holland. After the Dutch lost power in North America, their hold
on the trade declined, and New Englanders—together with enterprising
merchants in New York and Philadelphia—dominated the coastal trades of
North America.

In terms of the money value of products exchanged, coastal commerce
was less than foreign trade with either Britain or the West Indies, but in
physical volume it was equal to each of these major trade branches. As the
scholarship of James Shepherd and Samuel Williamson has shown, just
before the Revolution, coastwise trade comprised about one-third of the
volume of total overseas trade. Compared to the North, the coastwise commerce of the South was much less important, but even there it comprised
perhaps one-fifth of the tonnage that entered and cleared southern ports.[6]

With regard to commerce within the interior and between the countryside and towns, we can say little in quantitative terms. Thanks to recent
work by a host of scholars including James A. Henretta, Winifred B. Rothenberg and Thomas M. Doerflinger, much of it based on probates, tax lists,
and other original sources, we know much more about the rich diversity of
rural trade and activity.[7] Statistical estimates of volume still elude us, however. Back-country people traded their small agricultural surpluses for the
necessities they could not produce themselves—salt, medicines, ammunition, cotton yarn, tea or coffee, and the like. In the villages and towns,
households were less self-sufficient, although even the wealthiest homes
produced some goods for everyday consumption.

In the complex of colonial domestic trade between country and town, it
became common practice for the town merchant to extend credit to farmers, either directly or through the so-called country traders who served as
intermediaries. Advances were made for the purposes of obtaining both
capital equipment, such as tools and building hardware, and the supplies
necessary for day-to-day existence. At the end of the growing season, farmers brought their produce to town to discharge their debts. In times of

---

[6] E. R. Johnson et al., *History of Domestic and Foreign Commerce of the United States* (Washington,
D.C.: Carnegie Institution of Washington, 1915), pp. 171–72.
[7] For examples, see their papers in Ronald Hoffman et al. (eds.), *The Economy of Early America:
The Revolutionary Period, 1763–1790* (Charlottesville: Univ. Press of Virginia, 1988).

Boston's natural endowments helped the city attain a place of prominence as a trading and shipping center; but the mountains to the west inhibited access to the hinterland, and Boston ultimately fell behind New York in the commercial rivalry between these two great ports.

seriously depressed agricultural prices, farmers might be substantially in debt by the end of the year, and two or three bad years in a row could result in foreclosure and the loss of a farm with its improvements. The outcome was that many farmers gave up and moved farther west, and merchants or other propertied people who were able to withstand the vicissitudes of crop failures and wide swings in agricultural prices took the titles to these farms. As we will learn in Chapter 5, this changed the distribution of wealth in colonial times in some important ways.

MONEY AND TRADE

One of the most persistent problems in the colonies was establishing and maintaining an acceptable currency. Among friends and acquaintances especially, barter trade and credit were common, but money was needed as a unit of account, a liquid form of wealth, and to facilitate exchange. One of the earliest solutions—borrowed from the Indians by the first New England settlers—was to use wampum for money. The black and white polished beads made from clam shells, which circulated for several decades after the founding of the colonies, were legal tender for private debts in Massachusetts until 1661 and were used as money in New York as late as 1701.

In Maryland and Virginia, tobacco remained the principal medium of exchange long after its value had declined from three shillings to a penny or two a pound; indeed, the monetization of tobacco actually stimulated its production and thereby furthered its depreciation in value. Other colonies designated as "country pay" (acceptable for taxes) such items as hides, furs, tallow, cows, corn, wheat, beans, pork, fish, brandy, whiskey, and musket balls. Harried public officials were endlessly swindled because they received such a poor quality of "country pay," but just as serious was the cost of transporting the commodities received for taxes and loss through shrinkage and deterioration.[8] What public treasuries would accept, private merchants could not refuse. Until his death in 1764, Thomas Hancock, John's uncle, in conducting business with the country merchants of New England, had to accept commodities and pass them on to reluctant creditors in turn.

Clearly, one of the major problems in using commodity money, besides inconvenience, spoilage, and storage difficulties, was quality control. Gresham's law—that bad money (low quality) drives out good (high quality)—applied because it was in an individual's self-interest to make payments whenever possible with low-quality goods (money).

One of the earliest domestically initiated regulations, the Maryland Tobacco Inspection Act of 1747, addressed the issue of quality control. The intent of the Act was to increase the value of tobacco exports from Maryland, and came in response to a tobacco inspection law of 1730 in Virginia. In effect, British importers had been discounting Maryland tobacco relative to Virginia tobacco in 1730–47, because Virginia's inspection system eliminated the widespread practice of including damaged or "trash" tobacco in shipments. As Marylanders continued this practice, after 1730, the prices of Maryland tobacco slipped relatively. The adoption of the 1747 Act reversed that trend, and closed the price gap abruptly.[9]

Not only did this move to quality control raise the value of Maryland's tobacco exports, it also set firm standards of quality control for tobacco as money. In fact, because paper certificates, called inspection notes, were given on inspected tobacco, the circulation of money became easier, thus increasing the velocity of money.

---

[8]Charles J. Bullock, *Essays on the Monetary History of the United States* (New York: Macmillan, 1900), p. 11.

[9]For an excellent analysis of the impact of the Act, and evidence on tobacco prices see: Mary McKinney Schweitzer, "Economic Regulation and the Colonial Economy: The Maryland Tobacco Inspection Act of 1747," *Journal of Economic History* 40 (1980): 551–70.

One planter from Virginia commented in 1747 in the *Maryland Gazette*: "The very circulation of the inspection notes in the country is a great advantage to the people, for perhaps they will pass from one to another fifty times before they return to the Inspector again."[10]

Another planter, from Maryland, reported in 1753: "the Advantage of having Tobacco Notes in my pocket, as giving me credit for the quantity mentioned in them wherever I went, and that I was thereby at large to dispose of them when, to whom, and where I pleased; whereas, before this Act, my credit could not be expected to go beyond my own Neighborhood, or at farthest, where I might be known."[11]

Despite these and other problems, commodity money was extensively used in the colonies, especially in the seventeenth century whenever specie and paper substitutes were scarce. By the time of the eighteenth century, both specie (gold or silver) and paper currency were common in the major seaboard cities, and by the end of the century, commodities—particularly furs—were accepted as a medium of exchange only in communities along the western frontier.

Due to the sizable trades with many overseas areas, the gold and silver coins of all the important commercial countries of Europe and their dependencies in the Western Hemisphere were freely exchanged throughout the eastern seaboard. More important than English coins, which could not be legally exported from Britain to the colonies, were the silver coins of the Spanish mint. These were struck for the most part in Mexico City and Lima and introduced into the colonial economy via vigorous trading with the Spanish colonies. English-speaking people referred to the "piece of eight" (as the old Spanish peso was called) as a "dollar," probably because it was about the size of the German *thaler*. Spanish dollars were so common in the colonies that the coin was eventually adopted as the monetary unit of the United States. The fractional coin, known as the "real" or "bit," was worth about 12½ cents, or one-eighth of a Spanish dollar, and was important in making change.[12]

Although Massachusetts first attempted to mint coins of low bullion content as early as 1652, it is not surprising that the colonies turned to paper to increase their meager and undependable money supply, and settlers became accustomed to paper money at an early date. The promissory notes of well-known individuals often exchanged hands for several months. Bills of exchange drawn on English merchants or various government officials in London also circulated widely. Treasurers of the different colonies began to issue promissory notes in advance of tax collection or to issue written

---

[10]*Maryland Gazette*, May 1747, as reported in Schweitzer, pp. 563–64.

[11]*Maryland Gazette*, April 5, 1773, as reported in Schweitzer, p. 564.

[12]The "piece of eight" was so called in colloquial language because of the numeral *VIII* impressed on one side to indicate its value of eight *reales*. In many parts of the United States, the expressions *two bits*, *four bits*, and *six bits* are still used today.

orders to town officers requiring the payment of obligations from local stores; like other negotiable instruments, these pieces of paper were exchanged on endorsement as money.[13]

In 1690, Massachusetts issued the first bills of credit to pay soldiers who had returned from an unsuccessful military expedition. During the next 65 years, at least eight other colonies followed this example to meet financial emergencies, especially payments of war-related efforts. Bills of credit were issued with the proviso that they were to be redeemed in specie at some future date; in the meantime, they were accepted for taxes by the issuing colony. Such redemption provisions, although restricted, facilitated the free circulation of these bills as money. In some states—notably Rhode Island, Massachusetts, Connecticut, and South Carolina—the bills were commonly overissued, thereby depreciating their value relative to specie. The same difficulty was encountered with the paper of the publicly owned "banks" established by colonial governments. These institutions, unlike anything we call a bank today, issued "loan bills," lending to individuals, usually based on the security of land or houses. Borrowers used the bills to meet their obligations and were usually required to repay the debt, with interest, in annual installments.

Occasionally, despite public issues of paper, private remedies were still undertaken as exemplified by one merchant's announcement in April 1761 in the *Maryland Gazette:*

> As I daily suffer much inconvenience in my Business for Want of small Change, which indeed is a universal Complaint of almost everybody in any Sort of Business, I intend . . . to Print . . . a Parcel of small Notes, from Three Pence to Two Shillings and Six Pence each, to pass Current at the same Rate as the Money under the Inspecting Law, and to be Exchanged by me . . . for good Spanish Dollars at Seven Shillings and Six Pence each Dollar.[14]

In this fashion, transaction costs were lowered, especially on retail and small-lot exchanges.

MONEY, DEBTS, AND CREDITORS

During the eighteenth century, there was continuing conflict—especially in New England—over the currency question. As in every community throughout recorded history, there were advocates of "sound" money, who took the position that efforts to increase the money supply beyond the quantity of coin in circulation were both unethical and dangerous. On the

---

[13]See Curtis P. Nettels, *The Money Supply of the American Colonies Before 1720* (Madison: Univ. of Wisconsin Press, 1934), pp. 250–51.

[14]From Joseph A. Ernst, *Money and Politics in America, 1755–1775* (Chapel Hill: Univ. of North Carolina Press, 1973), pp. 154–155. For more on this issue see: John R. Hanson II, "Small Notes in the American Colonies," *Explorations in Economic History* 17 (1980): 411–20.

whole, however, American colonists were disposed toward an expansive supply of money. Primarily farmers and exporters of raw materials, most Americans wanted prices to rise to increase money incomes and to provide relief from debt. Farmers clearly favored the establishment of banks so that they could obtain money at low interest rates by offering their land as security. And many merchants, themselves debtors, joined with the agrarians to urge continuing issuances of paper.

Historically, most paper issues in the colonies invited little attention from England, but over time debtors more frequently attempted to pay off old obligations with depreciated paper. To use paper currency as legal tender, not just in tax payments, but in private transactions as well, became well established by custom and law in New England.

Figure 4-1 illustrates the problem and traces the exchange rate of Pennsylvania paper currency for English sterling in London. In the late 1740s, nearly £180 Pennsylvania currency were needed to equal £100 sterling. The discrepancy between the currency's face value and its market value was the source of the conflict between colonial debtors and English creditors. English merchants were normally willing to accept currency at market value, but debtors pointed to colonial laws stating that creditors had to accept paper money at face value (one pound currency for one pound debt in sterling). Ultimately the Crown and Parliament were forced into the controversy. In response to complaints by British creditors, the Currency Act of 1751 prohibited the New England colonies from issuing further bills of credit and from organizing new public banks. Furthermore, existing paper note issues, which because of depreciation normally did not exceed 5 percent of New England's purchasing power of money, were to be retired as they fell due. More important, from the point of view of its ultimate political consequences, was the Currency Restraining Act of 1764, which extended the

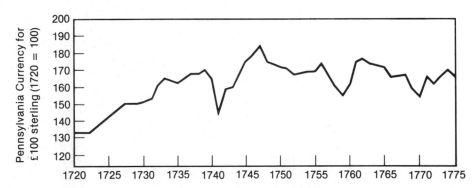

FIGURE 4-1   Annual Rate of Exchange in London for Pennsylvania Currency: The exchange rates between English sterling and Pennsylvania's paper currency moved upward, 1720–39, taking more Pennsylvania money to buy an English pound. Later there were periods when the sterling rate fell.

Source: *Historical Statistics of the United States* (Washington, D.C.: GPO, 1976), series Z 585.

provision of the Currency Act to all the colonies. Precipitated by events in Virginia, which after 1755 had issued £250,000 in bills of credit with full legal tender provisions, the act brought loud protests from residents in the southern colonies. Meanwhile British merchants, who objected that debts due in specie were being paid in paper money issued in great quantity during the French and Indian War, nodded approval. Coming as it did during a postwar recession, the Restraining Act aroused much animosity. By 1773, amidst growing antagonism, Parliament relented and permitted the colonies to use currency issues as legal tender at face value for public payments, but not for private ones.

It is important to emphasize that paper money at that time was uniquely American. Although invented and used in ancient China, paper money was not used anywhere in the world after 1500 until reintroduced by the mainland colonists. It stands as one of the great legacies of the colonists.

One of the most perplexing problems to later confront the nation's founding fathers, as in colonial times, was the establishment of a uniform, efficient currency. Indeed, the conflict between the advocates of "cheap" and "sound" money has continued throughout our history and is still an important issue today.

SELECTED REFERENCES AND SUGGESTED READINGS

Andrews, Charles M. *The Colonial Period of American History,* Vol. 4 of *England's Commercial and Colonial Policy.* New Haven, Conn.: Yale Univ. Press, 1938.

Barrow, Thomas. *Trade and Empire: The British Customs Service in Colonial America, 1660–1775.* Cambridge: Harvard Univ. Press, 1967.

Becker, Robert A. *Revolution, Reform, and the Politics of Taxation in America: 1763–1783.* Baton Rouge: Louisiana State Univ. Press, 1980.

Beer, George L. *British Colonial Policy, 1754–1765.* Gloucester: Peter Smith, 1958.

Breen, Timothy H. *Tobacco Culture: The Mentality of the Great Tidewater Planters on the Eve of the Revolution.* Princeton: Princeton Univ. Press, 1985.

Brock, Leslie. *The Currency System of the American Colonies, 1700–1764.* New York: Arno Press, 1975.

Bruchey, Stuart. *The Colonial Merchant: Sources and Readings.* New York: Harcourt Brace, 1966.

––––––. *The Roots of American Economic Growth 1607–1861: An Essay in Social Causation.* London: Hutchinson Univ. Library, 1965.

Burnstein, M. L. "Colonial and Contemporary Monetary Theory." *Explorations in Entrepreneurial History* 3, no. 3, 2nd series (Spring 1966).

Coleman, D. C., ed. *Revisions in Mercantilism.* London: Methuen, 1969.

Dickerson, Oliver M. *American Colonial Government 1696–1765.* Cleveland: Arthur H. Clark, 1912.

––––––. *The Navigation Acts and the American Revolution.* Philadelphia: Univ. of Pennsylvania Press, 1951.

Ernst, Joseph. *Money and Politics in America, 1755–1775.* Chapel Hill: Univ. of North Carolina Press, 1973.

Evans, Emory. "Planter Indebtedness and the Coming of the Revolution in Virginia, 1776 to 1796." *William and Mary Quarterly* 19, 2nd series (1962): 511–33.

Greene, Jack P., and Richard M. Jellison. "The Currency Act of 1764 in Imperial-Colonial Relations, 1764–1776." *William and Mary Quarterly* 18, no. 4, 2nd series (Oct. 1961).

Gwyn, Julian. "British Government Spending and the North American Colonies, 1740–1775." *Journal of Imperial and Commonwealth History* 8 (1984):74–84.

Hacker, Louis M. "The First American Revolution." *Columbia University Quarterly,* part 1, Sept. 1935. Reprinted in Gerald D. Nash. *Issues in American Economic History.* New York: Heath, 1972.

Hanson, John R. "Money in the Colonial American Economy: An Extension." *Economic Inquiry* (1979):281–86.

_____. "Small Notes in the American Economy." *Explorations in Economic History* 21 (1984):411–20.

Harper, Lawrence A. *The English Navigation Laws.* New York: Columbia Univ. Press, 1939.

_____. "Mercantilism and the American Revolution." *Canadian Historical Review,* March 1942. Reprinted in Gerald D. Nash. *Issues in American Economic History.* New York: Heath, 1972.

Hughes. J. R. T. *Social Control in the Colonial Economy.* Charlottesville: Univ. Press of Virginia, 1976.

Kulikoff, Allan. "The Economic Growth of the Eighteenth-Century Chesapeake Colonies." *The Journal of Economic History* 39 (1979):275–88.

Lester, Richard A. *Monetary Experiments: Early American and Recent Scandinavian.* Princeton, N. J.: Princeton Univ. Press, 1939.

_____. "Currency Issues to Overcome Depressions in Pennsylvania, 1723 and 1729." *Journal of Political Economy,* 71 (1963):324–75.

Neal, Larry. "Interpreting Power and Profit in Economic History: A Case Study of the Seven Years' War." *Journal of Economic History* 37 (1977):20–35.

Nettels, Curtis C. "British Policy and Colonial Money Supply." *Economic History Review* 3 (1931).

_____. *The Money Supply of the American Colonies Before 1720.* Madison: The Univ. of Wisconsin Press, 1934.

Perkins, Edwin J. *The Economy of Colonial America.* 2nd ed. New York: Columbia Univ. Press, 1988. Chs. 2 and 7.

Price, Jacob. *Capital and Credit in British Overseas Trade: The View from the Chesapeake, 1700–1776.* Cambridge: Harvard Univ. Press, 1980.

_____. "Economic Function and the Growth of American Port Towns in the Eighteenth Century." In *Perspectives in American History,* ed., D. Fleming and B. Bailyn, vol. 8. Cambridge: Harvard Univ. Press, 1974.

_____. "The Economic Growth of the Chesapeake and the European Market, 1697–1775." *The Journal of Economic History* 24 (1964):496–511.

_____. "A Note on the Value of Colonial Exports of Shipping." *Journal of Economic History* 36 (1976):704–24.

Rosenberg, Nathan, and L. E. Birdzell, Jr. *How the West Grew Rich.* New York: Basic Books, 1986. Ch. 4.

Schwertzer, Mary McKinney. "Economic Regulation and the Colonial Economy: The Maryland Tobacco Inspection Act of 1747." *Journal of Economic History* 40 (1980):551–70.

Shepherd, James F., and Samuel Williamson. "The Coastal Trade of the British North American Colonies 1768–1772." *Journal of Economic History* 32 (1972):783–810.

Smith, Bruce. "Some Colonial Evidence on Two Theories of Money: Maryland and the Carolinas." *Journal of Political Economy* 93 (1985):1178–1211.

Studenski, Paul, and Herman Krooss. *Financial History of the United States.* New York: McGraw-Hill, 1952.

Thomas, Peter A. G. "The Cost of the British Army in North America, 1763–1775." *William and Mary Quarterly* 45 (1988):510–16.

Ver Steeg, Clarence. *The Formative Years, 1607–1763.* New York: Hill & Wang, 1964.

Walton, Gary M., and James F. Shepherd. *The Economic Rise of Early America.* Cambridge: Cambridge Univ. Press, 1979.

Weiss, Roger. "The Issue of Paper Money in the American Colonies, 1720–1774." *Journal of Economic History* 30 (1970):770–785.

_____. "The Colonial Monetary Standards of Massachusetts." *Economic History Review* 27, no. 4, 2nd series (Nov. 1974).

Wicker, Elmer. "Colonial Monetary Standards Contrasted: Evidence from the Seven Years' War." *The Journal of Economic History* 45 (1985):860–84.

C H A P T E R 5

Economic Progress and Wealth

GROWTH AND CHANGE IN THE COLONIAL ECONOMY

The many local and regional economies that comprised the total colonial economy were always in a state of flux. Because they began literally as settlements in the wilderness and because war and other frontier disturbances were frequent, it is particularly difficult to systematically portray the economic growth of the colonies. Economic growth, of course, refers to the rate at which a society's material standard of living advances over an extended period of time. It implies more than a mere increase in inputs which enlarge output. Economic growth means an advance in output relative to population in the long run. This can be accomplished by an increase in the labor-population ratio, by the movement of inputs from lower- to higher-value uses, or from other sources of productivity gains—such as technological change, economies of scale, improvements in business organization and economic institutions—and from skill-enhancing investments—such as education and on-the-job training. Furthermore, labor productivity, namely output per unit of labor input, can be increased by raising the capital-labor ratio or the land-labor ratio, as well as the above general sources of productivity advance. These in turn raise the standard of living for the total population.

In 1964, George R. Taylor, president of the Economic History Association, triggered a debate that has not yet run its course. In his presidential address he argued that before 1710 very little economic growth occurred in the colonies—it was "slow and irregular," but then between 1710 and 1775 it averaged "slightly more than one percent per annum."[1] Was this in fact the case? Did such an early eighteenth-century acceleration really take place, and did per capita incomes really double between 1710 and 1775 as the 1-percent rate implies? Did such economic advances continue indefinitely thereafter, or did periods of stagnation reappear?

---

[1]George R. Taylor, "American Economic Growth Before 1840: An Exploratory Essay," *Journal of Economic History* 24 (1964):437.

Firm answers elude us because the yardstick of economic growth is the trend rate of growth of real per capita income,[2] and we lack the needed time series on yearly income or output. Fragments of information have appeared through recent scholarly efforts, however, to significantly advance our understanding of the timing and pace of growth in the colonies.

Productivity Change in Agriculture

The major economic activity in the colonies was agriculture, and progress in this sector had a particularly strong bearing on total colonial production. Because agriculture was such a significant part of total output, total average gains were significantly influenced by advances (or lack of advances) in this sector. Moreover, it is important to reemphasize that economic progress in real per capita terms stems primarily from human efforts to raise productivity—the increase of output relative to the inputs of labor, capital, and land. Therefore, we will devote particular attention to periods of change in productivity and to the causes of the agricultural improvements that were introduced.

Tobacco in the Upper South   An obvious starting point is the dominant colonial staple—tobacco. Information on tobacco prices in the Chesapeake Bay area as shown in Figure 5-1 suggests that throughout the late seventeenth century and almost all of the eighteenth century, only minor agricultural improvements were made. Most of the increases in the productivity of tobacco occurred very early in the colonial period. Ranging between 20 and 30 pence sterling per pound in the early 1620s, tobacco prices fell to almost 3 pence per pound around 1630. A second phase lasting approximately four decades followed that precipitous decline. This time the average price decreased to approximately a penny per pound. Of course, short-term periods of cyclical variations occurred, but normally tobacco prices stayed at that low level throughout most of the remaining peacetime years.

There can be little doubt that these two early periods of declining tobacco prices represented major surges in productivity, and, according to Allan Kulikoff, tobacco output per worker doubled in 1630–70. The demand for tobacco in Europe was persistently growing, and the costs of the labor and land required to produce tobacco did not decrease over these years. Since declining wages or rents cannot explain the lower costs of tobacco they must have been largely due to advances in output per unit of input (land, labor, and capital in combination); that is, to gains in productivity. Terry Anderson and Robert Thomas also estimate very high productivity advances in tobacco: over the last three quarters of the seventeenth century, it was nearly 1.5 percent per year on average. Very little productivity advance occurred in

---

[2]It is important to remember that in measuring changes of income, we often neglect other factors that affect the quality of life, such as the amount of leisure time enjoyed, conditions of health, environment, personal attributes, even the distribution of wealth.

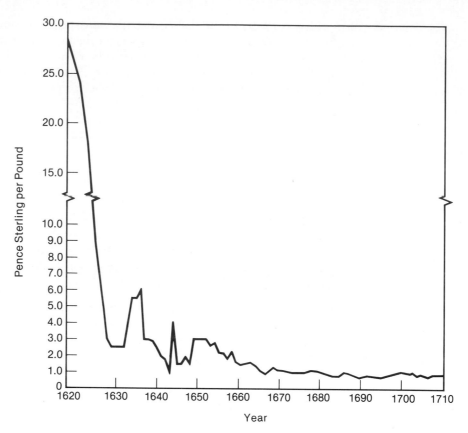

FIGURE 5-1   Price of Chesapeake Tobacco, 1618–1710

Source: Russell R. Menard, "A Note on Chesapeake Tobacco Prices, 1618–1660," *Virginia Magazine of History and Biography* (1976): 401–10, and "Farm Prices of Maryland Tobacco, 1659–1710," *Maryland Historical Magazine* 58 (Spring 1973): 85.

tobacco in the eighteenth century, however, and undoubtedly, the major period of progress in tobacco cultivation was in the seventeenth rather than the eighteenth century.

This characteristic of rapid early gains and subsequent periods of relative stagnation has always been common to the growth patterns of production in firms and industries. In colonial times, before the age of widespread technological advances, productivity gains stemmed primarily from trial and error and learning by doing. In agriculture, the fruits of these efforts generally materialized within a few decades of crop introduction. Sometimes, as in the case of tobacco, the introduction of a new seed type generated a surge of crop productivity. Also, in the early phases of experimentation, the colonists found ways to combine and adjust soils, seeds, labor, implements, and other agricultural inputs to their optimum uses. In later stages of agricultural development, improvements were more gradual, due

Additions of capital and the specialization of tasks raised productivity per worker in colonial tobacco production.

to a slower-paced accumulation of knowledge about the most productive uses of available soils and resources. Of course, in some instances such as wine production and silk cultivation, these futile efforts ceased in the experimentation phase.

Grain and Livestock in the Middle Colonies Similarly in grain and livestock production, gains in productivity appear to have been modest, indeed low, throughout most of the eighteenth century. At least the evidence on changes in Pennsylvania's agriculture suggests only limited progress over that century (see Table 5-1).

The most visible change in Pennsylvania farms was the sharp decline in average farm size from about 500 acres around 1700 to about 140 acres at the end of the century. But this decrease did not indicate a fall in the "effective land"–labor ratio. Instead it was the consequence of population expansion and the subdivision of uncleared acres as new farms evolved. Because the amount of uncleared land per farm exceeded the minimum needs for fuel and timber, these acreage reductions had no noticeable effect on agricultural output. Because the average number of cleared acres per farm changed little, the effective input of land per farm remained almost constant over the entire eighteenth century. This reasoning explains the nearly constant land index of 100 shown in Table 5-1, column 1.

TABLE 5-1   Indexes of Inputs, Outputs, and Productivity in Pennsylvania Agriculture, 1714–90

YEARS	(1) LAND	(2) CAPITAL	(3) LABOR	(4) COM-BINED INPUTS[a]	(5) LIVE-STOCK	(6) GRAIN	(7) TOTAL OUTPUT[b]	(8) (7)/(4) OUTPUT INPUT
1714–31	100	100	100	100	100	100	100	100
1734–45	100	114	91	95	103	100	101	106
1750–70	106	126	91	97	106	103	107	110
1775–90	106	121	88	97	87	110	103	109

[a]The combined inputs index is obtained by weighting land, capital, and labor at 14, 10, and 76, respectively.
[b]Total output is adjusted to include some nonagriculture output after 1750, therefore influencing the total output index slightly in the last two periods.

Source: Duane Ball and Gary M. Walton, "Agricultural Productivity Change in Eighteenth Century Pennsylvania," *Journal of Economic History* 36 (1976), Tables 4, 5, and 7.

Alternatively, additional implements, structures, and accumulated inventories raised the amount of capital inputs per farm (see column 2). On the other hand, average family size was shrinking. Consequently, in the predominantly family farm areas such as Pennsylvania, the amount of labor per farm decreased (column 3). Therefore, both the capital–labor ratio and the cleared land–labor ratio rose. Given the increase of inputs per worker, we would expect output per worker to expand.

Indeed, the evidence reveals that output per farm was increasing (column 7). Not only were farms producing more livestock and grains (mainly wheat and maslin, a combination of wheat and rye), but by the late colonial period, a small but growing portion of farm labor time was being diverted to nonagricultural production, including milling, smithing, cabinet making, chair making, and tanning. Overall, average output per farm increased by about 7 percent between the first and third quarters of the eighteenth century. When the gain in output is compared to the change in total input,[3] it appears that total productivity advanced approximately 10 percent during these decades. Expressed in terms of rates of change, total productivity expanded 0.1–0.2 percent per year, with the most rapid change (0.3 percent) occurring in the first decades of the eighteenth century. Finally, the growth of output per worker was somewhat higher—approximately 0.2–0.3 percent per year—over the first three-quarters of the century.[4]

---

[3]With land per farm nearly constant, labor per farm declining, and capital per farm rising, total input per farm changed according to the relative importance of labor and capital and the relative degree of change of each. Because labor comprised such a high percentage of total costs, total combined input per farm actually declined by a few percentage points during the eighteenth century.

[4]It should be noted that labor productivity (output per worker) increased more than total productivity (output per total combined input), because the amounts of capital and cleared land per worker increased during this period. Increases in these other inputs enabled labor to produce more.

Specific evidence as to the precise sources of these advances is almost entirely lacking. The low measured rate of advance, however, does reinforce historical descriptions. For instance, in their classic study of agriculture, Bidwell and Falconer assert that in the colonies north of the Chesapeake, "The eighteenth century farmers showed little advance over the first settlers in their care of livestock," and "little if any improvement had been made in farm implements until the very close of the eighteenth century."[5] Another study of Pennsylvania agriculture specifically concludes that "economic conditions throughout the century prohibited major changes and encouraged a reasonably stable and uniform type of mixed farming that involved fairly extensive use or superficial working of the land."[6] It seems reasonable to conclude that farmers were probably beginning to learn to use the soil and their implements more effectively. But there is little indication of input savings, either from technological improvements or from economies of scale in terms of larger farms. Better organized and more widespread market participation, however, may have contributed somewhat to gains in agricultural productivity.

These findings and conclusions come as no surprise when examined in the light of agricultural developments in later periods. For instance, investigations by Robert Gallman indicate total productivity gains of approximately 0.5 percent per year over the nineteenth century.[7] However, in the first half of the century, output per unit of land, labor, and capital combined advanced at a rate of 0.1–0.2 percent. In the second half of the century, the productivity rate rose to 0.8 percent. Undoubtedly, the lower-paced first half of the nineteenth century—before the transition to animal power and increased mechanization—would have been more suggestive of the eighteenth-century experience. In short, agricultural progress throughout most of the late colonial period and probably all of the eighteenth century was limited and slow-paced.

Productivity Gains in Transportation and Distribution

Although productivity advances in agriculture were slow and gradual, substantially higher gains were registered in the handling and transportation of goods. Such gains were extremely important because transportation and other distribution costs comprised a large portion of the final market price of products. This was especially true of the bulky colonial products, which

---

[5]P. W. Bidwell and J. I. Falconer, *History of Agriculture in the Northern United States, 1620–1860* (Washington, D.C.: Carnegie Institute of Washington, 1925), pp. 107, 123.
[6]James T. Lemon, *Best Poor Man's Country: A Geographical Study of Early Southwestern Pennsylvania* (Baltimore: Johns Hopkins Univ. Press, 1972), pp. 150–51.
[7]See Robert E. Gallman, "Changes in Total U.S. Agricultural Factor Productivity in the Nineteenth Century," *Agricultural History* 46 (1972):191–210; and Gallman, "The Agricultural Sector and the Pace of Economic Growth: U.S. Experience in the Nineteenth Century," in *Essays in Nineteenth Century Economic History,* ed. David C. Klingaman and Richard K. Vedder (Athens: Ohio Univ. Press, 1975), pp. 35–76.

were normally low in value relative to their weight or volume (displaced cargo space). For example, transportation and handling costs would double the value of a barrel of pitch between Maryland and London. Even the distribution costs of expensive lightwares represented a significant fraction of their value.

During the eighteenth century, the differential between English and colonial prices for manufactures shipped to the colonies was declining at a fairly steady rate. In the early decades of the century, it was not uncommon for English goods to sell for 80–140 percent more in the colonies than in England. By mid-century, prices on British wares were 45–75 percent higher in the colonies. Finally, just prior to the Revolution, this price spread had been reduced to a range of only 15–25 percent. However, as late as the 1770s, colonial staples such as pitch, tar, lumber, rice, and other space-consuming exports were still commanding more than double their domestic price in normal English and European markets.

Evidence of improvements in the marketing and distribution of transatlantic tobacco shipments reveals the declining average differential between the Amsterdam price and the colonial price of tobacco (given as a percentage of the Amsterdam price):[8]

Years	Price Differences
1720–24	82%
1725–29	76%
1730–34	82%
1735–39	77%
1740–44	77%
1745–49	76%
1750–54	67%
1755–59	72%
1760–64	70%
1765–69	65%
1770–72	51%

A series of advances in transatlantic tobacco distribution stemmed from improvements in packaging and merchandising, from declining costs of information on prices and markets, and from reductions in risk in trade. However, by far the most important improvements were in shipping. Although freight rates fluctuated and varied according to route, the long-run trend was persistently downward. During the 100 years preceding the Revolution, the real costs of shipping were almost halved. Expressed in terms of productivity gains, shipping advanced at a rate of approximately 0.8 percent per year. For that period in general—and specifically compared to changes

---

[8]James F. Shepherd and Gary M. Walton, *Shipping, Maritime Trade, and the Economic Development of Colonial North America* (Cambridge: Cambridge Univ. Press, 1972), p. 60.

in agriculture—these increases suggest that shipping was a strategic factor in the overall economic advance of the colonies.

Sources of Productivity Change in Shipping   What caused these productivity gains? Where trades were well organized and markets reasonably large and safe, economies of scale in shipping were usually realized. For instance, in such commerce as the Baltic timber trades, the use of large vessels generated labor savings per ton shipped. Although larger ships necessitated larger crews, the increased cargo capacity more than compensated for the additional labor costs. As vessels increased in size, their carrying capacity per unit of labor also increased. In other words, on larger ships, fewer men were needed to transport a given volume of goods.

Despite these possibilities, the average size of vessels employed in the western Atlantic and in the Caribbean failed to increase significantly over the 100-year period. The potential labor savings of the larger ships were offset by greater occurrences of low utilization in these waters. In fact, in those numerous small and scattered markets, the port times of large vessels were usually as much as twice as long as those for small vessels. Therefore, in colonial waters, schooners and sloops normally traveled a greater number of miles per ton than large ships or brigs did.

Nevertheless, the number of tons per man increased, because crew sizes decreased as vessels remained unchanged in size. For example, a Boston vessel of 50 tons employed an average of seven men early in the eighteenth century; but by the late colonial period, the same ship required only five crew members. Over this same time span, the crew size of a typical New York vessel of 50 tons decreased from eleven to seven members. Paralleling this reduction in labor was the reduction or elimination of armaments on vessels that traded in colonial waters. Guns had been commonplace on seventeenth-century vessels trading in the western Atlantic, but cannons had all but disappeared on ships there by the end of the colonial period.

Although the average useful life of vessels changed little over the period, insurance rates decreased due to the declining risks in ocean travel. In contrast to earlier times, insurance rates for most one-way transatlantic passages had reached the rock-bottom common peacetime level of 2 percent by 1720. Of course, rates for voyages into pirate-infested waters were quite another matter. Between New York and Jamaica, for example, the prevailing rate of 5 percent in 1720 had dropped to 4 percent by the 1770s. On routes from New England to various other islands in the West Indies, peacetime insurance rates were halved between 1700 and 1775.

These changes were accompanied by others of similar importance. Curiously, however, faster ship speed was not a positive force in raising productivity. Vessels from New England and the Middle colonies that sailed to the West Indies and back showed no gains in speed on either leg of the journey over this period, as shown in Figure 5-2.

Despite the constancy of ship speed, however, round-trip voyage times declined from 1700 to 1770. As Figure 5-3 shows, with the single exception

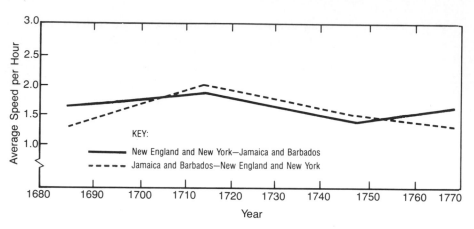

FIGURE 5-2 Average Ship Speeds (Knots)

Source: Gary M. Walton, "Sources of Productivity Change in American Colonial Shipping," *The Economic History Review* 20: 1, (April 1967), p. 74.

of Boston, layover times fell markedly in many key ports in the New World. Because a very large portion of a sailing ship's life was spent in port, such declines contributed greatly to higher productivity. For example, in the Chesapeake trade, vessels were in port more than twice as long at the end of the seventeenth century as they were in the 1760s. An important contributor to this change was the introduction of Scottish *factors* (representatives of Scottish merchant firms) into the Chesapeake Bay area after 1707. Undoubtedly their methods of gathering and inventorying the tobacco crop in barns and warehouses for quick loading significantly shortened port times in the Chesapeake Bay.

Similarly, in Barbados, port times were more than halved during this period. In the early colonial days, port times were extraordinarily long because exchanges were costly to transact. The many scattered markets were small and remote, and prices varied widely among islands and even within the same island. The shipmaster, acting on behalf of a merchant, might have to visit several islands on one trip to find the best market for his cargo. Difficulties in negotiating prices and determining the medium of exchange, as well as possibly settling past debts, all tended to lengthen the transaction period. Often bartering was practiced, but even when money was used, prices were not easy to determine because different currencies and bills of exchange (with varying degrees of risk) were afforded no set value. Finally, the problem of collecting cargoes extended port times, especially when harvests were poor.[9] Nevertheless, long layovers in the Caribbean became less common as a more systematic market economy evolved.

---

[9] As discussed in Chapter 4, many of these factors also explain the generality of shuttle patterns of shipping and of route dominance by the colonists, vis-à-vis the British on particular routes.

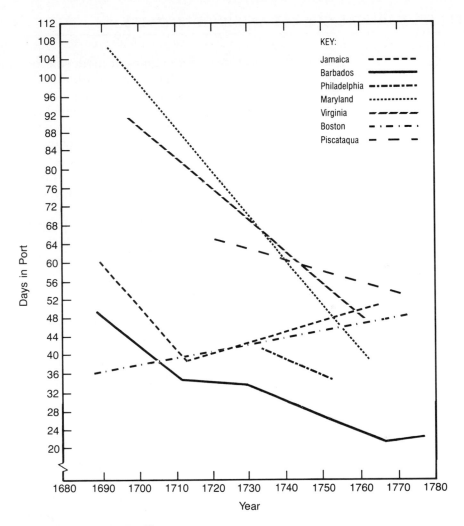

FIGURE 5-3 Average Port Times

Source: Walton, "Sources of Productivity Change in American Colonial Shipping," p. 75.

It should be emphasized that decreasing port times produced savings not only in capital but also in labor costs, since crews were customarily fed and paid while they were in foreign ports.

Such savings more than offset other sources of cost increases. Although wages and ship repair costs remained fairly constant over the period, the costs of shipbuilding and victualing (obtaining food for the crew) increased. Overall, however, the productivity gains countervailed, and freight costs were cut in half between 1675 and 1775.

TECHNOLOGICAL CHANGE AND PRODUCTIVITY

One of the most powerful engines of modern economic growth has been technological changes that have raised output relative to inputs. But compared to the nineteenth century, technological changes remained minor and sporadic in the colonial period. It preceded the era of the cotton gin, steam power, and the many metalurgical advances that vastly increased the tools available to workers. Even in iron production, we learn from Paul Paskoff that in the late colonial period learning by doing and adapting was the key source of labor and fuel savings in iron production. In the decade preceding the Revolution, iron output per man increased nearly 50 percent, and charcoal use per ton decreased by half. Learning to reduce the fuel input to minimal levels saved on labor needed to gather charcoal and work the forges. Technology remained static and forge sizes constant, however. The evidence in agriculture also indicates no significant leaps in technology. Old ways prevailed and as James Lemon stressed, farming was typically "stable and uniform".

In shipping, the same conclusion is reached. This period preceded the era of iron ships and steam, and both ship materials and the power source of ships remained unchanged. Even increasingly complex sails and rigs and the alterations of hull shapes failed to increase ship speed and, in any case, did not stem from fundamental advances in knowledge.

Of course, it might be argued that crew reductions stemmed from advances in knowledge. However, during the early seventeenth century, Dutch shipping had already displayed many of the essential characteristics of design, manning, and other input requirements that were found on the most advanced vessels in the western Atlantic in the 1760s and 1770s. In fact, the most significant technological change in seventeenth- and eighteenth-century shipping occurred in approximately 1595, when the Dutch first introduced the flyboat, or flute. The flyboat as a specialized merchant vessel designed to carry bulk commodities. It was exceptionally long compared to its width, had a flat bottom, and was lightly built (armament, gun platforms, and reinforced planking had been eliminated). In addition, its rig was simple and its crew size was small. In contrast, English and colonial vessels were built, gunned, and manned more heavily to meet the dual purpose of trade and defense. Their solid construction and armaments were costly—not only in materials but in manpower. Larger crews were needed to handle the more complex riggings on these vessels as well as their guns.

It quickly became evident that the flyboat could be used advantageously in certain bulk trades where the danger of piracy was low. However, in the rich but dangerous trades into the Mediterranean and the West Indies, more costly ships were required. In general, high risks in all colonial waters led to one of the most notable features of seventeenth-century shipping— the widespread use of cannons and armaments on trading vessels. Such characteristics were still observed in certain waters throughout much of the eighteenth century. Until around 1750 in the Caribbean, especially near Jamaica, vessels weighing more than 100 tons were almost always armed, and even small vessels usually carried some guns.

The need for self-protection in the Caribbean was self-evident:

> There the sea was broken by a multitude of islands affording safe anchorage and refuge, with wood, water, even provision for the taking. There the colonies of the great European powers, grouped within a few days' sail of one another, were forever embroiled in current European wars which gave the stronger of them excuse for preying on the weaker and seemed to make legitimate the constant disorder of those seas. There trade was rich, but settlement thin and defense difficult. There the idle, the criminal, and the poverty-stricken were sent to ease society in the Old World. By all these conditions piracy was fostered, and for two centuries throve ruinously, partly as an easy method of individual enrichment and partly as an instrument of practical politics.[10]

Privateering also added to the disorder. As a common practice, nation-states often gave private citizens license to harass the ships of rival states. These privateering commissions or "letters of marque" were issued without constraint in wartime, and occasionally even in peacetime, they were given to citizens who had suffered losses due to the actions of subjects from an offending state. Since privateers frequently ignored the constraints of their commissions, privateering was often difficult to distinguish from common piracy.

Other government policies also tended to aggravate existing sea hazards. Adding to the supply of privateers and pirates, some of the islands were deliberately peopled with convicts. Even as late as 1718, the governor of Jamaica complained of this policy:

> Several People have been lately sent over out of the gaols [jails] in England, upon the Encouragement of An Act of Parliament pass'd the last sessions . . . those people have been so farr from altering their Evil Courses and way of living and becoming an Advantage to Us, that the greatest part of them are gone and have Induced others to go with them a Pyrating and have Inveglied and Encouraged Severall Negroes to desert from their Masters and go to the Spaniards in Cuba, the few that remains proves a wicked Lazy and Indolent people, so that I could heartily wish this Country might be troubled with no more of them.[11]

Earlier in 1700, Colonel Quary of Virginia wrote to the Council of Trade and Plantations that "all the news of America is the swarming of pirates not

---

[10]Violet Barbour, "Privateers and Pirates in the West Indies," *American Historical Review* 16 (1911):529.
[11]Letters to the Board of Trade (Sept. 1, 1718, C. O. 137:13, 19), printed in Frank W. Pitman, *The Development of the West Indies, 1700–1763* (New Haven: Yale Univ. Press, 1971), pp. 55–56.

Acts of piracy in the western Atlantic, the Caribbean, and elsewhere thrived before 1720. The long-term effects of actions by the Royal Navy to eliminate piracy were to change the characteristics of ships and reduce freight rates on ocean transport.

only on these coasts, but all the West Indies over, which doth ruin trade ten times worse than a war."[12]

Of course, piracy was not confined to the Caribbean. Pirates lurked safely in the inlets of North Carolina, from which they regularly raided vessels trading at Charleston. In 1718, it was exclaimed that "every month brought intelligence of renewed outrages, of vessels sacked on the high seas, burned with their cargo, or seized and converted to the nefarious uses of the outlaws."[13] Local traders, shippers, and government officials in the Carolinas repeatedly solicited the Board of Trade for protection. In desperation, Carolina's Assembly appropriated funds in 1719 to support private vessels in the hope of driving the pirates from their seas. These pleas and protective actions were mostly in vain, but finally the Royal Navy took action. By the early 1740s piracy had been eliminated from the western Atlantic.

---

[12] Barbour, p. 566.
[13] S. C. Hughson, "The Carolina Pirates and Colonial Commerce," *John Hopkins University Studies in Historical and Political Science* 12 (1894):123.

The fall of piracy was paralleled by the elimination of ship armaments and the reduction of crew sizes. As such, this was a process of technical diffusion. Without piracy, specialized cargo-carrying vessels similar to the flyboat were designed, thereby substantially reducing the costs of shipping.

In summary, the main productivity advances in shipping during the colonial period resulted from (1) economies of scale in cargo handling, which reduced port times, and (2) the elimination of piracy, which stood as an obstacle to technical diffusion permitting the use of specialized low-cost cargo vessels.[14]

THE TREND RATE OF GROWTH

All such measures of productivity advance suggest that while improvements in colonial standards of material well-being occurred, the pace was slow and irregular, as George Taylor proposed. However, they do not support his assertion of an acceleration of growth of real income per capita to 1 percent annually in 1710–75. Before the modern age of rapid technological change and widespread investments in schooling to generate a highly skilled and adaptive labor force, the effective sources of growth were much more limited. This is revealed in the analysis of sources of productivity advance, emphasizing the importance of learning by doing, adapting and utilizing economies of scale where possible, and the diffusion of existing technologies.

Additional evidence, based on probated wealth holdings of deceased colonists, also portrays slow and irregular growth rates throughout the period 1630–1775. Per capita wealth included land, buildings, physical possessions, money, debts receivable minus debts owed, and often slaves and indentured contracts. Allan Kulikoff's analysis of wealth holdings in Maryland over the eighteenth century suggests a long-run trend rate of growth of 0.4 per year.[15] His evidence shows contrasting periods, a slight fall in the

---

[14]Other similar productivity gains deserve at least a brief mention here. As port times decreased, so did inventory times. This reduced the time in which a planter's capital (crop) lay idle in storage barns or warehouses. Decreased inventory times, of course, saved colonial capital. Similarly, declining risks and insurance rates reduced the costs to owners of insuring their shipments or bearing the risks of personal shipments. And there was considerable progress in packaging, as tobacco and sugar hogsheads, rice barrels, and other containers increased in size as the colonial period progressed. Although larger hogsheads and barrels demanded more input in construction, their carrying capacity grew relatively more because the surface area of such containers expanded less in proportion to their capacity. Finding the point at which increased difficulties in handling roughly offset the productivity gains from using larger containers provides us with a good example of the learning by doing, trial-and-error procedure.
[15]Deceased people's wealth exceeded average wealth per capita substantially, and not everyone who died had their estates probated. However, if the distribution of wealth did not change dramatically over the period, trends of probated wealth holdings probably reflected the trend in wealth holdings per person. Further, if the ratio of output (or income) to physical non-human wealth (capital) stayed fairly consistent, trends in such wealth per person would mirror trends in income per person.

first quarter of the century, a sharper decline in the second, with a very strong advance in the third quarter. Recalling the strong productivity growth period of 1630–1670 in the tobacco colonies, with little or no change in the late seventeenth century, suggests most of the growth bracketed a long period of no growth (or possibly some decline) in per capita well-being in the upper South. Work by Terry Anderson on New England also shows very strong advances in wealth holdings per person from 1650 to 1680, then very little growth up to 1710. The trend from 1650 to 1710 was unusually high, perhaps 1.6 percent per year.

Recent evidence provided by Gloria and Jackson Main on southern New England in 1640–1774 is shown in Table 5-2. This evidence of growth in total wealth per male indicates a trend in yearly average income advance of 0.35 percent in this region. Note, however, the spurt in the 1638–55 period, relative stagnation until the turn of the century, and then another 20-year spurt followed by another 20-year flat period, and finally another rapid spurt. This evidence further supports the view that regions differed greatly in the timing of their growth phases. Over a very long period, however, the trend growth rates of regions were probably fairly similar.

It seems reasonable to conclude that over the last 100 to 150 years of the colonial period, the growth rate trend was slightly below 0.5 percent per year. Based on evidence of wealth gathered from samples of probated estates for all the colonial regions, Alice Hanson Jones recently concluded, "Despite possible local or regional spurts or lags or even declines in some subperiods after 1650, it seems likely that, for all regions combined, fairly steady intensive growth accompanied accumulating experience in the New World, learning by doing, increasing knowhow in shipping within the Atlantic community, and the enlargement in size of the market that came with growth

TABLE 5-2   Components of Male Per Capita Probate Wealth in Southern New England, 1640–1774

YEARS	TOTAL WEALTH
1638–1654	£227.3
1655–1674	251.9
1675–1694	263.5
1695–1714	248.9
1715–1734	272.4
1735–1754	275.8
1765–1774	364.7

Note: For estates of males only; weighted for age and area. Estates from 1755–1764 were not included due to incomplete sample for area weighting.

Source: Adapted from Gloria L. Main and Jackson T. Main. "Economic Growth and the Standard of Living in Southern New England, 1642–1774," *Journal of Economic History* (1988):27–46.

of population and trade."[16] By her calculations she suggests growth rates for three distinct periods that are 0.3 percent, 1650–1725; 0.4 percent, 1725–50; and 0.5 percent, 1750–75.[17] Although the acceleration of growth implied by her figures may be challenged, the range seems reasonable in light of the improvements we have already noted and also in light of England's estimated annual economic growth rate of 0.3 percent throughout most of the eighteenth century.[18]

PER CAPITA WEALTH AND INCOME, 1774

Reflecting upon the ordeals of first settlement, such as "the lost colony" at Roanoke and the "starving time" in early Jamestown, projects stark contrast to the economic conditions of colonial life on the eve of the Revolution. From distant Scotland in 1776, Adam Smith's *Wealth of Nations* was published and on page 538 he said

> There are no colonies of which the progress has been more rapid than that of the English in North America. Plenty of good land, and liberty to manage their affairs their own way, seem to be the two great causes of the prosperity.

Contemporaries in the colonies also supported this view. Even as early as 1663 the Reverend John Higginson of Boston could observe, "We live in a more plentifull and comfortable manner than ever we did expect." And by the 1740s Benjamin Franklin could remark, "The first drudgery of settling new colonies, which confines the attention of people to mere necessities, is now pretty well over; and there are many in every province in circumstances that set them at ease . . . ."[19] Indeed, by most any standards of comparison, the quality of life and standards of material well-being were extraordinarily high for free Americans by the end of the colonial period. They lived longer and better than populations of other nations and places at the time, and better than most people throughout the world today.

The basis for these sweeping conclusions, derived from the work of Alice Jones, is shown in Tables 5-3 and 5-4. Table 5-3 shows the non-human physical wealth holdings (excluding financial debts and slavery and indenture contracts) per capita and per free person in the separate regions. Table 5-4 shows several income estimates per capita and per free person derived from the wealth figures in Table 5-3. Actual incomes would depend on the

---

[16]Alice Hanson Jones, *Wealth of a Nation to Be* (New York: Columbia Univ. Press, 1980), p. 305.
[17]Jones, p. 78.
[18]See Phyllis Deane and W. A. Cole, *British Economic Growth, 1688–1959: Trends and Structure* (London: Cambridge Univ. Press, 1964), p. 80.
[19]Stuart Bruchey (ed.), *The Colonial Merchant: Sources and Readings* (New York: Harcourt Brace Jovanovich, 1966), p. 1.

TABLE 5-3   Private Non-Human Physical Wealth, 1774 (in pounds sterling)

(1) REGION	(2) PER CAPITA	(3) PER FREE CAPITA
New England	36.4	38.0
Middle Colonies	40.2	44.1
Southern Colonies	36.4	61.6
Thirteen Colonies	37.4	48.4

Source: Adapted from Alice Hanson Jones, *Wealth of a Nation to Be* (New York: Columbia Univ. Press, 1980), pp. 54 and 58.

TABLE 5-4   Estimates of Regional Incomes, 1774 (in pounds sterling)

	Capital Output Ratios					
	PER CAPITA			PER FREE CAPITA		
REGION	(3:1)	(3.5:1)	(4:1)	(3:1)	(3.5:1)	(4:1)
New England	12.1	10.4	9.1	12.7	10.9	9.5
Middle Colonies	13.4	11.5	10.0	14.7	12.6	11.0
Southern Colonies	12.1	10.4	9.1	20.5	17.6	15.4
Thirteen Colonies	12.5	10.7	9.4	16.1	13.8	12.1

Note: These estimates of income per capita and for the free population are derived from Alice Hanson Jones' wealth estimates by using her assumption of a capital-to-income ratio of 3.5:1 and two others (3:1 and 4:1) to widen the analysis somewhat. It bears remembering that these income estimates are only approximate. Estimates of wealth stocks can be converted into income flows by dividing the wealth estimates by a capital-output ratio, but the relationship between capital and output (the capital-output ratio) is influenced by many different factors and varies both over time and among countries and regions. Nevertheless, under normal peacetime conditions, the capital-output ratio is seldom lower than 3 or higher than 5.

Source: Adapted from Jones, p. 63.

prevailing ratio of capital to output but the range of ratios (3 to 1, 3.5 to 1, and 4 to 1) very likely allow us to bracket the true incomes earned in 1774.

Using a capital-output ratio of 3.5:1 generates an estimate of income per free person in 1774 of £13.8 or £12.1 if the ratio was 4:1. These estimates compare approximately to $1,380 and $1,210 in 1989 prices, but obviously the range of goods and other conditions of life and errors of estimation make any comparison extremely crude. Nevertheless, we can safely guess that measured income per white person today has grown by a multiple of 11 to 13 times over those of free Americans in 1774 (99.2 percent of whom were white). In contrast according to Edwin Perkins, after considering food, clothing, housing, and other maintenance costs, an average slave's income probably approached £7 ($700).[20] Therefore, incomes for blacks living today have also increased on average by multiples of 11 to 13 since 1774.

---

[20]Edwin Perkins, *The Economy of Colonial America*, 2nd ed. (New York: Columbia Univ. Press, 1988).

In short, free colonials enjoyed surprisingly high standards of living for the world at that time; because taxes in the colonies were much less than in England, after-tax incomes of free persons in the colonies were probably above those in the mother country on the eve of the Revolution.

Even today, relatively few countries generate average income levels that approach the earnings of free Americans on the eve of the Revolution. In fact, more than one-half of the present world population lives in countries where the average income is below the level of the typical free American's income of over 200 years ago. This is true of most people of the "Third World," including mainland China, India, Pakistan, Indonesia, and large parts of Africa and South America. Relatively speaking, free colonial Americans lived very well, both by today's standards in many areas of the world and in comparison to the most advanced areas of the world in the late eighteenth century.

THE DISTRIBUTION OF INCOME AND WEALTH

As Tables 5-3 and 5-4 illustrate, the high levels of material well-being for colonial Americans were not equally distributed regionally. By far the richest area was the South, where wealth and incomes per free capita were far above those in the Middle colonies and in New England.

Evidence from probate records of the times also permits us to estimate the distribution of wealth among individuals. It is widely believed that wealth and income were fairly equitably distributed until the onset of industrialization in the early nineteenth century. However, the estimates in Table 5-5, which includes holdings in slaves and indentured contracts, suggest that widespread inequalities of wealth and income existed. For instance, the wealthiest 20 percent of all New Englanders owned 66 percent of the total wealth there. In the Middle colonies, the wealthiest 20 percent held 53 percent of the total wealth. In the South, 70 percent of the wealth was held by the top fifth. In short, the South had the most concentrated distribution of wealth, the Middle colonies had the least. The greater southern concentration was due primarily to the dominance of wealthy plantations enjoying advantages of economies of scale in production. Slavery also added to the South's high concentrations of wealth, but note that New England had concentrations almost as high, and wealth inequalities were notably high in the port towns.

Thanks to the pioneering efforts of Jackson T. Main and James Henretta, we have learned that a growing inequality in wealth and income accompanied the very process of colonial settlement and economic maturity. As development proceeded, frontier areas were transformed into subsistence farming areas and finally, in some instances, into urban areas. In Main's

TABLE 5-5   Total Physical Wealth, 1774: Estate Sizes and Composition for Free Wealth Holders
(in pounds sterling)

	ALL COLONIES	NEW ENGLAND	MIDDLE COLONIES	SOUTH
Mean average	£252.0	£161.2	£189.2	£394.7
Median Average	108.7	74.4	152.5	144.5
Distribution				
Bottom 20%	0.8%	1.0%	1.2%	0.7%
Top 20%	67.3%	65.9%	52.7%	69.6%
Composition				
Land	53.0%	71.4%	60.5%	45.9%
Slaves and servants	22.1%	0.5%	4.1%	33.6%
Livestock	9.2%	7.5%	11.3%	8.8%
Consumer-personal	6.7%	11.2%	8.4%	5.1%

Source: Adapted from Alice Hanson Jones, *American Colonial Wealth: Documents and Methods,* 2nd ed., 3 vols. (New York: Arno Press, 1978); presented in Edwin Perkins, *The Economy of Colonial America,* 2nd ed. (New York: Columbia Univ. Press, 1988), p. 219.

opinion, this increasing commercialization resulted in greater inequality in the distribution of colonial wealth and income.[21]

Other studies, by James Henretta and, more recently, by Bruce D. Daniels, also suggest a growth in the inequality of colonial wealth distribution within regions over time.[22] Comparing two Boston tax lists, Henretta found that the top 10 percent of Boston's taxpayers owned 42 percent of its wealth in 1687, whereas they owned 57 percent in 1771.[23] Daniels surveyed many New England probate records and therefore was able to tentatively confirm Main's contention that as economic activity grew more complex in the colonies it tended to produce a greater concentration of wealth. Apparently, as subsistence production gave way to market production, the interdependence among colonial producers generated or at least was accompanied by a greater disparity in wealth. This was true both in older and in more newly settled agricultural areas. Alternatively, large established urban areas, such as Boston and Hartford (Connecticut) exhibited a fairly stable distribution of wealth throughout the eighteenth century until 1776. These urban centers also reflected the greatest degree of wealth inequality in the colonies.

---

[21]Jackson T. Main, *The Social Structure of Revolutionary America* (Princeton: Princeton Univ. Press, 1965).

[22]James Henretta, "Economic Development and Social Structure in Colonial Boston," *William and Mary Quarterly* 22 (1965): 93–105; and Bruce D. Daniels, "Long-range Trends of Wealth Distribution in Eighteenth-Century New England," *Explorations in Economic History* 11 (1973–74):123–35.

[23]Henretta's 1771 estimate was revised downward to 48 percent by Gerard Warden due to historical inconsistencies in the evaluation of assets in the tax lists on which Henretta's study was based. This adjustment modifies substantially the argument for rapidly rising inequality in Boston, but not the overall picture of substantial inequality of wealthy holdings there.

Smaller towns showed less inequality, but as towns grew, their inequality also increased.

Particularly high levels of affluence were observed in the port towns and cities where merchant classes were forming and gaining an economic hold. Especially influential were the merchant shipowners who were engaged in the export-import trade and who were considered to be in the upper class of society. In addition, urbanization and industrialization produced another class group: a free labor force that owned little or no property.

Probably one-third of the free population possessed few assets (according to estate records and tax rolls), but as Jackson Main has argued, and Mary Schweitzer's work supports, these were not a permanent underclass of poor white people. These were mostly young people in their twenties, and still dependent on parents or relatives. Through gifts and savings and other sources, marriage usually tripled household wealth almost immediately. There were wandering poor, but their numbers grew more slowly than the total population.

Not only occupation, marriage, and property ownership, but also circumstances determined by birth greatly influenced a person's social standing. Race and sex were major factors. Some women were wealthy, but typically they owned far less property than men and very few owned land. The rise of slave labor after 1675 furthered the overall rise of wealth inequality in the colonies.

It is a statistical curiosity, however, that throughout most of the colonial period up to 1775, growing wealth concentration did not occur among free whites in the thirteen colonies as a whole. Although growing inequality occurred within specific regions and localities, this did not occur in the aggregate. This is because the lower wealth concentration areas, the rural and especially the new frontier areas, contained over 90 percent of the population. These grew as fast or faster than the urban areas, therefore offsetting the modest growth of inequality of the urban centers.[24] As an added statistical oddity, although rural wealth holdings (per free person) were less than urban holdings within each region, in the aggregate rural wealth holdings averaged above urban holdings. This reversal in order happened because of the very high wealth holdings per free person in the South, which actually exceeded the average wealth holdings of northern urban residents. In any case, despite these peculiarities of aggregation, substantial wealth inequality was a fact of economic life long before the age of industrialization and the period of rapid and sustained economic growth that occurred in the nineteenth century. The absence of growing inequality of wealth among free Americans implies that the growth of per capita income and wealth was shared widely among these nearly 1.8 million people.

---

[24]Jeffrey G. Williamson and Peter H. Lindert, *American Inequality: A Macroeconomic History* (New York: Academic Press, 1980), pp. 21–31.

On the eve of the Revolution, their sense of well-being and economic outlook was undoubtedly positive. British interference and changing taxation policies were threats that a powerful young emerging nation was willing and able to overcome.

SELECTED REFERENCES AND SUGGESTED READINGS

Anderson, Terry. "Economic Growth in Colonial New England: 'Statistical Renaissance.' " *Journal of Economic History* 39 (1979):243–57.

———. *The Economic Growth of Seventeenth-Century New England: A Measurement of Regional Income.* New York: Arno Press, 1975.

Anderson, Terry, and Robert Paul Thomas. "Economic Growth in the Seventeenth Century Colonies." *Explorations in Economic History* 15 (1978):368–87.

———. "White Population, Labor Force, and Extensive Growth of the New England Economy in the Seventeenth Century," *Journal of Economic History* 33 (1973):634–61.

Ball, Duane, and Gary M. Walton. "Agricultural Productivity Change in Eighteenth-Century Pennsylvania." *Journal of Economic History* (1976):102–17.

Carr, Lois G., and Lorena S. Walsh. "Changing Life Styles in Colonial St. Mary's County." In *Economic Change in Chesapeake Colonies,* ed. G. Porter and W. Mulligan. Greenville, Delaware: Regional Economic History Research Center, 1978.

Daniels, Bruce. "Economic Development in Colonial and Revolutionary Connecticut: An Overview." *William and Mary Quarterly* 37 (1980):427–50.

———. "Long Range Trends of Wealth Distribution in Eighteenth-Century New England." *Explorations in Economic History* 11 (1973/74):123–35.

Doerflinger, Thomas. *A Vigorous Spirit of Enterprise: Merchants and Economic Development in Revolutionary Philadelphia.* Chapel Hill: Univ. of North Carolina Press, 1986.

Egnal, Marc. "The Economic Development of the Thirteen Continental Colonies, 1720 to 1775." *William and Mary Quarterly* 32 (1975):191–222.

Galenson, David, and Russell Menard. "Economics and Early American History." *Newberry Papers,* No. 77-4E. Chicago, 1978.

Hanson, John R. "The Economic Development of the Thirteen Colonies, 1720 to 1775: A Critique." *William and Mary Quarterly* 37 (1980):165–72.

Jones, Alice H. *American Colonial Wealth: Documents and Methods,* 3 vols. New York: Arno Press, 1978.

———. *Wealth of a Nation to Be: The American Colonies on the Eve of the Revolution.* New York: Columbia Univ. Press, 1980.

Jones, Douglas L. "The Strolling Poor: Transiency in Eighteenth-Century Massachusetts." *Journal of Social History* (1975):28–54.

Kulikoff, Allan. *Tobacco and Slaves: The Development of Southern Cultures in the Chesapeake, 1680–1800.* Chapel Hill: Univ. of North Carolina Press, 1986.

———. "The Economic Growth of the Eighteenth-Century Chesapeake Colonies." *Journal of Economic History* 39 (1979):275–88.

Maddison, Angus. "A Comparison of Levels of GDP Per Capita in Developed and Developing Countries, 1700–1980." *Journal of Economic History* (1983):27–41.

McCusker, John J., and Russell R. Menard. *The Economy of British America, 1607–1789.* Chapel Hill: The Univ. of North Carolina Press, 1985. Chapters 3 and 12.

Main, Gloria. "The Standard of Living in Colonial Massachusetts." *The Journal of Economic History* 43 (1983):101–108.

———. *Tobacco Colony: Life in Early Maryland.* Princeton: Princeton Univ. Press, 1982.

Main, Gloria, and Jackson T. Main. "Economic Growth and the Standard of Living in Southern New England, 1640–1774." *The Journal of Economic History* 48 (1988):27–46.

Main, Jackson T. "Standard of Living and Life Cycle in Colonial Connecticut." *Journal of Economic History* 43 (1983):159–65.

Paskoff, Paul. "Labor Productivity and Managerial Efficiency against a Static Technology: The Pennsylvania Iron Industry, 1750–1800." *Journal of Economic History* (1980):129–35.

Pencak, William. "The Social Structure of Revolutionary Boston: Evidence from the Great Fire of 1760." *Journal of Interdisciplinary History* (1979):267–78.

Perkins, Edwin. *The Economy of Colonial America,* 2nd ed. New York: Columbia Univ. Press, 1988. Ch. 9.

———. "The Material Lives of Laboring Philadelphians, 1750 to 1800." *William and Mary Quarterly* 38 (1981):163–202.

Smith, Billy G. "Inequality in Late Colonial Philadelphia: A Note on Its Nature and Growth." *William and Mary Quarterly* 41(1984):629–45.

Schweitzer, Mary. *Custom and Contract: Household Government and the Economy in Colonial Pennsylvania.* New York: Columbia Univ. Press, 1987.

Walsh, Lorena S. "Urban Amenities and Rural Sufficiency: Living Standards and Consumer Behavior in the Colonial Chesapeake, 1643–1777." *Journal of Economic History* 43(1983):109–17.

CHAPTER 6

Three Crises and Revolt

THE OLD COLONIAL POLICY

Being part of the British Empire, colonists in British North America were subject to the laws of England, and they established colonial governments patterned after England's governmental organization. Although originally there were corporate colonies (Connecticut and Rhode Island) and proprietary colonies (Pennsylvania and Maryland), most eventually became Crown colonies and all had similar governing organizations. For example, after 1625, Virginia was a characteristic Crown colony, and both its governor and council (the upper house) were appointed by the Crown. But only the lower house could initiate fiscal legislation, and this body was elected by the propertied adult males within the colony.

Although all laws could be vetoed by the governor and the Crown, power gradually shifted to the lower houses as colonial legislative bodies increasingly tended to imitate the House of Commons in England. The colonists controlled the lower house—and therefore the purse strings—thereby generating a climate of political freedom and independence in the colonies. Governors, who were generally expected to represent the will of the Empire and to veto legislation contrary to British interests, were often not only sympathetic to the colonists but also dependent on the legislature for their salaries (which were frequently in arrears). Consequently, the actual control of civil affairs generally rested with the colonists themselves, through their representatives.

Of course, the power that permitted this state of affairs to exist rested in England, and the extent of local autonomy was officially limited. After the shift in power in England from the Crown to Parliament in 1690, the Privy Council reviewed all laws passed in the colonies as a matter of common procedure. In the process, the Council vetoed a small percentage of the legislation passed in the colonies. But even this restriction could be avoided. Time, distance, and bureaucratic apathy often permitted colonial laws to become effective long before they were even reviewed in England. If vetoed, a piece of legislation that was highly desired by the colonists could be reworded and reimplemented.

In short, day-to-today events in the colonies were influenced only modestly by British directives. Government activity—whether British or colonial—was a relatively minor aspect of colonial affairs. The colonists themselves held the power to resolve issues of a local nature and therefore of greatest importance to the colonies. In this way, British subjects in the New World enjoyed extensive freedom of self-determination throughout most of the colonial period.

The main provisions of the early Navigation Acts, which imposed the most important restrictions on colonial economic freedom, formed the basis of the old colonial policy. Recall that these laws epitomized British mercantilism, and their aim was threefold: (1) to protect and encourage English and colonial shipping; (2) to ensure that major colonial imports from Europe were shipped from British ports; and (3) to make sure that the bulk of desired colonial products—the enumerated articles—were shipped to England.

The first Acts of Trade and Navigation in 1651, 1660, and 1663 introduced these concepts concerning the colonies' relationship with the Empire. Colonial settlers and investors had always been aware of the restrictions on their economic activities. Rules were changed gradually and, until 1763, in such a way that American colonists voiced no serious complaints. Articles were added to the enumerated list over a long period of time. At first, the list consisted entirely of southern continental and West Indian products, most important of which were tobacco, sugar, cotton, dyewood, and indigo. Rice and molasses were not added until 1704; naval stores, until 1705 and 1729; and furs and skins, until 1721. Whenever enumeration resulted in obvious and unreasonable hardship, relief might be granted. For example, the requirement that rice be sent to England added so much to shipping and handling costs that the American product, despite its superior quality, was priced out of southern European markets. Consequently, laws passed in the 1730s allowed rice to be shipped directly to ports south of Cape Finisterre, a promontory in northwestern Spain.

Commodities were listed because they were especially important to English manufacturers or because they were expected to yield substantial customs revenue. However, the requirements of shipping to English ports were less onerous than we might initially suppose. First, the Americans and the English shared general ties of blood and language and, more specifically, because their credit contacts were more easily established, the colonists would have dealt primarily with English merchants anyway. Second, duties charged on commodities that were largely reexported, such as tobacco, were remitted entirely or in large part to the colonies. Third, bounties were paid on some of the enumerated articles. Fourth, it was permissible to ship certain items on the list directly from one colony to another for the purpose of furnishing supplies. Finally, the laws could be evaded through smuggling, and with the exception of molasses, such evasion was probably neither more nor less common in the colonies than it was in Europe during the seventeenth and eighteenth centuries.

With respect to imports, the effect of the Navigation Acts was to distort somewhat—but not to influence materially—the flows of trade. The fact that goods had to be funneled through England probably added to costs and restricted trade. Again, however, traditional ties would have made Americans the best customers of British merchants anyway. Furthermore, hardship cases were relieved by providing direct shipment of commodities like salt and wine from ports south of Cape Finisterre to America.

If English manufacturers were to be granted special advantages over other European manufacturers in British American markets, should restrictions also be placed on competing colonial manufacturers? Many British manufacturers felt that such "duplicate production" should be prohibited and tried to convince Parliament that colonial manufacturing was not in the best interest of the Empire. In 1699, a law made it illegal to export colonial wool, wool yarn, and finished wool products to any foreign country or even to other colonies. Later, Americans were forbidden to export hats made of beaver fur. Toward mid-century, a controversy arose in England over the regulation of iron manufactures; after 1750, pig and bar iron were admitted into England duty free and the colonial manufacture of finished iron products was expressly forbidden. The fact that these were the only prohibitive laws directed at colonial manufacture indicates Britain's lack of fear of American competition.

After all, the colonies' comparative advantage in production lay overwhelmingly in agriculture and other resource-intensive products from the seas and forests. Note that the important shipbuilding industry in the colonies was not curtailed by British legislation; indeed, it was supported by Parliament. Therefore, any piecemeal actions to prevent colonial manufacturing activities appear largely to have been taken to favor particular vested interests in England, especially those with influence and effective lobbying practices.

Nevertheless, as we will emphasize later in this chapter, the laws prohibiting colonial manufactures were loosely enforced; they were restrictive and a cause of annoyance, but they did not seriously affect the course of early American industrial development or the colonial quest for independence. Also, the economic controls that England imposed on the colonies were less strict than the colonial controls other European countries imposed, and these controls were less harsh for Americans than for Ireland and other colonies within the Empire. We should not misapprehend the trend of enforcement of the old colonial policy. Regulation of external colonial trade was progressively strengthened. Beginning in 1675, governors were supplied with staffs of officials to aid in enforcing trade regulations; after the general reorganization of 1696, the powers of these officials were sufficient to provide considerable surveillance and commercial regulation.

The only trade law flaunted with impunity was the Molasses Act of 1733—an act that, if enforced, would have disrupted one of the major colonial trades and would have resulted in serious repercussions, especially in New England. Before 1700, New England had traded primarily with the British possessions in the West Indies. In time, however, British planters failed to provide a sufficient market for northern colonial goods, and sugar and molasses from the increasingly productive French islands became cheaper than the English staples. During the same period, British planters in the sugar islands were hurt by the requirement that cane products be shipped to England before being reexported. In an effort to protect British West Indian holdings, Parliament imposed high duties on *foreign* (predominantly French) sugar, molasses, and rum imported to the English colonies. The strict levying of these duties and the prevention of smuggling would have decreased the prices of northern staples in the British West Indies and would have seriously curtailed all trade involving rum. New Englanders appeared to have no feasible alternative, because they had to sell their fish, provisions, lumber, and rum to pay for their imports. Rather than face possible economic annihilation, they continued to trade as usual; instead of facing the issue resolutely, English officials, many of whom were routinely bribed, made no serious attempts to enforce trade regulations. Some 30 years later, after the matter had been raised time after time, the Sugar Act of 1764 ruled against the American colonists in favor of the British West Indian planters. This decision, as we will see, was a key factor in helping to bring on revolution.

THE NEW COLONIAL POLICY AND THE FIRST CRISIS

The events that led to the American Revolution fall more readily into order if we keep in mind its central underlying theme: new and rapid changes in the old colonial policy that had been established and imposed on an essentially self-governing people for 150 years precipitated a series of crises and, ultimately, war. These crises were essentially political, but the stresses and strains that led to colonial fear and hatred of British authority had economic origins. Britain's "new" colonial policy was only an extension of the old, with one difference: the new enactments were adopted by a Parliament that had every intention of enforcing them to the letter of the law, thereby sharply changing the atmosphere of freedom in the colonies. Furthermore, high British officials insisted—at almost precisely the wrong moments—on taking punitive actions that only compounded the bitterness they had already stirred up in the colonies.

The series of critical events that generated the first crisis began with the English victory over the French in 1763. The Seven Years' War had been a struggle for empire, of course, but it had also been a fight for the protection of the American colonies. And the colonials had not been of much help in furnishing England with either troops or material—to say nothing of the hurtful trade they carried on with the French in both Canada and the West Indies. The English were in no mood to spare the feelings of an upstart people who had committed the cardinal sin of ingratitude. Besides, the war had placed a heavy burden on the English Treasury, and British taxes per capita, according to Lance Davis, and Robert Huttenback, were probably the highest in the world.[1] Interest on the debt had soared to $5 million annually (nearly $500 million in today's values), and land taxes in England had doubled during the war. It seemed just that American colonists be asked to contribute to the support of the garrisons that were still required on their frontier.

Despite their substantial wealth, the colonists at this time were still free riders of protection, receiving British defense at almost no cost. Taxes per capita in the colonies were among the lowest in the world, nearly 20–25 percent of taxes paid by English residents.

George Grenville, England's prime minister, proposed stationing a British force of some 10,000 men in the North American possessions. Although the actual number realized was closer to 6,000, their costs were over £350,000 annually. To meet these costs, Parliament passed two laws to generate approximately one-tenth of this revenue. Of the two laws, the Sugar Act of 1764 had more far-reaching implications for the colonists, because it contained provisions that served the ends of all major English economic interests and at the same time threatened American business in the colonies. But the Stamp Act of 1765, although really much less inclusive, incited political tempers to a boil that in a very real sense started the first step towards rebellion.

The most important clauses of the Sugar Act levied taxes on imports of non-British products of the West Indies. Although the duty on foreign molasses was actually *lowered* from 6d. to 3d. a gallon—a marked reduction from the rate set by the old Molasses Act—*provision was made for strict collection of the tax* in the belief that the smaller tax, if strictly enforced, would produce a larger revenue. (This argument is similar to today's proponents of supply-side economics.) A more important goal, however, was the protection of British West Indian planters—who were well represented in Parliament—from the competition of New England rum makers. Actually, more than half of the molasses imported by colonials was used for kitchen purposes (Boston baked beans, shoofly pie, apple pandowdy, and molasses jack—

---

[1]Lance E. Davis and Robert A. Huttenback, "The Cost of Empire," in Explorations in the New Economic History, ed. Roger L. Ransom, Richard Sutch, and Gary M. Walton (New York: Academic Press, 1982), p. 42.

a kind of home-brewed beer). But the chief fear of the English sugar planters was that cheap molasses imports from the French West Indies would enable the New England rum distilleries to capture the rum market on the mainland as well as in the non-British islands.[2] And their concern was probably more than justified, despite the alleged inferiority of the New England product. Moreover, the Sugar Act added to the list of enumerated articles several raw materials demanded by British manufacturers, including some important exports of the northern and Middle colonies. Finally, this comprehensive law removed most of the tariff rebates (drawbacks) previously allowed on European goods that passed through English ports and even placed new duties on foreign textiles that competed with English products.

The Stamp Act, on the other hand, was simply designed to raise revenue and served no ends of mercantile policy. The law required that stamps varying in cost from half a penny to several pounds be affixed to legal documents, contracts, newspapers and pamphlets, and even playing cards and dice.

According to Benjamin Franklin's argument against the tax to Parliament, the colonists objected on the grounds that the act levied an "internal" tax, distinguished from the traditional "external" taxes or duties collected on goods imported to the colonies. When English ministers refused to recognize this distinction, the colonists further objected that the tax had been levied by a distant Parliament that did not contain a single colonial representative. And they complained that both the Sugar Act and the Stamp Act required the tax revenues to be remitted to England for disbursement—a procedure that further drained the colonies of precious specie and constantly reduced the amount of goods that could be imported to America. When it became apparent that strict enforcement would accompany such measures, severe resistance arose in the colonies. Lawyers and printers—who were especially infuriated by the Stamp Act—furnished articulate, able leadership for anti-British agitation.

The decade of trouble that followed was characterized by alternating periods of colonial insubordination, British concession, renewed attempts to raise revenues, further colonial resistance, and, at last, punitive action—taken by the British in anger at what was felt to be rank disloyalty. The so-called Stamp Act Congress met in New York in 1765, passed resolutions of fealty, and organized a boycott of English goods. "Nonimportation associations" were established throughout the colonies, and the volume of imports from Britain declined dramatically as docks and warehouses bulged with unsold British goods. A concerted effort to boycott English goods did not develop in all regions, however. The Middle colonies—where the boycotts first centered—exhibited the greatest decrease in trade. The upper South contributed effectively to the boycott, largely because of the Restraining Act

---

[2]For the details of this controversy, see Gilman M. Ostrander, "The Colonial Molasses Trade," *Agricultural History* 30 (1956):77–84. See also Stuart Bruchey, *The Colonial Merchant* (New York: Harcourt Brace Jovanovich, 1966), pp. 67–78.

of 1764 which curtailed Virginia's paper money issues, as discussed in Chapter 4. But New England gave only slight support to these first nonimport agreements, and the lower South failed to join in the boycott. Yet overall, colonial efforts to boycott British imports were very effective. In fact, English merchants were so sharply affected that they demanded the repeal of the Stamp Act. They were joined by such political leaders as Edmund Burke and William Pitt, whose sympathies lay with the colonists. Parliament repealed the Stamp Act and reduced the duty on foreign molasses from 3d. to 1d. per gallon. Thus the first major confrontation between American and England ended peacefully, and a profound lesson had been learned. In the mercantilist scheme of things, the Empire that tilted. The American mainland colonies ultimately had become as important—perhaps even more important—as a market for English wares as they were a source of raw materials. Americans as consumers had found a new and powerful economic weapon.

MORE CHANGES AND THE SECOND CRISIS

Although Parliament had responded to economic pressure from America by repealing the Stamp Act, England obstinately maintained its *right* to tax the colonies. The other sugar duties remained, and a Declaratory Act affirmed the right of Parliament to legislate in all matters concerning Americans. Nevertheless, there was rejoicing in both the colonies and England, and it was generally believed that their differences would be reconciled. But even then, the Quartering Act of 1765 had been on the statute books a year, with its stipulations that the colonial assemblies provide barracks, some provisions, and part of the military transport for British troops stationed within the colonies. This law was to prove especially problematic to New York, where soldiers were to be concentrated on their way to the West. Much worse was to come, however. George Grenville had been dismissed from the British ministry in 1765, largely because Kind George III disliked him. He was replaced as Chancellor of the Exchequer by Charles Townshend, who in 1767, secured the passage of several measures identified with his name. Because the great English landowners were persistently clamoring for relief from their heavy property taxes, Townshend tried once again to raise revenues in America. He felt that if the colonials objected to "internal" taxes, he would provide them with some "external" duties levied on such important articles of consumption as tea, glass, paper, and red and white lead (pigments for paint).

Although they were definitely important to colonial life, the colonists might have accepted taxation on these items calmly if the British had not adopted measures to put real teeth into the law. One of the Townshend Acts provided for an American Customs Board; another, for the issuance by colonial courts of the hated general search warrants known as *writs of assistance;* and another, for admiralty courts in Halifax, Boston, Philadelphia, and Charlestown to try smuggling cases. With a single stroke, the British ministry succeeded once again in antagonizing a wide cross section of the American populace, and again resistance flared— this time in the form of both peaceful petitions and mob violence, culminating in the Boston Massacre, which left five dead. Once more, the nonimportation agreements, especially effective in the port towns, were imposed. Only in the Chesapeake colonies—the one major colonial region spared of a court of admiralty—was this boycott fairly unsuccessful.[3] Nevertheless, by late 1769, American imports had declined to perhaps one-third of their normal level. The value of lost English sales in the colonies exceeded £1 million in 1768 and 1769 combined, and once again the English exerted pressure to change trade policy. For the second time, Parliament appeared to acquiesce to colonial demands. In 1770, all the Townshend duties except the duty on tea were repealed, and although some of the most distasteful acts remained on the books, everyone except a few colonial hotheads felt that a peaceful settlement was possible. Trade was resumed, and a new level of prosperity was reached in 1771.

THE THIRD CRISIS AND REBELLION

Reasonable calm prevailed until 1773, when resistance flared again over what now seems to have been an inconsequential matter. The English East India Company, in which many politically powerful people owned an interest, was experiencing financial difficulties. Parliament had granted the company a loan of public funds and had also passed the Tea Act of 1773, which permitted the company to handle tea sales in a new way. Until this time, the company, which enjoyed a monopoly of the trade with India, had sold tea to English wholesalers, who in turn sold it to jobbers, who sent it to America. There the tea was turned over to colonial wholesalers, who at last distributed it to American retailers. Overall, many people had received income from this series of transactions; besides, duties had been collected on the product when it reached English ports and again when it arrived in America. The new Tea Act allowed the East India Company to ship tea directly to the colonies, thereby eliminating the British duty and some handling costs. Consumers were to benefit by paying less for tea, the company would presumably sell more tea at a lower price, and everybody would be happy. Only everybody was not happy. Smugglers of Dutch tea were now undersold, the colonial tax was still collected (a real sore point), and most importantly, the American importer was removed from the picture, thus alarming American

---

[3] Another contributing factor may have been that trade in the Chesapeake region was relatively decentralized, thereby reducing the possibility of blacklisting or boycotting colonial importers and others who failed to join the effort.

Angered colonists disguised as Indians, invited themselves to a "tea party"—as they called it—to show the British how they felt about English mercantile policies. The damage to property was nearly £9,000 (about $900,000 in 1989 values).

merchants. If the tea wholesaler could be bypassed, couldn't the business of other merchants also be undercut? Couldn't other companies in Great Britain be granted monopoly control of other commodities, until eventually Americans were reduced to keeping small shops and selling at retail what their foreign masters imported for them? Wouldn't just a few pro-British agents who would handle the necessary distribution processes grow rich while staunch Americans grew poor? The answers seemed clear to almost every colonist engaged in business. From wealthy merchants in Boston to shopkeepers in the hamlets, there was a swift and violent reaction. Tea in the port towns was sent back to England or destroyed in various ways—the most spectacular of which was the Boston Tea Party, a well-executed, three-hour affair involving 30 to 40 men. Many colonists were shocked at this wanton destruction of private property, estimated at nearly £9,000 (or nearly $900,000 in 1989 prices), but their reaction was mild compared with the indignation that swelled in Britain.

The result was the bitter and punitive legislation known as the Intolerable Acts. Passed in the early summer of 1774, the Intolerable Acts (1) closed the Port of Boston to all shipping until the colonists paid the East India Company for its tea, (2) permitted British officials charged with crimes committed while enforcing British laws to be tried in another colony or in Britain, (3) revised the charter of Massachusetts to make certain cherished rights dependent on the arbitrary decision of the Crown-appointed governor, and (4) provided for the quartering of troops in the city of Boston, which was especially obnoxious to the citizens after the events of the Boston Massacre four years earlier. In the ensuing months, political agitation reached new heights of violence, and economic sanctions were again invoked. For the third time, nonimportation agreements were imposed, and the delegates to the First Continental Congress voted not to trade with England or the British West Indies unless concessions were made. By this time, however, legislative enactments were of little importance. The crisis had become moral and political. Americans would not yield to the British until their basic freedoms were restored, and the English would not make peace until the colonists relented. The possibilities for peaceful reconciliation ebbed as the weeks passed. Finally, violence broke out with the shots of April 19, 1775, which marked a major turning point in the history of the world.

Support in the Countryside

Although the events leading to the Revolution centered primarily on the conflicts between British authority and activities concerning colonial merchants, the vast rural populace played an essential supporting role in the independence movement. But how can we explain the willingness of wealthy southerners and of many poor farmers to support a rebellion that was spearheaded by an antagonized merchant class? There were certainly no apparent allied economic interests among these groups. Nevertheless, coincidentally, each group had its individual motives for resisting British authority. In rural America, antagonisms primarily stemmed from English land policy.

Before 1763, British policy had been calculated to encourage the rapid development of the colonial West. In the interest of trade, English merchants wanted the new country to be populated as rapidly as possible. Moreover, rapid settlement extended the frontier and thereby helped to strengthen opposition to France and Spain. By 1763, however, the need to fortify the frontier against a foreign power had disappeared. By this time, too, other considerations had become more important. First, the British felt it was wise to contain the population well within the seaboard area, where the major investments had been made and where political control would be easier. Second, the fur trade was now under the complete control of the British, and it was deemed unwise to have frontier pioneers moving in and creating trouble with the Indians. Third, wealthy English landowners were purchasing western land in great tracts, and pressure was exerted to "save" some of the good land for these investors. Finally, placing the western lands under the direct control of the Crown was designed to obtain revenues from sales and quitrents for the British Treasury.[4]

For several reasons, then, many in England urged conservatism in the disposition of unsettled lands. Finally events on the frontier forced a temporary decision. Angry over injustices—real and imagined—and fearful that the settlers would encroach on their hunting grounds, the northern Indians rebelled under the Ottawa chief, Pontiac. Colonial and British troops put down the uprising, but only after seven of the nine British garrisons west of Niagara were destroyed. Everyone knew that the "Indian problem" would be a continuing threat unless the natives were pacified. Primarily as a temporary solution, the king issued the Royal Proclamation of 1763, which in effect drew a line beyond which colonials could not settle without express permission from the Crown (see Map 6-1). Governors could no longer grant patents to land lying West of the sources of rivers that flowed into the Atlantic; anyone seeking such a grant had to obtain one directly from the king. At the same time, the fur trade was placed under centralized control, and no trader could cross the Allegheny Mountains without permission from England.

A few years later, the policy of keeping colonial settlement under British supervision was reaffirmed, although it became apparent that the western boundary line would not remain rigidly fixed. In 1768, the Proclamation Line was shifted westward, and treaties with the Indians made large land tracts available to speculators. In 1774, the year in which the Intolerable Acts were passed, two British actions made it clear that temporary expedients had evolved into permanent policies. First, a royal proclamation tightened the terms on which land would pass into private hands. Grants were no longer to be free; instead, tracts were to be sold at public auctions in lots of 100–1,000 acres at a minimum price of 6d. per acre. Even more serious was the passage of the Quebec Act in 1774 (see Map 6-2), which changed the boundaries of Quebec to the Ohio River in the East and the Mississippi River in the West, thus destroying the western land claims of Massachusetts, Connecticut, and Virginia. The fur trade was to be regulated by the governor of Quebec, and the Indian boundary line was to run as far south as Georgia.

Not all colonists suffered from the new land policy. Rich land speculators who were politically powerful enough to obtain special grants from the king found the new regulations restrictive but not ruinous. Indeed, great holders of ungranted lands *east* of the mountains, such as the Penns and the Calverts, or of huge tracts already granted but not yet settled, stood to benefit from the rise in property values that resulted from the British embargo on westward movement. Similarly, farmers of old, established agricultural areas would benefit in two ways: (1) the competition from the produce of the new

---

[4]Quitrents were an old form of feudal dues seldom paid in any of the colonies except in Virginia and Maryland. In Virginia the quitrents went to the Crown (about £5,000 annually after 1765); in Maryland they went to Lord Baltimore, the proprietor.

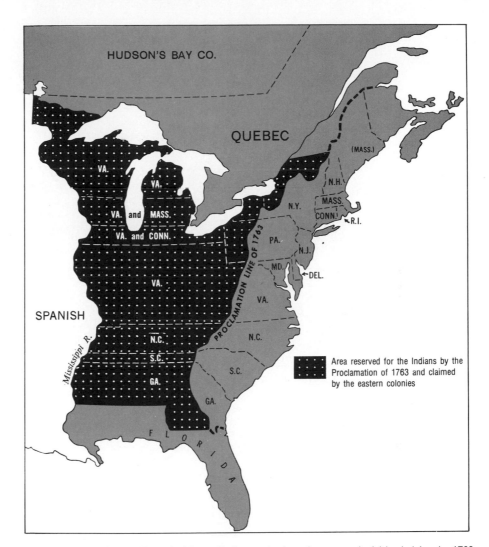

MAP 6-1 Land Claims: The colonial appetite for new land was huge, as colonial land claims by 1763 demonstrated. The Royal Proclamation of that year was designed to stop westward movement.

lands would not be so severe, and (2) since it would be harder for agricultural laborers to obtain their own farms, hired hands would be cheaper. Moreover, many of the restrictions on westward movement were necessary, at least for a time, because of Indian resistance on the frontier.

Nevertheless, not everyone benefited from these restrictions. The withdrawal of cheap, unsettled western lands particularly disillusioned many young adults who had planned to set out on their own but now could not. Recall that from 1720 to 1775 about 225,000 Scotch-Irish and Germans immigrated mostly to the Middle colonies. They were men of fighting age with no loyalties to the English Crown. Similarly, even established frontier

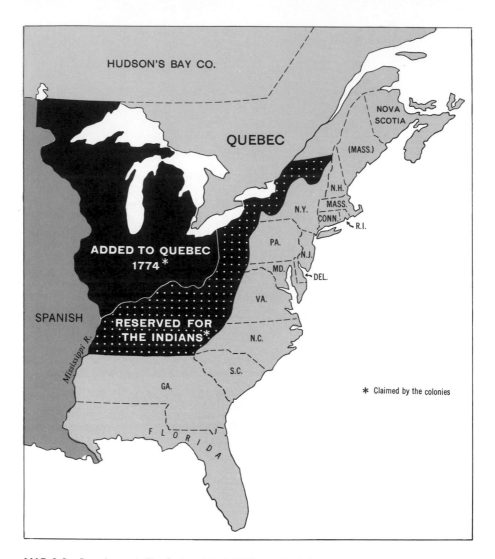

MAP 6-2   Reassignment: The Quebec Act of 1774 gave the Indians territorities that had earlier been claimed by various colonies and, at the same time, nearly doubled the area of Quebec.

farmers usually took an anti-British stand, because they thought that they would be more likely to succeed under a government that would be liberal in disposing of its land. Although poor agrarians did not have dollar stakes in western lands that were comparable to those of large fur traders, land speculators, and planters, they were still affected. Those who were unable to pay their debts sometimes lost their farms through foreclosure, and a British policy that inhibited westward movement angered the frontiersmen and tended to align them against the British and with the aristocratic Americans, with whom they had no other affiliation. The Currency Act (Restraining Act) of 1764 also frustrated and annoyed this debtor group, because although prices actually rose moderately in the ensuing decade, farmers were persuaded that their lot worsened with the moderate contraction of paper money that occurred. Finally, the repeated trade stoppages that followed the nonintercourse agreements worked against the small farmers by lowering the prices of the surpluses they had to sell. As much as anything, a vague, scarcely articulated feeling that any change would be an improvement encouraged most farmers to support the Revolution.

ECONOMIC EXPLOITATION RECONSIDERED

It is sometimes alleged that the American Revolution was the result of the inevitable clash of competing capitalisms and also of England's exploitation of the colonies. In long-run perspective, such conjectures defy empirical testing. After all, how can we judge whether independence or British rule offered more promise for economic progress in North America?

Of course, the short-run consequences of independence can be assessed—a task that awaits us in Chapter 7. But at this point, it is important to reconsider the question of colonial exploitation as a motive for revolt. Did British trade restrictions drain the colonial economy?

First, manufacturing restrictions had been placed on woolens, hats, and finished iron products. Woolen production in the colonies was limited to personal use or local trade, but this imposed no hardship. The colonists were quite satisfied to purchase manufactures from England at the lower costs made possible by the large-scale production methods employed there. This situation continued even after independence was achieved, and American woolens provided no competition for imported English fabrics until the nineteenth century.

A small portion of colonial manufacturing activity (predominantly New York producers) was hurt by the passage of the Hat Act in 1732. This one-sided legislation benefited London hatters by prohibiting the colonial export of beaver hats. For the overall American economy, however, the effects of the Hat Act were negligible. Similarly, Parliamentary restrictions of iron proved moderately harmless. Actually the colonial production of raw pig and bar iron was encouraged, but the finishing of iron and steel and the use of certain types of equipment were forbidden after 1750. Nevertheless, like the Molasses Act of 1733, restrictions on the manufacture of colonial iron were ignored with impunity: 25 iron mills were established between 1750 and 1775 in Pennsylvania and Delaware alone. Furthermore, the legislative freedom enjoyed by the colonists was amply displayed when the Pennsylvania assembly—in open defiance of the law—appropriated financial aid for a new slitting mill (nail factory). No matter how distasteful these British regulations were to the colonists, they were either superfluous (woolen restrictions), ignored (the slitting mill), or inconsequential (hat production).

The generally liberal British land policy was designed to encourage rapid settlement. Only after the war with Chief Pontiac and the resulting Royal Proclamation of 1763 did land policy suddenly become less flexible. When land controls were tightened again by the Quebec Act of 1774, important political issues emerged. Western lands claimed by Massachusetts, Connecticut, and Virginia were redistributed to the Province of Quebec, and land was made less accessible. Territorial governments were placed entirely in the hands of British officials, and trials there were conducted without juries.

We have already assessed the economic implications of these land policies. Some people gained; others lost. But clearly the climate of freedom changed swiftly, and the political implications of these new policies were hard for the colonists to accept. Apparently, however, those land policies were largely necessary, and the same basic restraints were prescribed and adopted by the federal government after American independence was achieved. It seems unlikely that the new government would have adopted these restraints if they had been economically burdensome on the colonists. The major issue appears to have been who was to determine the policy, rather than what the policy itself was to be.

The same thing was true of currency restrictions. After independence, the new government adopted measures similar to those England had imposed earlier. For instance, in 1751, Parliament passed the Currency Act, which prohibited New England from establishing new public banks and from issuing more paper money. A similar and supplemental Restraining Act appeared in 1764, in the wake of events in the Chesapeake area. Planters there were heavily in debt because they had continued to import goods during the Seven Years' War even though their own exports had declined. When Virginia issued £250,000 in bills of credit, to be used as legal tender in private transactions as well as for public sector payments (mainly taxes), British creditors stood to lose. When the planters began to use cheap money to repay the debts they had incurred in hard sterling, Britain countered by extending the original Currency Act to all the colonies. This enactment certainly hurt the hard-pressed Chesapeake region and stimulated its unusual support for the boycott of English imports in 1765. But the adoption of similar controls after independence indicates that the economic burden of currency restriction could not have been oppressive overall. The real point at issue was simply whether England or the colonists themselves should hold the reins of monetary control.

It appears that only with respect to the Navigation Acts was there any significant exploitation in a strict economic sense. In the words of Lawrence A. Harper:

The enumeration of key colonial exports in various Acts from 1660 to 1766 and the Staple Act of 1663 hit at colonial trade both coming and going. The

Acts required the colonies to allow English middlemen to distribute such crops as tobacco and rice and stipulated that if the colonies would not buy English manufactures, at least they should purchase their European goods in England. The greatest element in the burden laid upon the colonies was not the taxes assessed. It consisted in the increased costs of shipment, transshipment, and middleman's profits arising out of the requirement that England be used as an entrepôt.[5]

These burdens of more costly imports and less remunerative colonial exports may have amounted to as much as 1 percent of total colonial income.[6] But on the other side of the coin, the colonies were provided with bounties and other benefits such as naval protection and military defense at British expense.

In any case, the colonists had lived with these restrictions for over a century. Even those hardest hit—the producers of tobacco and other enumerated products—almost never mentioned them in their lists of grievances against England. It is especially noteworthy that *the acts of trade are not even mentioned in the Declaration of Independence.*

Rather than exploitation, it was the rapidly changing and severely administered new colonial policies that precipitated the American Revolution. Before 1763, the colonists had been free to do pretty much as they pleased. An occasional new enactment or veto of a piece of colonial legislation by Britain had caused little or no discord. After the Seven Years' War, however, conditions suddenly changed. A host of new taxes and regulations were effected and strictly enforced by Britain. Though minor in terms of financial impact, they gave almost every colonist a grievance: debtors objected to the Currency Act; shippers and merchants, to the Sugar Act; pioneers, to the Quebec Act; politicians, printers, and gamblers, to the Stamp Act; retailers and smugglers, to the Tea Act. As colonial resentments flared, Committees of Correspondence pressed forward to formally claim the rights they had long held de facto before 1763. In many ways, it appears that the growing economic maturity of the colonies would soon have made American independence inevitable. Indeed, the gross product of the colonies was nearly £25 million at the time, or nearly one-third of England's gross national product, as compared to only about 4 percent at the turn of the eighteenth century. Clearly the colonies had matured economically to a point where an independent course was feasible.

But was Revolution necessary to break away from the Empire? After all, other English colonies subsequently gained independence without resort-

---

[5]Lawrence A. Harper, "The Effect of the Navigation Acts on the Thirteen Colonies," in *The Era of the American Revolution*, ed. Richard B. Morris (New York: Columbia Univ. Press, 1939).
[6]For an assessment of the several studies and estimates of these costs, see Gary M. Walton, "The New Economic History and the Burdens of the Navigation Acts," *Economic History Review*, 2nd series, 24 (1971):33–42.

ing to armed warfare. By 1775, according to Charles Andrews, the colonies had reached a point where they were

> qualified to cooperate with the mother country on terms similar to those of a brotherhood of free nations, such as the British world is becoming today (1926). But England was unable to see this fact, or to recognize it, and consequently America became the scene of a political unrest which might have been controlled by a compromise, but was turned to revolt by coercion. The situation is a very interesting one, for England is famous for her ability to compromise at critical times in her history. For once, at least, she failed.[7]

The nature of that "failure" is nicely summarized by Harper:

> As a mother country, Britain had much to learn. Any modern parents' magazine could have told George III's ministers that the one mistake not to make is to take a stand and then to yield to howls of anguish. It was a mistake which the British government made repeatedly. It placed a duty of 3d. per gallon on molasses, and when it encountered opposition, reduced it to 1d. It provided for a Stamp Act and withdrew it in the face of temper tantrums. It provided for external taxes to meet the colonial objections and then yielded again by removing all except one. When finally it attempted to enforce discipline, it was too late. Under the circumstances, no self-respecting child—or colonist—would be willing to yield.[8]

It would appear that the lessons the English learned from their failures with the American colonies served them well in later periods, because other English colonies subsequently won their independence without widescale bloodshed. This colonial legacy was of paramount importance in the centuries to follow.

SELECTED REFERENCES AND SUGGESTED READINGS

Barrow, Thomas. *Trade and Empire: The British Customs Service in Colonial America, 1660–1775.* Cambridge: Harvard Univ. Press, 1967.

Becker, Robert A. *Revolution, Reform, and the Politics of Taxation in America: 1763–1783.* Baton Rouge: Louisiana State Univ. Press, 1980.

Beer, George L. *The Old Colonial System 1660–1754.* New York: Macmillan, 1912.

Davis, Lance E., and Robert A. Huttanbeck. "The Cost of Empire." In *Explorations in the New Economic History,* eds. Roger L. Ramson, Richard Sutch, and Gary M. Walton. New York: Academic Press, 1982.

Ernst, Joseph, and Marc Egnal. "An Economic Interpretation of the American Revolution." *William and Mary Quarterly* 29 (1972):3–32.

Hacker, Louis M. "The First American Revolution." *Columbia University Quarterly,* part 1, Sept. 1935. Reprinted in Gerald D. Nash. *Issues in American Economic History.* New York: Heath, 1972.

---

[7]Charles Andrews, "The American Revolution: An Interpretation," *American Historical Review* 31 (1926):232.

[8]Lawrence A. Harper, "Mercantilism and the American Revolution," *The Canadian Historical Review* 25 (1942):14.

Harper, Lawrence. "The Effects of the Navigation Acts on the Thirteen Colonies." In *The Era of the American Revolution*, ed., Richard Morris. New York: Columbia Univ. Press, 1939.

————. "Mercantilism and the American Revolution." *Canadian Historical Review*, March 1942. Reprinted in Gerald D. Nash. *Issues in American Economic History*. New York: Heath, 1972.

McClelland, Peter D. "The Cost to America of British Imperial Policy." *American Economic Review: Papers and Proceedings* 59, no. 7 (May 1969):370–81.

Miller, John C. *Origins of the American Revolution*. Stanford, Ca.: Stanford Univ. Press, 1959.

Morgan, Edmund S. *The American Revolution: A Review of Changing Interpretations*. Washington, D.C.: Service Center for Teachers of History, 1958.

Morgan, Edmund, and Helen Morgan. *The Stamp Act Crisis: Prologue to Revolution*. Chapel Hill: Univ. of North Carolina Press, 1963.

Nash, Gary. *The Urban Crucible*. Cambridge: Harvard Univ. Press, 1979.

Nettels, Curtis P. "British Mercantilism and the Economic Development of the Thirteen Colonies." *Journal of Economic History* 12 (1952): 105–14.

Ostrander, Gilman M. "The Colonial Molasses Trade." *Agricultural History* 30 (1956):77–84.

Perkins, Edwin J. *The Economy of Colonial America*, 2nd ed. New York: Columbia Univ. Press, 1988. Chs. 7 and 8.

Ransom, Roger. "British Policy and Colonial Growth: Some Implications of the Burdens of the Navigation Acts." *Journal of Economic History* 27(1968):427–35.

Reid, Joseph D. "On Navigating the Navigation Acts with Peter D. McClelland." *American Economic Review* 60 (1970):949–55.

————. "Economic Burdens: Spark to the American Revolution?" *Journal of Economic History* 38 (1978):81–120.

Thomas, Robert P. "British Imperial Policy and the Economic Interpretation of the American Revolution." *Journal of Economic History* 28 (1968):436–40.

————. "A Quantitative Approach to the Study of the Effects of British Imperial Policy on Colonial Welfare: Some Preliminary Findings." *Journal of Economic History* 25 (1965):615–38.

Tucker, Robert W., and David Hendrickson. *The Fall of the British Empire: Origins and the Fall of the British Empire*. Baltimore: Johns Hopkins Univ. Press, 1982.

Ver Steeg, Clarence. "The American Revolutionary Movement Considered as an Economic Movement." *Huntington Library Journal* 20 (1957).

Walton, Gary M. "The New Economic History and the Burdens of the Navigation Acts." *Economic History Review* 24, 2nd series, no. 4, (1971):533–42.

Walton, Gary M., and James F. Shepherd. *The Economic Rise of Early America*. Cambridge: Cambridge Univ. Press, 1979. Ch. 8.

PART

2

THE REVOLUTIONARY, EARLY NATIONAL, AND ANTEBELLUM ERAS

1776–1860

1. Industrializing Great Britain and the newly revolutionized France under Napoleon stood as the two leading powers, Britain dominant in Naval forces and leading in per capita income, France dominant in land forces and strong in total output and with a larger population.

2. In 1793, war broke out between Britain and France and lasted until 1815. Napoleon sold the Louisiana territory to the United States, doubling the land size of the nation. Trade and commerce soared in American ports as U.S. shippers served as neutrals to the belligerents until the suppression of U.S. shipping entangled the United States into a second war with Britain in 1812–15.

3. The Northwest Land Ordinances of 1785 and 1787 assured that new U.S. territories could progress toward statehood and enter the union with full equality of the older states, strong testimony to the lessons learned from the colonial status the Americans fought to overcome.

4. The U.S. Constitution adopted in 1789 is a landmark document, historically unprecedented for its scope and simplicity, for its constraint on government power, and as a model of political compromise. It provided assurances of protection of property consistent with individual freedoms with the telling exception of slavery, which persisted in the South.

5. The cotton gin, invented in 1793 by Eli Whitney, allowed the seeds of short staple cotton to be economically removed. Thereafter, U.S. cotton production as a share of world production increased from 0.5 percent in 1791 to 68 percent in 1850. Southern slavery became increasingly entrenched and a growing threat to the Union as western migrations brought the proslavery and antislavery forces into continual dispute.

6. As the industrial revolution spread from England to the United States in the early nineteenth century, a transportation revolution also unfolded to create a strong national market linking the industrializing Northeast with the agrarian West (Midwest) and the Southern Cotton Kingdom.

7. By 1860 the United States was the second leading industrial power in the world.

CHAPTER 7

Hard Realities
for a New Nation

THE WAR AND THE ECONOMY

The War of the Revolution, which began officially on April 19, 1775, dragged on for more than six bitter years. From a vantage point two centuries later, we can see that the war foreshadowed a massive upheaval in the Western world—a chain reaction of revolutions, great and small, that would transform the world. But to the embattled colonials, it was simply a conflict fought for the righteous cause of securing freedom from intolerable British intervention in American affairs. Paradoxically, the Revolution was never supported by the substantial popular majority. Perhaps one-third of the colonists remained loyal to England; another third did little or nothing to help the cause, often trafficking with the enemy and profiteering by selling provisions and supplies to American troops at exorbitant prices. In varying numbers and in widely scattered theaters, foot soldiers slogged wearily back and forth in heartbreaking campaigns that produced no military gains. Although there were relatively few seamen and sea battles were for the most part militarily indecisive, it is an irony of history that the Revolutionary War was finally won with naval strength, as the French fleet under DeGrasse drove off the British men-of-war and bottled up Cornwallis at Yorktown.

Of course, maritime commerce was always an important factor in the war effort, and trade linkages were vital to the supply of arms and ammunitions. When legal restrictions were implemented by both the British and the colonists in 1775, nearly all American overseas commerce abruptly ceased. By mid-1775, the colonies faced acute shortages in such militarily essential items as powder, flints, muskets, and knives. Even salt, shoes, woolens, and linens were in short supply. Late in 1775, Congress authorized limited trade with the West Indies, mainly to procure arms and ammunitions, and trade with other non-British areas was on an unrestricted basis by the spring of 1776.

Nevertheless, the British maintained a fairly effective naval blockade of American ports, and the amounts of wartime trade were at their lowest

127

levels in 1776 and 1777. Boston was pried open late in 1776, but most of the other major ports in New England and the Middle colonies were tightly sealed until 1778. But as the British relaxed their grip on the North, they tightened up on the South. Savannah was taken late in 1778, as was Charleston by 1780.

Formal treaties of commerce—first with France in 1778 and with Holland and Spain shortly thereafter—stimulated the flows of overseas trade, and between 1778 and early 1782, American wartime commerce was at its zenith. During those years, France, Holland, and Spain and their possessions all actively traded with the colonies.

Although the wartime flows of goods in and out of the colonies were highest before 1782 they were still well below prewar levels. Smuggling, privateering, and legal trade with France, Holland, and Spain and their possessions only partially offset the drastic trade reductions with Britain. Even the coastal trades were curtailed by a lack of vessels, by blockades, and by sky-rocketing freight rates. British-occupied ports, such as New York, generated some import activity but little or nothing in the way of exports.

As a result, the colonial economy became considerably more self-sufficient. In Philadelphia, for instance, nearly 4,000 women were employed to spin materials in their homes for the newly established textile plants. There was also a sharp increase in the number of artisan workshops and a similar stimulus to the production of beer, whiskey, and other domestic alcoholic beverages in the colonies. As these facts suggest, an increasing amount of American resources was being channeled into import-competing industries, especially along the coast and in the major port cities. Only the least commercialized rural areas remained little affected by the serpentine path of war and the sporadic flows of wartime commerce.

Overall, the stringencies of war imposed a distinct economic and social hardship on the new nation. Although war had slightly lessened the degree to which the rebelling states depended on Britain, most goods had risen in cost and were much more scarce in America. Markets were greatly disrupted during wartime, making trade very uncertain. Encouraged by temporarily high prices and facing severe commercial difficulties, some investors turned from commerce to manufacturing to vent their capital. But once the trade lanes reopened with the coming of peace, even those who profited from the war were stung by the tide of imports that swept into American ports and sharply lowered prices. Although many Americans escaped the direct ordeals of war, few Americans were untouched by it—at least indirectly.

THE LEGAL AND POLITICAL FRAMEWORK

The strains of war and economic declines were complemented by the critical problem of forming a government. The thirteen colonies were bound together by the Articles of Confederation; established initially for the pressing issue of uniting to engage the enemy, it took from 1777 to 1781 for the individual states to ratify them. The articles had merit, and were effective as a source of early political agreement among the colonies. As a permanent framework of national government however, they were too weak. For example, the power to tax was left to the individual states, thus allowing individual states to act as freeriders on revenues supplied by others. These and other problems too great to be surmounted by the states acting individually pressed inexorably for strong rather than weak union. For example, after independence was won the great powers treated the new nation with a disdain that bordered on contempt. Britain—annoyed because Americans refused to pay prewar British creditors and to restore confiscated Tory property as provided in the peace treaty—excluded the United States from valuable commercial privileges and refused to withdraw troops from its frontier posts on American soil. Spain tried to close the lower Mississippi to American traffic. Even France refused to extend the courtesies traditionally offered a sovereign government.

Internally, the most pressing problems were financial. Fortunately for postwar Confederation officials, the money cost of the Revolutionary War had been largely written off. Between 1775 and 1781, the war was financed by the issue of paper money in amounts great enough to result in a galloping inflation—the only one ever experienced in America except in the Confederate South. Nearly $400 million in continental money, quartermaster and commissary certificates of the central government, and paper money of the states were issued to defray wartime expenses. For all practical purposes, these various issues were repudiated by the middle of 1783, the effect being that of a tax on those who held the depreciating currency while it declined in value. Only a relatively small foreign and domestic debt totaling less than $40 million remained; but the question of the responsibility for its repayment remained a thorny issue, because political leaders assumed that the political units that paid the debt would ultimately hold the balance of power. More important was the fact that Congress had no independent income and had to rely for funds on catch-as-catch-can contributions of the states that were levied roughly in proportion to their several populations. Nor were the states without their own fiscal problems. By 1786, no less than seven states were issuing their own paper, and debtor groups in the other six states were clamoring for similar issues. Although the issuing states, with the exception of Rhode Island, acted responsibly, perhaps no other course of events so frightened conservatives as the control of the money supply by the states. Indeed the legacy of hyperinflation left a general distrust of government monetary management.[1]

As these experiences and the long period leading up to ratification of the Articles of Confederation suggests, American leaders remained divided

---

[1]See Charles W. Calomiris, "Institutional Failure, Monetary Scarcity, and the Depreciation of the Continental," *Journal of Economic History* 48 (1988): 47–68.

on what kind of government should ultimately be adopted. One group wanted no stronger central government than the Articles provided, preferring to cast its lot and fortune with the individual states. Another group, made up on the whole of less fiery revolutionaries, took the view that a strong central government, with power to coerce the states, should be quickly established. Until the end of the war, those who preferred a strong government were largely in control of the nation's affairs; but when news of a favorable peace arrived in 1783, many of the strongest leaders went home to their own pursuits, leaving the administration largely in charge of the weak-government advocates.

Even as early as 1783, however, supporters of a weak central government had begun to make concessions that would strengthen the power of Congress, and by 1786, most of the vehement opponents of a strong central government knew that genuine union was inevitable. Virginia called the Annapolis Convention ostensibly to settle questions of trade regulations among the states. As the delegates came to Annapolis, only to recommend to Congress that another convention be called to examine a broader range of problems, it was clear that American leadership was moving toward unity. The convention that met in Philadelphia in 1787 could ignore its instructions to amend the Articles of Confederation and create a new government instead only because the great constitutional questions debated so heatedly since 1775 were at last settled in the minds of the majority.

In a little over four months from the first meeting of the delegates, George Washington, president of the convention, sent the completed document to the states for ratification.[2] Delaware ratified it almost immediately, on December 7, 1787, and on June 21, 1788 New Hampshire cast the crucial ninth vote in favor. Congress declared the Constitution in effect beginning March 4, 1789 and two years later the Bill of Rights was passed and also put in effect.

THE CONSTITUTION

With the adoption of the Constitution, the power to tax was firmly delegated to the federal government, which was empowered to pay off past debts, even those incurred by the states. The assurance that public debts will be honored has proven critical to the development of a sound capital market in the United States. Even today, the United States benefits from this heritage and is viewed as a haven by major investors seeking safety for their capital.

---

[2] For an analysis assessing the economic vested interests of the delegates, see Robert A. McGuire and Robert L. Ohsfeldt, "An Economic Model of Voting Behavior over Specific Issues at the Constitutional Convention of 1787," *Journal of Economic History* 46 (1986): 79–82.

Second, the central government was granted the sole right to mint coins and regulate the money supply. Such rights were not allowed the states. Having just emerged from monetary chaos and hyperinflation, a stable dollar was highly desired and viewed as on answer to the conflicting interests of creditors and debtors.

Both of these powers, to tax and to regulate money, brought into sharp focus the delegates' concern over conflicting factions and the limits of majority rule.[3] Consequently, federal taxes had to be uniform among all the states, and of course, U.S. dollars were exchangeable throughout the states. These concerns urging barriers to prevent significant and radical changes in the distribution of wealth through government formed the basis for a major section of the Fifth Amendment: "nor shall any persons be deprived of life, liberty, or property without due process of law; nor shall private property be taken for public use without just compensation."

Another matter of great political and economic significance was the regulation of trade among the states. Although no substantial barriers to interstate commerce had emerged in the 1780s, the possibility for them was evident. With the Constitution the states were forbidden to enact tariffs—the toll-free movement of goods was thus assured. The important "interstate clause" not only established a great common market, nationally, in later decades it permitted the extension of federal authority to many areas of interstate economic activity.

The Constitution promoted trade and economic specialization in other ways. Besides its provisions for security against foreign and domestic threats (hence, to maintain an army and navy) it was authorized to establish post offices and roads, to fix standards of weights and measures, and to establish uniform bankruptcy laws. It also gave Congress the authority to set laws on

---

[3]In Paper 10 of the Federalist Papers, James Madison brings into sharp focus his preoccupation with these important matters and his concern about "factions" and the limits of majority rule: "The most common and durable source of factions has been the various and unequal distribution of property. Those who hold and those who are without property have ever formed distinct interests in society. Those who are creditors, and those who are debtors, fall under a like discrimination. A landed interest, a manufacturing interest, a mercantile interest, a money interest, with many lesser interests, grow up of necessity in civilized nations, and divide them into different classes, actuated by different sentiments and views. The regulation of these various and interfering interests forms the principal task of modern legislation, and involves the spirit of party and faction in the necessary and ordinary operations of the government. . . .The interference to which we are brought is, that the causes of faction cannot be removed, and that relief is only to be sought in the means of controlling its effects.

If a faction consists of less than a majority, relief is supplied by the republican principle, which enables the majority to defeat its sinister views by regular vote. It may clog the administration, it may convulse the society; but it will be unable to execute and mask its violence under the forms of the Constitution. When a majority is included in a faction, the form of popular government, on the other hand, enables it to sacrifice to its ruling passion or interest both the public good and the rights of other citizens. To secure the public good and private rights against the danger of such a faction, and at the same time to preserve the spirit and the form of popular government, is then the great object to which our inquiries are directed."

patents: "To promote the progress of science and useful arts by securing for limited times to authors and inventors the exclusive right to their respective writings and discovers." With greater assurances to the gains of their own ideas and creations, creative people would hasten technical change.

Another transfer of authority to the federal government was foreign affairs. It alone could negotiate treaties or set tariffs. The power to regulate tariffs became a powerful lever in negotiations with foreign nations to reduce or eliminate duties on American goods abroad. Before this shift of power, competition among the states minimized the possibility of this leverage and U.S. tariffs were very low as well. Throughout most of the nineteenth century tariffs were the chief source of federal revenues.

For the delegates at the Philadelphia convention (and the individual states) to voluntarily release such powers to the central government was unprecedented, and compromise was vital, especially as epitomized in the question of how to deal with slavery. The Constitutional compromise on slavery allowed slavery to continue, but limited the importation of slaves to only 20 years, until 1808. A tax, up to a maximum of $10 per imported slave, was allowed. Furthermore, each state was ordered to recognize the laws and court orders of other states; thus runaway slaves escaping to another state were to be returned, like stolen property. Oddly, the Constitution viewed slaves in two respects, first and foremost as property, just as in colonial times. Second, each slave was counted as three-fifths of a person for the purpose of determining the number of representatives to the House of Representatives from each state, which was based on population.

The debates of the Convention focused carefully on the question of state versus national interests and it was temporarily left implicit that powers not delegated to the federal government, or forbidden to the states, were reserved to the states (or the people). To strengthen these reserved rights, the Tenth Amendment was attached as the last one completing the Bill of Rights. These reserved rights included the rights to set local and state laws such as licensing, regulation of business, taxes, zoning laws, civil conduct and the like and to use police powers to enforce them.

In respect to relations among people the new nation preserved the treasured English common law. This long string of rules based on court decisions had worked well for centuries, and the First Continental Congress of 1774 formally proclaimed the Common Law of England as the right of Americans. Many states repeated this claim and legal interpretations were left to the states, as long as legal statutes and interpretations were consistent with the Constitution, the supreme law of the land. Any conflict or challenge was to be judicated by the courts and if necessary ultimately by the Supreme Court.

These and many other special features of the Constitution laid the foundation of private property rights we enjoy today. It curbed the arbitrary powers of government, and fostered personal security required for the pursuit of all varieties of productivity-enhancing activities. Amazingly brief and clear, the Constitution has proven flexible through court interpretation, and on 16 occasions since the Bill of Rights, through amendment.

There probably was no single original source from which the essential concepts of the Constitution were derived. And yet, in 1776, the same year that the Declaration of Independence rang its message of political freedom around the world, an odd-looking Scot, whose professorial mien belied his vast knowledge of economic affairs, offered a similarly clarion rationale of economic freedom. *The Wealth of Nations* became a bestseller, and Adam Smith almost at once found himself admired and famous. Educated people everywhere, including American leaders, read his great work, marveling at the lucid language and its castigation of mercantilist constraints on economic processes. It does not deny Adam Smith's great influence to say that he was the articulate commentator on forces that existed long before he began to write. Chief among these forces were a growing regard for the advantages of private property arrangements and the abiding conviction that law and order were essential to the preservation of property rights and to the opportunity for all people to acquire the things of this world. It follows, therefore, that equaling the political guarantees of the Constitution in their ultimate assurance of freedom were the fundamental economic guarantees of protection of private property and enforcement of contracts, essential to the stability necessary to a market economy. Smith himself could not have designed a state better tailored to his concept of an economic order directed by self-interest, of a system unshackled by governmental rules and regulations but assured the domestic tranquility and freedom from foreign interference that only a strong central government could provide.

AMERICAN INDEPENDENCE AND ECONOMIC CHANGE

The adoption of the Constitution in 1789 and the emergence of a stronger federal government did not have dramatic immediate effects. The economy remained basically of the same structure that had existed in colonial times. The important political, legal, and institutional changes that ensued during the critical years of war and throughout the entire 1780s were paralleled and influenced by economic adjustments. As we have noted, that period was not a time of prosperity. Indeed, the trials and tribulations of a government functioning under the Articles of Confederation and the rising pressures that led to the ratification of the Constitution only partially convey the many painful new circumstances that the struggling young nation faced. In short, the crucial political decisions of that time were matched by challenging economic problems.

The most central problem was independence itself, because this conversion was unlike previous adjustments to peacetime. All at once the young nation found itself outside the walls of the Empire, and soon even the wartime trade alliances with France and Spain began to crumble.

In the Caribbean, U.S. ships were excluded from direct trade with the British West Indies. American merchants who tried to evade the law faced possible seizure by officials. Spain added to American woes by withdrawing the wartime privilege of direct U.S. trade with Cuba, Puerto Rico, and Hispaniola. In addition, Spain reinstituted its traditional policy of restricting trade with its possessions, permitting them to import goods only from Spain. There was an increase in U.S. trade with the French West Indies, but this was not enough to offset the other declines in commercial trade with the Caribbean islands. Even in its lively trade with the French, the United States was not allowed to carry sugar from French islands, and only in times of severe scarcity did the French import American flour. In addition, the French imposed high duties on U.S. salted fish and meat, and these products were banned entirely from the British islands.

Restrictions and trade curtailments were not limited to the Caribbean. Now Americans were also cut off from direct trade with the British fisheries in Newfoundland and Nova Scotia. As a result, New England suffered severe losses in trade to the north in provisions, lumber, rum, and shipping services. To the east and into the Mediterranean, American shipping faced harassment by the Barbary pirates. The United States was no longer protected by the British flag and by British tribute to the governments of Tunis, Tripoli, and Algeria.

While American shipping rocked at anchor, American shipbuilding and the supporting industries of lumber and naval stores remained unengaged. Of course, Britain now labeled all American-built vessels as foreign, thereby making them ineligible to trade within the Empire even when they were owned by British subjects. The result was the loss of a major market for American shipbuilders, and the U.S. ship production declined still further because American whale oil faced prohibitively high British duties after 1783. In fact, nearly all of the activities that employed American-built ships (cod fishing, whaling, mercantile and shipping services) were depressed industries, and New England—the center of these activities—suffered disproportionately during the early years of independence.

The Middle colonies were also affected. Pennsylvania and New York shared losses in shipbuilding. Moreover, their trades in wheat, flour, salted meat, and other provisions to the West Indies were well below those in colonial peacetime years. By 1786, that region had probably reached the bottom of a fairly severe business cycle, but conditions began to improve in the late 1780s as these products were reaccepted into the traditional West Indian and southern European markets. Similar problems plagued the South. For instance, British duties on rice restricted planters of the lower South primarily to markets in the West Indies and southern Europe. As the price of rice declined, further setbacks resulted from the loss of bounties and subsidies on indigo and naval stores. Having few alternative uses of its productive capacity, the lower South faced special difficulties. Its overall economic future did not look bright. Similarly, the upper South faced stagnating markets for its major staple—tobacco. In Britain, a tax of 15d. sterling was imposed on a pound of foreign tobacco. In France, a single purchasing monopoly—the Farmers-General—was created to handle tobacco imports into France. Meanwhile, Spain and Portugal prohibited imports of American tobacco altogether.

Offsetting these restrictions were a few positive forces. Goods, which previously had been "enumerated," could now be traded directly to continental European ports. This lowered the shipping and handling costs on some items such as tobacco, so that American exporters and planters received higher prices. Meanwhile, the great influx of British manufactures sharply reduced prices on these goods in American ports. Although American manufacturers suffered, U.S. consumers were pleased; compared to the late colonial period, the terms of trade—the prices paid for imports relative to the prices paid for exports—had improved. This was especially true in 1783 and 1784 when import prices were slightly below their prewar level and export prices were higher. Thereafter, the terms of trade became less favorable, and by 1790, there was little advantage in the adjustments of these relative prices compared with the prewar period.

To convey these many changes more systematically and in a longrun perspective, it is essential to compare the circumstances of the late colonial period with the circumstances surrounding the time of the adoption of the Constitution. Of course, this does not entirely isolate the impact of independence on the economy, because forces other than independence contributed to the shifting magnitudes and patterns of trade and to the many other economic changes that occurred. Nevertheless, comparisons of the late colonial period with the early 1790s provide important insights into the new directions and prospects for the young nation.

In Table 7-1, we see that by 1790, the United States had taken advantage of its new freedom to trade directly with other northern European countries. Most of this trade was in tobacco to France and the Netherlands, but rice, wheat, four, and maize (Indian corn) were also shipped there in large amounts. The emergence of this new trade pattern must be attributed largely to independence, but it should be emphasized that the lion's share of American exports continued to be sent to Great Britain, including items that were then reexported to the Continent. Many have speculated on the reasons for this renewal of American–British loyalties. Part of the explanation may be that Britain offered the greatest variety of goods at the best price and quality, especially woolens, linens, and hardwares. Moreover, British merchants enjoyed the advantages of a common language, established contacts, and a knowledge of U.S. markets. Because American imports were handled by British merchants, it was often advantageous to use British ports as dropping off points for U.S. exports, even those destined for the Continent.

In addition to these changes, new patterns of trade were emerging in

TABLE 7-1   Average Annual Real Exports to Overseas Areas: The Thirteen Colonies, 1768–72, and the United States, 1790–92 (in thousands of pounds sterling: 1768–72 prices)

Destination	1768–72	Percentage of Total	1790–92	Percentage of Total
Great Britain and Ireland	1,616	58	1,234	31
Northern Europe	—	—	643	16
Southern Europe	406	14	557	14
British West Indies }	759	27	402	10
Foreign West Indies }			956	24
Africa	21	1	42	1
Canadian Colonies	NA	—	60	2
Other	—	—	59	1
Total	2,802	100	3,953	100

Source: James F. Shepherd and Gary M. Walton, "Economic Change after the American Revolution: Pre- and Postwar Comparisons of Maritime Shipping and Trade," *Explorations in Economic History* 13, no. 4 (Oct. 1976): 397–422.

the Caribbean. Before the Revolution, trade with the British West Indies had been greater than trade with the foreign islands, but by 1790 the situation was reversed, largely due to the exclusion of American shipping from the British islands. Undoubtedly, many American ships illegally traversed British Caribbean waters, and Dutch St. Eustatius remained an entrepôt from which British islands were supplied, as they had been during the war. Consequently, the statistics in Table 7–1 exaggerate this shift. Nevertheless, it would appear that U.S. trade with non-British areas of the Caribbean grew substantially during these years. This trend had been underway before the Revolution, but postwar restrictions on American shipping undoubtedly hastened that shift.

Lastly, it is worth noting that no new trades to romantic faraway places emerged in any significant way during this period of transition. The changes in trade patterns that were effected were actually rather modest.

As trade patterns changed, so did the relative importance of the many goods traded. For instance, Table 7-2 shows that the great prewar staple—tobacco—was no longer the single most valuable export by the early 1790s, despite some recovery in the 1780s. Actually, tobacco production may have equaled or perhaps even exceeded prewar levels as early as the mid-1780s. This, along with rising tobacco prices, aided the recovery of the tobacco-producing areas of Virginia and Maryland. However, such good fortune failed to touch the other important southern staples, and the lower South in particular lapsed into more self-sufficiency. Later in the 1780s, the rising prices for rice offset the diminishing quantity exported, but indigo and naval stores both fell in value and in quantity. This decline was due, of

TABLE 7-2 Annual Average Exports of Selected Commodities from the Thirteen Colonies, 1768–72, and the United States, 1790–92.

Commodity	THIRTEEN COLONIES, 1768–72			UNITED STATES, 1790–92		
	(1) Quantity	(2) Value (thousands of current pounds sterling)	(3) Value (thousands of dollars: 1790–92 prices)	(4) Quantity	(5) Value (thousands of current dollars)	(6) Value (thousands of pounds sterling: 1768–72 prices)
Beef }	26,036 bbl	51	209	60,457 bbl	367 }	159
Pork }				29,741 bbl	285 }	
Bread }	38,634 tons	410	2,534	3,823 tons	221 }	712
Flour }				63,256 tons	4,178 }	
Cotton	29,425 lb	1	7	163,822 lb	41	8
Fish, dried	308,993 quintals	154	740	375,619 quintals	900	187
Flaxseed	233,065 bu	42	189	352,079 bu	286	64
Grain: Indian Corn	839,314 bu	83	424	1,926,784 bu	974	191
Rice	140,254 bu	311	1,971	129,367 bbl	1,818	287
Wheat	599,127 bu	115	654	998,862 bu	1,090	192
Indigo	547,649 lb	113	567	493,760 lb	511	101
Iron: Bar	2,416 tons	36	195	300 tons	24	4
Pig	4,468 tons	22	116	3,667 tons	95	18
Livestock: Cattle	3,433	21	63	4,861	89	29
Horses	6,048	60	240	7,086	282	71
Naval Stores: Pitch	11,384 bbl	5	21	7,279 bbl	13	3
Tar	90,472 bbl	34	135	68,463 bbl	102	25
Turpentine	19,870 bbl	9	42	51,194 bbl	108	24
Oil, whale	3,841 tons	46	212	1,826 tons	101	22
Potash	1,381 tons	35	134	4,872 tons	472	123
Rum, American	342,366 gal	22	132	441,782 gal	170	28
Tobacco	87,986 hhd	776	3,093	110,687 hhd	3,891	964
Wood Products						
Pine boards	38,991 M ft	70	228	45,118 M ft	264	81
Staves and headings	21,585 M	65	275	31,554 M	401	95
Total, above commodities		2,471	12,181		16,683	3,388
All exports		2,802			19,465	

Source: Shepherd and Walton, "Economic Change," pp. 397–422.

course, to the loss of the bounties (and to increased British production of indigo in the West Indies after the war).

The most striking change of the period, however, was the increase in the export of foodstuffs such as salted meats (beef and pork), bread and flour, maize, and wheat. Of course, these accompanied the relative rise of the trades to the West Indies. Because the uptrend in food shipments to the West Indies was underway before the Revolution, not all of this shift in commodities can be attributed solely to independence.

Because of these changing patterns and magnitudes of trade, some states improved their economic well-being while others lost ground. Table 7-3 shows exports per capita for each state during this period, after adjusting for inflationary effects. Compared to prewar levels, New England had returned to about the same per-capita position by the early 1790s. The

TABLE 7-3   Average Annual Exports from Colonies and Regions of the Thirteen Colonies, 1768–72, and States and Regions of the United States, 1791–92 (in thousands of pounds sterling; 1768–72 prices)

	1768–72			1791–92		
Origin	Total exports	Percentage of total	Per capita exports	Total exports	Percentage of total	Per capita exports
New England						
New Hampshire	46	2	0.74	33	1	0.23
Massachusetts	258	9	0.97	542	14	1.14
Rhode Island	81	3	1.39	119	3	1.72
Connecticut	92	3	0.50	148	4	0.62
Total, New England	477	17	0.82	842	22	0.83
Middle Atlantic						
New York	187	7	1.15	512	14	1.51
New Jersey	2	—	0.02	5	—	0.03
Pennsylvania	353	13	1.47	584	16	1.34
Delaware	18	1	0.51	26	1	0.44
Total, Middle Atlantic	559	20	1.01	1,127	30	1.11
Upper South						
Maryland	392	14	1.93	482	13	1.51
Virginia	770	27	1.72	678	18	0.91
Total, upper South	1,162	41	1.79	1,160	31	1.09
Lower South						
North Carolina	75	3	0.38	104	3	0.27
South Carolina	455	16	3.66	436	12	1.75
Georgia	74	3	3.17	97	3	1.17
Total, lower South	603	22	1.75	637	17	0.88
Total, all regions	2,802	100	1.31	3,766	100	0.99

Source: Shepherd and Walton, "Economic Change," pp. 397–422.

Middle Atlantic region showed improvement despite the depression felt so sharply in Pennsylvania in the mid-1780s.

As indicated in Table 7-3, the trade of the southern regions did not keep pace with a growing population. Although the South's prewar absolute level of exports had been regained by the early 1790s, its per-capita exports were significantly below those in colonial times. The lower South was the region most severely affected. However, once again, this was not entirely due to independence; it was probably due more to a decline in growth of demand in Europe for southern staples.

The wide variety of changes among the states makes it extremely hazardous to generalize nationally. Overall, there was a 30 percent decline in real per-capita exports (per year). Total exports had climbed by 40 percent, but this fell far short of the 80 percent jump in population. Accompanying this change was a slowing in urbanization. The major cities of Philadelphia, New York, and Boston grew only 3 percent over this period, despite the large increase in the total population of the states. Both of these adjustments—the decline in per-capita exports and the pause in urban growth—were extremely unusual peacetime experiences. Yet, as emphasized, such aggregate figures hide as much as they reveal. The southern declines were sharp; only New York and the New England states (except New Hampshire) more than fully recovered from trade disruptions.

The western movement and the persistence of self-sufficient activities cushioned the downfall of incomes per capita. Undoubtedly, per-capita internal trade did not decline to the same extent as per-capita exports. Unfortunately, we have no statistics on domestic trade during that hectic period. Nevertheless, the external relations probably exaggerated the overall setbacks of the period. It is safe to conclude, however, that the political chaos of the Early National Era was accompanied by severe economic conditions. Indeed, the problems of government contributed to the weakness of the economy, and in turn, economic events clarified government failings under the Articles of Confederation.

These were the circumstances shortly before 1793—the year in which the Napoleonic Wars erupted and Eli Whitney invented the cotton gin. The sweeping consequences of those events could never have been foreseen in colonial times. The colonies, however, had already developed a commercial base that now would prove crucial to further development. Because of its early efforts at overseas trade, the new nation was ready to take quick advantage of the economic possibilities of a neutral nation in a world at war.

WAR, NEUTRALITY, AND ECONOMIC RESURGENCE

As we have seen, the economic setbacks experienced by the United States throughout the late 1770s and most of the 1780s were followed by years of halting progress and incomplete recovery. Then in 1793, just four years after the beginning of the French revolution, the French and English began a series of wars that lasted until 1815. During this long struggle, both British and French cargo vessels were drafted into military service, and both nations relaxed their restrictive mercantilist policies. Of all nations most capable of filling the shipping void created by the Napoleonic Wars, the new United States stood at the forefront.

Due to these developments, the nation's economy briskly rebounded from the doldrums of the preceding years. The stimulus in U.S. overseas commerce is graphed statistically in Figure 7-1. As indicated, per-capita credits in the balance of payments (exports plus other sources of foreign exchange

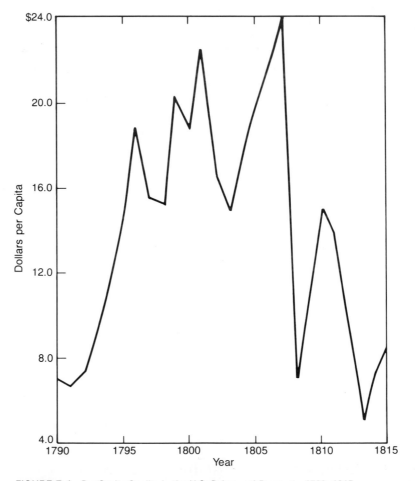

FIGURE 7-1 Per Capita Credits in the U.S. Balance of Payments, 1790–1815.

Source: Douglass C. North, "Early National Income Estimates of the United States," *Economic Development and Cultural Change* 9 (1961): 390.

earnings) more than tripled between 1790 and the height of war between the French and English. There can be little doubt that these were extraordinary years—a time of unusual prosperity and intense economic activity, especially in the eastern port cities. It was a time characterized by full employment and sharply rising urbanization, at least until 1808. Famed entrepreneurs of New England and the Middle Atlantic region, such as Stephen Girard, Archibald Gracie, E. H. Derby, and John Jacob Astor, amassed vast personal fortunes during this period. These and other capital accumulations added to the development of a well-established commercial sector and eventually contributed to the incipient manufacturing sector.

It is important to recognize the significance of the commercial sector of the economy as well as the role of the merchant class during these decades. The growing merchant class, of course, had played an active role in helping to spearhead the move for national independence. Now the merchant class supplied the entrepreneurial talents required to take full advantage of the new economic circumstances. As the spreading war opened up exceptional trade opportunities, the well-developed commercial sector provided the needed buildings and ships, as well as know-how. In short, both the physical and human capital were already available, and in many ways the success of the period stemmed from developments that reached back to colonial times. It was exactly that prior development that singled out the United States as the leading neutral nation in time of war. Rather than the ports of the Caribbean, Latin America, or Canada, the leading ports of the United States emerged as the entrepôts of trade in the western Atlantic.

The effects of war and neutrality on U.S. shipping earnings are shown in Figure 7-2. In general, these statistics convey the same picture that we saw in Figure 7-1, namely that these were exceptionally prosperous times for the commercial sector.

Although the invention of the cotton gin stimulated cotton production and U.S. cotton supplies grew in response to the growth of demand for raw cotton in English textile mills, commercial growth was by no means limited to products produced in the United States. As Figure 7-3 shows, reexports comprised a major portion of the total exports from U.S. ports, especially in such tropical items as sugar, coffee, cocoa, pepper, and spices. Because their commercial sectors were relatively underdeveloped, however, the Caribbean islands and Latin America depended primarily on American shipping and merchandising services rather than on their own.

Of course, such unique conditions did not provide the basis for long-term development, and—as Figures 7-1, 7-2, and 7-3 all show—when temporary peace came between late 1801 and 1803, the U. S. commercial boom quickly evaporated. When hostilities erupted again, the United States experienced another sharp upswing in commercial activity. This time, however, new serious problems arose with the expansion. In 1805, the British imposed an antiquated ruling, the Rule of 1756, permitting neutrals in wartime to

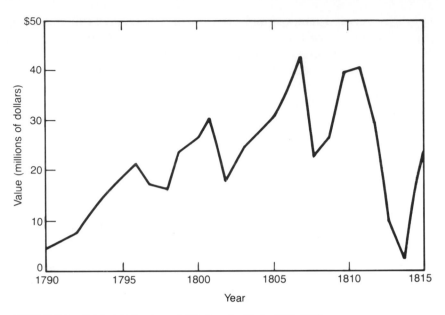

FIGURE 7-2   Net Freight Earnings of U.S. Carrying Trade, 1790–1815.

Source: Douglass C. North, *The Economic Growth of the United States, 1790–1860* (Englewood Cliffs: Prentice-Hall, 1961), pp. 26,28.

carry only those goods that they normally carried in peacetime. This ruling, known as the Essex Decision, was matched by Napoleon's Berlin Decree, which banned trade to Britain. As a result, nearly 1,500 American ships and many American sailors were seized, and some were forcefully drafted into the Royal Navy. The Congress and President Jefferson, fearful of entangling the United States in war, declared the Embargo Act of 1807, which prohibited U.S. ships from trading with all foreign ports.

Basically, this attempt to gain respect for American neutrality backfired, and as the drastic declines in Figures 7-1, 7-2, and 7-3 show, the cure was almost worse than the disease. As pressures in the port cities mounted, political action led to the Non-Importation Act of 1809. This partially opened up trade, with specific prohibitions against Great Britain, France, and their possessions.

Nevertheless, continuing seizures and other complications between the United States and Britain along the Canadian border finally led to war— the second with England within 30 years. The War of 1812 was largely a naval war, however, and the British seized more than 1,000 additional ships and blockaded almost the entire U.S. coast.

As exports declined to practically nothing, new boosts were given to the tiny manufacturing sector. Actually, stirrings there began with the Embargo of 1807, which quickly altered the possibilities for profits in commerce

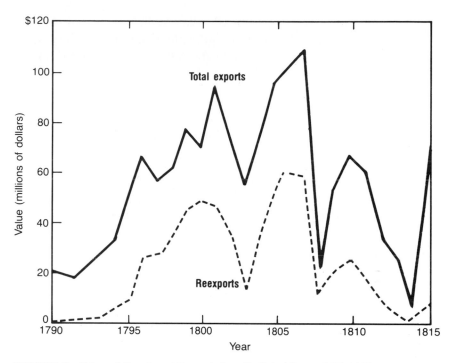

FIGURE 7-3   Values of Exports and Reexports from the United States, 1790–1815.

Source: North, *The Economic Growth of the United States, 1790–1860*, p. 28.

relative to manufactures. As prices on manufactures rose, increasing possibilities for profits encouraged capital to flow into manufacturing. From 15 textile mills in 1808, new additions raised the number to almost 90 by 1809. Similar additions continued throughout the war period, but when the Peace of Ghent in 1814 brought the war to a close, the textile industry faltered badly. Once again, British imports arrived in massive amounts and undercut prices, which were temporarily inflated by supply shortages resulting from the embargo and the war. Only large-scale U.S. concerns weathered the competitive storm, and there were few of these—most notably the Lowell shops using the Waltham system (discussed in Chapter 11) of cloth weaving. Nevertheless, these war-related spurts in manufacturing provided an important basis for further industrial expansion, not only in textiles—the main manufacturing activity of the time—but in other areas as well. This marked a time when the relative roles of the various sectors of the economy began to shift. Agriculture was to dominate the economy for most of the century, but to a lesser and lesser degree as economic growth continued.

The economic surge of the Napoleonic War period, 1793–1807, was unique, not so much by comparison to later decades in the nineteenth century, as by its striking reversal and advance from the two decades following

1772. Work by Claudia Goldin and Frank Lewis shows that during the decade and a half after the beginning of the Napoleonic Wars, the growth rate of per-capita income averaged almost 1 percent per year, with the foreign sector accounting for over 25 percent of the underlying sources of growth.[4]

In contrast, during the two decades preceding 1793, per capita exports fell (Table 7-3), and productivity in Pennsylvania agriculture suffered modest declines (see Table 5-1, for review). Claudia Goldin and Frank Lewis estimate that per capita income declined by a rate of 34 percent annually from 1774 to 1793.[5] Wealth holdings per capita also declined substantially over this period.[6]

There is little doubt that the several decades following independence were exceptionally unstable, not merely two decades of bust, and then one and a half of boom. There were ups and downs within these longer bust and boom periods. Because of the importance of foreign trade at the time, export instability had strong leverage effects throughout the economy. Although external forces were always an important factor in determining business cycles, just as the influence of OPEC reminded us in the 1970s, their almost total dominance was now beginning to wane. By the turn of the century, internal developments—especially those in the banking sector—had assumed a more pivotal role in causing economic fluctuations. As we shall see in Chapter 12, both external forces (acting through credit flows from and to overseas areas) and internal forces (acting through changes in credit availability and the money stock) came to bear on the economy during the early nineteenth century. And some of the biggest challenges and opportunities for young Americans were settling and working new lands in the West.

SELECTED REFERENCES AND SUGGESTED READINGS

Adams, Donald R., Jr. "American Neutrality and Prosperity, 1793–1808: A Reconsideration." *The Journal of Economic History* 40(1980): 713–38.

Beard, Charles A. *An Economic Interpretation of the Constitution.* New York: Macmillan, 1913.

Bjork, Gordon C. "The Weaning of the American Economy: Independence, Market Changes, and Economic Development." *Journal of Economic History* 24 (1964): 541–60.

Colomiris, Charles W. "Institutional Failure, Monetary Scarcity, and the Depreciation of the Continental." *Journal of Economic History* 48 (1988): 47–68.

Gilbert, Geoffrey. "The Role of Breadstuffs in American Trade, 1770–1790." *Explorations in Economic History* 14 (1977): 378–87.

---

[4]Claudia D. Goldin and Frank D. Lewis, "The Role of Exports in American Economic Growth during the Napoleonic Wars, 1793–1807," *Explorations in Economic History* 17 (1980): 6–25, especially p. 22. For an alternative interpretation of the role of neutrality, see Donald R. Adams, Jr., "American Neutrality and Prosperity, 1793–1808: A Reconsideration," *The Journal of Economic History* 40(1980): 713–38.

[5]Goldin and Lewis, pp. 22–23.

[6]Alice H. Jones, *Wealth of a Nation to Be* (New York: Columbia Univ. Press, 1980), p. 82.

Goldin, Claudia D., and Frank D. Lewis. "The Role of Exports in American Economic Growth during the Napoleonic Wars, 1793–1807." *Explorations in Economic History* 17 (1980): 6–25.

Jensen, Merrill. *The New Nation: A History of the United States during Confederation.* New York: Knopf, 1958.

Jones, Alice H. *Wealth of a Nation to Be.* New York: Columbia Univ. Press, 1980.

McGuire, Robert A., and Robert L. Ohsfeldt. "Economic Interests and the American Constitution: A Quantitative Rehabilitation of Charles A. Beard." *Journal of Economic History* 44 (June 1984): 509–19.

———. "An Economic Model of Voting Behavior over Specific Issues at the Constitutional Convention of 1787." *Journal of Economic History* 46 (1986): 79–112.

Nettels, Curtis P. *The Emergence of a National Economy, 1775–1815.* New York: Holt, Rinehart and Winston, 1962. Chs. 3 and 4.

North, Douglass C. *American Economic Growth 1790–1860.* Englewood Cliffs, N. J.: Prentice-Hall, 1960.

———. "Early National Income Estimates of the United States." *Economic Development and Cultural Change* 9, no. 3 (April 1961).

Shepherd, James F., and Gary M. Walton. "Economic Change after the American Revolution: Pre-War and Post-War Comparisons of Maritime Shipping and Trade." *Explorations in Economic History,* 13 (1976): 397–422.

CHAPTER 8

Land and the Early Westward Movements

THE ACQUISITION AND DISPOSAL OF THE PUBLIC DOMAIN

One of the first truly national issues for the new government, aside from waging war and financing it, was the disposition of new lands in the West. The Articles of Confederation held that western lands could not be unwillingly taken from the states by the central government, and seven of the colonies held claims on western lands. These claims were based on their original grants from England and from dealings with the Indians. Many people argued, however, that the new western territories should belong to the national government and held or disposed in the national interest. Maryland, a state without western claims, brought the issue to a head by refusing to ratify the Articles until the land issue was resolved. In 1781, Maryland finally signed, after New York voluntarily gave its claims, based on treaties with the Iroquois Indians, to the national government. Virginia promptly followed suit and relinquished its claims on western lands. The other five states having claims soon followed their lead.

What the new nation obtained from the British in 1783 is portrayed in the darkened area of Map 8-1. Thus, the United States began with a solid mass of land extending from the Atlantic coast to the Mississippi River and from the Great Lakes to, but not including, Florida.

Between 1802, when Georgia, the last of the states to do so, relinquished its rights to western land, and 1898, when the formal annexation of Hawaii occurred, the United States very nearly assumed its present physical form as the result of eight main acquisitions (shown in Map 8-1):

1. The Territory of Louisiana, acquired in 1803 by purchase from France.
2. Florida, acquired in 1819 by purchase from Spain. A few years previously, the United States had annexed the narrow strip of land that constituted west Florida.

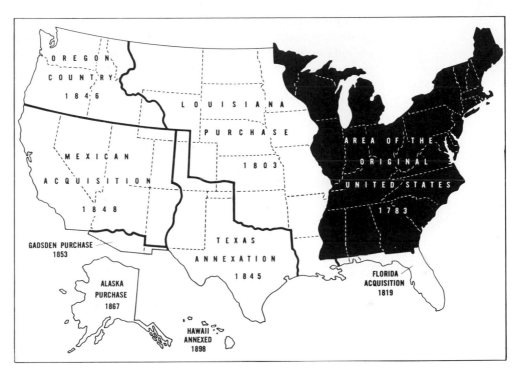

MAP 8-1   Land Growth: The purchase of Louisiana marked the beginning of the continental expansion of the United States, which culminated in the purchase of nonadjacent Alaska in 1867 and the annexation of Hawaii in 1898.

3. The Republic of Texas, annexed as a state in 1845. The Republic of Texas had been established nine years previously after the victory of the American settlers over the Mexicans.

4. The Oregon Country, annexed by treaty with Great Britain in 1846. Spain and Russia, the original claimants to this area, had long since dropped out. By the Treaty of 1818, the United States and Great Britain agreed to a joint occupation of the Oregon Country and British Columbia; the Treaty of 1846 established the dividing line at the forty-ninth parallel.

5. The Mexican Cession, acquired by conquest from Mexico in 1848.

6. The Gadsden Purchase, acquired from Mexico in 1853.

7. The Alaskan Purchase, acquired from Russia in 1867.

8. The Hawaiian Annexation, formally ratified in 1898.

In half a century, the United States obtained a continental area of 3 million square miles, of which 1.4 billion acres, or 75 percent, constituted the public domain.[1] In 1862, two-thirds of this vast area was still in the possession of the government, but the method of disposal had been agreed on long before. The decisions of our forebearers regarding federal land policy have their consequences in the present.

The Land Ordinances of 1785 and 1787

After victory in the Revolution, the Congress of the Confederation had to make three decisions regarding the disposal of public land:

1. How were land holdings and sales to be administered?
2. Should the government exact high revenues from the sale of land, or should cheap land be made available to everyone?
3. What was to be the political relationship between newly settled areas and the original states?

Two major land systems had developed during the colonial period. The New England system of "township planning" provided for laying out townships, for the subdivision of townships into carefully surveyed tracts, and for the auction sale of tracts to settlers. In the eighteenth century, it was usual to establish townships, which often were 6 miles square, in tiers. The opening of new townships proceeded with regularity from settled to unsettled land, gaps of unsettled land appeared infrequently, and no one could own land that had not been previously surveyed. In contrast, the southern system provided for no rectangular surveys. In the South, a settler simply selected what appeared to be a choice plot of unappropriated land and asked the county surveyor to mark it off. Settlers paid no attention to the relationship of their tracts to other pieces of property, and the legal description of a tract was made with reference to more or less permanent natural objects, such as stones, trees, and streams.

Two fundamentally different points of view also emerged about the terms on which land should be made available, and a debate ensued that was not to end for several decades. Those who advocated a "conservative" policy were in favor of selling the public lands in large tracts at high prices for cash. The proponents of a "liberal" policy were in favor of putting land within the reach of everyone by making it available in small parcels at low prices on credit terms.

The decision regarding the status of areas to be settled in the future also involved a great political principle. Were these areas to remain in colonial dependence, subject to profitable exploitation by the original thirteen states? Or were they to be admitted into a union of states on a basis of equality? The answers to these questions would test the foresight and selflessness of Americans, who had themselves escaped the dominance of a ruling empire.

---

[1]In addition, Alaska contains more than 586,400 square miles, most of it still in the public domain, and Hawaii added 6,423 square miles, none of it in the public domain.

There was no pressure on the Congress of the Confederation to provide a system for regulating public lands until 1784, by which time Virginia and New York had relinquished their claims to the southern part of the territory lying northwest of the Ohio River. In that year, a congressional committee of five, headed by Thomas Jefferson, proposed a system based on a rectangular survey. It is noteworthy that three of the five members were southerners who, despite their origins, recognized the value of the New England method of settlement. No action was taken in 1784, but a year later another committee, composed of a member from each state, reworked the report from the previous year and offered a carefully considered proposal. With minor changes, this proposal was passed as the Land Ordinance of 1785.

Insofar as the ordinance set a *physical* basis for disposing of the public lands, its effects were permanent. Government surveyors were to establish on unsettled land horizontal lines called *base lines* and vertical lines called *principal meridians*. The first of the principal meridians was to be in what is now the state of Ohio, and the first surveys covered land north of the Ohio River. Eventually, all the land in the United States was included in the survey except the original thirteen states and Vermont, Kentucky, Tennessee, parts of Ohio, and Texas. As the survey moved westward, other principal meridians were established, the second in what is now Indiana, the third in what is now Illinois, and so on. Map 8-2 indicates the other principal meridians and the base lines perpendicular to them. The insets show how tiers of townships, called *ranges,* were laid out to the east and west of a principal meridian. The ranges were designated by a number and a direction from the meridian, and the townships within each range were numbered north and south from the base line. Each township, being 6 miles square, contained 36 square miles numbered as shown in Map 8-2. In the Ordinance of 1785, a square mile was called a *lot*, but in later acts the term *section* was used.

The ordinance reflected the prevalent conservative view that public land should be a major source of revenue. Provisions relating to minimum size of tracts, prices, and terms were severe. Alternate townships were to be sold as a whole; the other half of the townships were to be sold by sections. All sales at public auction were to be for a minimum price of $1 per acre in cash. Thus, the smallest possible cash outlay was the $640 necessary to buy a section—an expenditure beyond the means of most pioneers. Moreover, a square mile of land was more than the small farmers wanted; they could barely clear and cultivate 10 acres in their first year, and a quarter-section was the most a settler could handle without the aid of grown children. Only individuals of means and land companies formed by large investors could purchase land under the first law.

Two years later, the Congress addressed the problem of establishing the *political* principles under which the settlement of the West was to take place. The Ordinance of 1787 provided that the Northwest Territory should be organized as a district to be run by a governor and judges appointed by the

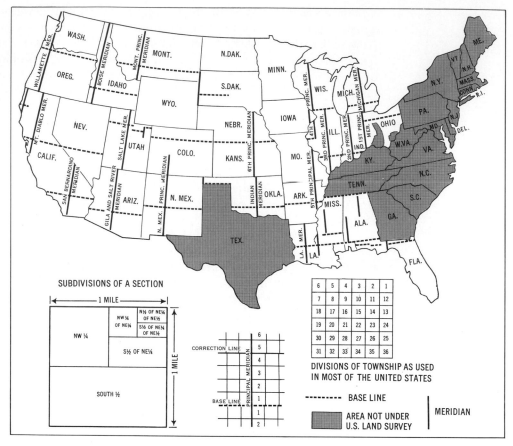

SUBDIVISIONS OF A SECTION

DIVISIONS OF TOWNSHIP AS USED IN MOST OF THE UNITED STATES

- - - - - - -   BASE LINE

AREA NOT UNDER U.S. LAND SURVEY

MERIDIAN

MAP 8-2   Land Survey: Principal meridians and base lines made possible precise apportioning of newly opened territories into sections, and easily described subdivisions of sections, thus simplifying later property transfers.

Congress. As soon as it contained 5,000 male inhabitants of voting age, a territorial legislature was to be elected and a nonvoting delegate was to be sent to the Congress. At least three and not more than five states were to be created from this territory; when any one of the established divisions of the territory contained a population of 60,000 inhabitants, it was to be admitted to the Union as a state on a basis of complete equality with the older states. Contained in the ordinance were certain guarantees of civil and religious liberties, together with a prohibition of slavery in the territory. *The main principle, however, was the eventual equality of status for the new areas.* The age-old source of trouble between colony and ruling country was thus removed by a simple, although unprecedented, device—making the colonies extensions of the empire that would be allowed to become socially and politically equal.

The Land Acts, 1796–1862

For a decade after the passage of the Land Ordinance of 1785, pioneering in the area north of the Ohio River was restricted by Indian trouble as well as by the high price of government land. The British, who persisted in maintaining posts on American territory in the Northwest, for years incited the Indians to make war on American settlers. By a treaty of 1794, the British agreed to evacuate the posts in the Northwest, and in August of that year "Mad Anthony" Wayne and his forces defeated the Indians at the Battle of Fallen Timbers. The time was then ripe for the establishment of new land policies by the Congress of the United States.

The Land Act of 1796 represented another victory for the conservatives. A system of rectangular surveys substantially the same as the one established by the Ordinance of 1785 was made permanent. The minimum purchase allowed by the Act of 1796 was still 640 acres, but the minimum price per acre was raised to $2—the only concession to the cheap-land advocates being a credit provision that permitted half of the purchase price to be deferred for a year. Only a small amount of land was sold under this act before Congress changed the minimum acreage to 320 in 1800 and permitted the buyer, after a cash payment of one-half the value, to pay one-fourth the value in two years and the final fourth in four years. A law of 1804 further lowered the minimum purchase to 160 acres. In 1820, the minimum purchase was reduced to 80 acres and the price per acre to $1.25, but the credit provisions, which had resulted in losses to the government, were repealed. By 1820, the liberal forces had clearly won the battle. Twelve years later, the minimum purchase was reduced to 40 acres, so in 1832 a pioneer could purchase a piece of farmland for $50. By this time, pressures for *free* land, which had been exerted from the first, were beginning to produce legislative results.

The settler who was brave enough to risk his life and the lives of his family in a pioneering venture was not usually deterred from action by legal niceties. From the beginning, pioneers tended to settle past the areas that had been surveyed and announced for sale. As the decades passed and the West became "crowded," this tendency to pick a tract in an unopened area increased. Unauthorized settlement, or "squatting," resulted from the attempts of the pioneers to find better soils and the hope that they could settle on choice land and make it a going proposition before they were billed for it.

Squatting was illegal, of course, but it was an offense that was hard to police. Moreover, there were those who argued that by occupying and improving the land, a squatter gained the rights to it—"cabin rights" or "corn rights" or "tommyhawk rights," as they were variously called on the frontier. At first, federal troops tried to drive squatters from unsurveyed land, but successes were only temporary. Gradually, the government came to view this pioneer lawbreaking less and less seriously. Against those who would purchase the squatter's land when it became available for public sale, informal but effective measures were taken by the squatters themselves, who formed protective associations as soon as they settled in a particular locality. When the public auction of land in that locality was held, the members of the protective association let it be known that there was to be no competitive bidding for land preempted by them. The appearance of well-armed frontiersmen at the auction ordinarily convinced city slickers and big land buyers that it would be unwise to bid. Even in places where there was no organized action, squatters who found their farms bought out from under them could often charge handsomely for the "improvements" they had made, and frontier courts were inclined to uphold their "rights."

As early as 1820, Congress began to give relief to squatters, and scarcely a year went by after 1830 in which preemption rights were not granted to settlers in certain areas. In 1841, a general Preemption Act, called the "Log Cabin Bill" by its proponents, was passed. This law granted to anyone settling on land that was surveyed, but not yet available for sale, the right to purchase 160 acres at the minimum price when the auction was held. No one could outbid the settler and secure the land, provided the squatter could raise the $200 necessary to buy a quarter section. Technically, squatting on *unsurveyed* land was still illegal; because of this and because there was still no outright grant of land, the westerner (and anyone else who could make money by buying land and waiting for it rise in value) was not satisfied. Nevertheless, the land policy of the country was about as liberal as could be consistent with the demand that the public domain be a continuing source of revenue.

Pressure remained on Congress to reduce the price of "islands" of less desirable land that had been passed over in the first surges to the West. In 1854, the Graduation Act provided for the graduated reduction of the minimum purchase price of such tracts, to a point where if the land remained unsold for as long as 30 years, it could be purchased for as little as 12½ cents an acre. Settlers quickly purchased these pieces of land, attesting to the fact that people were willing to gamble a little on the probable appreciation of even the most unpromising real estate.

In the 1850s, as agitation for free land continued, it became apparent that the passage of a homestead law was inevitable. Southerners, who had at one time favored free grants to actual settlers, became violently opposed to this as time went on. The 160-acre farm usually proposed by homestead supporters was not large enough to make the working of slaves economical, and it seemed obvious to southern congressmen that homesteading would fill the West with antislavery people. On the other hand, many northern congressmen, who would normally have had leanings toward a conservative policy, joined forces with the westerners because they also knew that free land meant free states.

In 1860, a homestead act was passed, but President Buchanan, fearing that it would precipitate secession, vetoed it. Two years later, with southerners out of Congress, the Homestead Act of 1862 became law. Henceforth, any head of a family or anyone over 21 could have 160 acres of public land on the payment of small fees. The only stipulation was that the home-

In the nineteenth century, wagon trains like these brought a steady stream of migrants to western America and its expansive lands.

steader should either live on the land or cultivate it for five years. An important provision was that settlers who decided not to meet the five-year requirement might obtain full title to the land simply by paying the minimum price of $1.25 an acre.

Although much land was to pass into private hands under the Homestead Act of 1862, it was not the boon that it was expected to be. Most of the firstclass land had been claimed by this time. Furthermore, it was so easy to circumvent the provisions of the law that land-grabbers used it, along with the acts that still provided for outright purchase, to build up great land holdings. By 1862, the frontier had reached the edge of the dry country, where a 160-acre farm was too small to provide a living for a settler and his family.

THE MIGRATIONS TO THE WEST

In discussing the colonial period, we noted that pioneers were moving across the Appalachian Mountains by the middle of the eighteenth century. By 1790, perhaps a quarter of a million people lived within the mountain valleys or to the west, and the trickle of westward movement had become a small stream. There were two eighteenth-century routes to the West. The more important one passed through the Cumberland Gap and then into either Kentucky or Tennessee; the other ran across southern Pennsylvania to Pittsburgh and on down the Ohio River. Even as the movement to the West was gaining momentum, pioneers were still settling in Pennsylvania and New York and to the north in Vermont, New Hampshire, and Maine.

An overview of population growth and the distributional impact of western migration and other demographic effects are shown in Table 8-1 and Figure 8-1. On the eve of the second war with Great Britain, just over 1 million people lived west of the Appalachians. From this 15 percent proportion, the western population grew to over 40 percent of the total by 1860. On the eve of the Civil War the center of the population was near Chillicothe, Ohio. The western population grew from 1 to 13 million as the total grew from 7.2 to 31.4 million. In short, the rate of population growth was twice as high west of the Appalachian Mountains as in the East, 5.1 percent annually compared to 2.2 percent.

As the population expanded and pushed westward, the Nation's frontier was pressed outward. The frontier, as technically defined in the census reports, was any area in which there were more than two and less than six people per square mile. In Map 8-3, the frontier lines for 1800, 1820, 1840, and 1860 have been drawn from census data. The line for 1800 indicates

TABLE 8-1   Population of Various Sections of the Trans-Appalachian West, 1810–60 (in thousands)

Region	1810	1820	1830	1840	1850	1860
Ohio	230.8	581.3	937.9	1,519.5	1,980.3	2,339.5
Indiana	24.5	147.2	343.0	685.9	988.4	1,350.4
Illinois	12.3	55.2	157.4	476.2	851.5	1,712.0
Michigan	4.8	8.8	31.6	212.3	397.7	749.1
Wisconsin				30.9	305.4	775.9
Iowa				43.1	192.2	674.9
Missouri	20.8	66.6	140.5	383.7	682.0	1,182.0
Kentucky	406.5	564.1	687.9	779.8	982.4	1,155.7
Tennessee	261.7	422.8	681.9	829.2	1,002.7	1,109.8
Arkansas		14.3	30.4	97.6	209.9	435.5
Mississippi	40.4	75.4	136.6	375.7	606.5	791.3
Louisiana	76.6	152.9	215.7	352.4	517.8	708.0
Trans-Appalachian West	1,078.3	2,088.5	3,363.0	5,786.2	8,716.8	12,984.1
United States	7,239.9	9,633.8	12,866.0	17,069.5	23,191.9	31,443.3
West as percent of United States	14.9%	21.7%	26.1%	33.9%	37.6%	41.4%

Source: U.S. House of Congress, House Executive Documents 133, Serial Set 2030, pp. 150–52.

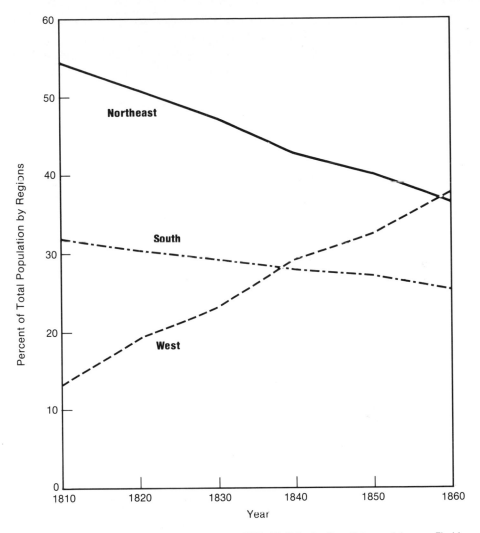

FIGURE 8-1   Population Distribution by Regions: 1810–60. Note: South—Alabama, Arkansas, Florida, Georgia, Louisiana, Mississippi, North Carolina, South Carolina, Texas and Virginia; West—Illinois, Indiana, Iowa, Kansas, Kentucky, Michigan, Minnesota, Missouri, Nebraska, Ohio, Tennessee, Wisconsin, California, Nevada and Oregon; Northeast—Connecticut, Delaware, Maine, Maryland, Massachusetts, New Hampshire, New Jersey, New York, Pennsylvania, Rhode Island, and Vermont.

Source: U.S. Census Bureau, *A Compendium of the Ninth Census, June 1, 1870,* by Francis A. Walker, Superintendent of Census (Washington, D.C.: 1872), pp 8–9. Reprinted from Douglass C. North, *The Economic Growth of the United States, 1790–1860* (Englewood Cliffs: Prentice-Hall, 1960), p. 121.

a wedge driven into the West, with its point in western Kentucky. Sixty years later, the line ran in a southerly direction from a point in the middle of Minnesota, with a noticeable bulge into the Nebraska and Kansas territories and a definite drift into Texas.

MAP 8-3   Moving Frontier: Census data from 1800 onward chronicled the constant westward flow of population. The "frontier," its profile determined by natural attractions and a few man-made and physiographic obstacles, was a magnet for the venturesome.

THE NORTHWESTERN MIGRATION AND HOGS, CORN, AND WHEAT

As shown in Table 8-1 and in Map 8-3, during the early 1800s the movement across the top of the country gained momentum and an initial lead over migration from the southern states. During the first quarter century, people from the New England and Middle Atlantic states were pouring into the northern counties of Ohio and Indiana and later into southern Michigan. By 1850, lower Michigan was fairly well settled, and the best lands in northern Illinois and southern Wisconsin had been claimed. On the eve of the Civil War, pioneers were pushing the northwestern tip of the frontier into central Minnesota, most of Iowa was behind the frontier line, and the hand-

The morning of the opening of the Oklahoma land rush.

some country of eastern Kansas was being settled. Only in Texas did the frontier line of 1860 bulge farther to the west than it did in Kansas. By this time, California had been a state for a decade, and Oregon had been admitted the year before, but the vast area between the western frontier and the coast was not to be completely settled for another half-century.

Southerners, then, moving across the Ohio River, were the chief influence in the lower part of the old Northwest. New Englanders, when the Erie Canal made transportation easy, were dominant in the Great Lakes region, but they were joined by another stream that originated in the Middle Atlantic states. For the most part, families moved singly, although sometimes as many as 50–100 would move together. As the frontier pushed westward, the pioneers on the cutting edge were frequently the same people who had broken virgin soil a short way back only a few years ago. Or they were the grown children of men and women who had once participated in the conquest of the wilderness.

Land speculation—"holding for a rise"—became a lively offshoot of the westward population surge. Here, a Kansas land office provides a center for speculative activity.

Throughout this early period of westward expansion, there was an ever-increasing influx of land-hungry people from abroad. From 1789 to the close of the War of 1812, not more than 250,000 people immigrated from Europe. With the final defeat of Napoleon and the coming of peace abroad, immigration resumed. From 500,000 people in the 1830s, the flow increased to 1.5 million in the 1840s and to 2.5 million in the 1850s. For the most part, the newcomers were from northern Europe; Germans and Irish predominated, but there were many immigrants from England, Scotland, Switzerland, and the Scandinavian countries. Of these peoples, the Germans

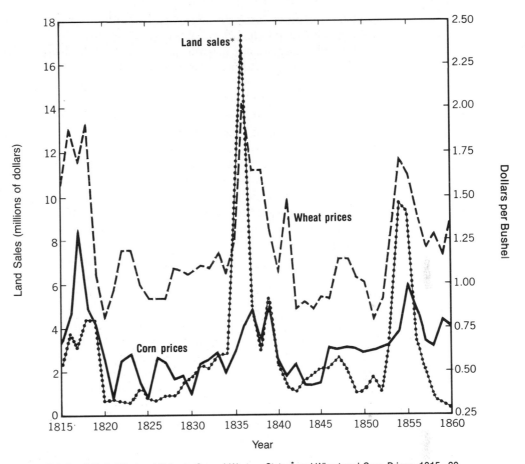

FIGURE 8-2   U.S. Public Land Sales in Several Western States* and Wheat and Corn Prices, 1815–60.

Source: North, *The Economic Growth of the United States, 1790–1860*, p. 137.

*Ohio, Illinois, Indiana, Michigan, Iowa, Wisconsin, and Missouri.

tended more than any others to go directly to the lands of the West. They proved to be a fairly well-educated and extremely able population and had a pronounced effect on the economic life of the states of the northwest and of Iowa and Missouri. Some immigrants from the other groups entered into the agricultural migration, but most of these were absorbed into eastern city populations.

Although the absolute numbers of western migrants from the eastern states and from abroad continued to swell, in terms of percentage, the years 1810 through the 1830s were the sharpest growing decades for the West. In large measure these surges are explained by the exceptional economic opportunities in the West. Hogs, corn, and wheat became the great northwestern staples, and as shown in Figure 8-2, corn and wheat prices were unusually high in these decades. People came in response to the profits to be made in the production of these great staples.

The resulting surges in production in the Northwest—the Midwest as we know it today—did not immediately dislocate agriculture in the older states. Over the decades, however, the leading producers of hogs, corn, and wheat became western states.

Early in the 1800s, western hog production was greatly limited by high transportation costs; hogs were driven overland from Ohio to the urban centers of the East or were sent south by boat for sale to the plantations. Cattle, too, were driven in great herds to the East, where they were sold for immediate slaughter or for further fattening. But it was not long before pioneer farmers could market their hogs fairly close to home. Slaughtering and meat-packing centers arose in the early West, and by the 1830s Cincinnati was the most important pork-processing city in the country.

Commercial hog raising required corn growing. For a while, hogs were allowed into the forest to forage on the mast (acorns and nuts that fell from the trees). But feeding is necessary to produce a good grade of pork, and corn is an ideal feed crop. Corn can be grown almost anywhere, provided there is adequate rainfall. It had been cultivated in all the original colonies and throughout the South. As late as 1840, Kentucky, Tennessee, and Virginia were first in corn production. But within 20 years, it was apparent that the states to the northwest would be the corn leaders.[2] On the eve of the Civil War, Illinois, Ohio, Missouri, and Indiana led in corn production, and it appeared that Iowa, Kansas, and Nebraska would one day rank ahead of Kentucky and Tennessee, then in fifth and sixth place, respectively.

The attraction of new lands for wheat was tremendous. Wheat also could not come into its own, however, until facilities were available for transporting it in quantity to the urban centers of the East, and as late as 1850, Pennsylvania and New York ranked first and third, respectively, in its production. Ohio, which had become a commercial producer in the 1830s, was second. During the next decade, the shift of wheat production to the West was remarkable. By 1860, Illinois, Indiana, and Wisconsin were the leading producers, and the five states carved from the Northwest Territory produced roughly half the nation's output of the bread grain. The major wheat-growing areas were still not finally established, however; further shifts to the West in the production of this important crop were yet to come.

Ultimately the northern migration forced changes on the agriculture of the northeastern states. For a quarter of a century after the ratification of the Constitution, agriculture in New England, except in a few localities, was

---

[2]For the advantages of corn growing to the western pioneer, see Paul W. Gates, *The Farmer's Age: Agriculture, 1815–1860* (New York: Holt, Rinehart & Winston, 1960), p. 169. Only a peck of seed corn, yielding as much as 50 bushels, planted an acre and could be transported far more easily than two bushels of wheat seed, weighing 120 pounds, that might bring in only 15 to 18 bushels to the acre.

exceptionally primitive; the individual farm unit produced practically everything needed for the household. With the growing industrialization of New England after 1810, production for urban markets became possible, and the result was a great improvement in the farmer's lot. Between 1810 and 1840, farmers in the Middle Atlantic states continued to grow the products for which their localities had traditionally been suited, and Pennsylvania and New York remained major wheat producers until mid-century. But the arrival of the steamboat in the West in 1811, the opening of the Erie Canal in the 1820s, and the extension of the railroads beyond the Alleghenies in the 1840s meant that products of the rich western lands would flow in ever-increasing amounts to the East. Western competition caused the northeastern farmer to reduce grain cultivation, and only dairy cattle remained important in animal production. Specialization in truck gardens and dairy products for city people and hay for city horses came to characterize the agriculture of this region, and those who could not adapt to the changing demand moved to the city or went west.

THE SOUTHWESTERN MIGRATION AND COTTON

As discussed in Chapter 7, the lower South suffered serious setbacks during the early years of independence. Even the market for tobacco stagnated, especially after the Embargo Act of 1807 and the War of 1812 allowed tobacco from other regions to enter the world market.

The hope of the South was in cotton. Obtaining their supplies of raw cotton from the Orient, the English increasingly turned to the manufacture of cotton cloth instead of wool in the late seventeenth century. The inventions that came 100 years or so later—the steam engine, the spinning jenny, the water frame, the spinning mule, and the power loom—all gave rise to an enormous demand for cotton fiber. The phase of the industrial Revolution that made it possible to apply power to textile manufacturing occurred at just the right time to stimulate and encourage the planting of cotton wherever it could be grown profitably. In the southern United States, the conditions for a profitable agriculture based on cotton were nearly ideal. Only some way of separating the green seed from the short-staple "upland cotton" had to be devised. One of the contributions of Yankee genius Eli Whitney was the invention of a gin that enabled a good worker to clean 50 pounds of cotton a day instead of only 1 pound by hand. With the application of power to the gin, the amount of fiber that could be produced appeared almost limitless.

On the humid coasts of Georgia and South Carolina, planters who had grown indigo turned to cotton. Even some rice fields were recultivated to produce the new staple. The culture moved up to North Carolina and Virginia and over the mountains to the beautiful rolling country of middle

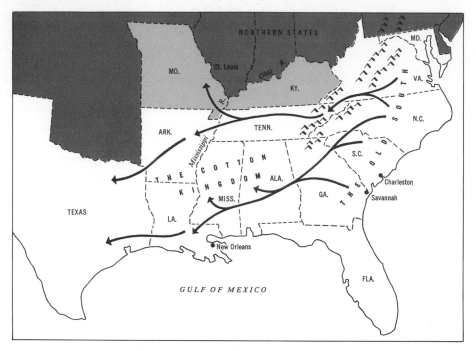

MAP 8-4   Shifts in Cotton Cultivation: The tremendous growth of the world demand for cotton propelled the westward movement of cotton civilization after the War of 1812 and up to the onset of the Civil War.

Tennessee. In the early 1800s, the piedmont of Georgia and South Carolina became the important cotton center, and these states were vying for first place by 1820, with South Carolina slightly in the lead.

Beginning with the end of the War of 1812, the really important shift in cotton production was to the West (see Map 8-4). Almost unerringly, the settlers first planted the loamy, fertile soils that extended in an arc from Georgia through Alabama in to northeastern Mississippi. A second major cotton-growing area lay in the rich bottom land of the lower Mississippi River and its tributaries. In this extremely fertile soil, the cotton even tended to grow a longer fiber. The culture spread into western Tennessee and eastern Arkansas. A jump into Texas then foretold the trend of cotton production.

By 1840, the early cotton-producing states had been left behind. In 1860, Alabama, Mississippi, and Louisiana were far in the lead, with Mississippi, then in the lead position, producing more cotton than Georgia and South Carolina combined. This shift in the realm of King Cotton was to have the most far-reaching consequences on the economy of the South.

Just before the Civil War, there could be no doubt that cotton was indeed king. As Douglass North has remarked,[3] it is difficult to exaggerate the role of cotton in American economic growth between 1800 and 1850. The great staple accounted for more than half the dollar value of U.S. exports—a value nearly ten times as great in U.S. foreign trade as its nearest competitor, the wheat and wheat flour of the North. At home, cotton planters furnished the raw materials for textile manufacturers in the North, who by 1860 were selling half again as much cotton cloth as wool cloth. The amount of the national income generated by cotton manufactures was greater at this time than that generated by the iron industry. It was not surprising that aristocratic southerners could scarcely envisage a North, or even a world, without their chief product.

There was both a slight push and a major pull to the new lands of the South. The push had begun in colonial times, as tidewater lands began to lose the natural fertility the staples grown there required. The small farmer, impelled by hardship, had moved into the piedmont. The shift had been especially pronounced in Virginia and North Carolina, from which struggling families tended to sift through the Cumberland Gap into Tennessee and Kentucky. The frontiersman—the professional pioneer—was then pulled into the rich new cotton country, mostly from Georgia and South Carolina, but partly from Tennessee and even from Kentucky. Following closely, came the yeoman farmer; almost simultaneously—and this is what clearly distinguishes the southern migration—came the planter, the man of substance, with his huge household establishment and his slaves. It was, of course, the expected return on the cotton that brought the great, irregular surges of movement into the southwest, and as shown in Figure 8-3, there is a close correlation between the price of cotton on the one hand and the volume of public land sales in Alabama, Florida, Louisiana, Mississippi, and Arkansas on the other.[4] The planter had sufficient means to acquire large acreages, and the small householder could compete in the best agricultural areas only with difficulty. The rich were at an obvious advantage in the public land auctions; the pioneer and the farmer with a slave or two were continually tempted to sell out to the plantation owner, because the price the latter could offer netted a profit for "improving" the land.

A farmer class of some numerical importance nevertheless developed in the South, even though many farmers sold out to planters and moved on across the Mississippi River, sometimes going north as well as west. Some of the least able retreated to the mountains or drifted into the barren pine belts that constitute much of the land area in the deep South. But it was the plantation owner, so unimportant numerically and so very important

---

[3]See Douglass C. North, *The Economic Growth of the United States 1790–1860* (Englewood Cliffs: Prentice-Hall, 1961).

[4]North, pp. 124, 129.

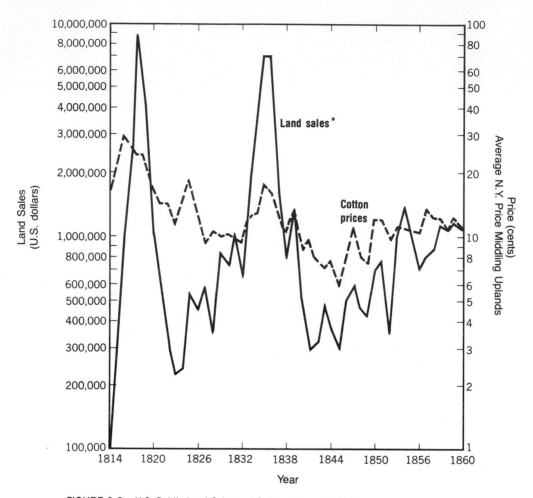

FIGURE 8-3   U.S. Public Land Sales and Cotton Prices, 1814–60.

Source: North, *The Economic Growth of the United States, 1790–1860* p. 124.
*Alabama, Florida, Louisiana, Mississippi, Arkansas.

as the aristocratic determiner of southern economic development, who was to take charge of the South's destiny.

THE FAR WESTERN MIGRATION

Although of only minor importance when compared with the southern and northwestern migrations, we should not forget one of the most widely discussed and emotionally charged of all the migrations, namely the California Gold Rush. On January 24, 1848, just nine days before the war with Mexico

THE FAR WESTERN MIGRATION

ended, James W. Marshall discovered gold while he was building a sawmill for John Sutter on the South Fork of the American River (presently called Coloma).

Sutter and Marshall attempted to keep the discovery a secret while trying to secure stronger property rights on the area. However, a young boy told of the discovery to a man bringing supplies to the mill, and coincidentally the boy's mother gave the driver a small nugget as a present. When the man later used the nugget to buy a drink back at "Fort Sutter" the word was out.

The rush had not yet begun, however, not even after the story first appeared in a San Francisco newspaper on March 15. As John Umbeck, one of the leading authorities on the Gold Rush, reports:

> Short notices continued to appear in both San Francisco newspapers, but few people took it seriously. As late as May 6, 1848, the editor of the *California Star* wrote:
>
>> After a very pleasant, but brief sojourn in the Great Valley of the Sacramento, we have returned and resumed our labors, settled down in our chair again, physically refreshed and invigorated, and in mind abounding with reminiscences of all that we have seen and done while absent. Great country—fine climate. Visit this Great Valley, we would advise all who have not yet done so. See luxuriant clover, fragrant flowers, gold and silver.
>
> But two weeks later people were taking notice, as indicated by the following which appeared in the *California Star* on May 20, 1848.
>
>> El Dorado Anew—A terrible visitant we have had of late—a FEVER which has well nigh depopulated a town—a town hard pressing upon a thousand souls.
>
> The rush for gold had begun in full force by mid-May.

While Marshall is generally accredited with the discovery of gold, the honor of starting the "rush," if it belongs to any one person, must go to Samuel Brannan. It was Brannan who, on about the 12th of May, went down the streets of San Francisco waving a bottle of gold dust and yelling, "Gold! Gold! Gold from the American River." Why would a miner announce publicly the existence of gold on land to which he has no exclusive rights? The answer, in this particular case, appears to be that Brannan, as the leader of the Mormons, had been collecting from his brothers a tithe of 30% on all the gold they discovered. This was done on the pretext of building a shrine for their God. The money, instead of going directly to God, went to stock a small store and trading post co-owned by Brannan at Sutter's Fort. A large "rush" of people to Sutter's Fort could have benefited his business.[5]

If the great San Francisco announcement was not for religious purposes, neither was the rush that ensued. As gold fever swept the land, people

---

[5] See John Umbeck, "The California Gold Rush: A Study of Emerging Property Rights," *Explorations in Economic History* 14 (1977): 209–10.

poured across the country. In the first several months of 1849, almost 20,000 left the east coast by boat destined for California, and nearly 40,000 arrived in San Francisco throughout 1849.[6] From a total population of about 107,000 near the end of 1849, California grew to over 260,000 within three years.

Perhaps the most fascinating aspect of the California Gold Rush was the initial absence of property rights in land or a government capable of enforcing law and order.[7] Despite this initial absence, violence in the gold fields was surprisingly low. As Umbeck summarizes:

> During 1848, . . . nearly 10,000 people rushed to mine gold on property to which no one had exclusive rights. Futhermore, although nearly every miner carried a gun, little violence was reported. In July, when Governor Mason visited the mines, he reported that the miners were respecting Sutter's property rights and that "crime of any kind was very infrequent, and that no thefts or robberies had been committed in the gold district . . . and it was a matter of surprise, that so peaceful and quiet a state of things should continue to exist."
>
> In the first 6 months after the initial discovery by Marshall, the size of the known gold fields increased from a small area around Sutter's mill to an area covering over 10,000 square miles. For the early miners, it was apparently less costly to move to a new discovery than to use violence to acquire someone else's mining rights. As long as gold land remained relatively abundant, small groups of miners found the sharing arrangement to be the most economical.[8]

Only after new waves of miners entered the fields did gold land become troublingly scarce, thereby urging exclusive property rights or claims. Several first-hand accounts indicate the nature of those rights:

> When the mines in and around Nevada City were first opened they were solely in the ravines . . . and there was no law regulating the size of a miner's claim, and generally a party that first went into a ravine had the exclusive right there too, . . . As population increased that rule did not long maintain. The miners saw that something must be done, and therefore a meeting was called and a rule was established that each miner could hold thirty feet square as a mining claim.
>
> All these bars on the Middle Fork of the American River, from Oregon Bar upwards, after the lowest estimate, employed in the summer of 1850 not less than 1,500 men; originally working on shares, and the assessment on the share paid out daily, so that those who had been drunk or absent did not get any part of it; but this after a while caused dissatisfaction and was the reason of breaking up the co-operative work and commencing work on claims. A claim was a spot of ground fifteen feet wide on the river front.
>
> In a comparatively short time we had a large community on that creek, which led to rows and altercations about boundaries, that eventuated in an

---

[6] Umbeck, p. 214.

[7] Despite stiff penalities for desertion, U.S. soldiers in California who typically earned $7.00 a month (plus room and board) numbered almost 1,059 in 1847, but only 660 in 1848. See Umbeck, p. 205.

[8] Umbeck, p. 214.

agreement, entered into by unanimous agreement, that each person should have 10 square feet.

Wood's Creek was filled up with miners, and I here for the first time after the discovery of gold, learned what a miner's claim was. In 1848, the miners had no division of the ground into claims—they worked where it was richest, and many times four or five could be seen at work in a circle of six feet in diameter; but . . . here they were now measuring the ground off with tape measures so as to prevent disputes arising from the division.[9]

It was at the "miners' meetings" that contract specifications were determined. Each "field" held their own meetings and afterwards each miner marked his claim boundary with wooden stakes, and frequently a notice such as this:

All and everybody, this is my claim, fifty feet on the gulch, cordin to Clear Creek District Law, backed up by shotgun amendments.

any person found trespassing on this claim will be persucuted to the full extent of the law. This is no monkey tale butt I will assert by rites at the pint of the sicks shirter if legally necessary so taik head and good warnin.[10]

In this fashion, property rights first emerged in the gold fields of California, and with them an outpouring of millions of dollars in gold.

The great California Gold Rush had effects far beyond the bossless mass employment and wealth creation it generated. It was a tidal wave of hope to people who no longer were forced to know their place and be resigned to it. And the timing! Ireland's potato famine, China's Taiping Rebellion, political uprisings in France and Germany—all added great numbers to young Americans, many discharged from service at the end of the U.S.-Mexican War, who sought their fortunes in the gold fields. Not everyone struck it rich like Leland Stanford, formerly a failed lawyer, or Lucius Fairchild, a store clerk from Wisconsin who returned home rich and became Wisconsin's governor. But the Gold Rush did guarantee dreams and adventure to match the towering Sierras.

SELECTED REFERENCES AND SUGGESTED READINGS

Berry, Thomas. *Western Prices Before 1861*. Cambridge: Harvard Univ. Press, 1943.

Bidwell, Percy, and John Falconer. *History of Agriculture in the Northern United States 1620–1860*. Washington, D.C.: The Carnegie Institute, 1925.

Billington, Ray A. "The Origin of the Land Speculator as a Frontier Type." *Agricultural History* 9 (Oct. 1945).

———. *Westward Expansion: A History of the American Frontier*. New York: Macmillan, 1949.

Bogue, Allan C. "Farming in the Prairie Peninsula 1830–1890." *Journal of Economic History* 23 (March 1963).

———. *From Prairie to Cornbelt: Farming on the Illinois and Iowa Prairies in the Nineteenth Century*. Chicago: Univ. of Chicago Press, 1963.

---

[9]As quoted in Umbeck, p. 215.
[10]As quoted in Umbeck, p. 216.

Bogue, Allan C., and Margaret Bogue. "Profits and the Frontier Land Speculation." *Journal of Economic History* 37 (March 1957).

Carstensen, Vernon. "Introduction" to *The Public Lands: Studies in the History of the Public Domain.* Madison: Univ. of Wisconsin Press, 1963.

Carstensen, Vernon, ed. *The Public Lands: Studies in the History of the Public Domain* Madison: Univ. of Wisconsin Press, 1963.

Cole, Arthur H. "Cyclical and Sectional Variations in the Sale of the Public Lands, 1816–1860." *Review of Economics and Statistics* 9 (1927). Reprinted in Carstensen, *The Public Lands.*

Danhof, Clarence. *Change in Agriculture: The Northern United States, 1820–70.* Cambridge: Harvard Univ. Press, 1969.

———. "Farm Making Costs and the Safety Valve, 1855–60." In *The Public Lands,* ed. Vernon Carstensen. Madison: Univ. of Wisconsin Press, 1963.

Freund, Rudolf. "Military Bounty Lands and the Origin of the Public Domain." *Agricultural History* 20 (1946). Reprinted in Carstensen, *The Public Lands.*

Gates, Paul W. "Charts of Public Land Sales and Entries." *Journal of Economic History* 24 (March, 1964).

———. *History of Public Land Law Development.* Washington, D.C.: Public Land Law Review Commission, 1968.

———. "The Role of the Land Speculator in Western Development." *Pennsylvania Magazine of History and Biography* 66 (1942). Reprinted in Carstensen, *The Public Lands.*

Hughes, Jonathon R. T. "The Great Land Ordinances: Colonial America's Thumb Print on History." In *Essays on the Economic Significance of the Old Northwest,* ed. David C. Klingamen and Richard K. Vedder. Athens, OH: Ohio Univ. Press, 1987, pp. 1–18.

Lebergott, Stanley. "'O Pioneers': Land Speculation and the Growth of the Midwest." In *Essays on the Economy of the Old Northwest,* ed. David C. Klingamen and Richard K. Vedder. Athens, OH: Ohio Univ. Press, 1987, pp. 37–58.

Merk, Frederick. *History of the Westward Movement.* New York: Knopf, 1978.

North, Douglass C. *The Economic Growth of the United States 1790–1860.* Englewood Cliffs, N.J.: Prentice-Hall, 1961.

———, and Andrew R. Rutten. "The Northwest Ordinance in Historical Perspective." In *Essays on the Economy of the Old Northwest,* ed. David C. Klingamen and Richard K. Vedder. Athens, OH: Ohio Univ. Press, 1987, pp. 19–36.

Parker, William. "Agriculture." In *American Economic Growth: An Economist's History of the United States,* ed. Lance E. Davis et al. New York: Harper & Row, 1972. Chapter 11.

Parker, William, and Judith Klein. "Productivity Growth in Grain Production in the United States." In *Output, Employment and Productivity in the United States after 1800,* vol. 30, ed. Dorothy Brady. National Bureau of Economic Research, Studies in Income and Wealth. New York: Columbia Univ. Press, 1966.

Primack, Martin. "Land Clearing Under 19th Century Techniques." *Journal of Economic History* 22 (Dec. 1962).

Riegel, Robert E., and Robert G. Athearn. *America Moves West.* New York: Holt, 1964.

Rohrbough, Malcolm. *The Land Office Business: The Settlement and Administration of American Public Lands, 1789–1837.* New York: Oxford Univ. Press, 1968.

Rothenberg, Winifred B. "The Market and Massachusetts Farmers, 1750–1855." *Journal of Economic History* 41 (1981): 283–314.

Steckel, Richard. "The Economic Foundations of East-West Migration During the 19th Century." *Explorations in Economic History* 20 (1983): 14–36.

Treat, Payson J. "Origin of the National Land System Under the Confederation." *American Historical Association Report, 1905.* Reprinted in Carstensen, *The Public Lands.*

Turner, Frederick Jackson. *The Frontier in American History.* New York: Holt, Rhinehart, Winston, 1921.

Umbeck, John. "The California Gold Rush: A Study of Emerging Property Rights." *Explorations in Economic History* 14 (1977): 192–226.

Wyman, Walker D., and Clifton B. Kroeber, eds. *The Frontier in Perspective.* Madison: Univ. of Wisconsin Press, 1957.

C H A P T E R   9

Transportation and
Market Growth

THE TRANSPORTATION REVOLUTION, 1811–1860

Once the western migrations were unleashed, the demand for improved transportation systems grew dramatically. Investments in watercraft, especially the steamboat, in canals, and in railroads were the most far-reaching and effective transportation developments of the antebellum era. There can be little doubt that the host of improvements in transportation and the precipitous decline in freight rates in the early and middle part of the nineteenth century, as shown in Figure 9-1, were truly revolutionary in impact as well as in form. Not only did they directly propel the process of westward expansion and the relocation of agriculture and mining discussed in Chapter 8, but they also greatly altered the regional comparative advantages in production. Indeed, they set the stage for the New England region to concentrate increasingly in manufacturing and to further the advance and application of new technologies and organizational forms of production in a factory setting. In turn, these changes set the stage for heightening urban problems and labor unrest. Moreover, the falling costs of transport—and communication—boosted market efficiency and responsiveness and forged a national market for goods and services. Whereas the pattern of general price declines in the western markets of Cincinnati and St. Louis had followed those in New York and Philadelphia by 12 months near the turn of the century, the lag was reduced to only 3 or 4 months by the 1830s. By the 1850s, this lag had fallen even further to a mere week or so. Lastly, the transportation linkage by water and rails between the East and West would prove significant in binding these two regions—politically as well as economically—as interregional tensions mounted in the years preceding the Civil War. The term *transportation revolution* consequently implies far more than a mere series of new technological forms rapidly introduced.

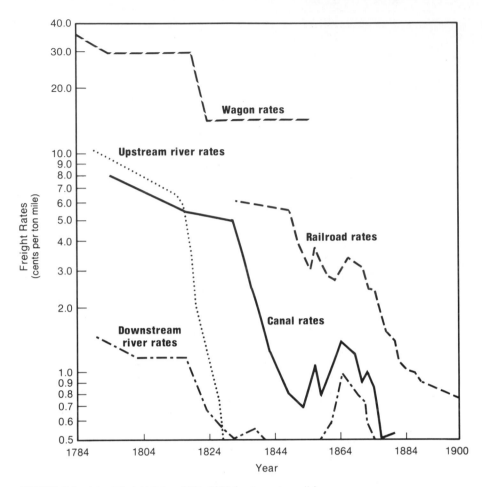

FIGURE 9-1   Inland Freight Rates, 1874–1900 (cents per ton mile)

Sources: Douglass C. North, *Growth and Welfare in the American Past* (Englewood Cliffs, Prentice-Hall, 1973), p. 108; and Douglass C. North, "The Role of Transportation in the Economic Development of North America," a paper presented to the International Congress of the Historical Sciences, Vienna, August 1965, and published in *Les Grandes Voies Maritimes dans le Monde XVᵉ–XIXᵉ Siecles*, © 1965 by Ecole des Hautes Etudes en Sciences Sociales, Paris.

From the advantage of hindsight we can recognize that the economic growth of the United States in the nineteenth century was strategically influenced by the spread of a market economy. But Adam Smith and early nineteenth-century contemporaries knew that levels of productivity were vitally dependent on the size of the market, especially in manufacturing. Of course, market size was limited by the costs of moving goods and negotiating exchanges. In this early era, transportation costs were the most important component of these costs. For these many reasons, special concentration on transportation is warranted, and indeed, vital to our understanding of long-term economic growth and the location of people and economic activity.

THE ROUTES OF WESTERN COMMERCE

During the antebellum period, three natural gateways linked the western territories and states with the rest of the nation and other countries. The first ran eastward, connecting the Great Lakes to New York. The main arteries to this Northern Gateway were down the St. Lawrence River or along the Hudson or Mohawk River valleys. Major investments on this route included the opening of the Erie Canal in 1825 and the completion of the New York Central and the New York and Erie Railroads in 1852.

The second gateway, called the Northeastern Gateway, was a network of roads, canals, and later rail systems that connected the river launching points at Pittsburgh on the Ohio River to Philadelphia, and Wheeling, also on the Ohio River, to Baltimore. The National Road was completed west to Wheeling in 1817 and the Pennsylvania Turnpike—a toll road—reached Pittsburgh the next year. Competing canals on these two links sustained this rivalry in the 1830s. Then in the 1850s the rivalry of these cities was boosted again through rail linkages.

Bustling inland shipping points like Cincinnati soon became major markets for an increasing variety of goods and services.

The third gateway, at New Orleans, was the main southern entrepôt. The key event on the trunk rivers of the Mississippi, Missouri, and Ohio, and other western river arteries to this gateway was the introduction of the steamboat in 1811.

Figure 9-2 shows the volume of shipments from the western interior to the east and abroad by each gateway.[1] The growth of total outbound shipments, from 65,000 tons in 1810 to nearly 4.7 million tons in 1860, documents the impressive development that was taking place in the West. We also see that the Northeastern Gateway played only a minor role, typically carrying less than 5 percent of the shipments from the West. The Northern Gateway was far more significant, but not until the late 1830s. Prior to 1825 and the opening of the Erie Canal, this gateway handled no outbound shipments. Even in the early 1830s most of the shipments on the Erie Canal were from upstate New York. Therefore, it was primarily the Southern Gateway that handled western produce shipments, at least until the last couple of decades of the antebellum period. It was the dominance of the natural waterways, encompassing 16,000 miles of western rivers, that led the contemporary James Lanman to say in 1841:

> Steam navigation colonized the west! It furnished a motive for settlement and production by the hands of eastern men, because it brought the western territory nearer to the east by nine tenths of the distance. . . . Steam is crowding our eastern cities with western flour and western merchants, and lading the western steamboats with eastern emigrants and eastern merchandise. It has advanced the career of national colonization and national production, at least a century![2]

STEAMBOATS AND THE NATURAL WATERWAYS

Before the coming of the steamboat in the West, river travel was especially difficult, hazardous, and costly. Rafts and flatboats allowed downriver passage at reasonable cost, but the return upriver on foot or horseback was costly in time and dangerous. Typical voyages of 1,000 miles took one month downstream and three to four months to return. The keelboat, which made upstream journeys possible, was based on labor-intensive, back-breaking work. As shown in Figure 9-1, upstream costs were typically more than five times downstream costs.

In 1807, Robert Fulton, with the assistance of Robert R. Livingston, built the steamboat *Clermont,* which completed a historic voyage up the Hudson

---

[1] The evidence on inbound shipments is more fragmentary and less complete, but it does not change the relative positions of each gateway in the movement of freight.
[2] James H. Lanman, "American Steam Navigation," *Hunt's Merchants' Magazine and Commercial Review* 4 (1841): 124.

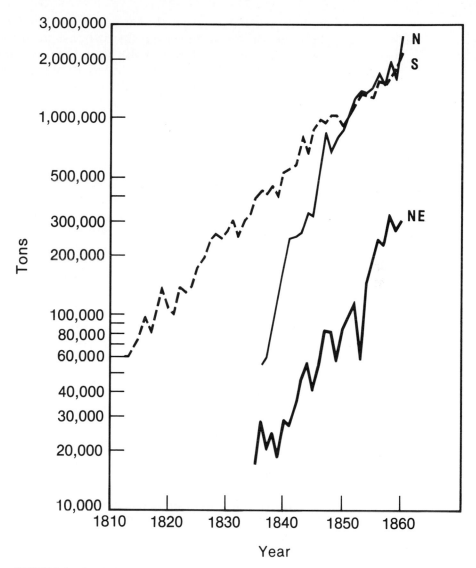

FIGURE 9-2   Freight Shipments from the Interior by the Western Gateways, 1810–60.

Source: Erik F. Haites, James Mak, and Gary M. Walton, *Western River Transportation* (Baltimore: Johns Hopkins Univ. Press, 1975), p. 7 and Appendix A.

River from New York to Albany, a distance of 150 miles, in 32 hours. Following the initial trip, regular passenger service from New York to Albany was inaugurated and the dependability of the steamboat was quickly demonstrated. A new era of transportation on the rivers of America had begun.

The steamboat's beginning in the West came at the northern terminus of Pittsburgh, which is situated where the junction of the Allegheny and the Monongahela forms the Ohio River. Plentiful supplies of timber and the local iron industry were the basis for a flourishing shipbuilding industry there, and it was at Pittsburgh that the first steamboat to ply the inland waters was constructed by Nicholas Roosevelt under the Fulton-Livingston patents. Named *The New Orleans,* it left Pittsburgh on October 20, 1811, and completed its voyage to the Gulf, despite an earthquake at New Madrid, Missouri, in a little over two and one-half months. Six years passed before regular service upstream and downstream was established, but by 1819 the tonnage of steamboats in operation on the western rivers already exceeded 10,000 and this figure grew to almost 200,000 tons by the late 1850s. The periods of the most rapid expansion were the first two decades following 1815, but significant gains occurred throughout each decade. It was not until the 1880s that steamboating in western rivers registered an absolute decline.

The appearance of the steamboat on inland waterways did not, by any means, solve all problems of travel. Variations in the heights of the rivers still made navigation uncertain, even dangerous. Ice in the spring and sand bars in the summer were ever-present hazards, and snags, rocks, and sunken vessels continually damaged and wrecked watercraft. In addition to these problems, the steamboat exposed westerners to some of the earliest hazards of industrialization; high-pressure boilers frequently exploded, accidentally killing thousands over the decades. This prompted the federal government to intervene; in 1838 and again in 1852, some of the first U.S. laws concerning industrial safety and consumer protection were legislated. Although these laws were widely evaded, steamboat designs eventually were improved, and better boilers and engines produced safer vessels. Also, the federal government sporadically engaged in the removal of snags (trees lodged in the rivers) and other obstacles from the rivers.

Competition, Productivity, and Endangered Species

One of the most significant characteristics of western river transportation was the high degree of competition among the various craft. This meant that the revolutionary effects of the steamboat, which were critical to the early settlement of the West, were transfused through a competitive market. Fulton and Livingston attempted to secure a monopoly via government restraint to prevent others from providing steamboat services at New Orleans and throughout the West. Their quest for monopoly rights was ultimately beaten in the courts. These and other associations failed to limit supply and block entry, and without government interference, the modest capital requirements needed to enter the business assured a competitive market.

From the early period of bonanza profits on the major routes, a normal rate of return on capital of about 10 percent was common by 1820. Only on the remote and dangerous tributaries, where trade was thin and uncertain, could such exceptional returns as 35 or 40 percent be obtained.

TABLE 9-1   Average Freight Rates (per 100 Pounds) by Decade Between Louisville and New Orleans, 1810–60

	Upstream	Downstream
Before 1820	$5.00	$1.00
1820–29	1.00	0.62
1830–39	0.50	0.50
1840–49	0.25	0.30
1850–59	0.25	0.32

Source: Erik F. Haites, James Mak, and Gary M. Walton, *Western River Transportation: The Era of Early Internal Development, 1810–1860* (Baltimore and London: Johns Hopkins Univ. Press, 1975), p. 32

Because the market for western rivercraft services was generally competitive, the series of productivity-raising improvements ushered in by the steamboat were passed on to consumers. And the cost reductions were significant, as the evidence in Table 9-1 illustrates.

Of course, a major cause of the sharp decline in freight costs was simply the introduction of steam power. However, the stream of modifications and improvements that followed the maiden voyage of *The New Orleans* provided greater productivity gains than the application of steam power. The decrease in rates after 1820 was greater, both absolutely and relatively, than the decline from 1811 to 1820, especially in real terms.[3]

Major modifications were made in the physical characteristics of the vessels. Initially like seagoing vessels, steamboats evolved to meet the shallow-water conditions of the western rivers. These boats became increasingly lighter in weight, with many outside decks for cargo (and budget-fare accommodations for passengers), and their water depth, or draft, became less and less, despite increased vessel size. Consequently, the amount of cargo carried (per vessel ton) greatly increased. In addition, the season of normal operations was substantially extended, even during shallow-water months. This, along with reductions in port times and passage times, greatly increased the number of round trips averaged each year.[4] Lastly, as noted earlier, government activity to clear the rivers of snags and other natural obstacles added to the time of normal operations and made river transport a safer business, as evidenced by a decline in insurance costs over the decades.

On reflection, it is clear that most of the improvements did not result from technological change. Only the initial introduction of steam power

[3] In the purchasing power of 1820 dollars, the real cost decline upstream on the New Orleans–Louisville run was from $3.12 around 1815 to $2.00 in 1820 to $.28 in the late 1850s. Downstream, the real cost changes were from $.62 around 1815 to $.75 in 1820, to $.39 in the late 1850s.

[4] The decline in passage times was only partially due to faster speeds. Primarily, this decline resulted from learning to operate the boats at night. Also, shorter stopovers at specified fuel depots instead of long periods spent foraging in the woods for fuel contributed as well.

stemmed from advances in knowledge about basic principles. The host of modifications evolved from the process of learning by doing and the restructuring of known principles of design and engineering to fit shallow-water conditions. In effect, they are a tribute to the skills and ingenuity of the early craftsmen and mechanics.

In sum, the overall record of achievement gave rise to productivity advances that averaged more than 4 percent per year during the period 1815–60. Such a rate exceeded that of any other transport medium over an equal length of time in the nineteenth century.[5]

The labor-consuming keelboat felt the strongest sting of competition from the new technology and was quickly eliminated from the competitive fray on the main trunk river routes. Only on some of the remote tributaries did the keelboat find temporary refuge from the chugging advance of the steamboat.

Surprisingly, quite a different destiny evolved for the flatboat, which showed a remarkable persistence throughout the entire antebellum period. Because the reductions in downstream rates were more moderate, the current-propelled flatboat was less threatened. In addition, spillover effects from steamboating aided flatboating. First, there was the tremendous savings in labor that the steamboat generated by providing quick upriver transport to returning flatboatmen. Not only were they saved the long and sometimes perilous overland journey, but access to steamboat passenger services led to repetitive journeys and thus to the acquisition of skills and knowledge. This resulted in the adoption of larger flatboats, which economized greatly on labor per ton carried. Because of these gains, there were more flatboats on the western rivers near the middle of the nineteenth century than at any other time.

In combination, these western rivercraft gave a romantic aura to the drudgery of day-to-day freight haulage and commerce. Sumptuously furnished Mississippi riverboats were patronized by rich and poor alike. Yeomen farmers also contributed their adventuresome flatboating journeys. However, such developments were regional in character, and their impact was mainly on the Southern Gateway. On the waterways of the East as well as on the Great Lakes, the steamboat never attained the importance that it did in the Midwest. Canals and turnpikes furnished alternative means of transportation, and the railroad network had an earlier start in the East. Steamboats in the East were primarily passenger carriers—great side-wheelers furnishing luxurious accommodations for people traveling between major cities. On the Great Lakes, contrary to what might be expected, sailing ships successfully competed for freight throughout the antebellum years. Where human comfort was a factor, however, the steamship gradually prevailed. Even so, the number and tonnage of sailing vessels on the Great Lakes in 1860 were far greater than those of steamboats.

---

[5] See Haites, Mak, and Walton, pp. 60–63.

THE CANAL ERA

Although the natural waterways provided a substantial web of transport facilities, many productive areas remained regionally and economically disconnected until the canals were built and other internal improvements were made to link them together. The first major undertaking began in 1817, when the New York legislature authorized the construction of the Erie and Champlain canals. With powerful DeWitt Clinton as the guiding spirit, the Erie Canal was promoted with enthusiasm, and sections were opened to traffic as they were completed. It quickly became apparent that the canal would have great success, and even before its completion in 1825, "canal fever" seized promoters throughout the country. In the tremendous building boom that followed, canals were constructed to link three types of areas. Some ran from the "back country" to the tidewater regions; some traversed, or attempted to traverse, the area between the older states and the Ohio Valley; and some—the western canals—linked the Great Lakes with the waterways running to the East. The principal canals of the antebellum period are shown in Map 9-1. They were vital in developing the Northern and Northeastern Gateways.

The Erie was the most important of the early canals, although it was by no means the only profitable one.[6] It was a massive undertaking. Beginning at Albany on the Hudson River, it traversed the state of New York westward to Buffalo on Lake Erie, covering a distance of 364 miles. The work cost approximately $7 million and took about nine years to complete. The builders overcame countless difficulties, not the least of which was their own ignorance. Hardly any of the engineers had ever worked in canal construction, and much experimentation was necessary in the process. Some sections of the canal did not hold water at first and had to be lined with clay after work had been completed. The locks presented a special difficulty. But ingenuity and the timely discovery of water-resistant, or hydraulic, cement led to the solution of the problems of lock construction.

The Erie system, in its final form, reached a fair portion of New York state. The Cayuga and Seneca, the Chemung, and the Genesee extensions connected important territory to the south with the canal. A branch to Oswego provided access to Lake Ontario, and the Champlain Canal gave access to the north. The system not only furnished transportation to much of the state but tapped the Great Lakes areas served by the St. Lawrence route and the vast Ohio Territory as well. Beginning about 1835, a large part of the traffic from the West that had formerly traversed the Ohio and Mississippi rivers to New Orleans was diverted over the Erie Canal to the port of New York. Lumber, grain, and meat products were the chief commodities to move eastward; textiles, leather goods, machinery, hardware,

---

[6]This system still exists in an expanded and improved form as the New York Barge Canal.

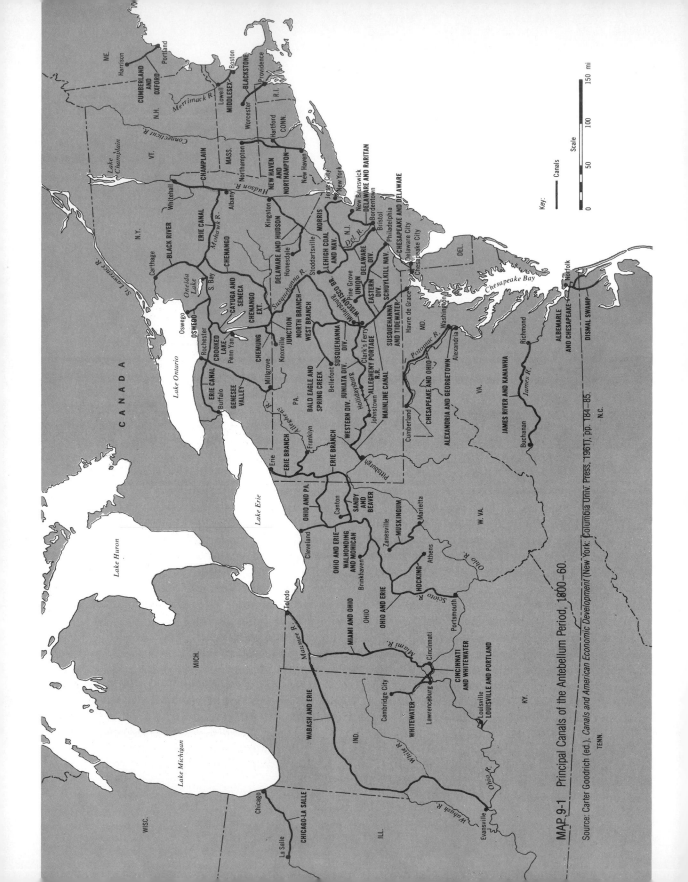

MAP 9-1 Principal Canals of the Antebellum Period, 1800–60.

Source: Carter Goodrich (ed.), *Canals and American Economic Development* (New York: Columbia Univ. Press, 1961), pp. 184–85.

and imported foods and drugs went west in exchange. Passengers, too, rode the horse-drawn boats in great numbers, with speeds of 100 miles in a 24-hour day compensating in part for the discomfort of cramped and poorly ventilated cabins.

Pennsylvania's answer to the competition of the Erie Canal was the Main Line of the Pennsylvania Public Works—a system of railroads *and* canals chartered in 1826 by the state legislature. The terrain traversed by the Erie to reach the western frontier was difficult enough for canal construction, and at its highest point it rose 650 feet above the Hudson at Albany. But the terrain of western Pennsylvania proved to be insurmountable by canal. The Main Line crossed the mountains, lifted passengers and freight to an altitude of over 2,000 feet, and deposited both travelers and goods, west-bound from Philadelphia, at Pittsburgh some 400 miles away. All this was accomplished by as fantastic a combination of transport as the country had ever seen. From Philadelphia, at tidewater, to Columbia, 81 miles westward on the Susquehanna River, a horsedrawn railroad carried both passengers and freight.[7] At Columbia, the railroad joined the Juniata, or Eastern Division of the Pennsylvania Canal, from which passengers and freight were carried up a river valley by canal 173 miles to the Portage Railroad at Holidaysburg. Here intrepid passengers saw their boat separated into front and rear sections, which were mounted on cars and run on underwater rails into the canal. A 36-mile trip on the Portage Railroad then began. The inclined tracks, over which cars were pulled by stationary steam engines winding cables on drums, accomplished a lift of 1,399 feet on the eastern slope to the summit and a descent of 1,172 feet on the western slope to another canal at Johnstown. From Johnstown to Pittsburgh, a distance of 105 miles, the water journey was comparatively easy.

The completion of this colossal work in 1834 was heralded by a celebration at Liberty Hall in Philadelphia. An old print depicts one of the halfboats decked with bunting and flags being drawn away from the hall by teams of prancing horses. In the sense that it carried all the traffic it could, the Main Line was successful, but the bottleneck of the Portage Railroad plus the fact that the system had twice as many locks as the Erie kept it from becoming a serious competitor for western business. Over the years, the Main Line carried 5–10 percent of the traffic volume of the Erie Canal, to the great disappointment of the people of a state that had spent more on waterways than any other.

Other states expended large sums of money on canals to draw the trade of the new West. The Chesapeake and Ohio Canal was projected up the valley of the Potomac to Cumberland, Maryland, and on to the Ohio River. The canal company was chartered by the state of Virginia with the assent

---

[7]Although the steam locomotive was not employed in the United States until 1829, rails to permit smooth haulage had been used in both America and Europe for several years.

This painting shows the junction of the Champlain Canal and the Erie Canal—an important point on the trade route that was to become the preeminent link between Midwest and East Coast urban centers.

of the Maryland legislature, and the federal government contributed heavily to the venture. But, despite the political blessings of two states and the federal government, the generous financial backing of all three, and the aid of some local governments, due to technical difficulties the project was completed only to Cumberland.

The dazzling success of the Erie Canal and the competitive rivalry among cities and regions for commercial traffic and economic growth generated many unprofitable investments in canals. The great canal-building era, 1815–43, totaled $31 million in investments, nearly three-quarters from government sources, mostly state governments. By comparison, government investment in support of steamboats, mainly by clearing the rivers, was only a few percent of the total investment on operating costs. Despite the lack of profitability, regional competitiveness spurred a wave of investment during 1843–60, totalling $66 million. Nearly two-thirds of the financing was from the government, again mainly from state treasuries. More might have been invested. However, the commercial crises of 1837 and 1839 and the deep depression of the early 1840s caused financial chaos and nine states had to suspend payments on their debts (mainly bonds, many sold to foreigners). Major canals in Pennsylvania, Maryland, Indiana, and Illinois never recovered.

Although most of the canal investments were not financially rewarding, they did support the natural waterways in opening up the West. Some that have been considered preposterous mistakes might have turned out to be monuments to human inventiveness if the railroad had not developed at almost the same time. The canals posed problems, it is true. The limitations on horse-drawn vehicles for cargo transport were great except with regard to a few commodities. Canals were supposed to provide a *system* of waterways, but as often as not the boats of larger canals could not move through the smaller canals. Floods and droughts often made the movement of the barges uncertain. Yet the chief reason for the eventual failure of the canals was the railroad, which could carry a wide variety of commodities at a much greater speed—and speed was requisite to a genuine transportation revolution.

THE IRON HORSE

Despite the clear-cut advantages of the railroad, the natural waterways remained the primary means of transportation for nearly 20 years after the first pioneering American railroads were introduced in the early 1830s. Besides the stiff competition of water transport, an important hindrance to railroad development was public antipathy, which had its roots in ignorance, conservatism, and vested interest. People thought that speeds of 20–30 miles per hour would be physically harmful to the passenger. At least one city in Massachusetts directed its representatives in the state legislature to prevent "so great a calamity to our town as must be the location of any railroad through it." Many honestly believed that the railroad would prove to be impractical and uneconomical and would not provide service as dependable as that of the waterways.

Unsurprisingly, the most vigorous opposition to railroads came from groups whose economic interests suffered from the competition of the new industry. Millions of dollars had been spent on canals, rivers, highways, and plank roads, and thousands of people depended on these transportation enterprises for their livelihood. Tavern keepers feared their businesses would be ruined, and farmers envisioned the market for hay and grain disappearing as the "iron horse" replaced the flesh and blood animal that drew the canal boat and pulled the wagon over turnpike and plank road. Competitive interests joined to embarrass and hinder the railroads, causing several states to limit traffic on them to passengers and their baggage or to freight hauled only during the months when canal operations ceased. One railroad company in Ohio was required to pay for any loss in canal traffic attributed to railroad competition. Other railroads were ordered to pay a tonnage tax to support the operation of canals.

These sentiments, however amusing today, were seriously espoused by national leaders as shown here by a letter from Martin Van Buren, governor of New York, to President Andrew Jackson, dated January 31, 1829[8]:

To: President Jackson

The canal system of this country is being threatened by the spread of a new form of transportation known as 'railroads.' The federal government must preserve the canals for the following reasons:

One. If canal boats are supplanted by 'railroads,' serious unemployment will result. Captains, cooks, drivers, hostlers, repairment and lock tenders will be left without means of livelihood, not to mention the numerous farmers now employed in growing hay for horses.

Two. Boat builders would suffer and towline, whip and harness makers would be left destitute.

Three. Canal boats are absolutely essential to the defense of the United States. In the event of the expected trouble with England, the Erie Canal would be the only means by which we could ever move the supplies so vital to waging modern war.

As you may well know, Mr. President, 'railroad' carriages are pulled at the enormous speed of 15 miles per hour by 'engines' which, in addition to endangering life and limb of passengers, roar and snort their way through the countryside, setting fire to crops, scaring the livestock and frightening women and children. The Almighty certainly never intended that people should travel at such breakneck speed.

Martin Van Buren
Governor of New York

Despite the opposition of those who feared the railroads, construction went on. In sections of the country where canals could not be built, the railroad offered a means of cheap transportation for all kinds of commodities. In contrast to the municipality that wished to exclude the railroad, many cities and towns, as well as their state governments, did much to encourage railroad construction. At the time, the federal government was restrained by the prevailing political philosophy from financially assisting and promoting railways. It did, however, make surveys to determine rights of way and provided tariff exemptions on railroad iron.

By 1840, railroad mileage in the United States was within 1,000 miles of the combined lengths of all canals, but the volume of goods carried by water still exceeded that transported by rail. After the depression of the early 1840s, rail investments continued, mostly government assisted, and by 1850 the country had 9,000 miles of railroads. Referring back to Figure 9-2 we see the Northern Gateway had surpassed the Southern and by 1850 the railroad's superiority was clear.

---

[8] As quoted in "No Growth," *The American Spectator,* January 1984, p. 31. Our thanks to R. L. Sexton for bringing this letter to our attention.

TABLE 9-2   Productivity Change in Railroads, 1839–1859 (1910 = 100)

Year		Inputs				
	(1) Output	(2) Labor	(3) Capital	(4) Fuel	(5) Total Input[a]	(6) Total Factor Productivity[b]
1839	.08	.3	.8	.07	.5	16.0
1859	2.21	5.0	10.1	1.50	6.6	33.5

[a]Weighted average of labor, capital, and fuel; weights are proportions of costs.
[b](column 1 ÷ column 5) 100.

Source: Adapted from Albert Fishlow, "Internal Transportation," in *American Economic Growth* ed. Lance E. Davis et al. (New York: Harper & Row, 1972), p. 499.

With the more than 20,000 miles of rails added to the transportation system between 1850 and 1860, total trackage approached 30,000 miles at the end of the decade, and the volume of freight traffic equaled that of canals.[9] All the states east of the Mississippi were connected during this decade. The eastern seaboard was linked with the Mississippi River system, and the Gulf and South Atlantic states could interchange traffic with the Great Lakes. Growing trunk lines like the Erie, the Pennsylvania, and the Baltimore and Ohio completed construction of projects that had been started in the 1840s, and combinations of short lines provided new through routes. By the beginning of the Civil War, the eastern framework of the present rail-transportation system had been erected, and it was possible to travel by rail the entire distance from New York to Chicago to Memphis and back to New York.

But the United States was still a long way from establishing an integrated railroad system. Although the "Stephenson gauge" of 4 feet 8½ inches was preponderant in 1860, its final selection as the "standard gauge" for the country was still a quarter-century away. A multitude of gauges prevented continuous shipment, as did the lack of agreement among companies on such matters as the interline exchange of rolling stock, through bills of lading and passenger tickets, the division of through rates, and standard time.[10]

Many modifications and improvements occurred, however, and, as shown in Table 9-2, total factor productivity in railroads more than doubled in the two decades before the Civil War. Alternately stated, railroad output grew relative to inputs by a factor of two. Technological advances, according to Albert Fishlow, were reflected in the fact that the average traction force of

---

[9]Railroads had won from canals almost all passenger business, except that of poor immigrants coming across New York state, and the carriage of nearly all light, high-value goods.
[10]George R. Taylor and Irene Neu, *The American Railway Network, 1861–1890* (Cambridge: Harvard Univ. Press, 1956), pp. 6–7, 12–14.

locomotives more than doubled in these two decades. Freight car sizes also increased with eight-wheel cars being common by 1859. Most of the productivity rise, however, was the result of increased utilization of the existing facilities. The stock of capital—and other inputs—grew, but output grew much faster as the initial inputs became more fully utilized.

TRAILS AND ROADS

Though technologically undramatic, our account of the transportation revolution would be incomplete without the story of trails and routes. Thanks to Hollywood and western movies, we are familiar with the trails followed by western settlers. These "highways" of long-distance land travel are shown in Map 9-2. The routes of westward emigration, settlement, and commerce usually followed the old Indian hunting and war paths, which in turn had followed the stream valleys providing the easiest lines of travel. One of the most important was the Wilderness Road, pioneered by Daniel Boone. Penetrating the mountain barrier at Cumberland Gap, near present-day Middlesboro, Kentucky, it then went north and west into the Ohio Territory. Over this road, which in many places was only a marked track, poured

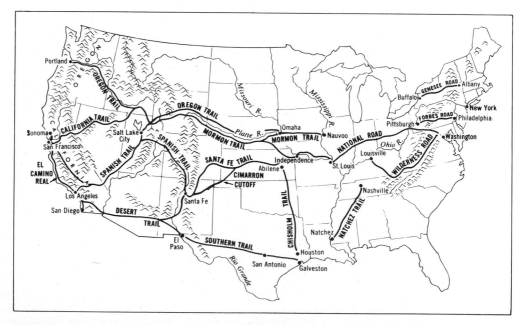

MAP 9-2   Westward Travel: The massive physical barriers faced by the pioneers could be circumvented by following such famous routes as the Oregon Trail and the Santa Fe Trail.

thousands of emigrants.[11] Other trails west of the mountains followed the Holston and the Watauga rivers as they flowed from their Appalachian sources into the Tennessee. Thus, geography in part directed the flow of emigration to the Southwest. As a rule, both transport and migration routes followed the natural drainage basins and the easiest, least obstacle-ridden paths overland.

Although most of the overland roads turned into quagmires in the rainy season and into billowing dust clouds in the dry season, some of them were well constructed and well maintained through portions of their length. The most notable surfaced highway was the Cumberland Road, or "National Pike," built by the federal government after much controversy. Begun at Cumberland, Maryland, in 1811, the road was opened to Wheeling on the Ohio River in 1818 and was later completed to Vandalia, Illinois.

The national government did not repeat its success with the Cumberland Road. As early as 1808, Albert Gallatin had proposed a plan for a system of federal roads, and progressive, enlightened people generally urged a comprehensive program of internal improvements. Opposition was based ostensibly on the assertion, repeated endlessly, that federal participation in such an activity was unconstitutional. Actually, sectional rivalries prevented the much-needed construction. The West persistently and loudly called for a national road system. At first, the Middle Atlantic states were inclined to agree, but after New York and Pennsylvania developed their own routes to the West, they did not wish to promote federally financed competition. New Englanders, with fairly good roads of their own, were even less inclined to encourage further population drains or to improve the commercial positions of Boston's rivals. The South, although mired in the mud, was bitterly antagonistic to any program that would add to the government's financial needs or facilitate access to nonslave portions of the West. Despite all the opposition, Congress could not avoid appropriating increasing sums for post and military roads, but sectional rivalries over the geographic allocation of internal improvements permitted an incredibly primitive road system to survive well into the twentieth century.

Turnpike Companies

When for some reason a unit of government refused to undertake construction, roads were often built by private turnpike companies, which then collected tolls for their use. Gates consisting of pikes or spears were turned

---

[11] This same type of road or marked track appeared during the overland migration to the West Coast. The Oregon Trail, over which travel began in the early 1840s, was 2,000 miles long and carried settlers to the Pacific Northwest and to California. The Mormon Trail, broken by Brigham Young in the late 1840s, paralleled the Oregon Trail along the south bank of the Platte for some distance. Earlier trails marked by the Spaniards, such as the Santa Fe Trail into present-day New Mexico and Arizona and *El Camino Real*, or the King's Highway in California, were valuable to early explorers and traders.

or lifted to let the tollpayer pass to and from the road at selected points. The turnpike era began in 1789 with the construction of the Philadelphia and Lancaster Turnpike; it ended about 1830, after which date only a few private highways were attempted as business ventures. During this period, Pennsylvania chartered 86 companies that built over 2,000 miles of road. By 1811, New York had 1,500 miles of highways constructed by 135 companies, and in New England by this date, some 180 companies had been granted the right to build turnpikes. Few of the companies that constructed roads for public use were profitable ventures; in fact, it is doubtful that even one earned close to the going rate of return on its capital. Teamsters avoided the tolls if at all possible, and the receipts were often pocketed by dishonest gatekeepers. But the chief difficulty—one unforeseen by most promoters—was that the only long-distance trade the roads attracted was stagecoach passengers and emigrants. Freight would not, for the most part, stand the cost of land carriage over great distances, and without freight traffic, turnpikes simply could not earn a profit. They were eventually faced with extensive competition from steamboats, canals, and railroads, but this competition did not appear until returns on invested capital had already proved disappointing. Some turnpikes were abandoned and later acquired by the states for the rapidly growing public road system; others were purchased by local governments and made into toll-free highways.[12]

Plank Roads

Another kind of toll road, the plank road or "farmer's railroad," developed shortly after the decline in turnpike construction. Plank roads were built by laying wide, heavy planks or "rails" on stringers or ties placed in the direction of travel. The first plank road in the United States was built at Syracuse in 1837; within the next 20 years or so, several thousand miles of plank roads were in use throughout the country, the heaviest concentration being in the Middle Atlantic states. So important did they seem that some were subsidized by the states, although most were privately financed.

OCEAN TRANSPORT

Besides the many developments in internal transportation, great strides were being made in the long-traditional merchant marine. Thanks to bold entrepreneurship, the Black Ball line of New York instituted regularly scheduled transatlantic sailings in 1818. Beginning with just four ships, a

---

[12] A few private roads continued into the twentieth century, but all that now remains of them is the name *turnpike* given to some important arteries of the highway system. These throughways differ from the older turnpike in that the modern enterprises are owned by public corporations.

Plank roadways proved important wherever heavy military or commercial traffic was concentrated.

vessel sailed from New York bound for Liverpool, in the first week of each month, and a ship began the Liverpool–New York passage at the same time. Considerable risk was involved in pledging ships to sail "full or not full," as the line's advertising declared, because a ship might make three round trips a year (instead of the usual two made by the regular traders) with its hold far from full.[13] But by specializing in passengers, specie, mail, and "fine freight," the packets managed to operate successfully for more than 100 years. In the 1820s, the Black Ball line increased its trips to two a month each way, and other packet lines between New York and European ports were soon established. Henceforth, passengers could count on sailing at a particular hour on a given day, and merchants could book freight with something more than a vague hope that it would arrive in time to permit a profitable transaction.

The transatlantic packets fully established New York as the predominant port in the United States. Coastal packets, running primarily to New Orleans, but also to Charleston, Savannah, and Mobile, brought cotton to New York for eastbound ocean shipment and carried southward a considerable portion of the European goods brought from England and the Continent.

---

[13] Robert G. Albion, *The Rise of the New York Port, 1815–1860* (Hamden, Conn.: Archon Books, 1961), p. 4.

In fact, trade between the cotton ports and New York was greater in physical and dollar volume than the ocean trade during most of the antebellum period.[14] These packets significantly complimented developments in the western rivers, which funneled produce from the interior through New Orleans, the Southern Gateway.

Between 1820 and 1860, remarkable design changes in sailing ships led to increases in tonnage and efficiency. From an average of 300 tons in the 1820s, American sailing ships increased to 1,000 tons in the 1850s, and vessels of 1,500 tons burden were not uncommon. There was a marked increase in length-to-beam ratios and spread of sail for the ordinary packet ship, and the centuries-old practice of making the widest part of the vessel forward of the center was abandoned. Borrowing from French designers, Yankee shipbuilders produced a special type of ship that was to dominate the seas for the three decades before the Civil War. This was the famed clipper ship, which, at some sacrifice of carrying capacity, attained unheard-of speeds. The clipper was a graceful ship with three masts, square-rigged but equipped with abundant fore-and-aft sails that gave it a great advantage going into the wind, thus increasing its speed. Manned by fewer hands than vessels of foreign register, a clipper was to be driven 24 hours a day, not put to bed for seven or eight hours at night.

The first American, or "Baltimore," clipper was the *Ann McKim,* launched in 1832. Her builder, Donald McKay, became a legendary figure, and some ships of his design bore names that are remembered even now: the *Flying Cloud,* the *Sovereign of the Seas,* the *Great Republic,* and the *Lightning* were spectacularly beautiful, with concave sides and bow and sail towering 200 feet above the deck. On its maiden voyage across the Atlantic, the *Lightning* logged a record 436 miles in one day for an average speed of 18 miles an hour. Even today, many ocean vessels do not approach this speed.

Clippers were designed for the express purpose of carrying passengers and high-value cargo long distances. On the Atlantic runs, they were not profitable due to their limited capacity. But they dominated the China trade, and after 1849 they made fortunes for their owners by carrying passengers and freight in the gold rushes to California and Australia. On the New York–San Francisco trip around Cape Horn, a distance of 16,000 miles, the *Flying Cloud* set a record of just over 89 days, when a little over 100 days was about par for the clipper voyage.[15] This meant a time saving over ordinary ocean travel of up to three months, for which some merchants and travelers would pay a good price.

Clippers, however, were not the only vessels in the American merchant fleet. Broad-beamed and full-bowed freighting ships, much slower vessels

---

[14]Robert G. Albion, *Square-Riggers on Schedule* (Princeton: Princeton Univ. Press, 1938), pp. 49–50.
[15]This record was not broken until 1988.

New York's rapid ascendancy as a port city is captured in this picture of the South Street Pier in 1850.

than the clippers, were the backbone of the nation's merchant marine. Officered by men to whom seafaring was a tradition and a career of considerable social prestige, manned by crews of Americans bred to the sea, and owned by merchants of vision and daring like Stephen Girard of Philadelphia, the cheaply and expertly built ships from the marine ways of New York, Boston, and the Maine coast were the great ocean-freight carriers until the Civil War.

In the meantime, the British were making technical advances that enabled them to challenge American maritime supremacy and finally to overcome it. The major British innovation was the adaptation of the steamboat, originally invented for use on rivers and protected waters, to navigation on the open sea. The two principal changes made by the British were the use of iron instead of wood for the hull and the employment of the Archimedean screw principle for propulsion instead of paddles. Iron hulls were necessary to transport the heavy machinery of the early steam era safely, but they also had greater strength, buoyancy, and durability than wood. From the 1830s on, the British rapidly solved the problems of iron-ship construction. The composite ship—with a frame of iron and a hull of wood—was tried for a while, but the acid in the oak timber corroded the iron. Once the British had perfected the techniques of riveting and working with sheet iron and steel, they had an absolute advantage in the construction of iron ships—as great an advantage as the United States had enjoyed in the making of wooden ones.

The inefficiency and slow speeds of the early steam engines were a source of unending difficulty. For a long time, steamships had to carry a greater weight of coal than of cargo, and low engine speeds made the inefficient paddle wheel necessary despite its theoretical inferiority.

After nearly 20 years of development, however, transatlantic steamships were making six voyages a year—twice as many as their sailing-packet competitors. Ten years later, Samuel Cunard's success in starting a line service was not entirely fortuitous; by 1848, engines were designed that could maintain higher speeds. The screw propeller was then rapidly adopted, and fuel consumption was cut greatly. During the 1850s, both the number and registered tonnage of steamships increased by leaps and bounds, and they almost entirely captured the passenger and high-value freight business.

In 1860, sailing ships still carried the greater part of the world's international freight. Yet by this time the shape of the future was clear to all except diehard American entrepreneurs, who—unable to comprehend the rapid obsolescence of their beautiful wooden ships—failed to take vigorous steps to compete with Britain. Although government subsidies to American steamship builders began as early as 1845, they were both insufficient and poorly administered. Under the most favorable circumstances, however, builders in the United States could scarcely have competed on a cost basis with the vastly superior British iron industry. The signs were there for those who chose to read them. During the 1820s, American ships had carried close to 90 percent of the foreign trade of the United States; by the 1850s, this figure had declined to about 70 percent. The times had changed, and fortune's hand was laid on other shoulders.

A NATIONAL MARKET

These many surges of transportation development solidly linked the interior western regions to the seaboard and abroad. Also contributing to market unification and falling costs of trade was the telegraph, invented by Samuel F. B. Morse in the 1830s. Telegraph wires were strung parallel to the railroads across the nation. By 1852 there were 23,000 miles of wire in operation, speeding communications and reducing uncertainties. In 1866 an undersea cable was laid to Europe, internationalizing further the U.S. and European economies.

Although economic unification was far from complete, dramatic gains had been realized by the eve of the Civil War. As stated earlier, regional price movements portrayed these strides toward economic unification. As Thomas Berry states:

> It is difficult to point to any consistent lag of the West behind the East during this early period (1788–1817) because of such diversity in general behavior; it is safe to state, however, that in such first-magnitude movements as those of 1793–1797 and 1810–1817 there was a lag measuring somewhat more than a year in length. . . . Taking a later interval (1816–1860) weighted general indices of monthly prices in New York, New Orleans, and Cincinnati show agreement with each other to a surprising degree. . . . Cincinnati prices lagged the greater part of a year in their decline in 1819–1820, but they were only three or four months behind the seaboard markets in the turning-point of 1839 and reacted simultaneously at the time of the panic of 1857.[16]

A viable transportation system was vital in perfecting a national market and linking regions. First the steamboats on the western rivers, then the canals, and finally the railroad revolutionized the costs of transport between the West and the seaboard. As Table 9-3 shows, western prices as a percentage of eastern prices grew dramatically. Farmers gained larger and larger shares of the selling price of their crops. Moreover, consumers paid decreasing shares of the purchase price for transportation and other marketing costs. As freight costs fell, new unsettled areas were profitably cleared and added to the nation's economic activity. As Peter Lindert has shown, average land prices, adjusted for quality, more than doubled and possibly tripled from 1810 to 1860.[17] Improvements in transportation increased economic specialization and raised living standards dramatically.

The Antebellum Interregional Growth Hypothesis

Another perspective on the importance of falling transportation costs to the early growth of a national market is provided by the antebellum interregional growth hypothesis. Douglass C. North advanced the argument with quantitative evidence derived from earlier works and added theoretical specifications and structure. Briefly stated, North has argued that U.S. growth in 1815–43 was propelled primarily by the growth of British demand for Southern cotton, which encouraged southern regional specialization in cotton. In turn, this raised the demand in the South for western foodstuffs

---

[16]Thomas S. Berry, *Western Rivers before 1861* (Cambridge: Harvard Univ. Press, 1943), pp. 97–99.
[17]Peter H. Lindert, "Long-run Trends in American Farmland Values," *Agricultural History* (Summer 1988): 60.

TABLE 9-3 Cincinnati Wholesale Prices as a Percentage of Philadelphia, New York, and New Orleans Wholesale Prices, 1816–60

Period	Flour (bbl.)			Wheat (bu.)			Corn (bu.)			Mess Pork (bbl.)			Lard (lb.)			Whiskey (gal.)		
	Phil.	N.Y.	N.O.	Phil.	N.Y.	N.O.	Phil.	N.Y.	N.O.	Phil.	N.Y.	N.O.	Phil.	N.Y.	N.O.	Phil.	N.Y.	N.O.
1816–20	63	66	72	45	48	—	51	48	—	56	58	63	65	69	68	—	—	—
1821–25	52	52	56	39	38	—	38	32	30	63	67	76	59	65	68	68	70	67
1826–30	68	67	67	50	48	—	49	41	29	67	68	78	56	65	66	80	79	75
1831–35	73	74	76	57	56	—	55	49	36	77	77	85	69	71	78	89	89	83
1836–40	73	73	77	59	61	90	56	51	47	87	85	86	83	82	87	91	91	79
1841–45	77	73	86	68	65	88	53	47	65	82	79	84	79	83	91	80	77	87
1846–50	78	71	87	68	63	90	51	48	62	81	90	88	80	86	93	74	73	90
1851–55	82	79	90	73	61	86	61	59	74	85	90	92	82	93	94	78	78	88
1856–60	88	95	89	79	70	86	70	66	72	91	94	93	86	96	94	85	83	87

Source: Erik F. Haites, James Mak, and Gary M. Walton, *Western River Transportation* (Baltimore: Johns Hopkins Univ. Press, 1975), p. 7 and Appendix A.

and cheap northeastern manufactures, mainly boots and shoes and coarse-fiber clothing for slaves. Growth in the size of the national market, through falling transport costs, realized economies of large-scale productions, and greater regional economic specialization. As the Northeast became more specialized in manufacturing and more urbanized, the growing demand of the South for western foodstuffs was reinforced. Each region advanced along lines dictated by their respective comparative advantages in production and each demanded goods produced in the other regions in greater and greater amounts. After 1843, the primary initiating role of foreign demand for cotton diminished and internal market forces ascended in importance. The railroad, linking the West to the North, also contributed to the lessening initiative forces of the South.

The evidence on the timing and waves of western migrations, land sales, and prices of key regional staples supports North's argument. Evidence on southern food productions, however, for the years after 1840—the only years providing us with reliable food-production data—suggests that the South was relatively self-sufficient in food.[18] And yet, as Lloyd Mercer has shown, pockets of food deficits in the South may have been sufficient to have had a significant impact on western food production for market, especially before 1840.[19] Despite the inconclusiveness of this lively debate, the hypothesis provides a useful framework of analysis and an international perspective on the advances and linkages of the regions and of the formation of a national economy in that vital period of the transportation revolution.

SELECTED REFERENCES AND SUGGESTED READINGS

Albion, Robert G. *The Rise of the New York Port, 1815–1860.* Hamden, Conn.: Archon Books, 1961.

———. *Square-Riggers on Schedule.* Princeton: Princeton Univ. Press, 1938.

Chandler, Alfred D., Jr. (1969). *The Railroads.* New York: Harcourt Brace Jovanovich, 1965.

Cootner, Paul. "The Role of the Railroads in the United States Economic Growth." *Journal of Economic History* 23 (1963).

David, Paul. "Transport Innovation and Economic Growth; Professor Fogel On and Off the Rails." *Economic History Review,* 2nd series, 22, no. 3 (1969).

Fishlow, Albert. "Antebellum Interregional Trade Reconsidered." *American Economic Review* 54 (May 1964): 352–64.

———. "Internal Transportation." In *American Economic Growth: An Economist's History of the United States.* ed. Lance E. Davis et al. New York: Harper & Row, 1972, Chapter 13.

Gallman, Robert E. "Self-Sufficiency in the Cotton Economy of the Antebellum South." *Agricultural History* 44 (1970): 5–23.

---

[18] Albert Fishlow, "Antebellum Interregional Trade Reconsidered," *American Economic Review* 54 (May 1964): 352–64; also see the "Discussion," by Robert W. Fogel in the same source, pp. 377–89. In addition see Robert E. Gallman, "Self-Sufficiency in the Cotton Economy of the Antebellum South," Agricultural History 44 (1970): 5–23.

[19] Lloyd Mercer, "The Antebellum Interregional Trade Hypothesis: A Reexamination of Theory and Evidence," in *Explorations in the New Economic History,* ed. Roger L. Ransom, Richard Such, and Gary M. Walton (New York: Academic Press, 1982), pp. 71–96.

Goodrich, Carter H. *The Government and the Economy, 1783–1861*. Indianapolis: Bobbs-Merrill, 1967.

Goodrich, Carter H. et al. *Canals and American Economic Development*. New York: Columbia Univ. Press, 1961.

———. *Government Promotion of American Canals and Railroads, 1800–1890*. New York: Columbia Univ. Press, 1960.

———. "Internal Improvements Reconsidered." *Journal of Economic History* (June 1970): 289–311.

Haites, Erik F., James Mak, and Gary M. Walton. *Western River Transportation: The Era of Early Internal Development, 1810–1860*. Baltimore: Johns Hopkins Univ. Press, 1975.

Hunter, Louis. *Steamboats on the Western Rivers*. Cambridge: Harvard Univ. Press, 1949.

Jenks, Leland H. "Railroads as a Force in American Development." In *Enterprise and Secular Change*, ed. Frederic C. Lane and Jelle Riemersma. Homewood, Ill.: Irwin, 1953.

Lindstrom, Diane L. "Demand, Markets and Eastern Economic Development, Philadelphia, 1815–1840." *Journal of Economic History* 25 (1975): 271–73.

Lindstrom, Diane L., and John Sharpless. "Urban Growth and Economic Structure in Antebellum America." In *Research in Economic History*, vol. 3. Greenwich, Conn.: JAI Press, 1978.

Mak, James, and Gary Walton. "Steamboat and the Great Productivity Surge in River Transportation." *Journal of Economic History* 33 (1972): 619–40.

McIlwraith, Thomas F. "Freight Capacity and Utilization of the Erie and Great Lakes Canals Before 1850." *Journal of Economic History* 36 (Dec. 1976).

Mercer, Lloyd. "The Antebellum Interregional Trade Hypothesis: A Reexamination of Theory and Evidence." In *Explorations in the New Economic History*, ed. Roger L. Ransom, Richard Such, and Gary M. Walton. New York: Academic Press, 1982, pp. 71–96.

Niemi, Albert W., Jr. "A Closer Look at Canals and Western Manufacturing in the Canal Era: A Reply." *Explorations in Economic History* 9 (1972): 423–26.

———. "A Further Look at Regional Canals and Economic Specialization: 1820–1840." *Explorations in Economic History* 7 (1970): 499–522.

North, Douglass C. *The Economic Growth of the United States, 1790–1860*. Englewood Cliffs, N.J.: Prentice-Hall, 1961.

———. "The Role of Transportation in the Economic Development of North America." A paper presented to the International Congress of the Historical Sciences, Vienna, August 1965, and published in *Les Grandes Voies Maritimes dans le Monde XVe–XIXe Siecles*. Paris: Ecole des Hautes Etudes en Sciences Sociales, 1965.

Ransom, Roger L. "Canals and Development, A Discussion of the Issues." *American Economic Review* 54 (1964): 365–76.

———. "A Closer Look at Canals and Western Manufacturing in the Canal Era." *Explorations in Economic History* 8 (1971): 501–10.

———. "Interregional Canals and Economic Specialization in the Antebellum United States." *Explorations in Economic History*, 2nd series, 5 no. 1 (Fall 1967).

———. "Social Rates of Return from Public Transport Investment: A Case Study of the Ohio Canal." *Journal of Political Economy* 78 (1970): 1041–60.

Scheiber, Harry. *Ohio Canal Era*. Athens, Ohio: Ohio Univ. Press, 1969.

Stover, John F. "Canals and Turnpikes: America's Early-Nineteenth-Century Transportation Network." In *An Emerging Independent American Economy, 1815–1875*. ed. J. R. Frese and J. Judd. Tarrytown, N.Y.: Sleepy Hollow Press, 1980.

Taylor, George R. *The Transportation Revolution, 1815–1860*. New York: Holt, Rinehart and Winston, 1951.

Taylor, George R., and Irene Neu. *The American Railway Network, 1861–1890*. Cambridge: Harvard Univ. Press, 1956.

Thompson, Robert. *Wiring a Continent: The History of the Telegraph Industry in the United States, 1832–1866*. Princeton: Princeton Univ. Press, 1947.

Walton, Gary M. "River Transportation and the Old Northwest Territory." In *Essays on the Economy of the Old Northwest*, ed. David C. Klingaman and Richard K. Vedder. Athens, OH: Ohio Univ. Press, 1987, pp. 225–42.

CHAPTER 10

Market Expansion and Industry in First Transition

The pre-Civil War transportation revolution resulted from remarkable technological advances and gains in productivity from many sources. As we have emphasized, however, the most revolutionary aspects of these advances were the far-reaching effects of diminishing costs for transport that linked together many isolated places and regional markets, transforming them into national and international market participants. Improvements in transportation played the main role in increasing regional specialization, and in many ways transportation developments were instrumental to economic unification. What made them all the more remarkable is that the westward movement, the rise of King Cotton, and industrialization were all unfolding simultaneously. Inexpensive transport, more than any other force, was responsible for moving the domestic market to center stage and giving it the position of prominence that it occupies today.

Between the time of the adoption of the Constitution and the outbreak of the Civil War, the economy of the United States was structurally transformed by these events, and the foundation was laid for the United States to become an economic power. From only a few small factories, mostly lumber mills, the new nation emerged by 1860 with a manufacturing sector second only to that of Great Britain, the world's industrial leader. In 1860 the United States was still predominantly an agricultural country, and the sizes of industrial firms were small by today's standards. Nevertheless, many important changes occurred that marked the advent of the industrial state. Most significant was the evolution of a new way of combining factors of production, resulting in the substitution of capital for labor and requiring new forms of business organization.

Table 10-1 provides an overview of the state of U.S. manufacture on the eve of the Civil War. The leading industries are ranked by value added (total product value minus raw material costs). As we can easily see, cotton manufacture, with New England leading the way, ranked first, having grown from infancy in 50 years. Lumbering was a close second; moving from its

TABLE 10-1   United States Manufactures, 1860

Item	(1) Number of employees	(2) Cost of raw material	(3) Value of total product	(4) (3)–(2) Value added by manufacture	Rank by value added
Cotton goods	114,955	$ 52,666,701	$107,337,783	$54,671,082	1
Lumber	75,595	51,358,400	104,928,342	53,569,942	2
Boots and shoes	123,026	42,728,174	91,889,298	49,161,124	3
Flour and meal	27,682	208,497,309	248,580,365	40,083,056	4
Men's clothing	114,800	44,149,752	80,830,555	36,680,803	5
Iron (cast, forged, rolled, and wrought)	48,975	37,486,056	73,175,332	35,689,276	6
Machinery	41,223	19,444,533	52,010,376	32,565,843	7
Woolen goods	40,597	35,652,701	60,685,190	25,032,489	8
Carriages, wagons, and carts	37,102	11,898,282	35,552,842	23,654,560	9
Leather	22,679	44,520,737	67,306,452	22,785,715	10

Source: *Eighth Census of the United States: Manufactures,* 1860.

old seat in the New England and Middle Atlantic states to the West and the South, it was the most important processing activity in these new areas. Of the first ten industries, the milling of flour and meal was the only other one in the West and South with a significant output. Iron manufactures were underrated due to the narrow definitions of the census; if all iron products and machinery had been combined in a single category, they would have formed the most important group of manufactures. Between 1850 and 1860, the doubling of the output of primary iron products and machinery forecast the shape of America's industrial future.

The sectional figures in Table 10-2 testify to the primacy of the East in early manufacturing. Because the census counted the smallest sawmills and gristmills as "manufacturing establishments," the West and the South showed a large number of these establishments. By any other criterion, New England and the Middle Atlantic states were the leading regions. The figures for the Midwest reflect in part the rapid antebellum industrial growth of the Ohio Valley and the burgeoning of the Chicago area.

During the period 1810–60, the total value of manufactures increased from about $200 million to just under $2 billion, or roughly tenfold. Farming was still in first place as a means of earning a livelihood, because the value added by manufacture in 1860 was markedly less than the value of America's three major crops—corn, wheat, and hay—and total capital investment in industry was equal to less than one-sixth the value of farm land and buildings. However, as already stated, the United States was even then second only to Great Britain in manufacturing. Soon it would be the

TABLE 10-2   Manufacturing, by Sections, Census of 1860

Section	Number of establishments	Capital invested	Employment		Annual value of products	Value added by manufacture
			Male	Female		
New England	20,671	$257,477,783	262,834	129,002	$468,599,287	$223,076,180
Middle Atlantic	53,287	435,061,964	432,424	113,819	802,338,392	358,211,423
Midwest	36,785	194,212,543	194,081	15,828	384,606,530	158,987,717
Southern	20,631	95,975,185	98,583	12,138	155,531,281	68,988,129
Pacific	8,777	23,380,334	50,137	67	71,229,989	42,746,363
Territories	282	3,747,906	2,290	43	3,556,197	2,246,772
Totals	140,433	$1,009,855,715	1,040,349	270,897	$1,885,861,676	$854,256,584

Source: *Eighth Census of the United States: Manufactures,* 1860.

industrial leader of the world, as well as its agricultural leader.[1] How was this remarkable achievement accomplished?

EARLY CHANGES IN U.S. MANUFACTURING

Household Production

When Alexander Hamilton delivered his *Report on Manufacturers* in 1791 to Congress, he estimated that from two-thirds to four-fifths of the nation's clothing was homemade. Most food processing was also done in the home. Water power had not yet been harnessed for textile production and was used mainly for milling grain, cutting lumber, and other uses. Artisans in the towns worked by hand, producing shoes, hats, pots, pans, and tools.

By 1830 household manufacture exhibited a marked decline in the East. Thereafter, home manufacture declined dramatically in all but the most inaccessible places. The major causes of the decline of household manufacture were the development of industrial organization and modern means of transportation. Wherever steamboats ran or canals, highways, and railroads were built, home manufacture declined quickly. Even on the frontier, most households had access to the products of domestic or European factories after the middle of the nineteenth century. The importance of transportation is illustrated in Map 10-1. The shaded areas in the two maps of New York show the third of the counties in the state having the highest per

---

[1] The *Twelfth Census of the United States,* quoting Mulhall's *Industries and Wealth of Nations,* placed the United States in fourth place after Great Britain, France, and Germany. But Douglass C. North, *The Economic Growth of the United States, 1790 to 1860* (Englewood Cliffs: Prentice-Hall, 1961), p. v, shows convincingly that the United States was second.

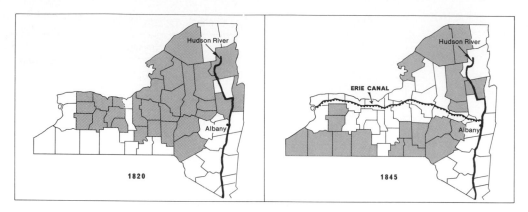

MAP 10-1   Canal Impact: Household manufacture of woolen cloth (an index of isolation from commercial routes) underwent a drastic change between 1820 and 1845 along the Erie Canal. The shaded areas indicate the one-third of the counties with the highest home production of woolen goods during this period.

Source: Arthur A. Cole, *American Wool Manufacture*, I (Cambridge: Harvard Univ. Press, 1926).

capita output of woolen goods made in the home in two different years—1820 and 1845. Note that in 1820 no county lying along the Hudson below Albany was in the top third. In 1845, the counties lying along the Erie Canal had similarly dropped in amount of home manufacture. But V. S. Clark reports that as late as 1865, nearly all the country people of Tennessee, especially those living in the mountain areas, wore clothing made at home.

The Craft Shop and the Putting-Out System

Until approximately 1850, the substantial increases in manufacturing output were effected by craftsmen operating independently or in a craft shop. The former did "bespoke" work, making commodities only to order, maintaining the highest standards of quality, and selling through their own small retail outlets. But the production of independent craftsmen declined rapidly after 1815. More important at that date and for some time afterward was the craft shop run by a master who employed several journeymen and apprentices. Sometimes, as in the case of the hatters of Danbury, Connecticut, an agglomeration of craft shops sold a quantity output to merchant wholesalers for distribution over wide market areas.

The putting-out or domestic system cannot be readily classified. In some ways, it is a unique form of organization, and yet it cuts across the categories of both household and craft production. For example, before 1830, the enterprising merchant frequently distributed cotton yarn among families for hand looming but employed skilled craftsmen to loom the yarn for finer fabrics in their shops. Until somewhat later, woolen yarn might be spun in a mill and put out to households for hand looming; the finishing processes of bleaching and dyeing were finally carried out by workmen assembled under one roof. In the boot and shoe industry, the leather might be cut under the supervision of a merchant, the pieces distributed to craft shops for sewing, and the nearly finished shoes returned to the shop for final processing. As people who bought ready-made shoes became more exacting in their demand for quality and fit and as machinery was developed for making a better product in quantity, the industry slipped easily into factory methods. Straw hats and galluses, on the other hand, were made by women and children in the home and sold by enterprising merchant employers in a wide market up to 1860.

Mill Industries

As in colonial days, the small mill was to be found everywhere from 1815 to 1860. In nearly all localities, a restricted but profitable market existed for the processed products of agriculture, forest, and mine. The census of 1860 reported nearly 20,000 sawmills and 14,000 flour mills in the country. With few exceptions, tanneries, distilleries, breweries, and iron forges also produced for local markets. The decentralization of American industry before 1860, favored by the use of water power and many times protected by high short-haul transport costs, produced small firms that often constituted effective local monopolies.

Before 1860, some mills had achieved large-scale production, using methods of manufacture typical of the factory. Furthermore, large mills in two industries tended to concentrate in certain rather well-defined areas. The flour-milling industry, which even in colonial days had been attracted to the Chesapeake area, continued to cluster there as farmers in Maryland and Virginia substituted wheat for tobacco. As cities grew larger and the demand for building materials increased, it became profitable for large lumbering firms to exploit timber areas located some distance from the markets; typical were those situated by 1850 on the upper reaches of streams flowing through New England, New York, and Pennsylvania.

PREREQUISITES TO FACTORY PRODUCTION

Machines and Technology

Not until after 1845 did it become clear that the methods of production we have just described would soon be outmoded. Yet the developments of the 1850s were such that even the most casual contemporary observer could not fail to be impressed by the rapid coming of the "factory system."

The Industrial Revolution that had already begun in England by no means guaranteed the immediate establishment of the factory system in America. In fact, the English sought to prevent dissemination abroad of the details of the new inventions. Parliament passed laws in 1774 and 1781 prohibiting the export of new industrial machinery, not unlike our laws today prohibiting high-tech exports to Soviet block countries. In 1782, a law was passed to prevent labor-pirating—the luring abroad of highly skilled British mechanics. Although these efforts possibly slowed the introduction of new machines and technologies to the United States, technology transfers occurred despite these laws. For example, on the eve of the Napoleonic Wars, the Scofield brothers arrived from Yorkshire and built water powered wool-carding machinery. They were preceded by Samuel Slater, who in 1789 came to the United States and in cooperation with the Brown family of Providence, Rhode Island, built the first American spinning mill powered by water. Over a dozen small prototypes of their mill were built during the next decade in New England.

Largely because of the relatively high cost of labor in the United States, American managers always tended to use the most nearly automatic machines available in a particular application. More importantly, they successfully innovated new ways of organizing production that saved labor expense per unit of output. Their chief contributions—the two basic ideas that led to American preeminence in nineteenth-century manufacturing—were interchangeable-parts manufacture and continuous-process manufacture. Both advances were inevitably allied with the development of machine tools and with changes in techniques of applying power.

Standardized Interchangeable Parts

The idea of standardizing a product and its various parts originated in Sweden in the early eighteenth century and before 1800 had been tried at least once in France, Switzerland, and England. Through standardization, the parts of one product could be interchanged for the parts of a like product, facilitating manufacture and repair. The first permanently successful application of the idea in a nontrivial use was made in the American armament industry. At the turn of the nineteenth century, Eli Whitney and Simeon North almost simultaneously obtained contracts from the government to manufacture firearms by the interchangeable-parts method. Records suggest that North was using the "uniformity principle" as early as 1807 in making his pistols. It has long been customary to credit Whitney with the first successful manufacture by interchangeable parts, but the evidence does not substantiate his claim to priority. Perhaps the first application of the idea in a modern sense was made by John H. Hall, inventor and engineer at the Harper's Ferry Armory, who by 1817 was installing his system using metal-cutting and woodworking machines.[2] In any case, it took

---

[2] See Robert S. Woodbury, "The Legend of Eli Whitney and Interchangeable Parts," *Technology and Culture*, II:1 (1960), pp. 235–53. In Professor Woodbury's view, interchangeable-parts manufacture involves four elements: (1) precision machine tools, (2) precision gauges or other measuring instruments, (3) uniform measurement standards, and (4) techniques of mechanical drawing.

more than two generations to make the essential innovations in the arms industry. Captain Hall's pattern-turning greatly reduced the number of man-hours needed to shape unsymmetrical rifle stocks. Drop-forging with dies was successfully introduced about 1827. By 1855, Samuel Colt, who had long since invented his six-shooter, could establish an armory in which machine work of a high degree of accuracy was accomplished by skilled operators. From approximately mid-century on, the ultimate tool of precision was no longer the hand file.

Continuous-Process and Assembly Lines

Although milling processes did not require assembly operations, continuous-process manufacture—production in which the plant is so arranged that the manufacture is done with facility and as nearly in order as possible—had its first successful application in the mills. Discussed in Chapter 3, the American inventor Oliver Evans in 1782 built a flour mill in Philadelphia run by gravity, friction, and water power that moved the grain through its processing without human intervention other than guiding and monitoring. Continuous-process manufacture in its most significant present-day form, with motor-driven moving assemblies like those introduced by Henry Ford for automobile production, was an outgrowth of the successful interchangeable-parts production of firearms, clocks and watches, sewing machines, and agricultural implements. In the 1850s, agricultural-implement companies actually used conveyor belts to assemble the parts of major subassemblies in sequence, thus foreshadowing "mass production" techniques of the early twentieth century.

Power and Energy

During the early years of manufacturing in the United States, water wheels furnished most of the motive power. Plentiful steadily moving rivers and streams assured this dependable source of power, but readily available water power was enhanced further by technological improvements in water wheels.

A water wheel is always placed in a vertical position on a horizontal shaft and is moved at a comparatively low speed by direct action of the water. Wheels are classified by the way water is applied to turn them (see Figure 10-1). The kind used in colonial times and for a while thereafter in frontier areas was the *undershot* wheel, which was placed in the stream so that its blades were moved by the water passing underneath it. The undershot wheel, although easy to install, was inefficient, transmitting no more than 40 percent of the power applied to it. The *overshot* wheel was moved by water running from a flume across the top of the wheel into buckets covering its surface; the weight of the water in the buckets moved the wheel in the direction of the steam flow. The overshot wheel was more efficient, easy to install, and satisfactory wherever there was a good head of water, but the power it developed was not great enough for heavy industrial purposes. Consequently, the large manufacturing concerns almost invariably

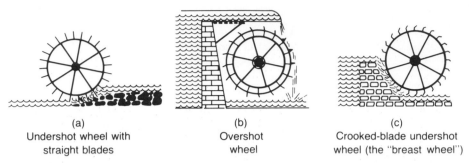

(a)	(b)	(c)
Undershot wheel with	Overshot	Crooked-blade undershot
straight blades	wheel	wheel (the "breast wheel")

FIGURE 10-1   Water Wheels Used to Power Textile and Woodworking Machinery: The three main engineering designs of waterwheels that powered early textile and woodworking machinery are displayed here.

used the *breast* wheel. This type, too, was equipped with buckets, but the water struck the wheel short of its highest point so that it rotated in an upstream direction; both the impulse of the water and its weight in the buckets enabled the wheel to utilize up to 75 percent of the power applied to it. Installed in multiples, the breast wheel developed a sufficient horsepower to serve the largest early nineteenth-century industrial firms. The machinery of the Merrimack Manufacturing Company, for example, was run by eight breast wheels, each 30 feet in diameter with buckets 12 feet long.

The slow-moving and cumbersome water wheels could develop several thousand horsepower, but they had marked disadvantages. Power from a wheel was transmitted by wooden shafts and cogwheels and was limited by the strength of the entire mechanism. Furthermore, industrial location was restricted to stream sites, and the problem of finding sites, especially in industrialized areas, became a serious one. The first difficulty was partially overcome by making wheels and transmission parts of metal; the second, by the improved engineering of dams and canals. The water turbine, which revolved on a vertical shaft, was much more efficient than a wheel and by the 1850s was adding rapidly to the power potential of the country.

Finally came steam power, although its introduction into U.S. manufacturing was slow for several reasons. In the beginning, the steam engine was extremely costly to operate. Breakdowns were frequent, and expert repair technicians were rare. In transportation, the steam engine could pull such heavy loads at such increased speeds that these disadvantages were more than offset, but in industry water power remained cheaper than steam power for a long time. It has been estimated that in 1812 only 11 engines of the high-pressure type developed by Oliver Evans were in use in this country.[3]

---

[3] Victor S. Clark, *History of Manufactures in the United States, 1607–1860* (Washington, D.C.: The Carnegie Institution, 1916), p. 409.

During the next two decades, steam engines became more common in the South and West, but most of them were used in ironworks and glass factories that required fuel for other purposes or in mills that could not conveniently be located near water. Around 1840, manufacturers in New England and the Middle Atlantic states estimated the annual cost per horsepower for steam to be five or six times that of water. Within the next 20 years, improvements in metal-working technology lowered the cost of steam engines and improved both their efficiency and reliability. By the 1850s, steam engines were replacing water wheels in the heat-using industries and wherever stream flows were highly variable as they were along the Ohio River. In New England, steam engines were being installed to power textile mills due to the serious lack of adequate power sites. As of 1860, water was still the chief source of power, but the years of the water wheel were clearly numbered.

Paralleling the rise of steam power, with a lag, was coal, and coal eventually became a major new source of energy. Because wood and hence charcoal were so cheap in the United States, however, coal use was slowed by comparison to its rapid adoption in England. Coal, like water, had a major impact on the location of manufacturing. With adequate transportation facilities, coal power increasingly allowed factories to be built in urban centers, and after 1830 coal powered factories increasingly became a feature of the rise of manufacturing in the United States.

FACTOR PROPORTIONS AND BORROWING AND ADAPTING TECHNOLOGY

Britain's head start in making machines gave the British a great advantage in manufacturing. Their machines typically embodied specific technological forms that reflected their relative costs of labor, capital, and raw materials. The relative costs of these inputs were different in the United States. Nineteenth-century Americans were short on labor and capital and were long on raw materials, like leather and wool by-products, and also natural power sources (water). American industrialists, as runners-up to British producers, had not only to copy English machines, but to adapt them as well, to economize on labor, perhaps at the sacrifice of raw material usage. One example of their success is reflected in the comparison of the textile industries in each country. English textile firms averaged 17,000 spindles and 276 looms compared to 7,000 spindles and 163 looms in the United States. Robert Zevin's study of textiles reveals that the American cotton textiles industry had 20 percent of Britain's spindles and 25 percent of its workers but processed 40 percent as much cotton. Clearly, the Americans had successfully adapted their equipment to save on scarce U.S. labor and capital.

The work of William Lazonick on the choice of techniques and their adaption reveals that there was not a uniform technology on both sides of the Atlantic. The British became increasingly labor intensive and lowered the quality of their raw material inputs. Americans conserved labor, especially scarce unskilled labor, by upgrading machines and adopting higher grades of raw cotton or wool materials. Because Americans did not unionize as did British workers and were more mobile than British workers, American management could more easily substitute new machines to reduce its labor dependence and labor costs. Claudia Goldin and Kenneth Sokoloff add another consideration; early manufacturers depended primarily on women and children. Where the opportunity costs of this labor were low, as in New England where farming produced a poor livelihood, children and women were relatively more available to supply scarce labor. This encouraged the location of manufacturing there and supplied a labor force accepting of technological changes.

In textiles, firearms, clocks and watches, and many other items, the ideas of standardization, interchangeable parts, and division of labor in assembly production processes were being widely applied. In 1851, at the Great Exhibition in London—in many ways like the World's Fair today—American products were a primary attraction. Though simple in design, not elegant, or long lasting, they were practical, cheap, and functional. After all, they reflected the characteristics in products demanded by a population dominated by masses of farmers, pioneers, and workers who were for the most part unpretentious, practical people. In 1855 a British Parliamentary Committee visited the United States to determine the secret of the success of the "American System" as it became known. This "American System" flourished in America's new factories.

The Emergence of U.S. Factories

The word *factory* has been used customarily to designate manufacturing units with the following characteristics:

1. A substantial output of a standardized product made to be sold in a wide, rather than a strictly local, market.
2. Complex operations carried on in one building or a group of adjacent buildings. Implied is a considerable investment in fixed plant, the mechanization of processes, and the use of power.
3. An assembly of workers under a definite organizational discipline.

The factory developed first in the United States in the cotton-textile industry. Due to the unusual nature of its founding, we think of the mill of Almy, Brown, and Slater, in operation by 1793, as the first American factory. Moses Brown and William Almy were men of wealth in the New England mercantile tradition. Like many other American enterprisers, they had tried and failed to duplicate English spinning machinery. As we said earlier, in 1790, there came to Rhode Island a young mechanical wizard, Samuel Slater, who had worked for years in the firm of Arkwright and Strutt in Milford, England. Having memorized the minutest details of the water frames,

The complexity of mechanized factories and the substantial economies of scale related to them, are illustrated here with a cotton manufacturing plant (circa 1839) where cotton is being carded, drawn, and roven (twisted into strands).

Slater emigrated to the United States, where he hoped to obtain a fortune for his information. Getting in touch with Almy and Brown, Slater agreed to reproduce the equipment for a mechanized spinning mill. Although small, the enterprise served as a training ground for operatives and as a pilot operation for managers.

A number of small mills like the Slater mill soon followed, but most of them failed by the turn of the century because their promoters did not aim for a wide market. Not until the Embargo Act of 1807 and the consequent scarcity of English textiles stimulated demand for domestic manufactures did spinning mills become numerous. Between 1805 and 1815, 94 new cotton mills were built in New England, and the mounting competition led Almy and Brown to push their markets south and west. By 1814, 70 percent of all consignments were to the Middle West via Philadelphia. Only two decades after Arkwright machinery was introduced into this country, the market for yarn was becoming national and the spinning process was becoming a true factory operation as it was in England.

The Lowell Shops and the Waltham System

Two events propelled these changes. One was the successful introduction of the power loom into American manufacture; the other was the organization of production so that *all four* stages of the manufacture of cotton cloth could occur within one establishment. After closely observing the workings of textile machinery in Great Britain, Francis Cabot Lowell, a New England merchant, gained sufficient knowledge of the secrets of mechanized weaving to enable him, with the help of a gifted technician, to construct a power loom superior to any that had been built to date. It was as an enterpriser, however, that Francis Lowell made a more significant contribution. He persuaded other men of means to participate with him in establishing a firm at Waltham that had all the essential characteristics of factory production. This was the famed Boston Manufacturing Company, the forerunner of several similar firms in which the so-called Boston Associates were interested. Specializing in coarse sheetings, the Waltham factory sold its product all over America. Consolidating all the steps of textile manufacture in a single plant lowered production costs. A large number of specialized workers were organized into departments and directed by executives who were not necessarily technical supervisors. The factory, by using power-driven machinery, produced standardized commodities in quantity.

At Lowell, where the Merrimack Manufacturing Company followed the Waltham pattern, and at Manchester and Lawrence, the factory system gained a permanent foothold. In the other great center of New England textile manufacture—the Providence–Pawtucket region—there was a similar trend, although the factories there were fewer and smaller. The third great district, located about Paterson and Philadelphia, contained mainly small mills that performed a single major process and turned out finer weaves. But by 1860, New England's industry had nearly four times as many spindles as the Middle Atlantic industry and accounted for nearly three-fourths of the country's output of cotton goods. The factory had demonstrated its superiority in the textile field.

It was simply a matter of time until other industries adopted the same organization. Because technological changes were slower, the production of woolen cloth tended to remain in the small mill longer than cotton production did. But after 1830, woolen factories began to adopt the characteristics of the Waltham system, and by 1860 the largest textile factories in the United States were woolen factories. Again, New Englanders far surpassed the rest of the country in combining factors of production in large units; two-thirds of America's woolen output in 1860 was made in New England.

Iron and Other Factories

In most other industries, the decade of the 1830s was one of expansion and experimentation with new methods. In the primary iron industry, establishments by the 1840s dwarfed those of a quarter-century earlier, and even in the pre-steel era, some of them had passed beyond what we have called the mill stage. By 1845, the Brady's Bend Iron Company in western Pennsylvania owned

> nearly 6,000 acres of mineral land and 5 miles of river front upon the Allegheny. It mined its own coal, ore, limestone, fire-clay, and fire-stone, made its

own coke, and owned 14 miles of railway to serve its works. The plant itself consisted of 4 blast furnaces, a foundry, and rolling mills. It was equipped to perform all the processes, from getting raw materials out of the ground to delivering finished rails and metal shapes to consumers, and could produce annually between 10,000 and 15,000 tons of rails. It housed in its own tenements 538 laboring families. This company, with an actual investment of $1,000,000, was among the largest in America before the Civil War, though there were rival works of approximately equal capacity and similar organization.[4]

In the anthracite region to the east, factory operation of furnaces and rolling mills had been achieved by 1850.

By the 1850s, factories were manufacturing arms, clocks and watches, and sewing machines. How one industry could adopt new methods as a consequence of progress in another industry is shown by the fact that, as the sewing machine was produced on a quantity basis, the boot and shoe industry developed factory characteristics. Carriages, wagons, and even farm implements were eventually produced in large numbers. Finally, where markets were more extensive, where there was a substantial investment in fixed plant, and where workers were subjected to formal discipline, some firms in the traditional mill industries other than the textile and iron industries achieved factory status. The great merchant flour mills of Baltimore and Rochester fell into this category, as did some of the large packing plants in New York, Philadelphia, Baltimore, and, after 1840, Cincinnati.

THE QUESTION OF PROTECTION

It will be recalled that after the peace of 1815, imports of English manufactured goods reached alarming proportions from the viewpoint of American businesses. Before 1815, duties on foreign goods had been set at rates that, although originally intended to protect, maximized governmental revenues in a hit-or-miss fashion. Growing protectionist sentiment in the Northeast gained enough support from the West and South to secure passage of the Tariff Act of 1816, which established the philosophy that was to guide framers of the tariff acts of 1824, 1828, 1832–1833, 1842, 1846, and 1857.

Ironically, John C. Calhoun was a leading advocate of the passage of the tariff of 1816, which levied ad valorem duties of 20–25 percent on most manufactured goods and 15–20 percent on raw materials. In general, the level of duties on manufactures did not prevent the entry of many goods at that time, although cheap cottons were shut out of the home market by specific duties (that is, duties of so much per yard). Moreover, the tax on raw materials, particularly raw wool, lowered the expansion potential of some domestic industries.

---

[4]Clark, p. 446.

From 1816 until 1832, the protectionist tide rose; cottons, woolens, glass, and iron products received the greatest favors, with raw wool and hemp garnering their share. However, the tariff enthusiasm of southerners began to abate shortly. They saw that the American market for southern staples, especially cotton, would not soon replace the European market damaged by a high U.S. tariff; industrialization simply could not take place fast enough. Meanwhile, the terms of trade would weigh heavily against the South, who would have to buy dear and sell cheap. Offsetting the defection of the South, however, was the growing tendency of the New England merchant class to align itself with the manufacturers in favor of taxes on imports.

The political shenanigans leading to the high tariff of 1828—the Tariff of Abominations—precipitated agitation in the South and necessitated a compromise within only a few years. In fact, a severe threat to the Union was South Carolina's Nullification Ordinance, which was legislated even after downward revisions in import duties had been made in 1832. The Compromise Tariff of 1833 provided that all duties would be reduced to a maximum of 20 percent ad valorem within a decade. But only two months after the 20-percent maximum level was reached in 1842, the Whigs passed a bill in which rates reverted to about the protective level of ten years before, and President Tyler, a Southerner, accepted it because he felt this action would provide more revenue for the government. With the return of the Democrats to power, more moderate tariffs were rapidly secured, and the Walker Tariff of 1846 set an example that was followed until 1861. The principle of protection of domestic industry was maintained, but the classification of commodities, the removal of specific prohibitive duties, and the introduction of a system of warehousing of imports until duties were paid all indicated a more liberal attitude toward tariffs by the United States.[5] The good times of the 1850s and the consequent increase in imports so swelled the revenues from tariffs that the government achieved great surpluses. The piling up of cash in U.S. Treasury vaults led to a general reduction in rates and many items were placed on the free list. Just before the Civil War, it appeared that the United States might join the United Kingdom as a free-trade country. In 1860, tariffs averaged less than 20 percent of the value of dutiable imports and 15 percent of the value of all imports—levels that had only moderate protective significance.

---

[5] By classifying dutiable articles into a number of schedules, Secretary of the Treasury Walker wished to discriminate among imports according to luxuries, semiluxuries, necessities, and so on. Brandy, for example, was placed in a schedule carrying a 100-percent duty, whereas most raw materials were in a schedule carrying a 5-percent duty. Schedule C, the main category, levied an ad valorem tax of 30 percent on iron and other metals, metal manufactures, wool and woolens, and manufactures of leather, paper, glass, and wood. Cotton manufactures, in Schedule D, were taxed at 25 percent. The warehousing provision enabled importers to keep goods in a government warehouse up to one year without having to pay duties until goods were withdrawn for sale.

It is hard to estimate the effects of tariff legislation on the economy of a country, for strands of causality are not easily separated. Yet most writers on the period agree on certain points. First, during the years 1816–32, when the protectionist sentiment was waxing, duties on cheap cottons and woolens reserved the American market for the Americans. But finer textiles continued to be imported from England, and after 1825, instead of selling coarse textiles to American consumers, England sold textile machinery to U.S. manufacturers. After 1833, the reduction of import duties lightened the burden on importers and, in turn, on the American consumer. In the depressed early 1840s, as in the 1820s, tariffs probably kept industrial output and employment from declining as much as they would have in a free market. On the other hand, the high tax on imported raw wool, together with the inferiority of the American product, accounts in large part for the slow development of American woolen manufacturing before 1850. In sum, however, American manufactures were stimulated and the dollar value of foreign commerce was reduced by tariffs. Second, the South suffered insofar as tariffs cut American imports and therefore the amount of American exports that foreigners, particularly the English, could buy. Southerners were probably also bothered by the higher prices of imported implements, hardware, housewares, and cheap clothing for slaves. But when all was said and done, southern planters were prosperous during the period despite protective tariffs. What people *think* is bad, though, may frequently lead to trouble, and the question of the tariff was one of the causes of sectionalism and eventual civil strife.

One fact is clear. Receipts from customs constituted the major source of income for the federal government before the Civil War. Nevertheless, tariffs probably did not alter the course of early industrial and commercial development very much because there is little evidence that tariffs seriously changed the direction of investment. Some industries, like the iron industry, refused to grow up and remained inefficient infants for a long time, protected as much by high transportation costs into the interior as by duties on English iron. Tariff protection, especially in textiles before the 1840s, did spur an industrial foothold and generate subsequent cost reductions in textiles through learning-by-doing effects.[6] Moreover, the *rate* of growth of the manufacturing industry was probably stimulated by tariffs, and in that sense the economic progress of the country was thereby hastened. In addition, tariffs altered the distribution of income in favor of owners of industrial property and to the disfavor of consumers.

---

[6]For a careful presentation of the complexities of tariff analysis, see Paul A. David, "Learning by Doing and Tariff Protection: A Reconsideration of the Case of the Antebellum United States Cotton Textile Industry," *Journal of Economic History* 30 (1970): 521–601. David tentatively concludes that after the Tariff of 1824, tariffs implied blanket subsidies for cotton textile manufacturers and offered them a means of redistributing income in their favor.

THE RISE OF CORPORATE ORGANIZATION

We must finally consider the change that was taking place in the legal concept of the business firm—the change from sole proprietorship and partnership organization to corporate organization. The corporation gained prominence chiefly because some businesses required more capital that one person or a few people could provide. By 1810, the corporate form was commonplace for banks, insurance companies, and turnpike companies, but in ensuing decades, canals and railroads could be financed only by tapping various sources of funds from small merchants and professionals along proposed routes to English capitalists thousands of miles away.

The corporation, a legal entity with privileges and responsibilities distinct from those of the people associated with it, evolved over centuries. In England, corporations followed two major lines of development. Municipalities and universities were established under corporate charters granted by the sovereign, and the great trading companies, formed for the purpose of exploiting foreign lands, were organized as "joint-stock associations" that borrowed many of the features of the corporation.

So the development of the corporation was in reality the transformation of an instrument of communal service to accommodate the demands of a new industrial age. It is a convention of economic historiography to begin the corporate cycle with Chief Justice Marshall's *Dartmouth College* opinion, reading into it the legal foundation of modern capitalism. It is true that Marshall implied as much when he made Dartmouth's royal charter a contract between the college and New Hampshire and, as such, placed it beyond the constitutional power of that state to repeal or amend. Nevertheless, this was only an implication; Marshall's explicit references concerned only municipal bodies and private charities. It is in Justice Joseph Story's concurring opinion that we find the principle extended to business enterprises. Contemporary opinion, both pro and con, recognized Story's analysis as novel and significant.

This creative revisionism, as a few historians have noted, produced a radical change in traditional analysis. The mere fact that a public authority had granted a charter meant that the corporation had, in some sense, a "public" purpose; taken at face value, this characteristic suggested the ability of the chartering authority to regulate, revise, or even revoke the privilege it had granted. But Story discarded purpose and substituted property as a starting point, achieving a two-fold division in result: on the one hand, private corporations holding private property and, on the other, public corporations charged with government or administration. The state could regulate the latter group without restraint; the state could approach the former group only with the deference due vested right and private interest.

An equally significant development was Story's grafting of the ancient law of trusts onto the emerging form of business enterprise. Here the consequence was a separation of ownership and control. Under this division, the capital of a corporation became a trust fund for the successive benefit of creditors and stockholders, the directors became trustees, and the corporation itself increasingly assumed a character and personality distinct from the persons who had provided its resources. The end result was an ideal apparatus of capital formation that involved both permanent contributions of resources and transferable, judicially protected claims.

When it first appeared in the United States, the corporation lacked many of its present-day characteristics. Charters were granted by special acts of legislatures, and the question of the liability of stockholders was far from settled. Nevertheless, the corporation had a number of advantages over the sole proprietorship and the partnership, and its legal status came to be better defined than that of the joint-stock company. Of its unquestioned advantages, the most notable—in addition to the obvious one of attracting greater numbers of investors—were permanence and flexibility. The partnership and the sole proprietorship have one inescapable drawback: If one partner or the proprietor dies, the business is dissolved. The business can go on, of course, under a new partnership or proprietorship, but continuity of operation is contingent on the lives of particular individuals. Furthermore, a partnership is dissolved when one partner's interest is sold. But the shares of a corporation can be transferred, and investors, whether small or large, can enter and leave the business without destroying the structure of the corporation.

Early corporations did not have certain advantages that corporations have today. Take the question of liability, for example. What the liability of the shareholders for the debts of the corporation should be was difficult to determine. Stockholders of the English joint-stock companies had finally come to assume "double liability"—that is, the stockholders were liable to the extent of their investment plus a like amount—and some states experimented with charters specifying either double liability or unlimited liability. After 1830, however, statutes were passed in various states providing for limited liability, and by 1860 this principle was generally accepted. Under limited liability, stockholders could lose, on the failure of a corporation, only the money they had invested in the venture.

The early requirement that incorporators of banks, insurance companies, canals, and railroads obtain their charters by the special act of a state legislature was not always a disadvantage. For those who had the political connections, this involved little uncertainty and expense, and there was always the possibility of obtaining a charter with exceptionally liberal provisions. Nevertheless, the politically unfavored could spend years lobbying futilely for corporate charters. As early as 1800, those who looked on incorporation by special act as "undemocratic" were agitating to secure "general" acts of incorporation—laws making it possible for any group, provided it observed and met prescribed regulations and requirements, to obtain a charter. Others, fearful that the corporation would spread too rapidly if their elected representatives did not pass on *each* application for charter, opposed general acts. In 1837, Connecticut passed the first general act that made incorporation the right of anyone.[7] From that date, *permissive* general acts (acts allowing, but not requiring, incorporation under their provisions) were gradually placed on the statute books of most of the chief manufacturing states, and before 1861 the constitutions of thirteen states *required* incorporation under general laws. In those states where permissive legislation had been enacted, incorporators continued until about 1870 to obtain special charters, because they enabled the incorporators to secure more liberal provisions than they could under general laws.

After 1837, mercantile and manufacturing firms were organized as corporations with growing frequency. There was, especially during the 1850s, a rapid increase in the number of manufacturing corporations. *Yet in 1860, the greater portion of resources devoted to manufacturing was under the control of proprietorships and partnerships.* At that time, a rolling mill of the most modern design could be built for $150,000, and the largest textile factory did not require an investment beyond the means of a single very wealthy person. The course of commerce and industry would not have been very different before 1860 if the privilege of incorporation had been given only to financial and transportation firms. Nonetheless, contemporary observers were aware that the corporate form would be inseparable from the enterprise of the future; bigness obviously lay ahead. For technical reasons alone, the size of the firm had to become larger, and, as the railroad companies had already demonstrated, enterprisers had to choose the corporate type of business organization when huge capital outlays were required.

SELECTED REFERENCES AND SUGGESTED READINGS

Ames, Edward, and Nathan Rosenberg. "Changing Technological Leadership and Industrial Growth." *Economic Journal* 73 (1963).

Atack, Jeremy. "Fact or Fiction? The Relative Costs of Steam and Water Power: A Simulative Approach." *Explorations in Economic History* 16 (1979): 409–37.

———. "Returns to Scale in Antebellum United States Manufacturing." *Explorations in Economic History* 14 (1977): 337–59

Atack, Jeremy, Fred Bateman, and Thomas Weiss. "The Regional Diffusion and Adoption of the Steam Engine in American Manufacturing." *Journal of Economic History* 40 (June 1980).

Bateman, Fred, and Thomas Weiss. "Comparative Regional Development in Antebellum Manufacturing." *Journal of Economic History* 35 (1975).

Bateman, Fred, James Forest, and Thomas Weiss. "Profitability in Southern Manufacturing: Estimates for 1860." *Explorations in Economic History* 12 (1975): 211–32.

Brito, D. L., and Jeffrey G. Williamson. "Skilled Labor and Nineteenth Century Anglo-American Managerial Behavior." *Explorations in Economic History* 10 (1973): 235–52.

Chandler, Alfred D. "Anthracite Coal and the Beginnings of the Industrial Revolution in the United States." *Business History Review* (1972): 141–81.

Clark, Victor S. *History of Manufactures in the United States 1607–1860.* Washington, D.C.: The Carnegie Institute, 1929.

[7] In 1811, New York had passed a law that permitted incorporation, without special act, of certain manufacturing concerns with capitalization of under $100,000.

Cochran, Thomas. *Frontiers of Change: Early Industrialism in America.* New York: Oxford Univ. Press, 1981.

Cole, A.H. *The American Wool Manufacture.* Cambridge: Harvard Univ. Press, 1926.

David, Paul. "The Horndal Effect in Lowell, 1834–1856: A Short-Run Learning Curve for Integrated Cotton Textile Mills." *Explorations in Economic History* 10 (1973): 131–50.

———. "Learning by Doing and Tariff Protection: A Reconsideration of the Case of the Antebellum United States Textile Industry." *Journal of Economic History* 30 (1970): 521–601.

Davis, Lance E. "The New England Textile Mills and the Capital Markets: A Study of Industrial Borrowing, 1840–1860." *Journal of Economic History* 20 (1960): 1–30.

———. "Sources of Industrial Finance: The American Textile Industry, A Case Study." *Explorations in Economic History,* 1st series, 60 no. 4 (1957).

Field, Alexander James. "Sectoral Shift in Antebellum Massachusetts: A Reconsideration." *Explorations in Economic History* 15 (1978): 146–71.

Goldin, Claudia, and Kenneth Sokoloff. "The Relative Productivity Hypothesis of Industrialization; The American Case, 1820 to 1850." *The Quarterly Journal of Economics* 69 (Aug. 1984).

Habakkuk, H. J. *American and British Technology in the Nineteenth Century: The Search for Labor Saving Inventions.* New York: Cambridge Univ. Press, 1962.

Halsey, Harlan I. "The Choice Between High Pressure and Low Pressure Steam Power in America in the Early Nineteenth Century." *Journal of Economic History* 61 (1981): 723–44.

Hughes, Jonathan. *Industrialization and Economic History: Theses and Conjectures.* New York: McGraw-Hill, 1970.

———. *The Vital Few: American Economic Progress and Its Protagonists.* New York: Oxford Univ. Press, 1986.

James, John. "The Welfare Effects of the Ante-Belum Tariff: A General Equilibrium Analysis." *Explorations in Economic History* 15 (1978): 231–56.

Lazonick, William H. "Production Relations, Labor Productivity, and Choice of Technique: British and U.S. Cotton Spinning." *Journal of Economic History* 41 (1981): 491–516.

Lindstrom, Diane. *Economic Development in the Philadelphia Region, 1810–1850.* New York: Columbia Univ. Press, 1978.

Livesay, Harold. "Marketing Patterns in the Antebellum American Iron Industry." *Business History Review* (1971): 269–95.

Livesay Harold, and Glen Porter. "The Financial Role of Merchants in the Development of U.S. Manufacturing, 1815–1860." *Explorations in Economic History* 9 (1971): 63–88.

North, Douglass C. *The Economic Growth of the United States 1790–1860.* Englewood Cliffs, N.J.: Prentice-Hall, 1961.

Passell, Peter, and Marie Schmundt. "The Financial Role of Merchants in the Development of U.S. Manufacturing, 1815–1860." *Explorations in Economic History* 9 (1971): 35–48.

Pope, Clayne. "The Impact of the Antebellum Tariff on Income Distribution." *Explorations in Economic History* 9 (1972): 375–422.

Rosenberg, Nathan. "Factors Affecting the Diffusion of Technology." *Explorations in Economic History* 10 (1972): 3–34.

———. *Technology and American Economic Growth.* New York: Harper & Row, 1972.

Sokoloff, Kenneth L. "Inventive Activity in Early Industrial America: Evidence from Patent Records, 1790–1846." *Journal of Economic History* 48 (1988): 813–50.

———. "Was the Transition from the Artisanal Shop to the Nonmechanized Factory Associated with Gains in Efficiency? Evidence from the U.S. Manufactures Censuses of 1820 and 1850." *Explorations in Economic History* 21 (1984): 351–82.

Temin, Peter. "Manufacturing." In *American Economic Growth: An Economist's History of the United States,* ed. Lance E. Davis et al. New York: Harper & Row, 1972.

———. "Steam and Water Power in the Early 19th Century." *Journal of Economic History* 26 (1966): 187–205. Also reprinted in *The Reinterpretation of American Economic History,* ed. Robert Fogel and Stanley Engerman. New York: Harper & Row, 1971.

Terrill, Tom E. "Eager Hands: Labor for Southern Textiles, 1850–1860." *Journal of Economic History* 36 (1976): 84–99.

Uselding, Paul. "Factor Substitution and Labor Productivity Growth in American Manufacturing, 1839–1899." *Journal of Economic History* 32 (1972): 670–81.

―――. "Henry Burden and the Question of Anglo-American Technological Transfer in the Nineteenth Century." *Journal of Economic History* 30 (1970): 312–37.

―――. "A Note on the Inter-Regional Trade in Manufactures in 1840." *Journal of Economic History* 35 (1976): 428–37.

Uselding, Paul, and W. Douglas Morgan. "Technical Progress at the Springfield Armory." *Explorations in Economic History* 9 (1972): 269–90.

Williamson, Jeffrey. "Urbanization in the American Northeast." *Journal of Economic History* 25 (1965): 592–608.

Williamson, Jeffrey, and Joseph Swanson. "The Growth of Cities in the American Northeast, 1820–1870." *Explorations in Entrepreneurial History,* 2nd series, 4 (Supplement) (1966).

Zevin, Robert B. "The Growth of Cotton Textile Production After 1815." In *The Reinterpretation of American Economic History,* ed. Robert Fogel and Stanley Engerman. New York: Harper & Row, 1971.

―――. *The Growth of Manufacturing in Early Nineteenth-Century New England.* New York: Arno Press, 1975.

CHAPTER 11

Economic Change and Labor's First Stirrings

Although the greater part of the U.S. population before 1860 was rural and self-employed on farms and in craftshops, the rapid industrialization, urbanization, and technological and organizational changes of the preceding decades foreshadowed a massive transformation in the way people earned their livings. The change to working for an employer had serious consequences, and the depersonalization of relations between employer and employee created tensions that would one day lead to serious disruption. But before the Civil War most workers were disposed to accept their status, even while the more aggressive stirred the beginnings of the "labor movement." To relate to these developments, we must study the early American workers at work. But before we do that, it is necessary to briefly reassess the economic background and demographic profile in which labor's first stirrings began in the United States.

ECONOMIC GROWTH AND WEALTH CONCENTRATION

Of course, periods of prosperity or hardship for the worker were effected both by short-term fluctuations and by the secular trend of economic progress. Sometimes reinforcing the secular trends and sometimes running counter to them were cyclical fluctuations ranging in duration from several months to several years. It should be recalled from Chapter 7 that in the period from the end of the Revolution to the end of the War of 1812, oscillations were frequent and wide, reflecting the changing fortunes of the European belligerents and the vagaries of international politics. The 1816–57 period contained two crises of great severity; the panics of 1819 and 1837. Each crisis was followed by years of deflation and distress.[1] Yet the boom

---

[1] After the contraction of 1837–38, there was a substantial recovery that peaked in 1839 and then disappointingly vanished.

of 1834–37, with its rapidly rising incomes, full employment, inflation, and speculation (in land rather than in securities), foreshadowed the recurrent upward surges of activity that characterized the growth of the economy. In 1843, a long period of prosperity began, marred by a brief crisis in 1854 and a short, nasty depression from 1857 to 1858. These years just preceding the Civil War nevertheless provided evidence of the kind of sustained forward movement of which the economy was capable.

Did these components of business cycles, the periods of surges and of stagnation or decline, counterbalance each other or was there a positive long-run trend to the growth of income per capita? Was there a unique turning point, such as 1843, when economic growth clearly accelerated?

Reflecting on the evidence of colonial growth in Chapter 5, we recall that incomes per capita in the various regions revealed different periods of advancing surges and years of stagnation. And there was a modest upward secular trend, probably around 0.5 percent per year overall, 1700–75. Further, in Chapter 7, the evidence indicated economic decline, or at the very best stagnation, in per capita incomes from the 1770s to the early 1790s. Thanks to the pioneering work of Paul David we have substantial and persuasive evidence to show that real gross domestic product per capita did grow quite substantially from 1790 to 1860 at a rate of nearly 1.3 percent yearly.[2]

By 1840, per capita real GDP was probably 60 percent greater than it had been at the turn of the century. To be sure, growth in per capita income did not proceed steadily during these years. As emphasized in Chapter 7, per capita incomes increased substantially from 1793 to the embargo of 1807. They subsequently fell somewhat, but then at least regained their 1800 levels by the depression of 1818–19. From 1820 to the middle 1830s, per capita real GDP may have grown at an average rate of 2.5 percent, only to fall to an average rate of 0.6 percent per annum from the middle 1830s to the middle 1840s.

Before David's work, W. W. Rostow had popularized a view that the American economy experienced a unique "take-off" of economic growth from 1843 to 1860 followed by a "sustained drive to maturity."[3] David's evidence has demolished this view. The acceleration of per capita income that began about 1843 "was part of a broader pattern of recurring variations of the per capita product growth rate and had been anticipated by a similar,

---

[2] Paul A. David, "New Light on a Statistical Dark Age: U.S. Real Product Growth Before 1840," *American Economic Review* 57 (1967):294–306, and "The Growth of Real Product in the United States Before 1840: New Evidence, Controlled Conjectures," *Journal of Economic History* 27 (1967):151–97.

[3] W. W. Rostow's *The Stages of Economic Growth* (Cambridge: Cambridge Univ. Press, 1961), esp. pp. 7–10, 36–58, was an extraordinarily influential book, and offered a stage model of growth different from Karl Marx's. Policy makers in many underdeveloped countries were particularly influenced by it.

possibly more pronounced surge of growth which came to an end in the mid-1830s. . . . When this approach is adopted, very serious doubts arise regarding the occurrence of any 'sharp break in the trend,' let alone an 1843–1860 'take-off,' or the putative upward shift 'not very long before 1839.' " [4]

In any case, the overall progress of labor during this period was largely the result of the many diverse forces that propelled economic growth and raised the standard of living and the conditions of work and employment. The gains of the period were broadly felt, but they were not shared equally. There was a sharp advance in the concentration of wealth between 1774 and 1860, denoting a distinct break with the pattern of stabilized aggregate wealth concentration prevalent during the colonial period. In 1774, 12.6 percent of total assets were held by the top 1 percent of free wealth holders, and the richest 10 percent held slightly less than one-half of total assets. By 1860 the wealthiest 1 percent held 29 percent of U.S. total assets, while the top 10 percent held 73 percent.[5] In short, the share held by the richest 1 percent more than doubled, and that of the top decile jumped by almost one-half of its previous level. There are no statistical peculiarities to these measures and Jeffrey Williamson and Peter Lindert emphasize their broad impact: "the movement toward wealth concentration occurred within regions, just as it seems to have occurred within given age groups, among native and foreign born, and within rural and urban populations." [6] Further work by Jeremy Atack and Fred Bateman adds to this perspective. They show that in 1860 wealth was more equally distributed in northern rural areas than in the cities or in the rural South.

Changes in the distribution of wealth and income occurred among regions as well as among people. Table 11-1 shows estimates of income levels by region in 1840 and 1860. It shows the industrializing Northeast growing more rapidly than the other regions. The Old South was poorer relatively and stagnating. The new cotton South, the West South Central area, was

---

[4]David, "The Growth of Real Product," p. 156. For another assessment of growth in post-colonial years, see Lance E. Davis, Richard E. Easterlin, and William N. Parker, et al., *American Economic Growth* (New York: Harper & Row, 1972), esp. pp. 19–35. Over the period 1710–1840, Robert Gallman concludes, "the performance of the American economy, as measured by per-capita product, was probably increasing at a rising rate."

David's estimates, we should note, have not gone unchallenged. Gallman considers David's growth estimates too high, and Diane Lindstrom's regional study of the Philadelphia area reveals that growth was lower there in the pre-1840 period than David's figures show. See Robert Gallman, "The Statistical Approach," in *Approaches to American Economic History*, ed. George R. Taylor and Lucias Ellsworth (Charlottesville: Univ. of Virginia Press, 1971); and Diane Lindstrom, "American Economic Growth Before 1840: New Evidence and New Directions" *Journal of Economic History* 39 (1979):289–302.

[5]Jeffrey G. Williamson and Peter H. Lindert, *American Inequality, A Macroeconomic History* (New York: Academic Press, 1980), p. 36.

[6]Williamson and Lindert, p. 46

TABLE 11-1   Per Capita Income Before the Civil War in 1860 Prices

	Total Population		Free Population	
	1840	1860	1840	1860
National Average	$ 96	$128	$109	$144
North	109	141	110	142
Northeast	129	181	130	183
North Central	65	89	66	90
South	74	103	105	150
South Atlantic	66	84	96	124
East South Central	69	89	92	124
West South Central	151	184	238	274

Source: Robert W. Fogel and Stanley L. Engerman, "The Economics of Slavery," in *The Reinterpretation of American Economic History* (New York: Harper & Row, 1971), p. 335.

the richest region in 1840 but slipping somewhat relative to the new industrializing Northeast. These conclusions hold for comparisons using either the total population or only the free population to determine income per capita.

Thomas Jefferson's egalitarian dream of a strong, free democratic nation of contented individualistic small farmers was only a dream. The forces of the industrial revolution had leaped the Atlantic from Great Britain. The famed traveler and commentator Alexis de Tocqueville (1839) warned of the growing concentrations of wealth. He feared that the rise of an industrial elite would destroy the basis of American egalitarianism:

> I am of the opinion . . . that the manufacturing aristocracy which is growing up under our eyes is one of the harshest that ever existed . . . the friends of democracy should keep their eyes anxiously fixed in this direction; for if a permanent inequality of conditions and aristocracy . . . penetrates into [America] it may be predicted that this is the gate by which they will enter.[7]

POPULATION AND IMMIGRATION, 1790–1860

Changes in the U.S. population were dramatic during the early national and antebellum periods. Population data in Table 11-2 show an underlying rate of advance that measures 3.3 percent per annum. No European nation showed any such increase over this period, not even by half. The average (median) age was increasing from about 16 to 19 years, but still youthfully dominated. Consequently that population could sustain exceptionally high

---

[7] As quoted in Williamson and Lindert, pp. 37–38.

TABLE 11-2   Basic Population Data, 1790–1860

Year	Population (in millions)			Percentages	
	Total	White	Nonwhite	Nonwhite	Urban
1790	3.9	3.2	0.7	17.9	5.2
1800	5.3	4.3	1.0	18.9	6.1
1810	7.2	5.9	1.3	18.1	7.3
1820	9.6	7.9	1.8	18.8	7.2
1830	12.9	10.5	2.3	17.8	11.7
1840	17.1	14.2	2.9	17.0	10.8
1850	23.3	19.6	3.6	15.5	15.2
1860	31.5	26.9	4.5	14.3	19.4

Source: *Historical Statistics,* 1960, series A 2, 45, 46, 195.

birth rates (50 to 55 births per 1,000 before 1850 compared to 15 per 1,000 today). Because American death rates were similar to those in Europe at this time, it was largely the birth rate that powered this exceptional rate of population growth.

This high rate of natural increase was most powerfully felt between 1790 and the mid-1820s when only about 250,000 new settlers arrived from foreign shores. In the decade of the 1820s, the influx from abroad was still less than 150,000, but as shown in Figure 11-1, immigration grew substantially in the 1830s. In the mid-1840s it skyrocketed. Immigration accounted for 2–3 percent of the total U.S. population growth in 1820–25, and between 25 and almost 33 percent in 1845–60. Table 11-3 shows the origin of this large wave of immigration. As shown, nationals of three countries constituted the overwhelming majority of newcomers. A steady stream of immigrants from England flowed into the United States until a decade after the Civil War. The Irish and the Germans came in ever-increasing numbers, repelled by conditions at home and attracted by economic opportunities in a new land. Thanks to the California Gold Rush, which drew hundreds of thousands West, attractive opportunities opened up for the new arrivals. The tragic potato famine of 1845–47 precipitated the heavy Irish emigration that lasted well into the 1850s. Fleeing starvation and the oppression of hated absentee landlords, the Irish found employment as common laborers and factory hands. The census of 1850 reported nearly 1 million Irish in the United States, 40 percent of them in large cities, where their "shanty towns" became the notorious slums of the era. The Germans came only a little later, following the failure of the democratic and nationalistic revolutions of 1848. Within 15 years, 1.3 million had arrived. Most Germans, having a little capital, settled on farms in the Midwest, but almost one-third of them swelled the populations of booming cities like Cincinnati, Chicago, Milwaukee, and St. Louis. Between 1820 and 1860, the population of the

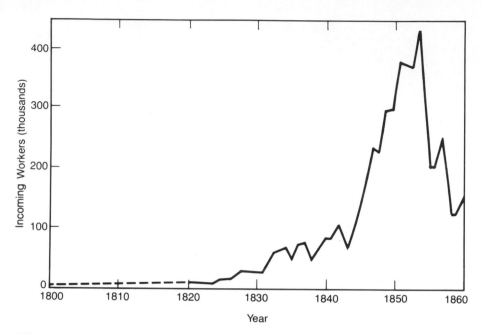

FIGURE 11-1   Additions to the U.S. Labor Force from Migration, 1800–1860: Laborers came in huge numbers during the post-1845 period to a nation rich in land and rapidly increasing its stock of capital. Famine in Ireland and domestic unrest in Germany sent millions of immigrants across the ocean to America.

country tripled to 31.5 million. The density of the population—only four and a half persons per square mile in 1790—was almost eight persons per square mile in 1850.

The distribution of the labor force was markedly different in 1860 than in 1810, as we observe from evidence provided by Stanley Lebergott, shown in Table 11-4. Mining took one of the biggest jumps, but more importantly, by 1860 there were over 1.5 million workers in manufacturing, a 20-fold increase in a half century. Agricultural employment continued to be the predominant occupation, but it grew only threefold in 1810–60. Immigration was also having its effects on the composition of the labor force. By

TABLE 11-3   Average Yearly Immigration by Origin, 1845–60 (in thousands)

Years	Total	Great Britain	Ireland	Germany	Other
1845–50	233	34	107	66	26
1851–55	350	47	139	129	35
1856–60	170	38	44	61	27

Source: *Historical Statistics*, 1958, Series C, pp. 88–114.

TABLE 11-4   Labor Force Distribution, 1810–60 (in thousands)

Year	Total	Agriculture	Fishing	Mining	Construction	Manufactures	Transportation	Trade	Services
1810	2,330	1,950	6	11	—	75	60	—	82
1820	3,135	2,470	14	13	—	—	50	—	130
1830	4,200	2,965	15	22	—	—	70	—	190
1840	5,660	3,570	24	32	290	500	112	350	285
1850	8,250	4,520	30	102	410	1,200	155	530	430
1860	11,110	5,880	31	176	520	1,530	225	890	715

Source: Adapted from Stanley Lebergott, *Manpower in Economic Growth: The American Record Since 1800* (New York: McGraw-Hill, 1964), p. 510.

1860 women constituted only one-fifth of the manufacturing labor force, indicating the lessening *relative* importance of textile manufacture and the competition of cheap immigration labor, most of which was male. Like today, this was a period of significant change in women's social roles, but then the trend was toward domestic pursuits. The cotton-textile industry still employed the most females (many of whom were children), and the clothing and boot and shoe industries were second and third in this respect, ahead of woolen textiles.

WAGE DIFFERENTIALS

When American industry started to develop in the early nineteenth century the wages of adult laborers were much higher in the United States than in England or other countries. Table 11-5 is based on work by Nathan Rosenberg and shows pay differentials classified by various skills for 1820–21. By and large these pay differentials are attributable to the fact that a floor under the remuneration of labor in industry was set by rewards in agriculture. Well into the 1800s, there were no insuperable obstacles, either of distance or expense, to obtaining a fertile farm. Output per worker in agriculture was relatively high, and the course of agricultural technology in the early nineteenth century increased output per person. Moreover, farmers in America, who ordinarily owned their own land, received, in addition to their own wages and those of their families, elements of rent and profit that in England went to the landlord and the tenant farmer, as distinguished from the agricultural laborer. Finally, American farmers always stood to gain from appreciation in land values as the country's population moved westward and transportation improvements brought more farmlands closer to market.

However hard the lot of antebellum laborers by today's standards, workers in the United States continued to be well-off compared to workers in England. Sharp increases in immigration during the 1830s and 1840s, along with the drift of settlement opportunities ever farther from the urban East,

TABLE 11-5   Wage Differentials Between England and the United States, 1820–21
(English wage = 100)

Workers	U.S. Wage
Skilled	
Carpenter	150
Mason	147
Best machine makers, forgers, etc.	77 to 90
Ordinary machine makers	114 to 129
Unskilled	
Common laborer	135
Farm laborer	123 to 154
Servant maid	149 to 224
Common mule spinners in cotton mills	106 to 137
Common mule spinners in woolen mills	115
Weavers on hand looms	122
Women in cotton mills	102 to 153
Women in woolen mills	128
Boys—10 to 12 years old	115

Source: Adapted from Nathan Rosenberg, "Anglo-American Wage Differences in the 1820s," *Journal of Economic History* 27 (1967): p. 226.

led to a narrowing of the wage differential between American and British labor; even so, the floor for U.S. industrial wages was, by consensus of voluminous testimony, relatively high until 1860.

More importantly perhaps from the perspective of free American workers was the change in relative wages among various "grades" or skill levels of workers. During the first decades of the nineteenth century, as throughout most of the colonial period, the premiums paid for artisan skills in the United States were typically less than those paid in England. Note, however, the evidence in Table 11-5 shows that this was not uniformly true. By "premiums" we mean the extra compensation paid to skilled labor above earnings to unskilled labor. Skilled U.S. workers typically earned more than skilled British workers, but the skilled to unskilled U.S. wage ratio was lower than the skilled to unskilled English wage ratios as revealed in Table 11-5. This is most clearly evident in the machinists skill category when compared to common or farm labor.

The relatively low premium paid for skilled labor in early nineteenth-century America resulted particularly from such causes as the greater pulling power of agricultural expansion on unskilled labor and the higher proportion of skilled British migrants entering the United States before mass migration began.[8] By the 1820s, however, this premium began to advance,

---

[8]See H. J. Habakkuk, *American and British Technology in the Nineteenth Century* (Cambridge: Cambridge Univ. Press, 1962).

TABLE 11-6   Ratios of Daily Wages of Machinists and Common Laborers in Urban
             Massachusetts, 1825–1860

Year	Percent
1825	150
1831–40	155
1837	185
1845	169
1841–50	190
1851–60	220

Source: C. D. Wright, *Comparative Wages, Prices, and Cost of Living* (Boston: Wright and Potter, 1889), pp. 22, 54, and 55. As quoted in Williamson and Lindert, p. 71.

thus significantly widening the U.S. pay differential between skilled and unskilled workers. For example, Table 11-6 shows the ratio of machinists' daily wages to those of common laborers in urban Massachusetts during the antebellum period. Although these alterations in pay differentials may have differed somewhat regionally, they were generally representative of a broad pattern of advance.[9]

Such advancing pay differentials disfavoring the unskilled, probably contributed to a growing sense of class consciousness. They certainly contributed to a widening in the distribution of income and wealth, noted previously. Most important perhaps, the workplace and work environment changed; gains in greater manufacturing productivity, to the customer's satisfaction, was at the cost of lost product identification for the worker.

THE FACTORY AND THE WORKER

As the urban centers grew and economic unification progressed, output was sold in larger, more integrated markets. Pressures were great to achieve volume at the expense of artistry, and as Table 11-7 shows, the size of firms grew, as reflected in the number of employees per firm. The small artisanal shops were increasingly giving way to the factory. This growth was apparent in both mechanized, or mechanizing industries (cotton and wool textiles) and in nonmechanized industries (hats, books, and shoes). So mechanization was only part of the story of this trend. The key changes were marked by a minute division of labor, diminishing the proportion and role of workers with general skills. More intense works under careful supervision aimed

---

[9]For further evidence in this point see Williamson and Lindert, pp. 70–75. For work challenging this view and based on labor contracts at military installations, see Robert A. Margo and Georgia C. Villaflor, "The Growth of Wages in Antebellum America: New Evidence," *Journal of Economic History* 47 (1987):837–96.

TABLE 11-7   Number of Employees per Northeastern Manufacturing Firm, 1820 and 1850

	1820		1850		Ratio of Firm Size in 1850 to that In 1820
	Number of Employees	Number of Firms Observed	Number of Employees	Number of Firms Observed	
Boots and shoes	19.1	15	33.6	72	1.76
Cotton textiles	34.6	92	97.5	856	2.82
Flour and grist milling	2.4	90	1.8	5,128	0.75
Glass	56.9	8	64.6	76	1.14
Hats and caps	8.4	32	17.0	812	2.02
Iron and iron products	19.5	73	24.2	1,562	1.24
Liquors	2.7	165	5.0	633	1.85
Paper	14.3	33	22.4	12	1.57
Tanning	3.8	126	4.2	3,233	1.11
Wool and mixed textiles	10.6	107	24.5	1,284	2.31

Source: Adapted from the 1820 and 1850 Census of Manufactures, as provided in Kenneth L. Sokoloff, "Was the Transition from the Artisanal Shop to the Nonmechanized Factory Associated with Gains in Efficiency? Evidence from the U.S. Manufactures Censuses of 1820 and 1850," *Explorations in Economic History* 21 (1984): 354.

for standardized products, an early form of quality control on a large scale. This transition in a nonmechanized shop is described in a study by B. E. Hazard:

> He [Gideon Howard, a manufacturer of shoes in South Randolph, Massachu-setts] had a "gang" over in his twelve-footer who fitted, made and finished: one lasted, one pegged and tacked on soles, one made fore edges, one put on heels and "pared them up," and in cases of handsewed shoes, two or three sewers were needed to keep the rest of the gang busy. . . . These groups of men in a ten-footer gradually took on a character due to specialization demanded by the markets with higher standards and need of speed in output. Instead of all the men working there being regularly trained shoemakers, perhaps only one would be, and he was a boss contractor, who took out from a central shop so many cases to be done at a certain figure and date, and hired shoe-makers who had "picked up" the knowledge of one process and set them to work under his supervision. One of the gang was a laster, another a pegger, one an edgemaker, one a polisher. Sometimes, as business grew, each of these operators would be duplicated. Such work did away with the old seven-year apprenticeship system.[10]

Another characteristic of this transition to larger firms, at least in most manufacturing firms, was the increase in the proportion of the labor force composed of women and children. Larger firms typically exhibited a pro-portionately large share of simple and relatively narrowly defined tasks,

---

[10] Kenneth L. Sokoloff, "Was the Transition from the Artisanal Shop to the Nonmechanized Factory Associated with Gains in Efficiency? Evidence from the U.S. Manufactures Censuses of 1820 and 1850," *Explorations in Economic History* 21 (1984):357.

such as machine tending, starting materials in machines, carrying materials, and other simple tasks. The key problem for many firms was hiring unskilled but able workers, especially before the large waves of immigration in the late 1840s and 1850s. As Pamela Nickless has shown, despite the transition in the late 1840s from predominately women workers to Irish workers, the advance of labor productivity in the mills remained high and steady, averaging 4.5 percent annually in 1836–60.[11]

The Rhode Island and Waltham Systems

Mill and factory owners in the textile industry solved employment problems in two ways. Under one system, called the Rhode Island system, they hired whole families, assigned father, mother, and children to tasks suitable to their strength and maturity, and housed the families in company-constructed tenements. South of Boston, the Rhode Island system was used almost exclusively, partly because child labor was first introduced there in imitation of English methods, and partly because the mule-spinning typical of the area required both heavy and light work. Francis Cabot Lowell and the Boston Associates introduced the Waltham system, under which women in their late teens and early twenties were brought together to form the nucleus of a labor force for large factories. Housed in dormitories—or boarding houses—they remained under the careful supervision of matrons who kept any taint of disreputability from the young women.

What about the conditions under which these early factory people worked? Hours of work were unbelievably long. A 12-hour day was not considered at all unreasonable, and half an hour off for meals was standard. From sunrise to sunset, it was possible to operate machinery without artificial light, and in wintertime candles furnished enough illumination to permit operation on into the evening. Because of the slow speeds of the early machines, the work pace was not great; for this reason women and children could work a 72-hour week without physical breakdown. By mid-twentieth-century standards, wages were pitifully low, but a family under the Rhode Island system earned enough to keep alive and enjoy a few comforts.

Young women under the Waltham system were better off; they spent half their weekly wage of $2.50 to $3.00 on room and board and were able to save money. Both families and single people worked under a paternalistic regime in which the concern of the employers was largely for the morals and behavior of the workers. As long as the level of living kept workers reasonably efficient, it was considered proper, and in the interests of strengthening character, to keep luxuries and leisure time to a minimum.

The life of a New England textile worker was tiresome and drab, although it was no worse than the life of a poor New England farmer, whose dawn

---

[11]Pamela J. Nickless, "Changing Labor Productivity and the Utilization of Native Women Workers in the American Cotton Textile Industry, 1825–1860," *Journal of Economic History* 38 (1978):288.

The factory labor force—as this photo and the drawing opposite suggest—was in significant part composed of women and children. Judging from the expression on their faces, the prospect of such work was no reason to rejoice.

to dusk regimen left little time for pleasure or intellectual growth in the household. Young women might find escape from the boredom and isolation of farm life by going to work in a factory; or they might join their mothers in handweaving or making straw hats, palmleaf hats, or shoes. The domestic system provided part-time or even full-time work for both villagers and farmers of the Northeast right up to the end of the 1850s. Pay was low, sometimes only $.25 a day or less, but the work was leisurely, and the income kept many families from penury. Also, work was done at home, so the sociological strains of taking the young out of the home were avoided.

New England factory workers generally escaped the harshness to which their English counterparts were subjected during the first decades of the factory system. Undoubtedly, this was largely because American manufacturers were compelled to maintain a certain standard of decency to attract and hold the labor they required. Nor does evidence show that American factory owners were cruel to children, as some English employers were.

An early start for crowds of factory workers of all ages. For them a 12-hour day was not considered at all unreasonable and half an hour off for meals was standard.

It was in the cities that the most negative aspects of industrialization were first witnessed, both in England and the United States. America's city employees fared less well than country people; unable to eke out an existence by farming or fishing in the cities, they were subject to the artful exploitation of merchant employers.[12] "Sweated" workers slaved 14–16 hours a day in the garment industries of New York, Philadelphia, and Boston, and common laborers sold their services for a pittance to transportation companies and urban building contractors. Factory and mill workers found themselves in an unenviable position as competition from immigrant labor

---

[12] The word *exploitation* is one commonly used in socialist writing, and there is some point in making its technical, economic meaning clear here. Workers are said to be "exploited" when they do not receive, in any time period, an amount equal to the "value of their marginal product"; that is, a worker is exploited when he or she does not receive wages equal to what he or she, in combination with the other agents of production, contributes to the value of the output. This contribution can be determined by holding all the conditions of employment constant, removing the worker from the combination, and observing how much output (and consequently, its value) declines. To Marxians, of course, the word is more sinister, meaning the failure of labor to receive the combined product of *all* the factors.

retarded the growth in real wages. Whatever the long-run benefits of immigration, its immediate effect was to dilute the gains domestic American workers had obtained from rapidly increasing industrial productivity.

THE EARLY LABOR MOVEMENT

Many economists argue that the original labor-management problem sprang from the separation of workers from their tools.[13] Like most generalizations, this one has its uses, but it may lead the unwary interpreter to make false inferences. The Industrial Revolution placed great numbers of laborers in a position of uncertainty and insecurity, making them dependent on the vagaries of economic fluctuations and the mercy of employers. Yet the first impetus to a genuine labor movement was furnished by craftsmen who were by no means separated from their tools. The ever-increasing numbers of factory workers became articulate and powerful only with the passage of time. At first, factory workers were little more adept at organizing than were day laborers, and their bargaining strength was slight. In the first half of the nineteenth century, factory operatives, except for the influence they could exert at the polls, served labor's causes chiefly by demonstrating how rising industrialism might create permanent class distinctions.

Organization: Economic Motivation

In colonial days, craftsmen of the same trade banded together in benevolent and protective guild associations, but until just before the Revolution there seem to have been no organizations that could be called unions. Beginning in the 1790s, craftsmen in Philadelphia, New York, and Boston founded the prototypes of the modern unions. Most of the societies were established in the vain hopes of securing increases in real wages (that is, of pushing up money wages faster than the prices of consumer goods), although attempts were made to gain shorter working hours, to establish and maintain a closed shop, and to regulate the conditions of apprenticeship. Invariably, there was considerable fraternal motivation; people who made a living in the same way easily forged a social bond. In nearly all the major cities, shoemakers (cordwainers) and printers were among the first to form "workingmen's societies," and carpenters, masons, hatters, riggers, and tailors also found it worthwhile to organize.

   The early craft societies were transitory. Many of the unions of the 1790s were established to meet particular objectives and, succeeding or failing, passed quickly out of existence. Apparently, the Philadelphia cordwainers,

---

[13]Artisans, no matter how inexperienced, had always owned the customary implements of their trade. When the artisans became factory workers, the capitalists furnished their equipment.

who maintained a union from 1794 to 1806, were the first to keep their organization in operation for more than a few years. Two influences worked against permanence. One was the cyclical nature of economic activity; the other was the attitude of the courts, which before 1850 were uniformly hostile toward union activity.

Union membership always rose rapidly during prosperous periods and declined just as rapidly with the onset of depression. On the economic upswing, everything was favorable to organizing endeavors. Price rises in commodities, and increases in rents and wages, invited collective action. Nor did workers fear the wrath of employers due to union activity, because when jobs were plentiful, employer tolerance was high. On the downswing labor's advantage was undone. As general unemployment prevailed, those fortunate enough to have jobs accepted wage cuts rather than go hungry. Attempts by unions to resist wage reductions were met by the counterefforts of belligerent employers, who themselves frequently banded together. Union members, when called on to strike rather than take lower wages, usually withdrew from the society, because they knew the employer could hire non-union labor to break the strike.

In good times as well as bad, there was always the threat and sometimes the actuality of court action to hinder and thwart organizational efforts. Conservative judges, in their instructions to juries, contended that union action per se was illegal. Societies of workers were considered conspiracies under English common law, a conspiracy being defined as "a confederacy of two or more, by indirect means to injure an individual or to do any act, which is unlawful or prejudicial to the community." A doctrine developed in England during the late Middle Ages was thus applied some 500 years later to restrict the unionization of craftsmen. In the famous case of the Pittsburgh Cordwainers in 1815, the judge contended that both the master shoemakers *and* the journeymen were coerced:

> "No shoemaker dare receive one who worked under price, or who was not a member of the society. No master workman must give him any employment, under the penalty of losing all his workmen." Moreover, "a conspiracy to prevent a man from freely exercising his trade, or particular profession, in a particular place, is endictable. Also, it is an endictable offense, to conspire to compel men to become members of a particular association, or to contribute towards it."[14]

The jury in this case agreed that the master shoemakers, the journeymen, and the public were endangered by the association of journeymen and returned a verdict of guilty of conspiracy, although the court fined the defendants only $1 each and the prosecution costs. Judgments against unions

---

[14] From Commons' *A Documentary History of American Industrial Society,* vol. 4 (Glendale: Arthur H. Clark), pp. 82, 83.

were not severe, and the climate remained favorable for unions until 1818. It took the depression of 1819–20 to wipe out most of the societies.

From 1824 until 1837 there was a gradual resurgence of craft unions. Gathering momentum after 1833, the movement reached substantial proportions, and had it not been for the devastating severity of the economic slump that began in the late 1830s and extended well into the 1840s, American labor might have attained a position at mid-century that, in fact, it was not to reach until around 1900. As it was, however, union members before 1860 never exceeded 1 percent of the total labor force. Nevertheless, in addition to the political gains made in these years, unions progressed in two directions:

1. *The technique of bargaining collectively was learned, and aggressive unions began to use the weapons of the strike and boycott with skill and daring.* The *closed shop*—an agreement whereby membership in a recognized union is made a condition of employment—was soon tested as an instrument for maintaining union security. The benevolent and protective aims of labor organizations tended to disappear, and militancy replaced early hesitance and reluctance to act.

2. *The rapidly increasing number of individual societies began to coalesce.* Local federations and then national organizations appeared. In 1827, unions of different crafts in Philadelphia federated to form a "city central" or "trades' union"—the Mechanics' Union of Trade Associations. Six years later the societies in New York established a General Trades' Union. In the next three years, city centrals were formed in several major cities—not, as might be supposed from the modern functions of such organizations, to exchange information or engage in political activities, but for the more pressing purpose of aiding individual unions engaged in battle with employers. Attempts at organization on a national scale followed. In 1834, the General Trades' Union, New York's city central, called a national convention of these city federations, which resulted in the foundation of a National Trades' Union. At the same time, some of the craft societies began to see the advantages to be gained from a national organization along strict craft lines, and in 1835 and 1836 no less than five national unions of this type were established. The strongest of these were formed by the shoemakers and the printers.

However remarkable these early gains were, labor's minority elite, the craftsmen, were the primary beneficiaries. *Factory workers and home workers under the domestic system were almost completely outside the union movement.* So too, of course, were all slaves, domestic workers such as housewives, and most other workers. There are records of occasional organizations of factory hands in the textile industry, but these embryonic unions were unstable. Spontaneous strikes occurred from time to time, even in the absence of formal organization, but they were easily broken. It was hard for a factory worker or a laborer and family if the wrath of an employer were incurred. The "blacklist," which was to have a long and dishonorable future, contained the names of those known to be disruptive influences, and its circulation in an area precluded the employment of those who were listed.

The shock of the long depression that began in 1837 brought to an abrupt end the trend toward unionism of the preceding ten years. As unemployment spread, city centrals and national organizations disappeared. So did all but the hardiest locals. For several years, there were only sporadic efforts to revive the unions, and activity was confined to the urban centers of the East. By the early 1840s, it looked as if the energies spent in bringing American trade unionism to some degree of maturity had been wasted.

As unions gathered strength toward the mid-1830s, people of property and their natural allies in the professional classes looked with alarm on what seemed to them a dangerous growth of labor's power. The courts concurred in this view. Two cases reminiscent of the older conspiracy trials were important in checking the union movement. The first was the trial of the Geneva Shoemakers. The journeymen shoemakers of Geneva, New York, had agreed not to work for any master who did not hire union workers. One master hired a nonunion member at below-union rates, and the other workers in the shop promptly struck. For refusing to work, the journeymen were indicted and convicted for criminal conspiracy. The case was appealed to the State Supreme Court, and Chief Justice Savage upheld the conviction on the grounds that such union action was harmful to trade. "It is important to the best interests of society," he said, "that the price of labor be left to regulate itself. . . . Competition is the life of trade." Meanwhile, in New York City, the Society of Journeyman Tailors had secured an increase in wage rates for its members only to have them later reduced by a combination of master tailors. A strike, accompanied by much strife, ensued. "Dungs," as scabs were then called, were hired by the masters to break the strike, with violent results. After Justice Savage handed down his decision in the Geneva Shoemakers case, the master tailors charged 20 of the journeymen with conspiracy. Again, the strike was the offense. The judge followed Justice Savage in his charge to the jury, and the journeymen were convicted and fined heavily. As a result of the trial judge's contention that American "trades and tradesmen" had hitherto flourished without the aid of combinations and that the unions must therefore have been "of foreign origin . . . and upheld by foreigners," there was much indignation among labor supporters over the outcome of the trial. In two similar cases, union members were acquitted, but the legality of union activity was still very much in question.

A definite turning point came in the now famous case of *Commonwealth v. Hunt*. In the fall of 1840, Hunt and other members of the Boston Bootmakers' Society were hauled into municipal court for attempting to enforce a closed shop. Again, after a strict charge from a judge who felt that such union activities could lead only to a "frightful despotism," the accused were convicted. The case was appealed to the Supreme Court of the Commonwealth of Massachusetts, and in 1842 Chief Justice Lemuel Shaw handed down a monumental decision that set a precedent on one point and opened the way to more liberal decisions on another. First he held that a combination of union members was not criminal unless the object of the combination were criminal; the mere fact of organization implied no illegal conspiracy. Second, he asserted the doctrine that union members were within their rights in pressing for a closed shop and in striking to maintain union security. Justice Shaw was not a radical, nor was he particularly sympathetic with labor's cause, but he was well aware of the economic realities that were pressing labor to act collectively. This decision did not mean that trade unions were free from further court confrontations, but there were no more serious efforts to make the mere fact of organization a criminal offense, and there would henceforth be some reticence about presuming that the use of any and all weapons of the trade unions were socially harmful.

After a tentative revival in the mid-1840s, workingmen's societies made a strong comeback during the 1850s. From 1850 to 1854, the rapidity with which craft unions organized was comparable to that of 20 years earlier, with inevitable retardation accompanying the depression of 1854. Another setback occurred in 1857, but the end of the period showed signs of definite growth. City centrals were back, as were national craft unions, and there were signs that the federations could do more than discuss matters of "mutual interest." Individual unions acquired members who were disposed to greater militance. Funds were accumulated to assist in the successful prosecution of strikes, and serious attempts were made by the stronger crafts to bargain with *all* employers in a particular locality.

Leaders who viewed the labor movement as a whole still had to face the problem presented by the growing masses of workers who had no particular skills. People who worked in factories had always been hard to organize. As the uneducated Irish, largely with agricultural backgrounds, swelled the ranks of industrial workers, the problem became increasingly difficult to solve. Yet the English and Germans were not without a tradition of labor solidarity, and they would be a source of strength in years to come.

Political Gains for Labor

Students of labor history are aware of a certain artificiality in distinguishing between the economic and political aspirations of labor. The two classes of ends merge and blend into one another and are indistinguishable at times. Yet there always have been certain goals that could be reached through the collective action of workers who make their living in the same way, and there have been others that could be achieved only through political processes. Many of labor's demands 100 years ago were for rights that today are considered matters of common decency. But these rights were then objects of desperate striving, and the struggle for them was carried on in an atmosphere of hostility and vindictiveness hardly imaginable today.

Political Suffrage   Labor's political awakening did not come until toward the end of the 1820s, and this awakening was not by mere chance. We do not disparage the founding fathers when we remark that the Constitution was not designed to give great power to the masses. State governments also favored people of wealth and property. During the first decades of our history as a republic, there was a persistent demand by the people for a greater voice in political affairs. The most significant gain in this regard was a broadening of suffrage. Requirements that a person own a minimum amount of real property or pay a certain amount of taxes were modified. The struggle for voting privileges took place in the original thirteen states; only four of the new states entering the Union placed no property or tax-payment qualifications on the right to vote. By the late 1820s, suffrage had been extended sufficiently to enable working men to participate in the elections of the populous states. First to disappear was the property-owning requirement; by 1821, only five states retained it. Five states still set a tax-paying restriction 30 years later, but it was purely nominal.[15] Generally speaking, by 1860 white male citizens of the United States could vote, black males could vote in New York and New England, and alien males could vote in the agricultural Northwest.

Public Education   Although she could not vote herself, Fanny Wright effectively strove for reforms in education. Except in New England, children of the poor received little or no education, and in New England the early training was of poor quality and exhibited a religious slant that was obnoxious to many. Fanny Wright and her followers proposed that the state establish boarding schools for the education of rich and poor children alike, where class distinction would be eliminated. Others, less radical, proposed a simple plan of free public schools. By the mid-1830s progress had been made to broaden educational opportunity, and Albert Fishlow has shown that by mid-century nearly 1 percent of GNP was spent on education (compared to almost 8 percent today). Public common schools were most prevalent in the North, where political concern and efforts were greatest.

Debts, Military Service, and Jail   In the minds of the working people, the most needed reform, next to that of the educational system, was the abolition of imprisonment for debt. Thousands of citizens were jailed annually for failure to meet obligations of a few dollars, and there was understandably fierce resentment against this injustice. The unfairness of the militia systems of the several states, which favored the rich, rankled in the hearts of the poor who were faced with the alternatives of a term in the service or a term in jail. These and other objectives—removing the competition of convict labor and obtaining the right to file liens on the property of employers for back wages—inflamed the spirits of great numbers of laborers, small

---

[15]Comparing the votes for President with the total population, we find that there were two large jumps in the electorate: from 1824 to 1828 (3.2 percent to 9.3 percent) and from 1836 to 1840 (9.6 percent to 13.6 percent).

businessmen, and professional people with a high degree of social consciousness. The militia system did eventually become less onerous, mechanics' "lien laws" were passed in many states, and imprisonment for debt was outlawed in most jurisdictions. But this first movement lost momentum after 1832, as labor turned its energies during the ensuing period of prosperity to advancing the cause of unionization, which in turn collapsed in 1837.

The Ten-hour Day   Although later movements and colorful episodes of the 1840s and 1850s were characterized by impractical utopian schemes (proposed and led by Robert Owen, Charles Fourier, and George Henry Evens) one movement of the mid-century gained quick relief for workers, the struggle for the ten-hour day. That goal was set as early as 1835, but there was then no serious prospect of attaining it. Hope rose in 1840 when Martin Van Buren[16] set a ten-hour day for federal employees. Craftsmen in some trades already worked no longer than ten hours, but factory operatives still labored 12–14 hours a day. In the mid-1840s, New England factory workers added to the agitation for shorter hours. In 1847, the New Hampshire legislature passed the first regulatory law setting a ten-hour upper limit for a day's work, but there was a loophole in it. The law provided that if workers *agreed* to work longer hours, the ten-hour limit might be exceeded. Threatened with discharge if they did not agree, factory hands found themselves no better off. Statutes passed by other state legislatures followed the same pattern, except that laws limiting the workday of children to ten hours did not contain the hated "contract" clause. Perhaps the most important effect of the agitation for regulatory acts was the pressure of public opinion thereby exerted on employers. Many large factories voluntarily established eleven-hour days. By 1860, a ten-hour day was standard in all the craft trades, and already a new standard of eight hours was being timorously suggested.

When we reflect on the temper of the era, this shortening of the workweek seems a notable advance. Labor had argued that acceleration of the working pace made a reduction in work hours mandatory and that a shorter workday would improve employee health and efficiency. To a considerable extent this was true. Given a long workweek of, say, 60 hours, a modest reduction in hours worked per week did not lead to a proportionate decline in output. Reductions in hours, then, were partly offset by a greater intensity of work per hour. Of course, employers did not always agree or consider hour reductions profit-enhancing, but competition for workers forced them to comply with labor's demands for a shorter workweek. It is a credit to the American laborers of more than a century ago that increased time for self-improvement was part of the progress of the period.

Of course, this progress was not shared with those still enslaved. That critical subject awaits us in Chapter 13.

---

[16]This is the same man, eleven years older and now President, who had feared the hazards of the railroad. See his letter to President Jackson in Chapter 9.

SELECTED REFERENCES AND SUGGESTED READINGS

Adams, Donald R., Jr. "Wage Rates in the Early National Period: Philadelphia, 1785–1830." *Journal of Economic History* 28 (1968):404–26.

——— . "Wage Rates in the Iron Industry: A Comment." *Explorations in Economic History* 11 (Fall 1973):89–94.

Crowther, Simon J. "Urban Growth in the Mid-Atlantic States, 1785–1850." *Journal of Economic History* 36 (1976):624–44.

David, Paul. "The Growth of Real Product in the United States Before 1840: New Evidence, Controlled Conjectures." *Journal of Economic History* 26 (1967):151–92.

Dawley, Allan. *Class and Community: The Industrial Revolution in Lynn*. Cambridge: Harvard Univ. Press, 1976.

Dublin, Thomas. *Women at Work: The Transformation of Work and Community in Lowell, Massachusetts, 1826–1860*. New York: Columbia Univ. Press, 1979.

Dunlevy, James A., and Henry A. Gemery. "Economic Opportunity and the Responses of Old and New Migrants to the United States." *Journal of Economic History* 38 (1978):901–17.

Fishlow, Albert. "The Common School Revival: Fact or Fancy?" In *Industrialization in Two Systems*, ed. Henry Rosovsky. New York: Wiley, 1966.

——— . "Levels of Nineteenth-Century American Investment in Education." *Journal of Economic History* 26 (1966):418–36.

Forster, Colin, and G. S. L. Tucker. *Economic Opportunity and White American Fertility Ratios, 1800–1860*. New Haven: Yale Univ. Press, 1972.

Gutman, Herbert. *Work, Culture, and Society in Industrializing America*. New York: Knopf, 1977.

Habakkuk, H. J. *American and British Technology in the Nineteenth Century*. Cambridge: Cambridge Univ. Press, 1962.

Higgs, Robert. "Mortality in Rural America." *Explorations in Economic History* 10 (Winter 1973):177–96.

Leet, Don R. "The Determinants of the Fertility Transition in Antebellum, Ohio." *Journal of Economic History* 36 (1976):359–78.

——— . "Interrelations of Population Density Urbanization, Literacy, and Fertility." *Explorations in Economic History* (Oct. 1977):388–401.

Lebergott, Stanley. "Labor Force." In *American Economic Growth: An Economist's History of the United States*, ed. Lance E. Davis et al. New York: Harper & Row, 1972.

——— . *Manpower in Economic Growth: The American Record Since 1800*. New York: McGraw-Hill, 1964.

Lindstrom, Diane. "American Economic Growth Before 1840: New Evidence and New Directions." *Journal of Economic History* 39 (1979):289–302.

Margo, Robert A., and Georgia C. Villaflor. "The Growth of Wages in Antebellum America: New Evidence." *Journal of Economic History* 47 (1987):873–96.

Neal, Larry, and Paul Uselding. "Immigration, A Neglected Source of American Economic Growth: 1790 to 1912." *Oxford Economic Papers*, 2nd series, vol. 24 (March, 1972).

Nickless, Pamela J. "Changing Labor Productivity and the Utilization of Native Women Workers in the American Cotton Textile Industry, 1825–1866." *Journal of Economic History* 38 (1978):287–88.

Pessen, Edward. *Most Uncommon Jacksonians: The Radical Leaders of the Early Labor Movement*. Albany: State Univ. of New York Press, 1967.

Potter, J. "The Growth of Population in America, 1700–1860." In *Population in History*, ed. D. V. Glass and D. E. C. Eversley. New York: Aldine, 1965.

Rosenberg, Nathan. "Anglo-American Wage Differences in the 1820s." *Journal of Economic History* 27 (1967):221–29.

Ross, Steven J. *Workers on the Edge: Work, Leisure, and Politics in Industrializing Cincinnati, 1788–1890*. New York: Columbia Univ. Press, 1985.

Rostow, W. W. *The Stages of Economic Growth*. Cambridge: Cambridge Univ. Press, 1961.

Rothenberg, Winifred B. "The Emergence of Farm Labor Markets and the Transformation of the Rural Economy: Massachusetts, 1750–1855." *Journal of Economic History* 48 (1988):537–66.

Smith, Merritt R. *Harpers Ferry Armory and the New Technology: The Challenge of Change.* Ithaca: Cornell Univ. Press, 1977.

Sokoloff, Kenneth L. "Was There a Transition from Artisanal Shop to the Nonmechanized Factory Associated with Gains in Efficiency? Evidence from the U.S. Manufactures Censuses of 1820 and 1850." *Explorations in Economic History* 21 (1984):351–82.

Soltow, Lee. "Economic Inequality in the United States in the Period from 1790 to 1860." *Journal of Economic History* 31 (1971):822–39.

Steckel, Richard H. "Antebellum Southern White Fertility: A Demographic and Economic Analysis." *Journal of Economic History* 40 (1980):331–50.

Taylor, George R. "American Economic Growth Before 1840: An Exploratory Essay." *Journal of Economic History* 24 (Dec. 1964).

Uselding, Paul. "Conjectural Estimates of Gross Human Capital Inflow to the American Economy." *Explorations in Economic History* 9 (Fall, 1971):49–62.

Vinovskis, Maris. "Mortality Rates and Trends in Massachusetts Before 1860." *Journal of Economic History* 32 (1972):184–213.

Williamson, Jeffrey. "American Prices and Urban Inequality Since 1820." *Journal of Economic History* 36 (June 1976).

Williamson, Jeffrey G., and Peter H. Lindert. *American Inequality: A Macroeconomic History.* New York: Academic Press, 1980.

Yang, Donghyu. "Notes on the Wealth Distribution of Farm Households in the United States, 1860: A New Look at Two Manuscript Census Samples." *Explorations in Economic History* 21 (Jan. 1984):88–102.

Zabler, Jeffrey F. "Further Evidence on American Wage Differentials, 1800–1830." *Explorations in Economic History* 10 (Fall 1972):109–18.

———. "More on Wage Rates in the Iron Industry: A Reply." *Explorations in Economic History* 11 (Fall 1973):95–99.

CHAPTER 12

Money, Banking, and the Young Economy

THE AMERICAN MONETARY UNIT

Independence from England along with the relinquishment by the states of the right to issue bills of credit (money), made the decision for a national monetary unit and the establishment of modern credit-granting institutions inevitable. Because the early flow of international trade made the Spanish dollar and its subdivisions more plentiful than any other coins in the commercial centers along the American seaboard, it became customary to reckon accounts in terms of dollars. Fortunately for all of us, and especially school children, a decimal system and the dollar was adopted as a unit of account rather than the arithmetically troublesome old English system of pounds, shillings (20 = one pound), and pence (12 = one shilling). The British finally changed to their decimal system in the late 1960s. Thomas Jefferson, who along with Robert Morris and Alexander Hamilton was most responsible for our coinage selection, made the following cogent argument in his 1783 report to Congress:

> The most *easy ratio* of multiplication and division, is that by ten. Everyone knows the facility of Decimal Arithmetic. Everyone remembers, that, when learning Money-Arithmetic, he used to be puzzled with adding the farthings, taking out the fours and carrying them on; adding the pence, taking out the twelves and carrying them on; adding the shillings, taking out the twenties and carrying them on; but when he came to the pounds, where he had only tens to carry forward, it was easy and free from error. The bulk of mankind are schoolboys through life. These little perplexities are always great to them. And even mathematical heads feel the relief of an easier, substituted for a more difficult process. Foreigners, too, who trade and travel among us, will find a great facility in understanding our coins and accounts from this ratio

of subdivision. Those who have had occasion to convert the livres, sols, and deniers of the French; the gilders, stivers, and frenings of the Dutch, the pounds, shillings, pence, and farthings of these several States, into each other, can judge how much they would have been aided, had their several subdivisions been in a decimal ratio. Certainly, in all cases, where we are free to choose between easy and difficult modes of operation, it is most rational to choose the easy.[1]

Jefferson then went on to point out that the dollar was in fact in general use in the states and that people everywhere would readily accept it as the monetary unit. The only difficulty, he said, was that Spanish dollars varied in their content of pure silver. He suggested that proper persons be appointed "to assay and examine with the utmost accuracy possible the Spanish milled dollars of different states in circulation with us" to determine the *average* number of grains in circulating Spanish dollars. This average would then be the number of grains of silver in the new U.S. dollar. Jefferson felt that silver ought to be accepted at the mint at the rate of 15 ounces of silver for one of gold.

These ideas were ultimately translated into law through the work of Secretary of the Treasury Alexander Hamilton. The coinage Act of 1792 stipulated that the dollar would be officially adopted as the American unit of account and defined in terms of both gold and silver. The silver dollar would contain by weight 15 times as much pure silver as the gold dollar would pure gold. This decision for a bimetallic standard proved troublesome over the three-quarters of a century it was legally maintained.

THE BIMETALLIC STANDARD

It is one thing to adopt a bimetallic monetary standard of value, and quite another to maintain it. The problem is that the relative values of gold and silver fluctuate. If the mint ratio always corresponded to the valuation placed on the two metals by those who trade in them, there would be no difficulty in maintaining a bimetallic standard. The mint ratio has never prevailed in the open market for long, however, and the experience of the United States and other countries furnishes plentiful evidence of the futility of trying to keep mint ratios and market ratios in correspondence. Thus, even though a *mint ratio* of 15 to 1 closely approximated the prevailing *market ratio* in

---

[1] Paul Leicester Ford, ed., *The Writings of Thomas Jefferson* (New York and London: Putnam's, 1894), pp. 446–47.

1792, world supplies of and demands for gold and silver were such that the ratio in the market rose gradually during the 1790s to about 15.5 to 1; by 1808 it was 16 to 1 as silver lost value. A *market ratio* of 16 to 1 and a *mint ratio* of 15 to 1, technically, is a relationship in which *silver is overvalued at the mint.* Under such circumstances people can get more for silver at the mint than they can by taking their silver "to market." If the *market ratio* were below the *mint ratio,* at, say 14 to 1, we would say that *gold is overvalued at the mint.* Indeed, if the mint ratio is 15 to 1 and the market ratio is 14 to 1, a profit can be made by melting down silver coins, selling the silver for gold, taking the gold to the mint, and using the newly minted gold coins to repurchase silver at 15 to 1.

For centuries observers had noted that debased coins (those overvalued at the mint) tended to remain in circulation, while full-bodied (or under-valued) coins were either hoarded or exported to pay for imported goods. One naturally paid out debased coins whenever it was possible to pass them off at their nominal value. Popular sayings to the effect that "bad money drives out good money" or "cheap money will replace dear" thus came into various languages. Sir Thomas Gresham, Queen Elizabeth I's master of the mint, is credited with analyzing this phenomenon, which has become known as Gresham's law. For our purposes we may best state the law as follows: *money overvalued at the mint tends to drive out of circulation money undervalued at the mint,* providing that the two monies circulate at face value.

Since silver was overvalued, gold coins soon disappeared from circula-tion. Oddly, it was also hard to keep American silver coins in circulation even when silver was overvalued at the mint. Merchants engaged in the West Indian trade soon discovered that shiny, new American dollars and subsidiary coins could be exchanged abroad for dull Spanish pieces con-taining a somewhat greater amount of silver. The Spanish money was even presented at the U.S. mint to be recoined into American pieces that were then exported. The problem became so bad that in 1806 coinage of the silver dollar was suspended by direction of President Jefferson; not until after the legislation of 1834 was it again struck at the mint. Thus Spanish silver coins and, subsequently, the French five-franc silver piece served as the chief "hard money" in circulation before 1834.

In June of 1834, two acts were passed changing the mint ratio to just a fraction over 16 to 1. Gold was then overvalued at the mint, and even though American coinage of silver had never been so high as it was in the years immediately after 1834, gold slowly began to replace silver, which was either hoarded or exported. Finally in 1857 a law was passed that repealed former acts authorizing the currency of foreign gold or silver coins as legal tender in the payment of debts.

In short, the dollar served very well as a unit of account, to calculate values and set prices. American coins often failed to serve as a medium of exchange, however, because of bimetalism and sound foreign coin substitutes.

BANK NOTES AS PAPER MONEY

Although the Constitution forbade the states to issue paper money, the states did retain the power to create corporations by special franchise. After the commercial boom beginning in 1793 a striking number of banks were established by special state charters. These were entirely new institutions on the American scene, for commercial banks had not existed in the colonies. From three banks before 1790, there were 28 banks in 1800, and 88 by 1811. All but two of these were private state-chartered banks empowered to issue their own paper money.

The bank notes issued by different institutions came to be accepted at widely varying rates. Notes of established, reputable, "specie-paying" banks were taken at their face value—that is, at par—over wide areas. Bills of other banks were received at discounts from 1 or 2 percent up to 50 percent or more. Distance from the city where the issuing bank was located tended to reduce the acceptability of notes. For example, the paper of Baltimore banks circulated at 1 to 2 percent discount in Washington, some 40 miles away, while Washington bills were at 1 to 2 percent discount in Baltimore. However, a bank that did not redeem in gold or silver in a period when specie payments were not generally suspended would find its bills circulating at a discount even in the immediate vicinity.

In many ways a bank note was similar to a bank deposit or check. When a bank made a loan to customers, it gave them the proceeds either in the form of its own (bank) notes, which then circulated as cash, or as a deposit credit against which they could draw checks. Nowadays, of course, banks no longer issue notes, and the paper money that passes from hand to hand is issued by the Federal Reserve; moreover, whenever a firm borrows money today it takes the proceeds as a credit to its account. But during the years before the Civil War, and even for some time after that in rural areas, a bank issued notes much more frequently than it made credits to a customer's account (checking).

In nearly every city there were dealers or brokers who bought and sold bank notes. These note-brokers, or "shavers," made profits by exchanging paper that did not circulate at par in a given area for paper that did. The fees they charged were the counterpart of the fees modern banks charge on deposit accounts. But the note brokers were frequently castigated by prominent citizens, and dissatisfaction with the currency system was widespread.

THE FIRST BANK OF THE UNITED STATES

The first American bank was organized by Robert Morris and established in 1781, with Congress' approval, to help finance the war effort and provide financial organization in those troubled times. However, we usually think of the nation's first central bank as being established ten years later.

Shortly after becoming Secretary of the Treasury, Alexander Hamilton wrote a *Report on a National Bank,* in which he argued for a Bank of the United States. His report shows remarkable insight into both the financial problems of the young country and the economic implications of banking. Hamilton asserted that a "National Bank" would augment "the active or productive capital of a country." By this, he meant that the notes issued by the banks would replace some of the gold and silver money in circulation, which could then be exported in exchange for real goods and services. In future years the United States would not be forced to export simply to acquire its money supply. Notes remained in circulation because of public confidence in them.

As important to Hamilton as the salutary effects of the proposed bank on the economy was the assistance the bank could give the government by lending money to the treasury in times of stress. Moreover, the institution could serve as a fiscal agent for the government by acting as a depository of government funds, making transfers of funds from one part of the country to another, and (Hamilton hoped) serving as a tax-collection agency. Finally, because the bank was to be jointly owned by the government and private shareholders, it would cement the relationship between the fledgling government and leading men of business.[2]

The bill creating the bank followed Hamilton's report closely. There was substantial opposition to it, even in the predominantly Federalist Congress, on the grounds that (1) it was unconstitutional, (2) it would create a "money-monopoly" that would endanger the rights and liberties of the people, and (3) it would be of value to the northern states but not to the agricultural South. The bill was carried on a sectional vote, and Washington signed it on St. Valentine's Day in 1791. But the charter of the bank was limited to 20 years, so further battles lay ahead.

Although the Bank was primarily a private corporation, operated for the profit of its stockholders, it performed invaluable services for the treasury—just as Hamilton had said it would. While it was not a central bank in the more fully developed sense in which its successor institution, the Second Bank of the United States, was to be, its directors showed a remarkable sense of responsibility for maintaining the stability of the banking system as a whole.

Because the Bank's conservative lending policy made it on balance a creditor of the state banks, it continually received a greater dollar volume

---

[2]The federal government bought one-fifth of the $10 million initial capital stock. The government paid for its shares with the proceeds of a $2 million loan extended by the Bank on the security of its *own* stock; the loan was to be repaid in ten equal annual installments. At the start of operations, then, the government participated in the earnings of a privately financed venture without contributing a penny to the original capital.

One of the chief architects
of the Constitution and
policy makers for the new
nation was Alexander
Hamilton, shown here in a
portrait by John Trumbull.

of state-bank notes than state banks received of its obligations. The Bank
was therefore in a position to present the notes of the state banks regularly
for payment in specie, discouraging them from issuing as many notes as
they would have liked. Notes of the United States Bank and its branches
circulated at, or very close to, par throughout the country.[3] At all times,
the Bank held a considerable portion of the gold and silver in the country—
its holdings during the last three years of its existence were probably close
to $15 million, which practically matched the amount held by all state banks.
It made specie loans to commercial banks; the second petition for renewal
of its charter asserted that the state banks generally had the use of at least
one-tenth of the Bank's capital. Although there was no established custom
of using deposits with the Bank of the United States as reserves and no
obligation on its part, legal or customary, to assist other banks in need, in
practice it became a lender of last resort. Thus, the Bank was clearly on its
way to being a central bank when Congress refused to recharter it in 1811.

The Bank also acted as fiscal agent for the government and held most
of the treasury's deposits; in return, the Bank transmitted government funds
from one part of the country to another without charge. After 1800, the

---

[3]By 1800, the Bank had branches in Boston, New York, Baltimore, and Charleston. Branches
were added in Washington and Savannah in 1802 and in New Orleans in 1805.

The first Bank of the United States issued these ten-dollar notes, which were canceled by inking three or four x's on their faces after they became worn.

Bank helped collect customs bonds in cities where it had branches. It further facilitated government business by effecting payments of interest on the public debt, carrying on foreign-exchange operations for the treasury, and supplying bullion and foreign coins to the mint.

In retrospect, the reasons for the continued operation of the United States Bank seem compelling. During the two decades of its existence, there was a well-ordered expansion of credit and a general stability of the currency. Compared to the difficulties before 1791, the money problems of the 1790s and early 1800s were insignificant. The first Bank of the United States helped to give the nation a better monetary system than it had had any reason to hope for in 1791.

But arguments based on cold economic facts are rarely as effective as arguments based on appeals to human emotion and prejudice. Those who opposed the recharter of the Bank made the same points that originally had been advanced when the matter was debated nearly 20 years earlier. They argued that the Bank was unconstitutional and that it was a financial monster so powerful it would eventually control the nation's economic life and deprive the people of their liberties. To these contentions was added a new objection: the Bank had fallen under the domination of foreigners, mostly Britishers. Foreign ownership of stock was about $7 million, or 70 percent of the shares, but about the same percentage of U.S. bonds was owned by foreigners. Only shareholding American citizens could be directors, and foreign nationals could not vote by proxy. Nevertheless, many people felt that the influence of English owners was bound to make itself felt through those American directors with whom they had close business contacts.

Personal politics also mattered. On a number of occasions, Thomas Jefferson had stated his abiding conviction that the Bank was unconstitutional and a menace to the liberties of the people. Although he was no longer

President when the issue of recharter arose, Jefferson's influence in Congress was tremendous. Many of his followers doubtlessly were swayed by his view. But the decisive votes were cast against the Bank as a result of personal antagonism toward Albert Gallatin, who, although a member of Jefferson's party, was a champion of the Bank. In the House, consideration of the bill for renewal of the charter was postponed indefinitely by a vote of 65 to 64. In the Senate, Vice-President George Clinton, enemy of both Madison and Gallatin, broke a 17–17 tie with a vote of nay.

Following the failure to recharter the first Bank of the United States, the number of state banks rose rapidly—from 88 in 1811 to nearly 250 in 1816. This almost threefold increase was not unexpected. There was opportunity to take over the business of the big Bank, and investors felt that without its controls bank profits would increase. The rise in the level of manufacturing activity brought about by the War of 1812 made possible the fulfillment of bank promoters' hopes of high earnings. The sharp increase in note issues, together with deficit financing by the government, led to an inflation that was at least temporarily stimulating to business ventures.

THE SECOND BANK OF THE UNITED STATES

Difficulties of financing the War of 1812 and the sharp inflation following the suspension of specie payments in 1814 convinced people of the need for a second Bank of the United States. It took two years of congressional wrangling and the consideration of no less than six separate proposals before a bill to charter such a bank was passed.

The charter of the second Bank of the United States resembled that of its predecessor. The capital was set at $35 million, four-fifths of it to be subscribed by individuals, firms, or states and the remaining one-fifth by the federal government. Most of the capital was to consist of government bonds, but one-fourth of the private subscription ($7 million) was to be paid in gold or silver coin. There were to be 25 directors, 20 elected by private stockholders and 5 appointed by the president. The main office of the Bank was to be located in Philadelphia, and branch offices were to be established on the initiative either of the directors or of Congress.

The greatest contributions of the second Bank came after 1823, the time of the appointment of Nicholas Biddle as its third president. Sophisticated, widely traveled, and well educated, Biddle typified the early American aristocrat. He had wealth, power, and a mind that enabled him to become not only a master of the business of banking but an economist as good as any in America in the first half of the nineteenth century.

Of course the mundane service functions of the Bank were continued. As an agent of the government, the Bank (1) received and kept all funds of the United States, (2) transferred funds on government account from

President of the second Bank of the United States, archfoe of Andrew Jackson and advocate of central-bank controls, was Philadelphia aristocrat Nicholas Biddle. Some argued that his hauteur cost the Bank its charter; others felt that Wall Street would have done-in Chestnut Street anyway.

one part of the country to another without compensation, and (3) made payments to owners of government bonds and to government pensioners. On several occasions, the Bank even lent money to the government on special terms.

Biddle made his mark in the function of control. Under his leadership there was both a full realization of the potential power of the Bank and a conscious attempt to regulate the banking system according to certain preconceived notions of what *ought* to be done. In the first place, the Bank under Biddle soon became the lender of last resort to the state banks. State banks did not keep their reserves as deposits with the Bank of the United States, but they did come to depend on the second Bank in times of crisis, borrowing specie from it to meet their obligations. *The second Bank was able to meet such demands because it kept a much larger proportion of specie reserve against its circulation than other banks did.* The second Bank also assisted in times of stress by lending to business firms when other banks could not or would not. Because of these practices, many came to regard the big Bank as *the holder of ultimate reserves* of the banking system.

In the second place, as an even more important means of control, the Bank under Biddle developed a policy of regularly presenting the notes of state banks for payment. In the course of business over the years, the Bank always took in more notes from state banks than the state banks received from the Bank. This net redemption against the state banks was no accident. The Bank had to keep its own note issues (including those of its branches) within bounds, so state banks had a reciprocal influence on the institution that was presumably doing the controlling. Nevertheless, the Bank of the United States was definitely in control, and by presenting the notes of state banks for payment in specie, it kept their issues moderate. The Bank not only furnished a currency of its own of uniform value over the entire country, but it reduced to a nominal figure the discount at which the notes of state banks circulated. By the late 1820s, the paper money of the country was, for the time being, in a very satisfactory state.

Nicholas Biddle tried to affect the general economic climate of the United States by alternate expansion and contraction of the Bank's loans. Furthermore, he made the Bank the largest American dealer in foreign exchange and was able to protect the country from severe specie drain when a drain would have meant a harmful contraction of monetary reserves. Moreover, in the 1820s, the problem of making payments over considerable distances *within the country* was not much different from the problem of effecting remittances *between countries*. There was a flourishing business in "domestic exchange," and the Bank obtained a large portion of it.

By 1829, the position of the second Bank of the United States seemed secure. It had grown and prospered. It had attained a shining reputation abroad—so much so that when the Bank of Spain was reorganized in 1829, the Bank of the United States was explicitly copied. Although it had made enemies, there was a wide acceptance of the idea of a "national institution," and there was grudging admittance by those who persistently opposed "the monster" that it had been good for business. Congress had made sporadic attacks on the Bank, but they had been ineffective. Yet the apparent permanence of the Bank was illusory. Its fate had already been sealed.

In 1828, Andrew Jackson was elected to the presidency. Beloved by the masses, Jackson had the overwhelming support of the people during two terms in office, and long ago he had decided against supporting banks in general and the big Bank in particular. As a young man in Tennessee, Jackson had taken in payment for 6,000 acres of land the notes of a Philadelphia merchant that passed as currency. When he gave these notes in payment of goods for his store, he found that they were worthless because the merchant had failed. To make his obligations good, Jackson consequently suffered years of financial difficulty in addition to the loss of his land. Later, he and his business partners often found themselves victims of exorbitant charges by bankers and bill-brokers in both New Orleans and the Eastern cities.[4] On one occasion, Jackson bitterly opposed the establishment of a state bank in Tennessee, and as late as 1826 he worked against the repeal of a law

---

[4]Claude A. Campbell, *The Development of Banking in Tennessee* (published by the author, 1932), pp. 27–29.

prohibiting the establishment of a branch of the Bank of the United States in his home state.

In his first annual message to Congress seven years before the charter of the Bank was to expire, Jackson called attention to the date of expiration, stated that "both the constitutionality and the expediency of the law creating this bank are well questioned by a large portion of our fellow citizens," and speculated that:

> If such an institution is deemed essential to the fiscal operations of the Government, I submit to the wisdom of the Legislature whether a national one, founded upon credit of the Government and its revenues, might not be devised which would avoid all constitutional difficulties and at the same time secure all the advantages to the Government and country that were expected to result from the present bank.

We have the great Democrat's word for it that his statement was toned down by his advisers. It was the beginning of the "Bank War."

We are forced to omit the detailed story of that war. It must be said that Biddle tried to win Jackson's support, but Biddle's efforts were unsuccessful. Henry Clay, charming and popular presidential candidate of the National Republicans (Whigs), finally persuaded Biddle to let him make the question of recharter a campaign issue in the election of 1832. In the summer of that year, there was enough pro-Bank power in the Congress to secure passage of a bill for recharter—a bill Jackson returned, as expected, with a sharp veto message prepared by presidential advisers Amos Kendall and Roger Taney. In that political document, the President contended that (1) the Bank was unconstitutional, (2) there was too much foreign ownership of its shares, and (3) domestic ownership was too heavily concentrated in the East. A central theme ran through the message: the Bank was an instrument of the rich to oppress the poor; an institution of such power and so little responsibility to the people could undo the democracy itself and should be dissolved. Agrarians of the West and South felt that the Bank's conservative policies had restricted the supply of credit to agriculture. But there was also opposition to the Bank from Wall Street, which wanted to overcome Chestnut Street as the nation's financial center. Economics makes strange bedfellows sometimes.

After a furious campaign, Jackson emerged the victor by a substantial margin. He considered his triumph a mandate from the electorate on the Bank question, and the acclaim he was receiving due to his masterful handling of the problem of nullification[5] strengthened his resolve to restrict

---

[5] The principle of nullification, first enunciated by John C. Calhoun in 1828, was that any state could refuse to be bound by a federal statute it considered unjust until three-quarters of the states had agreed to the statute. South Carolina tried to apply the principle in 1832–33 during a dispute over a tariff bill. Jackson's strong stand defeated the attempt.

In this cartoon, Andrew Jackson (left) attacks the many-headed serpent (the second Bank of the United States) with his walking stick (his veto). The largest head is Nicholas Biddle, the Bank's president. The remaining heads represent other officials of the Bank and its branches. Jackson is assisted by Martin Van Buren (center).

the Bank's activities at once. In the fall of 1833, the government discontinued making deposits with the Bank, and editor Greene of the Boston *Post* was moved to write its epitaph: "Biddled, Diddled, and Undone."

But Biddle was not through. Beginning in August 1833 and continuing into the fall of 1834, the Bank contracted its loans sharply and continued its policy of presenting the notes of state banks for payment in specie. Biddle maintained that his actions were necessary to prepare the Bank for liquidation, although there was doubtlessly a punitive motive in the vigor of his actions. In any case, his actions contributed significantly to the brief but definite panic of 1834.

The administration remained firm in its resolve to end the Bank, which became a state bank chartered under the laws of Pennsylvania in 1836. Although stripped of its official status, the United States Bank of Pennsylvania remained the most powerful financial institution in America for a few years. With its resources alone, Nicholas Biddle could still engineer a grandiose scheme to support the prices of cotton and other agricultural staples during the nation's economic troubles of 1837 and 1838. But this last convulsive effort started a chain of events that led to the Bank's failure in 1841, not two years after Biddle's retirement.

ECONOMIC FLUCTUATIONS AND THE SECOND BANK

During the time of Biddle's reign, the economy followed a relatively smooth course with no deep recessions or periods of significant inflation. As shown in Figure 12–1, during the 1820s, the price level slipped downward as the amount of specie in the economy remained roughly constant and the amount of money in the economy rose modestly. Undoubtedly, the growth in the stock of money was less than the growth of the volume of goods exchanged.

Then entirely new conditions began to prevail, and many historians blamed the inflationary bursts of the mid–1830s and ultimately the great depression of 1839–43 on the demise of the second Bank. Certainly, the increases in the money supply and in the price level at that time suggest that the absence of the second Bank may have unleashed irresponsible banking

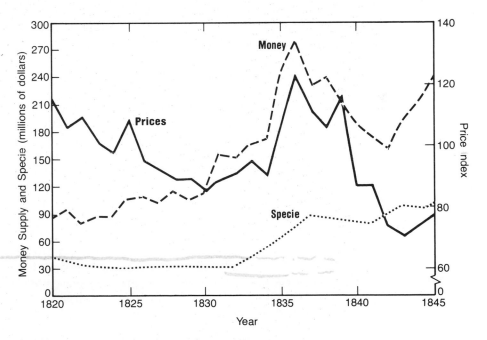

FIGURE 12–1   U.S. Prices, Money, and Specie, 1820–45.

Source: Hugh Rockoff, "Money, Prices, and Banks in the Jacksonian Era," in *The Reinterpretation of American Economic History,* ed. Robert W. Fogel and Stanley L. Engerman (New York: Harper & Row, 1971), Table 1, p. 451.

practices. Moreover, the number of state banks increased from 330 in 1830 to 901 in 1840. Shortly after Jackson's veto, he began withdrawing government funds from the second Bank and placing them in so-called "pet banks." Allegedly, as Biddle's powers ebbed, many "wildcat banks" began to take advantage of the new opportunities to expand credit and their paper note issues recklessly. Did the demise of the second Bank precipitate the economic fluctuations of the period? Did Jackson's politics ultimately lead to the depression of 1839–43?

The answer to both of these questions in the light of recent research is a qualified no. It must be remembered that the United States was still heavily involved in the international economy. The U.S. economy was still greatly influenced by external events. Coincidentally, at the time of the demise of the second Bank, the United States began to import substantial amounts of silver from Mexico, which was undergoing its own political and economic turmoil. These and other flows into the United States from England and France sharply raised the amount of specie in the United States. In addition, steady outflow of specie to China was substantially reduced at this time as Chinese merchants began to accept bills of credit instead of requiring payment in specie. As shown in Figure 12–1, there was a tremendous jump in specie between 1833 and 1837. Since banks generally held specie on reserve and only in fractional amounts of their paper-note issues, as the specie amounts increased, the amount of paper money expanded by a multiple. Therefore, to a considerable extent, the influx of specie explains much of the money increase and inflation. Clearly, then, external forces were very influential in instigating the business cycles of the period.

The banking sector does not appear to have acted irresponsibly during the 1830s, even after Jackson's veto. For instance, the ratio of bank-held reserves to credit outstanding (bank notes) did not decrease.[6] On the whole, banks remained fairly cautious and did not "wildcat," as some have claimed.

But the absence of the second Bank was also important. During Biddle's reign throughout the 1820s and early 1830s, people placed an increasing trust in banks, largely perhaps because of the leadership and sound banking practices of the second Bank. As a result, the proportion of money that people normally held in specie form declined.[7] Their confidence in paper money reached unusually high levels in the 1820s and early 1830s. Then events changed. First came Jackson's veto in 1832. This was followed by the Specie Circular in 1834, which required that most federal land sales must be paid in specie. As prices rose and people's confidence in paper monies waned, more and more people returned paper for specie at their banks. When large numbers of noteholders attempted to do this, the banks were

[6] For this evidence and a pathbreaking reinterpretation of the Bank War, see Peter Temin, *The Jacksonian Economy* (New York: W. W. Norton, 1969), p. 71.
[7] Temin, p. 159.

unable to make the exchanges and banking panics occurred. A strong second Bank might have been able to nip these panics in the bud by acting as a lender-of-last-resort. The final result was a sharp, but temporary, recession in 1837 and finally one of the worst depressions of the century in 1839–43.[8]

AN INDEPENDENT TREASURY

When Andrew Jackson and the Democrats were fighting the recharter of the second Bank of the United States, they seemed unconcerned about the prospect of keeping government funds in state banks. In fact, as we noted, Jackson began to place these funds in certain state institutions—his "pets," to use the opprobrious term coined by the president's critics—beginning in September 1833.[9]

In his view, banks in the hands of those who were "politically friendly" would have preference in receiving government deposits, but "opposition men whose feelings are liberal" might have to do. First of the pet banks was the Union Bank of Maryland, located in Baltimore. Six other selections, ranging from the little-known Moyamensing Bank of Philadelphia to the prestigious Bank of the Manhattan Company in New York, followed during September. By the end of 1833, 22 pets had been chosen, a number that rose to 35 by June 1836, when Congress passed a statute limiting the amount of deposits a bank could hold. The number of pet banks then increased to 96, and as the favored institutions grew in number, political loyalty became a less important consideration than the safety of treasury funds. Yet, of the first 35 deposit banks chosen, only the Bank of Louisville was clearly an opposition bank.

The idea was ultimately advanced to separate the federal treasury from the banking system. The opposition of the Whigs and Eastern Democrats, the private banks, and others, however, was so strong that an independent treasury was not established until the 1840s. More specifically an act was passed in 1840, repealed in 1841, and then finally re-established in 1846.

Henceforth, government officials were "to keep safely, without loaning, using, depositing in banks, or exchanging for other funds than as allowed by this act, all the public money collected by them, or otherwise at any time placed in their possession and custody, till the same is ordered . . . to be transferred or paid out." The federal government was to accept only gold

---

[8]In addition, the Bank of England, concerned over the continuing outflow of specie to the United States, began to call in specie (sell back bonds) in 1837 and thereafter.

[9]Frank Otto Gatell, "Spoils of the Bank War: Political Bias in the Selection of Pet Banks," *American Historical Review* 70 (Oct. 1964): 35. See also Harry N. Scheiber, "The Pet Banks in Jacksonian Politics and Finance, 1833–1841," *Journal of Economic History* 23 (1963): 196–214.

and silver in payment of sums due it. Government funds were to be kept only in the vaults of the treasury at Washington or in those of subtreasuries in various cities.

The difficulties foreseen by the opponents of this method of fiscal separation quickly materialized. During the 75 years or so in which the legislation was in effect, secretaries of the treasury rarely followed either the spirit or the letter of the law; violations began almost as soon as the law was in force. Frequently, treasury officials sought the aid of the banks in transferring funds about the country in order to avoid expensive and dangerous shipments of coin. The transfer of funds was a small problem, however, compared with that occasioned by treasury surpluses, which became usual during the 1850s. As the treasury year after year took in more than it expended, there was a withdrawal from the banks of the gold and silver that constituted their reserves. On occasion the Secretary of the Treasury would get coin back into the banking system by purchasing obligations of the federal government in the open market, though some restriction was placed on such action by a law preventing repurchase of government "stock" at a figure above par. During the financial stringencies of 1853 and 1857 the secretary had to take vigorous action to assist the banks; these open-market operations were only the beginning of varied kinds of manipulation to be required of secretaries in the next half-century. Within a few years of the passage of the law establishing an independent treasury, it became apparent that independence could *not* be maintained.

EXPERIMENTS IN STATE BANKING CONTROLS

The Suffolk System

Though not by conscious design, several important experiments in the states and regions complemented the activities of the second U.S. Bank to provide a more homogeneous currency. Urban banks were persistently confronted with the problem of competing with the circulation of country bank currencies (paper notes). For example, country bank note issues circulated widely in Boston. In 1824 six Boston banks joined with the Suffolk Bank of Boston to create a system for presenting country banks with their notes in volume, thus forcing them to hold higher reserves of specie. Soon after, the country banks agreed to keep deposits in the Suffolk Bank, resulting in the first arrangement of a clearing house for currencies of remote banks. These deposits, a costless source of funds, helped make the Suffolk Bank one of the most profitable in the country. The other Boston banks shared in this profit through their ownership of Suffolk stock. So the arrangement was hardly altruistic. But as a result the prevailing discounts on country bank notes fell. By 1825 country notes passed through this "Suffolk System" at par. Consequently, New England generally was blessed with a uniform currency.

The Suffolk Bank continued as the agency for the clearing of New England notes until 1858, when a rival institution was organized by some new Boston banks and by country banks that resented the dictatorial policies of the Suffolk. Shortly afterward, national banking legislation did away with state bank notes and with the need for such regional systems, but this system was the predecessor to our practice today of requiring reserve deposits of member banks in the Federal Reserve System.

In addition to this private regulatory effort, New York in 1827 envoked state regulatory power. To encourage conservation on bankers, the state passed a law holding bank stock holders responsible for debts equal to twice the value of their stock holdings. In 1827, New York passed the Safety-Fund Act, requiring new banks and those being rechartered to hold 3 percent of their capital stock in a fund to be used as reserves for banks that failed. This first state deposit insurance scheme failed in the panic of 1837, but others were tried again and again. State deposit insurance schemes were the forerunner of Federal Deposit Insurance initiated in the 1930s.

Free Banking

With the demise of the second U.S. Bank, a new era of free banking began. The first important free-bank law passed the New York Assembly in 1838. Actually, between the beginning of the agitation for the New York system and final passage of the act establishing it, a Michigan statute provided for a similar plan, but the chief influence on American banking derives from the New York law. The adjective *free* indicates the most important provision of the law. Under it, any individual or group of individuals, upon compliance with certain regulations, could start a bank in the state of New York.[10] Increased competition promised improved services and a reduction of legislative corruption. But in a few cases it led to wildcat banking. For instance, Michigan's free-bank act of 1837 provided that "any person or persons resident in the State . . . desirous of establishing a bank" might go into the business. Despite apparent safeguards, including a safety fund, the law permitted the poorest securities to be put up as a guarantee of note redemption. And enterprising bankers showed an amazing ingenuity in outwitting examiners. Since specie payments at the time were suspended, all a bank had to do to start operation was to show that it had specie on hand. Two commissioners noted a remarkable similarity in the packages of specie in the vaults of several banks on their examination list and later discovered that a sleigh drawn by fast horses preceded them as they went from place to place. In at least one instance a bank filled its specie kegs with glass, lead, and ten-penny nails, topping these materials off with a layer of silver. Nearly all banks operating on such a basis failed and disappeared by 1840, but not

---

[10]Under this law any person or group had a *right* to start a bank. Under the old rule, the *privilege* of starting a bank had to be granted by special legislative act.

before a victimized public had been stuck with their worthless notes. The kind of wildcat banking experienced in Michigan, and a few other states, however, was not typical.

The Forstall System

Reasonably sound banking systems usually developed in states achieving a degree of economic maturity. It was not by chance that the Louisiana law of 1842 set up a system, called the Forstall System, that became a model of sound and conservative banking.[11] With a port second only to that of New York, Louisiana had economic ties with both a great productive hinterland and the rest of the world. Legislators drafting the banking statute knew that any temporary gains resulting to some entrepreneurs from reckless creation of command over capital could not possibly equal the profits to be made by merchants *and* bankers through soundly financed trade.

The Louisiana law required banks chartered under it to keep a specie reserve equal to one-third of their *combined note and deposit liabilities*. Before 1863, several states came to require specie reserves against notes, ranging variously from 5 percent to 33⅓ percent, but except for Louisiana and Massachusetts they did not require reserves against *deposit liabilities* as well. Some banks everywhere, simply as matter of prudence, maintained reserves larger than those required by law.

In many states, then, both practice and legislation were bringing about improved banking. The heterogeneous state of the currency, however, was a matter of continuing concern.

The Chaotic Bank-Note Market

From 330 state banks in 1830, 901 in 1840, and 824 in 1850 there were by 1860 more than 1,500 state banks issuing, on an average, six different denominations of notes. Therefore, not fewer than 9,000 different types of notes were being passed. Some were as good as gold; but most were acceptable at a distance from the issuing bank only at a discount, and anyone ignorant of the actual worth of a note was open to loss. Notes of broken or liquidated banks sometimes remained in circulation for long periods, and counterfeiting was a continuing problem. Some gangs issued spurious counterfeits that imitated the notes of no particular bank, while others concentrated on careful imitations of genuine bills. Perhaps the most successful way of counterfeiting was to alter the notes of a broken bank to make them appear to be the issue of a solvent bank, or to change bills from lower to higher denominations. Some counterfeiters specialized in the *manufacturing* end of the business, while others, called utterers, were adept at *passing*

[11]It was named after the man who proposed it. See George P. Green, "The Louisiana Bank Act of 1842: Policy Making During Financial Crisis," *Explorations in Economic History* 7 (Summer 1970): 399–412. Irene D. Neu, "Edmund Jean Forstall and Louisiana Banking," *Explorations in Economic History* 7 (Summer 1970): 383–98.

the bogus money. To combat counterfeiters, banks formed anticounter-feiting associations, hiring men called snaggers to ferret out makers of spurious bills.

In the struggle to determine the genuineness of a bill and the discount at which a valid note should be accepted, it was everyone for himself. If a bill were much worn, or if it were perforated many times by the bank teller's needle-like staple, one might presume it to be genuine. Anyond who reg-ularly took in paper money had to have more assistance, however, usually in the form of a "bank-note reporter" and a "counterfeit detector." *Thomp-son's Bank Note and Commercial Reporter,* a weekly, contained alphabetical list-ings, by states, of the notes of banks and the discounts at which they should be received, together with descriptions of all known counterfeited bills. *Thompson's Bank Note Descriptive List,* published at irregular intervals, con-tained word descriptions of genuine bills of banks in the United States and Canada, while the *Coin Chart Manual* of the same firm furnished facsimile drawings of the most common gold and silver coins, both foreign and domestic, current in the United States.

Some of the services, like *Bicknall's Counterfeit Detector and Bank Note List,* specialized in counterfeit detection. *Nicholas' Bank Note Reporter* at one time listed 5,400 counterfeits known to be in circulation, and *Hodges' Bank Note Safeguard* contained 360 pages of facsimile reproductions of genuine notes. *Thompson's Bank Note and Commercial Reporter* used facsimiles only for certain bogus bills, and most of the others relied on word descriptions. None of the services achieved complete coverage, but some of them did a remarkably good job. For example, in 1859 *Hodges' Genuine Bank Notes of America* carried a listing of 9,916 notes of 1,365 banks, omitting the issues of fewer than 200 banks.

It is easy to exaggerate the difficulties caused by this state of affairs. Today merchants must still contend with bad checks, although credit cards and modern electronics have somewhat eased the problem. But there can be little doubt that money people of this period were dissatisfied with the currency and hankered for federal action to provide a uniform national currency. However, despite the chaotic heterogeneous conditions of the money supply, it bears remembering that the national economy grew sub-stantially during these antebellum years.

SELECTED REFERENCES AND SUGGESTED READINGS

Adams, Donald R. "The Role of Banks in the Economic Development of the Old Northwest." In *Essays in Nineteenth Century Economic History, The Old Northwest,* ed. David C. Klingaman and Richard K. Vedder. Athens, Ohio: Ohio Univ. Press, 1975.

Bordo, Michael, and Anna J. Schwartz. "Money and Prices in the Nineteenth Century: An Old Debate Rejoined." *Journal of Economic History* 40 (1980): 61–67.

Buck, Norman S. *The Development of the Organization of Anglo-American Trade, 1800–1850.* New Haven, Conn.: Yale Univ. Press, 1925.

Cattarall, Ralph. *The Second Bank of the United States.* Chicago: Univ. of Chicago Press, 1903.

Davis, Lance E., and Jonathan R. T. Hughes. "A Dollar-Sterling Exchange 1803–95." *Economic History Review* 13 (Aug. 1960).

Engerman, Stanley. "A Note on the Economic Consequences of the Second Bank of the United States," *Journal of Political Economy* 78 (July/August 1970): 725–28.

Fenstermaker, J. van. *The Development of American Commercial Banking, 1782–1837.* Kent, Ohio: Kent State Univ. Press, 1965.

———. "The Statistics of American Commercial Banking, 1782–1818." *Journal of Economic History* 25 (1965): 400–13.

Ferguson, E. James. *The Power of the Purse: A History of American Public Finance, 1776–1790.* Chapel Hill: Univ. of North Carolina Press, 1961.

Fraas, Arthur. "The Second Bank of the United States: An Instrument for an Interregional Monetary Union." *Journal of Economic History* 34 (1974): 447–67.

Green, George D. "The Louisiana Bank Act of 1842: Policy Making During Financial Crisis." *Explorations in Economic History* 7 (Summer 1970): 399–412.

Hammond, Bray. *Banks and Politics in America from the Revolution to the Civil War.* Princeton, N.J.: Princeton Univ. Press, 1957.

———. "Jackson, Biddle, and the Bank of the United States." *Journal of Economic History* 6 (Dec. 1946).

Hepburn, A. Barton. *History of Currency in the United States.* New York: Macmillan, 1915.

Hinderliter, Roger H., and Hugh Rockoff. "The Management of Reserves by Banks in Ante-Bellum Eastern Financial Centers." *Explorations in Economic History* 11 (Fall, 1973): 37–54.

Hughes, Jonathan R. T., and Nathan Rosenberg. "The United States Business Cycle Before 1860: Some Problems of Interpretation." *Economic History Review* 15, no. 3 (1963).

Lake, Wilfred S. "The End of the Suffolk System." *Journal of Economic History* 7 no. 2 (Nov. 1947).

Martin, David A. "The Changing Role of Foreign Money in the United States, 1782–1857." *Journal of Economic History* 37 (1977): 1009–27.

———. "1853: The End of Bimetallism in the United States." *Journal of Economic History* 33 (1973): 825–44.

———. "Metallism, Small Notes, and Jackson's War with the B.U.S." *Explorations in Economic History* 11 (Spring 1974): 227–48.

Neu, Irene D. "Edmond Jean Forstall and Louisiana Banking." *Explorations in Economic History* 7 (Summer 1970): 383–98.

North, Douglass. *The Economic Growth of the United States, 1790–1860.* New York: W. W. Norton, 1966.

Olmstead, Alan L. "Investment Constraints and New York City Mutual Savings Bank Financing of Antebellum Development." *Journal of Economic History* 32 (1972): 811–40.

Redlich, Fritz. "American Banking and Growth in the Nineteenth Century: Epistemological Reflections." *Explorations in Economic History* 10 (Spring 1973): 305–14.

———. *The Molding of American Banking: Men and Ideas.* New York: Hafner, 1947 and 1951, 2 vols.

Remini, Robert. *Andrew Jackson and the Bank War.* New York: W. W. Norton, 1967.

Rockoff, Hugh T. *The Free Banking Era: A Reexamination.* New York: Arno Press, 1975.

———. "Money, Prices and Banks in the Jacksonian Era." In *The Reinterpretation of American Economic History,* ed. R. W. Fogel and Stanley Engerman. New York: Harper & Row, 1971, ch. 33.

———. "Varieties of Banking and Regional Economic Development in the United States, 1840–1860." *Journal of Economic History* 35 (1975): 160–81.

Rogin, Michael. *Fathers and Children: Andrew Jackson and the Subjugation of the American Indian.* New York: Knopf, 1975.

Scheiber, Harry N. "The Pet Banks in Jacksonian Politics and Finance, 1833–1841." *Journal of Economic History* 33 (1963): 196–214.

Smith, Walter B., and Arthur H. Cole. *Fluctuations in American Business 1790–1860.* Cambridge: Harvard Univ. Press. 1935.

Studenski, Paul, and Herman Krooss. *Financial History of the United States.* New York: McGraw-Hill, 1952.

Summer, William G. *A History of American Currency.* New York: Putnam's Sons, 1878.

Taylor, George R., ed. *Jackson and Biddle: The Struggle over the Second Bank of the United States.* Boston: D. C. Heath, 1949.

Temin, Peter. "The Anglo-American Business Cycle, 1820–1860." *Economic History Review* 27 (May 1974).

———. "The Economic Consequences of the Bank War." *Journal of Political Economy* 70 (March/April 1968): 257–74.

———. *The Jacksonian Economy,* New York: Norton, 1969.

Timberlake, Richard H. *Money, Banking, and Central Banking.* New York: Harper & Row, 1965.

Trescott, Paul B. *Financing American Enterprise: The Story of Commercial Banking.* New York: Harper & Row, 1963.

Willett, Thomas D. "International Specie Flows and American Monetary Stability." *Journal of Economic History* 28 (1968): 28–50.

CHAPTER 13

The Entrenchment of Slavery and Regional Conflict

CONSTITUTIONAL LIMITATIONS

In 1780, the enslaved populations in the United States equaled nearly 575,000 blacks. Nine percent of these resided north of the Chesapeake; the remainder lived in the South. As part of one of the great constitutional compromises, the nation's forefathers agreed in 1787 not to allow the importation of slaves after 20 years. In 1807, therefore, pursuant to the authorizing Constitutional prohibition, Congress prohibited the foreign slave trade, effective the next year. In this way, the growth of slavery in the United States was limited, at least partially. Of course, the smuggling of human cargo was not uncommon, especially during years in which slaves brought high prices, and various estimates suggest as many as a quarter of a million blacks were illegally imported before 1860. But, illicit human importation was only a minor addition to the total numbers held in bondage. As shown in Figure 2-2 (p. 35), foreign-born blacks comprised a small percentage of the enslaved population in 1860. Natural sources of population expansion were predominant in increasing the number of slaves, and in 1863 their number equaled almost 4 million—all residing in the South.

NORTHERN EMANCIPATION

Even before the writing of the Constitution, some states were progressing toward the elimination of slavery. Between 1777 and 1804, the eight northeastern states individually passed measures to provide for the emancipation of their resident slave populations. In Vermont, Massachusetts, and New Hampshire, vague Constitutional clauses left the matter of emancipation to the courts. Unfortunately, little is known about the results of this process, but in any case, these three states domiciled only a very small fraction of

258

TABLE 13-1   Slave Emancipation in the North for the Free-Born

State	Date of Enactment	Age of Emancipation	
		Male	Female
Pennsylvania	1780[a]	28	28
Rhode Island	1784[b]	21	18
Connecticut	1784[c]	25	25
New York	1799[d]	28	25
New Jersey	1804[e]	25	21

[a]The last census that enumerated any slaves in Pennsylvania was in 1840.
[b]All slavery was abolished in 1842.
[c]The age of emancipation was changed in 1797 to age 21. In 1848, all slavery was abolished.
[d]In 1817, a law was passed freeing all slaves as of July 4, 1827.
[e]In 1846, all slaves were emancipated, but apprenticeships continued for the children of slave mothers and were introduced for freed slaves.

Source: Robert W. Fogel and Stanley L. Engerman "Philanthropy at Bargain Prices: Notes on the Economics of Gradual Emancipation," *The Journal of Legal Studies*, 3:2 (June 1974), p. 341.

the northern blacks—probably 10–15 percent in 1780. As shown in Table 13-1, Pennsylvania, Rhode Island, Connecticut, New York, and New Jersey each passed laws of emancipation well before the year prohibiting slave importations.

The process of emancipation used in these states was gradual, and the living population of slaves was not freed. Instead, newborn babies were emancipated when they reached adulthood.

Due to the form of the emancipation legislation it is apparent that many—perhaps most—of those who were politically dominant were more concerned with the political issue of slavery than with the slaves themselves. Besides not freeing the living slaves, there were no agencies in any of these states to enforce the enactments. In addition, the enactments themselves contained important loopholes, such as the possibility of selling slaves to the South.

The emancipation process, however, did recognize the issues of property rights and costs. These "gradual emancipation schemes" imposed no costs on taxpayers, and owners were not directly compensated financially for emancipated slaves. But curiously enough, owners were almost entirely compensated for their freed slaves. This was accomplished by maintaining the free-born in bondage until they had repaid their owner for their rearing costs. In most cases, these slaves were freed when they reached their mid-20s. In the first several years after birth, a slave's maintenance cost was in excess of the value of his or her services (or output). Near the age of 10, the slave's annual output usually just about matched the costs of food, clothes, and shelter. Thereafter, the value of output exceeded yearly maintenance costs, and normally by the age of 25 or 26 the slave had fully compensated the owner.

Most of the political rhetoric of the period was concerned with the problems of suddenly turning an uneducated and unskilled minority out into the world at large, as the ages in Table 13-1 suggest. But results and intentions are two quite different things. Perhaps the intentions of the legal designers were noble; perhaps they were not. In any case, we do know that the slaves themselves bore the lion's share of the costs of emancipation in the North. Newborn slaves who were eventually freed fully paid back their owners for their rearing costs. Owners of males who were born before the dates of enactment suffered no wealth loss. Owners of females who were born before the enactments and who could or eventually would reproduce incurred some minor wealth losses in that they lost the value of their slaves' offspring. About 10 percent of the value (price) of a young female slave was due to the value of her offspring, and perhaps as many as 30 percent of the total enslaved population was comprised of females in their fertile or prefertile years.[1] Consequently only 3 percent (10 percent of 30 percent) of the total slave wealth was lost to northern owners by abiding by these enactments, but the percentage was probably much closer to zero because of the loopholes of selling slaves to the South, working the slaves harder, and reducing maintenance costs.

THE PERSISTENCE OF SLAVERY

Despite the constitutional restrictions on slave imports and the "gradual emancipation schemes" of the northern states, slavery did not die. Table 13-2 profiles the growth of the southern population, showing the slave population increasing slightly more rapidly than the free southern population. Its proportion of the total grew from around 49 percent in 1800 to 53 percent in 1860. Also, the free black population was growing at a faster rate in terms of percentage than the total over this period.

After Eli Whitney's invention of the cotton gin in 1793, mechanical means replaced fingers in the separation of seed from short staple cotton varieties. The soils and climate of the South, especially the new Southwest, gave it a comparative advantage in supplying the massive and growing demand for raw cotton by the British, and later by New England textile firms. Cotton quickly became the nation's largest commodity export, and output expanded as the southwestern migrations discussed in Chapter 7 placed an army of slaves on new southwestern lands. According to estimates by Fogel and Engerman, nearly 835,000 slaves moved out of the old South (Maryland, Virginia, and the Carolinas primarily), most of them going to the cotton-rich lands of Alabama, Mississippi, Louisiana, and eastern Texas. Three

---

[1] Female slaves of all ages composed 37 percent of the total slave population.

TABLE 13-2   The Southern Population by Race, 1800–60 (in hundred thousands)

| Year | White | Black | | Slave as a Percentage of Free |
		Slave	Free	
1800	1.70	0.86	0.06	49%
1810	2.19	1.16	0.11	50
1820	2.78	1.51	0.13	52
1830	3.55	1.98	0.18	53
1840	4.31	2.43	0.21	54
1850	5.63	3.12	0.24	53
1860	7.03	3.84	0.26	53

Note: Amounts rounded off.

Source: *Historical Statistics,* 1960, Series A, pp. 95–122.

particular surges of movement and land sales occurred, first in the years right after the end of the War of 1812, a second in the mid-1830s, and finally a third surge in the early 1850s. These are graphically shown in Figure 8-2 (p. 159). The plantation based on slave labor was the organizational form that assured vast economical supplies of cotton.

Plantation Efficiency

In the heyday of King Cotton, the growth in the number and size of plantations in the South was dramatic. Of course, many small family farm units produced cotton and their related items for market. But the really distinguishing characteristic of southern agriculture in the antebellum period was the plantation. Based on forced labor, the plantations represented both the economic grandeur and the social tragedy of the southern economy.

Although most of the condemnation of slavery was confined to moral and social issues, some of the damnation was extended to strictly economic aspects. In some instances, the forced labor of blacks was condemned as inefficient, either on racial grounds or because slavery per se was considered economically inefficient and unproductive. For example, the white contemporary observer Cassius M. Clay noted that Africans were "far less adapted for steady, uninterrupted labor than we are,"[2] and another contemporary, Frederick L. Olmsted, reported that "white laborers of equal intelligence and under equal stimulus will cut twice as much wood, split twice as many rails, and hoe a third more corn a day than Negroes."[3]

[2]C. M. Clay in H. Greeley (ed.), *The Writings of Cassius Marcelius Clay: Including Speeches and Addresses (The New Yorker,* 1848), p. 204.
[3]F. L. Olmsted, *The Cotton Kingdom,* A. M. Schlesinger (ed.), *(The New Yorker,* 1953), pp. 467–68.

The technological break-through that revitalized the plantation economy was the cotton gin—a product of the innovative genius of Eli Whitney, a New England schoolmaster.

There are sound reasons and growing evidence to reject these contemporary assertions. For example, Gavin Wright has shown that 86 percent of the South's cotton crop was grown on farm units over 100 acres and owning 90 percent of the slaves.[4] We may, therefore, view the eleven- to twelvefold growth of cotton production in 1820–60 compared to the two and one-half-fold growth of the slave population as reflecting nearly a four- to fivefold increase in cotton output per slave. Clearly there was ample growth in agricultural productivity based on slave labor.

Another perspective is to directly compare plantations to free farms. Were plantations worked by masses of slaves more or less efficient than free-family farm units? Did the South face increasing economic retardation as slavery became more and more entrenched?

Before diving into the evidence, we must acknowledge certain caveats. The problems of measuring efficiency comparatively have been a source of intense scholarly debate. The agricultural output comparisons are really valued outputs rather than strictly physical output comparisons. Variations in soil type and location also pose problems of measurement when comparing farms and plantations.

Of course, due to their size, plantations produced more cotton and other goods and foodstuffs than the southern free-family farms. But when comparing output per unit of input (capital, labor, and land in combination, and after adjusting at least in part for variations in land quality, location, length of workday and work year, and other such factors), it is clear that

---

[4]Gavin Wright, *The Political Economy of the Cotton South: Households, Markets, and Wealth in the Nineteenth Century* (New York: W. W. Norton, 1978), p. 28.

TABLE 13-3   Comparisons of Efficiency in Southern Agriculture by Farm Type and Size (Index of free southern farms = 100)

Number of Slaves	Indexes of Output per Unit of Total Input
0	100
1–15	101
16–50	133
51 or more	148

Source: Robert W. Fogel and Stanley L. Engerman, "Explaining the Relative Efficiency of Slave Agriculture in the Antebellum South," *American Economic Review,* 67:3 (June 1977): p. 285.

the large plantations were considerably more productive than the small or slaveless farms.[5] Table 13-3 shows these productivity comparisons for southern farms and plantations as well as for plantations worked by different numbers of slaves. By far the most efficient units were those using 50 or more slaves. Small-scale farming was less productive per unit of input employed, and there was little difference in efficiency between southern free-family farms and small farms employing only a few slaves. Therefore, it appears that racial factors had an insignificant effect on productivity. Black workers with their complementary but white-owned capital and land were about as productive in small units as white workers on single-family farms. Alternatively, plantations with sizable numbers of slaves were extraordinarily efficient. Clearly economies of scale, or some other sources of productivity gains, provided advantages for large-sized plantations.

Final answers to why such differences existed still elude us. By and large, however, the main difference appears to be the organization of slaves into production units called gangs, the careful selection of slaves by skill for particular uses, and the intensity per hour with which the slaves were worked.

In many ways, the large antebellum plantations were more like factories than farms. Their organization of slave labor resembled that of assembly-line workers. Even contemporary reports stress these characteristics.[6]

The cotton plantation was not a farm consisting, as the farm does, in a multiplicity of duties and arrangements within a limited scope, one hand charged with half a dozen parts to act in a day or week. The cotton plantation labor was as thoroughly organized as the cotton mill labor. There were wagoners,

[5] For a lively but highly technical debate on the issues of measuring the relative efficiency of slavery see the exchanges in the March 1979 and September 1980 issues of the *American Economic Review* between Paul David and Peter Temin, Gavin Wright, Donald Schaefer and Mark Schmitz, and Robert Fogel and Stanley Engerman.

[6] These quotations by contemporaries are in reference to the Canebrake Plantation and the McDuffie Plantation, respectively. See Jacob Metzer, "Rational Management, Modern Business Practices, and Economies of Scale in Antebellum Southern Plantations," *Explorations in Economic History* 12:2 (April 1975), pp. 134–35 for complete citations and other examples.

An invoice of ten negroes sent this day to John
B Williamson by Geo Kremer named & cost as fol—
lows

    To wit Betsey Kackley $410.00
            Nancy Aulick 515.00
            Harry & Helen Miller . . 1200.00
            Mary Kootz 600.00
            Betsey Ott? 560.00
            Isaac & Fanny Brent . . 992.00
            Lucinda Luckett 467.50
            George Smith 510.00
Amount of my traveling expences & boarding 5254.50
of lot No 9 not included in the other bills .. 39.50
    Kremers expences Transporting lot No 9 to Richd 51..00
        Carryall hire .. .   6.00
                            $ 5357.00

    I have this day delivered the above named negroe
costing including my expences and other expences
five thousand three hundred & fifty dollars this May.
26th 1835—

                            John W Pittman

    I did intend to leave Nancy child but she made
such a damned fuss I had to let her take it I could
of got fifty Dollars for so you must add forty Dollars
to the above)

Invoice of a sale of slaves, 1835.

the plowmen, the hoe hands, the ditchers, the blacksmiths, the wheelwrights,
the carpenters, the men in care of work animals, the men in care of hogs and
cattle, the women who had care of the nursery . . . the cooks for all . . . [n]o
industry in its practical operation was moved more methodically or was more
exacting of a nice discrimination in the application of labor than the Canebrake Cotton plantation.

    When the period for planting arrives, the hands are divided into three
classes: 1st, the best hands, embracing those of good judgment and quick
motion; 2nd, those of the weakest and most inefficient class; 3rd the second

class of hoe hands. Thus classified, the first class will run ahead and open a small hole about seven to ten inches apart, into which the 2nd class [will] drop from four to five cotton seeds, and the third class [will] follow and cover with a rake.

The profitable exploitation of slave labor in the antebellum period was made possible principally by speeding up the work and greater work intensity, not longer hours, and the efficiency gains stemmed primarily from worker–task selection and the intensity of work per hour. In fact, slaves on large plantations typically took longer rest breaks and worked less on Sundays than their white counterparts did. Indeed, these conditions were needed to achieve the levels of work intensity imposed on the slaves. It is apparent that these productivity advantages were not voluntary. Essentially, they required slave or forced labor. No free-labor plantations emerged during the period. And as we will see, there was a significant reduction in labor participation and work intensity and organization after emancipation.

The Profitability of Slavery

Writing in the first decade of this century, noted historian Ulrich Phillips claimed that antebellum southern slavery had become unprofitable by the 1840s and 1850s, leading some to believe, incorrectly, that perhaps slavery eventually would have died out. His conclusions were widely accepted until two economists, Alfred Chandler and John Meyer, took the pains in the late 1950s to actually measure the rates of return to investments in slaves. Their calculations and a host of other estimates that followed showed a range of returns, typically 8 to 12 percent, that were competitive or above normal compared to alternative returns on investments at that time.

Phillips based his analysis on two time series: the prices of prime field hands shown in Figure 13-1 and the trend of cotton prices. Cotton prices varied year to year in real terms, 8 to 12 cents per pound, with 9 cents being typical in the 1840s and 10 cents being average in the 1850s. With slave prices soaring and cotton prices hardly increasing Phillips reasoned that investments in slaves increasingly were realizing losses. He further asserted that these losses surely occurred because a slave was no more productive in 1860 than in 1820 or 1830. But how then did the prices of slaves rise, if cotton prices did not? We now know the answer, more output per slave. Phillips erred in overlooking the productivity gains that arose over the period, from economies of scale as plantations grew, other organizational advances such as assigning tasks, and from moving into more productive areas (the southwestern migrations), and other sources. Phillips' observation, perhaps correct, that slaves worked no harder in 1860 than earlier and used the same technology, overlooked other sources of productivity advance.

Furthermore, there is no evidence to suggest that slavery would have died out. Not even temporary periods of overcapitalization of slaves—that

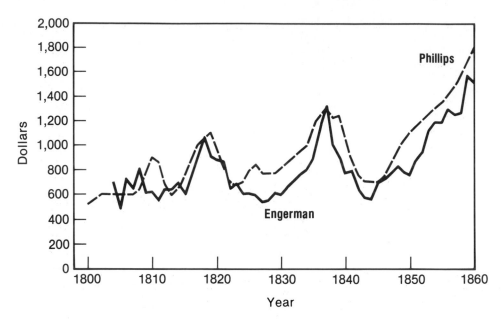

FIGURE 13-1   Price of a Prime Male Slave New Orleans, 1800–60

Source: Roger L. Ransom and Richard Sutch, "Capitalists without Capital: The Burden of Slavery and the Impact of Emancipation," *Agricultural History* (Summer 1988), p. 155. As reported there, the original sources to these two series are *Phillips:* Prices for 1800, 1801, and 1812 are estimated visually from Ulrich Bonnell Phillips, *Life and Labor in the Old South* (Little Brown, 1929), p. 177. All other figures are from Alfred H. Conrad and John R. Meyer, "The Economics of Slavery in the Antebellum South," *Journal of Political Economy* 66 (April 1958), reprinted in Alfred H. Conrad and John R. Meyer, *The Economics of Slavery and Other Studies in Econometric History* (Aldine, 1964), Table 17, column 6, p. 76. *Engerman:* Data were supplied by Stanley Engerman. They are mean values of the prices included in a sample of invoices of slave sales held in New Orleans. The sample size for each year ranged between 2.5 and 5 percent. The prices averaged refer to "males ages 18 to 30, without skills, fully guaranteed as without physical or other infirmity." Engerman "utilized only those cases in which there was an individual price listed for a separate slave." For most years there were about 15 to 20 observations used in preparing the averages given.

is, when prices were being bid too high—would support such a conclusion. The facts are that slaves produced more, much more, than it cost to rear and maintain them. Only if the value of slave output had fallen below subsistence costs, would owners have gained by setting slaves free.

ECONOMIC EXPLOITATION

It hardly needs to be stressed that black slaves were exploited. They had no political rights, and the law of the plantation and the whim of the taskmaster was the web of confinement the slave directly faced. Owners did not carelessly mistreat their slaves for obvious reasons. A prime male field hand was worth more than $13,000 in today's prices.

Various forms of punishments and rewards, however, pressured slaves to be obedient workers. Few failed to witness or feel the sting of the lash, and their lot was far from pleasant. Their relatively low standard of living certainly would have been much higher if the value of their total output had been returned to them. However, because the property rights to their labor and their product resided with the white owner, their output accrued to the owner.

Richard Vedder has attempted to measure the economic exploitation of slaves in the South. His measure is based on the fundamental economic proposition that workers in competitive industries like cotton production, tend to be paid amounts that are equal to what labor contributes at the margin. An additional worker adds a certain value of output. Any difference between the value of output the worker adds and what he or she receives may be reasonably termed economic exploitation. For the average slave, this difference (the value of output added minus maintenance costs) divided by the value of the output added was at least 50 percent and may have been as high as 65 percent.[7]

Of course, there was much more to the exploitation issue than simply taking one-half of the worker's earnings. The mere entrapment of workers blocked their advance materially and otherwise by taking away their incentive for self improvement and gain.

Perhaps the best thing that can be said about the economic conditions of American slavery is that it was not as bad as the conditions of slavery elsewhere. Figure 13-2 shows the percentage of slave imports to various parts of the Western Hemisphere (1500–1825) compared to the location of slaves in terms of percentages in 1825. Note the drastic declines in population, relatively, in the Caribbean and in Brazil. There conditions were especially brutal. By comparison, the southern United States offered treatment that was life-sustaining. Slaves in the antebellum South experienced standards of material comfort that were low by today's standards, but they were well above those of the masses in many parts of their contemporary world.

ECONOMIC ENTRENCHMENT AND REGIONAL INCOMES

Although the slave system proved efficient on the plantation, its economic advantages were not widely applicable elsewhere. As a result of this and other factors—especially its overwhelming comparative advantage in agriculture—the South experienced little structural change during the

---

[7]For further elaboration, see Richard Vedder, "The Slave Exploitation (Expropriation) Rate," *Explorations in Economic History* 12:4 (Oct. 1976), pp. 453–57. As Vedder notes, in New England cotton textile mills (a sample of 71 firms) in 1820, the comparable exploitation calculation was 22 percent; for iron workers in 1820 (101 firms), the rate was 28 percent (p. 456). Similar levels of exploitation (24 and 29 percent, respectively) have been computed in Roger L. Ransom and Richard Such, *One Kind of Freedom* (Cambridge: Cambridge Univ. Press, 1977), p. 3.

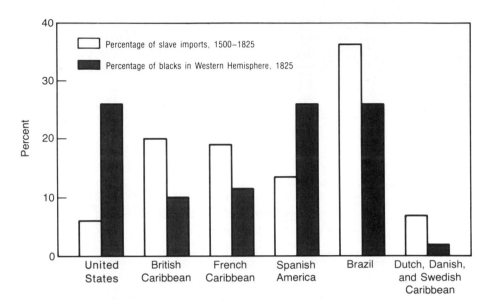

FIGURE 13-2   The Distribution of the Black Population (Slave and Free) in 1825 Compared to the Distribution of Slave Imports, 1500–1825.

Source: Robert W. Fogel and Stanley L. Engerman, *Time on the Cross: The Economics of American Negro Slavery* (Boston: Little, Brown, 1976), Figure 8, p. 28.

antebellum years. For instance, the South was slow to industrialize, partially due to the slave system. However, in pre-Civil War days, some slaves did become skilled craftsmen, and slaves were employed in cotton factories, coal mines, ironworks, lumber mills, and railroads. But there was no point in incurring the costs of training slaves for industrial occupations on a large scale when they could readily and profitably be put to work in agriculture.

In addition, the South experienced very little immigration from Europe or elsewhere. It was not the South's "peculiar institution" that kept European migrants away, because immigration did not increase after emancipation. Europeans tended to settle in latitudes where the climate was like that of their former home. But the main deterrent to locating in the South was that outsiders perceived a lack of opportunity there; the immigrant feared that he or she would become a "poor white." By 1860, only 3.4 percent of the southern population was foreign-born, compared with a foreign-born population in the central states of 17 percent and in New England of 15 percent.

As stated above, as vents for capital, there can be no doubt that plantation slavery was profitable throughout the South. Extremely high net returns in parts of the cotton belt and rewards at least equal to those of alternative employments of capital in most areas of the Deep South were the rule. Nor were there economic forces at work making the slave economy self-destructive. There is simply no evidence to support the contention that slave labor

The somberness of this group of slaves suggests their ill fortune.

was overcapitalized, and slaves clearly reproduced sufficiently to maintain a growing workforce. In addition, internal migration from the older southern states to the new cotton belt areas was on a large scale. The Southern economy did show signs of flexibility.

This flexibility, exhibited in the western migrations, was especially important to the South. Table 13-4 shows income figures for various regions in 1840–60. Note that the growth of income for the entire South, from $105 to $150, nearly 44 percent, was higher than the internal growth of any subregion in the South (about one-third for the old South, about 15 percent for the new South). The migrations from poorer to richer areas leveraged up the income growth for the South as a whole. As we shall see, the South was vitally concerned, for apparently sound economic reasons, with the rights to slavery expansion into western lands.

Moreover there were justifications for optimism. Note the relative position of the West South Central region, where King Cotton reigned supreme. This was by far the highest income region in the country. And these high relative standings remain whether or not slaves are included in the population figures. When the incomes per capita of only the free population are

TABLE 13-4   Per Capita Income Before the Civil War in 1860 Prices

	Total Population		Free Population	
	1840	1860	1840	1860
National Average	$ 96	$128	$109	$144
North	109	141	110	142
Northeast	129	181	130	183
North Central	65	89	66	90
South	74	103	105	150
South Atlantic	66	84	96	124
East South Central	69	89	92	124
West South Central	151	184	238	274

Source: Robert W. Fogel and Stanley L. Engerman, "The Economics of Slavery," in *The Reinterpretation of American Economic History* (New York: Harper & Row, 1971), Table 8, p. 335.

compared, even the older, less wealthy southern areas show levels that were quite high. There can be little doubt, that on the eve of the Civil War, the South was a very rich area indeed.

Yet from the moral, social, and political viewpoints, southern slavery imposed a growing source of self-destruction on the American people. The system epitomized a great barrier to human decency and social progress which was contrary to deeply felt ideals in many quarters. With almost religious fervor, abolitionist elements grew in strength and national disunity grew proportionately. It was highly unlikely that southerners would voluntarily free their own slaves. Without hope for compensation and fearing the social consequences of sudden emancipation, the South's oligarchical slave power stood firm. Meanwhile, the costs of emancipation to slave owners soared. As Figure 13-1 illustrates, the value of slaves continued to increase, primarily in response to the rising productivity of forced labor profitably employed in cotton and other staples. Steadily, the economic entrenchment of slavery grew in the southern states.

POLITICAL COMPROMISES AND REGIONAL CONFLICT

For a majority of Americans living at the time of slavery in the United States, the most significant issue was the containment of slavery, not its eradication. Indeed, the basis of political compromise on this issue was first established in the Northwest Ordinance, passed unanimously by Congress in 1787. Article six reads: "there shall be neither slavery nor involuntary servitude in the said territory . . . provided always, that any person escaping into the same, from whom labor or service is claimed in any of the original states, such fugitive may be lawfully reclaimed and conveyed to the person claiming his or her labor or service as foresaid." The 1787 ordinance, in effect, outlawed slavery in lands that became the states of Ohio, Indiana, Michigan,

Illinois, Wisconsin, and Minnesota. This set the stage for controlling the expansion of slavery in other territories, allowing some regions at least to be non-slave, but this important legislation did not provide a final solution.

The western migrations, both north and south, continued to bring the issue of slave containment to a head. The key problem for the South, as a political unit, was to maintain at least equal voting power in the Senate. The South accomplished this objective and won a series of compromises that enabled them to extend the institution of slavery and counter abolitionist threats.

In 1819, the political balance in the Senate was even; there were 11 slave and 11 free states. By the Missouri Compromise of 1820 (see Map 13-1), Missouri was admitted as a slave state and Maine as a free state, on the condition that slavery should thereafter be prohibited in the territory of the Louisiana Purchase north of 36° 30′. For nearly 30 years after this, states were admitted to the Union in pairs, one slave and one free, and by 1850 there were 15 free and 15 slave states. As of that year, slavery had been prohibited in the Northwest Territory, in the territory of the Louisiana Purchase north of 36° 30′, and in the Oregon Territory—vast areas in which an extensive slave system would not have been profitable anyway. Violent controversy arose over the basis of admission for prospective states contained in the area ceded to the United States by Mexico. The terms of the Mexican Cession required that the territory remain permanently free, yet

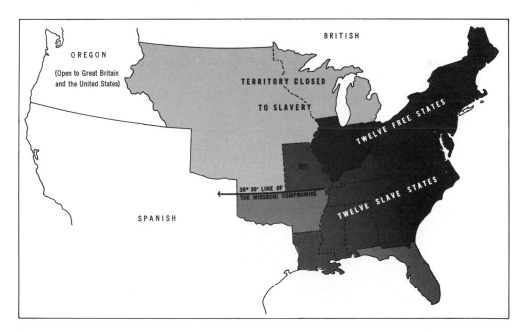

MAP 13-1   The Missouri Compromise of 1820: After this enactment, growing sectional acrimony was supposed to be a thing of the past. For a time, a truce did prevail.

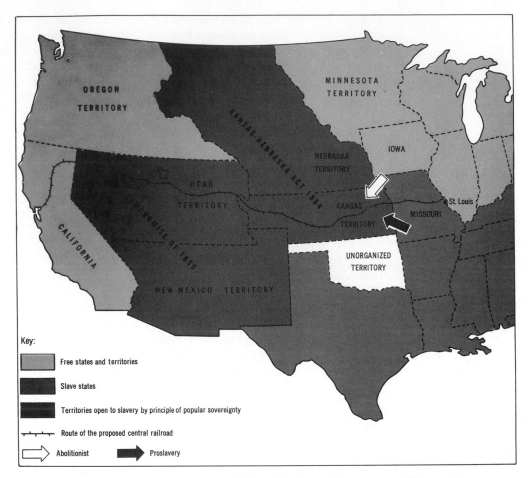

MAP 13-2   New Settlements: The Compromise of 1850 and the Kansas–Nebraska Act of 1854 were further attempts to keep sectional strife from erupting into warfare. The concept of "popular sovereignty" introduced in this act led to conflict in Kansas.

Congress in 1848 had rejected the Wilmot Proviso, which would have prohibited slavery in the Southwest, where its extention was economically feasible. In the end, California was admitted as a free state in 1850. The territories of Utah and New Mexico were organized, and slaveholding was to be permitted there; the final decision on the legality of slavery was to be made by the territorial populations on application for admission to the Union.

Further events of the 1850s for a time appeared to portend ultimate victory for the South in the matter of slavery extension. The Kansas–Nebraska Act of 1854 (see Map 13-2) in effect repealed the Missouri Compromise by providing for "popular sovereignty" in the hitherto unsettled portions of the Louisiana Purchase. The result was gunfire and bloodshed in Kansas. The Dred Scott decision of a states' rights Supreme Court went even further and declared that Congress could not prohibit slavery in the territories. And during this time, southerners, desperately eager to inhibit the movement of small farmers into territories where slavery could not possibly flourish, successfully resisted passage of a homestead act that would give free land to settlers.

Yet legislative successes could be achieved only as long as Democrats from the North and Northwest were willing to ally themselves with the South. Toward the end of the 1850s, the antislavery movement in the North became irresistible. In large part, the movement was led by those who opposed the servitude of anyone on purely ethical grounds, but altruistic motives were reinforced by economic interests. Northwest farmers resisted the extension of the plantation system because they feared the resulting competition of large units with their small ones. And as transportation to eastern centers improved, especially through the Northern gateway, the products of the Northwest increasingly flowed into the Middle Atlantic states and Europe. In this way, the people of the Northwest found their economic and other interests more closely tied to the eastern industrialist than to the southern planter. The large migrations of Irish and Germans, who had no stake in slavery, added to the shift in economic and political interests near mid-century. The Republican party, founded in the mid-1850s, capitalized on the shift in economic interests. As old political alignments weakened and ebbed, the Republican party rapidly gained strength, chiefly from those who opposed the extension of slavery into the territories.

In Abraham Lincoln's opening speech in his sixth debate with Stephen A. Douglas on October 13, 1858, in Quincy, Illinois, he elaborated on slavery:

> We have in this nation the element of domestic slavery. . . . The Republican party think it wrong—we think it is a moral, a social, and a political wrong. We think it is a wrong not confining itself merely to the persons or the State where it exists, but that it is a wrong which in its tendency, to say the least, affects the existence of the whole nation. . . . I suppose that in reference both to its actual existence in the nation, and to our constitutional obligations, we have no right at all to disturb it in the States where it exists, and we profess that we have no more inclination to disturb it than we have the right to do it. . . . We also oppose it as an evil so far as it seeks to spread itself. We insist on the policy that shall restrict it to its present limits. . . . We oppose the Dred Scott decision in a certain way. . . . We propose so resisting it as to have it reversed if we can, and a new judicial rule established upon this subject.

From the southern perspective, the election of Lincoln in 1860 presented only two alternatives: submission or secession. To a wealthy and proud people, submission was unthinkable.[8] To Lincoln, alternatively, the Union had to be preserved. The holocaust that maintained the Union cost the

---

[8]Recall the prewar scene from *Gone With the Wind* when anxious southern warriors were predicting a short war and a decisive southern victory. Rhett Butler, alone, cautioned to the contrary.

country more lives and human suffering than any war in the history of the United States. Although initially emancipation was not an objective of the northern war effort, it became, as we know today, a celebrated outcome matched only by the preservation of the Union itself.

SELECTED REFERENCES AND SUGGESTED READINGS

Aufhauser, R. Keith. "Slavery and Technological Change." *Journal of Economic History* 34 (1974): 36–50.

Blassingame, John. *The Slave Community: Plantation Life in the Antebellum South.* New York: Oxford Univ. Press, 1972.

Canarella, Georgio, and John A. Tomaske. "The Optimal Utilization of Slaves." *Journal of Economic History* 35 (1975): 621–29.

Conrad, Alfred, and John Meyer. "The Economics of Slavery in the Antebellum South." *Journal of Political Economy* 66 (1958): 95–130.

David, Paul, Herbert Gutman, Richard Sutch, and Gavin Wright. *Reckoning with Slavery.* New York: Oxford Univ. Press, 1976.

Douglass, Frederick. *Narrative of the Life of Frederick Douglass.* New York: New American Library, 1968.

Elkins, Stanley M. *Slavery: A Problem of American Institutional and Intellectual Life.* New York: Grosset & Dunlap, 1959.

Engerman, Stanley, and Eugene Genovese. *Race and Slavery in the Western Hemisphere: Quantitative Studies.* Princeton, N.J.: Princeton Univ. Press, 1978.

Fenoaltea, Stefano. "The Slavery Debate: A Note from the Sidelines." *Explorations in Economic History* 18 (July 1981): 304–8.

Fleisig, Heywood. "Slavery, the Supply of Agricultural Labor, and the Industrialization of the South." *Journal of Economic History* 36 (1976): 572–97.

Fogel, Robert W. "Three Phases of Cliometric Research on Slavery and Its Aftermath." *American Economic Review* 65 (May 1975): 37–46.

———. *Without Consent or Contract: The Rise and Fall of American Slavery.* New York: W. W. Norton, 1989.

Fogel, Robert W., and Stanley L. Engerman. "Explaining the Relative Efficiency of Slave Agriculture in the Antebellum South." *American Economic Review* 67 (June 1977): 275–96.

———. "Explaining the Relative Efficiency of Slave Agriculture in the Antebellum South: A Reply." *American Economic Review* 70 (Sept. 1980): 672–90.

———. "The Relative Efficiency of Slavery: A Comparison of Northern and Southern Agriculture in 1860." *Explorations in Economic History* 8 (Spring 1971): 353–67.

———. *Time on the Cross: The Economics of American Negro Slavery,* 2 vols. Boston: Little, Brown, 1974.

Genovese, Eugene. *From Rebellion to Revolution: Afro-American Slave Revolts in the Modern World.* Baton Rouge: Louisiana State Univ. Press, 1979.

———. *Roll, Jordan, Roll: The World the Slaves Made.* New York: Vintage Books, 1976.

Goldin, Claudia. *Urban Slavery in the American South.* Chicago: Univ. of Chicago Press, 1976.

Gray, Lewis. *History of Agriculture in the Southern United States to 1860,* 2 vols. Washington, D.C.: The Carnegie Institution, 1933.

Gunderson, Gerald. "The Origins of the American Civil War." *Journal of Economic History* 34 (1974): 915–50.

———. "Southern Ante-Bellum Income Reconsidered." *Explorations in Economic History* 10 (Winter 1973): 151–76.

Gutman, Herbert. *The Black Family in Slavery and Freedom.* New York: Pantheon Books, 1976.

Hutchinson, W. K., and Samuel H. Williamson. "The Self-Sufficiency of the Ante-Bellum South; Estimates of the Food Supply." *Journal of Economic History* 31 (1971): 591–612.

Kotlikoff, Laurence J., and Sebastian E. Pinera. "The Old South's Stake with Inter-Regional Movement of Slaves, 1850–1860." *Journal of Economic History* 37 (1977): 434–50.

Metzer, Jacob. "Rational Management, Modern Business Practice, and Economies of Scale in the Antebellum Plantations." *Explorations in Economic History* 12 (April 1975): 123–50.

Olmsted, Frederick L. *The Cotton Kingdom: A Traveler's Observations on Cotton and Slavery in the American Slave States.* New York: N.p., 1861.

———. *The Slave States.* New York: Capricorn Books, 1959.

Parker, William, ed. *The Structure of the Cotton Economy of the Antebellum South.* Washington, D.C.: The Agricultural History Society, 1970.

Passell, Peter, "The Impact of Cotton Land Distribution on the Ante-Bellum Economy." *Journal of Economic History* 31 (1971): 917–37.

Phillips, Ulrich B. "The Economic Cost of Slaveholding in the Cotton Belt." *Political Science Quarterly,* June, 1905.

Ransom, Roger L. *Conflict and Compromise: The Political Economy of Slavery, Emancipation, and the American Civil War.* New York and London: Cambridge Univ. Press, 1989.

Ransom, Roger L., and Richard Sutch. "Capitalists without Capital: The Burden of Slavery and the Impact of Emancipation." *Agricultural History* (Summer 1988): 133–60.

Schmitz, Mark D., and Donald F. Schaefer. "Slavery, Freedom, and the Elasticity of Substitution." *Explorations in Economic History* 15 (July 1978): 327–37.

Steckel, Richard H. "Slave Height Profiles from Coastwise Manifests." *Explorations in Economic History* 16 (Oct. 1979): 363–80.

Sutch, Richard. "The Treatment Received by American Slaves: A Critical Review of the Evidence Presented in *Time on the Cross.*" *Explorations in Economic History* 12 (Oct. 1975): 335–438.

Thomas, Robert P., and Richard N. Bean. "The Fishers of Men: The Profits of the Slave Trade." *Journal of Economic History* 34 (1974): 885–914.

Vedder, Richard K. "The Slave Exploitation (Expropriation) Rate." *Explorations in Economic History* 12 (Oct. 1975): 453–58.

Washington, Booker T. *Up from Slavery.* New York: Bantam Books, 1963.

Wright, Gavin. *The Political Economy of the Cotton South.* New York: W. W. Norton, 1978.

Wright, Gavin. "Slavery and the Cotton Boom." *Explorations in Economic History* 12, no. 4 (Oct. 1975): 439–52.

Zepp, Thomas M. "On Returns to Scale and Input Substitutability in Slave Agriculture." *Explorations in Economic History* 13, no. 2 (April 1976): 165–78.

PART

3

THE REUNIFICATION ERA

1860–1920

1. For nearly 100 years following 1815 there were no major wars between national coalitions. The U.S. Civil War, our bloodiest war ever, was a detached conflict in this long period of global peace.

2. After the war, rapid industrialization in the North and renewed western expansion sustained a high overall growth rate for the nation. The large absolute fall in output in the South due to the war and emancipation and the slow pace of growth in the cotton-belt states ushered in an era of southern backwardness and regional disparity.

3. Emancipation redistributed wealth and incomes sharply from white slaveowners to blacks, but a legacy of slavery sustained black poverty in the Deep South.

4. By the mid-1890s, after three decades of falling prices, the United States had become the world's leading industrial power, outproducing by nearly twice the nearest industrial rival, Germany, while England had slipped into third place.

5. Technological change, economies of scale, and mass-production methods became the main engines of sustained modern economic growth.

6. The U.S. population topped 100,000,000 during the First World War; 48 states were in the Union; and federal, state, and local expenditures combined reached a record high of nearly 10 percent of GNP.

CHAPTER 14

War, Recovery, and Regional Divergence

As the Democratic party split apart in mid-year of 1860, the Republican candidate for president, Abraham Lincoln, won the election in November with a mere 40 percent of the popular vote. He carried the North and West solidly, but so sectional was his victory that his name did not even appear on 10 state ballots in the South. The South's political strategy and source of success had been to control the senate and the presidency. Both were lost in 1860.

By the time of Lincoln's inauguration on March 3, 1861, ten southern states had followed South Carolina's decision to secede. One of Lincoln's first steps as president was to counter threats from South Carolina's troops in Charleston Harbor. His order to reinforce Fort Sumter gave South Carolinians the excuse they sought to begin shooting, and on April 10 the bombardment began. Within days all remaining slave states joined the Confederate states of America. The armed conflict exploded.

The nation's forefathers had equivocated on the slave issue both in 1776 and in 1790, by necessity to form a union of states. The last "slavery truce," in 1850, was based on popular sovereignty in the western territories and it ended within a decade. By 1860, the South was prepared to fight to save its social order, rooted in plantation slavery. The North was similarly prepared to fight, to save the union and the outcome of an election that "finally had contained the slave power within the political framework of the United States."[1] To allow independence to the southern states would have both divided the nation and allowed a separate southern course of foreign policy committed to the expansion of slavery. Lincoln understood this clearly, and wrote to Lyman Trumbull of Indiana why he opposed compromise with

---

[1] Roger Ransom, *Conflict and Compromise: The Political Economy of Slavery, Emancipation, and the American Civil War* (New York and London: Cambridge Univ. Press, 1989), p. 177.

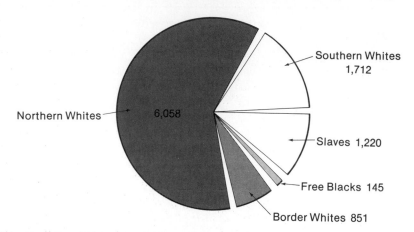

FIGURE 14-1   Population of Males 10 to 49 Years of Age in 1860 (in thousands)

Source: Roger Ransom, *Conflict and Compromise: The Political Economy of Slavery, Emancipation, and the American Civil War.* New York and London: Cambridge Univ. Press, Figure 6.2.

the South: "Let there be no compromise on the question of extending slavery. If there be, all our labor is lost, and ere long, must be done again . . . the Tug has to come, and better now than at any time hereafter."[2]

Lincoln's key miscalculation, like the South's, was his belief that a strong show of force would bring the fighting to a speedy end. The South's first victory under Generals Joseph E. Johnson and P. G. T. Beauregard at Bull's Run, the first great battle of the Civil War, only added to southern confidence and resolve to maintain the course of rebellion.

THE ECONOMIES OF WAR

Despite ample southern income, pride, talent, and faith, the South was woefully unprepared for a lengthy war against the North. Figure 14-1 provides a rough portrayal of the available human resources that each side possessed for potential combat. The reality of the situation, however, was that the 1.1 million military-aged slaves in the South could not be used for fighting on the front, and probably fewer than 30 percent of eligible whites in the border states sided with the southern cause.[3] By Ransom's estimate, the North could draw on a pool of 6.7 million men compared to the South's white total of only 2.1 million. Actual mobilization totaled 2.1 million in the North and 0.9 million in the South (1861–65). Conventional military wisdom of the day calculated a ratio of two to one for an offense to overcome

---

[2] As reported in R. Ransom from Allan Nevins, *Ordeal of the Union*, vol. 4 (New York: Scribners, 1950), p. 294.
[3] Ransom, p. 196.

a defending army. Ultimately those calculations proved valid, and the North had the capacity, if required, to out-man the South three to one.

In industrial capacity, the comparisons are even more lopsided. Value added in manufacturing in the North, according to Fred Bateman and Thomas Wiess, totalled $1.6 billion in 1860. It was merely $193 million in the South (half of it in Virginia). Initially neither side had any significant advantage in arms production and both sides depended heavily on imported arms. But the North was able to adjust quickly and produce its own armaments. The South was much less able to do this and the South's lack of domestic manufacture bore down heavily after the federal naval blockade of 1863–64 shut off foreign supplies. Particularly troubling to the South, especially after the North took control of the Mississippi River and various arteries, was the lack of a transport network sufficient to move food and supplies to the troops. The South's rail network was limited and strained to capacity, but the primary deficiency was the South's lack of horses and mules for moving men and supplies. As the fighting was largely on southern soil, the stocks of southern animals fell relatively to the North's as the war wore on.

SOUTHERN POLICIES

The South was tied to a limited range of production alternatives and was largely ineffective in its attempts to shift its resources out of agriculture and into manufacturing. With the exception of two new government built and operated munition factories, the South's agricultural emphasis was maintained much as in the antebellum period. The South's excessive self-confidence, either in the power of King Cotton, or the likelihood of a quick end to fighting encouraged it to adopt trade policies that sustained its poor preparation for war.

The northern naval blockade of the South was developed early, but it did not become really effective until 1863 and 1864. For nearly two years of the hostilities, it was feasible for the South to produce and export specialty crops like cotton to England in exchange for needed munitions and manufactures. However, the Confederate government discouraged exports in the hope of forcing England to support the southern effort, and only 13,000 bales of cotton from the 1861–62 crop of 4 million bales were exported. Also the southern government imposed a strict ban on cotton trade with the North. With the advantage of hindsight, it is clear that such policies weakened the southern war effort and helped to maintain a situation of inadequate supply. Meanwhile cotton was produced and wasted.

Besides production and trade problems, the South also faced financial difficulties. For the most part, foreigners were unwilling to lend sizable sums to the Confederacy, especially in the final years when the North's naval blockade was effective. The South's war materials and support, therefore,

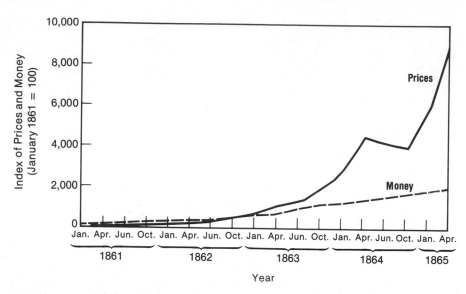

FIGURE 14-2   Inflation in the Confederacy: The rate of inflation was not very great in the beginning of the Civil War, but the value of a Confederate dollar had depreciated to about 1 percent of its original value by the end of the war.

Source: E. M. Lerner, "Money, Prices, and Wages in the Confederacy, 1861–1865," *Journal of Political Economy*, 63 (Feb. 1955), p. 29.

were financed primarily by inflationary means—by paper note issues. Only 40 percent of its expenditures were backed by taxes or borrowing.

Indexes of prices and money in the South given in Figure 14-2 show clearly that the final years were ones of hyperinflation. Whereas the stocks of money grew from an index of 100 in early 1861 to 2,000 by April 1865, the price level jumped from an index of 100 to 9,200. (Prices rose on an average of 10 percent every month.) Once people developed firm expectations about such increases, their spending patterns sped up.

A personal account of an exchange in 1864, by Mary Chesnut, reveals the uncertain and low value of Confederate dollars:

> She asked me 20 dollars for five dozen eggs and then said she would take it in "Confederate." Then I would have given her 100 dollars as easily. But if she had taken my offer of yarn! I haggle in yarn for the million the part of a thread! . . . When they ask for Confederate money, I never stop to chafer. I give them 20 or 50 dollar cheerfully for anything.[4]

Such reactions, of course, fueled the inflation even more, and once a Union victory appeared likely, the value of Confederate notes declined sharply.

---

[4]Dated March 7, 1864, from C. Vann Woodward, ed., *Mary Chesnut's Civil War* (New Haven: Yale Univ. Press, 1981), p. 749.

This precipitated the astronomical rates of inflation experienced in the final months of the war.

Valiant as the Confederate forces were, they could not preserve the economic strength of the South, and northern troops increasingly disrupted and occupied more and more southern territory. By late 1861, Union forces controlled Missouri, Kentucky, and West Virginia; union amphibious forces later took New Orleans in the spring of 1862. This strategic move cut off the major southern trade outlet. By 1863, the entire Mississippi River basin was under Union control, and Sherman's march through Georgia in 1864 splintered the Confederacy.

EFFECTS IN THE NORTH

The economic strain of the war on the North was not as severe as it was on the South, but the costs of the war were extremely high even there. A substantial portion of the labor force was reallocated toward the war effort, and the composition of production also changed with the disruption of cotton trade and growing default of southern debts. At the outset, in 1861, a sharp financial panic ensued and banks suspended payments of specie. With the federal treasury empty, the government quickly raised taxes and sold bonds. The tax changes included the first introduction of a small income tax, but the most significant increases were in tariffs and excise taxes. Yet bond sales brought in nearly three times the revenues of taxes. However, even these measures were inadequate, so the Union government also resorted to inflationary finance. Paper notes, termed "greenbacks" because of their color, were issued by the federal government. Unbacked by gold and silver, but based on the government's promise to redeem them, they fluctuated in value. In 1864, one gold dollar was worth two and one-half greenbacks, and the northern price level in 1864 was twice what it had been in 1860. Nevertheless, the North escaped the hyperinflation that confounded the South.

THE BEARD-HACKER THESIS

Writing in the years between the First and Second World Wars, Charles Beard and Louis Hacker provided a captivating interpretation of the Civil War to students of American history, namely that the war spurred industrial expansion. Their thesis emphasized the transfer of power from the southern agrarians to the northern industrial capitalists. With new power, the northerners passed legislation intended to propel the process of industrialization forward, including the establishment of the national banking system, the increase of tariffs, the adoption of contract labor law, and the grants of land to transcontinental railroads. We will discuss these pieces of legislation at length in later chapters; it is sufficient to note here that when the quantitative evidence is surveyed, it is clear that this war-torn decade was far from an industrial renaissance. Indeed, rather than being marked by rapid advances in industrialization and overall production, the Civil War decade was a definite departure from the trends in output, income, and productivity that had previously existed.

Perhaps this is less surprising when we realize that nearly 1 million men— or almost 15 percent of the labor force of 7.5 million—were normally involved in the fighting each year. Of these working-age soldiers, 259,000 Confederate men and 360,000 Union men were killed and another 261,000 southerners and 356,000 northerners were wounded. One person was killed and another wounded for every six slaves freed and for every ten southerners kept within the Union. These permanent losses of labor and human capital have been assessed by Claudia Goldin and Frank Lewis to have had economic values approaching $1.8 billion ($1.06 billion in the North; $787 million in the South—all lost). In addition, the North spent $2.3 billion directly on the war effort; the South spent $1 billion through direct government outlays. An additional $1.5 billion worth of property was destroyed, most of this in the South. These combined sums of $6.6 billion were probably more than twice the size of our national income in 1860, and exceeded eight times the value added of total U.S. manufacturing that year. Clearly, on the face of it the Beard–Hacker thesis appears unsupportable. The tragedy of the war is compounded by the fact that in 1860 the total value of slaves was approximately $3.06 billion.[5] The war costs of emancipation exceeded slave purchase costs by more than double. This is not to suggest that peaceful abolition was a realistic policy option shortly before the war. After 1845 peaceful abolition like that undertaken by the British in the West Indies was viewed in the U.S. South as a complete disaster. It was clear to all that the economy of the West Indies was in shambles and slaveowners lost fortunes in the process of emancipation.

The work of Stanley Engerman and Robert Gallman provide further ground for rejecting the Beard-Hacker thesis. For example, the growth rate of total commodity output in the Civil War decade was by far the lowest of any decade of the century after 1820. As shown in Table 14-1, the trends of total commodity production between 1840 and 1860 reveal average yearly growth rates of 4.6 percent. Between 1870 and 1900, these rates were 4.4 percent. The rates during the Civil War decade, however, were only 2.0 percent, less than half those during normal times before and after.

This same sharp decline occurred in the growth of manufacturing output in the 1860s, also as shown in Table 14-1. Agricultural output grew at a slower rate in the 1860s. Clearly, the Civil War decade was a sharp and costly break in the nation's long-run growth trend. The hypothesis of a direct

---

[5]Roger L. Ransom and Richard Sutch, "Capitalists without Capital: The Burden of Slavery and the Impact of Emancipation," *Agricultural History* 62, no. 3 (Summer 1988): 151.

TABLE 14-1   Average Annual Rate of Growth of Commodity Output, 1840–99

Years	U.S. Economy	Manufacturing Sector
1840–59	4.6	7.8
1860–69	2.0	2.3
1870–99	4.4	6.0

Source: Robert E. Gallman, "Commodity Output, 1839–99," in *Trends in the American Economy in the Nineteenth Century*, 24, Series on Income and Wealth (Princeton: Princeton Univ. Press, 1960).

short-run war-related demand stimulus that spurred economic growth must be rejected.

The Long-Run Effects

To test for the alleged stimulating long-run economic effects of the Civil War it is informative to compare prewar trends with postwar trends. Thanks to the efforts of Robert Gallman[6] such comparisons are possible. The following trend rates are for the two separate periods 1839–59 and 1869–99, respectively. First, the average decade rates of growth in value added in agriculture were 38 percent before the war and 32 percent afterwards.[7] In manufacturing, they were 133 percent and 80 percent; in mining, 112 percent and 99 percent; and in construction, 66 percent and 36 percent. The rates of growth per decade in employment in each of these sectors, except construction, also show much slower advances in the postwar decades than before the war.[8] Finally, taking growth rates per decade of real value added per worker, we observe in agriculture an advance from 7 percent in 1839–59 to 12 percent in 1869–99.[9] Alternatively, in mining and manufacturing combined there is little change in the rates of growth of labor productivity, averaging 25 percent and 24 percent. In construction, the rate fell from 27 percent before the war to 5 percent afterward.

Even within the various war industries of the North, there was no great spurt and by and large, the new dimensions of output in the North were modest adjustments in the various sectors. In fact, the most startling aspect of the war years was the minute stimuli to manufacturing. Iron production for small arms increased, but iron production for railroads declined. Although the demand for clothes and boots for servicemen stimulated manufactures, the loss of the southern market more than offset this. For example, in

---

[6]Robert E. Gallman, "Commodity Output, 1839–1899," in *Trends in the American Economy in the Nineteenth Century*, 24, Series on Income and Wealth (Princeton: Princeton Univ. Press, 1960); also see Stanley L. Engerman, "The Economic Impact of the Civil War," *Explorations in Economic History* (Spring 1966).
[7]Gallman, p. 24.
[8]Gallman, p. 30.
[9]Gallman, p. 31.

Massachusetts—the major state of boot and shoe production—employment and output in that important industry decreased almost one-third during the war period. Similarly, without raw cotton, the textile mills were underutilized. Nevertheless, the enlistment and conscription of men ameliorated the unemployment problem, and speculation offered opportunities for enrichment for a select few. Overall, however, expenditures by the federal government did not spur rapid industrialization or economic expansion. They were primarily a shifting of resources from the private sector into the war effort. This was a costly transfer, and as we noted, one that exceeded the total value of slaves freed by force.

THE INEQUITIES OF WAR

The war imposed inequities as well as resource allocation problems. Like the Vietnam War, where the actual fighting was improportionately carried by lower-income whites, blacks, and Hispanics, fighting in the Civil War was primarily waged by low-income whites. Once the need for mass mobilization was evident both sides turned to the draft to acquire men. From this time on the war was widely viewed as a "rich man's war and a poor man's fight." Both sides allowed conscripts to buy out their service by paying another to go in their place. Sons of wealthy families or high income earners, therefore, were often able to pay poor people in need to replace and fulfill their military obligation.[10] In the North, the most heated discontent was witnessed in the cities, especially in New York where large numbers of immigrants lived. The Irish, especially, felt that the burden of the draft was falling unfavorably on them. Mobs stormed through the streets of New York for four days in July of 1863 before order was restored by federal troops (20,000 strong); and 105 deaths resulted from these riots.

The problem of inequality was even more glaring in the South. In October 1862, the southern draft law was altered to allow an exemption for anyone owning 20 or more slaves. Although the numbers benefiting from this exemption were small, the resentment it created was great. Small farmers were infuriated as their farms, essentially dependent on their labor for operations and maintenance, deteriorated while rich plantations prospered. R. M. Radford of Virginia wrote the Secretary of War in October 1864:

> The people will not *always* submit to this *unequal, unjust,* and partial distribution of favor and wholesale conscription of the *poor* white able-bodied and healthy men of property are all occupying *soft* places.[11]

----

[10]While this policy option shifted the burden of fighting to the poor, it arguably had efficiency advantages. The exchanges were supposedly voluntary and without compulsion, and if those with higher labor opportunity costs were replaced by those with lower opportunity costs, the costs of the war effort were reduced overall. The inequities remained however.

[11]R. M. Radford to James Seddon, quoted in Paul Escott, *After Secession: Jefferson Davis and the Failure of Confederate Nationalism* (Baton Range: Louisiana State Univ. Press, 1978), p. 119.

TABLE 14-2   Commodity Output Per Capita by Region (in 1879 prices)

Year	Outside the South	South
1860	$ 74.8	$77.7
1870	81.5	47.6
1880	105.8	61.5

Source: Stanley Engerman, "The Economic Impact of the Civil War," *Explorations in Economic History* (Spring 1966), p. 181.

Earlier, in 1861, a Georgian also saw the looming fight as a rich man's war and a poor man's fight:

> Is it right that the poor man should be taxed for the support of the war, when the war was brought about on the slave question, and the slave at home accumulating for the benefit of his master, and the poor man's farm left uncultivated and a chance for his wife to be a widow, and his children orphan?[12]

Slaves were not used by the South for fighting because both masters and slaves knew the enemy provided a route to freedom.[13] Ironically, the efforts of slaves to grow cotton spurred on by the exceptionally high prices in the early 1860s was negated by the South's trade policies to England. Most of this vital labor was simply wasted, as high stockpiles of cotton rotted in the countryside and on the docks.

THE AFTERMATH OF THE CIVIL WAR

The outcome of the war was a distinct reversal in the relative income positions of the North and South. As shown in Table 14-2, the South's real commodity output per capita of $77.8 in 1860, slightly exceeded that of $74.8 in the North. By 1870, the North's per capita output exceeded the South's by nearly two-thirds ($81.5 compared to $47.6). This advantage remained in 1880 ($105.08 compared to $61.5). The major source of this reversal was not the northern and midwestern advance, but the absolute dramatic decline in southern output during and shortly after the war. The Civil War decade ushered in the roots of southern economic backwardness, another reflection of a costly war and incomplete recovery in the South.

It would be an error, however, to conclude that the southern economy remained stagnant. The commodity output per capita figures for 1870 and 1880 show the South's growth rate was initially rapid, and close to the North's growth rate of almost 2.6 percent yearly. Such high rates were not sustained,

---

[12]Letter to Rome, *Georgia Weekly Courier*, January 25, in Escott, p. 95.
[13]More accurately, slaves were not used by the South until the very end of the war when the South's desperate situation provided little choice. The North used greater numbers of blacks also toward the war's end.

TABLE 14-3   Annual Rates of Growth in Constant-Dollar Values of Per Capita Personal Income by State Between 1879 and 1899

State	Annual Percentage Rates of Growth Per Capita Personal Income
Louisiana	0.44
Georgia	0.81
Mississippi	0.96
South Carolina	0.98
Alabama	1.14
Five cotton states	0.86
North Carolina	1.38
Kentucky	1.42
Arkansas	1.43
Tennessee	1.89
Virginia	2.15
West Virginia	2.26
Texas	2.53
Florida	2.64
Total, 13 southern states	1.59
United States	1.59

Source: Derived from Richard Easterlin, "Regional Growth of Income: Long-Term Tendencies, 1880–1950," in *Population Redistribution and Economic Growth, United States 1870–1950*, vol. 2, *Analyses of Economic Change*, ed., S. Kuznets, A. R. Miller, and R. A. Easterlin (Philadelphia: American Philosophical Society, 1960), p. 185.

however, nor were they distributed evenly across the South. Table 14-3 shows estimates of the rate of growth of personal income per capita in real terms for the five most cotton-dependent states of the Deep South (Louisiana, Georgia, Mississippi, South Carolina, and Alabama), and for the remaining eight southern states from 1879 to 1899. Clearly there was great variation among the southern states, with several growing more than twice as fast as those comprising the Deep South.

As this evidence would suggest, and for other reasons discussed later, the economy of the South rebounded from the war more quickly in the area of manufacturing than in that of agriculture. Southern manufacturing output had approached prewar levels by the early 1870s, and the South's transportation network, based on steamboats, roads, and railroads, had been completely revitalized. This revitalization was accomplished with reasonable ease requiring little more than repairs and replacements and modest additions of capital. Actually, such rapid postwar recoveries have been quite common as noted explicitly by the astute contemporary observer J. S. Mill:

... the great rapidity with which countries recover from a state of devastation. ... An enemy lays waste a country by fire and sword, and destroys or carries away nearly all the moveable wealth existing in it; all the inhabitants are ruined, and yet in a few years after, everything is much as it was before. ...

The possibility of a rapid repair of their disasters, mainly depends on whether the country has been depopulated. If its effective population have not been extirpated at the time, and are not starved afterwards; then, with the same skill and knowledge which they had before, with their land and its permanent improvements undestroyed, and the more durable buildings probably unimpaired, or only partially injured, they have nearly all the requisites for their former amount of production.[14]

Rapid regeneration is propelled by investments in particular bottleneck areas—key capital resources devastated by the war, but which when restored initiate the reemployment of temporarily idled complementary resources. For example, the South's railroad network had nearly totally collapsed by the war's end, largely due to the lack of rolling stock and partially destroyed track; the roadbed, specialized labor expertise, and considerable track remained in good condition, but were unusable. Prompt investment in the essential complementary resources (rolling stock and damaged track) reemployed the other existing resources (in our example, the labor, roadbed, and usable track). This initiated a regenerative spurt, and other similar spurts in combination would lead to a temporary high-growth period. When these unusual investment opportunities had been fully exploited, the long-run slower rate of growth would resume.[15]

In agriculture, however, the prospects for southern recovery were quite different. Lincoln's Emancipation Proclamation altered the whole makeup of the South's agricultural society for whites and blacks. The highly significant "once and for all" change brought about great reductions in agricultural output, especially during the late war years and the immediate postwar years. In the absence of emancipation, the South's agricultural sector surely would have restored itself within a few years. But due to the political, social, and economic adjustments stemming from emancipation, regenerative growth was long delayed. Moreover, the decline in southern output, especially in the cotton states of the Deep South, was much deeper than that precipitated by war destruction alone. As indicated in Figure 14-3, the growth of agricultural output in the Deep South averaged *minus* 0.96 percent per year from 1857 to 1879.

DECLINE IN THE DEEP SOUTH

The five key cotton states of South Carolina, Louisiana, Georgia, Alabama, and Mississippi, which composed the Deep South, have been shown both

---

[14]J. S. Mill, *Principles of Political Economy*, 1848, Book I, Chapter 5, Section 7.
[15]For elaboration on the theory of regenerative growth see Donald F. Gordon and Gary M. Walton, "A New Theory of Regenerative Growth and the Post-World War II Experience of West Germany," in *Explorations in the New Economic History: Essays in Honor of Douglass C. North,* ed. Roger L. Ransom, Richard Sutch, and Gary M. Walton (New York: Academic Press, 1982), pp. 171–92.

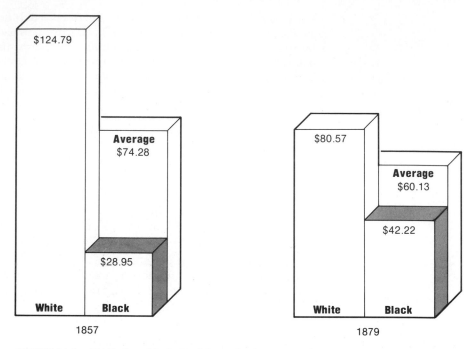

FIGURE 14-3   Distribution of Agricultural Output Per Capita by Race in the Deep South, 1857 and 1879.

Source: Roger L. Ransom and Richard Sutch, "Growth and Welfare in the American South," in *Market Institutions and Economic Progress in the New South 1865–1900*, ed. Gary M. Walton and James F. Shepherd (New York: Academic Press, 1981), p. 145.

in Table 14-3 and Figure 14-3 to have experienced the greatest setbacks of the period. There were three principal reasons for this precipitous decline. First, the highly efficient plantation system centered there was lost forever, and attempts to resurrect plantation methods proved futile. Assembly-line characteristics and old methods of driving gangs of workers were shunned by free blacks, just as they always had been by free whites. In place of the plantations, there arose smaller units—some owned, many rented, and many sharecropped. Table 14-4 shows the alteration in farm sizes between 1860 and 1870 in the Deep South. Whereas in 1860, 61 percent of the farms were less than 100 acres, in 1870, 81 percent were under 100 acres. Alternatively, the percentage of total land utilized by plantations over 100 acres was 81 percent in 1860, but only 50 percent by 1870. In short, economies of scale were lost.

Second, there was a significant withdrawal of labor from the fields, especially women and children. This reallocation of human effort undoubtedly raised household production, but as we know, this type of production is not tabulated in our national (or regional) income accounts. Measured per capita agricultural output in the Deep South fell 30–40 percent in 1860–70.

TABLE 14-4   Farm Size Distribution in Five Major Cotton States

Improved Acres	Percentage of Farms in Size Class		Percentage of Land in Size Class	
	1860	1870	1860	1870
3–49	36.9	60.9	7.4	20.2
50–99	24.2	19.8	12.0	19.6
100–499	32.0	17.2	47.6	49.1
500+	6.9	2.1	33.0	11.0

Source: Roger Ransom and Richard Sutch, *One Kind of Freedom* (Cambridge: Cambridge Univ. Press, 1977), p. 71.

The overall withdrawal of labor in percentage terms was similar.[16] This decline in labor input, however, was not matched by similar percentage reductions in capital and land. Consequently, the output reduction due to the labor withdrawal was less than the labor reduction itself.[17]

Finally, the world demand for cotton slowed in the late nineteenth century and this slowly growing market became more restrictive for U.S. cotton as new areas of the world (India, Brazil, and Egypt) gained on the South. The U.S. South dominated the world cotton market in 1860, commanding 77 percent of English imports.[18] In the war years 1862–65, however, when the door to the new competition was opened, it fell to 10 percent. The U.S. South's share rebounded well in the late 1870s, but not until over 15 years had passed, and even then it never reached its 1860 highmark.

In combination, the abandonment of plantation agriculture, the voluntary but steep withdrawal of labor, and the slow-up in the world market for cotton nullified the forces of regeneration in the Deep South. Moreover, the new social and economic structure that emerged there lacked flexibility. One of the peculiarities of the five most cotton-dependent states comprising the Deep South was the advance in concentration of cotton production on the smaller farms. Unlike the prewar small southern farm, the small postwar farms, especially the new ex-slave operated farms, became highly specialized in cotton production.

For example, in the five main cotton growing states, 82 percent of non-slave farms grew cotton in 1860 (85 percent of all farms) compared to 97

[16]See Roger L. Ransom and Richard Sutch, "The Impact of the Civil War and of Emancipation on Southern Agriculture," *Explorations in Economic History* 12:1 (Jan. 1975), p. 14.
[17]Output reduction would match labor reduction exactly only if capital, land, and labor inputs were combined in fixed and unalterable amounts.
[18]See Thomas Ellison, *The Cotton Trade of Great Britain* (Augustus Kelley, 1968) cited in Gavin Wright, "Cotton Competition and the Post-Bellum Recovery of the American South," *Journal of Economic History* 34 (1974): 611. Also see Gavin Wright, *The Political Economy of the Cotton South* (New York: W. W. Norton, 1978) and his *Old South, New South: Revolution in the Southern Economy* (New York: Basic Books, 1986).

percent of all farms there in 1870.[19] Moreover, a greater proportion of acres per farm was devoted to cotton production in the Deep South in 1870 than in 1860. Black farmers were the most cotton dependent, with 85 percent of their crop in cotton, compared to 60 to 70 percent for white farmers. White owners placed the smallest proportion of their land in cotton; white tenant farmers produced nearly twice that of white owners, and black tenants nearly four times that of white owners. This growing dependency on cotton, especially for tenant farmers, black and white, occurred despite declining cotton prices in the 1870s.

Why was the post-war Deep South so inflexible? So tied to cotton? The compelling argument by Roger Ransom and Richard Sutch is that the near absence of credit institutions in the Deep South and lack of collateral by most farmers forced them into cotton production. This "lock-in" resulted from the necessity of offering cotton crop liens for credit to buy food and other necessities. The source of rural credit was the white-owned country store.[20] The crop lien was a powerful means of control, and storekeepers, nearly 8,000 throughout the rural South, soon learned that by insisting on payment in cotton a secondary, but profitable, advantage befell them. Not only could they charge high interest on loans (40 to 70 percent per annum) but by insisting on repayment in cotton, borrowers became long-term debtors. Being less able to produce their own food by crop loan directives, debtor farmers had to buy food from the country stores at marked-up prices. Indeed, two sets of food prices were common in country stores, one for cash and one bought on time to be paid at the end of the season. This arrangement of credit locked in many farmers to cotton specialization and persistent hardship.[21]

The personalized nature of the rural credit system, poor roads, high information costs and poor means of communication added to the conditions of local credit monopoly in the countryside. The destruction of the old banking system in the South further prolonged these conditions. The market response to the credit vacuum created was woefully slow, a perplexing anomaly in the history of the American economy.

However, such problems were not endemic to the entire South, as we have noted. To recall the evidence from Table 14-3, such states as Virginia, West Virginia, Texas, and Florida showed remarkable recoveries and sustained advances following the war. Moreover, many areas of the South began to urbanize rapidly after 1880.[22]

---

[19]These figures are from Roger Ransom, *The House Divided,* Table 7-3, p. 257(s).

[20]As late as 1880 there were only 42 national banks in the Deep South out of 2,061 in the nation as a whole (126 in the 12 former Confederate states).

[21]For further discussion of these and other issues in the postwar South, see Gary M. Walton and James F. Shepherd, eds., *Market Institutions and Economic Progress in the New South 1865–1900* (New York: Academic Press, 1981).

[22]Kenneth Weiher, "The Cotton Industry and Southern Urbanization, 1880–1930," *Explorations in Economic History* (April 1977): 120–49.

The appearance then of southern backwardness in the early part of the second half of the nineteenth century, and its persistence thereafter, was not a result of prolonged stagnation in the South generally. Like the North, certain states in the South enjoyed sustained periods of economic progress throughout almost all of the nineteenth century. The Civil War decade, however, was a major economic watershed for the entire nation, and the Deep South suffered especially drastic setbacks from the war and its aftermath and King Cotton was transformed into the crop of poverty.

THE LEGACY OF SLAVERY

The Amendments to the Constitution that freed all slaves assured that no "state shall deprive any person of life, liberty or property, without due process of law," and guaranteed that "the right of citizens to vote shall not be abridged." These were passed soon after the war but were not sufficient to assure sustained progress for blacks. The first effects of the new freedoms surely helped blacks dramatically. As surely, many southern whites suffered in the late 1860s. Average wealth holdings of whites in the Deep South in 1860 were $81,400 for plantation owners, $13,300 for slaveowning small farmers, and $2,400 for non-slaveowning farmers. In 1870 the average for all white farmers in the Deep South was $3,200. White resentment against Yankees, and blacks, reflected their slide in wealth and hatred of the northern occupation.

The power of northern Republicans to assure a solid base of reconstruction in the South was limited by economic conditions nationally and by an absence of effective local support in the South. When President Johnson's executive order of total amnesty to anyone willing to take an oath of allegiance was upheld by the courts, the powers over state and local matters were swiftly transferred from the federal government into the hands of old Confederates. Ways to avoid the Constitutional Amendments were eventually found and blacks ultimately became disenfranchised for all practical purposes. By the turn of the century laws were being passed—commonly called "black codes" and "Jim Crow Laws," which segregated blacks and maintained their impoverishment. Such laws determined where blacks could work, live, eat and drink, ride on public transport, and go to school.

Up until the 1940s the southern economy, especially that of the Deep South, remained a low-wage economy distinctive for its absence of inward migration. Further, labor lost by outward migration was quickly replaced by rapid population growth spurred by high birth rates in the South.

Gavin Wright's book *Old South, New South* describes the South based on a prolonged legacy of slavery with a poorly educated black and white population pinned down by ignorance and by an absence of alternatives. The evidence supports his case. Ninety percent of freed slaves were illiterate, and public schools in the South and public expenditures per pupil remained

Typical of most blacks in the postwar South, the couple in this photograph taken in 1875—twelve years after emancipation—remained entrapped in poverty.

a mere fraction of those in the North. Wealthy influential southerners argued effectively that educating the poor merely encouraged their migration north in pursuit of higher wages. In addition, as we have seen, cotton became increasingly labor intensive as farm sizes fell in the Deep South. By the late nineteenth century southern farms were smaller than northern farms, the reverse of the antebellum years. Mechanization was thereby slowed in the South, and low wages and earnings were maintained. The northern victory did break up the plantation, but the postwar patterns of land ownership in the South changed little. Ransom and Sutch show that the wealthy fifth of the population owned 75 percent of the land in 1860[23] while in 1870 it was 73 percent. The war did little to distribute the land more evenly. A bill to give black heads of households 40 acres each passed by the House and Senate was vetoed by President Johnson. This perpetuated a large landless class of uneducated and largely unskilled workers in the rural South.

As shown in Figure 14-4, blacks occupied and operated about 30 percent of the land in crops; whites, worked 70 percent. Blacks were close to 70 percent of the agricultural work force in 1880 but owned less than 10

---

[23]Roger L. Ransom and Richard Sutch, *One Kind of Freedom* (Cambridge: Cambridge Univ. Press, 1977), p. 79.

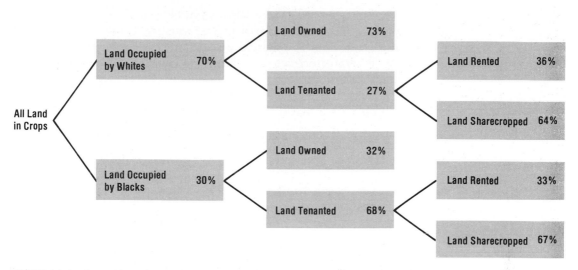

FIGURE 14-4   Ownership and Use of Farm Land in Crops in the Deep South by Race, 1880.

Source: Adapted from Roger L. Ransom and Richard Sutch, *One Kind of Freedom: The Economic Consequences of Emancipation*
(New York: Cambridge Univ. Press, 1977), p. 84.

percent of the land.[24] Given the resistance and hostility of white southerners and the absence of any federal redistribution program, it is a wonder that this much land was owned by blacks. Of the two-thirds of the land that was tenant occupied by blacks, two-thirds of that was sharecropped.

Sharecropping spread rapidly throughout the cotton South. Standard yearly contracts gave a fifty-fifty split to owner and tenant, thereby risks, were evenly split. Ex-slaves and poor whites were provided independence from day to day bossing and a chance to earn a living. It was a slow means to a fortune however, and, as the markets for cotton remained depressed, so did earnings. Meanwhile, the debtor status of sharecroppers and all tenants in cotton locked them into a sustained poverty trap.

Rather than southern industrialization, which progressed only painfully slowly,[25] it was ultimately northern industrialization and its growing demand for labor that allowed many southern blacks to break out of the southern poverty trap. As Wright emphasizes, northerners shunned investments in the South, and Ransom and Sutch show that wealthy southerners invested large amounts in the North in the postwar years. While wages converged within regions, a striking wage gap remained between the North and

[24]Specifically, 30 percent black occupied times 32 percent black owned equals 9.6 percent, the total percent of land owned by blacks (see Figure 14-4).
[25]See Fred Bateman and Thomas Weiss, *Deplorable Scarcity* (Chapel Hill: Univ. of North Carolina Press, 1981).

South. The separateness of these labor markets remained until blacks in great numbers began moving North to the industrial cities.[26] Before 1910, however, the Deep South remained a stagnant, relatively isolated region startling for its characteristics of relative retardation, poverty, and racial disadvantage.

SELECTED REFERENCES AND SUGGESTED READINGS

Aldrich, Mark. "Flexible Exchange Rates, Northern Expansion, and the Market for Southern Cotton, 1866–1879." *Journal of Economic History* 33 (1973): 399–416.

Andreano, Ralph, ed. *The Economic Impact of the Civil War.* Cambridge, Mass.: Schenkman, 1964.

Bateman, Fred, and Thomas Weiss. *Deplorable Scarcity.* Chapel Hill: Univ. of North Carolina Press, 1981.

Brown, William, and Reynolds Morgan. "Debt Peonage Reconsidered." *Journal of Economic History* 33 (1973): 862–71.

Cochran, Thomas. "Did the Civil War Retard Industrialization?" *Mississippi Valley Historical Review* 48 (Sept. 1961).

DeCanio, Stephen. "Cotton 'Overproduction' and Late Nineteenth-Century Southern Agriculture." *Journal of Economic History* 33 (1973): 608–33.

———. "Productivity and Income Distribution in the Post-Bellum South." *Journal of Economic History* 34 (1974): 422–46.

DeCanio, Stephen, and Joel Mokyr. "Inflation and Wage Lag During the American Civil War." *Journal of Economic History* 35 (June 1975).

Engerman, Stanley. "The Economic Impact of the Civil War." In *The Reinterpretation of American Economic History,* Robert Fogel and Stanley Engerman. New York: Harper & Row, 1971.

———. "Some Economic Factors in Southern Backwardness in the Nineteenth Century," in *Essays in Regional Economics,* eds. John F. Kain and John R. Meyer. Cambridge: Harvard Univ. Press, 1971.

Goldin, Claudia, and Frank Lewis. "The Economic Cost of the American Civil War." *Journal of Economic History* 35 (1975): 294–326.

Graves, Philip E., Robert L. Sexton, and Richard K. Vedder. "Slavery, Amenities, and Factor Price Equalization: A Note on Migration and Freedmen," *Explorations in Economic History* 20 (1983): 156–62.

Hacker, Louis. *The Triumph of American Capitalism.* New York: Columbia Univ. Press, 1940.

Higgs, Robert. *Competition and Coercion: Blacks in the American Economy, 1865–1914.* New York: Cambridge Univ. Press, 1977.

———. "Patterns of Farm Rental in the Georgia Cotton Belt, 1880–1900." *Journal of Economic History* 34 (1974): 468–82.

———. "Race, Tenure, and Resource Allocation in Southern Agriculture." *Journal of Economic History* 33 (1973): 149–69.

Lebergott, Stanley. "Through the Blockade: The Profitability and Extent of Cotton Smuggling, 1861–1865." *Journal of Economic History* 41 (1981): 867–88.

Lerner, Eugene. "Money, Wages and Prices in the Confederacy." *Journal of Economic History* 63 (Feb. 1955).

Mandle, Jay R. "The Plantation States as a Sub-Region of the Post-Bellum South." *Journal of Economic History* 34 (1974): 732–38.

McGuire, Robert A., and Robert Higgs. "Cotton, Corn, and Risk in the Nineteenth Century:

---

[26]See Richard Vedder, Lowell Gallaway, Philip E. Graves, and Robert Sexton, "Demonstrating their Freedom: The Post-Emancipation Migration of Black Americans," in *Research in Economic History* (Greenwich, CT: JAI Press, 1986), pp. 213–39.

Another View." *Explorations in Economic History* 14 (1979): 167–82.

——— . "A Portfolio Analysis of Crop Diversification and Risk in the Cotton South." *Explorations in Economic History* 17 (1980): 342–71.

Ransom, Roger L. *Conflict and Compromise: The Political Economy of Slavery, Emancipation, and the American Civil War.* New York and London: Cambridge Univ. Press, 1989.

Ransom, Roger L., and Richard Sutch. "Capitalists without Capital: The Burden of Slavery and the Impact of Emancipation." *Agricultural History* 62 (Summer 1988): 133–60.

——— . "The Ex Slave in the Post Bellum South." *Journal of Economic History* 33 (1973): 131–48.

——— . "The Impact of the Civil War and of Emancipation on Southern Agriculture." *Explorations in Economic History* 12 (Jan. 1975): 1–28.

——— . *One Kind of Freedom: The Economic Consequences of Emancipation.* New York: Cambridge Univ. Press, 1977.

Reid, Joseph. "Sharecropping as an Understandable Market Response: The Postbellum South." *Journal of Economic History* 33 (1973): 106–30.

Sellers, James L. "The Economic Incidence of the Civil War in the South." *Mississippi Valley Historical Review* 14 (Sept. 1927).

Stampp, Kenneth. *The Era of Reconstruction, 1865–1877.* New York: Knopf, 1966.

Temin, Peter. "The Post-Bellum Recovery of the South and the Cost of the Civil War." *Journal of Economic History* 36 (1976) 898–907.

Vedder, Richard, Lowell Galloway, Philip E. Graves, and Robert L. Sexton. "Demonstrating Their Freedom: The Post-Emancipation Migration of Black Americans." *Research in Economic History.* Greenwich, CT: JAI Press, 1986, 10:213–39.

Woodward, C. Vann. *The Strange Career of Jim Crow.* New York: Oxford Univ. Press, 1966.

Wright, Gavin. *Old South, New South: Revolutions in the Southern Economy.* New York: Basic Books, 1986.

——— . *The Political Economy of the Cotton South.* New York: W. W. Norton, 1978.

Wright, Gavin, and Howard Kunreuther. "Cotton, Corn, and Risk in the Nineteenth Century." *Journal of Economic History* 35 (1975): 526–51.

Walton, Gary M., and James Shepherd. *Market Institutions and Economic Progress in the New South, 1865–1900.* New York: Academic Press, 1981.

CHAPTER 15

Western Agriculture's Advance

During the 30 years following the Civil War, the western frontier was eclipsed. Spearheading the drive into the remaining vacant western territories were miners and cowboys. Gold and silver discoveries like those near Pikes Peak, Colorado, the famed Comstock Lode of silver in Nevada, and the last great gold rush in 1874 into the Black Hills of South Dakota, stampeded miners west.

Also after the war, the range cattle industry developed on the great plains, and cowboys came in vast numbers to spur cattle along the long drives to market. The origins of the long drives from Texas began in 1866, but by the 1880s cattle barons of great wealth spanned the territories from Texas to Montana. The long cattle drives were destined for the nearest rail heads, in the earliest years to Sedalia, Missouri, but later to Abilene and then Dodge City, Kansas (for transport to Chicago). The rise and decline of the great long-distance cattle drives is fascinating history and superb folklore.[1] Wild Bill Hickock, Wyatt Earp, Doc Holiday, and Bat Masterson were glorified in the cattle towns of Kansas. As David Galenson has shown, the long drives ended abruptly in 1885 not because of the advent of barbed wire as popularly believed. Rather, it was the over stocking of the northern ranges as well as the passage and enforcement of quarantine laws there to keep out the distant Texas herds.[2]

However important miners and cattlemen were as path-breakers, the abiding economic pattern of the West was set by the families who settled down on tracts of land. Most of the participants in the final opening of new

---

[1] The movie classic *Red River* starring John Wayne and Montgomery Cliff and the 1989 CBS TV special "Lonesome Dove" are recommended. Also see Lewis Atherton, *The Cattle Kings* (Bloomington: Indiana Univ. Press, 1961). Although the scions of wealthy eastern families like Richard Trimble and Teddy Roosevelt could not resist the West, the men who started from scratch and became fabulously successful were for the most part country boys from the Midwest and South or cowboys only a few years away from the hard-drinking, roistering life of Newton or Dodge City.

[2] For an in-depth account of the reasons long drives were abruptly ended in 1885, see David Galenson, "The End of the Chisholm Trail," *Journal of Economic History* 24:2 (June 1974), pp. 350–64.

TABLE 15-1 Total Number of Farms and Acres by Decade, 1860–1920

Year	Number of Farms (in hundred thousands)	Percent Increase	Number of Acres (in hundred thousands)	Percent Increase
1860	2.0		407	
		35		0
1870	2.7		408	
		48		31
1880	4.0		536	
		15		16
1890	4.6		623	
		24		35
1900	5.7		839	
		11		5
1910	6.4		879	
		2		9
1920	6.5		956	

Source: U.S. Bureau of the Census, p. 457, and *Historical Statistics,* 1976, Series K 2 and J 18.

land came from places that only a few years before had been the object of settlement. People who moved into Kansas, Nebraska, and the Dakotas, and later into Montana and Colorado, more often than not traveled only *short distances* to get there. They might have settled previously in Missouri or Iowa, Minnesota or Wisconsin, Indiana or Illinois. Or they might have been the sons and daughters of the pioneers of a previous generation. It was not uncommon for settlers to move from place to place within one of the new states. No matter how bitter previous pioneer experiences had been or how drab and unrewarding the life was on virgin land, the hope of better times always persisted if only new soil could be broken farther west.

Table 15-1 shows the total number of farms and farm acres by decade from 1860 to 1920. The decades of sharpest advance were the 1870s and 1890s. As discussed in Chapter 14, the 1860s were unusual because of the break up of southern plantations, which added significantly to the number of farms, but not to acreage. The addition of land input in the 1870s and 1890s was tremendous, however, more than doubling in 30 years, 1870–1900.

FEDERAL LAND POLICY

The absence of southern democrats in Congress, who had opposed a homestead act, allowed the Republican Congress to pass the Homestead Act of 1862. Recall from Chapter 8 that this Act, which provided 160 acres per homestead (320 per married couple), continued the federal government's liberalization of land policy. At the time of the Act, prime fertile lands remained unclaimed in western Iowa and western Minnesota and in the eastern parts of Kansas, Nebraska, and the Dakotas. But these were soon taken, leaving little except the unclaimed lands west of the hundredth meridian in the Great Plains (an area of light annual precipitation) or in the vast mountain regions. Consequently in most of the plains and mountain regions, a 160-acre homestead was impractical economically, being suitable only for grazing livestock, which required much larger areas. Between 1870 and 1900, less than one in five new acres added to farming were due to homestead entries.

Miners and timber magnets and other vested interest groups also pressed Congress to liberalize land policy, winning four more land Acts:

1. *The Timber-Culture Act of 1873.* This law, passed ostensibly to encourage the growth of timber in arid regions, made available 160 acres of free land to anyone who would agree to plant trees on 40 acres of it.

2. *The Desert Land Act of 1877.* By the terms of this law, 640 acres at $1.25 an acre could be purchased by anyone who would agree to irrigate the land within three years. (The serious defect of this Act was that there were no clearly defined stipulations as to what constituted irrigation.)

3. *The Timber and Stone Act of 1878.* This statute provided for the sale at $2.50 an acre of valuable timber and stone lands in Nevada, California, Oregon, and Washington.

4. *The Timber-Cutting Act of 1878.* This law authorized residents of certain specified areas to cut trees on government lands without charge, with the stipulation that the timber be used for agricultural, mining, and domestic building purposes.

The transfer of public lands into private hands also included purchases at public auctions under the Preemption Act. This act, as noted in Chapter 8, allowed first rights of sale to settlers who arrived and worked the land before public sales were offered.[3] Furthermore, huge acreages granted by the government as subsidies to western railroads and to states for various purposes were in turn sold to settlers. Nearly 100 million acres from the Indian territories were opened for purchase by the Dawes Act of 1887 and subsequent measures.

Under the first administration of Grover Cleveland, steps were taken to reverse policy and to tighten up on the disposition of public lands, but Congress did not pass any major legislation for several years. In a single bill, the General Revision Act of 1891, critical loopholes were closed. The Preemption Act, which had encouraged "squatting" was repealed, and to the Desert Land Act of 1877 were appended definite provisions regarding the irrigation of land secured under this law. The Timber-Cutting Act of

---

[3] As late as 1891, an individual could buy a maximum of 1,120 acres at one time under the public land acts. Unlimited amounts of land could be purchased from railroad companies and from states at higher, although still nominal, prices.

1878 was repealed, removing from the books one of the most flagrantly abused of all the land laws. Finally, the President was authorized by the 1891 Act to set aside forest preserves—the first step in the conservation movement that had been gaining popular support.

After the turn of the century, the Homestead Act itself was modified to enable settlers to obtain practical-sized farms and beginning in 1904, a whole section (one square mile or 640 acres) could be homesteaded in western Nebraska. A few years later, the Enlarged Homestead Act made it possible to obtain a half-section in many areas free of charge. Still later, residence requirements were reduced to three years, and the Stock-Raising Homestead Act of 1916 allowed the homesteading of 640 acres of land suitable only for grazing purposes. Whereas only one acre in five added to farming before 1900 was due to homesteaders, the ratio jumped to nine in ten in 1900–20.

The Distribution of Federal Lands

From the findings of a commission that reported to President Theodore Roosevelt on the pre-1904 disposition of public lands, we may see a recapitulation of U.S. land policy. The total public domain in the United States from 1789 to 1904 contained 1,441 million acres. Of this total, 278 million acres were acquired by individuals through cash purchase. Another 273 million acres were granted to states and railroads, about which more will be said in Chapter 16. Lands acquired by or available to individuals free of charge (mostly via the Homestead Act) amounted to 147 million acres. The rest of the public domain, aside from miscellaneous grants, was either reserved for the government (209 million acres) or unappropriated (474 million acres). Between 1862 and 1904, acres homesteaded exceeded cash sales by the government to individuals. If, however, we count purchases from railroads and states, ultimate holders of land bought twice as much between 1862 and 1904 as they obtained free.

After 1904, U.S. land policy became less generous, but by that time nearly all the choice agricultural land, most of the first-rate mineral land, and much of the timberland located close to market centers had been distributed. Between 1904 and 1920, over 100 million new acres of land were homesteaded in the dry and mountainous country, more than 90 percent of total new acres added. During this same short period, the government reserved about 175 million acres. Of the original public domain, 200 million acres of land that were yet to be disposed of were "vacant" in 1920.[4]

---

[4]Homestead entries were substantial in the 1920s and 1930s, but fell to practically zero by mid-century. Some homesteading continues today in Alaska.

The Impact of Federal Land Policy

The principal goals of federal land policy, namely (1) government revenues, (2) wide accessibility, or fairness, and (3) rapid economic growth, varied in importance over the century, with (2) and (3) gaining in importance over time. Clearly, one of the most outstanding features of American land policy was the rapidity with which valuable agriculture, mineral, and timber lands were transferred into private hands. In addition, the goal of making land widely accessible was largely achieved, especially in the second half of the nineteenth century.

By no means was the process, or result, egalitarian. As we just emphasized, large tracts of lands went to the states and to corporations and wealthy individuals. Special interests were favored, and for a time, the granting of land to railroads was considered normal public policy. In addition, large grants to the states were also rationalized as growth enhancing, either to support transportation ventures or educational purposes (that is, land-grant universities).

In the process, there were abuses. Frequently, good land was obtained fraudulently by mining and lumber companies and by speculators. Aided by the lax administration of the land laws, large operators could persuade individuals to make a homesteading entry or a purchase at a minimum price and then transfer the title for a song. With the connivance of bribed land officials, entries were occasionally made for people who did not even exist. In short, some chiseling was inevitable. Although the injustice of it rankles, it is not on a basis of fairness alone that we can decide whether federal land policy was good or bad. Rather we must focus on the direct effects of that land policy on economic growth and efficient use of resources.

For most of the twentieth century, the consensus among American historians has been that federal land policy was economically inefficient and reduced total output. Because people of all sorts and under greatly varied conditions settled on the land, there was a high rate of failure among the least competent—settlers who eventually lost their holdings and became either poor tenants or low-paid farm workers. More importantly it is alleged, the rapid distribution of the public domain laid the groundwork for modern agricultural problems by inducing too much capital and labor into agriculture, thereby impeding the process of industrialization.

There can be little doubt that specific errors were made and inefficiencies were imposed. And, yet, it is difficult to substantiate the case that federal policies were inefficient generally. Clearly, when factors of production such as land and other natural resources are added more rapidly to the production process, the growth of output and income will be greater. It should not be overlooked that partially as a result of this rapid addition of resources, the new West produced crops at such a rate that consumers of foodstuffs and raw materials enjoyed 30 years of falling prices. Furthermore, according to Robert Fogel and Jack Rutner, average rates of return on investments in land improvements, livestock, farm buildings, and machinery equaled or exceeded returns on other contemporary investments, and wages in the *new* agricultural areas outside the South grew at rates comparable to those in manufacturing.[5]

Nevertheless, as we shall see, there were numerous instances of hard times in rural America and political unrest characterized certain sections of the Midwest and the Plains in the late nineteenth century. Such events, however, were not the result of federal land policy. Though controversial and political, federal land policy was not generally inefficient or antidevelopment in its effect.[6]

GROWTH AND CHANGE IN AGRICULTURE

New Areas of Cultivation

Over time as various areas became settled, they tended to specialize and concentrate in certain select crops. These areas of geographic specialization are depicted for the principal crops in Map 15-1. The wheat and corn belt continued its western advance over the century, with spring wheat leading in western Minnesota and the Dakotas and winter varieties dominating the southern Midwest and Nebraska, Kansas, and Oklahoma.[7]

While tobacco remained tied to the Old South, cotton production leapfrogged the Mississippi River. By 1900, Texas was the leading cotton producer as well as a major source of cattle. Similar to earlier units in New England and New York, farmers around the Great Lakes found it profitable to turn from cereals to dairy farming. In California, Florida, and other warm climate areas, fruits, vegetables, and specialty crops became important—especially after the refrigerated rail car, introduced in the 1880s, created a national market.

In an era preceding chemical and biological improvements, output advances were approximately in proportion to acres added. Table 15-2 shows the growth of corn and wheat outputs and acreage harvested in each crop

---

[5]For the evidence and more discussion of these issues, see Robert Fogel and Jack Rutner, "Efficiency Effects of Federal Land Policy, 1850–1900," in *Dimensions of Quantitative Research in Economic History,* ed. William Aydelotte, et al. (Princeton: Princeton Univ. Press, 1972); and Susan Previant Lee and Peter Passell, *A New Economic View of American History* (New York: W. W. Norton, 1979), pp. 318–22.

[6]For an assessment of the politics of federal land policy see Paul Gates, "An Overview of American Land Policy," in *Two Centuries of American Agriculture,* ed. Vivian Wiser (Washington, D.C.: The Agricultural History Society, 1976), pp. 213–29.

[7]Winter wheat is sown in the fall and harvested in late spring and early summer, depending on the latitude. Where the climate is too cold, spring wheat is grown. Modern varieties of winter wheat are hardy enough to be grown in the southern half of South Dakota at least as far north as Pierre.

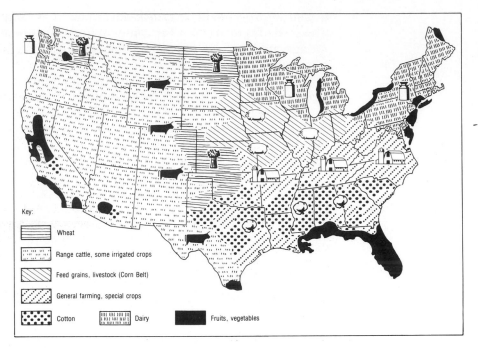

MAP 15-1   Geographic Areas of Specialization in Major Cash Crops in the late Nineteenth Century: It should be noted that the boundaries between sections did change and that many crops were and still are grown within various belts.

between 1870 and 1910. The evidence shows very little, if any, growth in land productivity as measured in bushels produced per acre. Nonetheless, labor productivity grew dramatically in wheat and corn over these decades. According to Robert Gallman, labor productivity in these two leading agricultural crops grew at a rate of 2.6 percent annually in 1850–1900.[8] In the first half of the nineteenth century, the comparable figure was 0.4 percent. Further evidence of output growth relative to inputs is shown in Figure 15-1, which measures total agricultural output relative to all inputs (land, labor, and capital), weighted respectively by output and input prices. Figure 15-1 clearly shows the "miracles" of the scientific chemical and biological advances that came in the 1920s and after. It also reveals the effects of mechanization that had such important influences, as Gallman's nineteenth-century findings reveal. In 1848 Lynn McCormick boldly moved his main implement plant to Chicago thereby assuring a steady supply of his harvesting machines to the burgeoning Midwest. The day of the hand scythe and the one-horse plow had passed, as this editorial from an 1857 *Scientific*

---

[8]Derived from Robert E. Gallman, "The Pace of Economic Growth: U.S. Experience in the Nineteenth Century," in *Essays in Nineteenth Century History*, ed. David C. Klingaman and Richard K. Vedder (Athens, OH: Ohio Univ. Press, 1975).

TABLE 15-2 Cereals Output and Land Input, 1870–1910

Year	Corn[a]	Land in Corn[b]	Bushels of Corn per Acre	Wheat	Land in Wheat	Bushels of Wheat per Acre
1870	1,125	38.4	29.3	254	20.9	12.1
1890	1,650	74.8	22.1	449	36.7	12.2
1910	2,853	102.3	27.9	625	45.8	13.7

[a]In millions of bushels.
[b]In millions of acres harvested.

Source: *Historical Statistics,* 1975. Series K 502, 503, 506, 507.

American suggests: "Every farmer who has a hundred acres of land should have at least the following: a combined reaper and mower, a horse rake, a seed planter, and mower . . . a thresher and grain cleaner, a portable grist mill, a corn-sheller, a horse power, three harrows, a roller, two cultivators, and three plows."[9]

Increased amounts of capital per worker, and new technologies embodied in the capital equipment, raised labor's productivity. Even though yields per acre changed little, mechanization allowed farmers to add more acres to their farms, thus expanding output per farm. The advent of new mechanized farms was not instantly introduced, however. Paul David's analysis of the mechanical reaper shows that in 1850 a minimum threshold size of 46 acres in grain was needed to profitably adopt a reaper.[10] This was well over the typical acreage per farm used for grain in most of the Midwest at that time. After the Civil War, wages paid to grain cradlers (hand harvesters) increased, lowering the threshold size for profitable adaptors. Meanwhile, acres per farm devoted to grains increased, hastening the introduction of mechanical reapers.

By 1857, John Deere was annually producing 10,000 steel plows at his new plant in Moline, Illinois, eclipsing the iron plow, which was so ineffectual in the tough clay-sod of the prairies. Seed drills, cultivators, mowers, rakes and threshing machines, and myriad attachments and gadgets for harvesting machines added to the mechanization of farming in the second half of the century. Between 1860 and 1920, the numbers of mouths fed per farmer nearly doubled, freeing up labor for industrialization, but not without economic dislocations and personal hardships.

---

[9]Quoted in C. Danhof, "Agriculture," in *The Growth of the American Economy,* ed. H. T. Williamson (New York: Prentice-Hall, 1951), p. 150.

[10]Paul David, "The Mechanization of Reaping in the Antebellum Midwest," in *Technical Choice, Innovation and Economic Growth, Essays on American and British Experience in the Nineteenth Century* (Cambridge: Cambridge Univ. Press, 1945). For an important study showing the dominance of supply-side effects on the relative price of harvesting equipment during this period, see Alan L. Olmstead, "The Civil War Was a Catalyst of Technological Change in Agriculture," in *Business and Economics History,* ed. Paul Uselding, 2nd series, vol. 5 (New York: Johnson and Associations, 1976), pp. 36–50.

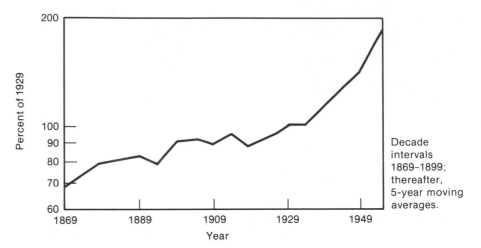

FIGURE 15-1   Total Factor Productivity in Agriculture, 1869–1955.

Source: John W. Kendrick, *Productivity Trends in the United States* (Princeton: Princeton Univ. Press, 1961), pp. 362–64.

Wheat harvesting in South Dakota, shown in this drawing, suggests the scale to which American agriculture had grown by the late 1800s and the innovative methods that were increasing farm productivity.

High horsepower became almost a logistical problem before the advent of steam and gasoline-powered tractors, as this scene indicates.

BAD TIMES ON THE FARM, 1864–1896

The years from the close of the Civil War to the end of the First World War comprise two contrasting periods in agricultural history. The first of these, from 1864 to 1896, was characterized by agricultural hardship and political unrest, whereas the second, from 1896 until about 1920, represented a sustained period of improvements in the lot of the farm population. This improvement, in part, is reflected quantitatively in Table 15-3, which traces average annual percentage growth rates in real farm income (per capita and per worker) for each decade over the last half of the nineteenth century.

American farmers, from the middle 1860s to the middle 1890s, knew that their lot was hard without being shown data to prove it. Farm people were living under frontier conditions, and the utter drabness of their surroundings combined with their physical hardship was not conducive to a cheerful acceptance of the difficulties of economic life, which included declining prices, indebtedness, and the necessity of purchasing many goods and services from industries in which there was a growing concentration of

TABLE 15-3   Trends in Farm Income and Productivity (average annual percentage change)

Years	Real Income per Capita	Real Income per Worker
1849–59	2.0	2.0
1859–69	0.8	0.9
1869–79	0.8	0.3
1879–89	0.7	0
1889–99	2.2	2.1
1849–99	1.3	1.0
1869–99	1.2	0.7

Source: Robert Fogel and Jack Rutner, "Efficiency Effects of Federal Land Policy, 1850–1900," in *The Dimensions of Quantitative Research in History,* ed. W. O. Aydelotte, A. G. Bogue, and R. W. Fogel, Copyright © 1972 by the Center for Advanced Study in the Behavioral Sciences. Table 2, p. 396, adapted by permission of Princeton Univ. Press.

economic power. Furthermore, farm prices, as shown in Figure 15-2, fell precipitously until 1896 (except for the early 1880s).[11] As also revealed in Figure 15-2, prices fell as supplies increased. The advance of agricultural production was especially sharp in the 1870s, however, and in that decade, the annual rate of increase was 6 percent, later leveling off at about 2 percent in the 1880s and 1890s.

As a consequence, in the 1870s crop prices fell below the average costs of production for many farm units, severely impacting certain high-cost regions. And all over the world, new areas were entering the competitive fray. In Canada, Australia, New Zealand, and the Argentine, as well as the United States, fertile new lands were becoming agriculturally productive. In the United States alone the number of acres in farming more than doubled between 1870 and 1900 (see Table 15-1). Reinforcing this trend was the increased output (per farm worker) made possible by mechanization and technological advances discussed earlier.

There were notable changes, too, on the demand side of farm production. One favorable influence on the domestic demand for food, feed, and fiber was the continued rapid increase in the population. After 1870, the *rate* of population growth in the United States fell, but until 1900 it was still high. In the decades of the 1870s and 1880s, the increase was just over 25 percent, and in the 1890s, it was more than 20 percent—a substantial growth in the number of mouths to feed. But there was an offsetting factor. In 1870, Americans spent one-third of their current per capita incomes on farm products. By 1890, they were spending just over one-fifth of those incomes on farm products, and in the next few years this proportion tended to drop a little more. Thus, although both the money and real incomes of the American population rose during the period, and although they did

[11] It is important to note that the general price level was also falling over this period. Indeed, the Wholesale Price Index actually fell more than agricultural prices, 1869–1900.

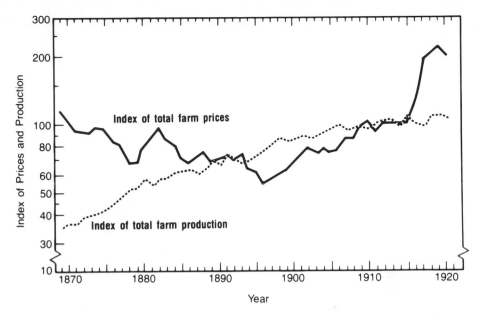

FIGURE 15-2   U.S. Farm Production and Prices, 1870–1920: From 1870 on, more acres and great advances in agricultural technology together greatly increased total output. After more than a quarter-century of downtrending prices, a quarter-century of generally rising prices followed. The period from 1896 to 1920 is often called the "Golden Age of American Agriculture."

Source: Strauss and Bean, *Gross Farm Income and Indices of Farm Production and Prices in the United States, 1869–1937.*

not spend less on food absolutely, the proportion of those incomes earned by farm people declined. Alternatively stated, as incomes increased the amounts spent on these items increased, but by a smaller percentage than the income increases. In short, the income elasticity of demand was less than one for most agricultural crops including wheat, corn, potatoes, beans, and other key crops.

Offsetting these effects in part was the rise in the demand abroad for U.S. crops after the Civil War. Export demand for farm products increased steadily until the turn of the century, when a drift began downward until the eve of the First World War. Wheat and flour exports reached their peak in 1901, at which time nearly one-third of domestic wheat production was sold abroad. Likewise, meat and meat products were exported in larger and larger quantities until 1900, when these exports also began to decline. Overall, the value of agricultural exports rose from $297 million in 1870 to over $840 million in 1900. Exports of farm products during these decades helped expand agricultural markets, but they were far from sufficient to correct the problems of oversupply, and they added to the cyclical fluctuations of the sector.

TABLE 15-4   Price Elasticity of Demand for Agricultural Commodities, 1875–1895

Sugar	− .38
Corn	− .71
Cotton	− .51
Wheat	− .03
Potatoes	− .68

Source: Adapted from Earl O. Heady, *Agricultural Policy under Economic Development.* (Ames: Iowa State Univ. Press, 1962), pp. 215–25.

Indeed, as Robert A. McGuire has shown, there was a strong correlation between political agitation in various western states and the economic instability of these states.[12] Price fluctuations were found by McGuire to have a particularly important bearing on the income instability of farmers. Given the very low price elasticity of demand of select agricultural crops, as shown in Table 15-4, we would expect modest swings in output to render sharp price variations. Moreover, output expansions, characteristic of the 1870s especially, generated sharp drops in relative prices and incomes in the agricultural sector.

Adding to agricultural discontent in this era was the entire process of commercialization. As emphasized by Ann Mayhew, in earlier decades farmers were less commercialized and less vulnerable to market fluctuations.[13] Reliance on the market was commonplace, but generally only on the periphery of farming activity. Most farmers marketed crops and livestock only to obtain essential tools and equipment. After the Civil War, however, the degree of market participation soared, paralleling the rapid rise of agricultural productivity. To keep abreast of progress, the farmer, whether a tenant or yeoman, needed more equipment—reapers, planters, harrows—as well as more land and irrigation facilities. This often meant greater indebtedness as extensions of credit became normal farming business practices. When agricultural prices fell, foreclosures or cessation of credit extensions brought ruin to many farmers.

As shown in Table 15-5, tenancy was on the rise, not only in the Deep South, already discussed in Chapter 14, but in the Midwest and other areas as well. Many yeoman farmers who owned and worked their own land were forced into tenancy in the late nineteenth century, and many hired hands who could not afford to buy land moved up to tenant status. Certainly it is to be expected that in distressed times farmers complained about those directly causing their ill fortune: bankers or railroads foreclosing on their

---

[12]See Robert A. McGuire "Economic Causes of Late Nineteenth Century Agrarian Unrest," *Journal of Economic History* 41 (1981) pp. 835–49.
[13]See Ann Mayhew, "A Reappraisal of the Causes of Farm Protest in the United States, 1870–1900," *Journal of Economic History* 32 (1972):464–75.

TABLE 15-5 Percentage of All Farms Operated by Tenants, by Geographic Region, 1880–1900

Region	1880	1890	1900
New England	8.5%	9.3%	9.4%
Middle Atlantic	19.2	22.1	25.3
East North Central	20.5	22.8	26.3
West North Central	20.5	24.0	29.6
South Atlantic	36.1	38.5	44.2
East South Central	36.8	38.3	48.1
West South Central	35.2	38.6	49.1
Mountain	7.4	7.1	12.2
Pacific	16.8	14.7	19.7

Note: Regions:
New England: CT, ME, MA, NH, RI, VT.
Middle Atlantic: NJ, NY, PA.
East North Central: IL, IN, MI, OH, WI.
West North Central: IA, KS, MN, MO, NB, ND, SD.
South Atlantic: DE, DC, FL, GA, MD, NC, SC, VA, WV.
East South Central: AL, KY, MS, TN.
West South Central: AR, LA, OK, TX.
Mountain: AZ, CO, ID, MT, NM, NV, UT, WY.
Pacific: CA, OR, WA.

Source: E. A. Goldenweisser and Leon E. Truesdell, *Farm Tenancy in the United States,* (Washington D.C.: GPO, 1924), p. 23. (U.S. Department of Commerce, Bureau of the Census, *Census Monograph IV*); as shown in Jeremy Atack, "Tenants and Yeomen in the Nineteenth Century," *Agricultural History* 62, no. 3 (Summer 1988):9.

lands, grain elevator operators changing to rates farmers could not afford, eastern monopolies charging high prices on industrial items, railroads charging "monopoly rates" on freight.

The evidence on these alleged sources of distress is largely unsupportive, suggesting these were symptoms rather than causes. Figures 15-3 and 15-4 show that the prices of industrial items in the West fell relative to the prices of farm products and that freight costs also fell as a percentage of farm prices.[14] Finally, both in nominal and in real terms, interest rates charged on midwestern farm mortgages declined over the decades, as shown in Table 15-6. Such rates were higher than in the East, where capital was more plentiful, and investments typically less risky, but they declined more rapidly in the West. It was primarily in the 1870s and to a lesser degree in the 1880s that high mortgage rates were especially burdensome to midwesterners.[15]

---

[14] Although long-haul railroad rates fell dramatically and relative to agricultural prices over the period, certain monopolized sections of railroad permitted discriminatory monopoly pricing on short hauls. This was a particular sore point with those affected. For more on this see Robert Higgs, "Railroad Rates and the Populist Uprising," *Agricultural History* 44 (July 1970).
[15] For more on this issue see Barry Eichengreen, "Mortgage Interest Rates in the Populist Era," *American Economic Review* (Dec., 1984):995–1015.

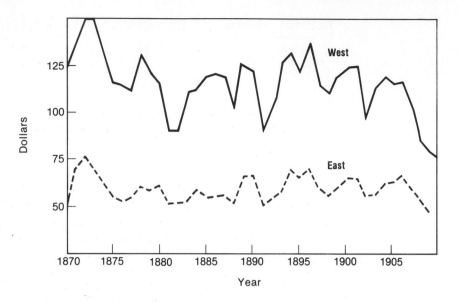

FIGURE 15-3   Price of Industrial Goods in Terms of Farm Products, West and East, 1870–1910.

Source: Derived from Jeffrey G. Williamson, *Late Nineteenth Century American Development, A General Equilibrium History.*
Cambridge: Cambridge Univ. Press, 1974, p. 149.

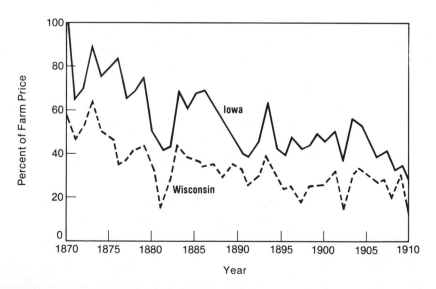

FIGURE 15-4   Freight on Wheat from Iowa and Wisconsin in New York as Percentage of Farm Price,
1870–1910.

Source: Derived from Jeffrey G. Williamson, *Late Nineteenth Century American Development, A General Equilibrium History.*
Cambridge: Cambridge Univ. Press, 1974, p. 261.

TABLE 15-6   Real (Nominal) Interest Rates on Midwestern Farm Mortgages, 1870–1900

Year	Illinois	Wisconsin	Iowa	Nebraska
1870	17.0 (9.6)%	15.4 (8.0)%	16.9 (9.5)%	17.9 (10.5)%
1880	11.4 (7.8)	10.8 (7.2)	12.3 (8.7)	12.7 (9.1)
1890	7.6 (6.9)	6.6 (5.9)	7.7 (7.0)	8.5 (7.8)
1910	4.3 (5.8)	3.4 (4.9)	4.0 (5.5)	4.8 (6.3)

Note: The real rate is the nominal rate plus the rate of deflation, or minus the rate of inflation.

Source: Derived from *Late Nineteenth Century American Development, A General Equilibrium History.* Cambridge: Cambridge Univ. Press, p. 152.

As farmers recognized, a big part of their problem was a falling price level that made real interest costs higher than the nominal rates charged at least before 1896. The apparent remedy was plain too. What the country needed was a larger and continually increasing stock of money, at least as they saw it.

AGRARIAN POLITICAL AGITATION, 1860–1920[16]

There can be little doubt that farmers of the late nineteenth century were painfully aware of the *symptoms* of their distress. Like people of any age and time who endure such distress, they reasoned back to particular causes; having discovered these causes, they wanted to remove them, one by one, by any means available.

In what has been called the "Thirty Years' War" against the princes of privilege, a number of organizations, large and small, were formed to fight for the farmers. Some organizations were influenced by urban industrial labor, and many of the ideas of the agrarians originated in the urban radicalism of the East.[17] The so-called agrarian revolt was not a purely agrarian agitation. It was neither closely knit nor well organized. There were four separate and rather clearly distinguishable movements, dominated—if not entirely motivated—by farmers in the West and South.

The Grangers

The first farm organization of importance was the National Grange of the Patrons of Husbandry. Formally organized in 1867, the order grew rapidly.

[16]For a most informative article providing a longer perspective on farm movements and political activity, see Morton Rothstein, "Farmers' Movements and Organizations, Numbers, Gains, Losses," *Agricultural History* 62, no. 3 (Summer 1988):161–88.
[17]For example, see Chester McArthur Destler, "Western Radicalism, 1865–1901: Concepts and Origins," *Mississippi Valley Historical Review* 31 (Dec. 1944):335–68.

In Granger Movement meetings like this one in Scott County, Illinois, members focused their discontentment on big-city ways, monopoly, the tariff, and low prices for agricultural products. From such roots grew pressures to organize support for agriculture.

By 1874, it had 20,000 local branches and a membership of about 1.5 million. After seven years of ascendancy, a decline set in, and by 1880 membership had largely disappeared except for a few strongholds such as the upper Mississippi Valley and the Northeast.

Although formal political action by the Grangers was strictly forbidden by the organization's bylaws, members held informal political meetings and worked with reform parties to secure passage of regulatory legislation. In several western states, the Grangers were successful (1) in obtaining laws that set an upper limit on the charges of railroads and of warehouse and elevator companies and (2) in establishing regulation of such companies by commission, a new concept in American politics. The Grangers developed a new weapon for fighting unfair business practices. If prices charged by businesses were too high, then, it was argued, farmers ought to go into business themselves. The most successful type of business organization established by the Grangers was the cooperative, formed for the sale of general merchandise and farm implements to Grange members. Cooperatives and stock companies were established to process farm products, and the first large mail-order house, Montgomery Ward and Company, was established to sell to the Granges.

The Greenback Movement

Some farmers, disappointed in the Grange for not making more decisive gains in the struggle to bolster farm prices, joined forces with a labor element to form an Independent National Party, which entered candidates in the election of 1876. This group was hopelessly unsuccessful, but a "Greenback Labor" party formed by the same people made headway in the election of 1878. To finance the Civil War, the government had resorted to the issue of fiat paper popularly known as "greenbacks," and the suggestion that a similar issue be made in the late 1870s appealed to poor farmers. The "Greenback Labor" platform, more than any other party program, centered on demands for inflationary (they would have said "reflationary") action. Although Greenback Labor candidates were entered in the presidential campaign of 1880, they received a very small percentage of the popular vote because labor failed to participate effectively. Greenback agitators continued their efforts in the elections of 1884 and 1888, but with continued indifferent success.

The movement is worth remembering for two reasons. First, Greenback agitation constituted the first attempt of farmers to act politically on a national scale. Second, the central tenets of the group were adopted by the later Populists as the most important part of their appeal to the electorate in the 1890s.

The Alliances

At the same time that the Granges were multiplying, independent farmers' clubs were being formed in the West and South. Independent clubs tended to coalesce into state "alliances," which in turn were consolidated into two principal groups—the Northwestern Alliance and the Southern Alliance. In 1889, an attempt to merge the Alliances failed, despite the similarity of their aims. The Alliances advocated money reforms similar to those urged by the Greenback parties and, like the Grangers, favored government regulation and cooperative business ventures. Alliance memberships favored actual government ownership of transportation and communication facilities. Each Alliance offered a proposal that had a highly modern ring. The Southern Alliance recommended that the federal government establish a system of warehouses for the storage of nonperishable commodities so that farmers could obtain low-interest loans of up to 80 percent of the value of the products stored. The Northwestern Alliance proposed that the federal government extend long-term loans in greenbacks up to 50 percent of the value of a farm. Due to their revolutionary nature, such ideas received little support from the voters.

The Populists

After the mild periods of prosperity of 1885–86 and 1888–90, there was another downturn in economic activity, and the hardships of the farmer and the laborer again became severe. In 1891, elements of the alliances met in Cincinnati with the Knights of Labor to form the People's Party. At the convention of 1892, held in Omaha, famed agrarian and formidable orator General James Weaver was nominated for the Presidency. Weaver, an old Greenback, won 22 electoral votes in the election of 1892. Two years later, the party won a number of congressional seats, and it appeared that greater success might be on the way.

Populism thus emerged from 30 years of unrest—an unrest that was chiefly agricultural but that had urban connections. To its supporters, Populism was something more than an agitation for economic betterment: it was a faith. The overtones of political and social reform were part of the faith because they would help to further economic aims. The old ferment against monopoly control—against the oppression of corporations, banks, and capitalists—had come to a head. Along with the key principle of anti-monopolism ran a strongly collectivist doctrine. Populists felt that only through government ownership of banks, railroads, and the means of communication and through government control of the monetary system could the evils of monopoly be put down. In fact, the "yardstick" operation of firms in basic industries was advocated by some Populists, so that the government could determine whether or not monopolistic prices were being charged.

In the older areas the extreme radicalism of the People's Party alienated established farmers who had a definite conservative bias. Had the leaders of the 1896 coalition of Populists and Democrats not chosen to stand or fall on the issue of free coinage of silver, there is no telling what the future of the coalition might have been. But inflation was anathema to the property owners with little or no debt, and when the chips were down, rural as well as urban property owners supported "sound" money.

THE BEGINNINGS OF FEDERAL ASSISTANCE TO AGRICULTURE

Although attempts by farmers to improve their condition through organization were unsuccessful as far as immediate goals were concerned, the way had been opened for legislation and federal assistance. Of course, the land acts of the nineteenth century worked to the advantage of new farmers, but they can scarcely be considered part of an agricultural "program." Similarly, much regulatory legislation passed late in the nineteenth and early in the twentieth centuries, although originating in agrarian organizations, produced effects that were not restricted to agriculture. In speaking of federal assistance to agriculture before the First World War, we refer to attempts to compile and disseminate information to help the individual farmer. Such efforts were calculated, however, to increase productivity; they were not designed to alleviate distress, as was later New Deal Legislation.

The Department of Agriculture

As early as 1839, an Agricultural Division had been set up in the Patent Office. In 1862, Congress created a Department of Agriculture, but its head, who was designated the Commissioner of Agriculture, did not have Cabinet ranking until 1889.

Until 1920, the Department of Agriculture performed three principal functions. These were (1) research and experimentation in plant exploration, plant and animal breeding, and insect and disease control; (2) distribution of agricultural information through publications, agricultural experiment stations, and county demonstration work; and (3) regulation of the quality of products consumed by human beings through the authority to condemn diseased animals, to prohibit shipment in interstate commerce of adulterated or misbranded foods and drugs, and to inspect and certify meats and dairy products in interstate trade. There was always pressure on the department to give "practical" help to the farmers, as evidenced by the fact that throughout this period it regularly distributed free seeds. In retrospect it seems that the chief contribution of the Department of Agriculture in these early years lay in its ability to convince farmers of the value of "scientific" farming.

Agricultural Education

Attempts to incorporate the teaching of agricultural subjects into the educational system began locally, but federal assistance was necessary to maintain adequate programs. Although colleges of agriculture had been established in several states by 1860, it was the Morrill Act of 1862 that gave impetus to agricultural training at the university level. The Morrill Act established "land-grant" colleges in the states and these colleges gradually assumed statewide leadership in agricultural research. The Hatch Act of 1887 provided federal assistance to state agricultural experiment stations, many of which had already been established with state funds. The Hatch Act also provided for the establishment of an Office of Experiment Stations in the Department of Agriculture to tie in the work of the department with that of the states. After 1900, as the quality of work accomplished by the agricultural colleges reached a university level, interest began to develop in secondary-school work. The Smith–Hughes Vocational Education Act of 1917 provided funds to states that agreed to expand vocational training at the high-school level in agriculture, trades, and home economics.

These and other measures were advanced by reformers nurturing the beginnings of federal involvement in the agricultural sector. As we shall see, such involvement would grow dramatically in the decades after 1920. Similarly, calls for reform, especially by scientific organizations and major periodicals, to "end the waste" of natural resources, advanced the role of government in the control and use of land, timber, and other natural resources.

NATURAL RESOURCE CONSERVATION: THE FIRST STAGES

The waste of natural resources in North America as perceived by Europeans, contemporaries, and others, dates as far back as Colonial times. For instance, it should be recalled that many Colonial dirt farmers ignored "advanced" European farming methods designed to maintain soil fertility. Instead they preferred to fell trees and plant around tree stumps and then move on if the land wore out. Because of land abundance, their concern was not with soil conservation, but rather with the shortage of labor and capital.

Similarly, in the early nineteenth century lumber was in great abundance, especially in the eastern half of the nation where five-sixths of the original forests were located. Indeed in most areas of new settlement, standing timber was often an impediment rather than a valued resource. As late as 1850 more than 90 percent of all fuel-based energy came from wood, primarily because of its abundance and accessibility.

By 1915, however, wood supplied less than 10 percent of all fuel-based energy in the United States, and in the Great Plains and in other western regions, timber grew increasingly scarce.[18] The western advance of the railroad, which devoured nearly one-quarter of the timber cut in the 1870s, along with the western shift of the population, brought new pressures on limited western and distant eastern timber supplies. Moreover, the price of stumpage on public lands was zero for all practical purposes. This and a lack of clear legal rights to timber on public lands provided incentive for individuals and logging concerns to cut as fast as possible on public lands. This, in turn, artificially lowered the value of timber on private lands and hastened cutting there, too. As a result, much waste occurred and various environmental hazards were made more extreme. These included the loss of watersheds, which increased the hazard of floods and hastened soil erosion. More importantly, the buildup of masses of slash (tree branches and other timber deposits) brought on severe fire hazards. In the late nineteenth century, large cutover regions became explosive timber boxes. For example, in 1871 "the Pishtigo fire" in Wisconsin devoured 1.28 million acres and killed more than 1,000 entrapped people. Similar dramatic losses from fire

---

[18] For an excellent account of the responsive process in the form and use of natural resources to changes in their costs and supplies see Nathan Rosenberg, "Innovative Responses to Material Shortages," *American Economic Review* 63 (May 1973).

occurred in 1881 in Michigan and in 1894 in Wisconsin and Minnesota. These and other factors, such as fraudulent land acquisitions, demanded legislative action and reform.[19]

Land, Water, and Timber Conservation

The first major step toward reform was the General Revision Act of 1891. As noted already, this law repealed measures that had been an open invitation to land fraud and made it more difficult for corporations and wealthy individuals to steal timber and minerals. Prevention of theft scarcely constitutes conservation, but one section of the 1891 Act, which empowered the President to set aside forest reserves, was a genuine conservation measure. Between 1891 and 1900, 50 million acres of valuable timberland were withdrawn from private entry despite strong and growing opposition from certain interests in the western states. Inadequate appropriations made it impossible for the Division of Forestry to protect the reserves from forest fires and from depredations of timber thieves, but a start had been made.

When Theodore Roosevelt succeeded to the presidency in 1901, there was widespread concern, both in Congress and throughout the nation, over the problem of conservation. With imagination, charm, and fervor, Roosevelt sought legislation during both his terms to provide a consistent and far-reaching conservation program. By 1907, he could point to certain major achievements:

1. National forests comprised 150 million acres, of which 75 million acres contained marketable timber. In 1901, a Bureau of Forestry was created, which became the United States Forest Service in 1905. Under Gifford Pinchot, Roosevelt's able chief adviser in all matters pertaining to conservation, a program of scientific forestry was initiated. The national forests were to be more than just locked-up preserves; the "crop" of trees was to be continually harvested and sold so that ever-larger future crops were assured.

2. Lands containing 75 million acres of mineral wealth were reserved from sale and settlement. Most of the lands containing metals were already privately owned, but the government was able to retain large deposits of coal, phosphates, and oil.

3. There was explicit recognition of the future importance of waterpower sites. A policy was established of leasing government-owned sites to private firms for a stipulated period of years, while actual ownership was reserved for the government.

---

[19]For further detail see Alan L. Olmstead, "The Costs of Economic Growth," *The Encyclopedia of American Economic History*, Glenn Porter (ed.), II (New York: Scribner's 1980), pp. 863–81; and Marion Clawson, "Forests in the Long Sweep of American History," *Science* 204 (June 15, 1979).

4. The principle was accepted that it was a proper function of the federal government to implement a program of public works for the purpose of controlling stream flows. Specifically, storage dams and irrigation works were to be constructed for the benefit of western settlers. The Reclamation Act of 1902 provided for the use of receipts from land sales in the arid states to finance the construction of reservoirs and irrigation works, with repayment to be made by settlers over a period of years. In this way, the idea of "reclamation" entered into the broader concept of conservation.

To students of the 1990s concerned with contemporary problems of the environment, such achievements seem modest enough. But in the first decade of the twentieth century, many people bitterly opposed any interference with the private explorations of the remaining public domain. Much of the growth of government expenditures in water control, dams, and irrigation systems awaited a second Roosevelt administration in the 1930s. But the precedents set by Theodore Roosevelt's administration set the stage for the engineering marvels of the present era that freed western agriculture from the shackles of dry-land farming of basic grains and livestock feeding. They also set a new direction, however haltingly, toward more prudent conservations of precious natural space, minerals, forests, and water.

SELECTED REFERENCES AND SUGGESTED READINGS

Arrington, Leonard. *Great Basin Kingdom.* Cambridge, Mass.: Harvard University Press, 1958.

Atack, Jeremy. "Tenants and Yeomen in the Nineteenth Century." *Agricultural History* 62, no. 3 (Summer 1988):6–32.

Bateman, Fred. "Improvements in American Dairy Farming, 1850–1910: A Quantitative Analysis." *Journal of Economic History* 23 (1968):255–73.

Bogue, Allan. *From Prairie to Cornbelt: Farming on the Illinois and Iowa Prairies in the Nineteenth Century.* Chicago: Univ. of Chicago Press, 1963.

Bogue, Allan, and Margaret Bogue. "Profits and the Frontier Speculator." *Journal of Economic History* 17 (March 1957).

Bowman, John. "An Economic Analysis of Midwestern Farm Land Values and Farmland Income, 1890 to 1900." *Yale Economic Essays,* Fall, 1965.

Bowman, John D., and Richard H. Keehn. "Agricultural Terms of Trade in Four Midwestern States, 1870–1900." *Journal of Economic History* 34 (1974):592–609.

Carstensen, Vernon. *Farmer Discontent, 1865–1900.* (New York: Wiley, 1974).

Coelho, Philip, and James Shepherd. "Differences in Regional Prices: The United States, 1851–1880." *Journal of Economic History* 34 (1974):551–91.

David, Paul. "The Agricultural Sector and the Pace of Economic Growth: U.S. Experience in the Nineteenth Century." In *Essays in Nineteenth Century Economic History,* ed. David Klingaman and Richard Vedder.

———. "The Mechanization of Reaping in the Antebellum Midwest." In *Technical Choice, Innovation and Economic Growth, Essays on American and British Experience in the Nineteenth Century* (Cambridge: Cambridge Univ. Press, 1975).

Eichengreen, Barry. "Mortgage Interest Rates in the Populist Era." *American Economic Review* 74 (Dec. 1984):995–1015.

Galenson, David. "The End of the Chisholm Trail," *Journal of Economic History* 24 (1974):350–64.

Gallman, Robert E. "Changes in Total U.S. Agricultural Factor Productivity in the Nineteenth Century." *Agricultural History* (January 1972).

Griliches, Zvi. "Hybrid Corn and the Economics of Innovation." *Science* 132 (July 29, 1960).

Harley, C. Knick, "Western Settlement and the Price of Wheat, 1872–1913." *Journal of Economic History* 38 (1978):865–78.

Hays, Samuel P. *Conservation and the Gospel of Efficiency: The Progressive Conservation Movement, 1890–1920.* Cambridge: Harvard Univ. Press, 1959.

Hicks, John D. *The Populist Revolt.* Lincoln: Univ. of Nebraska Press, 1961.

Higgs, Robert. *The Transformation of the American Economy, 1865–1914: An Essay in Interpretation.* New York: Wiley, 1971.

Jones, Lewis. "The Mechanization of Reaping and Mowing in American Agriculture: A Comment." *Journal of Economic History* 37 (1977):451–55.

Libecap, Gary D. "Bureaucratic Opposition to the Assignment of Property Rights: Overgrazing on the Western Range." *Journal of Economic History* 41 (1981):151–58.

———. "Economic Variables and the Development of the Law: The Case of Western Mineral Rights." *Journal of Economic History* 38 (1978):338–62.

Lindert, Peter H. "Long-Run Trends in American Farm Values." *Agricultural History* 62, no. 3 (Summer 1988):45–85.

Mayhew, Anne. "A Reappraisal of the Causes of Farm Protest in the United States, 1870–1900." *Journal of Economic History* 32 (1972):464–75.

McGuire, Robert A. "Economic Causes of Late Nineteenth Century Agrarian Unrest." *Journal of Economic History* 41 (1981):835–49.

Merk, Frederick. *History of the Westward Movement.* New York: Knopf, 1978.

Olmstead, Alan. "The Mechanization of Reaping and Mowing in American Agriculture, 1833–70," *Journal of Economic History* 35 (June 1975).

Parker, William. "Agriculture," In *American Economic Growth: An Economist's History of the United States,* ed. Lance E. Davis et al. New York: Harper & Row, 1972.

Petulla, Joseph M. *American Environmental History: The Exploitation and Conservation of Natural Resources.* San Francisco: Boyd & Fraser, 1977.

Ransom, Roger L., and Richard Sutch. "Capitalists without Capital: The Burden of Slavery and the Impact of Emancipation." *Agricultural History* 62, no. 3 (Summer 1988):133–60.

Rasmussen, Wayne D. "The Impact of Technological Change on American Agriculture, 1862–1962." *Journal of Economic History* 22 (Dec. 1962).

Rothstein, Morton. "Farmers Movements and Organizations: Numbers, Gains, Losses." *Agricultural History* 62, no. 3 (Summer 1988):161–81.

Shannon, Fred A. *The Farmer's Last Frontier, 1860–1897.* New York: Harper & Row, 1968.

Swierenga, Robert P. *Pioneers and Profits: Land Speculation on the Iowa Frontier.* Ames: Iowa State Univ. Press, 1968.

Turner, Frederick Jackson. *The Frontier in American History.* New York: Henry Holt, 1921.

Williamson, Jeffrey G. "Greasing the Wheels of Sputtering Export Engines: Midwestern Grains and American Export Growth." *Explorations in Economic History* 17 (July 1980).

Winters, Donald L. "Tenancy as an Economic Institution: The Growth and Distribution of Agricultural Tenancy in Iowa, 1850–1900." *Journal of Economic History* 37 (1977):382–408.

C H A P T E R   16

Railroads and Economic Change

Few developments, other than war and revolutions, have captured the attention of historians and contemporary observers quite like the railroad. That wonderful American creation, Superman, was described no less than "faster than a speeding bullet, more powerful than a locomotive." Fast, powerful, reaching everywhere, the railroad came to dominate the American landscape and the American imagination. The old pop song "I've been working on the railroad," was an all time hit. Trains were the symbol of modern America, epitomizing America's economic superiority in an industrializing world.

To stipulate the many important influences of the railroad would soon generate a list of unmanageable proportions. We will constrain our attentions to four main dimensions of the railroad's vast influence on late nineteenth-century American economic life:

1. First is the building of the railroad, especially the transcontinentals that in a timely way united the North American continent in the late 1860s. Were these continent-spanning investments built ahead of demand, or were railroads followers in the settlement process?

2. Second are the roles of finance and of government in building the railroad. Large land grants, both federal and state, and other means of financial assistance were given. Were these land grants needless giveaways or prudent uses of empty spaces? How did the builders get their capital?

3. Another factor of great importance was the growth of government intervention in the economy as manifested in railroad regulation, both at the state and federal levels. Key legal (re)interpretations paved the way for new economic controls by government. Did intervention and regulation ultimately assist management in avoiding runaway competition? Was there a capture of the regulatory process by railroad management, or did regulation primarily benefit users?

4. Finally, what impact did the railroad have on the overall growth rate of the economy? Was it only marginally superior to other modes of transport, or was it indispensable to American prosperity? Was the pace of

productivity advance that we observed for the railroad in Chapter 9 for the antebellum period sustained in the postbellum period?

THE TRANSCONTINENTALS

The Gold Rush of 1849 had produced knowledge of the fabulous West Coast and exciting stories about the vast spaces that separated East from West. Hard routes to the land of opportunity were open to adventurous people in the East. Wagon trails to California and the Pacific Northwest were beset with the dangers of blizzards in winter, thirst in summer, and Indian attacks in all seasons of the year. The trip via the Isthmus of Panama, with an overland trek through malarial and pestiferous jungles to board ship on the other side, was a nightmare of suffering.[1] The third route, around "Cape Stiff," was no less dangerous; the long voyage in slow sailing ships to the Cape, the storms encountered there, and the final reach to the California coast deterred all but the bravest. Thus, when the Civil War was over and the rich goal of far western lands was contemplated, a safe rail connection with the new West was eagerly sought.

From the outset government participation was viewed as essential to the project, and the first concrete proposal to Congress is attributed to Asa Whitney of New York, a merchant in the China trade. Finally, by 1853, Congress was convinced of the feasibility of a road to the West Coast and directed government engineers to survey practical routes. The engineers described five. Years passed before construction began because of rivalry for the eastern terminus of the line. From Minneapolis to New Orleans, cities on the Mississippi River vied for the position of gateway to the West, boasting of their advantages while deprecating the claims of their rivals. The outbreak of the Civil War removed the proponents of the southern routes from Congress, and in 1862 the northern Platte River route through uninhabited country was selected because it was used by the pony express, stages, and freighter wagons.

By the Pacific Railway Act of 1862, Congress granted a charter of incorporation to the Union Pacific Railroad, which was authorized to build a line from Omaha, Nebraska, to the western boundary of Nevada. The Central Pacific, incorporated under the laws of California in 1861, was at the same

---

[1]The shorter sea route via the Isthmus could cut the 6–8 month trip around Cape Horn to as little as six weeks. But from Chagres, a squalid eastern port on the Isthmus, to Panama City was a five-day journey by native dugout and muleback, and at Panama travelers might have a long wait before securing passage north. For those who could afford it, the best way to California was by clipper ship, which made the passage around the Horn in 100–110 days. The sailing record of 88 days was set in 1854 by the clipper *Flying Cloud* between New York and San Francisco. This was not broken until 1989 when a small ultramodern, high-tech sailboat named *Thursday's Child* with a crew of two made the passage in 80 days.

time given authority to construct the western part of the road from Sacramento to the Nevada border. Due to the uncertainty of the revenues to be derived from the undertaking, the government agreed to furnish financial assistance in two ways. Ten sections of public land (five alternate sections on each side of the right-of-way) were granted for each mile of track laid.[2] The government agreed further to lend the companies certain sums per mile of construction; the loans were to be secured by first-mortgage bonds. Because the Act of 1862 failed to attract sufficient private capital, the law was amended in 1864 to double the amount of land grants and to provide second-mortgage security on government loans, thus enabling the railroads to sell first-mortgage bonds to the public. To encourage speed of construction, the Central Pacific was permitted to build 150 miles beyond the Nevada line; later, it was authorized to push eastward until a junction was made with the Union Pacific.

The last two years of construction were marked by a race between the two companies as to which could lay the most track. With permission to build eastward to a junction with the Union Pacific, the directors of the Central Pacific wished to obtain as much per-mile subsidy as possible. The Union Pacific laid 1,086 miles of track; the Central Pacific, 689 miles. The joining of the Union Pacific and the Central Pacific occurred amidst great fanfare and celebration on May 10, 1869, at Promontory Summit, a few miles west of Ogden, Utah.[3] Two trainloads of dignitaries, one from the East and one from the West, approached the joining place of the rails. By telegraph, President Ulysses S. Grant gave the signal from Washington to drive in the last spike. The hammer blows that drove home the golden spike were echoed by Mr. Morse's telegraph to waiting throngs on both coasts. The hope was expressed that the fruits of the toil of farmer and laborer could now be transported swiftly and cheaply from coast to coast or from the interior to either coast. The continent had at last been spanned by rail; although transcontinental train travel was not without discomfort and even danger, the terrible trials of the overland and sea routes were over.

Yet the thin rails that crossed half a continent could not carry all the traffic to and from a growing West. New lines were quickly projected, but construction, although well under way, was halted by the Depression of 1873. In 1876, southern California was opened to transcontinental traffic by a line from San Francisco to Bakersfield and Los Angeles. Next, the Southern Pacific lines reached eastward from California to El Paso. The

---

[2]The land had little or no value without a means of access to it, but everyone knew that it would increase in value after the railroad was built. The fact that the companies had assets that would appreciate, in addition to the prospect of growing revenues, made private investment more attractive.

[3]By some strange quirk of historical writing, the meeting place of the two trains is usually designated Promontory Point. Professor Leonard Arrington, a resident of the area, assures us that Promontory Point extends well into the Great Salt Lake, where a railroad track would be most unlikely to be built, and that the 1869 news dispatches were filed from Promontory Summit.

At Promontory Summit, Utah, the "Rival Monarchs" nuzzled up to one another as hundreds cheered the completion of the transcontinental railroad line. The date was May 10, 1869.

Santa Fe and the Texas and Pacific soon provided connections from St. Louis and Kansas City to the Los Angeles area, and the Southern Pacific thrust on east from El Paso only a little later. These southern railroads provided the second of the three major transcontinental routes. The third route was the northern one from the Mississippi to the cities of Oregon and Washington. In 1883, the Northern Pacific, chartered nearly 20 years before, connected Portland with Chicago and Milwaukee and three years later reached Seattle.

TOTAL CONSTRUCTION: PACE AND PATTERNS

As the first transcontinentals pushed toward completion, settled regions were crisscrossed with rails for through traffic. All major lines tried to secure access to New York in the East and to Chicago and St. Louis in the West. On the more northerly routes, the New York Central achieved a through line from New York to Chicago by 1877, and the Erie did the same only a few years later. After the mid-1880s, the trunk lines filled the gaps, gaining access to secondary railroad centers and building feeder lines in a north–south direction.

From 1864 to 1900, the greatest percentage of track, varying from one-third to nearly one-half of the country's total annual construction, was laid in the Great Plains states. Chicago became the chief railroad terminus, extending north, west, and south, but a web of rails also surrounded such cities as St. Louis, Kansas City, Minneapolis, Omaha, and Denver.

The Southeast and the Southwest lagged both in railroad construction and in the combination of local lines into through systems. Sparseness of population and war-induced poverty accounted in part for the backwardness of the Southeast, but the competition of coastal shipping was also a deterrent to railroad growth. The only southern transmountain crossing utilized before 1880 was the Chesapeake and Ohio, and, except for the Southern, no main north–south line was completed until the 1890s.

Keeping in mind that the rate of growth of the main line railroad network varied in different regions, we turn to Table 16-1, which shows the expansion of total main line mileage nationally. One feature is unsurprising, the eventual slowing up in percentage jumps in mileage added. Nobel Laureate Simon Kuznets and Arthur Burns each revealed this typical feature of rapid industry expansion followed by a tapering off in the growth rate (and speed of productivity advance) in pioneering work done a half century ago.[4] All great innovations and industry growth patterns show these features, as we observed earlier in tobacco production, in cotton, and in steamboating, to name a few. It is interesting to note, however, that the total absolute mileage doubled in the 25 years preceding 1910. Work by Albert Fishlow reveals three major waves in the late nineteenth-century pattern of main track construction: 1868–73, 1879–83, and 1886–92.[5] These construction booms ended promptly with each of the major financial crises of the period: 1873, 1882, and 1893. As J. R. T. Hughes has argued, this is not terribly surprising when we recall that railroad construction was heavily dependent on borrowed money.[6] Alternatively, railroad construction had a strong influence on aggregate demand and business cycles. It was important enough to account for 20 percent of U.S. gross capital formation in the 1870s, 15 percent of the total in the 1880s, and 7.5 percent of the total in each of the remaining decades until 1920. These towering investments reinforced as well as responded to swings in the business cycle.

---

[4]Simon Kuznets, "The Retardation of Industrial Growth," *Journal of Economic and Business History,* August 1929; Arthur F. Burns, *Production Trends in the United States Since 1870* (New York: National Bureau of Economic Research, 1934), ch. 4, "Retardation in the Growth Industries."

[5]Albert Fishlow, "Internal Transportation," in *Economic Growth: An Economist's History of the United States* ed. Lance E. Davis et al. (New York: Harper & Row, 1972), p. 500.

[6]See his elegant and sophisticated book, *Industrialization and Economic History: Theses and Conjectures* (New York: McGraw-Hill, 1970), p. 120.

TABLE 16-1   Main Line Railroad Track in Operation (in thousands of miles)

Year	Miles	Percentage changes (in five-year intervals)
1860	31	13
1865	35	63
1870	53	42
1875	74	26
1880	93	38
1885	128	30
1890	167	8
1895	180	15
1900	207	15
1905	238	12
1910	266	

Source: Derived from *Historical Statistics,* 1960, series Q15, pp. 49–50.

RAILROAD BUILDING AND RAILROAD DEMAND

Joseph Shumpeter, one of the greatest scholars and economists of the early twentieth century, stated that many midwestern railroad projects "meant building ahead of demand in the boldest sense of the phrase" and that "Middle Western and Western projects could not be expected to pay for themselves within a period such as most investors care to envisage."[7]

To test Shumpeter's assertion, Albert Fishlow analyzed profits rates on railroad investments in the West in the antebellum period. He specified and tested the Shumpeter hypothesis rigorously, drawing the praise of fellow economists expert in the area.[8] Simply put, Fishlow reasoned that if railroads were built ahead of demand—in unsettled regions, let's say—the demand for the railroad's services (freight and passenger) must have been low, with prices below average costs. As settlement occurred, in time the demand curve would shift upward so that average revenues would eventually exceed average costs. This provided him with two tests:

1. Profit rates on new railroads should be less than profit rates in alternative (average) investments.

2. Railroad profit rates should grow as the railroad aged.

On both tests, Fishlow's findings for the antebellum western railroads did not support Shumpeter's assertion of railroads being built ahead of demand.

---

[7]Quoted in Albert Fishlow, *American Railroads and the Transformation of the Ante-Bellum Economy* (Cambridge: Harvard Univ. Press, 1965), pp. 165 and 167.
[8]Robert W. Fogel, "The Specification Problem in Economic History," *The Journal of Economic History* 27 (1967):296; and Meghnad Desai, "Some Issues in Econometric History," *The Economic History Review,* 2nd ser., 21 (1968):12.

Profit rates compared favorably to alternative investments and did not rise above rates earned early on. This evidence on profit rates led Fishlow to reject the hypothesis, and close analysis showed that early western construction was carried out in the most populous areas of early settlement. He concluded, however, that "a similar set of criteria casually applied to post-Civil War railroad construction in states farther West suggest that this constituted a true episode of building before demand.[9]

The work to determine whether or not Fishlow's tentative answer was right about the post-Civil War's transcontinentals was done by Lloyd Mercer. Using Fishlow's criteria, he showed that indeed the railroads were built ahead of demand; they had very low (below alternatives) initial profit rates, and their profit rates grew over time in the late nineteenth century. Finally, Mercer tested for another interpretation of the notion of the railroads being built ahead of demand. Did the transcontinentals *eventually* earn high enough profit rates on operations to justify private investment without government subsidy? Alternatively stated, was their average rate of return (excluding revenues from land sales) over several decades above or below average rates of return on alternative investments? Mercer's findings showed mixed results. The Central Pacific and the Union Pacific (which formed the first transcontinentals) and the Great Northern (the last) had private rates of return above rates on alternative investments. Three others, the Texas and Pacific, the Santa Fe, and the Northern Pacific, did not. Mercer's findings show that although the postbellum transcontinentals were built ahead of demand, in one sense the necessity of government subsidies for the three high-profit railroads could be questioned.[10]

LAND GRANTS AND RAILROAD FINANCING

It is noteworthy that before the Pacific Railway Act of 1862, the largest manufacturing plants rarely had more than $500,000 invested in capital, or as many as 1,000 employees. In contrast, five railroads at that time each had over $20 million invested and tens of thousand of employees. Building the transcontinentals was an especially huge undertaking, and the indivisibility of the fixed plant needed for operation added to the problems of attracting capital.

As we observed with canals and antebellum railroads, subsidies were not uncommon for major transportation projects. States and municipalities, competing with one another for lines they thought would bring everlasting

[9] Fishlow, *American Railroads and the Transformation of the Ante-Bellum Economy,* p. 204.
[10] Lloyd Mercer, "Building Ahead of Demand: Some Evidence for the Land Grant Railroads," *Journal of Economic History* 34 (1974):492–500.

prosperity, continued to help the railroads, but on a smaller scale than they had in the early days. They purchased or guaranteed railroad bonds, granted tax exemptions, and provided terminal facilities. Several states subscribed to the capital stock of the railroads, hoping to participate in the profits. Michigan built three roads, and North Carolina controlled the majority of the directors of three roads. North Carolina, Massachusetts, and Missouri took over failing railroads that had been liberally aided by state funds. Outright contributions from state and local units may have reached $250 million—a small sum compared to a value of track and equipment of $10 billion in 1880, when assistance from local governments had almost ceased.

In contrast to the antebellum period, subsequent financial aid from the federal government exceeded the aid from states and municipalities, although by how much we cannot be sure. Perhaps $175 million in government bonds were loaned to the Union Pacific, the Central Pacific, and four other transcontinentals, but after litigation most of this amount was repaid. Rights-of-way, normally 200 feet wide, together with sites for depots and terminal facilities in the public domain and free timber and stone from government lands, constituted another form of assistance. But the most significant kind of federal subsidy was the grant of lands from the public domain.

Congress simply invested a portion of the unsettled lands in the public domain in the railroads in lieu of money or credit. Following the precedent set by grants to the Mobile and Ohio and to the Ohio and Illinois Central in 1850, alternate sections of land on either side of the road, varying in size from 6 to 40 acres, were given outright for each mile of railroad that was constructed. The alternate-section provision was made in the expectation that the government would share in the increased land values that were expected to result from the new transportation facilities. Land-grant subsidies to railroads were discontinued after 1871 due to public opposition, but not before 79 grants amounting to 200 million acres, reduced by forfeitures to just over 131 million acres, had been given away.[11] This amounted to about 9 percent of the U.S. public domain accumulated between 1789 and 1904 and was slightly less than the amounts granted to the states.

It should be remembered, however, that aid to the railroads was not given unconditionally. Congress required that companies that received grants transport mail, troops, and government property at reduced rates. In 1940, Congress relieved the railroads of land-grant rates for all except military traffic; in 1945, military traffic was removed from the reduced-rate category. While land-grant rates were in effect, the government obtained estimated reductions of more than $500 million—a sum several times the value

---

[11]Five great systems received about 75 percent of the land-grant acreage. These were the Union Pacific (including the Denver Pacific and Kansas Pacific); the Atchison, Topeka, and Santa Fe; the Northern Pacific; the Texas and Pacific; and the Central Pacific system (including the Southern Pacific Railroad).

ILLINOIS CENTRAL RAILROAD COMPANY

OFFER FOR SALE

ONE MILLION ACRES OF SUPERIOR FARMING LANDS,

IN FARMS OF

40, 80 & 160 acres and upwards at from $8 to $12 per acre.

THESE LANDS ARE

NOT SURPASSED BY ANY IN THE WORLD.

THEY LIE ALONG

THE WHOLE LINE OF THE CENTRAL ILLINOIS RAILROAD,

For Sale on LONG CREDIT, SHORT CREDIT and for CASH, they are situated near TOWNS, VILLAGES, SCHOOLS and CHURCHES.

For all Purposes of Agriculture.

The lands offered for sale by the Illinois Central Railroad Company are equal to any in the world. A healthy climate, a rich soil, and railroads to convey to market the fullness of the earth—all combine to place in the hands of the enterprising workingman the means of independence.

Illinois.

Extending 380 miles from North to South, has all the diversity of climate to be found between Massachusetts and Virginia, and varieties of soil adapted to the products of New England and those of the Middle States. The black soil in the central portions of the State is the richest known, and produces the finest corn, wheat, sorghum and hay, which latter crop, during the past year, has been highly remunerative. The seeding of these prairie lands to tame grasses, for pasturage, offers to farmers with capital the most profitable results. The smaller prairies, interspersed with timber, in the more southern portion of the State, produce the best of winter wheat, tobacco, flax, hemp and fruit. The lands still further South are heavily timbered, and here the raising of fruit, tobacco, cotton and the manufacture of lumber yield large returns. The health of Illinois is hardly surpassed by any State in the Union.

Grain and Stock Raising.

In the list of corn and wheat producing States, Illinois stands pre-eminently first. Its advantages for raising cattle and hogs are too well known to require comment here. For sheep raising, the lands in every part of the State are well adapted, and Illinois can now boast of many of the largest flocks in the country. No branch in industry offers greater inducements for investment.

Hemp, Flax and Tobacco.

Hemp and flax can be produced of as good quality as any grown in Europe. Tobacco, of the finest quality is raised upon lands purchased of this Company, and it promises to be one of the most important crops of the State. Cotton, too, is raised, to a considerable extent, in the southern portion. The making of sugar from the beet is receiving considerable attention, and experiments upon a large scale have been made during the past season. The cultivation of sorghum is rapidly increasing, and there are numerous indications that ere many years Illinois will produce a large surplus of sugar and molasses for exportation.

Fruit.

The central and southern parts of the State are peculiarly adapted to fruit raising ; and peaches, pears and strawberries, together with early vegetables, are sent to Chicago, St. Louis and Cincinnati, as well as other markets, and always command a ready sale.

Coal and Minerals.

The immense coal deposits of Illinois are worked at different points near the Railroad, and the great resources of the State in iron, lead, zinc, limestone, potters' clay, &c., &c., as yet barely touched, will eventually be the source of great wealth.

To Actual Settlers

the inducements offered are so great that the Company has already sold 1,500,000 acres, and the sales during the past year have been to a larger number of purchasers than ever before. The advantages to a man of small means, settling in Illinois, where his children may grow up with all the benefits of education and the best of public schools, can hardly be over-estimated. No State in the Union is increasing more rapidly in population, which has trebled in ten years along the line of this Railroad.

PRICES AND TERMS OF PAYMENT.

The price of land varies from $7 and upward per acre, and they are sold on long credit, on short credit, or for cash. A deduction of ten per cent. from the long credit price is made to those who make a payment of one-fourth of the principal down, and the balance in one, two, and three years. A deduction of **twenty per cent.** is made to those who purchase for cash. Never before have greater inducements been offered to cash purchasers.

EXAMPLE.

Forty acres at $10 per acre on long credit, interest at six per cent., payable annually in advance ; the principal in four, five, six, and seven years.

	INTEREST.	PRINCIPAL.
Cash payment	$24.00	
Payment in one year	24.00	
" two years	24.00	
" three "	24.00	
" four "	18.00	$100.00
" five "	12.00	100.00
" six "	6.00	100.00
" seven "		100.00

Or the same farm, on short credit :

	INTEREST.	PRINCIPAL.
Cash payment	$16.20	$80.00
Payment in one year	10.80	80.00
" two years	5.40	80.00
" three "		80.00

The same farm may be purchased for $320 in cash.

Full information on all points, together with maps, showing the exact location of the lands, will be furnished on application in person or by letter to

LAND COMMISSIONER,

Illinois Central R. R. Co., Chicago, Ill.

Public land granted to the railroads as a subsidy and in turn sold to settlers was a continuing source of capital funds. Ads like this one appeared in city newspapers, luring thousands of Americans and immigrants westward.

of the land grants when they were made and about equal to what the railroads have received from their sale until now.[12]

Subsidies doubtlessly added to the profits and thus to the incentives of railroad builders until the early 1870s. But the great bulk of both new and replacement capital raised by the railroads came from private sources, both domestic and foreign. The benefits of railroad transportation to farmers, small industrialists, and the general public along a proposed route were described in glowing terms by its promoters. Investors responded with enthusiasm and generosity, if not with extravagance—their outlay of funds promoted in part by the realization that the growth of their communities and an increase in their personal wealth depended on the new transportation facility. Except in the industrial and urban Northeast, however, local sources could not provide sufficient capital, so promoters had to tap the accumulated wealth of eastern cities and the financial capitals of Europe.

Thus, as the first examples of truly large corporations, railroad companies led the way in developing fund-raising techniques by selling securities to sophisticated investors. Before 1860, first-, second-, and third-mortgage bonds were issued and traded, and convertible debentures and real estate bonds were introduced.[13] Preferred stocks were used to finance railroad construction, although this type of issue was not widely adopted until it was used as a substitute for bonds in the reorganizations of the 1890s. And although the common stock of the railroads was completely avoided by conservative investors, the proliferation of such issues added tremendously to the volume of shares listed and traded on the floor of the New York Stock Exchange.

The modern investment banking house appeared as an intermediary between seekers of railroad capital in the South and the West and eastern and European investors, who could not easily estimate the worth of the securities offered them. From the 1850s on, the investment banker played a crucial role in American finance, allocating capital that originated in wealthy old areas among those seeking it. J. Pierpont Morgan, a junior partner in the small Wall Street firm of Dabney and Morgan, joined forces in 1859 with the Drexels of Philadelphia to form Drexel, Morgan and Company. Along with Winslow, Lanier and Company and August Belmont and Company, Morgan's house grew rich and powerful through the placing of railroad securities, particularly in foreign markets.

European interests eventually owned a majority of the stock in several railroads, and English, Dutch, and German stockholders constituted impor-

---

[12]This comment is not intended to pass judgment on the wisdom of federal land grants to railroads but simply to suggest the magnitude of the sums involved. An estimate of the total cost to the federal government would have to include interest.

[13]For a detailed treatment of financial innovation by railroad promoters, see Alfred D. Chandler, Jr., *The Railroads—The Nation's First Big Business* (New York: Harcourt Brace Jovanovich, 1965), pp. 43–94.

tant minority groups in the others. In 1876, European holdings amounted to 86 percent of the common stock of the Illinois Central, and at one time two directorships of the Chicago and Northwestern were occupied by Dutch nationals. In 1914, Europeans who were largely English owned one-fifth of all outstanding American railroad securities.

UNSCRUPULOUS FINANCIAL PRACTICES

In a day when the issue of corporate securities was subject only to the cursory supervision of state authorities, promoters sometimes indulged in questionable, even fraudulent, practices. The most common method of getting around the law was the organization of "construction companies," which stood between the railroad corporation itself and the contractor who actually did the building.

The construction company was organized to permit the sale of stock below par value—a practice prohibited by law in some states. The railroad contracted with a construction company to build a certain number of miles of road at a specific amount per mile; payment was to be made in stocks and bonds. The contract price was set high enough to permit the construction company, when selling the stock, to offer real "bargains" to the investing public and still earn a profit.[14] Because the railroad corporation had issued the securities at par, no law was violated when they were sold at a discount by a second party, and the construction company obtained enough money from the transaction to build the road and make a profit. This method of financing, although it smacked of deceit, provided funds that might not have been obtained otherwise. It was in the "inside" construction company that the real evils of such financing were to be found. The owners of the construction company were often "insiders"—that is, officers and directors of the railroad corporation. It was common practice to sell railroad bonds to the general public for cash. The construction costs were then met by paying cash and issuing common stock to the construction company, in addition to passing the subsidies on to the construction company in the form of land grants and state and local bonds. The higher the price charged by the construction company, the greater, of course, were the profits that the insiders made at the expense of the railroad company itself.

Although not all railroad construction was financed through inside construction companies, this device was common—especially during the 1860s and 1870s—and all the transcontinentals made use of it. It was not unusual

---

[14]Although the value of a company's assets, plus its current and potential earning power, might determine prices for more sophisticated investors, rank-and-file buyers quickly become accustomed to receiving $2,500 or more in stocks and bonds for every $1,000 they paid out in cash. For 50 years or more after 1860, it was next to impossible to convince individuals to buy common stock in a new venture without sweetening the deal with a bond or two.

for the proceeds of security issues, plus the value of the subsidies, to exceed twice the actual cost of a railroad. The most notorious inside company was the Crédit Mobilier of America, chartered under Pennsylvania statutes, which built the Union Pacific. During President Grant's second term, when Americans were far from squeamish about conflicts of interest, this company's operations caused a national scandal: certain members of Congress were on the Union Pacific's directorate. By voting for land grants, some congressmen were indirectly voting themselves vast acreages in the western plains. Huge profits accrued to the Crédit Mobilier. A congressional committee reported in 1873 that over $23 million in cash profits had been realized by the company on a $10-million investment—and the cash take was over and above a $50-million profit in securities.[15]

MONOPOLISTIC AND COMPETITIVE RAILROAD MARKETS

Before 1870, a railroad usually had some degree of monopoly power within its operating area. However, as the railway network burgeoned, adding more than 40,000 miles in the 1870s and a fantastic 70,000 miles in the 1880s, the trunk lines of the East and even the transcontinentals of the West began to suffer the pangs of cut-throat rivalry. To be sure, major companies often faced no competition at all in local traffic and therefore had great flexibility in setting prices for relatively short hauls. But for long hauls between major cities there were usually two or more competing carriers. The consequence was a variance in the rates per mile charged between short and long hauls. Increasingly, this brought noisy cries of outrage.

Railroad managers were in charge of firms with high fixed costs, so they tried to set rates in ways that would assure the fullest possible use of plant and equipment. Where it was possible to separate markets, they did, and set rates in a discriminating way. For example, rates were set much lower on bulk freight such as coal and ore than they were on manufactured goods. If traffic was predominantly in one direction, shipments on the return route could be made at much lower rates, because receiving any revenue was better than receiving nothing for hauling empty cars. And lower charges for hauling carload lots than for smaller shipments were justified on the ground that it cost no more to move a loaded car than one that was half full.

Another more despised form of rate discrimination arose when the same railroad was in both a *monopolistic* and a *competitive* position, allowing rates

[15]The Crédit Mobilier scandal unquestionably turned both public and congressional opinion against further land-grant subsidy of railroads. Mercer's research indicates that profits from the Union Pacific and Central Pacific system were probably high enough to induce private venturing in such high-risk projects. See, for example, Lloyd J. Mercer, "Rates of Return for Land-Grant Railroads: The Central Pacific System," *Journal of Economic History* 30 (1970):602–26.

charged for equivalent distances to be anything but equal. Rates were then raised for shippers who lacked alternative rail or water routes to make up for the cut rates offered to shippers who did have alternative routes to choose from. Rates also were lowered more readily for favored firms that had real bargaining power. Shippers not favored by these discriminatory rates or by outright rebates were naturally indignant at the special treatment accorded their competitors. Railroads also discriminated among cities and towns—a practice especially resented by farmers and merchants of one locality who watched those in another area enjoy lower rates for the same service.

By 1873, the railroad industry was plagued by tremendous excess capacity. One line could obtain business by cutting rates on through traffic, but only at the expense of another company, which then found its own capacity in excess. Rate wars during the depressed years of the 1870s led to efforts to stop "ruinous competition." Railroad managers responded by banding together on through-traffic rates. They allocated shares of the business among the competing lines, working out alliances between competing and connecting railroads within a region. But more often than not the alliances were fragile agreements that were easily broken under the pressure of high fixed costs and excess capacity. To hide the rate cutting, shippers might pay the published tariff and receive a secret rebate from the railroad. But sooner or later, word of the rebating would leak out, with a consequent return to open rate warfare. To provide a stronger basis for maintaining prices, Albert Fink took the lead in forming regional federations to pool either traffic or profits. The first was the Southern Railway and Steamship Association, which was formed in 1875 with Fink as its first commissioner. Then in 1879, the trunk lines formed the Eastern Trunk Line Association. But despite their careful organization and competent leadership, even the federations eventually came unglued, as weak railroads or companies run by managers unconcerned about stability broke with the pool and began price cutting.[16] Moreover, both shippers and the general public resented pooling, as well as discrimination in any form. The result was both popular and industry-wide support of legislation directed toward government regulation of the railroad business.

State Regulation

The first comprehensive railroad regulation came in the early 1870s, largely in response to increasing evidence of discrimination against persons and places. As the decade progressed, agrarian tempers rose as farm incomes declined. As emphasized in Chapter 15, farmers in the Middle West attrib-

---

[16] Chandler, *The Railroads*, p. 161. Also see Chandler's *The Visible Hand: The Managerial Revolution in American Business* (Cambridge: Belknap Press of Harvard Univ. Press, 1977), especially Ch. 4.

uted a large measure of their economic difficulties to the railroads. Many farmers had invested savings in railroad ventures on the basis of extravagant promises of the prosperity that would result from better transportation facilities. When the opposite effect became apparent, farmers, particularly in the Middle West, initiated a move for legislation to regulate rates. Prominent in the movement were members of the National Grange of the Patrons of Husbandry, an agrarian society founded in 1867. Thus, the demand for passage by the *states* of measures regulating railroads, grain elevators, and public warehouses became known as the Granger movement, the legislation as the Granger laws, and the review of the laws by the Supreme Court as the Granger cases.

Between 1871 and 1874, regulatory railroad laws were passed by Illinois, Iowa, Wisconsin, and Minnesota. Fixing schedules of maximum rates by commission rather than by statute was a feature of both the Illinois and Minnesota laws. One of the common practices that western farmers could not tolerate was charging more for the carriage of goods over a short distance than over a longer distance in the same direction and by the same line. The *pro rata* clause contained in the Granger laws, which prohibited railroads from charging short shippers more than their fair share of the costs, was intended to rectify this alleged injustice and was the forerunner of the present-day *long-and-short-haul* clause of the Interstate Commerce Act. Both *personal* and *place* discrimination were generally outlawed. Finally, strong commissions were given power to investigate complaints and to institute suits against violators.

Almost as soon as the Granger laws were in the statute books, attempts were made to have them declared unconstitutional on the grounds that they were repugnant to the "due process" clause of the Fourteenth Amendment to the Constitution. Pleadings in the courts were based on the premise that limitations on rates and charges restricted the earnings of companies and deprived properties of their value. Six suits were brought to test the laws. The principal one was *Munn* v. *Illinois,* an action involving grain elevators. This case was taken to the U.S. Supreme Court in 1877 after state courts in Illinois found that Munn and his partner Scott had violated the state warehouse law in 1872 by not obtaining a license to operate grain elevators in the city of Chicago and by charging prices in excess of those set by state law. Although the Munn case involved grain elevators, the Supreme Court held that the principles expounded in the case also applied to the five railroad cases then before it; in each instance, the right of a state to regulate certain businesses was upheld. Chief Justice Morrison Remick Waite stated in the majority opinion that, when businesses are "clothed with a public interest," their regulation as public utilities is constitutional.[17] The Munn

---

[17] Associate Justice Stephen Johnson Field, in the dissenting opinion, objected to the vague language of the majority; he went on to say that the public is interested in many businesses and that to extend the reasoning of the majority might bring "calico gowns" and "city mansions" within the scope of such regulation.

case settled the constitutionality of the state regulation of railroads and certain other enterprises within the states—but not between states.

In 1886, a decision in the case of *Wabash, St. Louis and Pacific Railway Company* v. *Illinois* made a critical delineation of the sphere of state control as distinguished from that of federal control. The state had found that the Wabash was charging more for a shorter haul from Gilman, Illinois, to New York City than for a longer haul from Peoria to New York City and had ordered the rate adjusted because it violated the pro rata clause in the regulatory statutes. The Supreme Court held that Illinois could not regulate rates on shipments in interstate commerce even in the absence of federal regulation, because such regulation would inevitably restrict freedom of commerce among the states. This view was an extension of the opinion of the Court in the Granger cases, where the contention of the railroads had been that the Granger laws interfered with interstate commerce and therefore with the powers of the U.S. government. In the absence of federal legislation, the Wabash case left a vast area with no control over carrier operation; regulation would have to come at the national level or remain hopelessly inadequate. The public-policy answer was of more than passing importance, because it marked the first massive intervention of the federal government in the private economic sector outside the field of banking.

Federal Regulations[18]

Early in 1887, the Act to Regulate Commerce was passed by Congress and approved by President Grover Cleveland. Its chief purpose was to bring all railroads engaged in interstate commerce under federal regulation. The Interstate Commerce Commission, consisting of five members to be appointed by the president with the advice and consent of the Senate, was created and its duties were set forth. First, the commission was required to examine the business of the railroads; to this end, it could subpoena witnesses and ask them to produce books, contracts, and other documents of the carriers. Second, the commission was charged with hearing complaints that arose due to violations of the act and was empowered to issue "cease and desist" orders if unlawful practices were discovered. The third duty of the commission was to require railroads to submit annual reports based on a uniform system of accounts. Finally, the commission was required to submit annual reports of its own operations to Congress.

The Act to Regulate Commerce seemingly prohibited all possible unethical practices. Section 1 stated that railroad rates must be "just and reasonable." Section 2 prohibited personal discrimination; a lower charge could no longer be made in the form of a "special rate, rebate, drawback, or other

---

[18]For an excellent survey of the issues of regulation, see Thomas K. McCraw, "Regulation in America: A Review Article," *Business History Review* 49 (1975):159–83.

device." Section 3 provided that no undue preference of any kind should be accorded by any railroad to any shipper, any place, or any special kind of traffic. Section 4 enacted, in less drastic form, the pro rata clauses of the Granger legislation by prohibiting greater charges "for the transportation of passengers or of like kind of property, under substantially similar circumstances and conditions, for a shorter than for a longer distance, over the same line, in the same direction, the shorter being included in the longer distance." Pooling was prohibited.

The ICC was the first permanent independent federal regulatory agency. Its formation represented the beginning of direct government intervention into the economy on an expanding scale. The first decade and a half of the ICC, however, were filled with court challenges by the railroads. To clarify certain powers delegated by Congress, both the ICC and the railroads sought new legislation, especially regarding issues of price discrimination.

The Elkins Act of 1903 dealt solely with the practice of personal discrimination. There is convincing evidence that the Elkins Act, represented the wishes of a large majority of the railroad companies. It was drafted with their support, because this act protected them from demands for rebates by powerful shippers and brought the government to their aid in enforcing the cartel prices set by the trunk-line associates. The Elkins Act stated that railroad corporations should be liable for any unlawful violation of the discrimination provisions. Up to this time, only officials and employees of a company had been liable for discriminatory actions; henceforth, the corporation itself would be responsible, too. A second provision made the *receiver* of rebates guilty of violating the law, even though the rebate was given voluntarily by the carrier. But the most important provision of the act dealt with the practice of departing from published rates. Until this time, the courts had overruled the commission in the enforcement of published rates by requiring that discrimination against or injury to *other* shippers of similar goods had to be proved. The Elkins Act made *any* departure from a published rate a misdemeanor and authorized the courts to enjoin railroads from (1) continuing to depart from published rates and (2) unlawful discriminations.

To close remaining loopholes, especially regarding other discriminatory pricing practices, Congress passed the Hepburn Act of 1906. The Hepburn Act extended the jurisdiction of the ICC to private-car companies that operated joint express, tank, and sleeping cars. Such services as storage, refrigeration, and ventilation, furnished by the railroads in connection with transportation, were also made subject to the control of the commission. The extension of ICC jurisdiction over these phases of railroad transportation was necessary because the management of the railroads could use such services to discriminate among shippers in subtle fashion. For example, railroads normally charged for storage or refrigeration; if shippers were not charged for these services, discrimination resulted. Perhaps even more important that this extension of authority, however, was the change in the procedures for enforcement of the ICC's order. Until 1906 the ICC had to prove before the court the case it had adjudicated under the authority it had been granted by Congress. The Hepburn Act put the burden of proof on the carriers. Disobedience of commission orders carried a penalty of $5,000, and each day of violation constituted a separate offense. The right of judicial review was recognized, but the railroads—not the commission— had to appeal, and the presumption was for—not against—the commission.

The railroad industry was not pleased with the new regulatory agency, however. In 1892, Charles E. Perkins, president of the Chicago, Burlington and Quincy Railroad, wrote a letter to his lawyer Richard Olney, who later became Attorney General of the United States. Perkins was recommending that the embryonic five-year-old commission (the ICC) be abolished. Olney's reply is a masterpiece of impropriety and prophecy:

> My impression would be that looking at the matter from the railroad point of view it would not be a wise thing to undertake . . . The attempt would not be likely to succeed; if it did not succeed, and were made on the grounds of the inefficiency and uselessness of the Commission, the result would very probably be giving it the power it now lacks. The Commission, as its functions have been limited by the courts, is, or can be made of great use to the railroads. It satisfies the public clamor for a government supervision of railroads, at the same time that the supervision is almost entirely nominal. Further, the older such a commission gets to be, the more inclined it will be found to take the business and railroad view of things. It thus becomes a sort of protection against hasty and crude legislation hostile to railroad interests . . . The part of wisdom is not to destroy the Commission, but to utilize it.[19]

Capturing the Regulators   In 1905, noted historian Gabriel Kolko, proposed that railroad managers saw the ICC as a way of affecting stable profitable rates and other advantages of cartel management.[20] Although railroad managers openly supported the Elkins Act to assure through regulation fair pricing among competing carriers, the scholarship of Albro Martin shows that the work of the ICC was largely for the benefit of users—shippers and passengers.[21] As the long period of steadily falling prices reversed itself in 1896, the ICC disallowed rate increases sufficient to match rises in the general price level. Railroads reacted by slowing their repairs and

---

[19] Robert C. Fellmeth, *The Interstate Commerce Commission* [sic] (New York: Grossman, 1970), pp. xiv–xv.
[20] Gabriel Kolko, *Railroads and Regulation, 1877–1916* (Princeton: Princeton Univ. Press, 1965). For one of the first critiques of the Kolko thesis, see Robert Harberson, "Railroads and Regulation, 1877–1916: Conspiracy or Public Interest?" *Journal of Economic History* 37 (1964):230–42.
[21] For an analysis of the decline of railroads at the turn of the century see Albro Martin, *Enterprise Denied: Origins of the Decline of American Railroads, 1897–1917* (New York: Columbia Univ. Press, 1971). Although the decline was already underway, the troubled railroads were nationalized in World War I largely because of the war effort and inadequate responses by management to the needs of the military and government. This take-over contributed to increasing financial uncertainty for the railroads, even upon their return to private ownership.

replacement of capital stock and equipment. This helped to some extent to slow the rising costs of railroad operations. By the outbreak of the First World War, the railroads were physically decayed and financially strapped. If there was a management capture of the regulatory process, it is difficult to find in the events preceding the 1920s. Indeed, in 1917, the federal government scored the critical capture by nationalizing the railroads in the interests of the war effort. After the war the railroads were returned to private ownership. As we shall see in later chapters, the capture hypothesis pertains to other situations, but managers did not initially capture and control the regulation process in the case of early ICC activities.

RAILROADS AND ECONOMIC GROWTH

As the world turned from the ordeals of war to the problems of economic regeneration and economic growth in the late 1940s and the 1950s, the American experience was often held out as a model for low-income developing nations, and more advanced economies as well. The Soviet model of a planned economy was another. Joseph Shumpeter, an eminent economist in the pre-War period, held the view that railroads had led the transition to modern economic growth.[22] Growth to him was a dynamic process of applying major technological advances, both invention and innovation. To him, the railroad epitomized these growth-generating forces. Walt Rostow later added to this view by arguing that the railroad was a leading sector in the nation's take-off to modern economic growth.[23]

Within a calendar year of each other in the mid 1960s, Albert Fishlow and Robert Fogel produced books that generated an avalanche of debate.[24] Their objective was to quantify and pin down with actual numbers the contributions of the railroad to nineteenth-century U.S. economic growth. Although their classic works differed in style and approach, their methodology was essentially the same—to measure the social savings of the railroad, in 1859 (Fishlow) and in 1890 (Fogel). Fogel's work particularly drew fire, perhaps because of the enticing, charged rhetoric he used.[25]

Fogel began his study by reviewing the evolution of the "Axiom of Indispensability" a term that became widely accepted in describing the role of

---

[22] Joseph Shumpeter, *The Theory of Economic Development* (Cambridge: Harvard Univ. Press, 1949).

[23] W. W. Rostow, *The Stages of Economic Growth: A Non-Communist Manifesto* (Cambridge: Cambridge Univ. Press, 1960).

[24] Albert Fishlow, *American Railroads and the Transformation of the Antebellum Economy* (Cambridge: Harvard Univ. Press, 1965). Robert W. Fogel, *The Union Pacific Railroad: A Case of Premature Enterprise* (Baltimore: Johns Hopkins Univ. Press, 1965).

[25] See Donald McCloskey, *The Rhetoric of Economics* (Madison: Univ. of Wisconsin Press, 1985), Ch. 6.

the railroad. It was primarily in the late nineteenth-century battles over government control that "the indispensability of railroads to American economic growth was elevated to the status of an axiomatic truth."[26] Just prior to Fishlow's and Fogel's books, the most widely used texts in American economic history courses portrayed the railroads as having "the power of life and death over the economy," or "as essential to the development of Capitalism in America."[27] Because of the efforts of Fishlow and Fogel and other scholars, those views no longer hold.

Fishlow measured the cost of moving all the freight and passengers carried by rail in 1859 by the next best alternative to railroads. For example, the actual freight shipped by rail that year was cost estimated by water or wagon, or stage, depending on availability as if the railroad suddenly vanished. The higher costs of carrying railroad passengers and freight by these older technologies were figured by Fishlow to be about 4 percent of gross national product in that year.

Fogel selected 1890 to make his social savings estimate, in part, because the influence of the railroad was probably at or near its peak by then. He wanted to assure that his estimates were upperbound. He did, however, allow for resources to be reallocated and the economy restructured in the absence of the railroad. He argued that if there had been no railroad, production for market would have been closer to water transport modes and many more canals and roads would have been built if the railroad had never existed. His imaginary but plausible world was an especially lively part of the debate and analysis that followed. His results, however, did not differ too widely from Fishlow's. In short his social savings calculations for freight only, were about 4.7 percent of 1890 GNP. Subsequently others calculated the social savings of 1890 rail passengers, including the value of their time saved.[28] The total extra costs of rail passengers to travel by water or stage figured to 2.6 percent of 1890 GNP.

This measure of the direct effects of the railroad on economic output suggests that actual incomes (or output) per capita in 1890 would not have been as high as they were until 1892. In short, the railroad accounted for about two years of growth, or alternatively stated, equalled a postponement of all growth for two years.

Although Fishlow's and Fogel's pioneering classics debunked long held myths about the indispensability of the railroad, it is difficult to think of any other single innovation that rendered economic gains of a similar magnitude.[29] As students of this lively professional debate quickly learn however, it was not so much the final calculations that were Fishlow's and Fogel's

[26] Fogel, p. 7.

[27] See Fogel p. 9 for various examples.

[28] J. Hayden Boyd and Gary M. Walton, "The Social Savings From Nineteenth Century Rail Passenger Services," *Explorations in Economic History* 9 (1972):233–55.

[29] For a challenge to their studies, one that addresses various indirect effects such as greater scale economics in industry, higher rates of capital formation, and other effects, see Jeffrey,

TABLE 16-2 Productivity in the Railroad Sector, 1870–1910 (1910 = 100)

Year	Output	Labor	Capital	Fuel	Total Input	Total Factor Productivity
1870	7	14	17	5	14	47
1880	14	25	32	12	26	54
1890	33	44	62	29	49	67
1900	55	60	72	46	63	87
1910	100	100	100	100	100	100

Source: Adapted from Albert Fishlow, "Internal Transportation," in *Economic Growth* (New York: Harper & Row, 1972), p. 508.

main contributions, significant though they were. Rather it was their ability to focus the argument, to specify a testable hypothesis, and bring forth the evidence that narrowed the range of disagreement. In short, they advanced the level of analysis and the profession's understanding of an important issue in economic growth generally and in American economic history in particular.

Finally, as shown in Table 16-2 total factor productivity of the railroad somewhat more than doubled in the 40 years between 1870 and 1910. As in other maturing sectors and industries, the railroad experienced the usual phenomena of a continued but slowing advance. As observed in Chapter 9, the pace of total factor productivity advance was so rapid in 1840–60, that it doubled in this early 20 year period. The sustained rapid growth of output relative to inputs was due primarily to two sources of productivity advance. First, as concluded by Fishlow, were additional gains from economies of scale in operation. He accounts nearly half of the productivity advance of the railroads at this time as due to this source. The other half resulted from four innovations. In order of importance these were (1) more powerful locomotives and more efficient freight cars, which tripled in capacity; (2) stronger steel rails, permitting heavy loads;(3) automatic couplers; and (4) air brakes—these later two facilitating greater speed and safety.[30]

Despite the expected slowing up of the railroad's productivity advance, it continued throughout the period up to the First World War. It averaged 2 percent annually and exceeded the pace of economic growth and productivity advance for the economy as a whole, which was approximately 1.5 per unit per annum. There can be no doubt that the railroad was a leading sector, one of immense importance in the U.S. experience of modern economic growth. Although perhaps not indispensable, no other single industry could claim a greater role in America's economic growth during this period.

G. Williamson, "A General Equilibrium History," Ch. 9 of *Late Nineteenth Century American Economic Development* (Cambridge Univ. Press, 1974). For Fogel's response, see his article, "Notes on the Social Savings Controversy," *Journal of Economic History* 39 (1979):1–55.

[30] See Albert Fishlow,"Internal Transportation," p. 509–10 for a more detailed analysis of these sources of productivity advance.

SELECTED REFERENCES AND SUGGESTED READINGS

Boyd, J. Hayden, and Gary M. Walton. "The Social Savings from Nineteenth-Century Rail Passenger Services." *Explorations in Economic History* 9 (1972):233–54.

Chandler, Alfred D. *The Railroads: The Nation's First Big Business.* New York: Harcourt, Brace & World, 1965.

Cochran, Thomas C. *Railroad Leaders, 1845–1890, The Business Mind in Action.* Cambridge: Harvard Univ. Press, 1953.

David, Paul. "Transport Innovation and Economic Growth: Professor Fogel On and Off the Rails." *Economic History Review* (1969).

Dick, Trevor J. O. "United States Railroad Inventions, Investment Since 1870." *Explorations in Economic History* 11 (1974):249–70.

Engerman, Stanley. "Some Economic Issues Relating to Railroad Subsidies and the Evaluation of Land Grants." *Journal of Economic History* 32 (1972):443–63.

Fishlow, Albert. *American Railroads and the Transformation of the Antebellum Economy.* Cambridge: Harvard Univ. Press, 1965.

———. "The Dynamics of Railroad Extension into the West." In *Reinterpretation of American Economic History,* ed. Robert Fogel and Stanley Engerman. New York: Harper & Row, 1971.

———. "Productivity and Technological Change in the Railroad Sector, 1840–1910." In *Output, Employment and Productivity in the United States after 1800, Studies in Income and Wealth,* Vol. 30, National Bureau of Economic Research. New York: Columbia Univ. Press, 1966.

Fleisig, Heywood. "The Central Pacific Railroad and the Railroad Land Grant Controversy." *Journal of Economic History* 35 (1975):552–66.

Fogel, Robert W. "Notes on the Social Saving Controversy." *Journal of Economic History* 39 (1979):1–54.

———. *Railroads and American Economic Growth.* Baltimore: Johns Hopkins Univ. Press, 1964.

———. *The Union Pacific Railroad: A Case of Premature Enterprise.* Baltimore: Johns Hopkins Univ. Press, 1965.

Fogel, Robert W., and Stanley Engerman. *The Reinterpretation of American Economic History.* New York: Harper & Row, 1971.

Gates, Paul W. *The Illinois Central Railroad and its Colonization Work.* Cambridge: Harvard Univ. Press, 1934.

Greeves, William S. "A Comparison of Railroad Land Grant Policies." *Agricultural History* (1951).

Grodinsky, Julius. *Transcontinental Railway Strategy.* Philadelphia: Univ. of Pennsylvania Press, 1962.

Harbeson, Robert. "Railroads and Regulation, 1877–1916: Conspiracy or Public Interest?" *Journal of Economic History* 37 (1967):230–42.

Heath, Milton. "Public Railroad Construction and the Development of Private Enterprise in the South Before 1861." *Journal of Economic History* 9 (1949).

Hidy, Ralph, and Muriel Hidy. "Anglo-American Merchant Bankers and the Railroads of the Old Northwest, 1848–1860." *Business History Review* 34 (1960).

Hughes, Jonathan. *The Vital Few: American Economic Progress and Its Protagonists.* New York: Oxford Univ. Press, 1987.

Hunt, E. H. "Railroad Social Savings in Nineteenth Century America." *American Economic Review* 57 (1967):909–10. Also, P. R. P. Coelho, R. P. Thomas, and D. Shetter, "Comment." *American Economic Review* 58 (1968):184–89.

Jenks, Leland. "Railroads as an Economic Force in American Development." Reprinted in *Views of American Economic Growth,* ed. Thomas Cochran and Thomas Brewer. New York: McGraw-Hill, 1966, vol. 2.

Kolko, Gabriel. *Railroads and Regulation, 1877–1916.* Princeton, N.J.: Princeton Univ. Press, 1965.

Lebergott, Stanley. "United States Transport Advance and Externalities." *Journal of Economic History* 26 (1966):437–61.

Martin, Albro. *Enterprise Denied: Origins of the Decline of American Railroads, 1897–1917.* New York: Columbia Univ. Press, 1971.

Martin, Albro. *James J. Hill and the Opening of the Northwest*. New York: Oxford Univ. Press. 1976.

MacAvoy, Paul. *The Economic Effects of Regulation*. Cambridge: MIT Press, 1965.

McClelland, Peter D. "Railroads, American Growth, and the New Economic History: A Critique." *Journal of Economic History* 28 (1968):102–23.

McGraw, Thomas. "Regulation in America, a Review Article." *Business History Review* 49 (1975).

Mercer, Lloyd. "Building Ahead of Demand: Some Evidence for the Land Grant Railroads." *Journal of Economic History* 34 (1974):492–500.

———. "Land Grants to American Railroads: Social Cost or Social Benefit?" *Business History Review* (1969).

———. "Rates of Return for Land Grant Railroads, The Central Pacific System." *Journal of Economic History* (1970):602–26.

———. "Taxpayers or Investors: Who Paid for the Land Grant Railroads?" *Business History Review* (1972).

Ripley, W. Z. *Railroads: Rates and Regulations*. New York: Longmans, Green, 1912.

Rostow, W. W. *The Stages of Economic Growth: A Non-Communist Manifesto*. New York: Cambridge Univ. Press, 1960.

Stover, John. *American Railroads*. Chicago: Univ. of Chicago Press, 1961.

Ulen, Thomas S. "The Market for Regulation: The I.C.C., from 1887 to 1920." *American Economic Review* 70 (1980):306–10.

———. "Railroad Cartels Before 1887: The Effectiveness of Private Enforcement of Collusion." *Research in Economic History*. Greenwich, CT: JAI Press, 1986.

Weiss, Thomas. "United States Transport Advance and Externalities: A Comment." *Journal of Economic History* 28 (1968):631–34; and "Reply" by Stanley Lebergott, p. 635.

C H A P T E R 17

Industrial Expansion and Economic Concentration

STRUCTURAL CHANGE AND ECONOMIC GROWTH

During the half century that lay between the end of one great war and the beginning of another, the American economy assumed many of its modern characteristics. The most impressive change was the shift from an agricultural to an industrial economy. Although this shift had been underway throughout the entire nineteenth century, until the decade of the 1880s agriculture was the chief generator of income in the United States. The census of 1890, however, reported manufacturing output greater in dollar value than farm output, and by 1900 the annual value of manufactures was more than twice that of agricultural products. One set of most easily remembered numbers is the exact flip-flop between agriculture and manufactures in the percentage distribution of commodities produced between 1869 and 1899. In 1869 this distribution was 53 percent agriculture, 33 percent manufactures, and 14 percent mining and construction combined. Thirty years later it was 33 percent, 53 percent, and 14 percent.[1]

As emphasized in Chapter 15, agriculture expanded greatly in these years but fell relatively because of more rapid increases elsewhere. Table 17-1 shows the 1910 labor force in several employments as multiples of their 1860 employment level. For example, in 1910, the total labor force of 37,500,000 was approximately 3.4 times the 1860 level of 11,100,000. Agriculture's labor force grew only by a factor of two, however, from 5,900,000 to 11,800,000 between 1860 and 1910. By comparison, total labor in manufacturing grew by a multiple of 5.1, and in railroads by 23.2 in these 50 years.

---

[1] Robert E. Gallman, "Commodity Output, 1839–1899," in National Bureau of Economic Research Conference on Research in Income and Wealth. *Trends in the American Economy in the Nineteenth Century* (Princeton: Princeton Univ. Press, 1960), p. 26.

344

TABLE 17-1   Labor Force Expansion, 1860–1910: Select 1910 Multiples of 1860

Agriculture	2.0
Cotton textiles	3.0
Total labor force	3.4
Construction	3.7
Teachers	5.2
Total manufacturing	5.4
Trade	6.0
Mining	6.7
Primary iron and steel	7.1
Railroads	23.2

Source: Derived from Stanley Leberjott, *Manpower in Economic Growth: The American Record Since 1800* (New York: McGraw-Hill, 1964), p. 510.

TABLE 17-2   Output Expansion, 1860–1910: Select 1910 Multiples of 1860

Food and kindred products	3.7
Textiles and their products	6.2
Total manufacturing products	10.8
Iron and steel and their products	25.2
Bituminous coal	46.1
Cement	70.7
Railroad passenger miles[a]	17.1
Railroad freight ton miles[a]	98.1

[a]The railroad multiples are for 1859 to 1910.

Source: Derived from *Historical Statistics* (Washington, D.C.: GPO, 1960), series M, 178, Part 1; from Edwin Frickey, *Production in the United States, 1860–1914* (Cambridge: Harvard Univ. Press, 1947), pp. 38–43, 54; and from Albert Fishlow, "Productivity and Technological Change in the Railroad Sector, 1840–1910," in *Output, Employment and Productivity in the United States after 1800,* Studies in Income and Wealth, vol. 30, National Bureau of Economic Research, (New York: Columbia Univ. Press, 1966), p. 585.

Table 17-2 shows comparable multiples of output in several categories. The output expansion multiples are far larger than the labor multiples in comparable categories. For example, total manufactures output in 1910 was 10.8 times that of 1860. The labor force in manufactures had grown by only a multiple of 5.4. The coal and cement multiples suggest the vast devouring of natural resources needed to industrialize the nation and they were far larger than the mining labor multiple. All of these selected categories reveal output multiples higher than the total labor force multiple of 1860–1910.

Relative to the rest of the world, American gains in manufacturing output were also phenomenal. In the mid-1890s, the United States became the leading industrial power, and by 1910 its factories poured forth goods of nearly twice the value of those of its nearest rival, Germany. In 1913, the United States accounted for more than one-third of the world's industrial production.

TABLE 17-3   Population, National Income (1929 Prices), and National Income per Capita, 1869–1918 (annual averages for overlapping decades)

Decade	Population (in millions)	Real National Income (1929 prices)	National Income Per Capita (in dollars)	Per Capita Percentage Increases
1869–1878	43.5	9.4	$216	30.1
1874–1883	48.8	13.7	281	16.0
1879–1888	54.9	17.9	326	5.2
1884–1893	61.2	21.0	343	4.4
1889–1898	67.6	24.2	358	13.4
1894–1903	74.0	30.1	406	13.5
1899–1908	81.3	37.5	461	8.5
1904–1913	89.6	44.8	500	3.0
1909–1918	97.6	50.3	516	

Source: Simon Kuznets, "Changes in the National Incomes of the United States of America Since 1870," *Income and Wealth Series II* (London: Bowes & Bowes Ltd., 1952), p. 30. By permission of the publisher.

Productivity gains in agriculture, transportation, manufacturing, and other sectors powered an advance of total national income well above gains in population. Table 17-3 shows the growth of population, real national income, and real income per capita in overlapping decades. On the average, per capita income in real terms increased about 11 percent per decade. As the period progressed, there was a retardation in the rate of growth, but by World War I real per capita income was nearly 2½ times as great as it was during the 1869–78 decade.

According to Robert E. Gallman's estimates, real gross national product (GNP) grew at an average annual rate of somewhat more than 4 percent between 1865 and 1908—an increase of approximately eightfold for the period. A rate of real growth of this magnitude meant that per capita output advanced at an average annual rate of 2 percent. So between the Civil War and the First World War, real per capita GNP more than doubled.

Technological changes, investments in human capital, widening markets bringing new organizational business structures and economies of scale, and structural shifts in resources from lower to higher productivity uses (agricultural to manufacturing) combined to cause these exceptional long-run growth rates. They also led to a marked change in the composition of industries and how the world of business operated.

INDUSTRY COMPOSITION: THE LEADERS

A great number of industries comprised the totality of manufactures, but Table 17-4 lists the top ten industries (by value added) in 1860 and again 50 years later. It is clear from this evidence that the "make-up" of manu-

TABLE 17-4   The Ten Largest Industries in 1860 and in 1910, by Value Added

	1860 Value Added (in millions of dollars)		1910 Value Added (in millions of dollars)
Cotton goods	$55	Machinery	$690
Lumber	54	Lumber	650
Boots and shoes	49	Printing and publishing	540
Flour and meal	40	Iron and steel	330
Men's clothing	37	Malt liquors	280
Iron	36	Men's clothing	270
Machinery	33	Cotton goods	260
Woolen goods	25	Tobacco manufactures	240
Carriages and wagons	24	Railroad cars	210
Leather	23	Boots and shoes	180
All manufacturing	815	All manufacturing	8529

Source: U.S. Bureau of the Census, *Census of the United States: 1860,* vol. 3 (Washington: GPO, 1861), pp. 733–742 and U.S. Bureau of the Census, *Census of the United States: 1910,* vol. 8 (Washington: GPO, 1913), p. 40.

factures altered significantly as industrial expansion unfolded over the period. The push and tug of market forces and a high degree of resource mobility rendered such change possible. In addition, the industrial products of the United States were sold in markets that were expanding both at home and abroad as we shall see in detail in Chapter 20. Most American manufacturers, however, did not aggressively seek major foreign outlets until late in the nineteenth century since the nation itself provided an expanding free trade arena. For every dollar purchased in 1860 there were nearly six (in real terms) by the First World War.

A vast social transformation was reflected in the changes shown in Table 17-4. We see there that four entirely new industries—printing and publishing, malt liquor, tobacco, and railroad cars—were front runners by 1910, whereas flour and meal, woolens, wagons and buggies, and leather goods had slipped into lower positions. The low-income elasticity of demand for flour and meal, and woolens, plus new technologies (railroads cars for wagons) and other sources of productivity advance explain much of this transition. Also tastes were changing as cottons and linens, cigars and cigarettes, and store-bought alcoholic beverages, added to or replaced other items, many previously homemade. Mass communications and transportation based on technological advances helped spur social changes. Steel became the basic metal of manufactures, new forms and sources of power emerged like electricity and petroleum, and the scale of production grew to proportions unimaginable in 1860 or 1870. As big business grew, political pressures mounted to face the threat of monopoly power. Especially in the booming cities, where the factories grew, were changes in lifestyles so apparent.

We will address these and other forces affecting industrial progress in later chapters. Here our main concern is with the primary technological advances of the period, the expanding size and concentration of business enterprises, and the threat of monopoly that spurred new waves of government intervention and legal change. In short, we are looking primarily at changes on the supply side, in production, in business organization, and in the public policy responses. The issues of product distribution, urbanization, and other market changes are assessed in Chapter 20.

TECHNOLOGICAL ADVANCES IN LEADING MANUFACTURES

The technological changes that helped revolutionize industry after industry in this era are fascinating and often interrelated stories. No single industry is distinctly representative of the whole, but the advance of each was based on invention and innovation, the duel components of technological change. Invention signifies the discovery of something new, like steam power or electricity. Innovation denotes the many ways found to use and adapt the new ideas to products and service.

The avalanche of technological change, especially in the 1870s and 1880s, was pervasive as eloquently summarized by Anthony O'Brien.[2]

During the 1870s and 1880s the roller mill was introduced in the processing of oatmeal and flour, refrigerated cars in meat packing, the pneumatic malting process and temperature-controlled tank car in brewing, and food preparation and can-sealing machinery allowed for the mass production of canned meat, vegetables, fish, and soups. During the 1880s, the chemical industry saw the introduction first of the Solvay and then the electrolytic processes in the production of alkalis, and the discovery of the process of producing acetic acid and acetates as by-products of charcoal production. In the petroleum industry, John Merril's development of the seamless wrought-iron or steel-bottomed still allowed for a sharp increase in plant size between 1867 and 1873. The 1870s saw the development of the long-distance crude oil pipeline and the steel tank car. In the 1870s and 1880s the Bessemer and open-hearth processes were widely adopted in steel making. In the mid-1880s, new developments in electro-metallurgy made commercial mass production of aluminum possible. During the same period, a large number of mechanical and chemical innovations were devised that greatly facilitated the process of refining and working various metals. The development, beginning in 1880, of improved metalworking machinery based on the use of high-speed tool steel allowed for the production of a wide variety of better machines with finer tolerances. The typewriter, invented in the late 1870s, was mass produced during the 1880s. The electrical street railway car came into widespread use during the late 1880s. In addition, of course, the basic transcontinental railroad and national telegraph networks—infrastructure necessary for the rise

---

[2]Anthony P. O'Brien, "Factory Size, Economies of Scale, and the Great Merger Wave of 1898–1902," *Journal of Economic History* 48 (1988): 648–49.

of firms capable of distributing products on a national basis—were complete by 1880.

Technological change and labor productivity were closely linked indeed.

Table 17-5 shows the growth in value added per worker in those six industries that were among the ten largest in both 1860 and 1910. The cotton industry, which showed the slowest growth except for lumber in output per worker, was already maturing by 1860, and in no other field had power-driven machines already been so successfully applied. Therefore most of the post-Civil War period was merely one of innovation and achieving greater automaticity in cotton textiles. The industry listed in Table 17-5 with the most rapid advance per worker was men's clothing. During the Civil War, mechanization of the men's branch of the clothing industry increased rapidly as standardized sizes were derived from measurements of soldiers' uniforms taken by the Army, and the problem of achieving approximate fit was solved. Beginning in the 1870s, rotary cutting machines and reciprocating knives made it possible to cut several thicknesses of cloth at once. By 1895, sewing machines had been improved to the point that, power driven, they could operate at speeds of 1,600; 2,200; and 2,800 stitches per minute.

The boot and shoe industry, the second fastest growing in terms of value added per worker, was also markedly changed by invention and product standardizing innovations. It was only in the decade or so before the Civil War that manufactured shoes were shaped for the left and the right foot; consequently, many ladies and gentlemen had their footwear custom made and continued to do so for a long time. Manufacturers, however, eventually realized that design, finish, and attention to size and fit were necessary to secure a broad market for factory-made shoes. In 1875, they introduced the Goodyear welt process, which enabled soles to be attached to uppers without allowing nails and stitches to penetrate the inside of the shoe. Within

TABLE 17-5   Value Added per Worker in Leading Select Industries, 1860 and 1910 (in thousands of dollars)

	1860	1910	Percent Changed
Lumber	$.71	$ .93	31%
Cotton goods	.48	.68	42
Machinery	.81	1.29	59
Iron and steel	.72	1.37	90
Boots and shoes	.40	.91	128
Men's clothing	.32	1.18	269

Note: Value added measures the total value of output minus material costs; therefore, value added per worker reflects both labor and capital productivity.

Source: Simon Kuznets, "Changes in the National Incomes of the United States of America Since 1870," *Income and Wealth Series II* (London: Bowes & Bowes Ltd., 1952), p. 30. By permission of the publisher.

the next 20 years or so, machines were devised to do the work of lasting, eyeleting, heeling, and so on. By 1914, the industry was highly mechanized.

The first successful method of making steel in quantity was invented in the mid-1880s almost simultaneously by an Englishman, Henry Bessemer, and by an American ironmaster, William Kelly. Only a little while after Bessemer and Kelly invented substantially the same process, the open-hearth method reached experimental status. Inventors were trying to find a way of making cheap steel without infringing on Bessemer's patents. They were also trying to overcome some of the deficiencies of Bessemer's process— including the fact that the method was so quick there was not sufficient time to test the steel for carbon content, so that the manufacturer could never be certain for what purposes a given batch would be suitable. The best work in this new direction was accomplished by William and Friedrich Siemens in England and Émile and Pierre Martin in France. By 1868, the main features of the open-hearth or Siemens–Martin process had been developed. Instead of a cylindrical converter that could be tipped like a huge kettle, the open-hearth method employed a furnace with a shallow, open container holding a charge of molten pig iron, scrap iron, limestone, and even some iron ore.

Several considerations made the open-hearth process more economical than the Bessemer process. A large charge required about 12 hours compared to 10–15 minutes for a Bessemer "blow," but during the long refining period open-hearth steel could be sampled and its chemical composition could be adjusted to exact requirements. The open-hearth furnace also had a cost advantage over the Bessemer converter in that scrap iron and iron ore could be charged with the more expensive molten pig iron. The regeneration principle, by which the open-hearth furnace made use of hot gases drawn from nearby coke ovens or blast furnaces to melt and refine the charge, was highly efficient.

Increases in furnace size and efficiency of operation followed these changes. In 1860, good blast furnaces produced 7–10 tons of pig iron a day; 25 years later, 75–100 tons a day was the maximum, and by 1900 a daily output of 500 tons or more, with markedly less coke consumption, was common. During these years, methods of handling material improved greatly, regenerative heating of the blast was developed, blowing equipment was strengthened, and coke entirely superseded anthracite and bituminous coal as a fuel.

Perhaps the major accomplishment of the industry during that period was the integration of processes that led to great savings in heat. Coke ovens were eventually placed close to blast furnaces to avoid heat loss. Blast furnaces, in turn, were placed near steel furnaces (either Bessemer or open hearth), so that molten pig iron could be delivered directly to them. Finally, converters and open hearths were situated near the roughing mills, so that the first rolling could be accomplished as quickly as possible with a minimum of reheating. There were, to be sure, other economies resulting from inte-

TABLE 17-6   Steel Production, 1870–1910

Year	Total[a]	Bessemer[a]	Open Hearth[a]	Percentage Bessemer	Percentage Open Hearth
1870[b]	69	38	1	55	2
1880	1,247	1,074	101	86	9
1890	4,277	3,689	513	87	12
1900	10,188	6,685	3,398	66	33
1910	26,095	9,413	16,505	36	63

[a]Calculations are rounded in thousands of long tons.
[b]Still by 1872 a substantial proportion of steel was made by old technologies in pots and crucibles.

Source: *Historical Statistics* (Washington, D.C.: GPO, 1960), series P203–207.

gration—the most notable being a savings in the handling of materials and in the administration of the entire process.

As shown in Table 17-6, although introduced shortly after the Bessemer method, the open-hearth steel method actually lagged far behind until 1900. Bessemer steels were eminently satisfactory for rails, which constituted one of the first great demands for the new product. Eventually, however, as the engineers grew familiar with the characteristics of steel, they became convinced that plates and structural shapes made of Bessemer steel contained defects that did not appear in the open-hearth product. The consequence of this preference was that some rolling mills had to build open-hearth furnaces to meet the new demand. Furthermore, the costs of open-hearth processing were much lower than these costs of the Bessemer process, not only because scrap could be used but also because small operators could build and operate plants far smaller than those needed for a Bessemer operation. Moreover, small owners did not have to fear being "held up" by the large companies that controlled the Bessemer ores. By 1910, the open hearth had clearly won out over the Bessemer converter; of the 26 million tons of steel produced in that year, the open-hearth process accounted for 63 percent and the Bessemer process for only 36 percent; from this time on, the annual output of the Bessemer method decreased steadily.[3]

Improvements in steel processing and in nonferrous metals, especially copper and aluminum, made possible rapid advances in metalworking machinery, which jumped from the seventh largest to the largest manufacture between 1860 and 1910. Metalworking machinery consists of two main types of power-driven machines: (1) shaping or forming machines, which press, forge, hammer, and the like, and (2) machines that cut metal, such as gear-cutting, grinding, and milling machines. Early advances allowed greater accuracy, uniformity, and simplicity of design of metalworking

[3]For details of iron and steel output changes, see Peter Temin, *Iron and Steel in Nineteenth-Century America* (Cambridge: M.I.T. Press, 1964).

Steel manufacture required unprecedented amounts of capital in the form of great furnaces and mechanical aids as well as skilled workers who were able to judge when the time was ripe to tap Bessemer converters like these.

machinery. Particularly during the 1890s, there were two major technical advances: (1) machine tools became automatic or semiautomatic and (2) compressed air and electricity were used to drive high-speed cutting tools and presses. The demands of the automobile industry and of the armament and aircraft industries during the First World War brought the machine industry to maturity. Victor S. Clark reports that between the end of the Civil War and the end of the First World War, precision in metalworking increased from a tolerance limit of 0.01 inch to 0.001 inch, and tolerances of 0.0001 inch had been achieved, although not in quantity production. By 1919, metalworking machinery had increased greatly in power as well as in precision. Great electrically driven shears could cut steel slabs 12 inches thick and 44 inches wide, and huge presses could stamp out parts of automobile bodies rapidly enough to make "mass" production possible. Moreover, the industry played the central role in *diffusing* technical knowledge from its point of origin to other sectors of the economy that encountered similar problems. As Nathan Rosenberg has so cogently observed:

> The machine-tool industry, then, played a unique role *both* in the initial solution of technical problems and in the rapid transmission and application of newly learned techniques to other uses. In this sense, the machine-tool industry was a center for the acquisition and diffusion of the skills and techniques uniquely required in a machinofacture type of economy. Its role was a dual one: (1) new skills and techniques were developed here in response to the demands of specific customers, and (2) once acquired, the machine-tool industry served as the main transmission center for the transfer of new skills and techniques to the entire machine-using sector of the economy. A wide range of metalworking industries were continually being confronted with similar kinds of problems which urgently required solution and which, once solved by the machinery-producing sector, took their place in short order in the production of other metal-using products employing similar processes.[4]

FORMS AND SOURCES OF NEW ENERGY

Between 1860 and the First World War, there was a remarkable transition from reliance on the power of wind and water and the physical exertion of humans and animals to other sources of energy. The transition had begun only in the first half of the nineteenth century. In 1850, more than three-quarters of all power was furnished by animal energy, and human energy produced more power than machines did. As late as the eve of the Civil War, water power was far more important than steam power in the United States. Sometime during the decade of the 1870s, steam surpassed water as

---

[4]Nathan Rosenberg, *Technology and American Economic Growth* (New York: Harper & Row, 1972), p. 98.

a source of power. Then two major additional influences hastened the final phasing out of the ancient water wheel and the more recently developed water turbine. These were (1) the ever-increasing efficiency of the steam engine, along with the increased safety of high-pressure boilers, and (2) the opening up of vast and apparently inexhaustible supplies of coal as a result of the transportation revolution. This instance portrays the interdependence of resource availability and technological advances. By 1890, relatively few factories—mostly in the textile and paper industries—used direct water power, although gristmills and sawmills were still powered by this source.

But another way of utilizing the force of water flow was to be devised. At the time when steam engines had gained an unquestioned ascendancy, electricity appeared on the scene as a form of power. Like steam, electricity was not a new energy *source;* it was a new *means* of using energy generated either by the flow of water or the burning of fuel. But electricity brought about a remarkable improvement in the utilization of the older sources of energy. Because electric power is flexible and divisible, the power plant could be separated from the manufacturing establishment by long distances, and the cumbersome devices required to change the to-and-fro motion of the steam engine into rotary motion and then to transmit this motion were no longer necessary. Furthermore, the energy required to turn either a small motor or a large one was readily "on tap."

By the First World War one-third of the nation's industrial power was then provided by electricity, far more than in any other country. Nearly one-half of all urban dwellings had electric lights, although more than 98 percent of all farm families were burning kerosene lamps after dark.

The growing importance of electricity should not, however, divert our attention from the fundamental *sources* of energy. Before the First World War, the machines that generated power, whether electrical or not, were run either by the flow of water or by the burning of mineral fuels where wood had dominated earlier. In 1890, coal was the source of 90 percent of the energy furnished to manufacturing; in the years just before 1920, coal remained the source of at least 80 percent of all industrial energy. But petroleum was rapidly growing more important, and hydropower was recovering. Within 25 years, petroleum and natural gas would become strategic fuels, but the transportation and manufacturing industries were planted squarely in the age of coal as late as 1920.

MANAGERIAL CHANGES

Technological changes, new power sources, the development of the corporation based on multiple ownership of stock, and other forces brought forth the modern big business firm. Prior to the huge railroad companies, most businesses, even the largest, were typically managed by single owners, or partners, on a day-to-day basis. Often times supervisors were added but owners usually oversaw the business operations and made key managerial decisions. The railroads led the way to change all that.

Faced with unmanageable size and complexity, the railroads developed a host of new management practices and concepts. Managerial innovations and organizational changes were essential to better coordinate the activities of thousands of employees who ran the trains, sold the tickets, loaded freight, repaired track and equipment, and did endless other tasks. In the 1850s, Daniel McCallum of New York, president of the Erie Railroad, proposed a series of new management principles—with wide potential application. First, managers' authority to make decisions should match their level of responsibility. Internal reporting systems (accounting) should be used to identify trouble spots and allow prompt solutions. Performance evaluations, for employees and managers alike, should be routine. Today McCallum's concepts are routine in virtually all large business organizations, and other large businesses in the late nineteenth century soon adopted these and other concepts of better management and control.[5]

Two relatively new ideas spread like wildfire after the Civil War: mass production and scientific management. Mass production, that magical expression embracing all characteristics of modern industry, implies two basic production procedures: continuous process and interchangeable parts. Scientific management implies business procedures with a laboratory-like exactness. Entrepreneurs were constantly seeking more advanced production methods. Physically, it was necessary to devise mechanical means of systematically transporting materials from one stage of production to another. Intellectually, detailed planning and ordering of the assembly process by the managers was required. It was essential that management's goals be the minimization of the time consumed by workers in assembling a complex product.

Ever since Oliver Evans' first attempts at continuous-flow milling in the 1780s, entrepreneurs have sought new means of minimizing processing time. The concept of stationary assembly was applied successfully to the production of carriages and railroad cars, but it was Henry Ford, the great automobile entrepreneur, who devised the first progressive, moving assembly line systems for large complex final products. In 1914, a chassis, which had formerly been assembled in 12 hours, could be put together along a 250-foot line in a little over 1½ hours. Before 1920, motor-driven conveyors were moving motors, bodies, and chassis at optimum heights and speeds to workers along greatly lengthened lines. By this time, the moving assembly had spread throughout the automobile industry, the electrical industry, and the budding household-appliance industry, as well as to food processing and cigarette manufacture.

---

[5] For more on the early leadership of the railroads in these areas, see Alfred D. Chandler, *The Railroads: The Nation's First Big Business* (New York: Harcourt, Brace, and World, 1965).

With increases in size of plant and complexity of layout, the problems of efficiently handling a large labor force became apparent. Frederick W. Taylor, ultimately the most famous contributor in this regard, argued that worker efficiency could be improved by (1) analyzing in detail the movements required to perform a job, (2) carrying on experiments to determine the optimum size and weight of tools and optimum lifts, and (3) offering incentives for superior performance. From such considerations, Taylor went on to develop certain principles pertaining to the proper physical layout of a shop or factory, the correct routing of work, and the accurate scheduling of the production of orders.[6]

These productivity-enhancing improvements helped push real wages upward, softening somewhat workers' resentment to change and faster product processing. But competition kept the changes coming and the size of business growing.

FIRM SIZE AND INDUSTRY CONCENTRATION

Before the landmark legal decision of *Munn* v. *Illinois* (1877) and the creation of the Interstate Commerce Commission (1887), business firms were largely beyond the reach of federal government control. There were tariffs, but no income taxes; there were state chartered corporations, but not federal ones (banks excepted). The federal government imposed no business licenses nor did it limit the growth of firms. There were no antitrust laws.

Historians have referred to the period from 1880 to 1920 as the "rise of big business," or the "combination movement" or "merger movement." Central to the discussion of the rise of big business has been the debate on whether big business came about in response to technological changes and other advantages of economies of scale, or whether the pursuit of monopoly power and market control was also a fundamental force.[7]

Early Combinations

The first attempts at combination were two simple devices: (1) "gentlemen's agreements," usually used for setting and maintaining prices, and (2) "pooling"—dividing a market and assigning each seller a portion. In pooling, markets could be divided on the basis of output, (each producer to be free

---

[6]For a full account of the timing and dimensions of Taylor's influence on the managerial revolution, see the important book by Daniel Nelson, *Frederick W. Taylor and the Rise of Scientific Management* (Madison: Univ. of Wisconsin Press, 1980). For a critical assessment of "Taylorism" see David F. Noble, *America by Design: Science, Technology & the Rise of Corporate Capitalism* (New York: Knopf, 1977).
[7]Firms at this time typically grew in one or both of two ways: *horizontally* by building or acquiring a number of plants that turn out approximately the same product, or *vertically* to control a sequence of processes, or all of the sequences from raw materials to the final good. Firm growth through product diversification was not as common as it is today.

to sell so many units) or on a territorial basis (each producer to be free to sell within his own protected area). Or sellers could form a "profits pool," whereby net income was paid into a central fund and later divided on a basis of percentage of total sales in a given period. Although pools were formed even before the Civil War, they did not come into their own until after 1875. During the 1880s and 1890s, strong pooling arrangements were made in a number of important industries; producers of whiskey, salt, coal, meat products, explosives, steel rails, structural steel, cast-iron pipe, and certain tobacco products achieved great success with pooling agreements, as did the railroads in trunk-line territory. The pool corresponded to the European cartel; it differed from its European counterpart chiefly in the fact that, as a heritage from the English common law, such agreements were considered illegal in this country and were not enforceable in the courts among the agreeing parties.

Although both of these early forms worked temporarily, they typically were not durable for other reasons as well. First, insofar as they were successful in raising prices and achieving a "monopoly" profit, with price above cost, they encouraged new firms to enter the field. Second, one of the major objectives of collusion was the maintenance of prices in deflationary periods; yet it was in times of declining business activity that the temptation to violate business agreements was strongest. The very freedom allowed the several firms, although usually an advantage, made it possible for individual managers to exceed their assigned outputs or encroach on another's territory when the going was rough, and there was no legal recourse against violators.

Trusts and Holding Companies

To overcome this deficiency, a new combination device was created: the trust—a perversion of the ancient fiduciary device whereby trustees held property in the interest of either individuals or institutions. Under a trust agreement, the stockholders of several operating companies formerly in competition with one another turned over their shares to a group of trustees and received "certificates of trust" in exchange. The trustees therefore had voting control of the operating companies, and the former stockholders received dividends on their trust certificates. This device was so successful as a means of centralizing control of an entire industry and so profitable to the actual owners of stock that trusts were formed in the 1880s and early 1890s to control the output of kerosene, sugar, whiskey, cottonseed oil, linseed oil, lead, salt, rubber boots and gloves, and other products. But the trust form had one serious defect: Agreements were a matter of public record. Once their purpose was clearly understood, such a clamor arose that both state and federal legislation was passed outlawing them, and some trusts were dissolved by successful common-law suits in the state courts.

Alert corporate lawyers, however, thought of another way of linking managerial and financial structures. Occasionally, special corporate charters had permitted a company to own the securities of another company, such provisions having been inserted to allow horizontal expansion. In 1889, the New Jersey legislature revised its *general* incorporation statutes to allow any corporation so desiring to hold the securities of one or more subsidiary corporations. As trusts were declared illegal in several states, many of them simply obtained charters in New Jersey as "holding companies." The prime objective of centralizing control and at the same time leaving individual companies free to operate under their several charters could therefore be achieved by a relatively simple device. Theoretically, the holding company had to own more than 50 percent of the voting stock of its several subsidiaries. In practice, especially as shares became widely dispersed, control could be maintained with a far smaller percentage of the voting stock. The holding company was here to stay, although it would have to resist the onslaughts of Justice Department attorneys from time to time.

THE TWO PHASES OF THE CONCENTRATION MOVEMENT

Whatever the path to combination and whatever the form of organization finally selected, the large firm was typical of American manufacturing industry by 1905. Why was bigness inevitable? How can we account for the major transformation that occurred in the last few decades of the nineteenth and the early years of the twentieth centuries? We have suggested that one reason for the concentration of industry was a natural movement, encouraged by competitive pressures, toward larger more efficient sizes and that another reason was a conscious aiming for monopoly power. We now have to examine the forces that impelled entrepreneurs toward the control of a large part of the output of many major industries, for it is clear that a rapacious, overweening desire for monopoly profits did not suddenly sweep American entrepreneurs into great combinations.

We find a clue to the motivation toward combination in the reflection that the movement in this period occurred in two major phases. The first was the predominantly *horizontal* combination (1879–93) of industries that produced the old staples of consumption. The second was the predominantly *vertical* combination (1898–1904) of the producer-goods industries for the most part but also of a few consumer-goods industries that manufactured new products for growing urban markets.[8]

---

[8]The following analysis is based closely on the path-breaking work of Alfred D. Chandler, Jr., to whom we are indebted for a new interpretation of the concentration movement. For the initial version of the Chandler thesis at various stages and in alternative sources, see "The Beginnings of 'Big Business' in American Industry," *Business History Review* 33 (Spring 1959): 1–31; "Development, Diversification and Decentralization," in *Postwar Economic Trends in the United States*, ed. Ralph E. Freeman (New York: Harper & Row, 1960), pp. 235–88; and *Strategy and Structure* (Cambridge, Mass.: M.I.T. Press, 1962). For Chandler's more recent interpretation, see *The Visible Hand*, Part 4 (Cambridge: Harvard Univ. Press, 1977).

Phase One: Horizontal Combinations (1879–93)

During the 1870s and 1880s, as the railroads extended the formation of a national market, many existing small firms in the consumer-goods industries experienced a phenomenal increase in the demand for their products. This was followed by an expansion of facilities to take advantage of the new opportunities. Then, shockingly and distressingly, came the realization that in many areas there was great excess capacity and "overproduction." When this occurred, prices dropped below the production costs of some firms. To protect themselves from insolvency and ultimate failure, many small manufacturers in the leather, sugar, salt, whiskey, glucose, starch, biscuit, kerosene, and rubber boot and glove industries (to name the most important) combined horizontally into larger units.[9] They then systematized and standardized their manufacturing processes, closing down the least efficient plants and creating purchasing, marketing, finance, and accounting departments to service the units that remained. By 1893, consolidation and centralization were well under way in those consumer-goods industries that manufactured staple household items that had long been in use. Typical of the large firms created in this way were the Standard Oil Company of Ohio (after 1899, the Standard Oil Company of New Jersey), the Distillers' and Cattle Feeders' Trusts, the American Sugar Refining Company, and the United States Rubber Company.

Of the firms that became large during the first wave of concentration, the most spectacular was the Standard Oil Company. From its beginnings in 1860, the petroleum-refining business was characterized by a large number of small firms. By 1863, there were more than 300 firms in the industry, and although this number had declined by 1870 to perhaps 150, competition was vicious and the industry was plagued by excess capacity. "By the most conservative estimates," write Harold Williamson and Arold Daum, "total refining capacity during 1871–1872 of at least 12 million barrels annually was more than double refinery receipts of crude, which amounted to 5.23 million barrels in 1871 and 5.66 million barrels in 1872. At the same time, total demand approximated crude production at $4 per barrel."[10] An industry with investment in fixed plant and equipment that can turn out twice the volume of current sales is one inevitably characterized by repeated failures (usually in waves of the downswing of the cycle) and highly variable profits in even the most efficient firms.

In the oil industry, the Rockefeller firm—organized in 1869 as the Standard Oil Company of Ohio—was perhaps the best managed, with two great

---

[9]As we have already observed, in the various industries, pools and other loose forms of organization often preceded combination into a single large company.
[10]Harold F. Williamson and Arold R. Daum, *The American Petroleum Industry* (Evanston, Ill.: Northwestern Univ. Press, 1959), p. 344.

John D. Rockefeller, archetype of the nineteenth-century businessman, brought discipline and order to the unruly oil industry, parlayed a small stake into a fortune estimated at more than $1 billion, and lived in good health (giving away some of his millions) until 96 on a regimen of milk, golf, and riverwatching.

refineries, a barrel-making plant, and a fleet of tank cars.[11] Standard's holdings grew steadily during the 1870s, largely through the acquisition of refineries in Pittsburgh, Philadelphia, and New York, as well as in Ohio. Demanding and receiving rebates on oil shipments (and even drawbacks on the shipments of competitors), Standard had made considerable progress in absorbing independent refining competition by the end of 1876. By 1878, Standard either owned or leased 90 percent of the refining capacity of the country. The independents that remained were successful only if

[11] John D. Rockefeller got his start in business at the age of 19, when he formed a partnership with Maurice B. Clark to act as commission merchants and produce shippers. Moderately wealthy even before the end of the Civil War, Rockefeller entered the oil business in 1862, forming a series of partnerships before consolidating them as the Standard Oil Company.

they could produce high-margin items, such as branded lubricating oils, that did not require high-volume, low-cost manufacture.

To consolidate the company's position, a trust agreement was drawn up in 1879 whereby three trustees were to manage the properties of Standard Oil of Ohio for the benefit of Standard stockholders. In 1882, the agreement was revised and amended; stockholders of 40 companies associated with Standard also turned over their common stocks to nine trustees. The value of properties placed in the trust was set at $70 million, against which 700,000 trust certificates (par value $100) were issued. The agreement further provided for the formation of corporations having the name Standard Oil Company of New Jersey and New York as well as in other states. When the Supreme Court of Ohio ordered the Standard Oil Trust dissolved in a decree in 1892, the combination remained effective for several years by maintaining closely interlocking directorates among the major refining companies. Threatened by further legal action, company officials changed the Standard Oil Company of New Jersey from an operating to a holding company, increasing its capitalization from $10 million to $110 million, so that its securities might be exchanged for those of the subsidiaries it held. All the advantages of the trust form were secured, and, at least for the time being, no legal dangers were incurred. Thus, as the American Sugar Refining Company had done in 1891, Standard went from a trust to a holding company after successful combination had long since been achieved.

Phase Two: The Great Merger Wave (1898–1904)

The severe depression of 1893 brought acts of combination of all kinds almost to a standstill. But with the return of prosperity late in 1896, a new momentum developed. Over the span of years 1898–1904 more than 3,000 mergers were effected. In the four years before 1903 almost one-half of U.S. manufacturing capacity took part in active mergers, most of them vertically integrating. The underlying forces causing this merger wave was the growth of the market and urbanization, and a change in the law. First, how did urbanization affect firm size?

Urbanization and Firm Size In part, urbanization led to changes in both the demand for and the ways to supply consumer goods. Whereas in 1860 20 percent of the population resided in cities (or towns of 2,500 and more), by 1900 the figure was 40 percent; by the First World War it was almost 50 percent. This changing proportion, coupled with population growth, raised the numbers of city dwellers from 6.2 million in 1860 to 54.2 million in 1920.

As a consequence, there emerged a new kind of consumer-goods industry that produced *new* products (or old products in novel ways) for growing markets composed of city dwellers. Firms in these industries formed large organizations that were vertically integrated, except for the raw-material stage, to achieve economies of production and marketing. These industries were comprised of producers of fresh meat, cigarettes, and high-grade flour, as well as manufacturers of sewing machines and typewriters. Thus, Gustavus F. Swift and his brother Edwin, after experimenting with the shipment and storage of refrigerated meat, formed a partnership in 1878 that grew over the next two decades into a huge, integrated company. Its major departments—marketing, processing, purchasing, and accounting—were controlled from the central office in Chicago. Other meat packers, like Armour and Morris, built similar organizations, and by the late 1890s the meat-packing industry was dominated by a few firms with highly centralized, bureaucratic managements. In a similar manner, James B. Duke set out in 1884 to establish a national, even worldwide, selling organization to market his machine-made cigarettes. In 1890, he merged his company with five competitors to form the American Tobacco Company. Less than 15 years later, American Tobacco, after a series of mergers, achieved a monopoly in the cigarette industry.

But an even more spectacular result of the growth of the cities was the increased demand for producer goods and the consequent stimulation of output in the heavy industries (steel, copper, power machinery, explosives, and so on). Beginning in the 1840s, municipal authorities were shocked to discover what immense outlays were required to lay mains for water and sewer systems, which until then were provided by private companies only for the wealthy. The post-Civil War mushrooming of the cities meant a continually growing demand for such public-health facilities, which was followed by an expanded demand for gas lighting, telephone lines and exchanges, complex electrical lighting equipment, power lines, and street and elevated railways, to say nothing of construction materials to build the steel-skeletoned skyscrapers that made their first appearance in the late 1880s. These demands led in turn to the formation of large firms that emphasized vertical integration and highly centralized control over vast operations, extending from the mining of raw materials to the purveying of finished products.

In steel, for example, the Carnegie Company had by the early 1890s consolidated its several manufacturing properties into an integrated firm that owned vast coal and iron deposits. As the Carnegie interests grew, other businesspeople were creating powerful steel companies. In 1898, the Federal Steel Company was formed under the auspices of J. P. Morgan and Company. Its integrated operations and products greatly resembled those of the Carnegie Company, but it had the further advantage of having a close alliance with the National Tube Company and the American Bridge Company, producers of highly finished products. The National Steel Company, created by W. H. Moore, was the third largest producer of ingot and basic steel shapes and was closely connected with other Moore firms that made finished products—the American Tin Plate Company, the American Steel Hoop Company, and the American Sheet Steel Company. When Carnegie, strong in coal and (through his alliance with Rockefeller) iron ore,

Andrew Carnegie, a great salesman, built an integrated steel firm that combined with the Morgan and Moore interests to form the United States Steel Corporation in 1901. At that time, he sold out and became one of the world's leading philanthropists.

threatened to integrate forward into finished products, he precipitated action toward a merger by the Morgan interests. The result was the United States Steel Corporation, organized in March 1901 with a capital stock of over $1 billion and, by a substantial margin, the largest corporation in the world. Controlling 60 percent of the nation's steel business, United States Steel owned, in addition to its furnaces and mills, a large part of the vast ore reserves of the Lake Superior region, 50,000 acres of coking-coal lands, more than 1,100 miles of railroad, and a fleet of lake steamers and barges. While protecting its position in raw materials, the corporate giant was now able to prevent price warfare in an industry typified by high fixed costs.[12]

The Law and Firm Size As a legal statute, the Sherman Antitrust Act of 1890 seemed simple enough. It declared illegal "every contract, combination in the form of trust, or otherwise, or conspiracy in restraint of trade

---

[12]One more example was copper. Guggenheim's Philadelphia Smelting and Refining Company began a huge integrated operation that was soon imitated by Amalgamated Copper and the American Smelting and Refining Company. Another was in the explosives industry. After more than a generation of effective control of prices and production through the Gunpowder Trade Association—E. I. Du Pont de Nemours and Company bought a large number of independent companies in 1902 and consolidated them into a single, well-knit organization with centralized accounting, purchasing, engineering, and traffic departments. We could trace similar combinations with similar motives through a long list of "Americans," "Nationals," and even "Internationals," among them, American Locomotive, American Can, National Packing, and International Harvester.

among the several states." It prescribed punishment of a fine or imprisonment or both for "every person who shall monopolize, or attempt to monopolize, or combine or conspire . . . to monopolize any part of the trade or commerce among the several states." The Attorney General was charged with enforcing the Act by bringing either civil or criminal proceedings in the federal courts. Thus, how the law should be interpreted was left to federal judges.

The Supreme Court did much to discourage enforcement by its decision, rendered in 1895, in the case of *United States* v. *E. C. Knight Company*. The American Sugar Refining Company had acquired the stock of the E. C. Knight Company, along with that of three other sugar refiners in the Philadelphia area, raising American's shares of the refining market from 65 to 98 percent. The Attorney General brought an action against the sugar trust; but the Court would not apply the Sherman Act on the grounds that the company was engaged in manufacture—not in interstate commerce—and that Congress intended the prohibitions to apply only to interstate commerce. The business of sugar refining, the Court held, "bore no direct relation to commerce between the states or with foreign nations. . . . Commerce succeeds to manufacture, and is not a part of it." The Court further implied that the Sherman Antitrust Act did not preclude the growth of large firms by purchase of property—that is, *by merger or consolidation.*

Consequently, after 1895 mergers were widely viewed as legal and as the safer way to effectively eliminate cutthroat price competition. The post-1898 merger wave was launched in part by the 1898 ruling in the case of *United States* v. *Addyston Pipe and Steel Company.* Here the Court made it clear that the Sherman Act did apply to collusive agreements among firms supposed to be in competition with each other. But mergers were still apparently legal. George Bittlingmayer reports,

> The trade publication for the iron, steel, and hardware industry, *Iron Age,* ran a full-column editorial on the decision and concluded that merger might now replace price fixing. "The new decision is one which may gravely affect some of the arrangements now in force among manufacturers in different lines, in which some control over prices is sought by concerns otherwise acting independently in the conduct of their business. At first sight it looks as though this decision must drive them to actual consolidation, which is really more apt to be prejudicial to public interests than the losses and temporary agreements which it condemns." [February 17, 1898] A month later *Iron Age* reported that "quite a number of meetings of manufacturers have been held during the past week all looking to some scheme to take off the keen edge of unbridled competition." [March 17, 1898][13]

---

[13] George Bittlingmayer, "Did Antitrust Policy Cause the Great Merger Wave?" *Journal of Law and Economics,* April 1985, pp. 90–91.

As this trade publication suggests, the interest of the law and the effect of the law are not always consistent. The law itself, in this instance, was a strong force in bringing about the combinations—through merger—that people abhorred. Ironically, the available evidence strongly suggests that the first phase of the concentration movement (1879–93), which led to the 1890 Sherman Antitrust Act, was less spurred by monopoly power seeking than was the second phase (1898–1904). As O'Brien informs us, factories grew in size much more rapidly in the 1870s and 1880s than in later decades.[14] This was because the pace of technological change was so exceptional in those decades. Naomi Lamoreaux' research also concludes that the great merger wave, the second phase, was propelled mainly by the desire to suppress price competition.[15] O'Brien also concludes: "Increases in concentration during the merger wave were motivated more by the desire to reduce price competition than by the desire to exploit scale economies."[16] Whatever its primary source of motivation, the great merger wave of the turn of the century became an inviting political target.

Trust Busting   As early as 1902, Theodore Roosevelt sensed the political value of trust busting, and in the campaign of 1904 he promised vigorous prosecution of monopolies. During his administration, bills were filed against several great companies, the most important being against the American Tobacco Company and the Standard Oil Company of New Jersey. These firms were the archetypes of monopoly in the public mind, and the judgment of the Supreme Court in the cases against them would indicate the degree of enforcement that might be expected under the Sherman Act.

In decisions handed down in 1911, the Supreme Court found that unlawful monopoly power existed and ordered the dissolution of both the Standard Oil Company and the American Tobacco Company. But it did so on rather narrow grounds. First, it gave great weight to evidence of intent to monopolize. As an aid to discovering intent and purpose, the Court examined the *predatory practices* that had occurred during each company's growth period and the manner in which the companies exercised their monopoly power. The oil trust, so it was asserted, had achieved its powerful position in the market by unfairly obtaining rebates from the railroads and by acquiring refining companies brought to terms after price wars. Similarly, the tobacco trust was accused of bringing competing companies to heel by price wars, frequently closing them after acquisition by purchase. Moreover, the record showed that the old American Tobacco Company exerted a strong monopsonistic power, beating down the prices of tobacco farmers when the crop was sold at the annual auctions held throughout the tobacco-growing

---

[14]O'Brien, pp. 639–49.
[15]Naomi R. Lamoreaux, *The Great Merger Movement in American Business, 1895–1904* (Cambridge: Cambridge Univ. Press, 1985), esp. Chapter 4.
[16]O'Brien, p. 649.

states. Second, the Court adopted a "rule of reason" with respect to restraints of trade; since action against all possible violators was obviously impossible, it became necessary for the Court to exercise judgment:

> Under this principle, combinations which restricted competition were held to be lawful as long as the restraint was not unreasonable. Since there is no precise economic standard by which the reasonableness of a restriction on competition can be measured, the courts examined the practices pursued by a corporate giant in achieving and maintaining its position in the market. Predatory practices were indicative of an intent to monopolize the market, and a corporate combination which achieved dominance by indulging in them might be dissolved. Those which behaved in a more exemplary manner, even though their size gave them power over the market, did not transgress the law.[17]

Standard Oil and American Tobacco were the only companies that the Supreme Court dissolved, but even if the courts had continued ordering dissolution or divestiture, it is unlikely that competition in the classical sense would have been restored. The four major successor companies to the American Tobacco Company constituted a tight oligopoly with respect to cigarette manufacture. Stock in the 33 successor companies of the Standard Oil Company was ordered distributed pro rata to the stockholders of the holding company, but whatever the benefits of dissolution, an increase in price competition was not an obvious outcome.[18]

Legal Refinements   In two decisions handed down at the close of the First World War, large companies formed by merger were effectively freed from the threat of dissolution, provided that the actions of the dominant firm were not calculated to exclude competitors from the market. In the case of *United States* v. *United Shoe Machinery Company of New Jersey, et al.,* Justice Joseph McKenna took as the basis for his decision the finding of the trial court that the constituent companies had not been *competitors*—that they had performed supplementary rather than identical functions in making shoes. The Court did not deny the monopoly power of the United Shoe Machinery Company; it simply held that the company's power was not illegal, because the constituent companies had never been competitive. The decision in *United States* v. *United States Steel Corporation* made the position of merged companies even safer. Justice McKenna, who again spoke for the Court, found that the corporation possessed neither the power nor the intent to exert monopoly control. The majority of the Court was impressed by the fact that examination of the history of United States Steel revealed none of the predatory practices complained of in the oil and tobacco cases.

---

[17]George W. Stocking, "The Rule of Reason, Workable Competition, and the Legality of Trade Association Activities," *University of Chicago Law Review* 21:4 (Summer 1954), pp. 532–33.
[18]For an interesting account of growing price rigidity during these decades, see Austin H. Spencer, "Relative Downward Industrial Price Flexibility 1870–1921," *Explorations in Economic History* 14 (1977): 1–19.

The Court took cognizance of the splendid relations of the steel company with its rivals, noting that United States Steel's power "was efficient only when in cooperation with its competitors, and hence it concerted with them in the expedients of pools, associations, trade meetings, and finally in a system of dinners inaugurated in 1907 by the president of the company, E. H. Gary, and called 'The Gary Dinners.' "[19] But the corporation "resorted to none of the brutalities or tyrannies that the cases illustrate of other combinations. . . . It did not have power in and of itself, and the control it exerted was only in and by association with its competitors. Its offense, therefore, such as it was, was not different from theirs and was distinguished from theirs only in the leadership it assumed in promulgating and perfecting the policy. This leadership it gave up and it had ceased to offend the law before this suit was brought."[20]

Justice McKenna held that United States Steel had not achieved monopoly power despite its control of 50 percent of the industry's output. He decided that the pattern of regular price changes over time, clearly shown by the evidence, could have emerged from a competitive market just as easily as from collusion. The government's assertion that the size of the corporation made it a potential threat to competition in the industry was denied. On the contrary, said the Court, "the law does not make mere size an offense, or the existence of unexerted power an offense." After such a decision, only the most optimistic Justice Department attorneys could see any point in bringing action against a firm simply because it was big.

In 1914, during Woodrow Wilson's first administration, Congress passed the Clayton Act, which was intended to remove ambiguities in existing antitrust law by making certain specific practices illegal. Price discrimination among buyers was forbidden, along with exclusive selling and tying contracts if their effect was to lessen competition. Firms could not acquire the stock of a competitor, and interlocking directorates among competing firms were forbidden—again, if the effect was to lessen competition. A newly established Federal Trade Commission of five appointive members was to enforce the Act, and decisions of the FTC were to be appealed to the circuit courts. The Commission could also carry out investigations, acting on its own initiative or on the complaint of an injured party. If a violation was found, the Commission could issue a "cease and desist" order; offenders then had the right to appeal to the federal courts.

The Clayton Act was so weakly drawn that it added little to the government's power to enforce competition. Once the existence of listed illegal practices was determined, the courts still had to decide whether their effect was to lessen competition or to promote monopoly. As we have just observed, by 1920 about the only practice the courts would consistently consider in

---

[19]40 Sup. Ct. 251 U.S. 417, p. 295.
[20]40 Sup. Ct. 251 U.S. 417, pp. 295–96.

restraint of trade was explicit collusion among independent producers or sellers. "Reasonable" monopoly practices of huge firms on one hand and "weak" forms of collusion on the other were not subject to punishment. The useful functions of the Federal Trade Commission became the compiling of a massive amount of data helpful to economists and the elevation of the ethics of competition by acting against misbranding and misleading advertising. Not until it could take action on the basis of injury to *consumers* instead of on the basis of injury to a *competitor* would the public gain much advantage from the FTC's efforts.

Thus, the one great pre-1920 experiment in the social control of business achieved little. By the time a vigorous enforcement of the antitrust laws was undertaken late in the 1930s, it was too late to do much about the problem of bigness in industry. But by then it was clear that a kind of competition not envisioned by the framers of the Sherman Act protected consumers. The fall in communication and transportation costs wedded regional markets into national and international markets, thereby reducing local monopoly powers.[21] The effectiveness of these new competitive sources is examined in Chapter 20.

SELECTED REFERENCES AND SUGGESTED READINGS

Aduddell, Robert M., and Louis P. Caine. "Public Policy Toward the 'Greatest Trust in the World.'" *Business History Review* 55, no. 2 (Summer, 1981).

Allen, Robert C. "The Peculiar Productivity History of American Blast Furnaces, 1840–1913." *Journal of Economic History* 37 (1977): 605–33.

Asher, Ephraim. "Industrial Efficiency and Biased Technical Change in American and British Manufacturing: The Case of Textiles in the Nineteenth Century." *Journal of Economic History* 32 (1972): 431–42.

Atack, Jeremy. "Industrial Structure and the Emergence of the Modern Industrial Corporation." *Explorations in Economic History* 22 (1985): 29–52.

Averitt, Robert. *The Dual Economy: The Dynamics of American Industry Structure.* New York: W. W. Norton, 1968.

Berck, Peter. "Hard Driving and Efficiency: Iron Production in 1890." *Journal of Economic History* 38 (1978): 879–900.

Cain, Louis P. and Donald G. Paterson. "Factor Biases and Technical Change in Manufacturing: The American System, 1850–1919." *Journal of Economic History* 41 (1981): 341–60.

Chandler, Alfred D., and Louis Galambos. "The Development of Large-Scale Economic Organizations in Modern America." *Journal of Economic History* 30 (1970): 201–17.

Chandler, Alfred D., Jr. *The Visible Hand: The Managerial Revolution in American Business.* Cambridge, Mass.: Harvard Univ. Press, 1977.

Clark, V. S. *History of Manufactures in the United States 1607–1914,* 2 vols. Washington, D.C.: Carnegie Institution, 1928.

Feller, Irwin. "The Urban Location of United States Invention, 1860–1910." *Explorations in Economic History* 8 (1971): 284–304.

---

[21]See Jeremy Atack, "Industrial Structure and the Emergence of the Modern Industrial Corporation," *Explorations in Economic History,* 22 (1985): 29–52.

Floud, R. C. "The Adolescence of American Engineering Competition, 1860–1900." *Economic History Review* 37, no. 1 (Feb. 1974).

Frickey, Edwin. *Production in the United States, 1860–1914*. Cambridge: Harvard Univ. Press. 1947.

Galambos, Louis. *The Public Image of Big Business in America, 1880–1940*. Baltimore: Johns Hopkins Univ. Press, 1975.

Gallman, Robert. "Gross National Product in the United States, 1834–1909." *Studies in Income and Wealth*, National Bureau of Economic Research, vol. 30. New York: Columbia Univ. Press, 1966.

Gallman, Robert, and Edward S. Towle. "Trends in the Structure of the American Economy Since 1840." In *The Reinterpretation of American Economic History*, ed. Robert Fogel and Stanley Engerman. New York: Harper & Row, 1971.

Hughes, Jonathan. *The Governmental Habit: Economic Controls from Colonial Times to the Present*. New York: Basic Books, 1977.

———. *Industrialization and Economic History: Theses and Conjectures*. New York: McGraw-Hill, 1970.

———. "Industrialization: Economic Aspects." *International Encyclopedia of the Social Sciences*, 1968 edition, vol. 7.

———. *The Vital Few: American Economic Progress and Its Protagonists*. New York: Oxford Univ. Press, 1986.

Hurst, James Willard. *The Legitimacy of the Business Corporation in the United States, 1780–1970*. Charlottesville: Univ. Press of Virginia, 1970.

Josephson, Matthew. *The Robber Barons: The Great American Capitalists, 1861–1901*. New York: Harcourt Brace, 1934.

Kirkland, Edward. *Industry Comes of Age: Business, Labor, and Public Policy, 1860–1897*. New York: Holt, Rinehart and Winston, 1961.

Lamoreaux, Naomi R. *The Great Merger Movement in American Business, 1895–1904*. Cambridge: Cambridge Univ. Press, 1985.

Livesay, Harold. *Andrew Carnegie and the Rise of Big Business*. Boston: Little, Brown, 1975.

McCurdy, Charles W. "American Law and the Marketing Structure of the Large Corporation, 1875–1890." *Journal of Economic History* 38 (1978): 631–49.

McGee, John. "Predatory Price Cutting: The Standard Oil (N.J.) Case," *Journal of Law and Economics* (1958), 137–69.

Mulligan, William H., Jr. "Mechanization and Work in the American Shoe Industry: Lynn, Massachusetts, 1852–1883." *Journal of Economic History* 41 (1981): 59–63.

O'Brien, Anthony P. "Factory Size, Economies of Scale, and the Great Merger Wave of 1898–1902." *Journal of Economic History* 48 (1988): 639–49.

Porter, Glenn. *The Rise of Big Business, 1860–1910*. New York: Thomas Crowell, 1973.

Pratt, Joseph A. "The Petroleum Industry in Transition: Antitrust and the Decline of Monopoly Control in Oil." *Journal of Economic History* 40 (1980): 815–37.

Romer, Christina D. "The Prewar Business Cycle Reconsidered: New Estimates of Gross National Product, 1869–1908." *Journal of Political Economy* 97 (Feb. 1989): 1–37.

Rosenberg, Nathan. "American Technology: Imported or Indigenous?" *American Economic Review* 67 (1977): 21–26.

CHAPTER 18

The Emergence of America's Labor Consciousness

Between the bombardment of Fort Sumter and the devastation of the First World War, the conditions of working Americans changed dramatically. We have already assessed the upheavals in southern and western agriculture, and how the expansion of markets and new technologies and ideas brought about the rise of big business. No less affected during these years were those who primarily worked for others, in the mines, in transport, and in the shops and factories.

Paralleling America's industrial progress was the growth of America's labor consciousness. Class consciousness was never as deeply felt in the United States as in Europe, and American individualism as a concept generally triumphed over collectivism.[1] Nevertheless, in the 50 years following the Civil War, American labor slowly developed much stronger political clout. The first national unions emerged during this period, and "labor's perspective" became an important consideration for both politicians and employers.

DEMOGRAPHIC CHANGE

One reason laborers as a group became more important was simple arithmetic, based, of course, on economic change. In 1860 there were about three farmers per manufacturing worker; by 1910 the ratio was one to one.

---

[1]Recommended readings on this relative absence of radicalism in the American Labor movement include Gerald Friedman, "Strike Success and Union Ideology: The United States and France, 1880–1914," *Journal of Economic History* 48 (1988): 1–25; Sean Wilentz, "Against Exceptionalism: Class Consciousness and the American Labor Movement," *International Labor and Working Class History* 26 (Fall 1984): 1–24; Werner Sombart, *Why Is There No Socialism in America* (1906; 1st English ed., White Plains: 1976); Selig Perlman, *A Theory of the Labor Movement* (New York, 1928); and Seymour Martin Lipset, "Radicalism or Reformism: The Sources of Working Class Protest," *American Political Science Review* 77 (Mar. 1983), pp. 1–18.

TABLE 18-1   Population and Labor Force, 1860–1910 (in millions)

Year	(1) Population	(2) Labor Force
1860	32	11
1870	40	13
1880	50	17
1890	60	23
1900	76	29
1910	92	38

Source: *Historical Statistics of the United States, Colonial Times to 1970* (Washington, D.C.: GPO, 1975), pp. 8, 127, and 139.

Moreover, the number of workers as a percentage of the total population was going up from 33 to 40 percent. Table 18-1 shows this relative growth; the population grew by a factor of 2.9 and labor by 3.4, over the 50 years.

Live births per 1,000 people fell almost in half over the nineteenth century, from 55 in 1800 to 30 in 1900. This trend has continued, and in 1990 the birth rate is about half what it was in 1900. Urbanization has been a major source of this decline because the additional costs of raising a child are much higher in the city than in the countryside. Meanwhile death rates fell too (from 22 to 16 per 1,000 in 1870–1910) as health conditions improved, especially in the cities.[2]

Rather than natural increases, the tremendous growth of the labor force at that time was largely powered by immigration. Figure 18-1 reveals that close to 5 million people, most of working age, came to America between 1865 and 1880. Huge waves followed in the 1880s and after 1898. Between 1880 and 1920 more than 23 million immigrants came to form new homes in the United States.

As shown in Figure 18-1, the number of immigrants pouring in rose in good times and fell in bad times. Peak years of inflow coincided with or immediately preceded the *onset* of severe depressions. In times of rising economic activity and employment, the tug on immigrants increased tremendously; as depressions ensued and jobs disappeared, the attractiveness of American opportunity receded. Peaks were reached in 1873, 1882, 1892, 1907, and 1914. For obvious reasons, immigration declined greatly during the prosperous First World War years, as shipping lanes were cut and people were about sterner business.

The work of Brinley Thomas in the 1950s clarified underlying patterns. The inflow of immigrants—coupled with foreign capital inflows—helped push the American economy in its upswings and slowed the growth phase in the countries of departure. In effect, the growth surges in the United

_____

[2]Edward Meeker, "The Improving Health of the United States, 1850–1915," *Explorations in Economic History* 9 (1972): 353–74; and Robert Higgs, "Cycles and Trends of Mortality in 18 Large American Cities, 1871–1900," *Explorations in Economic History* 16 (1979): 381–408.

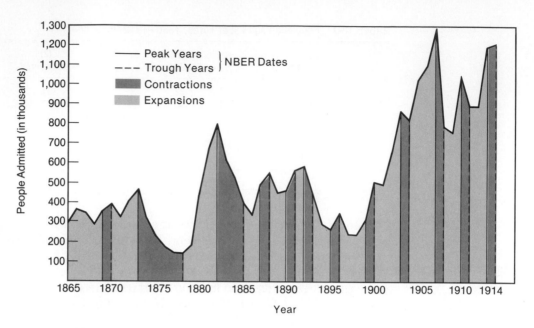

FIGURE 18-1   U.S. Immigration, 1865–1914

Source: Derived from *Historical Statistics* (Washington, D.C.: GPO, 1960), series C 88; business cycle dates: A. F. Burns and W. C. Mitchell, *Measuring Business Cycles* (New York: NBER, 1947), p. 78.

States coincided with slow expansion phases in much of Europe, and growth surges in Europe coincided with slower expansion periods in the United States. Though there were lags in information sent to the Old World, letters warning of poor times in America slowed the influx, and enthusiastic letters to relatives would encourage immigration in good times.

THE CHANGING COMPOSITION OF IMMIGRATION

Table 18-2 shows a striking alteration in the origins of immigrants from 1820 to 1920. In the 1880s, there was a decreasing influx of people from northern and western Europe and an increasing influx from southern and eastern Europe. It is usual to speak of the immigration from Great Britain, Ireland, Germany, and the Scandinavian countries as the "old" immigration, as distinguished from the "new" immigration composed of Hungarians, Poles, Russians, Serbs, Greeks, and Italians. In the 1870s, more than 80 percent of the immigrants came to America from northern and western Europe; by 1910, 80 percent of the total was arriving each year from southern and eastern Europe. It is reckoned that 1896 marked the point at which a majority of those arriving annually were no longer of the "old" nationalities.

TABLE 18-2   Origins of Immigrants, 1820–1920, (in percent)

	Northern and Western Europe	Central, Eastern and Southern Europe	Other
1821–1890	82%	8%	10%
1891–1920	25	64	11

Source: *Historical Statistics* (Washington, D.C.: GPO, 1960), Series C 88–114.

Much was once made of the presumed economic significance of these geographic shifts in the regions from which new Americans were drawn. In ethnic characteristics, the Swedes and Germans of the old immigration were not unlike the Anglo-Saxons who colonized America. Slovaks and Magyars, on the other hand, along with Russians and Italians and other people from the new areas, had unfamiliar customs and spoke odd languages—and they looked different. To native-born citizens of turn-of-the-century America, the new immigrants seemed inferior in skills, in cultural background, and in potentiality.[3]

The new immigrant supplanted the old for two reasons. As economic opportunity grew in England, Germany, and Scandinavia, America became less attractive to the nationals of these countries. Also important was the rapid improvement in transportation during the 1860s and 1870s. The steamship put the Mediterranean much closer to America, and railroads from the interior of eastern Europe to Mediterranean ports gave mobility to the southeastern Europeans. There was a vast difference between the economic opportunities offered an American laborer—even an unskilled one—and those available to the European peasant at home. The suction created by the removal of transportation barriers was irresistible; railroads, steamship companies, and American mill and factory managers hastened the movement by promotional advertising and financial assistance.

It is probably true that immigrants after 1880 were less skilled and educated than earlier immigrants had been. It may be that their different political and cultural history made their assimilation into American democracy and into the labor force more difficult. Nevertheless, the economic effects of the old and the new immigrations were roughly the same. New arrivals whatever their national origins, usually filled the ranks of unskilled labor. Slovaks, Poles, and Italians replaced Irish, Germans, and Swedes in the coal fields and steel mills and, like their predecessors, took the lowest positions in the social strata.

---

[3]*Each* immigrant group in its period of peak arrivals looked inferior; the "shanty Irish" and "dumb Swedes" of a previous generation were scorned as much as the "crazy Bohunks" who came later. But twentieth-century Americans seized on the assumed "inferiority" of southern and eastern Europeans as an argument for excluding them.

The great source of cheap labor was immigration. Densely packed ships brought millions of unskilled workers to America, often under contracts that specified no wage increases during the first year of employment.

Foreign Workers and American Labor

What was the impact of these foreigners on the American economy? Although 28 million people arrived between 1865 and 1920, the ratio of foreign born to the total U.S. population remained *"fairly constant,"* rising slightly from 13.1 percent to 14.6 percent.[4] But at the end of the period, more than one-third of the employees in manufacturing industries and almost one-half of the miners were foreign born. Moreover, the great majority of immigrants entered the labor markets of New England, the Middle Atlantic states, and the states of Ohio, Michigan, and Illinois, where they concentrated in the

---

[4]This rather curious fact is explained by the high rate of increase in the native population plus substantial *out*migration during periods of depression.

great industrial cities. Working for low wages in crowded factories and sweatshops and living in unsanitary tenements, immigrants complicated such urban social problems as slums, crime and delinquency, and municipal corruption. But their difficulties were not the result of discrimination in hiring or in wages. The relative earnings of native and foreign-born workers were approximately equal after adjusting for differences in schooling, experience, skills, and similar factors.[5]

American business profited greatly from an inexhaustible supply of unskilled and semiskilled workers. The steamship companies that brought these immigrants to America and the railroads that took them to their destinations were the first to benefit. But manufacturing and mining companies profited most; immigration enabled them to expand their operations to supply growing markets without any increase in the costs of low-grade labor. Moreover, the influx of immigrants meant more customers for American retailers, more buyers of cheap manufactured goods, and a greatly enlarged market for housing.

The rapidly increasing supply of unskilled labor kept wage levels for great numbers of workers from rising as fast as they would have otherwise. Therefore, some established American workers who could not escape from the unskilled ranks were adversely affected. But supervisory jobs and skilled jobs were given to native white Americans, and the number of better jobs available increased as the mass of unskilled new immigrants grew. As William Sandstrom has shown, by the turn of the twentieth century, U.S. firms methodically recruited and trained existing employees for more advanced and skilled positions. Promotion ladders were common, especially in large firms.[6] Moreover, the wages of those craftsmen engaged in making equipment to be used by the unskilled and semiskilled masses doubtlessly rose. And native American labor gained from the lower-priced manufactured products made possible by cheap labor.

Management was convinced that unrestricted immigration was necessary to the growth of American industry. Labor was equally certain that the influx of foreigners continually undermined the economic status of native workers. From the Civil War to the end of the First World War, there was a constant struggle between the proponents and adversaries of immigration restriction. In 1864, at the behest of the manufacturing interests, Congress passed the Contract Labor Law, which authorized contracts made abroad to import foreign workers and permitted the establishment of the American Emigrant Company to act as an agent for the American business sector.

[5]Martha Norby Fraudorf, "Relative Earnings of Native and Foreign-Born Women," *Explorations in Economic History* 15 (1978): 211–18. Peter J. Hill, "Relative Skill and Income Levels of Native and Foreign-Born Workers in the United States," *Explorations in Economic History* 12 (1975): 47–60. Peter R. Shergold, "Relative Skill and Income Levels of Native and Foreign-Born Workers: A Re-examination," *Explorations in Economic History* 13 (1976): 451–61.
[6]William Sandstrom, "Internal Labor Markets before World War 1: On the Job Training and Employee Promotion," *Explorations in Economic History* 25 (1988): 424–45.

An inevitable consequence of the urban crowding of workers was the appearance of slums. This photograph shows the litter and filth on Hester Street in New York City near the turn of the century.

The Contract Labor Law had the practical effect of bringing in laborers whose status could scarcely be distinguished from that of indentured servants, their cost of passage being repaid out of their earnings in the United States. The law failed, however, and was repealed in 1868. Few Europeans volunteered to work on contract; ocean passages had become much less costly, and many who did sign contracts, left their employment early. Wage earners fought effectively for the repeal of the Contract Labor Law and continued to struggle for immigration restrictions generally.

The first to feel the effects of the campaign for immigration restriction were the Chinese. The influence of the Chinese on the labor market was localized in California, and nearly 300,000 Chinese arrived on the West Coast from 1850 to 1882. Facing long-distance passage fares four times their annual wage, most of those laborers arrived in debt. Six large Chinese-owned and Chinese-controlled companies held title to most of the debts and used or rented out the immigrants' labor. It was just short of actual indentureship, but no formal contracts existed or were exchanged. These informal but carefully controlled arrangements were legal and were allowed.[7]

Other laborers, especially in California, feared and despised this cheap labor competition, and the Workingman's Party (also known as the "sand lotters") urged the exclusion of all Orientals. By the Chinese Exclusion Act of 1882, the first victory of the restrictionists was won. Successful in their first major effort, the restrictionists pressed on to make illegal the immigration of anyone who could neither read or write. Acts requiring literacy tests passed Congress, but President Cleveland, and later President Taft, vetoed them. For many years, labor had to be content with whittling away at the principle of the free movement of all immigrants who came into the United States. In succeeding laws, further restrictions were imposed on the immigration of the physically and mentally ill, vagrants, and anarchists. In 1917, Congress finally passed a literacy requirement—this time over President Wilson's veto—and permanent bars to the free flow of migrants into the United States were erected in 1920.

LABOR ORGANIZATIONS, 1860–1914

Although the first couple of years of the Civil War eroded the strength of labor unions, craft unions increased markedly in numbers and membership after 1862. By late 1864 there were about 300 local unions with a membership of 200,000 concentrated in the industrial states of New York, Pennsylvania, and Massachusetts. City centrals reappeared, as did national unions organized along craft lines. At least eleven national unions, some of them having a continuous history down to the present, were formed by 1865.

Business activity slackened after the war, and labor's position was weakened further by the return of soldiers to their jobs. Moreover, the downward pressure exerted on wages by immigrants was not relieved by the westward movement stimulated by the Homestead Act. But the economy (except for agriculture), after hesitating, moved on to good years in the

---

[7]For a fascinating account of this labor market, see Patricia Cloud and David W. Galenson, "Chinese Immigration and Contract Labor in the Late Nineteenth Century," *Explorations in Economic History* 24 (1987): 22–42.

early 1870s, and by 1872, there were 41 national craft unions with an estimated membership of 300,000–400,000.

A type of craft union had always been advocated by conservative labor
leaders, who were concerned primarily with wages, hours, and working
conditions. These men knew that national organization was essential, for
the great improvements in communication and transportation had given
labor a mobility it had never had before. There was no point in organizing
in New York City if Philadelphia workers in the same trade who were not
abiding by union rules could come to New York to take the jobs of the
strikers. On the other hand, while they recognized the need for a national
association of workers in a single craft, these leaders did not advocate an
all-inclusive union seeking broad social and political ends. But the depression that followed the downturn of 1873 revealed once more, and with
crushing finality, the inherent weakness of the pure national craft union.
One of the first to collapse was the numerically strongest of them all—the
shoemaker's association, known as the Knights of St. Crispin. Of the 41
national craft unions, only 8, greatly weakened, survived six years of hard
times after 1872.

Just prior to this collapse, the National Labor Union (NLU) was dissolved
after its policies were defeated at the polls in 1872. The NLU is noteworthy
as the first manifestation of U.S. labor's yearning to present a solid front
against the opposition of the business class. Originally seeking modest, purely
economic objectives, such as arbitration of disputes and advocating strikes
only as a last resort, radical leaders gradually injected more idealistic social
reforms into their purpose. Being 500,000 strong, and in coalition with
agrarian reformers, the National Labor Union entered politics on a platform that proposed an increase in the money supply, a weakening of the
"money monopoly" of the banks, and the establishment of producers' and
consumers' cooperatives. This "radicalism" alienated many local craft members and the NLU splintered in the wake of the 1872 elections.

The Knights of Labor

Meanwhile, in 1869, the most romantic of all American labor organizations
was formed as an association of poor Philadelphia tailors. Under the leadership of a Baptist preacher, Uriah S. Stephens, the Noble and Holy Order
of the Knights of Labor had an inauspicious beginning. With all the trap-
pings of a fraternal lodge, including a secret religious ritual, this group
offered a new appeal to workers and sought a new type of protection for
them. Besides having economic ends in common, the membership was to
be held together by bonds of brotherly love. Since the bitter opposition of
property owners had proved so damaging in the past, the new organization
extended the protection of anonymity to its members.

The Knights of Labor grew slowly during the first ten years. Its real rise
began in 1881, when its membership may have been as large as 20,000.

Within five years, membership reached the unprecedented total of 750,000—a huge increase in members occuring in 1885. Although the Knights were initially opposed to strikes, it was through a series of brilliant strike victories that their great membership was won. In 1884 and 1885, the Knights were successful in a series of work stoppages against the railroads—then the most powerful business firms in the country. The acclaim accorded the union was tremendous. When, in addition, the leadership announced the attainment of an eight-hour day as the next major objective, workers rushed to join.

A peak of membership and power was reached in the spring of 1886 and was followed by a decline almost as precipitous as the rise had been. Stretching their luck too far, the Knights lost a strike against one of Jay Gould's railroads as well as much of the prestige they had gained in a victory over Gould the preceding year. When a general strike to achieve an eight-hour day failed to materialize in May 1886, members lost faith. Membership slipped to 100,000 by 1890, the year in which the growing American Federation of Labor won a showdown fight against a group backed by the Knights to organize the cigar trade in New York City. Although the Knights remained in existence until 1917, they were of no importance after 1900.

The American Federation of Labor

In 1881, the year in which the Knights of Labor began its rise to short-lived eminence, the leaders of six of the country's strongest craft unions, meeting in Pittsburgh, Pennsylvania, proposed a federation of national unions. The new organization, composed of printers, glassworkers, iron and steelworkers, molders, and cigar makers, was to be known as the Federation of Organized Trades and Labor Unions. Its leaders were Adolph Strasser, then president of the International Cigar Makers Union, and Samuel Gompers, a former radical who rose to prominence as a colleague of Strasser. The original membership of the Federation was less than 50,000 and did not begin to increase until the Knights of Labor had expended itself. In 1886, strong national unions connected with the Knights withdrew in dissatisfaction and founded the American Federation of Labor. It was then a simple matter for the two federations to amalgamate—the new organization taking the name of the American Federation of Labor (AFL). Samuel Gompers became the first president of the group that was to dominate the labor movement for half a century.

Membership grew slowly during the next twelve years, reaching 250,000 by 1898. Then the first of two pre-1920 periods of remarkable AFL growth followed. By 1904, 1,676,000 workers had enlisted in the cause. A decade of slow increase ensued, and membership numbered approximately 2 million by 1914. Then came the second period of rapid additions to the ranks; by the end of the First World War, the Federation could legitimately claim 4 million workers, or 80 percent of all union members. Of the unions remaining outside the AFL, the most important were the four railroad brotherhoods, which were highly cooperative. The rest contended for jurisdiction with AFL affiliates or had disaffiliated.

Although labor leaders themselves might not place primary emphasis on the fortuitous onset of almost 25 years of good times, prosperity was a major element in the stability of the new organization. Between 1898 and the First World War, economic activity on the whole was quite high, exhibiting a rapidly growing rate of industrial output. There were only three depressed periods, and the country emerged from these without experiencing serious deflation or prolonged unemployment. But credit must also be given to those who planned the strategy. After long years of trial and error, labor leaders, including men with radical backgrounds like Strasser and Gompers, had discovered the principle of pushing for concrete gains in good times and strongly supporting what legislative action could be achieved without participating in politics as a labor party. Furthermore, their policy "to defeat labor's enemies and to reward its friends" meant that they played one major political party against another—a practice that probably maximized the number of bills favorable to labor that were passed by legislative bodies and minimized the risk of shattering defeats at the polls.

Certainly some credit for the American Federation of Labor's remarkable prewar success must be attributed to (1) its almost uncanny ability to make suitable modifications in structure without violating craft autonomy or permitting "dual" unionism, and (2) its promotion of the trade or collective-bargaining agreements as a means of stabilizing employer–employee relations.

From the experiences of the preceding 75 years, AFL leaders were convinced that stable unions had to be organized by self-governing crafts, that is, by workers with the same specific skills (such as printers). The one unifying principle of the Federation was to control job opportunities and job conditions in each craft. This principle implied an organizational unit comprised of workers who performed the same job and who, in the absence of collective action, would compete with one another to their economic detriment. Thus the craft union could act quickly to exert economic pressure on the employer.

But craft organization also meant that there could be no more than one union to a trade or skill. Two unions within a single craft (dualism) was unthinkable; dualism weakened solidarity and destroyed a "united front." Yet the disadvantages to rigorous adherence to the single-craft ideal became more pronounced after the turn of the century. First, there was the perplexing problem of setting the boundaries between different crafts; "demarcation" or "jurisdictional" disputes arose with increasing frequency. Second, problems of common interest to several crafts could not be solved because there was no basis of cooperative action. Finally, mechanization of industry and rapid immigration made it possible for employers to substitute unskilled for skilled workers, thereby weakening the control of single-craft unions.

To solve these problems by a wholesale turning to industrial unionism would have been to deny the principle of craft autonomy. Yet it quickly became apparent that there would have to be *some* exceptions to craft organization. As early as 1902, for example, the AFL granted a charter to an industrial union, the United Mine Workers. An industrial union includes all workers in the industry regardless of specific skills or craft. In this case, it was readily apparent that the numerical superiority of noncraftsmen in mining made organization on a basis of crafts altogether unrealistic. By 1915, however, only five industrial unions were affiliated with the AFL.

Meanwhile, AFL affiliates were assuring their own continued existence and the general stability of the labor movement by obtaining increased use of the written trade agreement. Written trade agreements were rare before the late 1880s; after 1890, they gradually became an accepted outcome of collective bargaining, whether on a local or national level. Such recognition was a great source of strength in the decade of slow growth that followed, and the footholds thus secured made possible a second period of increase in collective bargaining during the First World War.

Industrial Conflict and Employer Opposition

The organizational gains of labor were not obtained without a serious and prolonged struggle that was still unresolved by 1920. Strikes, though frequent, even in the late nineteenth century, were not sanctioned legally; nor were they always instigated by unions. Sometimes strikes erupted as simply the spontaneous responses of unorganized workers and on certain occasions successful strikes resulted in a union being formed. In any case, employers supported by middle-class opinion and by government authorities, took the position that their rights and the very institution of private property were threatened by the growing strength of the unions.

The most violent conflicts between management and labor occurred in the last quarter of the century. During the depressed years of the mid-1870s, much blood was shed when strikes were broken by force. The climax of that particular series of conflicts occurred in 1877, a zenith of turmoil that had begun with the railroad strikes in Pittsburgh and had spread throughout the country. The brutality was not all on one side. In the anthracite regions of Pennsylvania, a secret society known as the "Molly Maguires" terrorized the populace and committed murder and other outrages for years while fighting employers and strikebreakers. Generally, however, it was the laborer who had to fend off the physical assaults of paid thugs, state militiamen, and federal troops.

Three incidents, purposely spaced, it would seem, over time to do the maximum damage to labor's cause, stand out as examples of the most severe disputes. The infamous Haymarket affair on May 4, 1886, was the tragic climax of efforts of the Knights of Labor to secure a general strike of workers in the Chicago area. A bomb thrown at police officers attempting

This picture taken in New York's Lower East Side, *circa* 1920, changes the focus from the generalities of slum dwelling to the particular poignancy of children with a back alley for a playground.

to break up a mass meeting at Haymarket Square resulted in several deaths. Four men, who were probably innocent, were executed for murder. Although the injustice of the punishment aroused great resentment on the side of labor sympathizers, antilabor agitators used the incident as a horrible example of what radicals and anarchists would do to undermine American institutions by violence.

Six years later, just as antilabor feeling was subsiding, the management of the Carnegie Homestead Works at Pittsburgh decided to oust the Amalgamated Association of Iron and Steel Workers, which was trying to organize the Homestead laborers. A strike was called, ostensibly because the company refused to come to an agreement on wage matters, and Henry Frick, a close associate of Carnegie, brought in 300 Pinkerton detectives to disperse the strikers and maintain order. Turning the tables, the striking mob won a heated battle with the detectives, capturing several and injuring them severely. To restore order, the state militia was called out, and the union suffered a defeat that set the organization of labor in steel mills back several decades.

Simultaneous strikes by various Chicago unions were met by strong police action, resulting in the Haymarket Riot of May 4, 1886.

The adverse publicity received by the Homestead episode was exceeded only by that of the Pullman strike of 1894. Although the Pullman strike was led by mild-mannered Eugene V. Debs, who had not yet embraced socialist doctrines, the strife was attributed to the un-American ideology of radical leaders. Rioting spread over the entire Chicago area, and before peace was restored—this time by federal troops sent on pretext of protecting the U.S. mails—scores of people were killed and injured. Again the seriousness of the labor problem became a matter for widespread concern and the basis of much immoderate opposition to the labor cause in general. On the other hand, the Pullman strike served as a warning to conservative union leaders that violence would only disrupt unions and damage them in the public regard. Furthermore, the dispatch with which Debs and other labor leaders were jailed on contempt proceedings for disobeying a court injunction against inciting union members to strike was a sobering blow. Any long-run strategy would have to include efforts both to pacify voters and to strengthen labor's position in the courts. Pre-1920 successes along both lines were, to say the least, limited.

Beginning in 1902, employers changed their tactics. They began a serious drive to sell Americans on the benefits—to employers, workers, and the public—of the open shop. To further their propaganda, several organizations were formed. The most prominent were the National Association of Manufacturers and the American Anti-boycott Association, both of which were assisted materially by employers' trade associations. So effective were

Henry Clay Frick obtained coking coal properties that were vital to an integrated steel firm. Frick later became Andrew Carnegie's partner and an architect of the hard line that steel leaders took with the labor unions in the bitter Homestead Mill strike of 1892.

the employers' efforts that labor leaders of all shades of political belief experienced increasing pressure from their constituents to fight back.

Perhaps it was inevitable that a radical, activist left should emerge. A small group of extremists advocated the overthrow of the state itself and, in their militancy, tinged the leftist movement with the threat of violence. Socialism under various labels gained small followings; doctrines ranged from the utopian idealism of novelist Edward Bellamy to Marxist insistence on revolutionary seizure by the state of basic industries and services. Yet the only radical group that showed any signs of gaining a permanent place in the labor movement was the Industrial Workers of the World (IWW), which was formed about 1905. From 1909 to 1917, it was a militant organization, preaching doctrines of intimidation and sabotage, leading successful strikes against textile firms in the East, and keeping the mining and lumber industries of the Northwest in a continual state of upheaval. But the "Wobblies," as they were also called, opposed the First World War so vocally that they aroused public hostility and ultimately the bitter repression of police authorities everywhere. The small postwar remnant of the IWW membership apparently joined forces with the Communists.

Gompers, able young John Mitchell of the United Mine Workers, and others favored a counteroffensive against the employers through education and propaganda. Affiliating with the National Civic Federation—an association of people with an enlightened social outlook, including wealthy eastern capitalists, corporation officers, editors, professional people, and labor representatives—AFL leaders sought to elicit a more favorable attitude from the electorate. The National Civic Federation maintained a division for the mediation and conciliation of disputes, tried to secure wider acceptance of collective-bargaining agreements, and preached the doctrine that greater labor responsibility would mean fewer work stoppages and a better livelihood for all. How much good the National Civic Federation did is hard to say. It doubtlessly served in part to offset the organized efforts of employers, but the alliance may have lulled job-conscious unionists into ultraconservatism at a time when more aggressive policies were called for. At any rate, the core of employer opposition remained almost as solid as ever, particularly among the industrialists of the Midwest.

Overall, however, it must be stressed that union activity in the United States, especially in comparison to labor unrest in Europe, was largely unpolitical, at least at the national level. No national labor party as a political entity emerged and unions were seldom united in their stand on national issues. Instead, the main confrontation lay outside the political arena and was predominantly between employers and employees. For that reason, perhaps, strikes were longer in the United States than in Europe, even without the sanction of law.[8]

Reactions from the Bench

Nor did the judiciary show signs of increasing liberality toward statutory attempts to protect the rights of workers to organize. By the end of the nineteenth century, the right of labor unions to *exist* was established. Yet the right of employers to force employees to enter into anti-union contracts was upheld to the very end of this period. In this way nonunion status as a condition of employment was maintained by many employers. For example, in the case of *Adair* v. *United States* (1908), the Supreme Court declared unconstitutional a provision of the Erdman Act that made it unlawful for any carrier in interstate commerce to discharge an employee because he or she had joined a union. In the case of *Coppage* v. *Kansas* (1912), a state law, similar to many state laws passed to outlaw anti-union contracts, was declared invalid. Coppage, a railroad employee, had been fired for refusing to with-

---

[8]For an analysis of these and other historical features of strikes in the United States, see Poko Edwards, *Strikes in the United States 1881–1974* (New York: St. Martin's Press, 1981).

Labor leadership eventually became concentrated largely in the hands of Samuel Gompers who sat on the first Executive Council of the American Federation of Labor in 1881.

draw from a union. Because his withdrawal would have cost him $1,500 in insurance benefits, the Kansas Supreme Court held that the statute protecting him prevented coercion and was valid. But the Supreme Court of the United States reversed this decision, holding that an employer had a constitutional right to require an anti-union contract from employees; a statute contravening this right, the Court held, violated the Fourteenth Amendment in that it abridged the employer's freedom of contract.

It is important to keep in mind that these judicial decisions had widespread support. To grant security to unions in the form of, say, a closed shop was believed by many people to be an unconscionable interference with the rights of both the employers and those laborers who wanted to remain rugged individualists.

State and federal governments typically stood firmly on the side of business against labor unions. It was considered a legitimate use of police power to call out troops to break strikes. Such actions were condoned by the state and federal courts, which proved to be invaluable allies of management in the struggle to suppress collective action on the part of the laboring class. Especially effective as a device for restraining union action was the injunction. Employers could go to court to have labor leaders enjoined from calling or continuing a strike. Failure to comply with an injunction meant jail for the offenders, and "government by injunction" proved to be one of the strongest weapons in the anti-union arsenal.

As late as 1917, the U.S. Supreme Court decided that anti-union or "yellow-dog" contracts, whether oral or written, could be protected by injunction. The Hitchman Coal and Coke Company, after winning a strike, had hired back miners on the condition that they could not be members of the United Mine Workers while in the employ of the company. Later, union organizers tried to convince the miners to promise that after a certain time had elapsed they would again join the union. In a U.S. District Court, the company asked for and obtained an injunction stopping further efforts to organize. The Supreme Court affirmed the decision, holding that, even though the miners had not yet joined the union, they were being induced by organizers to break a contract with the employer and that the employer was entitled to injunctive protection.

LABOR'S GAINS IN THE POSTBELLUM PERIOD

Hours and Wages

Despite these odds, labor made progress as a class between the end of the Civil War and the end of the First World War. In 1860, the average number of hours worked per day in nonagricultural employment was close to 10.8. By 1890, the average workday in manufacturing was 10 hours—a decline of about 7 percent—and people normally worked a six-day week.[9] There were, of course, variations from the average. Skilled craftsmen in the building trades worked a 10-hour day in 1860 and probably no more than an average of 9.5 hours per day by 1890. On the other hand, in the textile mills outside New England, 12–14-hour days were still common in 1890, and workers in steel mills, paper manufacturing, and brewing stayed on the job 12 hours a day, seven days a week.

During the second 30-year period, there was continued gradual improvement in the standard workweek. By 1910, it was 55 hours in all industries; by 1920, it had dropped to about 50. A widespread weekly work pattern was comprised of five 9-hour days and 4–5 hours on Saturday morning. Again, the skilled trades fared better, having achieved a 44-hour week by 1920. Unskilled laborers, on the other hand, were still working 9-hour days, six days a week, and the 12-hour day persisted in the metal-processing industries.

Both daily wages and annual earnings in manufacturing increased by about 50 percent between 1860 and 1890. Prices rose so rapidly during the Civil War that real wages fell drastically between 1860 and 1865. But from then on, the cost of living declined, not steadily but persistently, eventually

---

[9]Clarence D. Long, *Wages and Earnings in the United States, 1860–1890* (Princeton: Princeton Univ. Press, 1960). See especially pp. 3–12 and 109–18.

returning the dollar to its prewar purchasing power. The consequence was that *real* wages and earnings in 1890 also increased by about 50 percent.[10] Daily wages in manufacturing rose from just over $1 in 1860 to $1.50 in 1890, and annual earnings increased from slightly under $300 in 1860 to over $425 in 1890. In the building trades, both real wages and real earnings rose a little higher, perhaps by 60 percent. It should be realized that wage differentials among industries were great in both 1860 and 1890. The highest-wage industry paid 2–2½ times more than the lowest. If we take into account the shortening of the workweek by about 7 percent, the net increase in hourly money or real wages over the 30-year period was about 60 percent, or 1.6 percent compounded annually.[11] Despite the tremendous immigration during these years, American workers made substantial gains.

Similarly, in the decades after 1890, real wages marched upward. The real earnings of manufacturing workers advanced 37 percent—or an annual compound rate of 1.3 percent—between 1890 and 1914.[12] Further gains were made during the war years, so that the annual rate between 1891 and 1920 was only slightly less than that recorded during the preceding 30 years.

Women and Children

In the pre-First World War years of industrial expansion, there was a sharp upward trend in the employment of children. In 1880, 1 million boys and girls between the ages of 10 and 15 were "gainfully occupied," and the number had risen to a high of nearly 2 million by 1910. In 1910, one-fifth of the youngsters between 10 and 15 had jobs, and they constituted 5.2 percent of the work force. But in 1920, the total number employed in this market was again less than 1 million, children made up only 2.6 percent of the workforce, and only one-twelfth of the 10–15-year age group was at work.

Since hours were long and working conditions were unsatisfactory, if not positively harmful, the decrease in the employment of children represented a social improvement. This improvement was primarily attributable to the successes of humanitarian groups in obtaining protective legislation at the state level. Massachusetts had a long history of ineffective child-labor legislation, and the first stringent regulation did not appear until 1903, when Illinois passed a law limiting child labor to an 8-hour day. State laws limiting hours of work, requiring minimum wages, and setting age limits were common by 1920, but additional protection was needed in certain states, such as the Cotton Belt and some industrial states in the mid-South and East.[13]

---

[10]Long, p. 109.
[11]Long, p. 109.
[12]Albert Rees, *Real Wages in Manufacturing, 1890–1914* (Princeton: Princeton Univ. Press, 1961), pp. 3–5.
[13]In these states especially, the fight against child labor was waged indirectly through increases in compulsory education ages.

When publicized, bad working conditions like these among very young slate pickers in Pennsylvania at the turn of the century won middle-class sympathy for labor's cause.

Efforts by Congress, however, to place *federal* restrictions on the use of child labor were declared unconstitutional by the Supreme Court on two occasions before 1920.

The role of women in the labor force had also changed dramatically by the First World War. The number of women gainfully employed increased remarkably after 1880. In that year, 2.5 million women, constituting 15 percent of the gainfully employed, were at work outside the home. This number doubled by 1900, when women comprised 18 percent of the workforce. By 1920, 8.5 million women, comprising one-fifth of the gainfully employed, were involved in some pursuit other than homemaking.

As with child labor, statutes prescribing maximum hours and minimum wages for women were common by 1920. There was growing legislative concern with the physical surroundings in which work was performed, and in the mill towns of the South and the industrial cities of the North, women gained further protection under the law.

In addition, the slow but inexorable forces of competition operated to open more pleasant and more lucrative occupations for women. The typewriter and other office equipment became generally accepted before the turn of the century, and young women found new fields in which they faced no major employment disadvantages.[14] Sales work in city stores became a more attractive occupation than degrading domestic service. Typing and sales work did contribute to a form of segregation by sex, to stereotyping of job classifications, and to aggregate wage differentials. Nevertheless, the new occupations opened up important new opportunities for women and changed traditional thinking about the role of women. The First World War, however, caused the greatest shake-up in hiring policies as employers, urged to employ women as replacements for men lost to the armed services, discovered that women performed a wide range of occupations as satisfactorily as men and that in some jobs their performance was often superior.

UNION GAINS

In 1920, the American factory worker could look back on 60 years of substantial improvement. Real wages were up, hours were shorter, and laborers, children and—to some extent—women were protected by law. The fundamental ideas of Social Security were being more generally discussed, and clear-cut legislative victories had been won to reduce the hardships caused by industrial accidents. In addition, urban dwellers of all kinds saw vast improvements that brought about sharp long-run reductions in mortality.

When viewed in the aggregate, however, union impact remained negligible throughout the entire nineteenth century. Without strong legal support, union membership remained small, as did the influence of organized labor. For instance, union membership in 1860 was merely 0.1 percent of the total labor force.[15] This figure had jumped to 2.3 percent by 1870, but then it slumped throughout the 1880s and 1890s. By 1900, it had regained its 1870 proportions at 2.7 percent. But not until the end of the First World War did union membership exceed 10 percent of the total labor force.

Although the labor movement would be much stronger in the twentieth century than in the nineteenth, unions could claim specific gains for their members, even by the turn of the century. For instance, as direct owner-supervision declined and management became more impersonal, the arbitrary power of foremen indulging their personal whims increased. Unions

---

[14]Clerical workers as a percentage of the nonagricultural work force grew from 1.2 to 9.2 percent in 1870–1920, while women as a percentage of all clerical workers grew from 2.5 to 49.2 percent over these 50 years. See Elyce J. Rotella, "The Transformation of the American Office: Changes in Employment and Technology," *Journal of Economic History* 41 (1981): 52.
[15]Stanley Lebergott, "The American Labor Force," in *American Economic Growth* ed. Lance Davis, et al. (New York: Harper & Row, 1971), p. 220.

helped offset and reduce arbitrariness in hiring and firing and other harsh treatment by supervising personnel. In addition, unions sometimes gained substantial wage differentials for their members, at least in certain industries. For unskilled workers and common laborers, the wages of union members over nonunion workers was slight, perhaps a few percentage points. Alternatively, a substantial differential was obtained by the unionization of bituminous coal miners, and near the eve of the First World War, they received wages some 40 percent above nonunion workers in that industry.[16] Finally, trade unions had become strong enough to weather future depressions without disintegrating. Labor Day as a national holiday was first celebrated in 1894, and the power of their political support for legislated advances was destined to grow. By 1913, a Department of Labor with cabinet-level officer status was established. For the most part, however, labor's nineteenth-century progress was reflected in rising standards of living and work stemming from economic growth and rising productivity—not from union strength.

SELECTED REFERENCES AND SUGGESTED READINGS

Bernstein, Irving. *The Lean Years: A History of the American Worker, 1920–1933*. Boston: Houghton Mifflin, 1960.

Brody, David. *Labor in Crisis: The Steel Strike of 1919*. Philadelphia: Lippincott, 1965.

———. *Steelworkers in America*. Cambridge: Harvard University Press, 1960.

Carlson, Leonard A. "Labor Supply, the Acquisition of Skills, and the Location of Southern Textile Mills, 1880–1900." *Journal of Economic History* 41 (1981): 65–71.

Commons, John R., and Associates. *History of Labour in the United States*. New York: Kelly, 1921.

Dubofsky, Melvyn. *Industrialism and the American Worker, 1865–1920*. Arlington Heights, Ill.: Harlan Davidson, 1975.

Dunlevy, James A., and Henry A. Gemery. "Economic Opportunity and the Responses of the 'Old' and 'New' Migrants to the United States." *Journal of Economic History* 38 (1978): 901–17.

Easterlin, Richard. "Economic-Demographic Interactions and Long Swings in Economic Growth." *American Economic Review* (1966): 1063–1104.

———. "Population Issues in American Economic History: A Survey and Critique." In *Research in Economic History*, ed. Robert Gallman. Greenwich, Conn.: JAI Press, 1977, supplement.

———. "Population." In *American Economic Growth: An Economist's History of the United States*, ed. Lance E. Davis et al. New York: Harper & Row, 1972.

———. *Population, Labor Force, and Long Swings in Economic Growth: The American Experience*. New York: Columbia Univ. Press, 1968.

Erickson, Charlotte. *American Industry and the European Immigrant 1860–1885*. New York: Russell and Russell, 1967.

Ermisch, John, and Thomas Weiss. "The Impact of the Rural Market on the Growth of the Urban Workforce, U.S., 1870–1900." *Explorations in Economic History* 11 (Winter 1973–74): 137–54.

Frauendorf, Martha Norby. "Relative Earnings of Native and Foreign-Born Women." *Explorations in Economic History* 15 (1978): 211–20.

---

[16] H. G. Lewis, *Unionism and Relative Wages in the United States* (Chicago: The Univ. of Chicago Press, 1963).

Galloway, Lowell, and Richard Vedder. "Emigration from the United Kingdom to the United States, 1860–1913." *Journal of Economic History* 31 (1971): 885–97.

Galloway, Lowell, Richard Vedder and Vishwa Shukla. "The Distribution of the Immigrant Population in the United States: An Economic Analysis." *Explorations in Economic History* 11 (1974): 213–26.

Galloway, Lowell, and Richard Vedder. "Population Transfers and the Post-Bellum Adjustments to Economic Dislocation, 1870–1920," *Journal of Economic History* 40 (1980): 143–50.

Goldin, Claudia. "The Work and Wages of Single Women, 1870–1920," *Journal of Economic History* 40 (1980): 81–88.

Grob, Gerald. *Workers and Utopia: A Study of the Ideological Conflict in the American Labor Movement, 1865–1900.* New York: Quadrangle Books, 1969.

Haber, Samuel. *Efficiency and Uplift: Scientific Management in the Progressive Era, 1890–1920.* Chicago: Univ. of Chicago Press, 1964.

Higgs, Robert. "Cycles and Trends of Mortality in 18 Large American Cities, 1871–1900." *Explorations in Economic History* 16 (1979): 381–408.

——— . "Landless by Law: Japanese Immigrants in California Agriculture to 1941." *Journal of Economic History* 38 (1978): 205–25.

——— . "Mortality and Rural America, 1870–1920." *Explorations in Economic History* 10 (1973): 177–96.

——— . "Race, Skills and Earnings: American Immigrants in 1909." *Journal of Economic History* 31 (1971): 420–28.

Hill, Peter. "Relative Skill and Income Levels of Native and Foreign-Born Workers in the United States." *Explorations in Economic History* 12 (1975): 47–60.

Jenks, Jeremiah, and Jeff Lauck. *The Immigration Problem.* New York: Funk & Wagnalls, 1926.

Jerome, Harry. *Migration and Business Cycles.* New York: National Bureau of Economic Research, 1926.

Kirk, Gordon W., and Carolyn J. Kirk. "The Immigrant, Economic Opportunity, and Type of Settlement in Nineteenth-Century America." *Journal of Economic History* 38 (1978): 226–34.

Kuznets, Simon. "Long Swings in the Growth of Population and Related Economic Variables." *Proceedings of the American Philosophical Society* 102, no. 1, (Feb. 1958): 000–00.

——— . "Notes on the Pattern of U.S. Economic Growth." In *The Reinterpretation of American Economic History,* ed. Robert Fogel and Stanley Engerman. New York: Harper & Row, 1971.

——— . "Two Centuries of Economic Growth: Reflections on U.S. Experience," *American Economic Review* 67, no. 1 (1977): 1–14.

Kuznets, Simon, and Ernest Rubin. *Immigration and the Foreign Born.* New York: National Bureau of Economic Research, 1954.

Lebergott, Stanley. "The American Labor Force." In *American Economic Growth,* ed. Lance E. Davis et al. New York: Harper & Row, 1972.

Livesay, Harold. *Samuel Gompers and Organized Labor in America.* Boston: Little, Brown, 1978.

McGouldrick, Paul F., and Michael B. Tannen. "Did American Manufacturers Discriminate Against Immigrants Before 1914?" *Journal of Economic History* 37 (1977): 723–46.

Meeker, Edward. "The Improving Health of the United States, 1850–1914." *Explorations in Economic History* 9 (1972): 353–74.

Neal, Larry, and Paul Uselding. "Immigration, A Neglected Source of U.S. Economic Growth, 1790–1913." *Oxford Economic Papers,* 2nd series, 24, no. 1 (March, 1972).

Nelson, Daniel. *Frederick W. Taylor and Scientific Management.* Madison, Wisconsin: Univ. of Wisconsin Press, 1980.

——— . *Managers and Workers: The Origins of the New Factory System in the United States, 1880–1920.* Madison, Wisconsin: Univ. of Wisconsin Press, 1975.

Nevins, Allan, and Frank Hill. *Ford: The Times, the Men, and the Company.* New York: Scribners, 1954.

Niemi, Albert W. "The Role of Immigration in United States Commodity Production, 1869–1929." *Social Science Quarterly* 52, no. 1 (June 1971).

Rotella, Elyce J. "The Transformation of the American Office: Changes in Employment and Technology." *Journal of Economic History* 41 (1981): 51–57.

Taylor, Phillip. *The Distant Magnet: European Emigration to the United States.* London: Eyre and Spottiswood, 1971.

Thomas, Brinley. *Migration and Economic Growth.* Cambridge: Cambridge Univ. Press, 1954.

Williamson, Jeffrey G. *Late Nineteenth Century American Development: A General Equilibrium History.* New York: Cambridge Univ. Press. 1974.

Williamson, Jeffrey D., "Migration to the New World: Long-Term Influences and Impact." *Explorations in Economic History* 11 (1974): 357–90.

CHAPTER 19

Money and Finance in the Postbellum Era

The Civil War and its aftermath, along with the structural changes of industrialization, repeatedly brought matters of money and finance center stage to the nation's attention. The 50-year span between the Civil War and the First World War contained vital episodes of conflict and learning in money, banking and finance. Inflation vs. deflation, paper money vs. specie, gold vs. silver, national and state banks, the national debt, financial panics and economic instability were issues and terms familiar to all engaged in the modernizing world of American trade and commerce.

The first issue of interest commanding our attention was the politics of money. Following the inflation of the Civil War years, when the money supply and prices had doubled, prices began a decline that persisted, with brief interruptions, for three decades. During this time various groups suffered from the protracted deflation. As emphasized in Chapters 15 and 18, farmers and silver miners in the West and various labor organizations were particularly vocal, and they supported a variety of measures to reverse the forces of deflation. Nevertheless, from the high inflations of the Revolutionary times and the Civil War, and from the hyperinflation in the South toward the end of the Civil War, Americans learned lessons they would not soon forget. With few exceptions, leaders in politics and finance insisted on "sound money" and were generally successful in resisting inflationary moves. As we shall see, these issues dominated national elections, especially in 1896 and 1900.

A second issue of great importance was the role of the federal government in banking. One outcome of the Civil War was the federal government's re-entry into the banking system, the first time since Jackson's veto of the bill to recharter the Second Bank of the United States. Congress passed a series of National Banking Acts, in 1863, 1864, and 1865 to help finance the Civil War, to administrate the issue of national-bank notes, and to systematize and establish a uniform currency. The 1863 Act and its revisions left a permanent imprint on the nation's economic system and provided the legal framework for national-bank charters that persists to the present day. Though not by design, the 1865 Act's heavy tax on state bank notes also encouraged the development of checking (bank deposits) as a major form of money exchange.

Third, the myriad complex of state and federal laws on banking perpetuated a system of thousands of local banks that were restricted in their growth and prevented from crossing state boundaries to engage in interstate branch banking. These legal restrictions had an important impact on the growth of U.S. firms hungry for financial capital. Many firms merged to accommodate their financial needs, and investment banking, essentially brokerage houses specializing in stocks and bonds, emerged to take positions of dominance in the world of U.S. finance. This was quite different from the financial world of England where large banking conglomerates were allowed and grew large enough to meet most of the financial needs of industrializing England.

Last but not least of the key issues were the problems of economic instability and bank insolvency during business downturns. In times of great financial crises, factories and banks closed, railroads went bankrupt, and millions lost their jobs. The depressions of the mid-1870s and mid-1890s were especially severe. Bread lines were long, and in April of 1894 "Coxey's Army" of the unemployed arrived in Washington, D.C., to vocalize demands for federal relief. It portended a different future for the nation, one where monetary reform alone would not do. But by Christmas of 1913, the nation once again had a central bank, one based on arrangements different from earlier versions. These were codified in the Federal Reserve Act signed by President Wilson. But as the Great Depression of the 1930s clarified, the Federal Reserve System was not the final answer to the nation's hard-earned lessons of bank panics, unemployment, and economic suffering.

CURRENCY AND THE POLITICS OF MONEY

Prior to the Civil War the amount of money in circulation was dominated by flows of specie into and out of the country through foreign trade and by changing flows from American mines. Federal revenues were obtained overwhelmingly from tariff collections, and these revenues declined markedly as trade fell when the fighting began. By 1862 gold was flowing out of the country so fast that the government and banks were obligated to suspend gold specie payments. Silver, which had been undervalued at the mint ever since the Currency Act of 1834, had virtually no circulation. Figure 19-1 traces the different forms of currencies in circulation from 1860 to 1915, and we will summarize the story of each, beginning with new paper money.

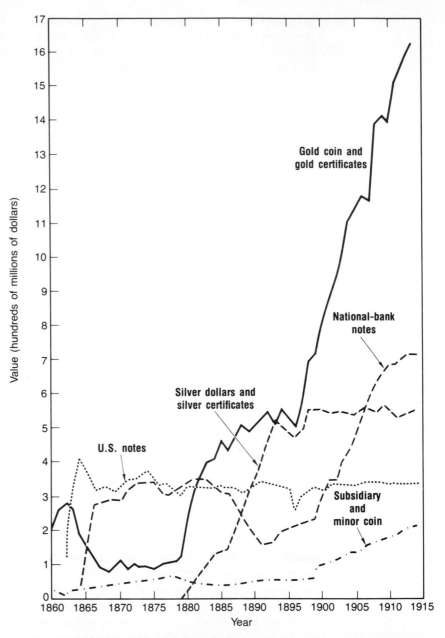

FIGURE 19-1 Forms of Money in the United States, 1860–1915: From the late 1870s to the early 1890s, there were substantial additions to the nation's monetary stocks of gold and silver, but the supply of paper money actually declined during these years.

Source: Board of Governors of the Federal Reserve System.

United States Notes (Greenbacks)

Because sufficient revenues to wage the War were not obtained from sales of U.S. Treasury bonds, the Treasury issued a new fiat currency in 1862 nicknamed "greenbacks." This avalanche of new paper money is shown in Figure 19-1, and the results are reflected in Figure 19-2, which shows the upward zoom of prices during the War years. People were legally bound to accept greenbacks during the Civil War, and the government accepted greenbacks for all payments except customs duties. Nevertheless, the value of greenbacks did not equal that of gold and silver. Gresham's law was at work and many people hoarded gold. Two sets of prices soon emerged for commodities and foreign exchange. On the gold market in New York,

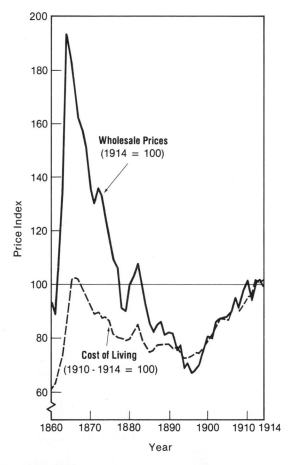

FIGURE 19-2   Prices, 1860–1914

Source: *Historical Statistics* (Washington, D.C.: GPO, 1960), series E 1, pp. 101, 157.

greenbacks at one time sold at a gold price as low as 35 cents on the dollar; on August 31, 1965, four and a half months after the assassination of Lincoln, $100 in gold exchanged for $144.25 in greenbacks or checks drawn on bank deposits. Stated another way, the gold price of a $100 greenback on this date was $69.32. Other types of paper money such as state-bank notes, which could be redeemed only in greenbacks, depreciated similarly; a further serious element of instability was injected because the paper currency fluctuated violently below the gold par.

Returning to the Gold Standard

At the end of the war, there was agitation to have the greenbacks retired. Businesses wanted to return to a gold basis as quickly as possible, and most authorities agreed that gold redemption would be possible only after the paper circulation was reduced. After the close of hostilities, Congress authorized the redemption of greenbacks at a rate of $10 million per month for six months and $4 million per month thereafter. As prices began to drop, however, Congress stopped the retirement and then later cautiously began again.

To bring greenbacks and other currencies onto a par with gold, and to eliminate the "gold premium," treasury officials had recourse to two practical courses of action:

1. The general price level could be forced down by contracting the supply of paper money. The greenback price of gold would decline with the general decrease of prices; when the mint price was reached, resumption could be proclaimed.

2. A slower less painful decline in prices could be achieved by holding the money supply constant and allowing the growth of the economy to bring about a gradual decline in prices. Once again, the market price of gold would fall relatively and ultimately reach the mint price.[1]

Actually, as shown in Figure 19-1, a severe policy of money contraction was initiated by Hugh McCulloch, appointed Secretary of the Treasury in the Johnson administration, and this strategy was approved by Congress in December 1865 by passage of the Contraction Act. But the deflationary medicine was too bitter, and Congress ended contraction in February 1868. Grant's Secretary of the Treasury, George S. Boutwell, followed a much

---

[1]Other alternatives included devaluation of metal dollars, abandoning the specie standard, and simply hoping and praying for a fortuitous increase in the supply of the money metals. See Richard H. Timberlake, Jr., "Ideological Factors in Specie Resumption and Treasury Policy," *Journal of Economic History* 24 (1964). See also James K. Kindahl, "Economic Factors in Specie Resumption: The United States, 1865–1879," *Journal of Political Economy* 69 (February 1961): pp. 30–48.

easier policy—a general *easing* of the money markets rather than a tightening of them.[2] After Boutwell's resignation in 1873, his Assistant Secretary, William Richardson, pursued a less vigorous policy that was nevertheless calculated to "grow into" resumption.

From 1868 to 1874, the Republican administration, while paying lip service to a return to gold, had taken the temperate course of not pressing for this return through severe contraction of the money stock. But when the Democrats won control of the Congress in the election of 1874, lame-duck Republicans, fearful of the antipathy of western and southern legislators toward resumption, hurriedly passed an act providing for a return to gold payments in four years. After January 1, 1879, the United States was to maintain strict convertibility between greenbacks and gold. Thanks to a favorable balance of trade in the latter years of the 1870s, gold stocks in this country increased at a rapid rate. The government removed the requirements that all customs duties be paid in gold to prevent discrimination against greenbacks, and on the appointed day the United States began to maintain specie payments. For a technical reason to be discussed presently, the United States was not finally and legally committed to a gold standard and would not be for another 21 years. Nevertheless, between 1879 and 1900, the government did *in fact* maintain parity of all other money forms with gold, and during these years America was on a *de facto* gold standard.

Silver and the Crime of '73

During the Civil War and for several years afterwards, silver coins had gone out of circulation, having been replaced at first by ungummed postage stamps and later by fractional currency—paper notes issued by the government in denominations of 5, 10, 25, and 50 cents. It is not surprising, then, that when Congress sought to simplify the coinage in 1873, the silver dollar was omitted from the list of coins to be minted. There was no agitation over the omission at the time, because at the mint ratio of approximately 16 to 1, silver was worth more on the market than at the mint, and little silver was brought to the mint for coinage. Yet, scarcely three years later, the failure to include the silver dollar in the Act of 1873 began a furor that was to last for a quarter of a century.

The reason for the subsequent agitation over the "demonetization" of silver lay in the fact that the price of silver began falling in international markets. Increasing output of western silver mines in the United States and a shift of the bimetallic countries of western Europe to the gold standard

---

[2]It was Boutwell who broke the dramatic corner on gold attempted by James Fisk and Jay Gould by selling $4 million of the money metal in the "Gold Room" of the New York Stock Exchange. See also Larry Wimmer, "The Gold Crisis of 1869: Stabilizing or Destabilizing Speculation Under Floating Exchange Rates," *Explorations in Economic History,* 12 (1975): 105–22.

When gold fluctuated wildly in 1869, the Gold Room of the New York Stock Exchange was the nerve-center of speculation. In its center, a bronze Cupid sprayed water quietly; on the dais, the secretary of the room had to cup his ears to hear and record transactions.

had led to a growing surplus of silver. When the price of the silver contained in a dollar actually fell below the price of $1 that the government, under the Coinage Act of 1834, had *formerly* paid, silver producers took silver to the mint for coinage.[3] To their dismay they discovered that the government would take only as much silver as the Treasury needed for small subsidiary coins. The cry that went up from the silver producers was horrendous.

A relatively small group like the silver producers would not appear to have much power in a large country like the United States. But during the 1870s and 1880s, a number of western states were being admitted to the Union, each with two U.S. senators to represent their small populations, and silver producers acquired political representation out of all proportion

---

[3]A dollar contained 371.25 grains of pure silver, or a little over three-quarters of an ounce. The *average* bullion value of that amount of silver in 1873 was $1.00368. The next year, the value dropped to $0.98909 and fell consistently from that year on.

to their numbers. The "reflationist" element in the West and South joined the silver producers in a clamor for the free and unlimited coinage of silver at the old mint ratio of 16 to 1. Silver advocates knew that at such a ratio silver would be brought to the mint in great quantities and that the monetary reserves of the country—and the general price level—would consequently be increased. The cry of the opposition that gold would be driven out of circulation meant nothing except relief to the unemployed, oppressed debtors or others who wanted to raise the general price level. To the supporters of the free coinage of silver, the act that had demonetized the metal became the "Crime of '73." Even though the silver dollar had been struck from the list of coins largely because no one thought the matter was of any importance, the slogan greatly helped to stir the emotions of the electorate.

Ultimately, the silver forces were able to push through Congress a compromise between the positions of the "sound-money" advocates and the free-coinage forces. The first of four major silver bills was the Bland–Allison Act of 1878. This law provided for the coinage of silver in *limited* amounts, and produced what Paul Studenski and Herman Krooss have termed "the limping standard," an odd sort of bimetalism.[4] The Secretary of the Treasury was directed to purchase not less than $2 million and not more than $4 million worth of silver each month *at the current market price*.[5] The conservative secretaries in office during the next twelve years purchased only the minimum amount of silver, but by 1890 the Treasury's monetary silver (not counting subsidiary coins) amounted to almost $380 million. According to the Bland–Allison Act and an amendment passed in 1886, the Treasury could keep the actual silver in its vaults and issue silver certificates, dollar for dollar, instead. Due to the bulkiness of silver dollars, nearly everyone except westerners preferred paper currency, and silver certificates circulated more than silver dollars.

But the silver question was by no means settled. After 1888, Republicans were in control of both the administration and Congress. To secure the passage of high-tariff legislation, it was necessary to have the votes of the silver senators. In exchange for their affirmative votes on the McKinley tariff bill, the Republican leadership agreed to further silver legislation. A new bill—the Sherman Silver Purchase Law of 1890—was carefully prepared to avoid the veto of President Harrison.

The Secretary of the Treasury was directed to make a *monthly* purchase, at the market rate, of 4.5 million *ounces* of silver. To pay for this quantity of

---

[4] Paul Studenski and Herman Krooss, *Financial History of the United States* (New York: McGraw-Hill, 1952), pp. 178–79.

[5] By 1878, the market price of silver in New York averaged a little over $1.15 per ounce for the calendar year; the average market value of the silver contained in a dollar in that year was just over $.89. For the next twelve years, silver prices consistently fell. Two points ought to be made in passing: the market price of silver was bolstered by government purchases, and the government later made quite a profit (about $70 million) on its silver purchases under the Act.

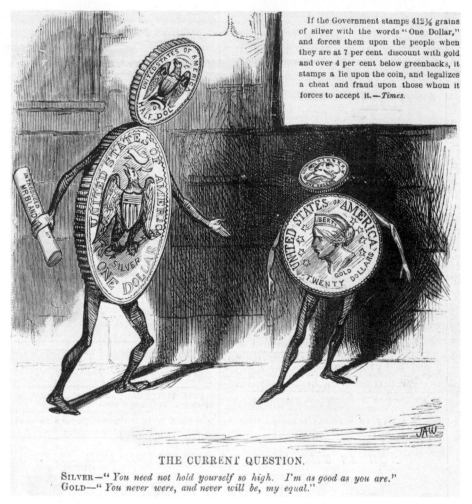

If the Government stamps 412½ grains of silver with the words "One Dollar," and forces them upon the people when they are at 7 per cent. discount with gold and over 4 per cent below greenbacks, it stamps a lie upon the coin, and legalizes a cheat and fraud upon those whom it forces to accept it.—*Times.*

THE CURRENT QUESTION.

SILVER—"*You need not hold yourself so high. I'm as good as you are.*"
GOLD—"*You never were, and never will be, my equal.*"

Friends of silver saw in its monetization relief from depression and persistent grief and agony if gold continued to reign as the sole monetary metal in America.

bullion, he was to issue a new type of paper to be known as Treasury notes; these notes were to be redeemable *in either gold or silver* at the discretion of the Secretary. At silver prices prevailing in 1890, the new law authorized the purchase of almost double the monthly amount of silver taken in under the previous law. But silver supplies kept expanding so rapidly that almost at once, the market price of silver resumed further sharp declines. Within three years, the *dollar amount* of silver being purchased was little more than it had been under the old act. In 1893, at the insistence of Democratic President Cleveland—a "sound-money" man at odds with his party on this issue—the Sherman Act was repealed. In over three years of purchasing under this law, more than $150 million of the Treasury notes of 1890 were issued and overall between 1878 and 1893, as shown in Figure 19-1, $500 million was added to the circulating currency by silver purchases. This was a victory of sorts for the silver forces. But, the treasury's silver purchases were insufficient to prevent silver prices from falling and, as shown in Figure 19-2, the general price level continued its deflationary spiral. When the Sherman Act was repealed in 1893, the nation was just entering a severe depression.

Gold and the Gold Standard Act of 1900

Thanks largely to the output of American mines, the gold stock increased significantly after 1875. As shown in Figure 19-1, in the 1880s the monetary gold stock doubled in quantity and between 1890 and 1914 it tripled. These advances did not free the Treasury authorities, however, from serious difficulties.

Although the silver acts of 1878 and 1890 made silver certificates redeemable in *either* gold *or* silver, in practice Treasury authorities redeemed them in gold if it were demanded. After 1879, Treasury secretaries felt that a minimum gold reserve of $100 million was necessary to back up the paper circulation. Just at the time when the Treasury notes of 1890 were authorized, the government's gold reserve began declining toward the $100 million mark as the public presented Treasury notes and greenbacks for payment in gold. To meet current expenses, the Treasury had to pay the paper money out again almost as soon as it was received. By early 1893, the gold drain had become serious, and the gold reserve actually dipped below the traditional minimum toward the middle of the year.

Several times during the next three years it appeared certain that the *de facto* gold standard would have to be abandoned. Two kinds of drains—"external" (foreign) and "internal" (domestic)—plagued the Treasury from 1891 to 1896. Today, abandonment of gold redemption hardly seems foreboding, but in the middle 1890s conservatives considered going off the gold standard equivalent to declaring national bankruptcy. The difficulty was that when the danger of abandoning gold became apparent, people rushed to acquire gold, thus making it even more likely that the Treasury *would* have to abandon the gold standard. Chiefly by selling bonds for gold, the administration replenished the government's reserve whenever it appeared that the standard was about to be lost. The repeal of the Sherman Silver Purchase Law of 1893 reduced the number of Treasury notes, which, along with greenbacks, the public was presenting for redemption. Increasing exports at last brought an influx of gold from abroad in the summer of 1896, improving public confidence to the extent that the "gold standard" was saved.

The election of 1896 settled the matter of a monetary standard for nearly 40 years. The money issue was clearly drawn. The Democrats, under the leadership of William Jennings Bryan, stood for free coinage of silver at a ratio of 16 to 1—even though the market ratio was then over 30 to 1. He

William Jennings Bryan on the political stump. Bryan was more than just a political leader; he also had a lively awareness of the need for economic and political reform. Although he was defeated on the money issue, Bryan's monetary prescriptions had a solid New Deal ring.

won the party's nomination, inspiring the inflationists with his famous "Cross of Gold" speech.

The Republicans, with McKinley as their candidate, stood solidly for the gold standard. The West and the South supported Bryan; the North and the East supported McKinley. Any attempt to stop the long years of deflation was anathema to the conservative East, and industrial employers—aided and abetted by the professional class (including Protestant clergy)—brought every possible pressure to bear on employee voters. Thus Bryan could not draw on the great urban vote, as Franklin Roosevelt was to do 36 years later, and when well-to-do farmers in the older agricultural states deserted him, the cause was lost. The Republican victory of 1896 was not followed immediately by legislation ending the controversy, because free silver advocates still had a majority membership in Congress. But the return of prosperity, encouraged by new gold discoveries, new methods of processing gold, and high levels of investment, made Congress receptive to definitive gold legislation.

Finally, in 1900, the Gold Standard Act was passed. The dollar was defined solely in terms of gold, and all other forms of money were to be convertible into gold. The Secretary of the Treasury was directed to maintain a gold reserve of $150 million, which was not to be drawn on to meet current government expenses. To prevent a recurrence of the difficulties of the

1890s, a provision was made to keep redeemed silver certificates and greenbacks in the Treasury during times of stress for borrowing to meet deficits that might occur from time to time.[6] The United States had at last committed itself *by law* to the gold standard.

National-Bank Notes and the Total Money Supply

A new set of banking institutions, called nationally chartered banks, were created by the National Bank Act in 1863; their currencies—known as national-bank notes—became important by 1865, grew steadily in amount for a decade, and then began to fluctuate. Originally, the total issue was limited to $300 million, this sum having been allotted among the states in proportion to the population and to the total national-bank capital within each state. Restrictions were removed by a clause in the Resumption Act of 1875, and from this year on national banks kept in circulation whatever amount of notes seemed profitable as shown in Figure 19-1. The low point of notes outstanding was reached in the early 1890s. A slow rise followed that changed in the early years of the century to a sharp increase, and a record high of more than $700 million was reached in 1914.

Collectively, greenbacks (U.S. Notes), national-bank notes, and silver and gold specie or their certificates plus small subsidiary coins made up the currency. As shown in Figure 19-1, first greenbacks (U.S. Notes) and then national-bank notes initiated the monetary increases that sent prices skyrocketing during the Civil War years. Later gold and silver provided other notable increases in the supply of hand-to-hand money. These types of currency provided, in order, the "dynamic" elements in the *supply of currency*. But as shown in Figures 19-3 and 19-4, most of the increase in the *total money supply* was by the growth of bank deposits—savings and checking deposits and deposits created by loans. The currency amounts were critical to the total, however. Cash, except for the national-bank notes, constituted the reserves of the banking system. The growth of these reserves allowed the growth of bank deposits and the total money supply.

Money and Prices

We shall discuss some of the implications of the development of checking below, but first it is important to note three rather distinct trends in the total money supply. The first is from 1860 to 1879; as shown in Figure 19-3, there was a sharp advance in 1862–65, a reverse to 1868 and then growth and leveling off in the mid-1870s. The trend overall is clearly slower than in the years after 1879. Also the sharp advance and then decline in the 1860s coincides with the sharp inflation and deflation of that decade (see Figure 19-2).

---

[6]The Treasury notes of 1890 were retired by the Gold Standard Act.

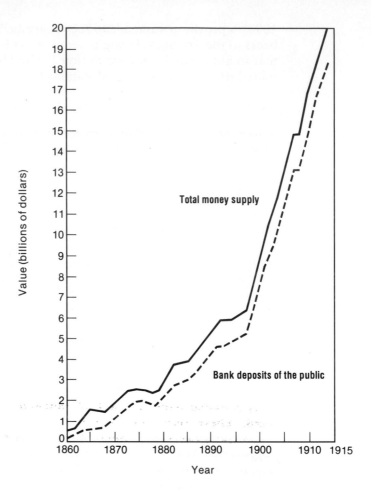

FIGURE 19-3   The U.S. Money Supply, 1860–1915: The total U.S. money supply grew in three trend surges of increasing speed, 1860–78, 1879–96, and 1897–1914, with greater instability before 1897.

Source: Albert G. Hart, *Money, Debt, and Economic Activity* (Englewood Cliffs: Prentice-Hall, 1948).

Later the rate of growth of the money supply turned dramatically upward, first in 1869 and then again in 1897. Specifically, Milton Friedman and Anna Jacobson Schwartz found that the growth rate of the money stock was "decidedly" smaller in the 1879–97 period than in the 1897–1914 period, averaging about 6 percent per year in the former and 7½ percent per year in the latter. Their contention is that different rates of monetary growth were "associated" with corresponding differences in price behavior. Prices *fell* at an annual rate of over 1 percent between 1879 and 1897 and *rose* at an annual rate of over 2 percent between 1897 and 1914. Furthermore, the growth rate of the money supply was much more uneven in the

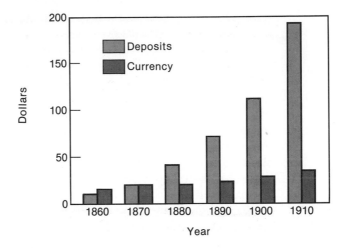

FIGURE 19-4 Per Capita Deposits and Currency in Circulation, 1860–1910.

Source: Data from *Historical Statistics of the United States, 1789–1945* (Washington, D.C.: GPO, 1947), pp. 25, 262, 263, and 274.

first period than in the second—a fact that accounts for the more unsteady pace of economic activity in the first period.[7]

The Banking System

The National Bank Act of 1863 initiated a new type of bank, a national bank. These were mainly existing state banks that took on a new charter from the federal government. Their operations continued to be limited within state boundaries. To make the national banks appear more sound than state banks, legal reserve requirements were required and double liability was imposed on the stock of national banks.[8] The federal government's underlying motive, under the guise of rationalizing the nation's currency, was to raise war revenues. To do this the Treasury tried to force-feed federal banks into the banking system. Getting the state banks to convert

---

[7]Milton Friedman and Anna Jacobson Schwartz, *A Monetary History of the United States, 1867–1960* (Princeton: Princeton Univ. Press, 1963), pp. 91–92.

[8]The National Bank Act recognized prevailing practice in many states by permitting new national banks to keep their reserves in two forms—cash in their vaults or deposits with a national bank in one of 17 "redemption" cities. Banks located in New York City (later called a "central reserve" city) were exceptions in that they had to keep *all* their reserves as cash in vault. Banks in the 16 other redemption cities (later redesignated "reserve" cities) had to keep half their reserves as cash in vault but could keep the other half as deposits with national banks in New York. Banks in all other cities and towns (country banks) had to keep two-fifths of their reserves as cash in vault but could deposit the remaining three-fifths in a national bank in a redemption city. Reserves, in whatever form they were maintained, were set at 25 percent for banks in redemption cities and at 15 percent for country banks. *Originally, reserves were to be calculated as a percentage of notes outstanding plus deposits.*

their charters was the key because national banks were required to buy bonds in order to issue bank notes.

To secure its note issue, each national bank was required to buy U.S. government bonds equal to one-third (later one-quarter) of the dollar amount of its paid-in capital stock, with the provision that no bank would have to buy more than $50,000 worth of bonds. Each bank was to deposit its bonds with the U.S. Treasurer and was to receive notes, engraved in a standard design but with the name of the issuing bank on the obverse side, in the amount of 90 percent of the par or market value (whichever was lower) of the bonds deposited. A national bank could have any amount of government bonds in its portfolio, but the amount of its notes outstanding could not exceed its *capital* in dollar amount.[9]

Because the early pace of conversion was so slow, a small tax of 2 percent was levied against state-bank notes in June 1864. Still bankers were slow to change charters and buy U.S. bonds so in March 1865 the tax on state bank notes was raised to 10 percent. Then the pace of conversion soared; as Table 19-1 indicates, the tax was indeed effective. A majority of the state banks immediately shifted to federal jurisdiction; in 1866, less than 300 state banks remained. For the most part, these state banks were large city banks that had long since discarded the practice of issuing notes when they extended loans. After the Civil War, bank deposits (checking) were far more important than notes in cities; by the mid-1870s, banks in all but the backwoods areas could extend loans simply by crediting the account of the borrower. As the practice of using and accepting checks for payment spread from the city to the country, the tax on state-bank notes no longer was a serious economic deterrent to operation under state charters.

By the early 1870s, then, it had become clear that a national charter was not essential to a profitable banking business. Moreover, for bank organizers who had no aspirations toward national or substantial regional operations, state charters had several positive advantages:

1. Lower amounts of capital were required in most state jurisdictions and under nearly all circumstances. Until 1900, the minimum amount of capital required for a national bank was $50,000. In the West and South, state minimum capital requirements of $10,000 were frequent, and some states prescribed no capital minimums at all.

2. Reserves required against deposits were lower under most state banking laws than under the National Bank Act. Furthermore, national banks had to observe substantially stricter rules regarding the amount of cash held in reserve—and the Comptroller of the Currency was generally

---

[9]National banks in towns of less than 6,000 inhabitants had to have a minimum capital of $50,000; those in towns of more than 6,000 but less than 50,000, a capital of $100,000; and those in cities of 50,000 or more, a capital of $200,000.

TABLE 19-1   Commercial Banks in the United States, 1860–1914

Year[a]	State banks[b]	National banks	Year[a]	State banks[b]	National banks
1860	1,562		1888	1,523	3,120
1861	1,601		1889	1,791	3,239
1862	1,492				
1863	1,466	66	1890	2,250	3,484
1864	1,089	467	1891	2,743	3,652
			1892	3,773	3,759
1865	349	1,294	1893	4,188	3,807
1866	297	1,634	1894	4,188	3,770
1867	272	1,636			
1868	247	1,640	1895	4,369	3,715
1869	259	1,619	1896	4,279	3,689
			1897	4,420	3,610
1870	325	1,612	1898	4,486	3,581
1871	452	1,723	1899	4,738	3,582
1872	566	1,853			
1873	277	1,968	1900	5,007	3,731
1874	368	1,983	1901	5,651	4,163
			1902	6,171	4,532
1875	586	2,076	1903	6,890	4,935
1876	671	2,091	1904	7,970	5,327
1877	631	2,078			
1878	510	2,056	1905	9,018	5,664
1879	648	2,048	1906	10,220	6,046
			1907	11,469	6,422
1880	650	2,076	1908	12,803	6,817
1881	683	2,115	1909	13,421	6,886
1882	704	2,239			
1883	788	2,417	1910	14,348	7,138
1884	852	2,625	1911	15,322	7,270
			1912	16,037	7,366
1885	1,015	2,689	1913	16,841	7,467
1886	891	2,809	1914	17,498	7,518
1887	1,471	3,014			

[a]All figures as of June 30, or nearest available date.
[b]Excludes unincorporated banks and mutual savings banks.

Source: *Banking Studies,* by members of the staff of the Board of Governors of the Federal Reserve System (Baltimore: Waverly Press, 1941), pp. 422–23. See also *Historical Statistics of the United States, Colonial Times to 1957* (Washington, D.C.: GPO, 1958), esp. pp. 623–32.

more severe in dealing with reserve deficiencies than were state counterparts. Finally, several state laws distinguished between time and demand deposits, permitting lower reserves to be maintained against both.

3. In general, national banks operated under much stricter lending and investment policies than did their state-chartered competitors. Before 1913, the National Bank Act for all practical purposes prohibited loans

on real estate, which in some areas constituted a major portion of competing banks' business. Until 1906, a national bank could not lend to a single borrower more than 10 percent of its paid-up capital—a limitation that became increasingly harmful in competing with other institutions. And although state banks and trust companies frequently had wide latitude in purchasing the stocks of banks and other corporations, national banks were barred from such activities.

4. Standards of bank supervision and examination were much higher in the national jurisdiction.

In summary, the rules governing the entry and operations of banks chartered by the states were far less onerous than those prescribed for national banks. From 1864 to 1914 (and, for that matter, to the present day), a dual banking system developed simply because one set of rules was easier than the other, and the data testified to the truth of the proposition.

As Table 19-1 shows, the revival of state banking began in the 1870s; by the early 1880s, the relative growth of the state-bank system was unmistakable. Between 1880 and 1900, the number of national banks increased from 2,076 to 3,731, while the number of state banks jumped from 650 to just over 5,000. In 1900, the resources of national banks were just less than double those of state banks. A few years later, in 1907, state banks outnumbered national banks by nearly two to one, and the resources of state banks were about the same as those of national banks.

FINANCIAL CAPITAL, INVESTMENT BANKING, AND THE NATIONAL DEBT

The National Bank Acts, as we have seen, were effective in curtailing the growth of state banking in the late 1860s and early 1870s. Barriers formed by high capital requirements of national banks, restrictions on mortgage loans, and limits on their note issues before 1875 also protected many country national banks from new entrants and increased competition. This allowed many rural national banks to effectively price discriminate. To do this, rural national banks restricted loans and charged higher interest rates to local borrowers; they also sent their reserves to city banks, usually above required limits. This practice, in combination with slower banking expansion rurally, helped finance urban-industrial growth. As Richard E. Sylla has concluded, the national banking system "raised barriers to entry into banking, and these had differential geographic impact which, when coupled with the increased mobility the National Banking System gave to interbank transfers of funds, worked very much to the advantage of industrial finance."[10] On

---

[10]Richard E. Sylla, "The United States, 1863–1913," in *Banking and Economic Development: Some Lessons of Economic History* ed. Rondo Cameron (New York: Oxford Univ. Press, 1972), p. 236.

the other hand, the interbank transfers only went part way. Nationwide branch banking systems were not allowed; hence the thousands of banks listed in Table 19-1.

As Lance Davis discovered in his comparative analysis of U.S. and British industrial finance, the American system was very different from the British one.[11] British industrialists could visit their local branch banks—Lloyds or Westminster or Barclays—and draw capital loans on a huge system, a capital pool built internationally. American firms, on the other hand, faced banks with more restricted capital pools. Typically, theirs were locally based funds plus some additional funds from interbank transfers.

Because of this limitation, a new form of banking—investment banking—emerged to serve the expansion of railroads, mining companies, and large-scale manufacturers. Unlike commercial banks, investment banks did not have the power to issue notes (money) or make deposits. Instead they acted as middlemen, bringing together investors (stock buyers) and borrowers (firms). J. P. Morgan and Company was a pioneer in investment banking, earning $3 million for services in advising and selling stocks for Vanderbilt and his New York Central Railroad in 1879. Charles Schwab, a yuppie-like employee of Andrew Carnegie in 1900, carried a note to Morgan with an asking price of over $400 million for Carnegie's steel holdings. Morgan, promptly replied, "I'll take it"—thus giving birth to the United States Steel Corporation; it was by far the largest merger ("buy out") ever at that time. Forty years earlier in 1860, when Carnegie had tried to raise financial capital of only a fraction of the sum Morgan promptly gave him, Carnegie had to go to England because no U.S. banks could supply his capital needs. Investment banking grew up in response to the huge demands for capital, and close links between investment bankers and big business were forged even more strongly by the practice of placing representatives of the large investment houses on the boards of directors of the firms.

Another important force helping to finance industrial growth was the rapid steady retirement of the national debt after 1865. To provide historical perspective, the national debt, accumulated from the Revolution through the War of 1812 peaked at $127 million in 1815. This was retired completely by 1835, the only time in our history this was accomplished. By 1865, the debt was $2,322 million; it was reduced to $648 million by 1877 before increasing for several years. By 1893, $1,732 million had been retired. High tariffs supplied government with continued surpluses that permitted the debt retirement. This inflow of government funds to buy up old bonds—a type of crowding in, as John James has called it—lowered yields on private assets and stimulated capital formation in the private sector.[12] How

---

[11]Lance E. Davis, "Capital Immobilities and Financial Capitalism: A Study of Economic Evolution in the United States," *Explorations in Entrepreneurial History* 1, no. 1 (Fall, 1963): 88–105.
[12]John A. James, "Public Debt and U.S. Economic Growth," *Explorations in Economic History* 21 (April 1984): 192–217.

different from the 1980s and today when huge federal deficits and treasury-bond sales have continually raised interest rates and "crowded out" corporate bond issues.

BANK PANICS AND THE ESTABLISHMENT OF THE FEDERAL RESERVE SYSTEM

Despite these gains from institutional change and refinement, the depression of the mid-1890s was followed by the severe panic and ensuing depression of 1907. Once again, the American people were aroused to the need for basic reforms.

One of the most painful manifestations of economic crises in pre-First World War days was the flight to obtain hand-to-hand money. As individuals and business firms became apprehensive about the economic future, they rushed to the banks to convert their deposits into cash. The banks, which operated on the "fractional reserve" principle, could not immediately meet the demands for their total deposit liabilities. A single bank could *gradually* convert its assets into cash; given time, any sound bank could even be liquidated in an orderly fashion, and its depositors and stockholders could be paid in full. But in periods of panic, an orderly shifting of assets into cash was difficult, if not impossible. Not only was there insufficient time, but as harried banks all tried to sell securities (their most liquid assets) at the same time, the prices of securities fell drastically. For some banks, the consequent losses on securities proved disastrous, even though "runs" were stopped. If, instead of selling its securities, a bank called its loans or refused to renew notes as they came due, pressure was transferred to the customers of the bank. And if these customers—business firms that had come to rely on the bank for loans in time of need—could not meet their obligations, they were forced into insolvency.

A common way of mitigating these difficulties was to "suspend" cash payments during crises. Before the Civil War, suspension meant that banks temporarily refused to redeem their notes or to pay out deposits in specie. After the Civil War, suspension meant that banks ceased to pay out cash in any form—gold or gold certificates, silver or silver certificates, greenbacks, national-bank notes, or subsidiary coins. Instead of suspending payments, a bank might restrict cash payments to a certain maximum sum per day or per withdrawal. During the panic of 1907, such suspensions were more general and for longer time periods (over two months in some cities) than they had ever been before. In the Southeast and Midwest, the resulting shortage of cash was so serious that local clearing houses even issued "script" against collateral pledged by cooperating banks so that people could carry on business. These small-denomination "clearing-house certificates" were not issued much elsewhere, but large-denomination certificates were used by banks in cities all over the United States to make up balances due one another.

In response, the Aldrich–Vreeland Act was passed in 1908. It provided for the organization of "national currency associations" to be composed of not less than ten banks in sound financial condition. The purpose of these associations was to enable the banks that formed them to issue emergency bank notes against the security of bonds and commercial paper in their portfolios. A secondary provision, which was really an attempt to postpone more positive action, established a National Monetary Commission. The report of the Commission in 1912 helped point out to the public the weaknesses of the American banking system. The report blasted the system:

> The methods by which our domestic and international credit operations are now conducted are crude, expensive and unworthy of an intelligent people. . . . The unimportant part which our banks and bankers take in the financing of our foreign trade is disgraceful to a progressive nation. . . . The disabilities from which our producers suffer in our foreign trade also apply largely to domestic transactions.[13]

The key recommendation was a new central bank. The Commission felt that what was needed was a central institution that could create reserves to stretch or contract the money supply, *a great central institution with the authority to hold the reserves of the commercial banks and to increase their reserves through its own credit-granting powers.*

A central bank was also needed to help the Treasury. After the demise of the second Bank of the United States, the federal government had to maintain its own fiscal agent in the form of the Treasury, which was by law required to remain aloof from the banking system. Impossibly antiquated methods of handling government funds resulted. Even in the early years of the twentieth century, the government had a sizable amount of banking business to conduct. The Treasury continuously received and disbursed tax monies in all sections of the United States and needed an institution to carry its principal checking accounts. Furthermore, an official institution was required to handle the myriad physical details involved in government borrowing, to advise Treasury officials regarding management of the public debt, and to act as the agent of the Treasury in gold and foreign-exchange transactions. By 1912 the need for a modern, central fiscal agent was too great to be postponed further.

Two days before Christmas in 1913, President Wilson signed the bill that established the Federal Reserve System. The system was composed of twelve Federal Reserve Banks, one in each of twelve districts in the country. Unlike the 20-year charter of the First and Second United States Banks, the charter of the Federal Reserve was permanent.

The system was to be headed by a Federal Reserve Board composed of seven members, including the Secretary of the Treasury, the Comptroller of the Currency *ex officio,* and five appointees of the President. Each Federal

---

[13]Report of the National Monetary Commission (Washington, D.C. GPO, 1912), pp. 28–29.

Reserve Bank was to be run by a board of nine directors. Three of the directors, representing the "public," were to be appointed by the Federal Reserve Board; the remaining six were to be elected by the member banks of the district. Three of the six locally elected directors could be bankers; the remaining three were to represent business, industry, and agriculture. Thus, the banking community had a minority representation on the Reserve Bank directorates in each district.

The Federal Reserve Act made membership in the system compulsory for national banks; state banks, on compliance with federal requirements, might become members. To join the system a commercial bank had to purchase shares of the capital stock of the district Federal Reserve Bank in the amount of 3 percent of its combined capital and surplus. (Another 3 percent *might* be required.) Thus, the member banks nominally owned the Federal Reserve Banks, although the annual return they could receive on their stock was limited to a 6-percent cumulative dividend. A member bank also had to deposit with the district Federal Reserve Bank a large part of the cash it had previously held as reserves. The Act originally provided that member banks might retain a part of their reserves as cash in vault, but in 1917 the requirement was changed; after 1917, *all* the legal reserves of member banks were to be in the form of deposits with the Federal Reserve Bank.[14]

It was expected that the Federal Reserve Banks, as a system of control, would operate almost automatically and that, if the Federal Reserve Act were carefully followed, monetary disturbances would be very nearly eliminated. To most people, prudent monetary control and the elimination of monetary disturbances were synonymous with the elimination of business fluctuations. But, as we will see in Part IV, despite the appropriate institutional arrangement provided by the Federal Reserve System, periods of inadequate leadership and resolve at the "Fed" permitted catastrophic monetary disturbances, bank panics, and sharp business cycles. Indeed, the Great Depression—America's darkest economic period—came in the modern era and left a New Deal legacy that lives with us today.

SELECTED REFERENCES AND SUGGESTED READINGS

Aghevli, Bijan B. "The Balance of Payments and Money Supply Under the Gold Standard Regime: U.S. 1879–1914." *American Economic Review* 65 (1975): 40–58.

Bloomfield, Arthur I. *Short-Term Capital Movements Under the Pre-1914 Gold Standard.* Princeton: International Finance Section, Dept. of Economics, Princeton Univ., 1963.

Davis, Lance E. "Capital Immobilities and Finance Capitalism: A Study of Economic Evolution in the United States." *Explorations in Entrepreneurial History* 1, no. 1 (Fall 1963): 88–105.

———. "The Investment Market, 1870–1914: The Evolution of a National Market." *Journal of Economic History* 25 (1965): 355–99.

---

[14]All required reserves were held on deposit with Federal Reserve Banks from June 21, 1917, until late 1959, when, after a series of transitional steps, member banks could once again count vault cash as reserves.

Friedman, Milton, and Anna J. Schwartz. *A Monetary History of the United States, 1867–1967*. Princeton: National Bureau of Economic Research, Princeton Univ. Press, 1963.

Gurley, J. G., and E. S. Shaw. "The Growth of Debt and Money in the United States, 1800–1950: A Suggested Interpretation." *Review of Economics and Statistics* (August 1957).

Hawtrey, R. G. *The Gold Standard in Theory and Practice*. London: Longmans, Green, 1939.

Hughes, Jonathan, and Nathan Rosenberg. "The United States Business Cycle Before 1860: Some Problems of Interpretation." *Economic History Review,* 2nd series, 15 (1963).

James, John A. "Cost Functions of Post-bellum National Banks." *Explorations in Economic History* 15 (1978): 184–95.

———. "The Development of a National Money Market, 1893–1911." *Journal of Economic History* 33 (1976): 878—97.

———. "Public Debt Management Policy and Nineteenth-Century American Economic Growth." *Explorations in Economic History* 21 (1984): 192–217.

———. *Money and Capital Markets in Postbellum America*. Princeton: Princeton Univ. Press, 1978.

Jenks, Leland H. *The Export of British Capital to 1875*. London: Cape, 1938.

Kindahl, James K. "Economic Factors in Specie Resumption: The United States, 1865–1879." In *The Reinterpretation of American Economic History*, ed. Robert W. Fogel and Stanley L. Engerman. New York: Harper & Row, 1971.

McGrane, R. C. *Foreign Bondholders and American State Debts*. New York: Macmillan, 1935.

Myers, Margaret. *The New York Money Market*. New York: Columbia Univ. Press, 1931.

Simon, Matthew. "The Morgan-Belmont Syndicate of 1895 and Intervention in the Foreign Exchange Market." *Business History Review* 42 (Winter, 1968).

Smiley, Gene. "Interest Rate Movements in the United States, 1888–1913." *Journal of Economic History* 35 (1975): 591–620.

Sobel, Robert. *The Big Board: A History of the New York Stock Market*. New York: Free Press, 1969.

Studenski, Paul, and Herman Krooss. *Financial History of the United States*. New York: McGraw-Hill, 1952.

Sushka, Marie Elizabeth, and W. Brian Barrett. "Banking Structure and the National Capital Market, 1869–1914." *Journal of Economic History* 44 (1984): 463–78.

Sylla, Richard. "American Banking and Growth in the Nineteenth Century: A Partial View of the Terrain." *Explorations in Economic History* 9 (Winter, 1971–72): 197–228.

———. "Federal Policy, Banking Market Structure, and Capital Mobilization in the United States, 1863–1913." *Journal of Economic History* 29 (1969): 657–86.

———. *The American Capital Market, 1846–1914*. New York: Arno Press, 1975.

Tanner, J. E., and B. Bonomo. "Gold, Capital Flows, and Long Swings in American Business Activity." *Journal of Political Economy* 76 (Jan.–Feb., 1968).

Timberlake, Richard. *The Origins of Central Banking in the United States*. Cambridge: Harvard Univ. Press, 1978.

Unger, Irwin. *The Greenback Era*. Princeton: Princeton Univ. Press, 1964.

West, Robert Craig. *Banking Reform and the Federal Reserve 1863–1923*. Ithaca, N.Y.: Cornell Univ. Press. 1977.

Williamson, Jeffrey G. *Financial Intermediation, Capital Immobilities and Economic Growth in Late Nineteenth Century American Development: A General Equilibrium History*. Cambridge: Cambridge Univ. Press. 1974.

———. "Watersheds and Turning Points: Conjectures on the Long-Term Impact of Civil War Financing." *Journal of Economic History* 34 (1974): 636–61.

Wimmer, Larry T. "The Gold Crisis of 1869: Stabilizing or Destabilizing Speculation Under Floating Exchange Rates?" *Explorations in Economic History* 12 (1975): 105–22.

CHAPTER 20

Commerce at Home and Abroad

The percentage of the total population that resides in cities has persistently grown since the days of the nation's beginning. By 1960 nine out of ten Americans lived in 160 metropolitan areas, and photographs from high-powered cameras aboard satellites taken on clear nights reveal brilliant clusters of light, especially around the Great Lakes and along the coasts, West, East, and South. These photos command the careful study of entrepreneurs seeking markets for their goods and services.

The long steady march to city dominance is revealed in Table 20-1, showing a near doubling in the percentage of the population living in urban centers in 1800–40, again in 1840–60, and again in 1860–1900. By 1910 nearly 10 percent of the total population lived in three cities, New York, Chicago, and Philadelphia, each with a million-plus residents.

Prior to 1860 the rapid pace of urbanization was due primarily to the rapid growth of interregional trade spurred by the transportation revolution. Urban centers emerged as "entropôts" of trade and trade more than industry was the magnet pulling people into cities and towns. Early industrial progress in the United States was largely a matter of "carrying labor to raw materials."[1] As Eric Lampard has shown, the 15 greatest cities in the nation in 1860 had relatively small shares of their population in manufactures. For the 1840–60 period he concluded, "It would be misleading to suggest that this explosion to American cities was due entirely to the growth of urban manufactures. It was much more the outcome of a continental development carried out with railroads—colonialism on a continental scale."[2] What the cities in this early period provided was primarily transport, commercial, and banking services for expanding long-distance trades.

Urbanization after the Civil War was different, however, a new age of the modern industrial city. Early industrial complexes, which had been tied

---

[1] V. S. Clark, *History of Manufactures in the United States,* vol. II (New York: McGraw-Hill, 1929), p. 2.

[2] Eric Lampard, "The History of Cities in the Economically Advanced Areas," *Economic Development and Cultural Change* 3 (Jan. 1955): 119, quoted in Jeffrey G. Williamson, "Antebellum Urbanization in the American Northeast," in *Journal of Economic History* 35 (1965): 603.

TABLE 20-1   Urban Proportions of the Population, 1800–1910

Year	Population in Towns over 2,500	Population in Towns over 100,000
1800	6%	0%
1840	11	3
1860	20	8
1880	28	12
1900	40	19
1910	46	22

Source: *Historical Statistics, 1975* (Washington, D.C.: GPO, 1976), Series A2 and A57–72.

to primary resources in city hinterlands, shifted to the city. The railroad and other advances in transportation and communication made factories and cities nearly synonymous by the late nineteenth century.

Populations poured into the centers of industrial activities, many from abroad. Between 1860 and 1910 over half of *new* city residents came from overseas. About 10 percent of the urban growth was due to natural increase, and a little over one-third came from domestic rural areas.

Cities in the Midwest and the South, long established as distributing centers for the manufactures of the East, grew phenomenally as industrial workers flocked to them. Chicago and Detroit, Cleveland and Cincinnati, St. Louis and Kansas City, Memphis and New Orleans, and Atlanta and Birmingham originated shipments that went far beyond their own trade areas in all directions. By 1910, the West and the South originated half as much railroad tonnage of manufactures as the East. Meanwhile, smaller cities within the trade areas of the metropolises and cities in the thinly populated region west of the Mississippi specialized in the mercantile functions. Trade eddied about these lesser centers, which distributed wholesale and retail goods over clearly marked, if overlapping, territories. As automobiles came into common use after 1910, large towns and cities gained business at the expense of small towns and villages; by 1920, retailers in urban centers were beginning to attract customers from distances which had been unimaginable during the previous decade. This change was reflected in new ways of distributing goods and in new marketing institutions.

MARKETING AND SELLING

The typical store on the eve of the Civil War, with rare exceptions, was more devoted to processing sales orders than to promoting and selling goods. Advertising was limited largely to local newspapers and some national magazines plus occasional outdoor ads in a few large cities. "Business getting" was not a part of advertisements; the information conveyed was simple and direct. Newspaper ads wasted no space, listing items for sale and the place, but usually not prices. Installment buying was known but rare. McCormick sold his reaper "on time" at 20 percent down and four months to pay. Edward Clark of the Singer Sewing Machine Company innovated consumer credit in 1856, selling $125 sewing machines for $5 down and $3 per month. But McCormick and Singer, who entrepreneured direct sales to consumers before the Civil War, were rare exceptions. Most manufacturers sold directly to wholesalers, or commission agents who marketed the wares. Many wholesalers, in turn, hired "drummers," traveling salesmen who "drummed up" trade and solicited orders in the towns and countryside.

Wholesaling

The full-service wholesale houses that evolved after 1840 bought goods on their own account from manufacturers and importers to sell to retailers, frequently on credit. In the growing cities of the Midwest, successful retailers began to perform some wholesale functions along with the business of selling to consumers. As these houses grew, they sometimes dropped their retailing activities altogether and concentrated on handling the output of manufacturing centers in the East. Occasionally, wholesale firms—especially those located in major distributing centers like Chicago and St. Louis— offered several lines of merchandise, but more often they specialized in a single "full line," such as hardware or dry goods.

From 1860 to 1900, full-line, full-service wholesale houses were without serious competitors in the business of distributing goods from manufacturers to retailers. But as transportation and communication facilities improved after the turn of the century, the power the wholesaler enjoyed began to shift, because some manufacturers—their financial capabilities increasing with size—could advertise their wares in great regional markets or even the national market and thus reach retail outlets directly.[3] Wholesale houses did not decline between 1900 and 1920; in fact, their sales continued to increase, but they handled an ever smaller *proportion* of goods in wholesale channels.

Retailing

In rural areas, where retail units remained characteristically small and independent, the wholesale house kept its customers. The general store was rapidly disappearing except in villages and hamlets, as retailers in towns with a surrounding trade area began to specialize in particular lines. But this specialization of retail functions did not bring about a reduction of the

---

[3] For discussion of several manufacturers' integration into marketing and distribution activities, see Alfred D. Chandler, Jr., *The Visible Hand: The Managerial Revolution in America* (Cambridge: Belknap Press of Harvard Univ. Press, 1977); and Harold Livesay and Glenn Porter, *Merchants and Manufacturers* (Baltimore: Johns Hopkins Univ. Press, 1971).

Manhattan residents purchased a great variety of groceries from vendors. In this photograph, an inspector is testing the accuracy of the scale of a downtown pushcart vegetable vendor in the early 1900s.

traditional wholesaler's business. What transpired was the development of new types of retail outlets, usually large ones, and the increasing ability of manufacturers to establish strong consumer preferences through advertising.

Department Stores   Of the new retailing organizations that gained definite acceptance by the First World War, the department store ran counter to the trend of greater specialization in handling merchandise. As cities became bigger and more congested, the convenience of being able to shop for all personal necessities in a single store had an increasing appeal. Furthermore, department stores offered delivery services and credit privileges that were conveniences in an ever more complex urban existence. The early department stores in large cities evolved after the Civil War from the efforts of dry-goods stores to replace business lost to the growing ready-to-wear trade. There was a definite division of the store into separate departments, each with its own manager, buyers, and clerks for a line of merchandise; the separation was once so distinct that departments were frequently leased to individuals or companies.

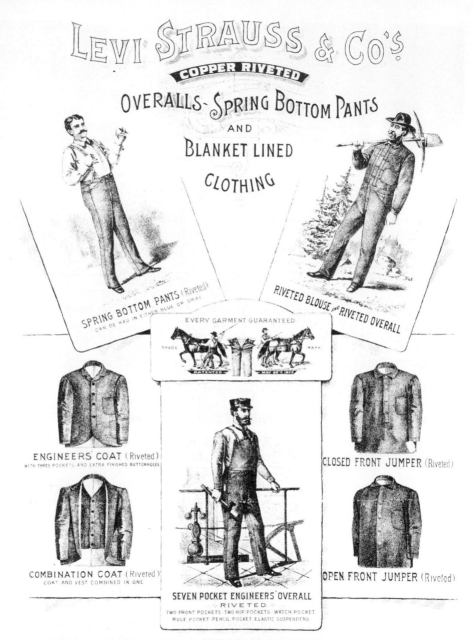

Measurements of American male sizes for Civil War uniforms marked the beginning of standardized clothing, and U.S. manufacturers of boots and shoes steadily improved the quality and fit of their product. Economies resulting from mass production techniques drove down the cost of clothing and mail-order solicitation helped to broaden markets.

At first, department stores bought merchandise through wholesalers. However, larger stores like Macy's in New York, John Wanamaker's in Philadelphia, and Marshall Field in Chicago took advantage of their growing size to obtain price reductions by going directly to manufacturers or their selling agents. Due to the size of their operations, large stores with numerous clerks had to set one price for all customers and the old practice of haggling with merchants over the price of an article was soon a thing of the past. So successful was the department store concept that by 1920 even small cities could usually boast one. Small department stores purchased merchandise through regular wholesale channels, and their departmentalization was so indistinct that they were very similar to the general store of an earlier day.

Chain Stores   It soon became apparent to some enterprisers that the costs of distributing goods in certain lines could be reduced by performing agency and brokerage functions in their own departments and by buying directly from manufacturers and processors. But to achieve the bargaining power to enable them to buy directly, enterprisers had to have retail sales of considerable magnitude. Such sales could be obtained by combining many spatially separate outlets in chains with a centralized buying and administrative authority. Additional savings could be made by curtailing or eliminating the major services of credit and delivery.

One of the early chains, still with us today, was the Great Atlantic and Pacific Tea Company, founded in 1859. From an original line restricted to tea and coffee, the company expanded in the 1870s to a general line of groceries. In 1879, F. W. Woolworth began the venture that was to make him a multimillionaire when he opened variety stores carrying articles that sold for no more than a dime. By 1900, tobacco stores and drugstores were often organized in chains, and hardware stores and restaurants soon began to fall under centralized managements. By 1920, grocery, drug, and variety chains were firmly established as a part of the American retail scene. A few companies then numbered their units in the thousands, but the great growth of the chains was to come in the 1920s and 1930s—along with innovations in physical layout and the aggressive selling practices that would incur the wrath of the independents.

Mail-Order Houses   It is difficult for the modern urban resident to imagine the thrill of "ordering by mail." Yet for many American families in the decades before the First World War, the annual arrival of a catalog from Montgomery Ward or Sears, Roebuck was an event that was anticipated with pleasure. Although Montgomery Ward started his business with the intention of selling only to Grangers, he soon included other farmers and many city dwellers among his customers. Both Montgomery Ward and Sears, Roebuck & Company experienced their great growth periods after they moved to Chicago—a vantage point from which they could sell, with optimum economies of shipping costs and time, to eager Midwestern agrarians

F. W. Woolworth—a pioneer in chain-store merchandising—opened his first store in 1879 in Lancaster, Pennsylvania.

and to both coasts as well. Rural free delivery and the establishment of a parcel-post system were godsends to mail-order houses. By 1920, however, towns were readily accessible to farmers and they could make their own purchases; if the mail-order houses were to remain important merchandisers, they would have to modify their selling methods.

Product Differentiation and Advertising

Merchants had advertised long before the Civil War. But as long as durable and semidurable goods were either made to order for the wealthy or turned out carelessly for the undiscriminating poor, and as long as food staples

Advertising helped to expand the consumer demand for new products like this all-purpose potion.

were sold out of bulk containers, the field of the advertiser was limited. In fact, the first attempts at advertising on more than a local scale were directed largely toward retailers rather than consumers. Notable exceptions were patent-medicine manufacturers—the first sellers in America to advertise on a national scale.[4]

Not until after the Civil War, however, did advertising on a national scale become a widely accepted business practice. With the trusts came truly national firms, whose brand names and trademarks became impressed on the minds of consumers. Where products such as tobacco, whiskey, kerosene, and rubber boots and shoes could be rationally differentiated in terms of buyer thinking, the trusts attempted an institutional advertising designed to reassure householders about the quality of the goods being purveyed. And as the quality of nondurables improved, particularly in the case of clothing, manufacturers of leather shoes, hosiery, underwear, and men's

---

[4]There is a suspicion that the popularity of patent medicines resulted in good part from their high alcohol content. Many, if not most, customers would not have touched liquor, and they may not have realized that the immediate sense of well-being derived from such medicines arose from alcohol instead of from other "beneficial ingredients."

suits and overcoats found that a loyal, nationwide following could be won through brand-name advertising.

By 1920, advertising was a billion-dollar industry. In some fields, the increasing size of the firm in American industry was an important factor in the growth of national advertising, but advertising itself helped firms to attain large sizes.

It became a well-accepted fact that a firm had to advertise to maintain its share of an industry's sales. It was also realized that as competing firms carried on extensive campaigns, the demand for a product might increase throughout the entire industry. Yet only a beginning had been made. Two changes were to loom large in the future of American advertising. One was the radio, which within a decade was to do the job of advertising far more effectively than it had ever been done before. The second was the change in the kind of consumer durables people would buy in the future. In 1869, half the output of consumer durables consisted of furniture and house furnishings; 30 years later, the same categories still accounted for somewhat more than half of the total. But after 1910, as first the automobile and then electrical appliances revolutionized American life, the share of furniture and household furnishings in the output of consumer durables declined rapidly. Household furnishings were articles that could not be differentiated in people's minds with any remarkable degree of success, although efforts were continually made to do so. On the other hand, automobiles and household appliances could be readily differentiated and presented a wonderful challenge to the American advertising account executive.

The First Steps toward Consumer Protection

It is widely believed that the Meat Inspection and the Pure Food and Drug Acts of 1906 were the first major interventions into the economy by the federal government to ensure quality standards of products for unwary customers. In 1906 Upton Sinclair's novel *The Jungle* was published and received the personal attention of President Theodore Roosevelt. Sinclair's descriptions of unsanitary production facilities for meat and his allegations of occasional processing of diseased animals stirred up sensational media and public reactions.

Sinclair's book was timely, coming on the heels of the 1898 "embalmed beef" scandal, an event of the Spanish-American War in which it was alleged that adulterated beef was provided to the army. Although these allegations, both in *The Jungle* and from the scandal, ultimately were found baseless in congressional testimony, the Acts were promptly passed.[5]

---

[5]See Gary D. Liebcap, "The First Consumer Quality Guarantees by the Federal Government: The Meat Inspection Acts of 1890 and 1891," Working Paper 88-12, Karl Ellen Centon, University of Arizona, Dec. 1988, fn. 2.

The Pure Food and Drug Act was initially quite trivial in effect, calling simply for the federal regulation of the content and labeling of certain food and medicinal products. The sum of $174,180 was allocated to the Bureau of Chemistry for its enforcement. In contrast, the Bureau of Animal Husbandry had its budget increased by the 1906 Meat Inspection Act for inspection purposes from $0.8 million to $3.0 million. This was a sizable jump but the 1906 Meat Act was not new. It was merely an amendment to the Meat Inspection Act of 1891.

The 1891 Act was passed in response to allegations by small local butchers and their organizations that dressed meat sent to distant markets by refrigerated railroad cars was unwholesome. Chicago meat-packing companies like Armour, Swift, Morris, and Hammond dominated the interstate dressed-beef trade. In 1890 their shares of the market were 27, 26, 24, and 12 percent (of cattle slaughtered in Chicago), respectively. Because the new refrigeration technology dramatically lowered the costs of shipments (dressed beef was roughly one-third of the weight of whole beef), local butchers' prices were vastly undercut. To fight back, local butchers attempted to discredit refrigerated beef, claiming it was unwholesome. Although their claims were unfounded, the big packers welcomed the governmental response.

The large Chicago packers had private quality controls for dressed beef and a substantial stake in protecting their brand-name reputations. But they welcomed federal inspection of beef in interstate markets, first, because federal inspection augmented their own quality assurances, and second, it gave each firm clear and accurate public information on the shipments of every other firm. This publicly provided inspection system allowed the firms to engage in pooling and market sharing arrangements with excellent assurances that no firm could cheat on sale-share agreements.

The 1891 Meat Inspection Act for interstate trade, moreover, was similar to an 1890 act on meat for export. Both acts largely benefited the producers by reinforcing each firm's quality-control standards for shipment to markets at home and abroad. Whether or not consumers benefited from the acts is unsubstantiated, but the grounds and precedents for consumer protection were established by these first inspection acts allegedly on the consumers' behalf.

FOREIGN TRADE

Between 1860 and 1920, the network of international trade underwent extensive changes and assumed its modern characteristics. From the new lands of the world came an ever-swelling flow of foodstuffs and raw materials to support the growing industrial populations and feed the furnaces and fabricating plants of industry. In exchange went the manufactured and semimanufactured products of the industrial countries—chiefly Great Britain, Germany, and the United States.

Two major forces dominated the great sweep of change. One was the rapid improvement in methods of communication and transportation. To take several instances: the first transatlantic cable began operations in 1866, a railroad line spanned the American continent in 1869, the Suez Canal was opened in the same year, and dramatic productivity gains in ocean transportation occurred over the last half of the nineteenth century. An extremely important improvement was the development of railroads in various parts of the world, making possible a flood of cheap grain from Canada, Australia, Argentina, Russia, and the Danube Valley, as well as from the midlands of the United States. In the late 1870s and early 1880s, refrigeration on vessels made possible the shipments of meats, then dairy products, and lastly fruits. To these were added the products of the tropics—rice, coffee, cocoa, vegetable oils, and tapioca. However, the shipment of grains was also of great importance in stimulating the worldwide distribution of foods.

But transportation was not the whole story. We have already described the second major force at work—improvements in metals processing. It was not by mere chance that Great Britain, Germany, and the United States rose to industrial supremacy during the nineteenth century. These were the countries that had coal and iron in abundance. England, which until 1875 was preeminent in manufactures, lost ground in the last quarter of the century to Germany and the United States. The volume of British trade increased, but England's chief role became that of a world financial leader. The United States forged to the front in iron and steel production; Germany and the United States quickly became leaders in the applied fields engendered by the scientific efforts—the electrical, chemical, and machine-tool industries.

Alternatively expressed, the United States gained new and evolving lines of comparative advantage in production as technological advances and changing factor proportions occurred. Slowly and persistently, resources at the margin were reallocated to new uses, where producers in the United States had a comparative advantage relative to foreign competitors. Figure 20-1 shows the changing composition of U.S. foreign trade between mid-century and 1900. This transition portrays the shift in U.S. comparative advantage internationally, away from agriculture and toward manufactures.

On the export side, Figure 20-1 shows that the most striking change was the decline of raw materials (for example, cotton), from three-fifths to one-fourth the total. Crude foodstuffs, which had swelled to nearly one-quarter of all exports in the late 1870s reflecting the piercing of the West by the railroad, declined to 17 percent by 1900, and continued to fall until 1915. Manufactured foodstuffs, which also had climbed to about 25 percent of the total, held fairly steady. As shown, another important trend was the rise of semimanufactures and finished manufactures. By 1915–20, together they accounted for almost half the total value of exports.

We find the opposite movements, although not as remarkable, on the import side. Crude materials rose from one-twelfth the value of imports in

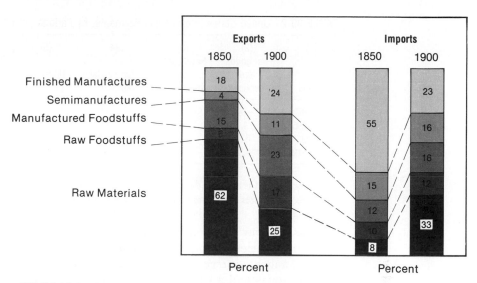

FIGURE 20-1   Composition of U.S. Foreign Trade, 1850 and 1900

Source: U.S. Department of Commerce.

1850 to one-third the value of imports by 1900. The chief crude materials imported—those that were necessary to a great industrial structure but that could not be found in the United States—were rubber, tropical fibers, and metals such as nickel and tin. Crude foodstuffs showed uneven ups and downs, but did not change materially over the half-century, as Americans imported coffee, tropical fruits, and olive and coconut oils that could be produced domestically only at great cost, if at all. Imports of semimanufactures increased somewhat, but finished manufactures declined greatly in importance as American productive capacity grew.

Finally, trade linkages altered as well. Although Europe became a more important customer of the United States than ever before after the Civil War, American exports to Europe began to decline relatively about 1885. During the 1870s and 1880s, Europeans were the recipients of more than four-fifths of all U.S. exports; by 1920, this figure had dropped to three-fifths. In the meantime, the United States remained Europe's best customer. But the sharp decline in the proportion of American imports from Europe during the years 1915–20, a result of wartime disruption, permanently injured this trade.

In the first 20 years of the twentieth century, American foreign traders found new customers in Asia and Canada, and an interest in the Latin American market was just beginning. On the import side, the Asiatic countries and Canada were furnishing a great part of the crude materials that were becoming typical U.S. imports. South America had already achieved a substantial position as a purveyor of coffee and certain key raw materials to Americans.

TABLE 20-2   United States International Payments, by Periods (in billions of dollars)

(1) Period	(2) Net goods and services	(3) Net income on investment	(4) Net capital transactions	(5) Unilateral transfers	(6) Changes in monetary gold stock[a]	(7) Errors and omissions
1850–1873	−.8	−1.0	1.6	.2		
1874–1895	1.7	−2.2	1.5	−.6	−.4	
1896–1914	6.8	−1.6	−.7	−2.6	−1.3	−.6
1915–1919	14.3	1.4	−14.1	−1.8	1.2	−1.0

[a]A minus sign indicates an addition to the U.S. monetary gold stock. Why?

Source: *Historical Statistics of the United States, Colonial Times to 1970* (Washington, D.C.: GPO, 1971), pp. 865–69.

The best way to summarize the history of American foreign trade is to examine a series of international balance-of-payments statements to see what changes occurred in the major accounts. As Table 20-2 shows, the United States had a slightly unfavorable trade balance between 1850 and 1873. Between 1874 and 1895, the balance of trade shifted to favorable, becoming markedly favorable between 1896 and 1914 and enormously favorable between 1915 and 1920. But, as we have learned, items other than merchandise enter into the international balance of payments. A persistently favorable balance of trade may be offset by "importing" the services, the securities, or the gold of other nations. It is important to understand how, as years went by, the people of the United States offset their consistently favorable balance of trade.

Table 20-2 shows that a total of $1.8 billion (columns 2 + 3) *net* was paid out by Americans over the period 1850–73. Residents of the United States could enjoy this net inflow of goods and services and pay interest and dividends on existing foreign investments largely because foreign nationals continued to make *new* investments in American businesses (column 4) usually in American railroads.[6] Another balancing item during this period was the $200 million in foreign currencies brought or sent to the United States and changed into dollars by immigrants and their families. Such payments are called *unilateral transfers* (column 5).

From 1874 to 1895, the American price level declined more than price levels abroad, so exports were stimulated more than imports. Moreover, American agricultural commodities were available to the world market in rapidly increasing quantities. When we consider that the manufacturing industries of the United States were also becoming progressively more efficient, it is hardly surprising to find that exports increased as they did.

---

[6]International investment can take one of two forms: *real* investment or *portfolio* investment. Real investment occurs when a foreign company builds a plant for operation in the domestic market of another country. Portfolio investment takes place when foreign nationals buy the securities (stocks and bonds) of firms in another country.

During these years, the favorable *trade* balance was reduced by the growing tendency of Americans to use the *services* of foreigners. Even so, Americans had net credits on current account of $1.7 billion (column 2), and foreign investors poured another $1.5 billion into this country (column 4). Offsetting the credits were more than $2 billion in interest and dividend payments to foreigners, and on balance unilateral transfers began to reverse themselves as immigrants sent substantial sums back to friends and relatives in their countries of origin. To make up the balance, the United States imported $400 million in gold (column 6).

During the prosperous years of 1896–1914, the United States came into its own as an economic power. The favorable balance of trade shot up to over $9 billion, but this figure was cut to less than $7 billion by purchases of services from foreigners. Interest and dividend payments to foreign investors, remittances of immigrants to their families, a slight reversal of the capital flow, and an inward gold flow secured a balance of payments.

Finally, the First World War brought a change in the balance of payments of the United States. The last rows of Table 20-2 show the great jump in the favorable balance of trade created by the prodigious demand for American war materials. Until the United States entered the war in 1917, European nations financed their purchases here by selling their American securities and by shipping gold. When the United States finally took its position on the side of the Allies, continued large purchases of American goods were made possible by U.S. government loans to the Allies of nearly $10 billion. At this stage in the progress of international relations, the United States did not think of *giving* assistance to its friends. It was expected that one day the loans would be repaid, but just how Europeans would earn the dollar exchange to repay the loans was not made clear. During the war, Americans, as private citizens, began to invest heavily in the fortunes of other countries; in these few years they received more income in the form of interest and dividends than they paid out. At last, the United States had shifted from a debtor position to the position of a major creditor. Although the capital flow reversal had preceded the First World War, the effect was to involve the United States in world matters on an unprecedented scale. As we will see in the following sections, to some we appeared to be a new imperialist country.

THE ACCEPTANCE OF PROTECTIONIST DOCTRINES

In a Victorian world that paid more than lip service to the ideal of laissez-faire, the untrammeled price system was allowed to allocate domestic resources more than ever before or ever since. But the United States, which—like most of Europe—had long been protectionist, became more so beginning with the Civil War. Setting up ever-higher tariff walls, Americans led the way in trying to control trade with other countries in the interests of national policy. To observe these changes systematically, Figure 20-2 traces a hundred-year history of tariffs, or customs duties as a percent of the value of (1) total imports and (2) dutiable imports. As revealed there, compared to earlier times, on the eve of the Civil War the nation traded in an atmosphere of limited protection.

In 1861, maximum U.S. tariffs were not more than 24 percent and averaged less than 20 percent on dutiable commodities. The national prosperity of the last 15 years before the Civil War seemed to refute protectionists' arguments that a healthy economy required high duties. Yet by 1864, the trend of nearly three decades was reversed so sharply and positively as to put the United States on a high protective-tariff basis for nearly three-quarters of a century. There was no widespread demand for such a change in policy; only in the manufacturing centers were the old arguments for protection advanced with enthusiasm. To win the votes of the industrial East, the Republicans advocated higher tariffs during the campaign of 1860. After the returns were in but before Lincoln's inauguration, Congress passed the Morrill Act of 1861—the first in a long series of laws levying ever-higher taxes on imports. Thus, the first step was taken before the war, but such major increases came only after the southern congressional opponents of the tariff were not in the Congress. The requirements of Civil War financing, at a time when import duties and domestic excises furnished the principal revenues, provided an excuse for raising tariffs to unprecedented highs. By 1865, the *average* level of duties was 48 percent, and protection was granted to nearly any commodity for which it was requested.

As Bennett Baack and Edward Ray have shown, the structure of tariffs and subsequent levels of protection throughout the late nineteenth century were explained largely by the profit motives of special interest groups.[7] While high tariffs were not in the national interest, Congress was besieged by special interests offering political support in exchange for market security and protection. No organized consumer groups existed to cry out against higher prices on imports, and congressmen found it to their individual advantage to trade higher tariffs for political capital.

For 25 years after the war, a few leaders in both political parties attempted to reduce the "war tariffs." In 1872, to ward off drastic downward reductions that appeared imminent, protectionist forces in Washington agreed to a flat 10-percent decrease in all protective duties. But in 1875, the earlier levels were restored, and it appeared for a time that consumers and the electorate were resigned to permanently high import rates. Yet people were increasingly persuaded that protective tariffs were, in effect, a tax that raised consumer-goods prices—and there was a growing suspicion that high levels

---

[7]Bennett D. Baack and Edward J. Ray, "The Political Economy of Tariff Policy: A Case Study of the United States," *Explorations in Economic History* 20 (1983): 73–93.

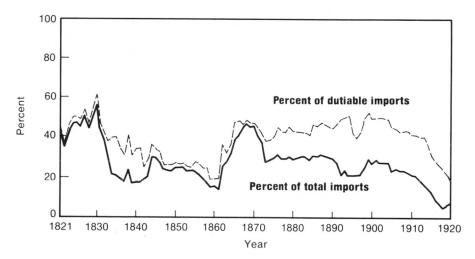

FIGURE 20-2   Customs Duties as a Percent of (1) Total Imports and (2) Dutiable Imports, 1821–1920. Tariffs slid steadily until the Civil War, then the new politics set forth a sharp increase and new level that was maintained until the turn of the century.

Source: *Historical Statistics of the United States, Colonial Times to 1970* (Washington, D.C.: GPO, 1971), p. 888.

of protection fostered the rapid growth of business combinations. During his first administration, President Grover Cleveland placed the Democrats squarely on the side of greater freedom of trade, but two Democratic assaults on the protective system produced disappointingly modest results. Cleveland's defeat in 1888 blasted hopes of genuine reform. The McKinley tariff of 1890 raised the average level of protection in the immediate following year to 50 percent, increased the articles on the dutiable list, and reaffirmed the Republican commitment to the support of high tariffs. Following insignificant reductions during Cleveland's second term, the Dingley Act of 1897 raised duties above 50 percent. More goods, by value, were now taxed as imports than were admitted free. As might be expected, free goods were mostly raw and semifinished commodities requiring further processing, but even some farm products, raw wool, and hides were placed in a protected category.

The prosperity of 1897–1914 made it easy to defend high-tariff policies. It was argued that the country was experiencing a high level of employment and economic activity *because* tariffs were high. Yet by 1900, American industry had obviously come of age. American manufacturers were competing in the markets of Europe; it was apparent, especially in the metal-processing industries, that most American firms needed no protection. The textile industries, which had enjoyed the benefits of high tariffs for a century, paid the lowest wages, had the highest unemployment, and suffered from the rigors of competition more than any other class of producers. Moreover, it was readily demonstrable by this time that import duties usually raised the prices of protected articles to consumers. As the populace felt the pressures of rising living costs in the first decade of the century, voters blamed the tariffs, and Democratic politicians exploited this political unrest. When the Payne–Aldrich bill of 1909 failed to bring any relief from high tariffs, there was widespread political protest.

In the campaign of 1912, the Democrats promised a downward revision of import duties—a revision that was carried out in the Underwood–Simmons bill of 1913. These reductions, while substantial, were not sufficient to satisfy everyone; however, iron and steel were placed on the free list, and duties on cost-of-living items like cotton and woolen textiles were sharply reduced. The result was a simplified tariff structure, still of protective significance, with average duties about one-half of what they had been for several decades. During President Woodrow Wilson's administration, the average level of the tariffs was slightly below 25 percent—almost the level that had prevailed just before 1860.

THE UNITED STATES IN AN IMPERIALIST WORLD[8]

The erection of trade barriers by European countries in the nineteenth century (Great Britain being a notable exception) marked a revival of national self-consciousness in the Old World. One manifestation of the revived nationalism was a "new" imperialism. During most of the nineteenth century, Europeans did not seek physical expansion, because the economically and politically powerful countries were not convinced that colonies were a paying proposition. But in the early 1880s, western Europeans became obsessed with a desire to own more of the earth's surface. Africa's interior, which before 1875 was almost entirely unexplored and unmapped, was partitioned among the major European powers. In Asia, the French took over all of Indochina, British India annexed Burma, and Britain extended its hold over the Malay states. China, although it avoided physical disintegration, nevertheless had to make humiliating economic concessions to the major European powers. By the end of the nineteenth century, there was not much of the world left to colonize.

Pressures built up by the Industrial Revolution encouraged this second expansion of Europe. By 1875, the productive output of the industries that were first mechanized was becoming very great. Industrialists and merchants thought that Asiatic and African markets would furnish an outlet for the rapidly increasing production of cheap manufactured goods. The centuries-old notion that a government ought to have command over its

---

[8]For a most interesting reinterpretation of the issue of American imperialism, see Stanley Lebergott, "The Return to U.S. Imperialism, 1890–1929," *Journal of Economic History* 40 (1980): 229–52.

sources of raw materials also played a strong part in the colonization. The most important of all the economic reasons, however, was the profit seeking of those who had capital to invest; the frantic efforts to seize thinly populated and apparently worthless land was stimulated by the hope of return from the fruits of the land or from mineral discoveries. Reinforcing the purely economic motives was a desire for national glory. Private citizens took personal pride in the fact that their country owned exotic territories and dominated weaker peoples. Nor could it be denied, in a day when sea power was still vital to a nation's military success, that national strength was buttressed by the ownership of naval stations in widely separated parts of the globe.

The importance of economic motives in the search for colonial possessions is suggested by the fact that the nations that industrialized first were the leaders in late colonization. Great Britain, France, Belgium, and the Netherlands obtained the prize possessions. Germany, Italy, and Japan— the last major powers except Russia to feel the full impact of the Industrial Revolution—came out of the competition with the poorest prizes.

At this time, the United States maintained its preoccupation with internal affairs. As long as great areas of unexploited land lay within its borders, there were no pressures for physical expansion; inside its large free-trade area, domestic markets developed rapidly enough to forestall concern for foreign markets. When America finally decided to expand, the decision had little to do with profits. U.S. imperialistic ventures were primarily the result of (1) a strong nationalist feeling engendered by a few politicians and vociferous newspaper editors and (2) the desire to achieve an impregnable military position in the Caribbean, the Central American Isthmus, and the Pacific.

But whatever its real motives, American expansion ostensibly sprang either from pure altruism or from accidents of history. The only territory outside the continental limits that the United States acquired before 1898 was Alaska, which was presumed at the time to be almost worthless. In 1893–94, there was agitation to annex Hawaii, but the American people would not stand for the high-handed methods proposed to depose the old Hawaiian government. Business interests generally were opposed to the needless and tragic Spanish-American War despite the chauvinist campaign of the Hearst newspapers, and there was little popular enthusiasm for the conflict until a martial spirit was whipped up by the destruction of the U.S. battleship *Maine* in Havana harbor on February 15, 1898. But the quick and favorable outcome of that "nice little war," as it was sometimes called, forced Americans to make decisions regarding expansion outside their continental borders.

The first decisions concerned disposition of the former Spanish colonies of Cuba, Puerto Rico, and the Philippines. Cuba was given nominal independence and Puerto Rico received territorial status, but the Platt Amendment of 1901 so restricted Cuban independence that Cuba, in effect, became a protectorate of the United States. Instead of granting independence to the Philippines, the United States claimed them as a colonial possession. With these islands in the Pacific (see Map 20-1) and a growing interest in trade with the Orient, the United States insisted on an "open-door" policy in China and, in general, on economic opportunities in East Asia equal to those of the European powers. By the Hay–Varilla Treaty of 1903, the United States acquired a perpetual lease of the Panama Canal Zone from the newly independent Republic of Panama, and the completion of the canal in 1914 assured a lasting American interest in the Caribbean and Central America.

Indeed, two years before construction of the canal began, the policy known as the "Roosevelt Corollary" to the Monroe Doctrine had been pronounced. In a message to Congress in 1904, President Theodore Roosevelt enunciated a principle that was to make the Monroe Doctrine an excuse for intervention in the affairs of Latin American countries. Because, Roosevelt argued, chronic weakness of a government might require some "civilized" nation to restore order and since, by the Monroe Doctrine, European interference would not be tolerated, the United States might be forced to exercise police power in "flagrant cases of wrongdoing or impotence." Europeans were not disturbed by such an assumption of international police power, but Latin Americans were. And they had reason to be apprehensive.

The United States did not take long to apply the Roosevelt Corollary. When the Dominican Republic could not meet its financial obligations, certain European states threatened to collect payments by force. Roosevelt's new doctrine required American intervention to forestall such moves. A treaty was signed in 1905 giving the United States authority to collect customs duties, of which 55 percent was to be paid to foreign creditors. In 1916, the Dominican government tried to escape American domination, and the U.S. Marines were sent in to quell the rebellion. In 1914, Haiti was made a protectorate of the United States, again with the aid of the Marines. American forces landed so often in Nicaragua that the succession of episodes became a standing joke.

After the 1910 revolution in Mexico against the old dictator, Porfirio Diaz, American and other foreign investors, who were heavily committed in railroads and oil, pressed for intervention and the restoration of order. For a time, President Wilson encouraged Latin Americans by failing to invade Mexico. But "watchful waiting" could last just so long amid the cries of outrage at the destruction of American property, and U.S. politicians were unable to tolerate these repeated affronts to American honor. Troops crossed onto Mexican soil in 1914 and 1917—the second time, under the leadership of Black Jack Pershing, to seize the "bandit" Pancho Villa. With the adoption of the Mexican Constitution in 1917, the turmoil subsided temporarily, only to begin again in the early 1920s.

The word "imperialism" has had a pejorative connotation in the American lexicon, even when the United States, flanked by the Atlantic and

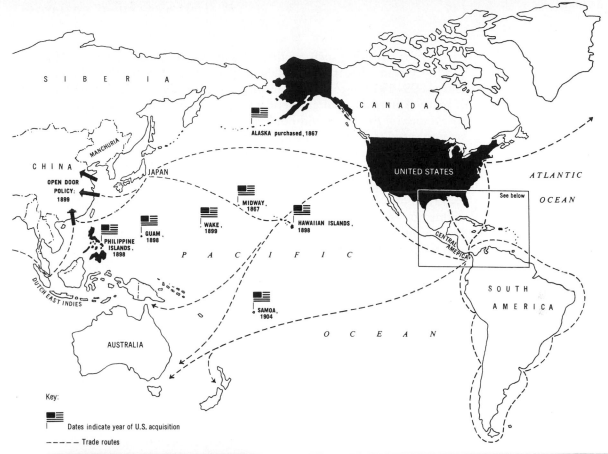

S I B E R I A

C A N A D A

ALASKA purchased, 1867

MANCHURIA

CHINA

OPEN DOOR
POLICY,
1899

JAPAN

UNITED STATES

A T L A N T I C

O C E A N

See below

CENTRAL AMERICA

MIDWAY,
1867

WAKE,
1899

HAWAIIAN ISLANDS,
1898

GUAM
1898

PHILIPPINE
ISLANDS,
1898

DUTCH EAST INDIES

P A C I F I C

O C E A N

SOUTH
AMERICA

SAMOA,
1904

AUSTRALIA

Key:

Dates indicate year of U.S. acquisition

- - - - Trade routes

U N I T E D   S T A T E S

A T L A N T I C

O C E A N

GULF OF MEXICO

BAHAMA
ISLANDS

CUBA

Guantánamo

U.S. NAVAL BASE

DOMINICAN
REPUBLIC

VIRGIN ISLANDS, 1916

MEXICO

BR.
HONDURAS

GUATEMALA

HONDURAS

EL SALVADOR

NICARAGUA

JAMAICA

HAITI

PUERTO RICO,
1898

CARIBBEAN SEA

COSTA RICA

PANAMA CANAL
ZONE, 1903

P A N A M A

VENEZUELA

BR. GUIANA

PACIFIC OCEAN

COLOMBIA

MAP 20-1 New Imperialism: A reluctant and sometimes uncertain America assumed colonial responsibility as a consequence of expanding world interests, wider-ranging trade, and growing industrial might.

Pacific, was annexing such exotic places as the Philippines, Samoa, Hawaii, and the Virgin Islands, which allegedly provided essential naval bases. The years 1898–1918 were marked by an uncomfortable conviction on the part of many Americans that euphemisms, including *manifest destiny* and *extending the areas of freedom,* could not long cover up such high-handed methods as those used to wrest the Panama Canal Zone from Colombia. Nor would it be possible to maintain approval for a diplomacy that was devoted largely to promoting or protecting the private financial or commercial interests of the United States. If American capital was willing to seek profits in the countries of Central America and the Caribbean, it should also have been willing to take the risks of venturing under unstable governments. Some Americans contended, of course, that the benighted Latins were better off with the improved sanitation, better educational facilities, and higher incomes that usually resulted from American intervention. Our friends to the south were not properly impressed, however—apparently preferring freedom to material gain.

The imperialistic ventures of the United States made the nation turn its attention outside itself and increase its military strength. Offsetting these gains were the fears and hatreds built up among natural allies in Central and South America, with whose aspirations Americans should have been in sympathy. It would take a new generation of Americans and a second world war to remove part of this emotional conflict. Even so, the harm of two decades of harsh diplomacy could not be undone. As the fires of world revolution were kindled among the disadvantaged peoples of the world, beginning in the 1950s, it was not hard to perceive the permanent injury to U.S. international relationships that was inflicted by America's early experiments with imperialism.

SELECTED REFERENCES AND SUGGESTED READINGS

Ashworth, William. *A Short History of the International Economy 1850–1950.* London: Longmans, Green, 1952.

Baack, Bennett D., and Edward John Ray. "The Political Economy of Tariff Policy: A Case Study of the United States." *Explorations in Economic History* 20 (1983): 73–93.

———. "Tariff Policy and Comparative Advantage in the Iron and Steel Industry, 1870–1929." *Explorations in Economic History* 11 (1973): 3–24.

Bullock, Charles J., John H. Williams, and Rufus S. Tucker. "The Balance of Trade of the United States." *Review of Economic Statistics* 1 (1919).

Chandler, Alfred D., Jr. *The Visible Hand: The Managerial Revolution in America.* Cambridge: Belknap Press of Harvard Univ. Press, 1977.

Clark, V. S. *History of Manufacturers in the United States,* vol. 1. New York: McGraw-Hill, 1929.

Galloway, Lowell E., and Richard K. Vedder. "The Increasing Urbanization Thesis: Did 'New Immigrants' to the United States Have a Particular Fondness for Urban Life?" *Explorations in Economic History* 8 (1971): 305–20.

Grauman, John V. "Population Growth." In *International Encyclopedia of the Social Sciences,* vol. 12. New York: Macmillan, 1968.

Hawke, G. R. "The United States Tariff and Industrial Protection in the Late Nineteenth Century." *Economic History Review* 28 (1975).

Lebergott, Stanley. "The Return to U.S. Imperialism, 1890–1929." *Journal of Economic History* 40 (1980): 229–52.

Lipsey, Robert. "Foreign Trade." In *American Economic Growth: An Economist's History of the United States,* ed. Lance E. Davis et al. New York: Harper & Row, 1972.

Livesay, Harold, and Glenn Porter. *Merchants and Manufacturers.* Baltimore: Johns Hopkins Univ. Press, 1971.

Pred, A. R. *The Spatial Dynamics of U.S. Urban-Industrial Growth, 1800–1914.* Cambridge: MIT Press, 1966.

Simon, Matthew. "The United States Balance of Payments, 1861–1900." *Studies in Income and Wealth,* vol. 24, National Bureau of Economic Research. Princeton: Princeton Univ. Press, 1960.

Smolensky, Eugene. "Industrial Location and Urban Growth." In *American Economic Growth: An Economist's History of the United States,* ed. Lance E. Davis, et al. New York: Harper & Row, 1972.

Taussig, Frank W. *The Tariff History of the United States.* New York: Putnam's, 1932.

Weiher, Kenneth. "The Cotton Industry and Southern Urbanization, 1880–1930." *Explorations in Economic History* 14 (1977): 120–40.

Weiss, Thomas. "Urbanization and the Growth of the Service Workforce." *Explorations in Economic History* 8 (1971): 241–58.

———. "The Industrial Distribution of the Urban and Rural Workforces: Estimates for the United States, 1870–1910." *Journal of Economic History* 32 (1972): 919–37.

Williamson, Jeffrey G. *American Growth and the Balance of Payments.* Chapel Hill: Univ. of North Carolina Press, 1964.

4

THE MODERN ERA, 1920 TO THE PRESENT

1. Two world wars engulfed the industrial nations with enormous costs in terms of labor, capital, and human suffering. The United States emerged from each conflict with its domestic capital intact, and with an enhanced position relative to its economic rivals.

2. The stock market boom of the roaring twenties ended abruptly in the great crash of 1929. The depression that followed was a cataclysm of unparalleled magnitude. At its height in 1933 one worker out of four was unemployed.

3. The federal government took a much larger role in the economic life of the nation than it ever had before. Regulation of economic activity increased, and welfare expenditures increased. In 1929 federal spending amounted to 3.0 percent of GNP; in 1985 it was 23.7 percent.

4. The world's monetary system was radically altered as the gold standard disappeared. Eventually, exchange rates were allowed to vary at least partly in response to market forces. Inflation became a chronic problem in the United States and many other industrial countries after the Second World War.

5. In the 1960s a civil rights revolution shook the nation. Efforts were made through the government to secure greater economic progress for women, blacks, and other disadvantaged groups.

6. Technological and economic progress continued to be rapid. In the U.S. economy agriculture and industry declined in relative terms and the service sector rose. U.S. living standards reached new heights. But in the 1970s signs of a slowdown emerged and Americans wondered whether a disturbing new trend had begun.

CHAPTER 21

The First World War

MOBILIZING FOR WAR

Europe in 1914 was ready for war; numerous fears and grievances gnawed at political leaders. European armed forces had been built up in a sustained arms race and European states had been linked together in military alliances. The assassination of Austrian Archduke Ferdinand by a Serbian on June 28, 1914, set off a chain reaction that soon engulfed Europe in war. A German advance into France quickly became bogged down in a trench war, a stalemate that could not be broken even with the loss of incredible numbers of men. In America the first economic reaction was a financial panic. The stock market was temporarily closed, and there was considerable pressure on the banks, as depositors tried to convert their money into gold. But the crisis soon passed. Under the Aldrich-Vreeland Act, passed after the crisis of 1907, banks were allowed to temporarily issue an emergency currency to substitute for gold, and the issue of this currency in 1914 put an end to the crisis. At the peak, this currency amounted to nearly one-quarter of the currency in the hands of the public before the war.[1]

As the period of American neutrality (from the outbreak of the war in 1914 until America's entry in April 1917) continued, it became clear that the war would be immensely profitable for American business. Reflecting this, the stock market gradually recovered. America supplied food and industrial products to the Allies, payments for which were made by extinguishing foreign holdings of American debt, by shipping gold across the Atlantic, and by incurring new debts in the United States. When the war began, the United States was a debtor, the normal status for a developing country. When the war ended, the United States was in the position of a mature creditor that held much of the world's stock of monetary gold.

---

[1]Milton Friedman and Anna J. Schwartz, *A Monetary History of the United States* (Princeton: Princeton Univ. Press, 1963), p. 172.

Throughout the period of "neutrality," the Wilson administration had tilted toward the Allies, partly no doubt due to our common cultural heritage, but also due to the continuing violence of Germany's policy of unrestricted submarine warfare. However, many in the United States felt considerable antiwar sentiment. President Wilson's Secretary of State William Jennings Bryan resigned in protest over what he considered Wilson's prowar stance, and Wilson ran for reelection in 1916 on the slogan that he kept us out of war. But in early 1917 Germany's resumption of submarine warfare, and other events, pushed America into the war.

America's involvement in the war would be short. General John J. Pershing arrived in Paris in June 1917 to direct the American Expeditionary Force, and the Armistice with Germany was signed on November 11, 1918, just 17 months later. Songwriter and performer George M. Cohan caught the spirit of the times with his patriotic song "Over There." The song warned that the "Yanks are coming" and promised, accurately, that "It will soon be over, over there." American forces were instrumental in turning back the last German offensives and breaking German resistance. But the song didn't warn about the deadly battles that lay ahead. The armed forces were increased from 179,000 in 1916 to 2,897,000 in 1918. Vast amounts of arms and weapons were produced, and a great shipbuilding program was launched, although the war ended before any ships came on line. Americans took part in bitter fighting, and 116,000 Americans died in military service. Financing that military effort was a tremendous increase in spending by the federal government, from 1.5 percent of GNP in 1916 to 24.2 percent in 1918.

American involvement began when the United States was operating close to full employment (the unemployment rate in 1916 was 5.1 percent). So, unlike beginning the Second World War, when America had reserves of underutilized labor and capital, greatly increasing the production of weapons and other military supplies was not possible without reducing civilian consumption.

FINANCING THE WAR

There are three basic ways of financing a war: (1) taxation, (2) borrowing from the public, and (3) creating money. And during the war the United States relied on all three. On October 3, 1917, after considerable wrangling, Congress passed the War Revenue Act. This act increased corporate and personal income taxes, and established excise, excess profits (for business) and luxury taxes. Table 21-1 shows the total financial cost of the war and how it was distributed among various sources of finance. Taxation was clearly an important source, but secondary to borrowing.

It is easy to see why Congress preferred borrowing to taxation. When taxes are raised, it is altogether too clear who is doing what to whom. Borrowing, however, produces less obvious costs. If interest rates rise as a result

TABLE 21-1   Financing the First World War, 1917–19

	Total (in thousands)	Percent
War Expenditures	$30,984,980	100.0%
Taxes	7,591,447	24.5
Borrowing from the Public	19,024,533	61.4
Creating New Money	4,369,000	14.1

Note: Total wartime expenditures are calculated as the sum of federal government expenditures in 1917 through 1919 less three times average expenditures in 1916. The deduction is an estimate of civilian expenditures. The figure for borrowing from the public is an upper bound estimate; see text.

Source: *Historical Statistics of the United States, Colonial Times to 1970* (Washington, D.C.: GPO, 1976), series Y336 (expenditures), Y335 (taxes), X594 (U.S. government obligations held by commercial banks), and X800 (U.S. government obligations held by the Federal Reserve).

of government borrowing, those hurt may blame the market or other private-sector borrowers. But it could also be argued that the war was an investment—"to make the world safe for democracy" in Wilson's phrase. If future generations would benefit, why should the current generation bear all the burden of the war?[2] As Table 21-1 shows, borrowing was the primary method Congress adopted for financing the war; borrowing from the general public accounted for 61.4 percent of total financing.

Secretary of the Treasury William Gibbs McAdoo had studied the financing of the Civil War and concluded that Salmon Chase, the Secretary of the Treasury during that conflict, had made a mistake in not linking the purchase of war bonds more closely to patriotism. So McAdoo launched an aggressive program to market bonds during the war, to "capitalize patriotism."[3] It is true that Jay Cooke had pushed government debt hard during the Civil War, but McAdoo had something else in mind. He organized huge bond rallies where the crowds were exhorted to buy war bonds by stars such as Mary Pickford and Douglas Fairbanks. Charlie Chaplin even made a film showing how the purchase of war bonds helped the government finance the war. Thrift stamps (at a cost of $.25) were sold in schools, post offices, and factories. How much all of this helped, however, is open to question. Despite all the hoopla, the government found that it could not issue bonds that paid much below the going market rate.[4]

As in wars past and wars to come, the government relied on the third means of financing the war: creating new money. In earlier wars this mechanism had been simpler and easier for the public to understand. In the

---

[2]A numerical example will make the difference between taxing and borrowing clear. If a middle-aged man is taxed $100 in 1918 to pay for the war, that is the end of the story; in later years his son pays nothing. But if the same man buys a bond for $100, then in later years he and his son will both be taxed to pay back the interest and principal on the bond.

[3]David M. Kennedy, *Over Here* (Oxford: Oxford Univ. Press, 1980), p. 105.

[4]Margaret G. Myers, *A Financial History of the United States* (New York: Columbia Univ. Press, 1970), pp. 280–83; Schultz and Caine, *Financial Development of the United States* (New York: Prentice-Hall, 1937), pp. 533–39.

In 1918 Douglas Fairbanks, Mary Pickford, and Charles Chaplin sell war bonds during a rally in Philadelphia.

Revolutionary War the government had printed Continental dollars; in the Civil War, Greenbacks. Now the mechanism was more complicated. When the Fed bought bonds on the open market, it did so by creating deposits that had not existed before. When put in the banking system, these new deposits became the basis for a further expansion of money and credit by the banks. The banks, of course, were not forced to invest these additional funds in government bonds, but to the extent that they did, further finance for the war was made available. All told, as Table 21-1 shows, the Fed and the commercial banking system acquired over $4 billion worth of government bonds, about 14 percent of total war finance. Even this figure understates the effect of money creation to some extent, because the banks made personal loans that were secured by government bonds to purchasers of bonds. Although such transactions show up on the books of the bank as a personal loan, they are really the indirect purchase of a government bond.

The net result of financing the war in part by creating money was a tremendous increase in the stock of money and the price level. As Table 21-2 shows, the stock of money about doubled during the war, and with it the level of prices. Note, however, that prices did not rise in the exact same proportion as money per unit of real output, as a naive version of the quantity theory of money would predict. Prices rose faster than money per

TABLE 21-2   Money and Prices during the First World War

Year	Stock of Money (in Billions)	Money per Unit of Real Net National Product (1914 = 100)	Implicit Net National Product Deflator (1914 = 100)
1914	$16.39	100.0	100.0
1915	17.59	104.1	103.1
1916	20.85	105.2	116.5
1917	24.37	126.3	143.9
1918	26.73	126.1	165.5
1919	31.01	140.5	168.0
1920	34.80	166.0	191.7

Source: Milton Friedman and Anna J. Schwartz, *Monetary Trends in the United States and the United Kingdom* (Chicago: Univ. of Chicago Press, 1982), pp. 123–24.

unit of output (velocity rose) during 1915–18, more slowly during 1918–19, and then more rapidly during 1919–20. This pattern can be explained in a fairly straightforward manner. During the years of threatened and actual war, the fear of inflation and expanding economic activity encouraged people to spend their money rapidly, thus causing the very thing they feared. The end of the war created expectations of a return to price stability that worked against rapid turnover of money balances. Finally, an unexpected postwar boom rekindled real economic activity and expectations of inflation, thus adding to the flow of spending.

Inflation is analogous to a tax on money: the cash in your pocket goes down in value while the government acquires real resources. But like deficit financing, money creation has the attractive political property that it may be a hidden tax. The public may blame profiteers for the inflation rather than monetary policy. This was true in earlier wars as well as this one. But here the complex ways in which the government could finance itself through money creation may have hidden the tax even better. All of this does not mean, of course, that there is no justification for financing war through money creation. If the government can tax houses, tobacco, automobiles, and alcohol, why not money? But it does suggest that money creation is likely to be overused. In a later section we will examine some of the ways the government tried to cope with the resulting increase in prices.

The Human Costs of the War

In adding up dollars we should not forget that federal spending paid for only part of the cost of the war. The major part of the cost was borne by the men and women in the armed forces. To some extent we can think of these costs in monetary terms. The draft (created in April 1917) can be thought of as another kind of tax. The tax paid is the difference between what the country would have had to pay a soldier to get his services voluntarily, and what it actually paid him. Offsetting this tax were veteran's benefits paid after the war. But in the end it is impossible to put dollar signs on all of the costs of the war. In all, as we noted, 116,516 died while in military service; 53,402, in battle. Another 204,002 received nonmortal wounds.[5]

CENTRAL CONTROLS

Unlike during the Civil War, a real attempt was made during the First World War to direct the economy from the top down. To a large extent this was due to the ideological temper of the times. The battle between those who favored and those who opposed organizing the economy through the market was particularly sharp in the Progressive Era. And there were strong antimarket factions in both the Democratic and Republican parties. Germany, which was widely perceived to be both powerful and organized along centralized lines, was also an example. By the end of the war, Washington, D.C., was bulging with agencies set up to cope with a vast array of problems that had emerged in the economy. The Capital Issues Committee limited issues of securities by the private sector; the War Trade Board had powers over imports and exports; and so on. Existing agencies were often also given new powers. We cannot examine all of these agencies here. But a closer look at a few of them will show how the government tried to manage the war economy.

In August 1917, Congress passed the Lever Food and Fuel Control Act. Herbert Clark Hoover was appointed the Food Administrator. Hoover enjoyed a reputation as a brilliant administrator—he was then serving as the director of the Commission for the Relief of Belgium—and his reputation grew with his performance as Food Administrator. His job was to try to maintain an adequate supply of food both to the domestic market and to the Allies, while at the same time preventing excessive increases in prices. The tools given to Hoover were limited, although his philosophy of voluntary cooperation with government would not have allowed him to seek greater authority. Direct control of prices, with penalties for violation, and formal rationing were out. But the Food Administrator was given the power to license food dealers. The license could then be revoked if the dealer failed to go along with Food Administration price policies. In place of formal rationing, Hoover called for various voluntary conservation measures. Retailers were encouraged (or permitted depending on how you look at it) to tie sales of wheat flour with less desirable substitutes such as rye or potato flour. The resulting mixture could be baked into a loaf of "Victory Bread."

---

[5] *Historical Statistic of the United States, Colonial Times to 1970* (Washington, D.C.: GPO, 1976), series Y879, Y880, Y882.

Herbert Hoover (at far right) was the brilliant director of the Commission for the Relief of Belgium and Food Administrator during the First World War.

Of course, it was really a hidden price increase. The true price of the wheat flour was the direct amount paid plus the difference between what the buyer paid for the less desirable flour, and what he would voluntarily pay for it. By such half measures, food prices were controlled and output rationed.

Harry A. Garfield, the Fuel Administrator, was not as successful. In the extremely cold winter of 1917–1918, parts of the country ran short of coal for a variety of reasons: unusual cold, unusual demands on the rail network, and perhaps the Fuel Administration's price and allocation policies. After Eastern factories were shut down for a brief period to reduce coal demand and give the railroads time to move more coal, the problem abated. But as a result, the Fuel Administration came in for considerable criticism, adding to already widespread criticism of Wilson's management of the war economy. One energy conservation measure introduced during the war, however, proved to be permanent—daylight savings time.

In response to the mounting criticism of the war effort, Wilson reorganized the most ambitious of the war agencies, the War Industries Board, in March of 1918 and placed at its head Bernard Baruch. Baruch was a successful Wall Street speculator. But perhaps because of his background (he was a Southerner and a Jew) he was something of an outsider on the Street.

He was also a Democrat. Baruch's stint at the War Industries Board was brief; the Armistice came eight months later. But he drew strong conclusions from his experience. In subsequent years he repeatedly argued that the wartime example of the War Industries Board pointed the way toward peacetime cooperation between business and industry. And he argued that it showed the importance of doing away with the market and relying on centralized administration in wartime.

In part, the War Industries Board relied on striking various deals with individual industries, Baruch's model for postwar cooperation. It also issued priorities. A contract was given a government priority rating—AA, A, B, C, and D—and if a conflict arose, a producer had to fill an A order before a B order and so on. It sounds good. Why rely on the market when a government planner could determine priorities in line with national goals? But when firms were given their own power to set priorities in order to save administrative resources, industry soon became choked with high priority contracts; the natural tendency was to give everything the highest priority. During the Second World War "priorities inflation" nearly wrecked the system. Although Baruch and other observers who saw the war as a triumph for central planning did not like to admit it, the market still provided the basic means for reallocating resources during the war. Manufacturers pursuing profitable war contracts stopped producing for the private sector and started producing only for the government.

LABOR DURING THE WAR YEARS

The war tightened labor markets as the demand for labor was increased by government contracts financed in part by borrowing and creating new money. The supply of labor was reduced by the end of immigration from abroad and by drafting men into the armed forces. Adjustments in the labor market, however, were far from smooth. Table 21-3 shows that money incomes rose yearly, but real incomes fluctuated. In the year 1917 in particular, money incomes were up 14.5 percent over 1916, but consumer prices were up 16.1 percent, so real wages had actually fallen. It is not surprising that 1917 was a year of strikes, a record 4,450 of them. Strikes were particularly acute west of the Mississippi where a combination of low wages, harsh working conditions, uncompromising employers, and radical labor unions caused bitter labor disputes.

The Wilson administration responded pragmatically. In a few cases it threatened strikers through the draft and in other ways. In most cases, however, it was more accommodating. War contracts generally included provisions calling for higher wages and better working conditions, although they did not provide the goal dearest to the heart of organized labor, the closed shop. When a strike of railroad workers threatened to disrupt the industry that was at the heart of the war effort, the administration nation-

TABLE 21-3   Annual Earnings, 1914–20

Year	Money Earnings of All Employees after Deduction for Unemployment	Real Earnings of All Employees after Deduction for Unemployment (in 1914 dollars)
1914	$ 555	$555
1915	547	541
1916	647	595
1917	748	586
1918	972	648
1919	1,117	648
1920	1,236	619

Source: *Historical Statistic of the United States, Colonial Times to 1970* (Washington, D.C.: GPO 1976), series D723, D725.

alized the railroads. Under government control the railroads provided improved working conditions and higher wages, while raising shipping costs only modestly. The result was an operating deficit made up by the government. The railroads were finally returned to private ownership in 1920.

As we can see in Table 21-3, money earnings leaped upward in 1918 by 22.6 percent, outrunning the cost of living; real earnings probably reached an all time high.[6] Organized labor was extremely optimistic in the immediate postwar period. Union membership was up, and the public's view of the conservative wing of the labor movement, under the leadership of Samuel Gompers, was also high. But the hopes of many labor leaders for a new era in labor relations soon came to an end. An Industrial Conference called by the President in 1919 with representatives from labor, management, and the public under Baruch's leadership ended in failure. More important, an attempt to organize the steel industry, then the leader of American industry, was beaten back after a long and bitter strike.

Women were one source of potential labor. On the political front the Wilson administration strongly supported the right of women to vote, calling the vote "vital to the winning of the war."[7] As a result the Nineteenth Amendment to the Constitution giving women the right to vote was finally adopted in 1920. Some women served with the armed forces in Europe, usually as nurses or telephone operators. Women also made important contributions in industry with about 1 million taking up war work. But the war did not mean a breakthrough in the economic role of women. Few took jobs in heavy industry. First time hires were relatively few. Many who entered the labor force were women who had been previously employed while single and returned temporarily to help their families cope with war and inflation.

---

[6] Price indices are not as accurate for these years as they normally are because of price controls.
[7] As quoted in Kennedy, *Over Here,* p. 284.

Women workers made important contributions to industry during the war years.

When the war ended, the role of women in the labor force returned to what it had been before. Partly this was due to pressure from labor unions and other sectors for women to make room for veterans; partly it was the result of older economic and social pressures. In 1920 fewer women, both married and single, were working in the labor force than in 1910.

Perhaps no group of workers seized the opportunities provided by the war more eagerly than blacks. Deprived of a steady stream of immigrants from Europe, northern industry at last looked to blacks in the South for a supply of labor. Beginning in 1914 agents for northern industries fanned out across the South to recruit workers. Transportation north was often free. A mass exodus of black workers began from the rural South to northern cities. New York, Detroit, St. Louis, Cleveland, and Chicago saw a steady stream of newcomers. In a few places in the South, the new shortage of labor actually led to improved race relations. But in others the white South reacted in the old way with harassment, detentions, and beatings.

Southerners also tried to prevent northern agents from recruiting in the South, but nothing the South could do could stem the flow of blacks north. Northern industry provided higher wages; and northern cities, greater freedom. But competition between blacks and white workers soon exploded in violent race riots; in one of the worst, in Chicago in 1919, 13 whites and 23 blacks were killed.

AFTER THE ARMISTICE

Demobilization followed the simplest possible path after the Armistice ended the war. Soldiers were mustered out of the Army as fast as possible; war contracts were canceled; government bureaus were closed. The War Industries Board was closed down so fast that Bernard Baruch ended up paying the way home for some of his employees out of his own pocket. It is tempting to argue that a more gradual winding down of affairs would have eased the transition to a peacetime economy. But this is far from obvious. The problem is much like that faced by modern-day countries trying to liberalize their economies: should they do it all at once or only gradually? Individuals can be helped by a gradual transition; life is a lot easier for a government bureaucrat, for example, if he can look for permanent employment while holding on to his old job. On the other hand, the longer resources are held in unproductive uses, the greater the loss of output for the economy as a whole.

Despite the rapid demobilization of the economy, things never quite returned to where they had been before. As economic historian Robert Higgs shows in his challenging book *Crisis and Leviathan,* the war left many legacies.[8] Some were financial, such as increased federal spending for interest on the national debt, veteran's benefits, and other long-term costs of the war. But perhaps more important was the ideological legacy. While most Americans were more than willing to return to the old patterns, some such as Bernard Baruch drew the lesson that the economy would work better if the government played a major role in coordinating economic activity. Such ideas lay dormant during the prosperous 1920s, but would become important in the depressed 1930s.

The immediate effect of the Armistice and the cancellation of war contracts was a slowdown in the economy. Although price controls had disappeared abruptly with the Armistice, there was no postwar burst of inflation. Instead, prices remained roughly level for some months. But then in 1919, a vigorous boom got underway and prices began to rise rapidly. The Fed realized that its policy of holding its discount rate below market rates was adding to inflationary pressures. Banks found it profitable to borrow from

---

[8] Higgs, *Crisis and Leviathan* (New York: Oxford Univ. Press, 1987), chapter 7.

the Fed and then expand their own lending. But the Fed was reluctant to raise its rates because higher interest rates might have depressed the values of the large amount of government war loans in the market.

But finally, possibly because its own reserves of gold were becoming depleted, the Fed acted. In late 1919 and early 1920 the Fed raised its discount rate. The increase in January 1920 from 4.75 percent to 6 percent was the sharpest single increase in the short history of the system. On June 1, the discount rate was raised again to 7 percent. These increases sent a strong signal to the market that credit would soon be tight. In addition, there were sharp breaks in other sectors of the economy. Agricultural prices, for example, fell throughout much of the world as European production recovered. As a result, the economy went into a severe recession. From 1920 to 1921 nominal net national product fell 18 percent and real net national product fell 4 percent. But the recession was also very brief; it resembled what has come to be called a "V-shaped" recession, straight down and straight back up again. One reason for this, perhaps, is that even though the number of bank failures rose substantially, there was no financial panic. As we will see later, the sharp contraction of 1929 to 1930 produced a financial panic that drove the economy even deeper into depression.

After the economy recovered from the recession of 1920–21, it entered a long period of economic expansion. So vigorous was the expansion that many people began to believe that a new age of continuous prosperity had arrived—the "Roaring Twenties."

SELECTED REFERENCES AND SUGGESTED READINGS

Clark, John Maurice. "The Basis of War-Time Collectivism." *American Economic Review* 7 (1917): 772–90.

———. *The Costs of the War to the American People.* New Haven: Yale Univ. Press, 1931.

Clarkson, Grosvenor B. *Industrial America in the World War.* Boston: Houghton Mifflin, 1923.

Coit, Margaret L. *Mr. Baruch.* Boston: Houghton, Mifflin, 1957.

Cuff, Robert D. *The War Industries Board: Business-Government Relations During World War I.* Baltimore: Johns Hopkins Univ. Press, 1973.

———. "We Band of Brothers—Woodrow Wilson's War Managers." *The Canadian Review of American Studies* 2 (1974): 135–48.

Cuff, Robert D., and Melvin I. Urofsky. "The Steel Industry and Price Fixing During World War I." *Business History Review* 44 (Autumn 1970).

Friedman, Milton. "Price, Income, and Monetary Changes in Three Wartime Periods." *American Economic Review* 42 (May 1952). Reprinted in *The Optimum Quantity of Money and Other Essays.* Chicago: Aldine, 1969.

Friedman, Milton, and Anna J. Schwartz. *A Monetary History of the United States.* Princeton: Princeton Univ. Press, 1963.

Fussell, Paul. *The Great War and Modern Memory.* New York: Oxford Univ. Press, 1975.

Gilbert, Charles. *American Financing of World War I.* Westport, Conn.: Greenwood, 1970.

Higgs, Robert. *Crisis and Leviathan: Critical Episodes in the Growth of American Government.* New York: Oxford Univ. Press, 1987.

Himmelberg, Robert F. "The War Industries Board and the Antitrust Question in 1918." *Journal of American History* 52 (1965): 378–402.

Johnson, James P. "The Wilsonians as War Managers: Coal and the 1917–1918 Winter Crisis." *Prologue* 9 (1977): 193–208.

Kennedy, David M. *Over Here: The First World War and American Society.* Oxford: Oxford Univ. Press, 1980.

Koistinen, Paul A. C. "The 'Industrial-Military Complex' in Historical Perspective: World War I." *Business History Review* 41 (1967): 378–403.

Kuznets, Simon. *National Product War and Prewar.* New York: National Bureau of Economic Research, Occasional Paper 17, 1944.

Litman, Simon. *Prices and Price Control in Great Britain and the United States during the World War.* New York: Oxford Univ. Press, 1920.

Leuchtenburg, William E. "The New Deal and the Analogue of War." In *Change and Continuity in Twentieth-Century America,* ed. John Braeman et al., New York: Harper & Row, 1966.

Mullendore, William Clinton. *History of the United States Food Administration, 1917–1919.* Stanford: Stanford Univ. Press, 1941.

Myers, Margaret G. *A Financial History of the United States.* New York: Columbia Univ. Press, 1970.

Rockoff, Hugh. *Drastic Measures: A History of Wage and Price Controls in the United States.* New York: Cambridge Univ. Press, 1984.

Samuelson, Paul A., and Everett Hagen. *After the War, 1918–1920: Military and Economic Demobilization of the United States.* Washington D.C.: GPO, 1943.

Scheiber, Jane Lang, and Harry N. Scheiber. "The Wilson Administration and the Wartime Mobilization of Black Americans, 1917–1918." *Labor History* 10 (1969): 433–58.

Schultz, William J., and M. R. Caine. *Financial Development of the United States.* New York: Prentice-Hall, 1937.

Stein, Herbert. *Government Price Policy in the United States During the War.* Williamstown, Mass.: Williams College, 1939.

Taussig, Frank W. "Price Fixing as Seen by a Price Fixer." *Quarterly Journal of Economics* 33 (1919): 205–41.

Urofsky, Melvin I. *Big Steel and the Wilson Administration: A Study in Business-Government Relations.* Columbus: Ohio State Univ. Press, 1969.

CHAPTER 22

The Roaring Twenties

IN THE AFTERMATH OF WAR

When the First World War ended, the promising young song writer, Harry Donaldson, cast his lot with the just-organized Irving Berlin Music Company to begin a long and mutually profitable association. His smash 1919 hit was at once a question and a prophetic answer: "How ya gonna keep 'em down on the farm after they've seen Paree?" How indeed? Millions of young Americans had been wrested from the placid boredom of country life, marking the beginning of the end of an agrarian society. To be sure, only a fraction of them ever saw Paris, and some got no farther than Camp Funston. But country boy, small-town bookkeeper, and city millworkers alike had a taste of travel that broke routine—although almost 120,000 of them died in military service.

The high pitch of wartime excitement eventually passed, of course, and there were signs that the old provincialism might return. Isolationist sentiment had prevailed in the congressional elections of 1918; and the press made it plain to all who could read that the intellectual in the White House would fight in vain for a genuine peace even if France and Britain could be persuaded from their vengeful course. In a dreadful intrusion on the rights of the individual, a moralistic minority secured passage of the Eighteenth Amendment, which took away a basic comfort of field hands, factory workers, and others, on the grounds that drinking was sinful and that poor people were not entitled to such a luxury anyway.[1] A swell of fear and hate was rising that would crest in the activities of the Ku Klux Klan, and by 1924 that wicked organization's anti-black, anti-Jewish, and anti-Roman Catholic persecutions had become a national scandal.

---

[1] The authors confess their prejudice on the issue.

454

The future nevertheless held a bright promise of prosperity and more leisure time for everybody. Women had at last gained an unequivocal right to vote, but their emancipation was broader than that. Young women in particular began to chisel away at the double standard of morality that had been typical of pre-1914 relations between the sexes; the flapper of the 1920s with her boyish bob and figure was already emerging in 1919 as the girl who could smoke men's cigarettes, drink men's whiskey, play men's games, and even work at men's jobs. There were many reasons why women gained their freedom, but a main one was that many men thought that life would be better that way. Not that freedom came easily or all at once! At least 50 years would go by before serious questions could be raised about the social wisdom of paying women less than men for the same work. In the meantime, productivity would suffer because bright women were not allowed to replace mediocre males in the workforce. The difficulties for women to move up into managerial or important administrative positions were particularly persistent.

Sometime near the end of the First World War, the number of Americans living in urban centers of 2,500 people or more passed the 50 million mark. As the Census of 1920 was to report, for the first time more than 50 percent of the population, over 54 million people, were urban dwellers. Leading the flight to the city were southern blacks who migrated northward in large numbers during the First World War. Especially magnetic to blacks were New York, Philadelphia, Washington, D.C., Chicago, St. Louis, and out west, Los Angeles. By 1930, Harlem was the concentration point of nearly 300,000 New York blacks.

Lured by the availability of jobs, the excitement of city life, and advances in transportation, nearly 15 million people were added to the number of American urbanites. Of course the number of workers in urban areas increased greatly as well, and between 1920 and 1929, the number of non-farm employees advanced from 27.4 million to 31.3 million.

Composer Donaldson's popular song implied that the upheaval of the war was moral and social rather than technological and economic. With the peculiar insight vouchsafed only to artists, he foresaw the era of speakeasies and bathtub gin, of the Untouchables and the Capone mob, of Harding's Ohio gang and Coolidge's servants of big business. It would be impossible to keep the boys down on the farm, yet in the next decades there would not really be a place for them in the city. For all their bright hopes, many who were young in 1919 would be the "lost generation" of Fitzgerald and Hemingway. The Great Depression would blight the most productive part of their lives, and the United States would not really enter the twentieth century as a world leader until the Second World War forced Americans to accept their international responsibilities. Nevertheless, the events that ensued in the 2½ decades following the First World War produced a great transformation in the U.S. economy. It began with the Roaring Twenties.

BUSINESS IN THE 1920s

The revolutionary social changes of that remarkable decade—the Noble Experiment of prohibition, the beginning of organized crime, the jazz age, the automobile and such lesser events of sheer wildness as marathon dances, flagpole sitting, and Lindberg's transatlantic flight were based on rapid economic advance and impressive economic flexibility. In the 1920s, the process of mass production accelerated and the administrations of Harding and Coolidge were openly dedicated to the principle that business should be free to grow without government meddling or interfering. With little hindrance from government, the process of mass production and marketing advanced, and businesses became even more consolidated than in earlier decades. Secretary of Commerce Herbert Hoover, among others, encouraged consolidations for reasons of production efficiency, and competing firms were allowed to form trade associations, not just to standardize tools and share technical information, but also to set prices. This movement was further solidified by the 1925 Supreme Court ruling in the Cement Manufacturer's Productive Association case. To the public's apparent delight, or disinterest, both Harding and Coolidge appointed men to the Federal Trade Commission who had little intention of enforcing the antitrust laws, either in letter or in spirit. As the years passed, banking, manufacturing, distribution, electronics, iron and steel, automobiles, and mining all became increasingly controlled by large conglomerates.

Such policies added to an environment that produced unparalleled business prosperity. Spectacular advances in the production of consumer durables, electric power, new appliances, suburban housing, and city skyscrapers highlighted the decade.

The Automobile

In many ways the automobile was the vital force of the economy of the 1920s. Annual automobile production rose from 1.5 million cars in 1921 to 4.8 million in 1929 while prices for the horseless carriage slipped steadily downward. By 1929, one American in six owned an automobile. The indirect effects of the automobile were very important for production in general. It provided important backward linkages to steel, rubber, plate glass, and petroleum, but not so much to spur them as to cushion and replace the fall in demand from cutbacks in railroad rolling stock, wagons, streetcars, and sleighs. Perhaps its main impact was on the landscape of America. The automobile not only changed the location of residences, portending the heyday of suburbia, but it also ushered in the activity of commuting to work. In addition, there were the recreational features of weekend trips and access to the country. The automobile combined travel with entertainment, and spotted the countryside with motels, hot dog stands, road signs, and gas stations.

Of course, the automobile also enlarged the demands on government—mostly for paved roads—as automobile clubs and especially farmers pressed for assistance to get out of the mud.

With the passage of the Federal Aid Road Act of 1916, the development of a national highway system began in halting, timorous fashion. The government committed itself to spending $75 million to build rural post roads; the money was to be expended by the Department of Agriculture over a period of five years. The national contribution was not to exceed 50 percent of the total construction cost, exclusive of bridges and other major structures, and was conditional on the organization of state highway departments with adequate personnel authority and sufficient equipment for initial work and subsequent maintenance. The Federal Highway Act of 1921 amended the original law by requiring that the Secretary of Agriculture, in dispensing aid, give preference to states that had designated a system of highways to receive federal aid. A designated state system was to constitute the "primary" roads of the state and was not to exceed 7 percent of the state's total highway mileage. Incidentally, in the Act of 1921, Congress appropriated as much money for a single year's construction (1922) as it had for all of the preceding five years.

Although state-legislature appropriations for roads were sporadic and uneven, they also increased from $70 million in 1918 to nearly $750 million by the end of the 1920s. In addition to this stimulus to government activity came the need for the bureaucracies to administer licensing, titles and registrations, and, of course, traffic courts.

Electricity and Appliances

A second major growth sector in the 1920s was the electric power industry. Its influence on residential living was dramatic and there was a remarkable growth of electric appliances, such as ranges, vacuum cleaners, and refrigerators. Over the decades, annual refrigerator production expanded by almost 50 times, reaching nearly 1 million units in 1930.

Accompanying these new items were marked changes in mass advertising and installment buying, which together created both a greater desire for goods and a greater ease of buying them. Whereas in 1910 advertising expenditures of all types amounted to nearly $1 billion, the figure was $2 billion by 1920 and over $2.5 billion by 1929. The age of consumer goods had arrived.

In 1922, 3 million homes had radios—to hear entertainment and advertisements—and by 1930 ownership reached 10 million. Mass entertainment (and advertisement) expanded still further through ticket sales to the movies, which doubled over the decade to almost 80 million tickets per week.

In response to this vast expanding market, the National Broadcasting Company (NBC) was formed in 1926, one year before the formation of the Columbia Broadcasting System (CBS). Predictably, a proliferation of radio

Domestic joy: Early radio appealed to listeners and had become the chief living-room enter-tainment by the late 1920s.

stations resulted and increased the outreach to mass audiences. Polling systems by telephone were used to determine program ratings, with low ratings leading to program abandonment. Certain goods became tied to particular programs, as producers sought any and all means to market their products and address the desires, fads, and fancies of the American public. For these and other reasons, the age of mass consumption, mass production, and the giant corporations became the trademark of the 1920s.

ORGANIZED LABOR

The twenties also profoundly affected Americans at work. During the First World War, the 48-hour workweek was accepted in many manufacturing industries, and by 1920 some agreements granted a half-holiday on Saturday. It was not until the very end of the decade, however, that a 48-hour week was standard for most occupations. Nevertheless, as revealed for production workers in Table 22-1, there was a fall in average hours worked by several hours per week. The implied advance in leisure for many American workers was one of the gains of the period.

Another gain was the relative absence of cyclical unemployment. Except for the hard years of 1921 and 1922, the 1920s were generally free of mass joblessness. In 1929, fairly typical of many years in the 1920s, the percentage of the civilian labor force that was unemployed by one measure was 3.2 percent. In short, the threat of unemployment was usually low, thereby contributing, along with added leisure, to the gaiety of the times.

The Paycheck

Observations on money wages are also given in Table 22-1. Although money wages failed to increase between 1920 and 1929, the impact of falling prices was to raise real wages during the decade by more than 10 percent. Further evidence on the monetary gains of nonfarm workers for a somewhat longer period are revealed in Table 22-2. Here, again, we see the important positive effects of falling prices and changes in the average price level on real earnings. The surge in prices accompanying the First World War and continuing until 1920 almost completely nullified the advances of money earnings. Real

TABLE 22-1 Average Weekly Earnings and Hours Worked of Production Workers in Manufacturing, 1920–29

Year	(1) Average Weekly Hours	(2) Average Weekly Money Earnings
1919	46.3	$21.84
1920	47.4	26.02
1921	43.1	21.94
1922	44.2	21.28
1923	45.6	23.56
1924	43.7	23.67
1925	44.5	24.11
1926	45.0	24.38
1927	45.0	24.47
1928	44.4	24.70
1929	44.2	24.76

Source: *Historical Statistics of the United States, Colonial Times to 1970* (Washington, D.C.: GPO, 1976), p. 170.

TABLE 22-2   Annual Earnings of Nonfarm Employees, 1914–29[a]

| | MONEY EARNINGS | | | REAL EARNINGS (in 1914 dollars) | | |
Year	When Employed	Income Loss from Unemployment	After Deduction for Unemployment	Consumer Price Index (1914 = 100)	When Employed	After Deduction for Unemployment
1914	$ 696	$ 65	$ 613	100.0	$ 696	$ 613
1915	692	93	597	101.1	684	591
1916	760	59	706	108.7	699	649
1917	866	76	805	127.7	678	631
1918	1,063	25	1,041	150.0	709	694
1919	1,215	26	1,174	172.5	704	681
1920	1,426	104	1,343	199.7	714	672
1921	1,330	230	1,105	178.1	747	620
1922	1,289	129	1,148	166.9	772	688
1923	1,376	44	1,313	169.7	811	774
1924	1,396	98	1,284	170.3	820	754
1925	1,420	61	1,336	174.8	812	764
1926	1,452	33	1,411	176.2	824	801
1927	1,487	64	1,399	172.8	861	810
1928	1,490	80	1,394	170.9	872	816
1929	1,534	74	1,462	170.9	898	855

[a]Excludes armed forces.

Source: Stanley Lebergott, *Manpower in Economic Growth: The American Record Since 1800* (New York: McGraw-Hill Book, 1964), p. 526. Used with the permission of McGraw-Hill Book Company.

incomes changed very little between 1914 and 1920. Alternatively, as prices began to recede after 1920, the gains in real earnings became quite pronounced. Moreover, the losses of income from unemployment, which averaged only 3.3 percent between 1923 and 1929, were comparatively small throughout the period, except from late 1920 to 1922[2]. Overall, labor's advance, at least for those in the city and in industry, was substantial.

Union Decline

Despite this surge, the 1920s were not years of advance for organized labor. As Table 22-3 shows, the number of workers holding union membership fell from over 5 million in 1920 to less than 3.5 million at the end of the decade. This fall is especially surprising in light of the rapid growth and concentration of the population and the labor force.

It is true that throughout the 1920s, employers continued their effective use of the anti-union instruments developed before the First World War.

---

[2]These unemployment rates from Stanley Lebergott, *Manpower in Economic Growth: The American Record Since 1800* (New York: McGraw Hill Book, 1964) were challenged and revised upward to 5.1 percent by R. M. Coen, "Labor Force Unemployment in the 1920's and 1930's: A Re-examination Based on Postwar Experience,"*The Review of Economics and Statistics* 55, (1973): 46–55. Such an adjustment, if accepted, would alter the level but not the trend in the progress of labor in the 1923-29 period.

TABLE 22-3 Union Membership, 1920–29 (in thousands)

Year	Number	Year	Number
1920	5,048	1925	3,519
1921	4,781	1926	3,502
1922	4,027	1927	3,546
1923	3,622	1928	3,480
1924	3,536	1929	3,461

Source: U.S. Bureau of Labor Statistics, "Handbook of Labor Statistics 1971," *Monthly Labor Review* Jan. 1972).

They discriminated, in hiring and firing, against employees who joined or organized unions. The hated yellow-dog contract, judged constitutional by the Supreme Court, was commonly employed to prevent union membership and to serve as a basis of civil suits against unions that persuaded employees to violate the contract. But the most useful weapon was the injunction by which a court could forbid, at least temporarily, such practices as picketing, secondary boycotts, and the feeding of strikers by the union. During the 1920s, except for legislation applying to railroads, government generally did not interfere with labor relations. Although such policies slowed organized labor's progress, it is difficult to accept such actions as the primary cause of an absolute decline in union membership.

It seems most likely that the upsurge in membership associated with the First World War was not firmly established. The wartime increase in membership resulted in part from agreements from the unions to a nonstrike pledge in return for lessened opposition to union organization. The sharp recession of 1921–22, which raised levels of unemployment to 11 percent undermined labor's bargaining power. In addition, beginning with the important strike against U.S. Steel in 1916, a host of postwar strikes failed, except perhaps to anger employers. It is pertinent to note from Table 23-3 that most of the membership decline had occurred by 1923, after which there was only minor further attrition. Company welfare programs designed to entice workers away from their own organizations also took their toll. But the inertia of the 1924–29 period must be attributed primarily to two other causes. The increase in real wages left the greater part of labor comfortable and generally satisfied. More importantly, the powerful AFL unions, whose members especially benefited during the building boom, took no interest in organizing the growing mass-production industries. Added to this was a generally tired and unimaginative leadership.

THE END OF FREE IMMIGRATION

Labor, however, finally did achieve one of its most cherished objectives in the 1920s—limiting immigration. Partially this was the result of growing hostility to the "new immigrants" from southern and eastern Europe who had constituted the bulk of the large influx of immigrants in the years leading up to the war. Racism, including the activities of the Ku Klux Klan, was on the rise. Sometimes racism was given a pseudo-scientific veneer by writers who claimed that the new immigrants were less able and intelligent than native Americans. But even as we take our stand against racism, we should not overlook labor's basic economic point that increasing the supply of labor, other things being equal, tends to lower the real wage.

The war, moreover, seemed to upset the balance in the world labor market. In the years preceding the First World War the economy of central Europe had developed rapidly; now it lay in ruins, saddled for years to come with heavy reparation payments. Farther east, the Russian economy, starting from a lower base, had also been exhausted by years of war and revolution. The war had also created a vast new supply of shipping that was now coming on line. Would not America, if it continued a policy of unlimited immigration, be swamped by immigrants from continental Europe once the war was over? That was the question haunting American policymakers. This fear seemed to be confirmed by the resumption of a high level of immigration immediately after the war. Slightly more than 800,000 immigrants entered the United States between June 1920 and June 1921.

The Emergency Immigration Act of 1921 restricted the number of people to be admitted from any country to 3 percent of that nation's share of U.S. population in 1910. In 1924 a new law limited immigration to 2 percent based on the 1890 U.S. population. This change made the restriction even more effective against the new immigrants from southern and eastern Europe. This law also completely eliminated immigration from East Asia, terminating President Theodore Roosevelt's informal "Gentleman's Agreement" of 1907 with the Japanese. The law also set a maximum limit of 150,000 immigrants with quotas based on 1920 to become effective in 1929. The effects of these restrictions on the flow of immigrants can be seen in Table 22-4. The contrast between the years before 1914 and the 1920s is obvious. The

TABLE 22-4   Immigration, 1910–29

Year	New Arrivals	Year	New Arrivals
1910	1,041,570	1920	430,001
1911	878,587	1921	805,228
1912	838,172	1922	309,556
1913	1,197,892	1923	522,919
1914	1,218,480	1924	706,896
1915	326,700	1925	294,314
1916	298,826	1926	304,488
1917	295,403	1927	335,175
1918	110,618	1928	307,255
1919	141,132	1929	279,678

Source: *Historical Statistics of the United States, Colonial Times to 1970* (Washington, D.C.: GPO, 1976), series C89.

limit on immigration was clearly effective in cutting down the number of legal immigrants.

How much did limiting immigration contribute to the rise in real wages, reduction in hours of work, and other benefits realized by labor in the 1920s? No one, as far as we know, has attempted the difficult task of answering this question. To answer it we would have to know the elasticity of the supply of immigrants and of domestic labor, and the elasticity of the demand for labor in the United States, among other variables.

THE ECONOMIC POSITION OF THE AMERICAN FARMER

Recall that for a quarter of a century before 1920, American agriculture was moving to a stronger position in the economy. Indeed, the 1896–1915 period—sometimes nostalgically referred to as "Agriculture's Golden Era"—was one of rapid improvement in the economic position of the American farmer. Although farm production slackened its rate of increase to approximately one-half of 1 percent per annum over these years, farm prices and gross farm income rose steadily. The agricultural population remained constant at 32 million, as the natural rate of increase (650,000 per year toward the close of the period) was offset by the movement of farmers to city occupations. Consequently, from 1911 to 1915, income per person employed in agriculture was approximately two-thirds that of those employed in industry—a remarkably favorable ratio that was not achieved again until the Second World War[3]. Moreover, farmers' assets—land, buildings, and livestock,—continually appreciated in value.[4] Many people on the land were still abysmally poor, but the economic position of large-scale producers was much improved. Then a worldwide surge in demand stemming from the war stimulated farm production, boosted prices, and amplified the rise in incomes even beyond that which had been underway for the previous 20 years. In short, the agrarian sector was extraordinarily prosperous in the years just preceding the 1920s.

Economic Distress in Agriculture

During 1919 and the early months of 1920, hopes for the future of farming continued to be bright. But in mid-1920, farm prices began a precipitous drop. From an index of 234 in June 1920 (1909–14 = 100), prices received by farmers fell to an index of 112 a year later. By the end of 1921, despite

---

[3] Due to the relatively favorable ratio of income per worker in agriculture to income per worker in industry, the quinquennium 1911–15 has ever since been urged as the basis of computing "parity" income for agriculture.

[4] See Theodore W. Schultz, *Agriculture in an Unstable Economy* (New York: McGraw-Hill, 1945), pp. 114–16.

a slight recovery, wheat was selling for $0.93 a bushel that 18 months previously had sold for $2.58, and corn was down to $0.41 from $1.86. Many commodities did not suffer quite so severe a decline, but prices seriously decreased in all lines of production. A gradual recovery followed and the farm price index stood at 159 in August 1925. After a small decline during 1926 and 1927, prices remained stable until the end of 1929.

The deflation of 1920 and 1921 was severe in the industrial sector and overall economy too, but it was not as great as in the agriculture sector. Prices *paid* by farmers fell until the end of 1921 and then remained stable until the close of the decade. The terms of exchange (the ratio of the prices received by the farmers to the prices they paid) ran against agriculture during the break in prices and then recovered, so that by 1925 they were not much below the figure of 1920. This index fell a little during the next few years, but in 1929 it was still not far from the level of prosperous prewar years. On the whole, then, it does not seem that agriculture should have suffered much in the middle and late 1920s. Moreover, recent research by Charles F. Holt suggests a rise in income for the average farmer in the 1920s. Yet, there was great agitation for remedial farm legislation during these years. Why?

The answer seems to lie in the fact that a large part of the farmers, especially in the Midwest, had incurred fixed indebtedness at what turned out to be the wrong time. During the decade 1910–20, land values had risen sharply; at the height of the boom, the best lands in Iowa and Illinois sold for as much as $500 an acre—a fantastically high figure for the time. In those ten years, many high-grade farms doubled in value. To buy such high-priced properties farmers often borrowed heavily, and farm-mortgage debt increased rapidly. Long-term debt rose from $3.2 billion in 1910 to $8.4 billion in 1920 and, along with the distress that accompanied the deflation of the early 1920s and the fall of farm land values in many areas, farm debt reached a high of nearly $11 billion in 1923. Although a majority of American farmers may not have been burdened with fixed debt payments during these years, such charges undoubtedly created difficulties for a large and extremely vocal minority. In any case, the number of farm mortgage foreclosures advanced sharply at the turn of the decade and then remained high throughout the entire 1920s. According to H. Thomas Johnson the rate increased from 3.8 per 1,000 mortgaged farms foreclosed in 1920 (2.8 in 1918) to 6.4 in 1921, 11.2 in 1922, and hovered between 14 and 17 per 1,000 in 1929.[5]

First Efforts at Farm Legislation

As early as 1919, Secretary of Agriculture David Franklin Houston, who was not as optimistic as most agricultural leaders, called for a conference

[5] H. Thomas Johnson, "Postwar Optimism and the Rural Financial Crisis of the 1920s," *Explorations in Economic History* 11 (Winter 1973–74) p. 176.

to discuss possible agricultural problems, but not until disaster struck in the form of sharply falling prices and incomes was this proposal seriously considered. Violent protests from farmers in the late months of 1920 led Congress to create a Joint Commission of Agricultural Inquiry in 1921. The Commission reported the obvious—that farm troubles were the result of general business depression and a decline in exports—and recommended measures to help cooperative marketing associations, improve credit facilities, and extend research activities by the Department of Agriculture. More important was the National Agricultural Conference, called early in 1922 by Secretary of Agriculture Henry C. Wallace. Despite the administration's attitude expressed by President Harding that "the farmer must be ready to help himself," many radical proposals were heard at this conference. In its report, the idea of parity for agriculture was first made explicit, and the slogan "Equality for Agriculture" was offered. There was recognition of the fact that in times of a decreasing demand for goods, manufacturers reduced production and lowered prices slowly, if at all, whereas farmers maintained or even increased production and took the consequences in the form of sharply falling prices. It was argued that agriculture as a whole was *entitled* to its fair share of the national income and that justice would be achieved if the ratio of the prices farmers received to the prices they paid were kept equal to the ratio that had prevailed from 1910 to 1914.

Throughout the 1920s, various ideas were proposed aimed at securing parity prices or "fair-exchange values" for agricultural products. Most readily acceptable to professional farm supporters and politicians were the McNary–Haugen bills, considered by Congress between 1924 and 1928. They were well received because they made use of traditional devices, including a high tariff on agricultural products. The fair-exchange value of each farm product was to be determined; the fair value was to be a price that would have pre-First World War purchasing power. This "fair" price was to be maintained in the domestic market in two ways. First, a tariff was to protect the home market from imports. Second, a private corporation chartered by the federal government was to buy a sufficient amount of each commodity to force its price up to the computed fair-value level. The corporation could in turn sell the acquired commodities. Obviously, if the purchases had been necessary to raise prices, the commodities could not be sold in the domestic market. Thus, it was proposed that they be sold abroad at the world price, which would presumably be lower than the supported American price. Administrative expenses and operating losses would be shared among the producing farmers. For every bale of cotton or bushel of wheat sold, a tax called an "equalization fee" would be charged to the grower. This tax would be used to defray all expenses of operating the price-support plan. The farmer would gain insofar as the additional amount of income resulting from higher prices exceeded the tax expense.

The McNary–Haugen bills were twice passed by Congress and twice vetoed by President Calvin Coolidge. But the agitation of the 1920s did secure special privileges for agriculture. For one, the Capper-Volstead law of 1922 exempted farmers' cooperatives from the threat of prosecution for violation of the antitrust laws. Also, the Federal Intermediate Credit Act of 1923 provided for twelve intermediate credit banks that would rediscount agricultural paper maturing within three years for commercial banks and other lending agencies.[6] To achieve the broader aims of price and income maintenance, there were two major efforts. A naïve belief in the tariff as a device to raise the prices of farm products, which had been traditionally exported *not* imported, led to "protection" for agriculture, culminating in the high duties of the Smoot–Hawley Act of 1929. More significant was the passage of the Agricultural Marketing Act of 1929, which was the outcome of Republican campaign promises of the previous year. The first law committing the federal government to a policy of stabilizing farm prices, the 1929 Act worked as much as possible through nongovernment institutions. The Act established a Federal Farm Board with the primary function of encouraging the formation of cooperative marketing associations. The board was also authorized to establish "stabilization corporations" to be owned by the cooperatives, which would use a $500 million fund to carry on price-support operations.

But the supply of farm output was highly elastic. Without the means to control output, or greatly increased financial backing, such price-support legislation was doomed to failure. Nevertheless, the policy discussions of the 1920s set the stage for the massive government interference in agriculture that was to follow in the 1930s.

REVERSALS IN CONSERVATION POLICY

Unlike new government advances in agriculture, but consistent with the "hands-off" policies afforded business, the 1920s witnessed setbacks in the role of government control of valued natural resources. Indeed, between the administrations of Woodrow Wilson and Franklin D. Roosevelt, the cause of conservation suffered under the public management of natural resources. The first blow to enthusiasm for public measures was dealt in the Presidency of Warren G. Harding. In 1915, President Wilson had set aside Naval Oil Reserve No. 3 in Wyoming. The reserve was named Teapot Dome after a butte located on it, and its supervision and that of the previously established California reserves were entrusted to the Secretary of the Navy. President Harding illegally transferred the administration of these reserves to Secretary of the Interior Albert B. Fall—a confirmed enemy of the conservation movement. Fall granted contracts to private oil companies, allowing them to take oil from the naval reserves to the point of exhaustion

---

[6]Nonemergency farm credit needs were pretty well taken care of with the passage of this act, for the Federal Farm Loan Act of 1916 had established twelve Federal Land Banks to provide long-term loans to farmers through cooperative borrowing groups.

in exchange for the construction of storage tanks on both coasts. When the fraud became known, control of the oil reserves was restored to the Secretary of the Navy, but "Teapot Dome" became a rallying cry for those who wished to oppose government ownership and control of natural resources.

The trend away from federal conservation activities that became established during the early 1920s was not lessened under Herbert Hoover. Both the President and his Secretary of the Interior, Ray Lyman Wilbur, flatly supported the transfer of all unappropriated and unreserved lands to the western states. A commission—appointed by President Hoover to make recommendations regarding future land policies—supported the proposal of ceding the remaining public domain to the states. But even westerners, including those with powerful livestock interests, were opposed to the idea, and Congress refused to enact a bill containing the Commission's recommendations.

The development of the Forest Service gained impetus during the 1920s. The policy was to cut and sell only mature timber from the national forests. Efforts were made to introduce the most up-to-date methods of cutting and planting, so that a substantial future supply of timber would be assured. There was a remarkable improvement in the administration of the range lands within the national forests. Essentially, however, nothing new was added to the conservation policy of Theodore Roosevelt that had been enunciated and practiced early in the twentieth century.

THE DISTRIBUTION OF INCOME

Our image of the wealthy during the 1920s as self-satisfied and self-indulgent is not kind. We see them drinking champagne and dancing the Charleston, ignoring the growing misery around them and the warnings of seers that such behavior could only end in tragedy. Early studies of the distribution of income to some extent confirm that the rich had grown relatively richer, and the poor poorer, during the 1920s. In his pioneering work published in 1953, Simon Kuznets shows, for example, that the share of disposable income received by the top 1 percent of the population increased from 11.80 percent in 1920 to 18.92 percent in 1929.[7] Furthermore, Charles Holt, working from Kuznets' data, argues that all of the increases in real income in the 1920s went to upper-income groups and that most of the population merely held firm or lost ground.[8]

---

[7] *Historical Statistics of the United States, Colonial Times to 1970* (Washington, D.C.: GPO, 1976), series G341. These series are drawn from Simon Kuznets, *Shares of Upper Income Groups in Income and Savings* (New York: National Bureau of Economic Research, 1953). Kuznets, the father of national income accounting, was later awarded the Nobel Prize.
[8] Charles Holt, "Who Benefited from the Prosperity of the Twenties?" *Explorations in Economic History* 14 (1977): 277–89.

More recent research, however, muddies the waters. Gene Smiley points out that the upward trend in the share of income going to the richest fractions of the population was biased upward because it was based on tax returns.[9] Tax rates for the rich were lowered substantially in the 1920s, encouraging people to shift their wealth into assets yielding taxable income and to report income that went unreported previously. Kuznets was aware of these problems but was unable to adjust his data for them. Jeffrey Williamson and Peter Lindert, in a landmark study of American inequality, draw attention to the long-run dimension of the problem.[10] A long trend toward increased inequality had been interrupted by the First World War. So some increase in inequality in the 1920s was to be expected. Whatever the increase was, it probably represented a return to the conditions before the war.

Stanley Lebergott in an imaginative study shifts the emphasis to the standard of living. He makes a strong case that whatever the changes in the distribution of income, it is nevertheless clear that increases in the standard of living were widespread in the 1920s. Here, for example, are three of his many homely examples: the percentage of families with electric lighting increased from 35 to 68 during the 1920s, the percentage of families with washing machines increased from 8 to 24, and the percentage of households with inside flush toilets increased from 20 to 51.[11] The distribution of income was far from equal in 1929, but the evidence that American policymakers should have been more concerned about it than in previous years is far from clear.

THE GREAT BULL MARKET

The premier economic event in the 1920s, at least in the mind of the general public, is the great stock market boom. Stock prices rose steadily in the 1920s, but in 1928 and the first three quarters of 1929 they rocketed upward. Table 22-5 shows what happened to two price averages between 1922 and 1929. In seven years prices more than tripled. Between 1928 and 1929 the average stock (column 1) rose 26.5 percent in value. It seemed that getting rich was easy; just put money in the stock market and sit back and wait. Typical of the times was an article by financier John Jacob Raskob in the *Ladies Home Journal* with the optimistic title "Everybody Ought to Be Rich."[12]

---

[9] Gene Smiley, "Did Incomes for Most of the Population Fall from 1923 through 1929?" *Journal of Economic History* 42 (1983): 209–16.
[10] Jeffrey Williamson and Peter Lindert, *American Inequality: A Microeconomic History* (New York: Academic Press, 1981), chapter 12.
[11] Stanley Lebergott, *The American Economy* (Princeton: Princeton Univ. Press, 1962), pp. 248–99, *passim.*
[12] As quoted in John Kenneth Galbraith, *The Great Crash of 1929* (Boston: Houghton Mifflin, 1961,) p. 57.

TABLE 22-5   The Stock Market, 1922–29

Year	(1) Standard & Poor's Common Stock Index (All Stocks)	(2) Standard & Poor's Common Stock Index (Industrials)	(3) Ratio of Stock Price to Dividend
1922	100	100	18.62
1923	102	103	18.52
1924	108	108	19.05
1925	133	137	21.05
1926	150	158	19.08
1927	182	197	21.19
1928	237	266	26.18
1929	309	336	27.40

Source: *Historical Statistics of the United States, Colonial Times to 1970* (Washington, D.C.: GPO, 1976), series X495, X496, X480.

What caused the great bull market? Various economic factors have been suggested. Earnings and dividends paid by corporations rose in the late 1920s, but stock prices rose even faster. Consider column 3 of Table 22-5 that shows the ratio of stock prices to dividends. In 1922 an investor had to pay $18.62 for each dollar of current dividends; by 1929 that figure had climbed to $27.40.

Of course, people do not invest on the assumption that dividends will remain the same forever. One of the favorites of the bull market was Radio Corporation of America (RCA), which had never paid a dividend. It was bought on the assumption (a valid one) that it would pay great dividends in the future. George Sirkin in an interesting comment on the bull market argues that if earnings growth in the years immediately preceding the stock market crash are projected forward, then only relatively few stocks could be considered overvalued at the market's peak. But Eugene White points out that Sirkin's result depends on projecting earnings from a very favorable period of years.[13] This begs the question. Why did the market choose to base its projections on the most favorable years?

If earnings did not drive the market, did credit conditions? At that time much stock was bought on margin. The buyer would put down, say, 50 percent of the value of the stock in cash and borrow the remaining 50 percent from the broker.[14] Consider what this "leverage" means to the buyer of stock. A speculator buys $1,000 worth of stock, putting down $500 and borrowing $500 at, say, 10 percent interest. Now suppose the price of the stock rises to $1,200, an increase of 20 percent, while it pays a dividend of

---

[13]Eugene White, "When the Ticker Ran Late: The Stock Market Boom and Crash of 1929," in *Panics and Crashes in Historical Perspective* (Homewood, IL.: Dow Jones-Irwin, 1989).

[14]It is sometimes assumed that margin requirements were extremely low in the boom, but most brokers required 45 to 50 percent down. See Galbraith, *The Great Crash,* p. 37.

5 percent. The speculator sells his stock, pays back the loan plus interest ($550) and keeps $700. He has earned a profit of 40 percent ($200 ÷ $500), even though the market has gone up only 20 percent, and the dividend was only 5 percent. But what is true going up is also true going down. Suppose the stock decreases in value to $800, a 20 percent loss in value. Then, after repaying the loan with interest, the speculator is left with only $300. He has suffered a 40 percent loss in value even though the value of his shares has gone down only 20 percent. Where did the brokers get the money to lend to stock speculators? The brokerage houses borrowed the money from banks in the form of "call loans" (loans that had to be repaid on demand and secured by the purchased securities).

Some historians have argued that it was the willingness of the banks to supply call loans that caused the bull market. But a sophisticated study of the supply and demand for loans by Eugene White shows that the supply of loans to the market did not shift outward.[15] Instead, the increasing demand for loans moved the market along the supply curve for loans. Credit was pulled into the stock market from other sectors by the rising interest rates being paid on call loans. The call loan rate rose dramatically during the boom, from 4.36 percent in 1922 to 7.74 percent in 1929, showing at the very least that the demand for loans grew faster than the supply.[16]

The true explanation for the boom, if there ever is one, will have to be provided by the social psychologists. It was an optimistic age. Business was booming. There seemed to be no reason why it could not keep on booming, providing an ever higher standard of living for the average American. The stock market reflected that optimism. And for the skeptical there was always the assumption that they would be able to beat the crowd out the door when the market began to tumble. The crash came in October 1929, but that story is more appropriate for the next chapter on the Great Depression.

INTERNATIONAL DEVELOPMENTS

Two problems dominated the international scene during the 1920s: German war reparations (and Allied war debts to the United States), and the reestablishment of the international gold standard. The Treaty of Versailles that ended the First World War called for Germany to make large payments to France and the other Allies to compensate for damages caused by German forces during the war. It quickly became apparent that Germany lacked the economic strength and political cohesion to make the payments on schedule. Part of the problem was that Germany would need to produce large surpluses in its balance of trade in order to make the reparations payments, but economic policies, tariff policy for example, in the United

[15] White, "When the Ticker Ran Late."
[16] *Historical Statistics of the United States, Colonial Times to 1970* (Washington, D.C.: GPO, 1976), series X447.

States and elsewhere were not helpful. Germany did benefit, however, from the surge in the stock market and the related willingness of Americans to buy foreign debt; Americans lent heavily to Germany in the 1920s.

In 1924 under the Dawes Plan, German debts were scaled down, and a large loan mostly from the United States was floated to help Germany restore its currency after the disastrous hyperinflation of 1923. Further reductions in payments were made under the Young Plan of 1929. In retrospect, most historians agree that trying to extract reparations from Germany was a mistake, and that the wiser policy, as after the Second World War, would have been to help restore the German economy as rapidly as possible.[17]

It was taken for granted in the 1920s that restoring the gold standard was necessary to achieve lasting prosperity. If each country made its currency convertible into gold, exchange rates would be fixed, and the free flow of capital across international borders would be assured. Monetary authorities, moreover, would be forced to be circumspect in the amount of money they created (to avoid an outflow of gold) and inflation would be prevented. Britain, and particularly its bankers, was anxious to return to the gold standard at the pre-war parity (the prewar price of pounds in terms of dollars) because it would help to restore the position of London as the world's leading financial center. Britain finally did return to the gold standard in 1924, but it appears that the pound was overvalued at the pre-war rate. (The new rate was $4.86 per pound but the equilibrium price where supply and demand for pounds would balance was probably less, say $4.40). The high rate made it hard to export British goods and contributed to a long period of hard times in Britain.[18]

To Americans, however, the problems of Europe seemed far away. American monetary and fiscal policy was influenced primarily by domestic considerations, and, with the exception of the agricultural sector, things seemed to be moving smoothly.

MONETARY AND FISCAL POLICY

The 1920s were a period of growing prestige for the Fed. It is not hard to see why. Table 22-6 shows that after the sharp but brief recession of 1920–21 the economy advanced smoothly. Real income rose steadily year after year as did the stock of money. Prices, judging by the net national product deflator, were stable after 1922.

What influenced the Fed's policy during these years? Surprisingly, one fact that did not influence policy was the large number of bank closings.

---

[17] John Maynard Keynes warned of the dangers of trying to extract reparations from Germany in *The Economic Consequences of the Peace* (New York: Harcourt, Brace & World, 1920).
[18] Once again Keynes warned against a mistaken policy, *The Economic Consequences of Mr. Churchill* (London: L. and V. Woolf, 1925).

TABLE 22-6   Money, Prices, and Real Income, 1920–29

Year	Stock of Money (in billions)	Implicit Price Deflator (1929 = 100)	Real National Income (in billions of 1929 dollars)
1920	$34.80	121.7	$62.208
1921	$32.85	103.7	$59.567
1922	$33.72	98.6	$63.859
1923	$36.60	100.9	$73.460
1924	$38.58	99.6	$75.559
1925	$42.05	101.6	$77.343
1926	$43.68	102.1	$82.807
1927	$44.73	99.4	$83.623
1928	$46.42	100.1	$84.918
1929	$46.60	100.0	$90.308

Source: Milton Friedman and Anna J. Schwartz, *Monetary Trends in the United States and the United Kingdom* (Chicago: Univ. of Chicago Press, 1982), p. 125.

Year after year in the 1920s closures numbered in the hundreds; the peak year was 1926 when 975 banks closed. The Fed concluded that these banks (mostly in rural areas) were plagued by bad management, unrealistic loans to farmers made during the war boom, and increased competition due to the rise of the automobile. (The automobile increased the ability of borrowers and depositors to shop for favorable terms). It followed that simply allowing these banks to close strengthened the banking system as a whole. Although it is hard to imagine the Fed taking such a callous position in today's political climate, there was probably a good deal of truth in the analysis. Unfortunately, this analysis was carried into the 1930s when high rates of bank failures under very different economic conditions undermined confidence in the banking system as a whole.

An important series of papers by Eugene White clarifies the nature of the weakness in the rural banking system and its role in the breakdown of the banking system in the early 1930s. To a large extent the problem was the product of legislation that prohibited branch banking. Small unit banks were unable to diversify their loan portfolios and had no resources to draw on during periods of temporary illiquidity. The states tried various deposit insurance schemes to protect their systems, but these ended in failure. Eventually, most states began to eliminate crippling prohibitions against branch banking, but only after the damage had been done.[19]

---

[19]Eugene N. White, "State-Sponsored Insurance of Bank Deposits in the United States," *Journal of Economic History* 41 (1981); "A Reinterpretation of the Banking Crisis of 1930," *Journal of Economic History* 44 (1984); "Before the Glass-Steagall Act: An Analysis of the Investment Banking Activities of National Banks," *Explorations in Economic History* 23 (1986).

The Fed, however, was deeply concerned about the growing speculation on Wall Street. Speculation diverted capital from more productive investments, the Fed believed, and the inevitable retrenchment might cause widespread disturbances in the economy. But it was not clear how to slow the flow of funds to the stock market without at the same time restricting the total supply of credit, thus risking a recession. At first the Fed tried pressuring the New York City banks into making fewer call loans—"moral suasion." This policy was partly effective, but other lenders quickly moved into the gap left by the banks.

Finally, frustrated by its inability to cool the market in any other way, the Fed raised its discount rate from 4.5 to 5.5 percent on August 9, 1929. The discount rate was still well below the call loan and other bank lending rates, so the increase itself did not remove the incentive to borrow, but it signalled the intention of the Fed to restrict the supply of credit. Other central banks were simultaneously taking similar actions; the Bank of England raised its discount rate from 5.5 to 6.5 percent in September. Perhaps as a result of these widespread harbingers of tighter credit, American stock prices reached their peak early in September. The exact role of the Fed's policy in subsequent events, as we will see in the next chapter, is a matter of considerable debate. But during the 1930s the Fed was given the power to set margin requirements because it was recognized that the Fed's policy had been distorted in the late 1920s by its efforts to control the stock market.

Fiscal policy in the late 1920s is best characterized by the phrase coined by President Harding, "a return to normalcy." Certain costs of the war continued into the postwar period—interest on the increase in the national debt, veteran's benefits, and so on. Nevertheless, demobilization created considerable scope for cutting the high level of taxes imposed during the war.[20] The White House favored reducing taxes by removing the steep progression in rates introduced during the war. Secretary of the Treasury Andrew Mellon (1921–31) argued that reducing high rates would encourage the wealthy to shift their assets from tax-exempt municipal bonds to taxable assets, thus minimizing the effect on total revenues. (Similar arguments would be made in the 1980s under the banner of supply-side economics.) Liberals in Congress, however, favored reducing taxes by increasing exemptions for those in lower-income groups. The outcomes of this fight were the revenue acts of 1924, 1926 and 1928 that swept away the system of wartime excise taxes, reduced the rates for personal and corporate taxes, and reduced estate duties. On the whole, the pride taken by successive administrations in their fiscal policies during the 1920s is understandable. A federal budget system was introduced in 1921. Tax rates were cut, but revenues grew, and a budget surplus was maintained.

---

[20]Taxes could have been maintained at a high level and the resulting surplus could have been used to pay off the national debt. But that had little political appeal, since the people who benefited, the bondholders, might attribute their good fortune to someone other than Congress.

Table 22-7 shows that federal spending was relatively small compared with the whole economy in the 1920s. Indeed, in 1927 the federal government was spending less than half of what was being spent by state and local governments. Table 22-8 shows how the federal and state and local budgets were divided among different categories. At the federal level most of the spending was accounted for by the traditional categories of national defense,

TABLE 22-7   Government Spending and Distribution of Expenditures by Level of Government, 1922 and 1927 (in percent)

	1922	1927
Share of GNP		
Total Government	12.6%	11.6%
Federal	4.9	3.5
State and Local	7.7	8.1
Expenditure Distribution by Level		
Federal	39.2	30.4
State	11.7	12.9
Local	49.1	56.7

Source: Albert W. Niemi, *U.S. Economic History* (Chicago: Rand McNally, 1975) p. 117; as derived from *Historical Statistics of the United States, Colonial Times to 1957* (Washington, D.C.: GPO, 1960), pp. 484–516.

TABLE 22-8   Distribution of Direct Expenditures, 1922 and 1927 (in percent)

	1922	1927
Federal		
National Defense	24.0%	18.1%
Postal Service	15.2	20.9
Education	0.2	0.2
Public Welfare	0.2	0.3
Natural Resources	2.2	3.3
Veterans Services	11.7	17.0
Interest	27.1	22.4
Other	19.4	17.8
State and Local		
Education	30.2	28.6
Highways	22.9	23.2
Public Welfare	2.1	1.9
Hospitals & Health	4.6	4.6
Police, Fire, Sanitation	9.5	10.1
Natural Resources	2.6	3.2
General Control	5.5	5.3
Utility & Liquor Store	6.4	6.3
Other	15.2	16.8

Source: Albert W. Niemi, *U.S. Economic History* (Chicago: Rand McNally, 1975), pp. 118–19; as derived from *Historical Statistics of the United States, Colonial Times to 1957* (Washington, D.C.: GPO, 1960), pp. 484–516 and 547–74.

the postal service, veterans' services, and interest on the national debt. Although more funds were being spent on the health and welfare of the people, these were still minor categories. The revolution in the budget was yet to come.

SHOULD THEY HAVE KNOWN BETTER?

In the uncommonly pleasant summer of 1929, Americans were congratulating themselves for having found a way to unending prosperity. The flow of U.S. goods and services had reached an all-time high, industrial production having risen 50 percent in a decade. Most businesses were satisfied with their profit positions, and workers were content with the moderate gains in wages and earnings that enabled them to enjoy the luxury of automobiles and household appliances. Farmers grumbled about price weaknesses in agricultural products, but it was traditional that they should; anyone could see that mechanical inventions had made life on the farm easier and more productive than ever before. Besides, anyone who really wanted to become rich had only to purchase the common stock of thriving enterprises and put the shares in safekeeping, secure in the knowledge that they would appreciate in value. The political climate was favorable to the business venturer, then held high in public esteem as the provider of material well-being. Herbert Hoover, a successful businessman and a distinguished public servant, had been elected to the presidency, and although some people considered him a bit inclined to the liberal side, it was generally felt that he would be a temperate and judicious leader. Equally reassuring was the stability of the economies of western Europe. War damage had been repaired, the gold standard had been restored, and the problem of reparations seemed to be near solution. Hope was high for a return to the freer international movement of goods and capital that had characterized the rapid economic growth of the two decades before the war.

The greatest American economist of the day was Irving Fisher. A remarkable figure, Fisher made important theoretical and empirical contributions in areas of economics ranging from index numbers to monetary theory. He was a prolific inventor; his invention of a card index system made him a fortune. He wrote books in support of Prohibition and on how to eat a healthy diet (the latter a best seller). When journalists wanted to know whether "Yes, we have no bananas" was good English, they asked Irving Fisher.[21] Fisher was not shy about making predictions about the stock market. Just weeks before the crash he argued that "stock prices have reached what looks like a permanently high plateau," adding that "there might be a

---

[21] The answer was yes, if the question was "Have you no bananas?"

recession in stock prices, but not anything in the nature of a crash." Even after the crash he was writing that for "the immediate future, at least, the outlook is bright."[22]

It is easy now to laugh at such optimism. But should Fisher and others have known better? Were there signs of the impending disaster that should have been heeded? The long history of panics and crises in U.S. history (which Fisher knew well) should, perhaps, have given pause. And there were, of course, weaknesses in the economy such as the banking system and the agricultural sector. But the economy had expanded rapidly for years despite these weaknesses. Ultimately, whether we believe that Fisher and other optimists were unwise or merely incredibly unlucky depends on what we believe caused the Great Depression, the subject of the next chapter.

SELECTED REFERENCES AND SUGGESTED READINGS

Coen, R. M. "Labor Force Unemployment in the 1920's and 1930's: A Re-examination Based on Postwar Experience." *Review of Economics and Statistics* 55 (1973): 46–55.

Field, Alexander J. "A New Interpretation of the Onset of the Great Depression." *Journal of Economic History* 45 (June 1984).

Galbraith, John Kenneth. *The Great Crash of 1929,* reissued with a new introduction. Boston: Houghton Mifflin, 1961.

Hawley, Ellis W. *The Great War and the Search for a Modern Order: A History of the American People and Their Institutions, 1917–1933.* New York: St. Martin's Press, 1979.

Holt, Charles. "Who Benefited from the Prosperity of the Twenties?" *Explorations in Economic History* 14 (1977): 277–89.

Hughes, Jonathan. *The Vital Few.* New York: Oxford Univ. Press, 1986.

Johnson, H. Thomas. "Postwar Optimism and the Rural Financial Crisis of the 1920's" *Explorations in Economic History* 11 (Winter 1973–74): 173–92.

Keller, Robert. "Factor Income Distribution in the United States During the 1920's: A Reexamination of Fact and Theory." *Journal of Economic History* 33 (1973): 252–73.

Lampman, Robert. *The Share of Top Wealth-Holders in National Wealth, 1922–1956.* Princeton: Princeton Univ. Press, 1962.

Lebergott, Stanley. *The American Economy: Income, Wealth and Want.* Princeton: Princeton Univ. Press, 1976.

Lorant, John H. "Technological Change in American Manufacturing During the 1920's." *Journal of Economic History* 27 (1967): 243–46.

Mercer, Lloyd, and Douglas Morgan. "Alternative Interpretations of Market Saturation: Evaluation for the Automobile Market in the late 1920's." *Explorations in Economic History* 9 (Spring 1972): 269–90.

———. "The American Automobile Industry: Investment Demand, Capacity, and Capacity Utilization 1921–1940," *Journal of Political Economy* 80 (Nov.–Dec. 1972): (214–31).

———. "Housing Surplus in the 1920's: Another Evaluation." *Explorations in Economic History* 10 (Spring 1973): 295–304.

Metzer, Jacob. "How New Was the New Era? The Public Sector in the 1920s." *Journal of Economic History* 45 (March 1985): 119–126.

Sirkin, Gerald. "The Stock Market of 1929 Revisited: A Note." *Business History Review* 49 (Summer 1975): 223–31.

Smiley, Gene. "Did Incomes for Most of the Population Fall from 1923 Through 1929?" *Journal of Economic History* 42 (1983): 209–16.

---

[22]As quoted in Galbraith, *The Great Crash,* pp. 91, 99, 151.

Soule, George. *Prosperity Decade: From War to Depression, 1917–1929*. New York: Holt, Rinehart and Winston, 1947.

Swanson, Joseph, and Samuel Williamson. "Estimates of National Product and Income 1919–1941." *Explorations in Economic History* 10 (Fall 1972): 53–73.

Vatter, Harold G. "Has There Been a Twentieth-Century Consumer Durables Revolution?" *Journal of Economic History* 27 (1967): 1–16.

White, Eugene N. "Before the Glass–Steagall Act: An Analysis of the Investment Banking Activities of National Banks." *Explorations in Economic History* 23 (1986): 33–53.

_____. "A Reinterpretation of the Banking Crisis of 1930." *Journal of Economic History* 44 (1984): 119–38.

_____. "State-Sponsored Insurance of Bank Deposits in the United States, 1907–1929." *Journal of Economic History* 41 (Sept. 1981): 537–57.

_____. "When the Ticker Ran Late: The Stock Market Boom and Crash of 1929." In *The Stock Market Crash in Historical Perspective*, ed., Eugene Nelson White. Homewood, IL.: Dow Jones-Irwin, 1989.

Williamson, Jeffrey, and Peter Lindert. *American Inequality: A Macroeconomic History*. New York: Academic Press, 1981.

CHAPTER 23

The Great Depression

As the decade of the 1920s drew to a close, Americans were confident in their well-being and in the prospects of even better times ahead. On the election trail in the summer of 1928, Hoover boasted of America's optimism with the words:

> We in America today are nearer to the final triumph over poverty than ever before in the history of any land. The poorhouse is vanishing from among us. We have not yet reached the goal, but, given the chance to go forward with the policies of the last eight years, we shall soon, with the help of God, be in sight of the day when poverty will be banished from this nation.

Hardly a voice in the wilderness, Hoover's words were typical of the confidence of the times; nearly everyone missed the emerging signs of a faltering economy. Indeed, many failed to recognize the magnitude of the decline even after the Great Depression was erupting in full force.

DIMENSIONS OF THE DEPRESSION

It is utterly remarkable, even in hindsight, that an economic catastrophe of such magnitude could have occurred. But in the four years from 1929 to 1933, the American economy (and all other industrialized economies as well) simply disintegrated. The U.S. gross national product in current prices declined 46 percent, from $104.4 billion to $56 billion; as shown in Figure 23-1, in constant (1929) prices, the decline was 31 percent. Industrial production declined by more than one-half, and gross investments, as revealed in Figure 23-2, fell to practically nothing. By 1933, gross investments were below levels of capital depreciation. The nation's capital stock was actually declining. In the process, wholesale prices dropped one-third and consumer prices one-quarter. But the most horrible statistics were those of employment and unemployment. Figure 23-3 graphically illustrates how

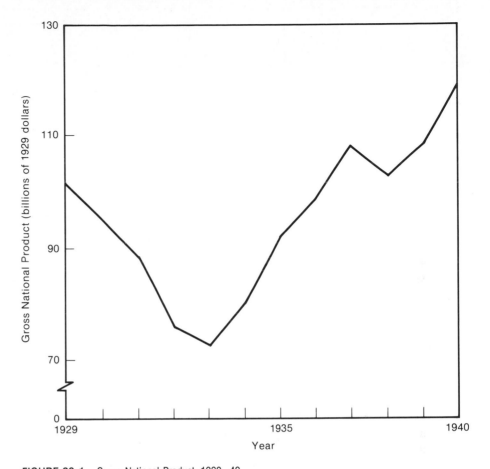

FIGURE 23-1 Gross National Product, 1929–40

Source: John W. Kendrick, *Productivity Trends in the United States,* National Bureau of Economic Research, No. 71 (Princeton: Princeton Univ. Press, 1961), p. 291.

unemployment soared. Civilian employment dropped by almost 20 percent, and unemployment rose from 1.5 million to at least 13 million. One-quarter of the civilian workforce was unemployed in 1933. The figures do count workers employed by government emergency programs as unemployed. But extensive part-time employment and underutilization of skills probably brought the real unemployment rate close to one-third. Fully one-half the nation's breadwinners were either out of work or in seriously reduced circumstances.

The profile of durable goods production since 1920 (as shown in Figure 23-4), reveals, in perspective, the magnitude of the decline in business in the early 1930s. From a peak of nearly 25 in 1929 (1967 = 100), the index of durable-goods output fell to 6 in 1932. At the trough of the Depression

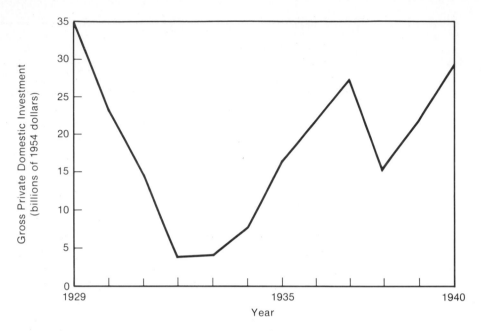

FIGURE 23-2   Gross Private Domestic Investment, 1929–40.

Source: U.S. Office of Business Economics, *U.S. Income and Output, 1958* (Washington, D.C.: GPO, 1959), p. 118.

in March 1933, the durable-goods index stood at 5; output of durables had fallen 80 percent. Nondurables dropped much less—from an index of slightly over 40 to about 28.

The intensity of the Depression was distressing, but its seeming endlessness brought frustration and despair. Forty years had passed since the long depression of the 1890s. The depression of 1920–21 had been sharp and nasty, with a decline in durables output of 43 percent. But it had behaved as a depression should—it had come and gone quickly, with complete recovery of manufacturing production in less than two years. In the Great Depression, on the other hand, manufacturing output did not reach the 1929 level until late 1936; it stayed somewhat above the 1929 level for nearly a year but dropped again and did not climb back to the pre-Depression peak until late 1939. Durable-goods production did not regain the 1929 peak until August 1940, more than 11 years after the beginning of the Depression.

It is difficult to overemphasize the deep imprint registered by the duration and depth of the collapse. Overall, the revolutionary impact—economically, politically, socially, and psychologically—of the events of that fateful decade were matched only by those of the Civil War decade.

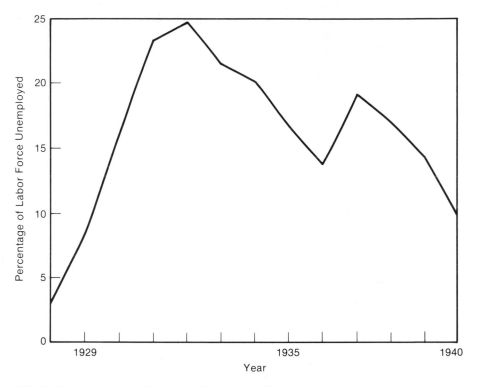

FIGURE 23-3   Percentage of Labor Force Unemployed, 1929–40.

Source: *Economic Report of the President* (Washington, D.C.: GPO, January 1955) p. 153.

CAUSES OF THE GREAT DEPRESSION

For nearly 50 years, economists have attempted to explain the greatest economic crisis to beset not only the United States but the entire world. A satisfactory explanation requires us to distinguish between the forces that brought a downturn in economic activity and those that turned a business recession into an utter disaster.

Hindsight enables us to detect two drags on the economy that prepared the way for a decline in economic activity. The most important was the decline from 1925 onward in both residential and nonresidential construction. The boom in building activity that began in 1918 had doubtlessly helped the economy out of the slump of 1920–21; the downward phase of the same building cycle, coinciding as it did with other economic weaknesses, was a major depressing influence. What was a gentle slide in construction from 1925 to 1927 became a marked decline in 1928.

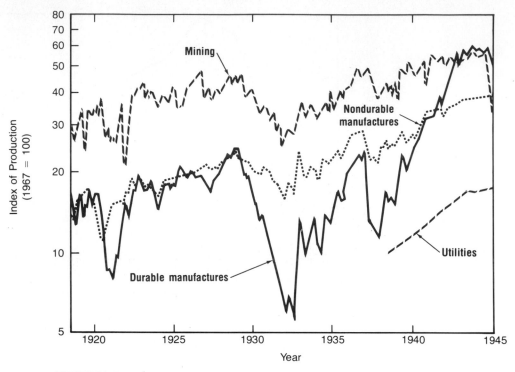

FIGURE 23-4   U.S. Industrial Production, 1920–45.

The second drag on the economy came from the agricultural sector, which was still important enough in the 1920s to exert a powerful influence on the total economy. During the 1920s, the trend of world agricultural prices was downward. As we noted in Chapter 22, in the farm belts, where indebtedness incurred for the purchase of land remained high, there were widespread complaints among businesses that sales to farmers were falling. In the great agricultural midlands, few manifestations of boom psychology appeared after 1926. A mild downturn in durables output in the spring of 1929 and a drop in nondurable production in the summer of that year could well have been expected. But nothing catastrophic was portended. The economy, however, was then hit by some devastating shocks.

The Stock Market Crash

The first emotional shock was the break in the stock market during the last week in October. Normally, economists do not consider fluctuations in the stock market to be a *cause* of business fluctuations, although many recognize the indirect effect of market swings on the attitudes of entrepreneurs and consumers; others consider the market an important leading indicator of the health of the economy. The 1929 break, however, must be viewed as an exception to the general rule due to the catastrophic magnitude of the

Wall Street on Black Thursday, October 24, 1929: Investors and the curious milled around in confusion in the planked street (subway construction was going on) as the extent of the disaster inside the New York Stock Exchange (at right) became clear.

decline. *The New York Times* index of 25 industrial stocks, which early in 1924 had stood at 110, by January 1929 had climbed to 338 and by September to 452. It was almost impossible to buy a common stock that did not rise rapidly in value, and investors quickly accumulated paper fortunes that many of them converted into real ones. The optimism engendered by these gains permeated the business community and led to the conclusion that permanent prosperity had been achieved. When the break came, the shock to the economy was indescribable. Paper fortunes disappeared; and so did a great many real ones, as people who had earned great profits on some issues were required to put up more collateral to save their other stock-holdings. The terrible realization that a new era had not dawned—that American business was not infallible—engendered a pervasive pessimism that no amount of cheerful public statements could relieve. After falling to 275 within a week of the first drop, the market recovered only to slide another 50 points by mid-November.

v York Times.

pyright, 1929, by The New York Times Company.

THE WEATHER
Rain today and probably tomorrow;
somewhat colder tomorrow.
Temperatures Yesterday—Max. 54, Min. 45.
U. S. Weather Forecast—For details see Page 83.

YORK, TUESDAY, OCTOBER 29, 1929.

TWO CENTS by Greater | THREE CENTS | FOUR CENTS Elsewhere
New York | Within 200 Miles | Except 7th and 8th Postal Zones

Memory Honored Day Fete on Ships

a and in port offi-
ted Navy Day yester-
gh major land cele-
held on Sunday, the
of the birth of Theo-
lt, similar ceremonies
were reserved for

e was kept by ships
he public was invited
. Flags appropriate
ere broken out on all
ships, and even some
craft in the harbor
ennants in honor of

ngeles and the new
irigible and other
air craft at Lake-
were ordered out and
along the Atlantic
over this city and

T. E. BURTON, DIES AT 77

man Had Served in
41 Years—First
to the House.

VOCATE OF PEACE

EUROPE IS DISTURBED BY AMERICAN ACTION ON OCCUPATION DEBT

London Urges an Explanation of Move for Direct Payments by Germany.

BANK'S PRESTIGE INVOLVED

Britain and Continent Feel That We Do Not Have Faith in Young Plan Institution.

SCHEME IS LAID TO HOOVER

President Is Said to Wish to Avoid Clash in Congress Over Linking of Reparations and War Debts.

By EDWIN L. JAMES.
Special Cable to The New York Times.

LONDON, Oct. 28.—There appears
to exist in London a certain absence
of understanding as to the significance of the conversations between
Washington and Berlin which now
are about to ripen into diplomatic
negotiations in the German capital
for the preparation of a treaty deal

STOCK PRICES SLUMP $14,000,000,000 IN NATION-WIDE STAMPEDE TO UNLOAD; BANKERS TO SUPPORT MARKET TODAY

Sixteen Leading Issues Down $2,893,520,108;
Tel. & Tel. and Steel Among Heaviest Losers

A shrinkage of $2,893,520,108 in the open market value of the
shares of sixteen representative companies resulted from yesterday's
sweeping decline on the New York Stock Exchange.
American Telephone and Telegraph was the heaviest loser,
$448,905,162 having been lopped off of its total value. United States
Steel common, traditional bellwether of the stock market, made its
greatest nose-dive in recent years by falling from a high of 202½ to
a low of 185. In a feeble last-minute rally it snapped back to 186,
at which it closed, showing a net loss of 17½ points. This represented for the 8,131,955 shares of common stock outstanding a total
loss in value of $142,293,446.
In the following table are shown the day's net depreciation in
the outstanding shares of the sixteen companies referred to:

Issues.	Shares Listed.	Losses in Points.	Depreciation.
American Radiator	10,096,289	10¼	$104,748,997
American Tel. & Tel.	13,203,093	34	448,905,162
Commonwealth & Southern....	30,764,468	3⅛	96,138,962
Columbia Gas & Electric......	8,477,307	22	186,500,754
Consolidated Gas.............	11,451,188	20	229,023,760
DuPont E. I.................	10,322,481	16⅝	169,030,625
Eastman Kodak	2,229,703	41⅞	93,368,813
General Electric	7,211,484	47½	342,545,490
General Motors................	43,500,000	6⅝	293,625,000
International Nickel..........	13,777,408	7⅝	108,497,088
New York Central............	4,637,086	22⅝	104,311,071
Standard Oil of New Jersey...	24,843,643	8	198,749,144
Union Carbide & Carbon......	8,730,173	20	174,615,460

PREMIER ISSUES HARD HIT

Unexpected Torrent of Liquidation Again Rocks Markets.

DAY'S SALES   9,212,800

Nearly 3,000,000 Shares Are Traded In Final Hour—The Tickers Lag 167 Minutes.

NEW RALLY SOON BROKEN

Selling by Europeans and "Mob Psychology" Big Factors in Second Big Break.

Newspapers reported in sterile statistics the painful events of Wall Street's collapse, in late October, 1929.

Using a broader measure of stock prices and over a longer period, Figure 23-5 reveals the "Great Crash" in full force. Much of the panic selling of stocks resulted from brokers selling stocks which had been purchased on margin. On Tuesday, October 29, 1929, 16.4 million shares were sold in record amounts generated by sheer panic. On that fateful Monday and Tuesday, an average stock lost almost 25 percent of its value. But note that, as Figure 23-5 shows, even well into 1930 share prices remained above the levels reached even a few years earlier. The unique psychological trauma produced by the crash was more significant for the economy than the direct effects of the loss of wealth. Similar to buying stocks on margin, in the 1920s consumer spending was done increasingly on credit, or installment loans, as they were popularly called. And this assistance to consumer buying, once slowed, also had sharp backlash effects. Within a year industrial production was down more than 25 percent.

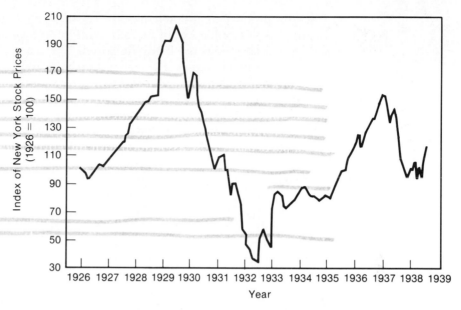

FIGURE 23-5 The Standard Statistics Index of New York Stock Prices, 1926–38. The rise and fall in stock prices shows the magnitude of speculative activity and the market crash. From an index level of 100 in 1926, the market soared to a high of 206 in September 1929, before collapsing to 34 in June 1932.

Source: Charles Kindleberger, *The World in Depression, 1929–1939* (Berkeley: Univ. of California Press, 1973), pp. 110–11. Reprinted by permission of the Univ. of California Press.

The Banking Crises

The devastating impact of the stock-market collapse and other faltering aspects of the economy came in the early stages of the Depression. Public morale might have improved and the market and the economy might have regained some buoyancy if it had not been for the structural weaknesses of the banking system and the international economy. In particular, three waves of bank failures, each timed to have a particularly unsettling effect, shook the economy.

Bank failures had been frequent in rural parts of the country throughout the 1920s, so the high rates of failure that occurred in early 1930 did not strike observers as unusual. But in October 1930 a wave of bank failures concentrated in the South and Midwest hit the country and produced something new. A general alarm about the banking system spread across the country, and people began converting bank deposits into currency.[1] Some-

---

[1] But while the response to the crisis was new, a sophisticated study by Eugene White has shown that the banks that failed were similar to those that had failed previously. See Eugene N. White, "A Reinterpretation of the Banking Crisis of 1930," *Journal of Economic History* 44 (1984): 119–38.

times this produced runs on banks, the classic sign of a panic. A rumor that a bank was in trouble would literally send people running to the bank to try to get their money out before it closed. The crisis continued in November and December, and on December 11, the Bank of the United States in New York failed. This failure was significant for several reasons. It was the largest failure, measured by deposits, in the history of the United States up to that time. And, although it was an ordinary bank (chartered by the state of New York), its name may have led some people to believe that a bank with a particularly close association with the government had failed.

The Fed at this point, most historians agree, should have acted as a *lender-of-last-resort*. It should have lent generously to the Bank of the United States and other failing banks to break the cycle of fear that was undermining the banking system. But for a variety of reasons it did not do so. It still seemed to the Fed that the banks that were failing were simply badly managed banks that should be eliminated to make the system more efficient. In retrospect we can see that with the economy in a downward spiral, permitting bank failures would only make matters worse, but this was not evident to the Fed at the time.[2]

For a few months things seemed to be calmer, but a second, more intense crisis began in March 1931. This time events abroad reinforced the sense of crisis. In May 1931 the Kreditanstalt, a major bank in Vienna, failed. Since gold was the root of the money supply in most of the industrial counties, failures such as this one convinced people worldwide that now was the time to convert paper claims to gold into the real thing. In September 1931, Britain left the gold standard: the British pound would no longer be convertible on demand into gold. This in turn increased the pressure on currencies such as the dollar that were still convertible into gold.

The final banking panic began in 1933. In the three years 1930 through 1932 over 5,000 banks containing over $3 billion in deposits (about 7 percent of total deposits in January 1930) had suspended operations. In 1933 another 4,000 banks containing over $3.5 billion in deposits would close. The weakened condition of the banks after years of deflation, uncertainties about how the new administration of Franklin D. Roosevelt would handle the crisis, and the general atmosphere of distrust and fear—all contributed to the final crisis. By the time that Roosevelt took office on March 4, 1933, the destruction of the financial system that had taken place was incredible.

One of the first acts undertaken by Roosevelt was to announce a nationwide bank holiday beginning on March 6, 1933. This action, which followed a number of state bank holidays, closed all of the banks in the country for

---

[2]An excellent example of how to handle a run on a bank (in this case a savings bank) occurs in the popular movie *It's a Wonderful Life,* which stars Jimmy Stewart as the president of a small savings bank. There is a run on the bank. But at the height of the panic the wife of the bank's president (played by Donna Reed) acts as a lender of last resort and offers the family's personal savings to allay the fears of depositors.

one week. How could such an action improve things? The public was told that during this period the banks would be inspected and only the sound ones allowed to reopen. Questions have been raised about the way this was handled. Probably many sound banks were closed, and unsound ones allowed to remain open. But the medicine seemed to work, even if it was only a placebo; the panic subsided.

In addition to the bank holiday, the federal government took a number of other actions that helped to restore confidence in the financial system. Gold hoarding was ended by the simple expedient of requiring everyone to turn monetary gold over to the Fed in exchange for some other form of currency. Perhaps most important, the Federal Deposit Insurance Corporation (FDIC) was set up to insure bank deposits. The insurance took effect on January 1, 1934, and within six months almost all of the nation's commercial banks were covered. Deposit insurance dramatically changed the incentives facing depositors. No longer would a rumor of failure send people rushing to the bank to try to be first in line, because they now knew that they would eventually be paid their deposits in any case. All of these factors together drastically changed the rate of bank failures. The number of bank failures fell from 4,000 in 1933 to 61 in 1934, and remained at double-digit levels through the rest of the 1930s. By way of contrast, the lowest number of bank failures in any year from 1921 to 1929 was 366 in 1922. Although the Great Depression was to drag on for the remainder of the decade, the banking crisis had been surmounted.

DID MONETARY FORCES CAUSE THE GREAT DEPRESSION?[3]

It's hard to believe that the financial collapse did the economy any good. But how significant was it as an independent factor? A sharp debate has occurred between those economic historians who believe that the Great Depression could have been prevented, or at least been made much less severe by timely Federal Reserve actions to prevent monetary contraction, and those who believe that the collapse of the banking system was merely another symptom of the overall collapse of the economy. Are we talking about the fever that accompanies the flu, or have we discovered the virus that causes it? The discussion has become extremely technical, but the basic points of disagreement can be understood by looking at Table 23-1.

To monetarists, such as Milton Friedman and Anna J. Schwartz, the decline in the money stock in column 1 of Table 23-1 was the primary cause of the Great Depression. They believe that money plays an independent causative role in the economy. According to the quantity theory of money, if the money supply contracts, people will try to restore the relation between

---

[3]This is the title of an important book by Peter Temin; (New York: W. W. Norton, 1976).

TABLE 23-1   Money, Income, and Interest Rates, 1929–33

Year	(1) Money Supply (in billions)	(2) Net National Product (in billions)	(3) Ratio of Net National Product to Money	(4) Commercial Paper Interest Rate (percent)
1929	$46.6	$90.3	1.94	5.78%
1930	45.7	76.9	1.68	3.55
1931	42.7	61.7	1.45	2.63
1932	36.1	44.8	1.24	2.72
1933	32.2	42.7	1.32	1.67

Source: Milton Friedman and Anna J. Schwartz, *Monetary Trends in the United States and the United Kingdom* (Chicago: Univ. of Chicago Press, 1982), p. 124.

their money balances and their income by spending less; the result is a fall in net national product.

Monetarists do not contend that the fall in the money supply was the only factor at work. Note that the ratio of net national product to money (the velocity of money, column 3) also fell. In the first year of the Depression in particular, the ratio of net national product to money fell dramatically (perhaps due to the stock market crash or other factors) while the money supply fell only slightly. But while allowing for these other factors, monetarists insist that any decline in the money supply (which normally grows from year to year) is significant. The decline in the money supply itself, might explain part of the decline in the ratio of income to money. People normally spend less freely in recessions, and, if prices are falling, people have another incentive not to spend since their money is worth more the longer they hold on to it.

To Keynesians, such as Peter Temin, the proper interpretation of the figures in Table 23-1 is just the reverse. Net national product fell because spending collapsed. (Temin believes that there was a sudden and unexplained collapse in consumer spending.) As a result, profits fell, workers were laid off, and many firms and individuals could no longer repay their bank loans. The result was the waves of bank failures and the decline in the money supply shown in column 1. This was a tragedy to be sure, but it was a symptom of the depression analogous to the problems in agriculture, consumer durable production, and other sectors of the economy.

To Keynesians, the key piece of evidence in support of their story is the behavior of interest rates as shown in column 4. They contend that the interest rate is determined by the supply and demand for money. If the decline in the supply of money was the initiating factor, interest rates should have been rising. In this case people would have begun selling financial assets to acquire money, and the prices of those assets would have fallen while the returns they yielded (relative to their prices) would have risen.

But we observe just the opposite, short-term interest rates fell from 5.78 percent in 1929 to 1.67 percent in 1933, indicating that the demand for money was falling even more rapidly than supply. If there is a shortage of wheat, we expect the price of wheat to rise, and, if there is a shortage of money, we expect the rate of interest to rise. Since it did not, we must conclude that there was no shortage.

The monetarists believe none of this. They contend that the rate of interest is the price not of money but of credit. The demand for credit declined because of the general decline in economic activity caused by the decline in the money supply. The price of money to the monetarists is the inverse of the price level, the purchasing power of money. That variable rose from 1929 to 1933, showing that the supply of money was contracting faster than demand.

And so it goes. The interested reader can explore subsequent rounds of the debate in the works referenced at the end of this chapter. The authors believe that recent research, on the whole, has tended to strengthen the monetarist position. But the debate is surely far from over. Recent research, moreover, has attempted to go beyond the confines of the monetarist-Keynesian debate. An influential paper by Ben Bernanke, for example, argues that the banking crisis deepened the economic crisis by interfering with the ability of the financial system to allocate capital efficiently.

What caused the Great Depression is one of the most studied and (presumably not for that reason) least understood questions in economic history. We can confidently expect further debate in the near future.

WHY DIDN'T THE FEDERAL RESERVE SAVE THE BANKING SYSTEM?

It would be hard to find an economic historian of any persuasion who would defend the actions of the Fed during the banking crisis. But there is little consensus on why the Fed remained so passive in the face of an unprecedented collapse of the banking system. In its defense the Federal Reserve Board maintained in its 1932 Annual Report that its use of open-market purchases of bonds (which pump reserves into the banking system) was inhibited by the requirement that Federal Reserve notes be backed by either gold or eligible paper (loans sold by the banks to the Fed). The Federal Reserve Board argued that if the Fed purchased government bonds in the open market, member banks would reduce their indebtedness and consequently the Fed's holdings of eligible paper. But this meant that more gold would be required as collateral for Federal Reserve notes at a time when only $416 million of gold was not committed to some legal reserve purpose. This was the so-called "free gold" problem. But it is not clear that the Fed made a determined effort to get the rules changed, as it undoubtedly could have. Nor should it be forgotten that in 1931 Fed officials refused to inject reserves for far less technical reasons. In his diary entries during August 1931, Charles S. Hamlin, then a member of the Board, tells us that the Open Market Committee voted 11 to 1 against open-market purchases of $300 million, substituting $120 million instead. The governors of the regional banks who were still in control of monetary policy, simply could not grasp the extent of the catastrophe, and Governor Meyer of the Federal Reserve Board was even worried about inflation.

Perhaps officials at the Fed were looking at the wrong indicators of monetary policy. If they felt that low interest rates are a certain sign of easy money, then they would have concluded (look again at column 4 of Table 23-1) that financial markets were awash with money, and that trying to pump in more could do little good. A power struggle within the Federal Reserve system identified by Friedman and Schwartz was also important. In the 1920s the Federal Reserve Bank of New York, under its charismatic president Benjamin Strong, had dominated the system. After Strong's death in 1928 the Federal Reserve Board in Washington tried to assert its authority by resisting pressures from New York. But this power struggle took its toll in the 1930s when the New York Bank pushed for more expansionary monetary policies and the Board in Washington resisted for internal political reasons. Other reasons for the passivity of the Fed have been given, but the important point is that the system, for whatever reason, failed to stop the greatest banking crisis in American economic history.

FISCAL POLICY IN THE 1930s

The common impression that the Hoover administration did nothing to combat the Depression is erroneous. Within the limits of economic orthodoxy, which called for trying to balance the budget, steps were taken to restore economic equilibrium. The Reconstruction Finance Corporation Act was passed in January 1932. This institution was set up to borrow money by issuing securities guaranteed by the federal government and to relend it to banks, insurance companies, railroads, and other businesses experiencing financial difficulties. The very formation of such an agency in peacetime (it was a revival of the War Finance Corporation of the First World War) marked a sharp break with tradition. Support of agricultural prices with production controls by the Federal Farm Board was equally revolutionary. The major deficiencies of the Hoover administration were the persistent refusal to establish a federal program of work relief and the failure to consciously carry out an aggressive fiscal policy of large deficits financed by borrowing from the banking system. Too much reliance was placed on maintaining confidence through the public testimonials of business and government leaders and not enough was placed on measures to raise incomes and correct the deflation.

Grim hopelessness descended on the quarter of the population that was out of work and the two-thirds that occasionally went hungry as the Great Depression deepened. "Hoovervilles" like this one in New York's Central Park tarnished the countryside.

It is true, as shown in Table 23-2, that the treasury began running small but growing deficits by the mid-1930s. But these deficits were not the result of bold spending programs (or cuts in tax rates) by government. Rather they were primarily due to the decline in tax revenues as incomes fell and they occurred despite efforts to prevent them.

Indeed, in 1932 a tax increase was enacted, partly over concern about the deficit and its effects on bond values. It should be remembered that declining bond values were contributing to the deteriorating capital holdings of banks, and this was especially important to those facing possible "runs." Of course, this policy move was counterproductive, not unlike taking a steambath to reduce a fever. What Hoover should have done was to cut taxes, vastly increase spending, and demand that the Fed buy bonds in great volume to finance the deficit, bolster bank reserves, and ease credit.

Franklin D. Roosevelt and his staff were not entirely comfortable with the idea of deficits. During the campaign of 1932, Roosevelt promised to cut spending 25 percent and balance the budget. But once in office the Roosevelt administration was willing to run fairly large deficits by historical standards to finance its many new programs. How large were these deficits?

TABLE 23-2   Governmental Expenditures and Revenues, 1927–40 (in millions)

| | Federal | | State and Local | | Private |
Year	Expenditures	Revenues	Expenditures	Revenues	Investment
1927	$2.9	$4.0	$ 7.8	$ 7.8	$14.5[a]
1932	4.8	2.0	8.4	7.9	3.4
1934	6.5	3.1	7.8	8.4	4.1
1936	7.6	4.2	8.5	9.4	7.2
1938	7.2	7.0	10.0	11.1	7.4
1940	9.6	6.9	11.2	11.7	11.0

[a]This is the 1929 figure.

Source: *Historical Statistics of the United States, Colonial Times to 1970* (Washington, D.C.: GPO, 1976), series F53, Y335, Y336, Y339, Y340, Y652, Y671.

Why didn't they lift the country out of the Depression as Keynesian economic theory predicts?[4] Some evidence is given in Table 23-2. The federal budget was steadily in deficit during the Depression. Relative to the traditional size of the federal government the level of spending and the deficits seemed large indeed. Note that by 1938 federal spending was two and a half times as high as it had been in 1927.

But compared with other parts of the economy, the federal government was still rather small. In 1938 the federal deficit was $.2 billion ($7.2 − $7.0), but this was more than offset by a surplus at the state and local level of $1.1 billion ($10.0 − $11.1). Remember, too, that tax revenues were down because of the Depression. At full employment the same tax rates would have produced much higher revenues.[5] Keynesian theory suggests that the role of government spending is to offset decreases in autonomous private spending such as investment (the traditional culprit) or consumption (Peter Temin's candidate). It is clear that the fall in investment spending, $7.1 billion between 1929 and 1938, was far greater than the increase in federal spending or the federal deficit. No wonder then that Keynesian economist E. Cary Brown concludes that "fiscal policy . . . seems to have been an unsuccessful recovery device in the thirties—not because it does not work, but because it was not tried."

In retrospect this should not surprise us. Orthodox economic opinion, although far from unanimous, still looked skeptically at large-scale federal deficits as a remedy for depression. Political constraints on spending, moreover, were significant. Recent research by Gavin Wright shows that New

---

[4]The famous book by John Maynard Keynes, *The General Theory of Employment, Interest and Money* was not published until 1936. Many economists, however, favored increased government spending financed by deficits. Some thought that increased spending would "prime the pump" and stimulate the natural expansionary powers of the economy.

[5]This point was first made by E. Cary Brown. Recent work by Larry Peppers has strengthened his original conclusions.

Deal spending was carefully allocated to maximize political support for the Roosevelt administration.[6]

The Great Depression and Laissez-Faire

Rexford Tugwell, a member of President Roosevelt's "brain trust" (a group of advisors who suggested many new programs to combat the Depression) remarked

> The Cat is out of the Bag. There is no invisible hand. There never was. If the depression has not taught us that, we are incapable of education . . . . We must now supply a real and visible guiding hand to do the task which that mythical, nonexistent, invisible agency was supposed to perform, but never did.[7]

Tugwell's forthright remark addresses the fundamental question raised by the Great Depression: doesn't the Depression prove that unguided by government a free-market economy has the potential to run off the rails and produce an economic disaster? And furthermore, doesn't the Depression prove that there is something wrong with Say's Law (the theory named after French economist J. B. Say that the balancing of supply and demand creates a tendency toward full employment)? And if the market cannot accomplish the simple task of balancing the supply and demand for labor, why should we trust it to allocate resources at the micro level? Should we leave the allocation of capital to a stock market that goes through ridiculous boom and bust cycles? Should we leave the allocation of agricultural products to Adam Smith's "invisible hand" when it drives farmers off the land while people in cities go hungry? To many thoughtful observers in the 1930s, the clear answer to these questions was the one given by Tugwell: do not leave things to the free market; common sense tells us that government regulation can make things better.

Most mainstream economists and economic historians, however, have not been entirely persuaded. John Maynard Keynes, who agreed that the Depression revealed fundamental weaknesses in the economic system, nevertheless concluded that the Depression did not justify across-the-board intervention in the market. He believed that the Depression was a problem of aggregate demand and that this was separate from the problem of individual markets. As he wrote,

> To put the point concretely, I see no reason to suppose that the existing system seriously misemploys the factors of production which are in use. There are, of course, errors of foresight; but these would not be avoided by centralizing decisions. When 9,000,000 men are employed out of 10,000,000 willing and

---

[6] For a less cynical view see Don Reading, "New Deal Activity and the States, 1933 to 1939," *Journal of Economic History* 33 (1973): 792–810.

[7] As quoted by Rebeca Brooks Gruver, *An American History* (New York: Appleton-Century-Crofts, 1972), p. 936.

able to work, there is no evidence that the labour of these 9,000,000 men is misdirected. The complaint against the present system is not that these 9,000,000 men ought to be employed on different tasks, but that tasks should be available for the remaining 1,000,000 men. It is in determining the volume, not the direction, of actual employment that the existing system has broken down.[8]

Monetarists have given the most negative answer. In their view the Great Depression was a monetary crisis. Government regulation had produced a weak, dependent banking system. The Fed, the agency created to prevent banking crises, pushed the economic system to the edge of the abyss and failed to save it when it plunged in. Eliminate these weaknesses by allowing the banking system to strengthen itself through competition and by forcing the Fed to maintain the stock of money, and a recurrence of the Great Depression could be prevented. But during the 1930s it was Tugwell's position that prevailed. As we shall see, the Depression led to a vast increase in the extent to which the federal government attempted to influence individual markets.

CAN IT HAPPEN AGAIN?

No one, unfortunately, can say for certain that it cannot happen again. But there are many reasons for thinking that a collapse on the scale of the Great Depression is a remote possibility under modern circumstances.

One reason is that we are not likely to repeat the same mistakes. The Federal Reserve with better data at hand, and with the experience of the Great Depression laid out in many books and articles, is unlikely to permit a complete collapse of the banking system. Remember, too, that we are no longer on a gold standard. Hence the ability of the Federal Reserve to create dollars during a crisis is virtually unlimited.

The same is true of fiscal policy, although here we cannot be quite so confident. Faith in a balanced budget seems to be hard to shake even under very dire circumstances. Nevertheless, it seems likely that conditions similar to those of the early 1930s would be met today with tax cuts and increased spending on a substantial scale. Many sorts of spending, such as unemployment benefits, would increase even without specific congressional actions—the so-called automatic stabilizers.

The private economy, too, may be less vulnerable to economic collapse. The industrial sector, particularly producers of consumer durables, seems to be the most vulnerable to sudden shifts in demand that lead to massive layoffs. But this sector is now relatively much smaller compared with the service sector than it was in the 1930s. The rapid increase in two-earner

[8]John Maynard Keynes, *The General Theory of Employment, Interest, and Money* (1936; reprint, New York: Harcourt, Brace & World, 1964), p. 379.

households has reduced the probability for many families that an economic downturn will deprive them completely of an income.

Lastly there exists a vast network of government programs that would alleviate suffering, and, by simply being there, reduce the chance of a paralyzing fear. These include the Federal Deposit Insurance Corporation, the Federal Savings and Loan Insurance Corporation, the Pension Guarantee Corporation, and so on. But however much we may be aware of these facts, it is nevertheless true that the nightmare of the Great Depression lies in the back of many minds and surfaces time and again when conditions in one sector or another take a turn for the worse.

SELECTED REFERENCES AND SUGGESTED READINGS

Bernanke, Benjamin. "Non-Monetary Effects of the Financial Crisis in the Propagation of the Great Depression." *American Economic Review* 73 (1983): 257–76.

Boughton, James and Elmus Wicker. "The Behavior of the Currency-Deposit Ratio during the Great Depression." *Journal of Money Credit and Banking* 1 (1979): 405–18.

Brown, E. Cary. "Fiscal Policy in The Thirties: A Reappraisal," *American Economic Review* 46 (Dec. 1956): 857–79.

Brunner, Karl., ed. *The Great Depression Revisited.* Boston: Martinus Nijhoff, 1981.

Eichengreen, Barry. "Central Bank Cooperation under the Interwar Gold Standard." *Explorations in Economic History* 21 (1984): 64–87.

Eichengreen, Barry, and Jeffrey Sachs. "Exchange Rates and Economic Recovery in the 1930s." *Journal of Economic History* 45 (1986): 925–46.

———. "Did International Forces Cause the Great Depression?" *Contemporary Policy Issues* 6 (April 1988): 90–114.

Epstein, Gerald, and Thomas Ferguson. "Monetary Policy, Loan Liquidation, and Industrial Conflict: The Federal Reserve and the Great Contraction." *Journal of Economic History* 44 (1984): 957–84.

Field, Alexander. "Asset Exchanges and the Transactions Demand for Money, 1919–1929." *American Economic Review* 74 (1984): 43–59.

———. "A New Interpretation of the Onset of the Great Depression." *Journal of Economic History* 44 (1984): 489–98.

Fisher, Irving. *Booms and Depressions.* New York: Adelphi, 1932.

Friedman, Milton. "Why the American Economy is Depression-Proof." In *Dollars and Deficits.* Englewood Cliffs, N.J.: Prentice-Hall, 1968.

Friedman, Milton, and Anna J. Schwartz. *A Monetary History of the United States,* (Princeton: Princeton Univ. Press, 1965), pp. 299–545.

Galbraith, John Kenneth. *The Great Crash.* Boston: Houghton Mifflin, 1972.

Gandolfi, Arthur, and James Lothian. "Review of 'Did Monetary Forces Cause the Great Depression.'" *Journal of Money Credit and Banking* 9 (1977): 679–91.

Gramm, William. "The Real Balance Effect in the Great Depression." *Journal of Economic History* 22 (June 1972): 499–519.

Kindleberger, Charles P. *Manias, Panics, and Crashes.* New York: Basic Books, 1978.

Mayer, Thomas. "Consumption in the Great Depression." *Journal of Political Economy* 86 (1978): 139–45.

———. "Money and the Great Depression: A Critique of Professor Temin's Thesis." *Explorations in Economic History* 15 (1978): 127–45.

Meltzer, Allan H. "Monetary and Other Explanations of the Start of the Great Depression," *Journal of Monetary Economics* 2 (1976): 455–71.

Muchmore, Lynn. "The Banking Crisis of 1933: Some Iowa Evidence," *Journal of Economic History* 30 (Sept. 1970): 627–39.

Peppers, Larry C. "Full Employment Surplus Analysis and Structural Changes: The 1930s." *Explorations in Economic History* 10 (Winter 1973): 197–210.

Schwarz, Jordan A. *The Interregnum of Despair: Hoover, Congress, and the Depression.* Urbana: Univ. of Illinois Press, 1970.

Stauffer, Richard. "The Bank Failures of 1930–1931." *Journal of Money, Credit and Banking* 13 (1981): 109–13.

Temin, Peter. *Did Monetary Forces Cause the Great Depression?* New York: W. W. Norton, 1976.

Trescott, Paul. "The Behavior of the Currency-Deposit Ratio during the Great Depression." *Journal of Money, Credit and Banking* 16 (1984): 362–65.

———. "Federal Reserve Policy in the Great Contraction: A Counterfactual Assessment." *Explorations in Economic History* 19 (1982): 211–20.

White, Eugene N. "A Reinterpretation of the Banking Crisis of 1930." *Journal of Economic History* 44 (1984): 119–38.

Wicker, Elmus. "Interest Rate and Expenditure Effects of the Banking Panic of 1930." *Explorations in Economic History* 19 (1982): 435–45.

———. "A Reconsideration of the Causes of the Banking Panic of 1930." *Journal of Economic History* 40 (1982): 435–45.

CHAPTER 24

The New Deal

The presidential campaign of 1932 was fought in an atmosphere of fear and discontent. Herbert Hoover, nominated for a second term, blamed events in Europe for the nation's troubles and promised that prosperity would soon return. Tampering with our basic economic institutions, Hoover argued, could only lead to even worse disasters. Franklin D. Roosevelt, the warm and yet forceful Democratic candidate, was generally not specific about what measures he would take if elected (although he did promise to balance the budget among other things). But there was no mistaking his willingness to use the power of the government directly to try to solve the nation's problems. In his acceptance speech at the Democratic convention he promised a "New Deal" if he was elected. Few people at the time realized how fully these words would be put into practice in the years to come.

Between the time of his election and the time he took office economic conditions deteriorated. No president since Abraham Lincoln had faced a greater crisis at the moment he assumed power. Industrial production was at about 40 percent of full potential, one-quarter of the nation's breadwinners had no work, and unknown numbers of people were literally starving to death. But in his inaugural address, delivered on March 4, 1933, Roosevelt rallied the nation's spirits declaring, "Let me assert my firm belief that the only thing we have to fear is fear itself—nameless, unreasoning, unjustified terror which paralyzes needed efforts to convert retreat into advance." In the famous "hundred days" that followed, the Roosevelt administration proposed many new, and for the time, radical pieces of legislation. Thus was born the New Deal. Although occupying only a brief span of time in the context of our history, we must consider it in detail, because it is the origin of many of the institutions and ideas that shape our daily lives today.

ROOSEVELT TAKES CHARGE

The most pressing problem for the new administration was to provide relief for destitute families. And the administration's New Deal responded with legislation on this and a host of other related problems during the famous "hundred days." The Federal Emergency Relief Agency (FERA) directed by Harry Hopkins pumped a half billion dollars into bankrupt state and local relief efforts. In 1935 the federal government set up the Works Progress Administration, later the Works Projects Administration (WPA), also under Hopkins's direction. This agency employed millions of people on road building, flood control projects, and similar programs. Its most famous and controversial projects employed writers, photographers, and other creative artists. Critics complained, with some justice, that these projects often had strong leftwing political messages. But some of the projects, for example recording the recollections of the last generation of former slaves, also had lasting value. Under Hopkins's direction the main emphasis of the WPA was creating employment; the contribution of these projects to the infrastructure of the economy was secondary. Another well-known agency with a similar purpose was the Civilian Conservation Corps (CCC), which hired young men to work on planting trees and other outdoor conservation projects. Thus began the creation of a myriad of federal agencies to deal with the problems created by the Depression. Critics of the administration complained that this "alphabet soup" was turning the United States into a bureaucratic state. But there can be no doubt, as revealed by Roosevelt's overwhelming reelection victories in 1936 and 1940, that a majority of the public approved of the administration's active and experimental response to the crisis.

The New Deal did not merely supply temporary relief. It reformed the economic system to try to prevent a recurrence of depression and to redress the imbalance between rich and poor that had existed even before the crash. And it experimented.

Reform of the financial system was an obvious and popular place to start. One of the first pieces of New Deal legislation was the Truth-in-Securities Act of 1933, which required issuers of new securities to register them with the Federal Trade Commission. Later this power, along with far more general regulatory authority, was transferred to the newly created Securities and Exchange Commission (SEC). The power to set margin requirements on stock purchases, however, was given to the Fed. The stock market boom had been attributed, in part, to the buying of stock on margin with very little money down. The Fed, moreover, had argued that its inability to stop the boom in time to prevent a collapse was due to the lack of an instrument aimed directly at the stock market.

Inevitably, much of this legislation was based on ill-conceived theories of what caused the Depression and the pleadings of special interests. The prohibition of interest payments on bank deposits is an example. Until the

1930s commercial banks were free to compete for deposits by offering to pay interest on them. But many bankers argued that this forced them to take unnecessary risks in order to maintain their deposits. It is not hard to see why Congress responded to this argument during the Depression by prohibiting interest payments on checking accounts. But the long-run effect of this legislation was simply to help some of the less competitive banks maintain their share of the market at the expense of consumers.

A fundamental readjustment of the industrial wage structure was attempted with the National Industrial Recovery Act (NIRA). The chief purposes of the act were to raise prices and wages, spread out work by reducing hours, and prevent price cutting by competitors trying to maintain volume. A National Recovery Administration (NRA) under the direction of General Hugh Johnson supervised the preparation of a "code of fair practice" for each industry. Deputy administrators, presumably assisted by representatives of employers, labor, and consumers, prepared the codes, which were really agreements among sellers to set minimum prices, limit output, and establish minimum wages and maximum hours of work. Pending the approval of basic codes, the President issued a "blanket code" in July 1933. Sellers signing the blanket code agreed to raise wages, shorten the maximum work-week, and abstain from price cutting. In return, they could display a "blue eagle" and avoid being boycotted for not doing their part. By 1935, 557 basic codes had been approved. In practice, labor representatives participated in the construction of less than 10 percent of the codes, and consumer representation was negligible. Employer representatives found it convenient to work through their national trade associations and manufacturers' institutes, with the consequence that prices were set with a view toward profit maximization in the manner of a European cartel.

Roosevelt's broad grin, in evidence above, center, at the 1936 Democratic convention, made his theme song, "Happy Days Are Here Again," believable to a shaken nation. His charm and buoyancy did much in itself to soften the Depression's psychological impact.

The possibility of such an outcome was recognized in the NIRA by suspending the antitrust laws.

The effectiveness of the NIRA and other New Deal measures, especially in the early phase of development, will forever be debated. For the most part, however, they redistributed rather than expanded incomes. Higher farm prices for farmers resulted in higher food costs for consumers, and higher prices may have reduced output levels in some sectors. Manufacturing output jumped after the institution of NRA, as merchants added to their inventories in anticipation of price increases. But industrial production lapsed again, and by mid-summer of 1935 the index was no higher than it had been after the first NRA spurt. Unemployment, although reduced, was still incredibly high, and most manufacturing firms were operating at far less than capacity.

Agricultural poverty sent thousands fleeing from the Midwest to California, with belongings piled in the family jalopy. A nation that "drove to the poor house in an automobile," as Will Rogers said, had to change some of its babies' diapers on the miserable highways of the time.

Early in 1935, there was a growing awareness that the lift the economy had experienced had come chiefly from income injections via deficit spending and money creation. It was with little regret, then, that New Dealers saw the passing of NRA, which was declared unconstitutional by the Supreme Court on the grounds that Congress had illegally delegated legislative powers to the president.

The Tennessee Valley Authority

A more conventional approach to the Depression was the construction of large-scale public works through a variety of agencies. But the most ambitious and controversial of all the New Deal public works was clearly the Tennessee Valley Authority (TVA). This was a multifaceted project designed to promote economic development in a large region that had been poverty stricken for decades. The TVA built dams in a seven-state area (see Map 24-1), supplied low-cost electric power to farmers (a policy that created con-

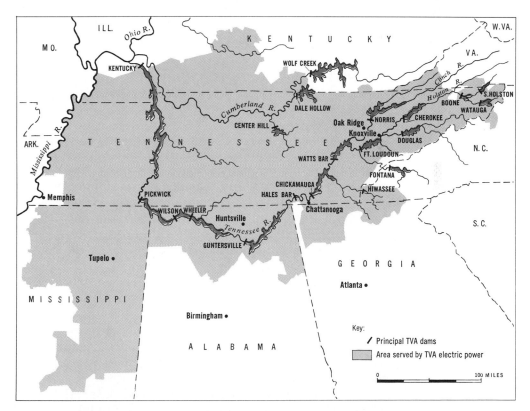

MAP 24-1   Public Power: The Tennessee Valley Authority—the New Deal's major experiment in publicly financed power—ranges through portions of seven states. Its supporters call the TVA a splendid monument to "regional planning;" its foes denounce it as a noxious example of "creeping socialism."

siderable opposition from private power companies), engaged in flood control, created inland navigation routes, and promoted farmer education and related projects.

Any judgment about the overall effect of the TVA would be hotly debated. But there is agreement that in the area of conservation, it has been a success. First, major floods are a thing of the past in the Tennessee Valley; this means that much of the bottom land in the valley is protected from the periodic dumping of erosion debris. Second, the TVA has done much to prevent upland erosion. Although a unified system of dams and reservoirs can prevent *major* floods and their consequent destruction of bottom land, the problem of erosion on the uplands remains. Silting from the uplands is the enemy of the reservoirs and the navigable channel; it must be stopped at the source—where the raindrop strikes the ground. Thus, TVA authorities have had no choice but to work hard to secure the general adoption of conservation practices. Their program includes reforestation and afforestation, the substitution of cover crops for row crops, contour plowing, and the building of check dams to prevent rapid runoff. Technical assistance and demonstration, in cooperation with other federal agencies and with state universities, has been the chief help to the landowner, but free seedlings and fertilizers have frequently swung the balance in securing the farmers' cooperation.

AGRICULTURE AND THE NEW DEAL

With the onset of the Great Depression, farm people began to suffer a severity of economic distress that only a few old timers would have believed possible. Yet in many ways, the rural communities, which had suffered through hardship and waves of bank failures in the 1920s, were perhaps the best prepared psychologically for the crisis.

The first signs of depression reality came with the downturn and then tumble of agricultural prices. From an overall farm price index of 147 in January 1930, there was a drop to 57 in February 1933 (1909–14 = 100). Individual price series from the Department of Agriculture show that in three years the average price of corn at central markets fell from $0.77 to $0.19 per bushel, and the average price of wheat dropped from $1.08 to $0.33 per bushel. At many local elevators, the selling point for farmers, 10-cent corn and 25-cent wheat were common, and 5-cent cotton similarly burdened southern planters.

In terms of farm income, the picture was just as bad. Gross farm income, which had reached a postwar high of almost $14 billion in 1929, slipped to $11 billion in 1930 and fell drastically to about $6.5 billion in 1932. Production expenses also declined during these years. But gross income fell more; therefore, in 1932 net realized income in agriculture was less than one-third of what it had been in 1929. Indeed, it was only one-half of that recorded in the exceptionally bad year of 1921.

Farmers with fixed indebtedness were particularly hard hit, and in 1932, 52 percent of all farm debts (45 percent of all farm debtors) were in default. The threat of foreclosure reached an all-time high and marred the lives of rural people everywhere. From the record high level of 17 farm foreclosures per thousand farms in 1926 (14.9 in 1929) foreclosures jumped to 18.0 per thousand farms in 1930, 27.8 per thousand in 1931, and peaked at 38.1 per thousand in 1932.[1]

Most devices to help farmers in earlier years had centered on the notion of price parity or "fair exchange" values as Senator George Norris had called them. Most acceptable to politicians had been the traditional devices of high tariffs, and high duties were imposed with the Smoot–Hawley Act of 1929. Far more important, however, was the passage of the Agricultural Marketing Act of 1929, which was the outcome of Republican campaign promises of 1928. This predepression law committed the government to a policy of farm price stabilization and established a Federal Farm Board to encourage the formation of cooperative marketing associations. The Board was also authorized to establish "stabilization corporations" to be owned by the cooperatives and to use an initial fund of $500 million for price-support operations.

With the onset of serious depression in 1930, the Federal Farm Board strove valiantly to support farm prices through its stabilization corporations, but between June 1929 and June 1932 the corporations bought surplus farm products only to suffer steadily increasing losses as prices continued to decline. The Board itself took over the operation and accepted the losses, expending in three years some $676 million in stabilization operations and loans to cooperatives. While all this was going on, however, farmers faced with catastrophically falling prices increased output. At the time it seemed that prices could not be supported in a sustained fashion without production controls.

The Crystallization of a Farm Policy, 1933–41

By the date of Franklin D. Roosevelt's inauguration, theories about farm policy had undergone fundamental changes. Proponents of dumping American farm products abroad were successful in securing the dollar devaluation of 1933–34, which made dollars cheaper in terms of foreign currencies, thereby stimulating the demand for U.S. commodities traded in world markets. But this solution to the farmer's dilemma was not satisfactory either, because the worldwide depression was accompanied by extremely low world prices, and other countries devalued their currencies,

---

[1] H. Thomas Johnson, "Postwar Optimism and the Rural Financial Crisis of the 1920s," *Explorations in Economic History* 11 (Winter 1973/74): 176.

too. American policymakers wished to devise a plan to raise farm prices substantially in the home market. It soon became clear that supports through purchases and loans, like those attempted by the Federal Farm Board, would require enormous outlays. Consequently, a scheme evolved that took the central idea of the domestic-allotment plan, a plan that had been widely discussed in the 1920s.

In May 1933, the Agricultural Adjustment Act was passed. One of the first major pieces of New Deal legislation, it provided for an Agricultural Adjustment Administration, popularly referred to as the AAA, which was given the responsibility of raising farm prices by restricting the supply of farm commodities. The most important weapon of the AAA was the "acreage allotment." Taking into consideration prospective demand and carry-over from the previous season, the AAA would determine a total acreage of certain major crops to be planted in the next growing season. The total acreage would then be subdivided into state totals, which were in turn to be allotted to individual farms on the basis of each farm's recent crop history. For example, the base acreage for each wheat farm was to be the average acreage in wheat from 1928 to 1932. To secure the cooperation of the individual farmer, a direct "benefit payment," later called an "adjustment payment," was made. In the beginning, wheat farmers who restricted acreage received about $0.30 a bushel on 54 percent of their average production in the base period. The payment was made by check from the federal Treasury, but in these early New Deal days it still seemed a little too much to expect the general taxpayer to foot the bill—at least directly. The benefit payments were financed, therefore, by processing taxes paid by the first processor of any product (millers, for example, had to pay a tax for each bushel of wheat that was ground into flour), although it was not expected that the processor would bear the burden of the tax. It was assumed that the processing tax would be shifted forward and be paid by the consumer.

The original AAA scheme experienced a setback in 1936 when the Supreme Court, in the Hoosac Mills case, declared that the Agricultural Adjustment Act was unconstitutional because it attempted to regulate agricultural production—a power reserved to the several states. The processing tax was specifically declared invalid. The adverse decision did not force a discontinuance of acreage allotments, but only changed the *basis* on which these allotments were made to one that presumably encouraged soil conservation.

The drought of 1936, with its attendant dust-bowl conditions, provided the needed loophole, focused attention on the need for vigorous soil-conservation measures, and prompted passage of the Soil Conservation and Domestic Allotment Act of that year.[2] Under this act, the Secretary of Agri-

---

[2]The migration of the "Okies" from the dust bowl of the Midwest to California is eloquently described by John Steinbeck in *The Grapes of Wrath*. A superb movie based on the novel stars Jane Darwell and Henry Fonda.

Adding to the farmer's woes during the depressed 1930s were several years of unprecedented heat and drought. The subsequent blowing of previously eroded land often left bleak landscapes, like this one in the Texas panhandle.

culture could replace the old type of specific contract between the government and the farmer with an open offer to make benefit payments to anyone who would reduce acreage of soil-depleting crops and take steps to conserve or rebuild the land withheld from production. But production in 1937 was very high, and there was pressure to supplement acreage reduction with even more vigorous measures.

The soil-conservation basis for acreage allotments was maintained. However, in 1938 Congress passed a new Agricultural Adjustment Act, which placed more emphasis than ever before on the principle of giving direct support to prices. Since 1933, the Commodity Credit Corporation (CCC) had operated as an independent agency, performing the minor function of "cushioning" the prices of corn, wheat, and cotton against adverse fluctuations in demand and supply. The CCC had carried out the cushioning process by making loans to farmers on the security of their crops. Most of these loans were made "without recourse." Nonrecourse loans were a heads-you-win, tails-I-lose proposition. If the CCC extended an advance against a commodity and the price of that commodity fell, the farmer could let the CCC take title to the stored product and cancel the debt together with the accumulated interest. If the price of the commodity against which the advance had been made rose, the farmer could sell the commodity, pay back the loan with interest, and keep any profit. Thus, loan rates became, in effect, minimum prices. From 1933 to 1937, CCC operations were carried out with reference to vague price objectives. In these early years, no loans were made on wheat because short crops kept wheat prices around $1 a bushel.

Lending on corn and cotton was nominal due to reasonably high loan rates combined with a strong tendency for prices to move upward.

The Agricultural Adjustment Act of 1938 greatly increased the power of the CCC by making it mandatory that the directors extend loans on corn, wheat, and cotton at favorable rates. From this point on, Congress was to specify support prices at a certain percentage of parity prices, parity prices being defined as farm prices adjusted to have the same purchasing power as those prevailing in a favorable base period. In 1938 and for many years thereafter, the base period for most products was 1910–14, derived from a time when farm prices relative to other prices were exceptionally high.

Mandatory supports went into effect after farm prices had dropped from their post-Depression "recovery" highs of 1937. From 1939 to 1941, the CCC accumulated great quantities of wheat, corn, cotton, and tobacco. Strengthened demand following the outbreak of the Second World War enabled the government to sell these stocks at a profit, but large holdings of wheat were stored into the war years, and vast amounts of low-grade, short-staple cotton were not disposed of until even later.

Two other means of restricting the supply of farm products came into use during the 1930s. One of these, the *marketing agreement,* was tried in the early experimental years, then fell into disuse, and finally after 1937 became important in the production of certain fruits and vegetables and in the chief milk areas. Marketing agreements are contracts between an association of producers of a raw product and the processors of that product; the contractual agreement is reviewed by a Department of Agriculture representative. Producers and processors may set minimum prices, total quantities to be marketed, and allotments of marketings among processors. Milk producers and the city milk companies, in addition to controlling the amounts of milk marketed, have made a profitable enterprise of establishing different prices in different markets for milk uses with different elasticities of demand—that is, by becoming discriminating monopolists.

Marketing quotas became important after 1936, when Congress empowered the Secretary of Agriculture to set an upper limit to the quantities that growers of certain crops could sell. Before such controls could be instituted, the Secretary had to determine that the current supply of a basic commodity exceeded a "reserve supply." A referendum was then held, and if two-thirds of the qualified producers approved, a quota was assigned to each grower. Any farmer who marketed amounts in excess of the quota was subject to a penalty or fine on the excess sold.

The Roosevelt administration, in its search for ways to increase farm income, introduced a number of "surplus removal" programs. The more acceptable operation has been the nutrition or direct-distribution programs. Nutrition programs have taken the form of food-stamp plans, low-cost milk distribution plans, and school lunch programs. School lunch programs were so readily accepted by the public that they have since been authorized by separate legislation without any implications of furnishing relief. The Food

Stamp Plan, in operation from 1939 to 1942, won enthusiastic support.[3] Stamps given to low-income families were (indeed, still are) used to purchase food from regular retail outlets; storekeepers, in turn, cashed the stamps in at the Treasury. Thus, surplus commodities were given to those who presumably had the greatest need for them. In addition to using up the excess stocks, they, in effect, helped offset the effect on the poor of artificially high prices created by the crop restrictions.

The second type of surplus-removal operation has been the *export subsidy*. This method of increasing the sales of farm commodities originated with the Agricultural Adjustment Act of 1933, but not until the passage of an amendment in 1935 (commonly referred to as Section 32) did sales become significant. In that year, the amendment provided that as much as 30 percent of annual customs revenues might be used to finance the disposal of farm surpluses at home and abroad.

The subsidization of exports by payments of bounties did not reach alarming proportions before the Second World War.[4] In the fiscal year 1939–40, bounties for wheat and cotton amounted to $26 million and $38 million, respectively. In the postwar period, however, expenditure of public funds on export subsidies would become an effective, if somewhat dubious, means of adding to American farm income.

The Impact on Farmers

The price-support programs of the Agricultural Adjustment Act and other New Deal legislation in agriculture succeeded in improving the relative price and income positions of farmers. Farm prices began to rise in April 1933, more than doubling and ultimately climbing to an index of 131 early in 1937. The recession of 1937–38 affected the agricultural sector, and the index of farm prices reverted back to 100, where it stood in both the first and last months of 1940. Meanwhile, prices *paid by* farmers recovered somewhat from a 1933 low and then remained almost stable through 1940; because farm prices recovered more than industrial prices, the terms of

---

[3] In 1961, advocates finally secured reactivation of this program—first on a pilot basis in eight economically distressed areas, and then on a permanent basis nationwide. The fiscal 1971 appropriation for the national food-stamp program was just over $1.4 billion, roughly three times the amount budgeted for school lunch and special milk programs. In 1981, the Food Stamp Program costs exceeded $10 billion.

[4] An export bounty is a payment to exporters of so much per unit of commodity to offset losses incurred in the process of buying in the artificially supported home market and selling at lower world prices. This kind of interference with international trade, a form of dumping, can be defended on the grounds that it offers the rest of the world an enhancement of real income: other countries can enjoy the goods that are dumped. But it adversely affects the income and marketing positions of producers of competing commodities, hurting friendly nations in a way the United States has always considered unfair. Matters of U.S. relationships with other countries aside, there are always other ways to give farmers as large an income as can be obtained with an export subsidy and taxes. For further details, see D. Gale Johnson, *Trade and Agriculture* (New York: John Wiley & Sons, 1950).

exchange (parity ratio) were definitely improved. From the low of 1932, gross farm income moved steadily upward to $11 billion in 1937, declined slightly for two years, and then rebounded to the $11 billion mark in 1940— about where it had been a decade earlier.

American preparation for war, which began in 1940, did not affect agricultural markets until the next year. However, in 1941, the demand for farm products for both export and domestic consumption increased noticeably, and the U.S.' entrance into the war late in the year further removed farmers from their troubled past.

Clearly, Roosevelt's New Deal for farmers was far removed from Harding's policy advice that "the farmer must be ready to help himself." But the most concrete step taken by government was its advance into production controls. To restrict output in agriculture and raise prices on food and fiber when the major national problems were economic depression, massive unemployment, and hunger, must certainly be viewed with suspicion if not outright alarm. As with other types of New Deal legislation aimed at helping particular groups, the primary outcome was to redistribute income. In that respect, Roosevelt's farm policy was more responsive to a powerful political block than it was counter-recessionary or stimulative on a broad economic front. Nevertheless, it had very broad consequences, for never again, except in temporary short periods, did agricultural production become guided by "free market" forces. The acceptance by the American people of the principle that the government ought to bolster the economic fortunes of particular occupational groups or classes was of momentous importance. Farmers have not been the only beneficiaries of this emerging philosophy; but we cannot find a better example of the way in which legislation, passed at first in an effort to relieve emergency distress, has become accepted as a permanent part of the economic mechanism. It is this monumental change in attitudes—away from reliance on markets and toward dependence on government—that marks the most significant characteristic of the Great Depression.

THE NEW DEAL AND THE UNIONS

Besides the advance of government relief agencies, further bonding between government and workers came about in the 1930s as new powers were given to unions. Most important of these were the right to strike and to organize, free of employer interference.

As noted in Chapter 22, union membership had declined sharply in the early 1920s, falling from over 5 million in 1920, to 3.5 million in 1923. It remained steady around this level until 1930, when it began falling again before reaching bottom in 1933. (See Table 24-1 and 22-3 for comparison.)

By this time, and before the new administration had been in power a year, the more vigorous union leaders sensed that the government would encourage organization and that the attitude of the nation toward unions had changed as people became disillusioned with business. Especially successful in their organizational efforts were the powerful and able leaders of the industrial unions that had evolved within the AFL: John L. Lewis of the United Mine Workers, Sidney Hillman of the Amalgamated Clothing Workers, and David Dubinsky of the International Ladies Garment Workers.

By the mid-1930s, a conflict within labor over the question of proper union structure had grown to major proportions. The move to organize the new mass-production industries (steel, automobiles, rubber, and electrical equipment) was inevitable; but the older unions hampered such organization by insisting that their craft jurisdiction remain inviolate and by raiding the membership of the new industrial unions. In 1935, eight industrial unions formed the Committee for Industrial Organization within the AFL, and in 1936 these unions were suspended from the federation. Three years later, the CIO became a separate entity, the Congress of Industrial Organization.

Conflict continued between these two great federations, but the competition seemed only to spur membership growth. There was defection, to be sure. After interminable controversy over policy, John L. Lewis resigned from the presidency of the CIO and withdrew the United Mine Workers from it. After unsuccessfully attempting to attract other unions to coalesce about him, Lewis rejoined the AFL in 1946 only to disaffiliate the next year. Meanwhile CIO leaders made no secret of their contempt for the AFL's lack of militancy and its failure to participate aggressively in political activities, and AFL leaders viewed the CIO's violent break with conservative unionism with concern. But complacency and inertia no longer beset the labor movement. In 1955, the AFL and the CIO, prodded into unity by hostile public opinion and punitive labor legislation, merged to form the AFL–CIO.[5]

As shown in Table 24-1, however, the period of most rapid union membership growth came in the mid-1930s not in the later years of greater leadership accord. Consequently, it was not so much from bold well-organized union leadership as from a new pro-labor attitude of government in the 1930s that barriers to organization were broken down. This is clearly revealed in the labor legislation of the New Deal.

New Legislation

Except for legislation that applied only to the railroad industry, Congress refused to interfere by statute with labor relations until 1932. The Norris–LaGuardia Act of 1932, however, created a first great step toward removing the barriers to free organization. Largely procedural in character, the act had the effect of eliminating or modifying the worst abuses of the labor

---

[5] Roughly 50 percent of the total membership was in AFL affiliates, 30 percent in CIO unions, and the remainder in unaffiliated unions.

TABLE 24-1   Union Membership, 1930–55 (in thousands)

Year	Number	Year	Number
1930	3,401	1943	13,213
1931	3,310	1944	14,146
1932	3,050	1945	14,322
1933	2,689	1946	14,395
1934	3,088	1947	14,787
1935	3,584	1948	14,300
1936	3,989	1949	14,300
1937	7,001	1950	14,300
1938	8,034	1951	15,900
1939	8,763	1952	15,900
1940	8,717	1953	16,948
1941	10,201	1954	17,022
1942	10,380	1955	16,802

Sources: U.S. Bureau of Labor Statistics, "Handbook of Labor Statistics 1971," *Monthly Labor Reviews* (Jan. 1972).

injunction. The yellow-dog contract was eliminated by making it nonenforceable in the federal courts, and the issuance of injunctions was greatly restricted. Moreover, as a result of a liberal definition of the term *labor dispute*, unions were freed to engage in organizational activity. Specifically, the term was defined in such a way as to permit *secondary* activity in the form of boycotting and picketing by nonemployees as distinguished from the narrower concept of *primary* activity only. By the act, the government granted to workers the opportunity to organize but did not positively intercede to assure that they could secure the benefits of collective bargaining.

The first positive assertion of the right of labor to bargain collectively was contained in Section 7a of the National Industrial Recovery Act, but no means of enforcing the statement of principle were provided. Two years later, the NIRA was declared unconstitutional on grounds that had nothing to do with the labor section, and Congress replaced Section 7a with a much more elaborate law of labor relations. This was the National Labor Relations Act, usually referred to as the Wagner Act after its sponsor, Senator Robert F. Wagner of New York.

The Wagner Act

The Wagner Act proceeded from the explicit premises that inequality of bargaining power between employees and large business units depresses "the purchasing power of wage earners in industry" and prevents "stabilization of competitive wage rates and working conditions," and that denial of the right to self-organization creates industrial strife. The act established the principle of collective bargaining as the cornerstone of industrial relations in the United States and stated that it was management's obligation to recognize and deal with a bona fide labor organization in good faith. The act further guaranteed workers the right to form and join a labor organization, to engage in collective bargaining, to select representatives of their own choosing, and to engage in concerted activity. In addition, the Wagner Act outlawed a list of "unfair" managerial practices that had the effect of denying worker rights. Henceforth, employers could *not*:

1. Interfere with, restrain, or coerce employees in the exercise of their rights of self-organization and collective bargaining.
2. Dominate or interfere with the formation or administration of any labor organization or contribute financial or other support to it.
3. Encourage or discourage union membership by discrimination in regard to hiring or tenure of employment or condition of work, except such discrimination as might be involved in a closed-shop agreement with a bona fide union enjoying majority status.
4. Discharge or otherwise discriminate against an employee for filing charges or testifying under the Act.
5. Refuse to bargain collectively.

The Wagner Act was no mere statement of principles. It established a National Labor Relations Board (NLRB), composed of three members with genuine powers of enforcement. After hearings regarding a union complaint, the board could issue cease-and-desist orders to employers who were judged guilty of unfair labor practices. If employers did not comply with these orders, the NLRB could turn to a U.S. Circuit Court of Appeals for enforcement. The board also had the power, on its own initiative or at the request of a union, to supervise a free, secret election among a company's employees to determine which union, if any, should represent the workers.

When the Supreme Court declared the law constitutional in 1937, there were no remaining barriers to the rapid organization of labor. But before the question of constitutionality was settled, many employers openly violated the act, producing increasing turbulence in labor relations. Animosity between the suspended CIO unions and the AFL grew, leading to jurisdictional conflicts that the NLRB had to spend much time settling. As industrial strife seemed to be increasing rather than decreasing, there were public demands for amendments to the act, and employers complained bitterly of the one-sidedness of the law. From labor's view, however, the Wagner Act was its Magna Charta.

The Wagner Act was never intended to be a comprehensive code of labor relations. It did not even define "collective bargaining," nor did it cover the problems of jurisdictional disputes, "national emergency" disputes, and secondary boycotts. If the Second World War had not intervened, basic amendments to the act would doubtless have been made sooner, but the war placed the national problem of labor relations almost in abeyance.

FURTHER QUESTS FOR SECURITY

Before 1932, loss of income from any cause other than industrial accident posed a great hardship, because workers had no economic protection except the buffer of their savings, organized charity, and payments from the relief agencies of states and their subdivisions. The burden of relief during the Great Depression soon overwhelmed charitable organizations and local government units, and the federal government, largely through the WPA and other emergency agencies, took over the job. This experience with federal relief convinced the majority of Americans, on both economic and ethical grounds, of the necessity of a permanent plan for coping with severe losses in income.

A few leaders in government, business, and the universities had long argued that a comprehensive program of social security was requisite to the adequate functioning of a modern industrial economy. Such programs had long been common in Europe. Yet as late as 1930, there was little public sentiment in favor of social-security legislation. Americans believed that the individual ought to be self-reliant and objected to compulsory supportive action by the government. In agriculture, where the need for social insurance was not so pronounced, there was understandable opposition to additional taxes for such insurance. The astonishing fact is that organized labor itself did not support social insurance (except worker compensation) before 1930; as late as 1931, a national AFL convention refused to endorse unemployment-insurance legislation. Not inconsequential opposition was also voiced by private insurance companies, which sought to prevent, or at least modify, government insurance of social risks.

Four years of economic disaster removed all serious obstacles to major legislation. Whatever the philosophical objection to a social security program may have been, certain hard facts of life were undeniable. Almost four out of every five income receivers depended on paid employment for their livelihood. There were many hazards to continuity of income, some of which seemed to be increasing in severity as the economy became more specialized. Income interruptions included being laid off, getting sick, being injured on the job, and becoming too old to meet the demands of modern industrial life. Finally, the *incidence* of income interruptions, although uncertain and uneven, fell most heavily on low-income people, who were the least able to prepare for them.

The Social Security Act of 1935

The Social Security Act of 1935, which has since been amended, has attacked social risks through application of the *insurance* principle and the *assistance* principle. Under social-insurance programs, the individual acquires a *right* to income because of premiums paid. The 1935 act in particular provided for a federal old-age and survivors' insurance program based on payments from workers of one percent of earnings up to $3,600 with the employers paying an equal share.[6] It further provided for *assistance* to the needy aged, needy and dependent children, and needy blind, and recent amendments have added other groups.

Under continuing pressure for ever-higher employee benefits, Congress has further increased substantially both individual and employer contributions and benefits. This fact reflects its strong appeal to Americans generally and to those who remember when social insurance first emancipated millions of workers from the fear of one day being "on the county."

The program of unemployment insurance was less extensive in its aim than Social Security, but it has been a powerful short-run help to discharged workers. Largely to circumvent legal difficulties, unemployment insurance is provided through state systems. The Social Security Act of 1935 secured state action by levying a 3-percent tax on the first $3,000 of wages paid by employers in all except a few business occupations. Similar to changes in Social Security, recent trends have been to make unemployment insurance laws more liberal—partly in recognition of the fact that unemployment compensation is a highly dependable automatic stabilizer. This automatic stabilizing effect occurs through the timely increase in unemployment compensation payments when unemployment increases. This lowers the fall in income and expenditures of displaced workers, thereby helping to stabilize the economy "automatically."

MONETARY AND FISCAL POLICY, 1934–1939

From a low of $42.7 billion in 1933, net national product rose to $75.1 billion in 1937, still well below the level of 1929, but sufficient to alleviate much hardship and to show the potential of the economy to recover. Unemployment fell from 20.9 percent to 9.2 percent. (Although over 5 percent of the labor force had jobs with emergency agencies.) Over the same period the implicit price deflator rose from 73.3 to 81 (1929 = 100). So the gain in real net national product was substantial. This boom was stimulated in part by the expansion of government spending for relief and other programs and by the expansion of the money stock from $32.2 billion in 1933 to $45.7 billion in 1937. The expansion of the stock of money was not, however, due to a deliberate policy by the Fed of increasing the stock of

---

[6] It should be emphasized that the premium payment by the employer is part of the wage cost to the employer. Therefore, this results in a lower wage being paid to the worker. It is an unfortunate but common misconception that the employer pays half the premiums; actually, the worker pays almost the entire amount. It is also important to understand that these payments are not saved or placed in a fund. Rather, they have been promptly spent by those receiving Social Security checks.

money to fight the Depression. Instead, it was due to an influx of gold. To see how this happened we need to take a close look at gold policy.

The New Deal changed the gold standard in two important ways. First, it prohibited banks from paying out gold to private citizens and prohibited Americans from owning and using gold in ordinary transactions. One of the first measures designed to carry out this policy was a proclamation issued on April 5, 1933, requiring American citizens to turn over all their gold (except for small amounts held for coin collections) to the Federal Reserve banks in exchange for Federal Reserve notes or bank deposits. The purpose of this policy was to help end the banking panic and prevent a recurrence. If all that one could draw out of a bank was Federal Reserve notes, there was less likelihood of a run; and if there was a run, there was no danger that the Federal Reserve could not supply enough notes.

The second change in the gold standard was to raise the dollar price of gold (now paid primarily to producers or foreigners, since U.S. citizens had surrendered most of their gold). Over less than a year, the U.S. Treasury raised the price it would pay for gold from $20.67 per ounce, to $35.00 per ounce. What good would this price change, known as a devaluation of the dollar, do? Potentially, it could lower the price of agricultural products sold on world markets and stimulate sales of U.S. exports. For example, suppose some other country, Britain for instance, had kept its currency fixed in relation to gold, say at 5 pounds per ounce. Then the effect of raising the price of gold would be to increase the exchange rate from about $4.13 per pound ($20.67 ÷ 5 pound) to $7.00 per pound ($35.00 ÷ 5 pound). Obviously, Britains then pay lower prices on goods from the United States.

Because the economic collapse was worldwide, however, the situation was not so simple. Other countries devalued their own currencies to offset, or more than offset, the devaluations undertaken by the United States or other trading partners; some countries such as Britain went off the gold standard altogether.

But by being willing to exchange dollars for gold at an even higher price than before the Depression, the Treasury did produce a substantial effect on the stock of money. When the Treasury purchased gold, it created gold certificates which it could use as cash or deposit with the Fed. In effect, when the Treasury bought gold, it was allowed to pay for it by printing new currency. So an inflow of gold increased the amount of money in the economy. Moreover, a number of factors tended to increase the flow of gold into the United States. For one, world production of gold was increasing. After all, gold was one of the few products whose price was increasing while the price of almost every other product was falling. In addition, the rise of fascism in Europe created a large outflow of capital seeking a safe haven.

As measures aimed at restoring confidence in the banking system such as Federal Deposit Insurance took hold, people began to redeposit Federal Reserve notes in the banking system. This process also led to an increase in the money stock because banks would create several dollars of loans and deposits on the basis of each additional dollar of currency redeposited. The fractional reserve system that had worked to destroy the monetary system in 1930–33 now ran in reverse. This influence was partly offset, however, by the tendency on the part of the banks to build up their excess reserves. (If a bank was legally required to hold, say, $15 in cash or deposits at the Fed for each $100 in deposits, and it actually held $20, then it would have $5 in excess reserves.)

By early 1937 total manufacturing output had exceeded the rate of 1929. But at that point the expansion came to an abrupt halt. Industrial production reached a post-1929 high in May 1937 and then turned downward. Commodity prices followed, and the weary process of deflation began again. Retail sales dropped off, unemployment increased, and payrolls declined substantially. Adding to the general gloom, the stock market started a long slide in August that brought prices in March 1938 to less than half the peak of the previous year. The important setbacks of 1937 are revealed graphically in each of Figures 23-1, 23-2, 23-3, 23-4, and 23-5 (pp. 479–85).

What had happened? Then, as now, many attributed the renewed onslaught of depression to the reform measures introduced and passed in 1935 and 1936. Social Security and the new freedom granted labor came in for some hard words. But most of the criticism was directed toward the hostile political climate in which, it was asserted, vigorous business expansion was impossible. In his state-of-the-union message of 1936 President Roosevelt had castigated "the royalists of the economic order" who opposed government intervention in economic affairs and received a disproportionate amount of national income. Tax legislation in 1935 and 1936, directed at preventing tax avoidance and making the tax structure more progressive, was especially resented by people of means. In addition, estate and gift taxes were increased, as were individual surtaxes, and taxes on the income of large corporations. The undistributed profits tax of 1936—a surtax imposed on corporations to make them distribute profits instead of holding them so that individual stockholders could avoid personal taxation—was also resented. Why would business undertake long-term investments, critics of the administration wondered, when the profits might all be taken away from them by future legislation?

But whatever merit there is in this argument, it is clear that fiscal and monetary policy also played a role in causing the downturn. Government officials were persuaded in early 1937 that full employment and inflation were just around the corner. Therefore, expenditures for relief and public works were cut. In conjunction with the new taxes (those discussed and the Social Security tax), the result was that the projected deficit for 1937 dropped significantly. Keynesian economists would not be surprised to find a recession.

Monetary policy also worked to create a recession. The excess reserves of the banks, as we noted, had risen steadily after the banking crises of the early 1930s. The Fed interpreted these reserves simply as money that could not be profitably invested at the low rates then prevailing. Money was just piling up in the banks because they didn't know what to do with it. The Fed then decided to raise legal reserve ratios to lock up the excess reserves and prevent them from being put into use during the not-too-distant inflation. This proved, however, to have been a disastrous mistake. In fact these reserves were not unwanted by the banks. The banks had been deliberately building up a cushion in the event of a replay of the banking crises. Their response to the Fed's decision to raise legal reserve ratios was to restore their margin above the legal reserve ratio. To do this they had to reduce their loans and deposits. The stock of money fell once again, although only slightly, in 1937.

The recession of 1937–38 unlike the great contraction of 1929–33, however, was quickly countered by expansionary fiscal and monetary policies. Following an explicit recommendation of the president to increase the national income through fiscal policy, Congress provided increased appropriations for the Works Progress Administration. The Fed also helped by reverting to an easy-money policy, and the stock of money soared in the latter half of 1938. No more tax reforms were introduced, and the only reform measure of any consequence passed in 1938 was the Fair Labor Standards Act. Business picked up in the summer of 1938, and recovery was well under way toward the close of the year.

Not until the end of 1939, however, was total industrial production back to 1937 peak levels, and the output of durables did not reach the 1937 level until well into 1940. Conventional estimates of the level of unemployment place the unemployment rate in 1939 at an incredible 17.2 percent of the labor force. Workers in the Civilian Conservation Corps and other emergency programs, however, were counted as unemployed. As Michael Darby shows in his important article, if these workers are counted among the employed, the unemployment rate in 1939 was 11.3 percent of the labor force. This was down considerably from the 22.0 percent reached in 1933, but still extremely disappointing after a decade of fighting the Depression.[7] The final cure for the Depression, as we will see in the next chapter, was the tremendous expansion of private investment, government spending, and the stock of money generated by the Second World War.[8]

SELECTED REFERENCES AND SUGGESTED READINGS

Allen, Frederick Lewis. *Since Yesterday: The Nineteen Thirties in America.* New York: Harper & Brothers, 1940.
Alston, Lee J. "Farm Foreclosures in the United States during the Interwar Period." *Journal of Economic History* 43 (1983): 885–903.

---

[7] See Michael Darby, "Three and a Half Million U.S. Employees Have Been Mislaid," *Journal of Political Economy* 84 (Feb. 1976): 1–16.

[8] The reader should be warned that our analysis follows the conventional approach that attributes stimulative effects to government deficits. An influential school of modern macroeconomists holds that deficit spending will not stimulate the economy because private citizens will increase savings in anticipation of higher future taxes.

———. "Farm Foreclosure Moratorium Legislation: A Lesson from the Past." *American Economic Review* 74 (1984): 445–57.

Bernstein, Michael. *The Great Depression: Delayed Recovery and Economic Change in America.* New York: Cambridge Univ. Press, 1988.

———. "A Reassessment of Investment Failure in the Interwar American Economy." *The Journal of Economic History* 44 (1984): 479–88.

Brunner, Karl, ed. *The Great Depression Revisited.* Boston: Martinus Nijhoff, 1981.

Chandler, Lester V. *America's Greatest Depression, 1929–1941.* New York: Harper & Row, 1970.

Darby, Michael. "Three and a Half Million U.S. Employees Have Been Mislaid: Or, an Explanation of Unemployment, 1934–41." *Journal of Political Economy* 84 (Feb. 1976): 1–16.

Hawley, Ellis W. *The New Deal and the Problem of Monopoly: A Study in Economic Ambivalence.* Princeton: Princeton Univ. Press, 1966.

Higgs, Robert. *Crisis and Leviathan: Critical Episodes in the Growth of American Government.* New York: Oxford Univ. Press, 1987.

Jones, Jesse H. *Fifty Billion Dollars: My Thirteen Years with the RFC.* New York: Macmillan, 1951.

Kindleberger, Charles P. *The World in Depression 1929–39.* Berkeley: Univ. of California Press, 1973.

Leuchtenberg, William E. *Franklin D. Roosevelt and the New Deal, 1932–1940.* New York: Harper Colophon Books, 1963.

———. "The New Deal and the Analogue of War." In *Change and Continuity in Twentieth Century America,* ed. John Braeman, Robert H. Bremner, and Everett Walters. Columbus: Ohio State Univ. Press, 1964.

Mitchell, Broadus. *Depression Decade: From New Era through New Deal, 1929–1941.* New York: Harper Torchbooks, 1969.

Reading, Don. "New Deal Activity and the States, 1933 to 1939." *Journal of Economic History* 33 (1973): 792–810.

Smiley, Gene. "Recent Unemployment Rate Estimates for the 1920's and 1930's." *Journal of Economic History* 43 (1983): 487–93.

Wallis, John Joseph. "The Birth of the Old Federalism: Financing the New Deal, 1932–1940." *Journal of Economic History* 44 (1984): 139–59.

Wallis, John Joseph, and Daniel K. Benjamin. "Public Relief and Private Employment in the Great Depression." *Journal of Economic History* 41 (1981): 97–102.

Walton, Gary M., ed. *Regulatory Change in an Atmosphere of Crisis: Current Implications of the Roosevelt Years.* New York: Academic Press, 1979.

Weinstein, Michael M. "Some Macroeconomic Impacts of the National Industrial Recovery Act, 1933–35." In *The Great Depression Revisited,* ed. Karl Brunner. Boston: Martinus Nijhoff, 1981.

Wright, Gavin. "The Political Economy of New Deal Spending: An Econometric Analysis." *Review of Economics and Statistics* 56 (1974): 30–38.

CHAPTER 25

The Second World War

MOBILIZING FOR WAR AGAIN

The Second World War began in September 1939, when German forces attacked Poland, and Great Britain and France, which had guaranteed Poland's independence, declared war on Germany. In the United States there was a brief surge in industrial production as manufacturers anticipated a repeat of the heady days of 1916 when a neutral America made enormous profits by supplying a Europe at war. But industrial production sagged during the period of the so-called "phony war" when it appeared that Britain, France, and Germany, although officially at war, would avoid a major clash of arms. The phony war ended in May 1940 when Germany launched a blitzkrieg (lightning war) attack against the Low Countries, swept around France's supposedly impenetrable Maginot Line, and conquered France. U.S. manufacturers began building up inventories in anticipation of future shortages, Britain and its remaining allies began placing large-scale orders for war supplies in the United States, and the U.S. government launched a vastly expanded program of military procurement.[1]

Initially, Great Britain was asked to pay for arms on a "cash and carry" basis. It paid by transferring gold and by requisitioning American bank deposits and securities owned by British nationals. When these sources of funds began to run out, President Roosevelt succeeded in establishing the lend-lease program in March 1941. The term *lend-lease* was calculated to deflect attention from the simple fact that now the U.S. government would be paying for the arms sent to Britain and its allies.

At first, prices remained relatively stable because there were still millions of unemployed and underemployed U.S. workers and much underutilized industrial capacity. The United States had not yet reached its production

---

[1] The best general survey of the American economy during the war is Harold G. Vatter, *The U.S. Economy in World War II* (New York: Columbia Univ. Press, 1985).

possibilities curve, to use the economist's term. By the fall of 1940, however, supply had become inelastic in many sectors and wholesale prices had begun to rise. In 1941 the U.S. economy was moving into high gear, although there were still pockets of unemployment. Production of steel ingots and castings, for example, had already reached 59.8 million long-tons in 1940, exceeding the previous peak of 56.4 million reached in 1929. In 1941 production reached 74.0 million long-tons. Sulfuric acid, a chemical used in a wide variety of industrial applications, was also being produced in unprecedented quantities, 6.8 million short-tons in 1941 compared with 5.3 million in 1929. But, the best indicator to look at is an index of industrial production that takes account of a wide variety of products. The Federal Reserve Board's index of industrial production reached a level of 162 in 1941 compared with 110 in 1929.

Although U.S. industry was moving into high gear, many Americans still doubted the wisdom of aiding Britain and its allies. But all doubts vanished on December 7, 1941. To quote President Roosevelt's famous war message:

> Yesterday, December 7, 1941—a date which will live in infamy—the United States of America was suddenly and deliberately attacked by the naval and air forces of the Empire of Japan. . . . The facts of yesterday speak for themselves. The people of the United States have already formed their opinions and well understand the implications to the very life and safety of our nation.

The United States was now fully committed to war against the Axis powers (Germany had quickly declared war against the U.S. after the Japanese attack), but many military and economic questions still had to be answered.

Under President Roosevelt's leadership, the United States adopted a bold plan of economic mobilization. It would become the "Arsenal of Democracy," and use its vast industrial might to mass-produce arms and overwhelm the Axis powers with sheer firepower. Characteristically, President Roosevelt called for the construction of an unprecedented 50,000 airplanes, although at the time no one knew how such a vast number of planes could be produced.

Economic mobilization involved many trade-offs. The most obvious and most important was how far civilian consumption would be reduced—the decision, as it was often put, between "guns and butter."[2] Because the United States entered the war, as we have noted, with considerable reserves of unemployed, and underemployed resources, to some extent it could divert those resources to the war effort without actually reducing civilian consumption. But as the economy became fully employed, achieving further increases in military production was possible only by diverting resources from the civilian sector.

---

[2]Civilian consumption of butter did fall during the war. But this appears to have been simply part of a long-run trend toward lower consumption. Consumption of ice cream, on the other hand, was higher during the war than it had been before, also part of a long-run trend.

Table 25-1 shows, in very broad terms, how these resources were allocated to the war effort. As we can see, in 1929 the federal government was
spending only a small fraction of GNP. Even in 1940, after years of government expansion under the New Deal, the government at all levels was
spending only about 19.4 percent of GNP. However, the war changed this
situation dramatically. The maximum expense occurred in 1944 when the
government spent some 790.8 billion at 1982 prices, some 57.3 percent of
total GNP, an impressive figure.

Another way of analyzing these figures is also of interest. Between 1940
and 1944 real government spending increased by 555.2 billion ($790.8 −
$235.6), while total real GNP increased by $471.2 billion ($1,380.6−$909.4).
So the increase in real GNP was 84.9 percent of the increase in government
spending ($471.2 ÷ $555.2). Only 15.1 percent of the increase in government spending on the war had to be offset by a decline in production for
the civilian sector. Thus the great bulk of the resources for the war effort
were obtained by using unemployed resources and by using more intensively resources that were underemployed. Other countries, where the capacity
to expand was less, were forced to sacrifice more of their current consumption or investment to make resources available for the military effort.

While the decision of how much to reduce civilian consumption and
investment was the most important, there were other and more subtle trade-
offs. One was industrial safety. Industrial accidents increased dramatically
during the war years, often resulting in serious injury or death. Of course,
to some extent this was to be expected when so many more men and women
were working so many more hours in dangerous jobs. But it also appears
that the rate at which accidents occurred increased, at least in manufacturing. The official figures show an increase in the number of disabling injuries

TABLE 25-1   Real Gross National Product, 1929−50 (in billions of 1982 dollars)

Year	GNP	Total Government Purchases of Goods and Services	Total Private Sector Purchases of Goods and Services
1929	$ 709.6	$ 94.2	$615.4
1940	772.9	150.2	622.7
1941	909.4	235.6	673.8
1942	1,080.3	483.7	596.6
1943	1,276.2	708.9	567.3
1944	1,380.6	790.8	589.8
1945	1,354.8	704.5	650.3
1946	1,096.9	236.9	860.0
1950	1,203.7	230.8	972.9

Source: *Economic Report of the President, 1987* (Washington, D.C.: GPO, 1987), pp. 246−47.

per million hours worked in manufacturing from 15.3 in 1940 to 20.0 in 1943, the all-time peak.

Should greater efforts have been made to maintain safety? Possibly, but the problem was always a matter of the trade-off between safety and production. Well-rested workers are safer workers, but more rest periods would lower output. More workspace in shipyards reduces the risk of accidents, but more workspace would mean higher construction costs and less resources available to build other facilities.

Another subtle trade-off lay between the quality of arms produced and the quantity. Changing technology and battlefield experience were constantly suggesting modifications of existing weapons. But making these modifications often meant tearing down and rebuilding an assembly line, and so losing valuable production time. This trade-off was often a bone of contention between the military, who argued for the most sophisticated weapons possible, and the civilians in charge of military production, who were more mindful of the potential loss in production. When Hitler's troops attacked the Allied invasion force during the Battle of the Bulge, German tanks, the famous Panzers, were as good or better than any tank used by the Allies, but the Panzers were vastly outnumbered.

On the whole, the U.S. decision to mass-produce the weapons of war turned out to be a brilliant success. America by itself, although starting behind, soon produced more arms than could the combined Axis powers.[3] Not only supplies such as small arms and ammunition were mass-produced, but also planes and even ships to carry the arms to the theaters of war were produced in record numbers. At Henry Kaiser's shipyards in Portland, Oregon, where some of the most innovative construction techniques were used, one of the famous liberty ships was produced in a record eight days.

MONETARY AND FISCAL POLICY

As we noted before, the three basic ways to finance a war are (1) by taxation (2) by borrowing money and (3) by printing money.[4] During the Second World War, the government relied on all three. Indeed, it financed a larger part of the war effort through taxation than it had during the Civil War or the First World War. Table 25-2 shows the relative importance of each form of finance.

---

[3]See Mark Harrison, "Resource Mobilization for World War II: The U.S.A., U.K., U.S.S.R., and Germany, 1938–1945, *Economic History Review* 2 (May 1988): 172.
[4]The government can also acquire the means of war simply by seizing them. The draft was, of course, the most important example of this during the war. It is analogous to a tax equal to the difference between what a soldier would need in pay to serve voluntarily and what he was actually paid.

TABLE 25-2   Financing the Second World War, 1941–46

Source of Funds	Total (billions) 1941–46	Percent
Total Federal Expenditure for war[a]	$326.3	100.0%
Tax Revenues	138.7	42.5%
Borrowing from the Public	109.8	33.7
Creating New Money	77.8	23.8

[a]Total expenditures 1941–46 less six times 1940 expenditures.

Source: *Historical Statistics of the United States, Colonial Times to 1957* (Washington, D.C.: GPO, 1960), p. 711; Milton Friedman and Anna J. Schwartz, *Monetary Statistics of the United States* (New York: National Bureau of Economic Research, 1970), pp. 33–37.

To do this, the government broadened the tax base in a variety of ways and increased the rate of taxation. The income tax was radically changed by the war. The exemption for single persons was lowered from $750 to $500 and the exemption for married persons was lowered from $1,500 to $1,200. Inflation, moreover, was proceeding apace. So the exemptions measured in real terms (divided by the price level) were falling even faster. These steps meant that many more low-income workers owed income tax for the first time. In 1943, the payroll deduction system for collecting income taxes was introduced, and the term *take home pay* entered the language. Together these innovations meant that the income tax had become a mass tax for the first time. (Some scholars have seen this transformation as the basis of the continued expansion of government after the war. Because the government could now skim off vast amounts of revenue without causing any one group of taxpayers to complain too bitterly, the total amount of government spending could be increased.)

Getting Congress to raise taxes is never easy, not even during a major war. To the tax legislation requested by the Roosevelt administration, Congressmen complained that high tax rates discouraged work and raised objections to the distribution of tax burdens. In general Congress supported only partial financing of the war through increased taxation.

The gap between spending and tax revenues then had to be covered by selling government bonds. When the war started in 1941, the federal debt stood at $49.0 billion. By 1945, it had reached $258.7 billion. To get a better perspective on the debt, we can compare it with GNP in 1945, $213.6 billion: the debt had reached 121 percent of the GNP. This fact is often cited as evidence that an economy *can* survive a huge deficit—in 1985 the debt was "only" 46.4 percent of GNP. But we must be careful in using such analogies. There were many differences between the economy in 1945 and the one we live in today, differences in the savings rate (it was higher in 1945), the expected future levels of government taxes and spending, the role of the United States in the world economy, and so forth. All of these must be taken into account before we can apply the lessons of history.

To have financed all of the wartime deficits by sales of securities to the general public might have been possible at some rate of interest. But, despite highly publicized war-bond drives, it appears likely that the interest rate required to market these bonds would have been very high by historical standards. So the Fed, in cooperation with the Treasury, took the extraordinary step of "pegging" the rate of interest on government securities. It accomplished this by pledging itself to buy government securities whenever their price fell below the predetermined support level.[5]

On the surface this action seems to give a free ride to the government because it minimizes the future interest costs the government incurs in raising a given sum of money. The fly in the ointment (or rat in the soup, depending on one's view of things) is that the Fed must create new money to purchase these securities, and this adds to the inflationary pressures facing the economy.

By 1945, some 24.3 billion bonds were owned by the Federal Reserve System, and some 84.1 billion by commercial banks. What happens when one part of the federal government (the U.S. Treasury) prints up pieces of paper, sells them, and then watches while they are bought by another arm of the federal government (the Federal Reserve System)? What has happened, ultimately, is that the Fed has created new money for the Treasury to spend. During the Civil War, the system by which the government created money was straightforward. It simply printed Greenbacks and spent them. During the two world wars, the system was more complex, but the results were similar. Instead of printing paper money, the Fed enlarged the Treasury's deposit balances. In all three cases, creating new money added to inflationary pressures.

When bonds were sold to commercial banks, however, the system became potentially more complex. To the extent that commercial banks reduced their lending to the private sector in order to buy more bonds, the sales were much like sales to the general public. But when the Fed supplied additional reserves to the banking system, or when commercial banks reduced their reserve ratios so that they could purchase bonds by creating new deposits, then sales to commercial banks could simply be regarded as another way in which the government financed the war by printing money.

Compared with financing earlier wars, the U.S. experience in financing the Second World War was "better" in the sense that more reliance was placed on taxes than on borrowing or creating new money. Indeed, as we can now see, there has been a steady upward trend in the proportion of wars financed by money taxation.

This massive increase in purchasing power brought the economy to full employment and created strong upward pressure on prices. By 1944, the

---

[5]The interest rate paid on a government security is determined by the relationship between the fixed annual payments on the security and its market value; low market values imply high interest rates.

civilian unemployment rate had fallen to 1.2 percent, one of the lowest on record. It is often argued that the experience of financing the Second World War helped to convince economists that Keynesian theory is correct—that high government spending would cure a depression. If this is so, and it appears to be, it is because economists were ready and willing to be convinced. The wartime experience also reinforces the monetarist argument that a large increase in the money supply would cure a depression, although perhaps causing inflation in the process. Indeed, the wartime financial system throws little light on the distinctively Keynesian proposition that GNP will increase when government spending increases even when financed by borrowing from the public or by higher taxes.

WAGE AND PRICE CONTROLS

Early in the war the Roosevelt administration decided that in addition to relying on taxation to control prices it would combat rising prices with direct controls. It would try to persuade firms not to raise prices by appealing to their patriotic instincts, and, if persuasion failed, it would simply make price increases illegal.

In May 1940, President Roosevelt set up the National Defense Advisory Committee and chose Leon Henderson—a crusty, cigar-smoking New Dealer—to head its Price Stabilization Division. Henderson attempted to obtain voluntary agreements from producers in key areas of the economy not to raise prices, a policy that met with very limited success. Prices continued to rise, although severe inflation was still concentrated in a few sectors. In April 1941, Roosevelt strengthened Henderson's hand by creating the Office of Price Administration and Civilian Supply (OPA). Eventually the OPA would become the civilian agency most familiar to the average American because it set the prices and determined the quantities of the goods and services consumed every day.

Of special interest to economists was the creation of the Price Division of the OPA under the direction of a young economist, John Kenneth Galbraith. In the postwar period, Galbraith—tall, urbane, and articulate—would become a leading advocate of the liberal view that America's social and economic problems could be solved by expanding the role of the federal government. Undoubtedly his experience at the OPA, with its enormous and in his view favorable effect on the economy, profoundly influenced his thinking.

Initially, the OPA hoped to control the general price level by applying controls only in selected sectors, but uncontrolled prices continued to accelerate. In April 1942, the OPA issued the General Maximum Price Regulation, affectionately known as "General Max," which put a ceiling on most prices. But even this measure was only partially successful. One problem was that each seller was responsible for setting his own prices according to the rules set by the government. Effective price-control measures would require that the agency responsible for enforcing price controls be the agency setting the price.

In April 1943, President Roosevelt issued his famous "hold-the-line" order requiring the OPA to refuse all requests for price increases except in very limited circumstances. And this approach, economically suspect but easy to defend in the court of public opinion, worked surprisingly well for the remainder of the war. The official consumer price index rose at only 1.6 percent per year from April 1943 to February 1946 when the hold-the-line policy began to come apart. Perhaps the main positive result of this policy was that it encouraged people to save rather than spend their high wartime earnings by creating expectations of future price stability.

But the official index alone does not tell the whole story. It is a basic proposition of economics that if a price ceiling is set below the free market equilibrium there will be a scramble for supplies that will very likely result in attempts to evade the ceiling. There were innumerable examples of this process during the war. In some cases evasion took the form of quality deterioration—fat was added to hamburger, coarse fabrics were substituted for finer ones, maintenance on rent-controlled apartments was reduced or eliminated. Quality deterioration could be limited by regulations that specified the exact content of a product, such as specifying the butterfat content of milk, for example. But such regulations tended to get longer and longer and became a problem in themselves. In one famous case, Lou Maxon, an OPA official, resigned in 1943 complaining about what he saw as the anti-business atmosphere at OPA. Many of his charges were exaggerated, but the six-page regulation specifying the content of fruit cakes that he used to dramatize his charges spoke to a real problem.

Quality deterioration was just one in a long list of techniques available to people who wanted to evade the controls. Another was *forced uptrading,* the term used to describe the problem caused by the elimination of lower-priced lines of merchandise. Before the war, manufacturers often offered buyers a choice between low-priced, low-quality items and higher-priced, higher-quality items. As demand in all lines exceeded supply, manufacturers eliminated the lower-priced lines. This was fine for consumers who wished to move up to the higher-priced item anyway, but it was a hidden price increase for those who were forced to trade up. The difference between what they would have voluntarily paid for the higher-priced good and what they were forced to pay because the cheaper line was eliminated is a measure of the hidden increase.

The most startling form of evasion, although not the most frequent, was the black market. Here buyers willing to pay more than the official price and sellers willing to sell for more would meet away from the prying eyes of the OPA to transact their illegal business. The black market took many forms depending on the product and the enforcement effort being made by the OPA. In New York there were "meateasys," much like the speakeasys that had flourished under prohibition, where one could buy extra meat at prices much above the legal price. After the production of automobiles resumed at the end of the war, evasion of automobile price controls was widespread. Some of it occurred in the dealer's showroom where cash payments were often made on the side while official documents showed that the car had been sold at the OPA ceiling. But a true black market in cars also developed. At Leesville, South Carolina, for example, there was a huge lot where cars recently purchased from dealers were brought from all over the country to be sold at black-market prices.

Rationing is one way to reduce evasion when prices are being held below their free-market equilibrium. A consumer who is assured at least of receiving a bare minimum is less likely to enter the black market than a consumer who is in danger of being left without anything in a mad scramble for limited supplies. The simplest form of rationing was a ticket entitling the holder to buy a certain quantity of a certain good. The ticket was surrendered when the good was purchased. Tires were the first commodity rationed in this way.[6] Moreover, a company that must be able to show the authorities ration tickets corresponding to the output it has manufactured and sold will find it harder to divert supplies to the black market.

Rationing was often necessary even when supplies were adequate by prewar standards because demand had increased and the price was being held below the new equilibrium. For certain food groups, more complicated systems were used. Under the red point system for meats and fats, the consumer was periodically supplied with a certain number of points. Each good was assigned a point price, and the consumer could choose among rationed items as long as he had enough ration points. In other cases rationing was undertaken to achieve particular policy goals.[7]

Balancing the supply of goods and the number of ration tickets or points outstanding was no easy matter. In order to make the red point system operate more smoothly, the OPA had issued red point tokens that could be taken as change and stored for use at a later date. However, by late 1944, surveys showed that consumers had stored up large quantities of these tokens, and the OPA became afraid of a run on the stores that would leave shelves bare and confidence in the rationing program shaken. In order to regain control, the OPA, after much soul searching, decided to cancel all

---

[6]The largest part of the tire supply consisted of tires already on automobiles. These could not be rationed. But tire wear was controlled indirectly by rationing gasoline, and this was one of the main purposes of the gasoline rationing program in areas of the country where gasoline was abundant.

[7]In a few cases the goals of the rationing program were debatable. A well-publicized fat salvage program led consumers to believe that the fat was needed to make a chemical crucial to the war effort. But the real motive was the fear on the part of soap manufacturers that a shortage of fat would lead to the rationing of soap, and that consumers accustomed to economizing on soap during the war would continue to buy less afterwards.

outstanding ration tokens, a decision that cost the agency a great deal of public support. In 1945, as the war came to a close, most of the rationing programs were discontinued, a highly popular decision. But few people appreciated the intimate connection between rationing and price control, and so few appreciated the problems that would soon afflict the price control system.

ORGANIZED LABOR DURING THE WAR

As we noted in the previous chapter, the war put normal labor relations on hold. The Roosevelt administration had been evolving a policy that would support labor's efforts to organize, bargain collectively, and strike; now labor was expected to cooperate with the effort to maximize production. And on the whole labor did so. Labor took a no-strike pledge, paralleling management's no-lockout pledge. The major exception was the United Mine Workers under their charismatic leader John L. Lewis. As the result of public indignation over strikes in the coalfields, the Congress passed the Smith-Connally War Labor Disputes Act in 1943. It provided for government takeover of plants in essential war industries that were hampered by strikes. Despite this case, however, the conflict between labor and management was generally kept in check during the war by labor's patriotism, and by the government's extraordinary powers.

The real crunch came at the end of the war. As workers' overtime disappeared and real earnings were eroded because of rising prices, labor leaders were under pressure to secure wage increases, which were not to be forthcoming without a struggle. Meanwhile, the widespread work stoppages of 1945 and 1946, shown vividly in Figure 25-1, alienated large segments of the electorate.

During this period of unusual strike proneness, employers complained loudly that they were being caught in the jurisdictional disputes of rival unions and that labor itself was guilty of unfair practices. There was a growing belief that union power was being used to infringe on the rights of individual workers.

In point of fact, employers often used strikes during the transition to their own advantage. They could put pressure on the OPA to grant a price increase to make possible a wage increase. Labor, of course, realized that this avenue was open to employers, and this entered their strike calculations. The OPA, in many cases, claimed that higher wages could be paid without granting higher prices. But the path of least resistance was often to grant a round of wage and price increases in an industry experiencing a strike. The end result was that it was increasingly difficult for OPA to maintain its line on prices.

After the Republicans won control of Congress in 1946, they lost no time in drawing up a long, technical bill that significantly amended the Wagner

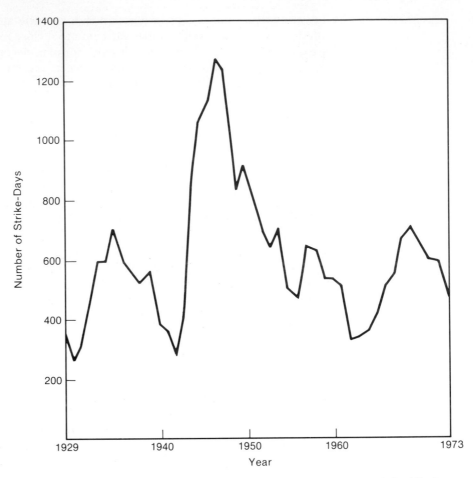

FIGURE 25-1   Five-year Moving Average of Number of Striker-days per Thousand Nonagricultural Employees, 1929–73.

Source: P. K. Edwards, *Strikes in the United States, 1881–1974* (New York: St. Martins Press, 1981), p. 18.

Act. The new law, passed in 1947 over President Harry S Truman's veto, was called the Labor-Management Relations Act and became known famil-iarly as the Taft-Hartley Act. The act reflected the belief that individual workers should be protected by public policy not only in their right to join a labor organization but also in their right to refrain from joining. The closed-shop agreement under which the employer hires only union mem-bers was outlawed. Union shop agreements, which permit nonunion mem-bers to be employed but require them to join the union within a certain time period after starting to work, were permitted. However, the enforce-ment of union-security provisions was limited to cases of nonpayment of dues, and, more importantly, the law permitted the states to outlaw *all* forms of union security, including the union shop.

The Taft-Hartley Act, unlike the Wagner Act, assumed that the interests of the union and individuals in the union are not identical, taking the view that many union members are "captives" of the "labor bosses"—a position especially offensive to a great part of organized labor. For example, the act provided that a union could not negotiate a union-shop provision in collective-bargaining agreements unless a majority of workers in the unit voted for it. In 1951, after 46,000 separate polls in which security provisions won 97 percent of the time, the requirement of NLRB-conducted union-security elections was dropped, and a large number of doubters became convinced that union leaders commonly reflect the wishes of their memberships.

The most important features of the Taft-Hartley Act were those purporting to regulate unions in the "public" interest. A union seeking certification or requesting an investigation of unfair labor practices had to submit to a scrutiny of its internal affairs by filing statements, and its officers were required to sign affidavits stating that they were not Communists. The right to strike was modified by providing a "cooling-off period" after notice of termination of contract, and the President was given authority to postpone strikes for 80 days by injunction. More significant in "evening up" the one-sidedness of the Wagner Act was the outlawing of certain unfair union practices. Since 1947, it has been unfair for a union

1. to restrain or coerce *employees* regarding their right to join or refrain from joining a labor organization, or to restrain or coerce *employers* in the selection of employer representatives for purposes of collective bargaining or adjustment of grievances.

2. to cause or attempt to cause an *employer* to discriminate against an employee.

3. to charge, under a valid union-shop agreement, an "excessive" initiation fee.

4. to refuse to bargain collectively with an employer when the union involved is the certified bargaining agent.

5. to "featherbed" the job—that is, to cause an employer to pay for services that are not performed.[8]

6. to engage in, or encourage employees to engage in, a strike where the object is to force one employer to cease doing business with another employer. This provision banned the secondary boycott.

After twelve years of almost complete freedom, labor found the Taft-Hartley Act harshly restrictive. Dire warnings were voiced about the coming decline of trade unionism in America. Labor's leadership was incensed at the offensive language and punitive spirit of the act. But many of the provisions looked worse in print than they proved in practice. The injunction clause, for example, stirred memories of the days when the courts granted

---

[8]Featherbedding continued to be a scandal in the railroad industry, which is not subject to the Taft-Hartley Act.

injunctions at the request of private parties; in the hands of a President of the United States, acting in an emergency, however, the injunction was no longer a destructive weapon. Moreover, although union problems persist, they have come primarily from sources other than the Taft-Hartley Act.

ROSIE THE RIVETER

One of the most dramatic developments during the war was the change in the role of women in the labor force. Some 200,000 women entered the military services. Mainly they served in the Women's Army Corps (WAC) and Women Accepted for Volunteer Emergency Service (Waves), with smaller numbers in the Marine Corps, Coast Guard, and the Women's Auxiliary Ferrying Service. Women also entered the civilian labor force in large numbers. Many entered jobs that women had filled before the war. But many others, as symbolized by Rosie the Riveter,[9] entered jobs traditionally filled by men; women became tool makers, crane operators, lumberjacks, and stevedores, and so on.

Women were encouraged to do this by market forces, since wages for women workers were rising rapidly, and by government propaganda urging women to take jobs in industry for the sake of the country. This propaganda also encouraged women to think of these as temporary jobs that would be turned back to returning soldiers after the war. But the wartime experience seems to have left a permanent imprint on the participation rates of women in the labor force. Table 25-3 shows how the participation rate of men and women in the labor force changed over the war years.

As we can see, the participation rate of men in the labor force (the ratio of employed and unemployed workers to the total relevant population) rose during the war and then, after a dip in 1946, remained at a somewhat higher level. The participation rate of women in the labor force also rose during the war, and also fell back after the war was over. But it did not remain there; instead it began to edge higher. The participation rate of women then continued to rise, and by the late 1950s it exceeded the wartime peak.

Perhaps more important than the participation rate, the types of jobs held by women also changed during the war years. Table 25-4 shows how the distribution of women in the labor force changed between 1940 and 1950. The number of women in low-paid service or farm-sector jobs remained about constant—actually falling in the category of private household work-

---

[9]The Second World War marked a major watershed in the conversion from the older technology of riveting to the then-newer technology of welding. Wanda the Welder might have been a more appropriate symbol.

TABLE 25-3   Participation Rate of Men and Women in the Labor Force, 1940–50 (in percent of the relevant population)

Year	Men	Women
1940	82.5%	27.9%
1941	83.8	28.5
1942	85.1	30.9
1943	87.4	35.7
1944	88.2	36.3
1945	87.6	35.8
1946	81.1	30.8
1947	86.8	31.8
1948	87.0	32.7
1949	86.9	33.2
1950	86.8	33.9

Source: *Historical Statistics of the United States, Colonial Times to 1970,* (Washington, D.C.: GPO, 1975), p. 132, series D30, D36.

TABLE 25-4   The Female Labor Force by Occupation, 1940–50 (in thousands)

Occupation	1940	1950
White collar workers	5,648	8,627
Professional, technical, etc.	1,608	2,007
Managers, officials, proprietors	414	700
Clerical	2,700	4,502
Sales	925	1,418
Manual and service workers	6,419	7,217
Manual	2,720	3,685
Craftsmen, foremen, etc.	135	253
Operatives	2,452	3,287
Laborers	133	145
Service workers	3,699	3,532
Private household	2,277	1,459
Service	1,422	2,073
Farm Workers	508	601
Farmers and farm managers	157	120
Laborers and foremen	351	481

Source: *Historical Statistics of the United States, Colonial Times to 1970,* (Washington, D.C.: GPO, 1975), p. 140, series D217–D232.

ers. The growth took place in the manual job category, and most of all in white-collar employment.

The war undoubtedly played a role in this transformation. It demonstrated to women that, depending on circumstances, they could improve their well-being by working outside the home, and it demonstrated to some employers that a female worker could add as much to their profits as a male worker. But, because we are dealing with an event as dramatic as the war, and with a character as memorable as Rosie the Riveter, we run the risk of exaggerating the importance of these short-term events relative to the long-run trend. The participation rate of women in the labor force had risen steadily, albeit slowly, through the decades leading up to the Second World War, and, to some extent, the higher level at the end of the war and the continued rise afterwards reflected these long-run trends rather than the unusual events of the war years.

THE MINORITY EXPERIENCE

The wartime boom accelerated the long-term movement of blacks out of southern agriculture. The ideal time to move to a new location is when unemployment is low in that area. This reduces the risk of a long and costly search for a new job. Altogether almost a million blacks moved from southern farms to industrial centers in the South, North, and West.[10] While the movement of the black population had the most dramatic political and social consequences, it should not be forgotten that the movement of poor whites out of southern agriculture was also massive during the war, as both whites and blacks responded to similar economic facts of life. The urbanization produced by these migrations is illustrated in Table 25-5. In 1940 the black population was about evenly divided between urban and rural areas; in 1950 it was predominantly urban. But just as clearly the movement of both whites and blacks to urban areas has been a long-term trend that accelerated during periods (like the war years) when unemployment in urban areas was relatively low.

TABLE 25-5   Urbanization: Proportion of the Population Living in Urban Areas, 1920–70 (in percent)

Year	Black	White
1920	34.0%	53.4%
1930	43.7	57.6
1940	48.6	57.5
1950	62.4	64.3
1960	73.2	69.5
1970	81.3	72.4

Note: The definition of urbanization changed over these years. With a constant definition the trends would be even more dramatic.
Source: *Historical Statistics of the United States, Colonial Times to 1970*, (Washington, D.C.: GPO, 1975), p. 12.

---

[10] Vatter, p. 127.

AGRICULTURE DURING THE WAR

As demand expanded to meet lend-lease agreements and growing domestic requirements, agricultural production, aided by exceptionally good weather, climbed at the remarkable rate of 5 percent per year.[11] Price controls during the war were purposely made less effective for agricultural than for non-agricultural commodities; consequently, the prices of farm products rose more rapidly during the war than the prices of the things that the farmer had to buy. To encourage such expansion, Congress passed three laws in May, July, and December of 1941. The first of these directed the Commodity Credit Corporation (CCC) to support the basic crops of wheat, corn, cotton, tobacco, rice, and peanuts at 85 percent of parity. The second, the Steagall Amendment, gave the Secretary of Agriculture authority to support the price of any *nonbasic* commodity at *not less than* 85 percent of parity if, in the opinion of the Secretary, support was necessary to increase the production of a crop vital to the war effort. The third law guaranteed the 85-percent loan rate on basic crops for the years 1942–46, inclusive, putting price floors into effect for six crops well into the future.

During 1942 emphasis was placed on the necessity for stimulating particular *kinds* of output, notably meats and the oil-bearing crops, and avoiding a repetition of the price collapse that followed the First World War. Legislation of October 1942 set final policy for the war period and for two postwar years. The 1942 act provided *minimum* support rates of 90 percent of parity for both basic and Steagall commodities; the supports were to remain in effect for two full years, beginning with the first day of January following the official end of the war. Finally price ceilings on farm products were set at a maximum of 110 percent of parity.[12]

Over the war period and during the first two postwar years, price supports were not generally required. Due to the great demand for most products, agricultural prices tended to push against their ceilings, but the Secretary found it necessary to set floors for some needed nonbasic commodities that were above minimum levels. Surplus supplies of eggs and certain grades of hogs created a problem for part of 1944, but farm prices on the whole were subject to upward pressure. For some meats and dairy products it was even necessary to roll back retail prices in an effort to "hold the line" against inflation. In such cases, to prevent a reduction in the floor prices received

---

[11]This figure may be compared with the average in the First World War when agricultural production increased at 1.7 percent per year.

[12]There were two other provisions of special interest. Cotton supports were set at 92.5 percent of parity. The Secretary of Agriculture, at his discretion, could leave wheat and corn supports at 85 percent of parity if he felt that higher prices would limit available quantities of livestock feed. It is not entirely beside the point to note that cotton and beef interests were strongly represented by Congressmen, some of whom had reached powerful positions through their seniority.

by farmers, meat packers and creameries were paid a subsidy equal to the amount of the rollback on each unit sold.

We have already noted that the war enabled the CCC to unload heavy inventories that had built up between 1939 and 1941. From 1944 to 1946, loans extended by the CCC were small. Beginning in 1944, however, egg purchases became so great as to cause embarrassment, and support to the production of eggs and potatoes received a fantastically unfavorable press in 1945 and 1946. But foreign demand through the United Nations Relief and Rehabilitation Administration (UNRRA) and military governments, an unexpectedly high domestic demand, and the removal of price ceilings led to highly favorable postwar prices and lightened CCC loan and purchase commitments. Indeed, contrary to the predictions of many experts, the demand for food, feed, and fiber was exceptionally high after the war. The removal of price controls in the summer of 1946 permitted all prices to shoot up, but similar to the war years, the rise in agricultural prices was steeper than the price rise in other areas. Most production restrictions on crops were canceled before or during the Second World War, and by the spring of 1948 only tobacco and potatoes were still controlled.

DEMOBILIZATION AND RECONVERSION

It was widely expected that the Great Depression would return once the war was over. After all, it seemed as if enormous levels of government spending during the war were the only thing that had gotten the country out of the Depression. Many, perhaps most, economists agreed with this analysis. They pressed for a commitment by the government to maintain the high level of employment after the war. The result was the Employment Act of 1946.

In 1945, Congress had considered a bill that would guarantee full employment by placing a $40 billion "annual investment fund" at the disposal of the Secretary of Commerce. Senator Murray, its author, said that the bill was a "legal acknowledgment that the national government assumes the responsibility for prosperity in peacetime. The federal government is the instrument through which we can all work to accomplish full employment and high annual income." After much argument and semantic juggling, a revised version of the original "full-employment" bill was passed as the *Employment Act of 1946*. Full employment was no longer explicitly required; instead it was to be the federal government's responsibility to "promote maximum employment, production and purchasing power." The adjective *maximum* was purposely ambiguous, but the entire statement was generally understood to mean that the government would act quickly to shore up the economy if a severe recession threatened. A Council of Economic Advisers, with an adequate professional staff, was added to the Executive Office of the President. The President, assisted by the Council, was directed to submit to Congress at least annually a report on current economic conditions, with recommendations for legislative action. The statute further provided that the House and the Senate were to form a standing Joint Economic Committee on the Economic Report (later simplified to the Joint Economic Committee), which would study the report of the President and the Council of Economic Advisers, hold hearings, and report in turn to Congress. Although no "investment fund" was provided, a watchdog agency was established to keep Congress and the President systematically informed of economic change. A compromise piece of legislation, the act acknowledged the government's role in maintaining full employment, but did not say how the government would prevent depressions.

But in fact it did not matter because the expected depression did not materialize. During the war people had accumulated large stores of money, government bonds, and other financial assets. They did so in part because they could not buy consumer durables during the war and in part because they were saving for the bad times they thought lay ahead. Once the war was over these savings were released and created a surge in demand that contributed to a postwar rise in prices and to the reintegration of millions of workers from the armed forces into the labor force without a significant increase in unemployment.

The postwar surge in demand ushered in a new consumer-oriented society that to some represented the fulfillment of the American dream, and to others represented the creation of an unthinking, materialistic culture. Builders like Arthur Levitt utilized mass-production techniques pioneered by Henry Kaiser and others during the war to mass-produce suburban homes. Balladeer Malvina Reynolds expressed the feelings of many critics of the new tract housing in a popular folksong that called the houses "little Boxes on the hillside, little boxes made of ticky tacky. . . . little boxes all the same." Defenders of the new construction techniques argued that by achieving the economies of long production runs, builders were able to lower the unit cost of housing and permit people to buy a home who could not otherwise afford one. No one, however, was able to put that idea into an enduring folksong.

These years witnessed the beginning of the "baby boom." Birth rates surged in the late 1940s and 1950s. The image of a baby boom following shortly after the reuniting of soldiers with their loved ones is romantic, and undoubtedly valid in many individual cases. But as Table 25-6 shows the baby boom was a much broader phenomenon, and owes its existence, sad to say, as much to economics as to romance. The birth rate plunged during the Great Depression, reaching a low point in 1936. It then recovered somewhat during the war years and actually reached a level in 1943 higher than any year since 1927. There was a substantial leap in the birth rate in 1946 and 1947 as the romantic theory predicts. But note that the boom continued beyond the late 1940s. The rate of live births per 1,000 women in the 15 to 44 age range actually peaked in 1957. The baby boom was a complex phenomenon, but economic conditions undoubtedly played a role. The

TABLE 25-6   The Birth Rate, 1929–59

Year	Live Births per 1,000	
	Total Population	Women, Age 15–44
1929	21.2	89.3
1930	21.3	89.2
1936	18.4	75.8
1939	18.8	77.6
1940	19.4	79.9
1941	20.3	83.4
1942	22.2	91.5
1943	22.7	94.3
1944	21.2	88.8
1945	20.4	85.9
1946	24.1	101.9
1947	26.6	113.3
1948	24.9	107.3
1949	24.5	107.1
1950	24.1	106.2
1951	24.9	111.5
1952	25.1	113.9
1953	25.0	115.2
1954	25.3	118.1
1955	25.0	118.5
1956	25.2	121.2
1957	25.3	122.9
1958	25.5	120.2
1959	24.0	118.8

Source: *Historical Statistics of the United States, Colonial Times to 1970*, (Washington, D.C.: GPO, 1975), p. 49.

1950s were the economic reverse of the 1930s; a strong economy and optimism about the future encouraged many Americans to start families.

The war, in short, ushered in a period in which millions of Americans could take part for the first time in a middle-class lifestyle. A helping hand was also furnished by government programs for veterans, such as the G.I. Bill (passed in 1944), that among other things provided financial aid for veterans attending college. However, the key factor was what didn't happen, a return to the depressed economic conditions of the 1930s.

SELECTED REFERENCES AND SUGGESTED READINGS

Alston, Lee J. and Joseph P. Ferrie. "The Bracero Program and Farm Labor Legislation in World War II." In Mills and Rockoff.
Blum, John Morton. *V was for Victory: Politics and American Culture During World War II.* New York: Harcourt Brace Jovanovich, 1977.

Cain, Louis, and George Neumann. "Planning for Peace: The Surplus Property Act of 1944." *Journal of Economic History* 41 (1981): 129–35.

Chandler, Lester Vernon. *Inflation in the United States, 1940–1948.* New York: Harper, 1951.

Clinard, Marshall B. *The Black Market: A Study of White Collar Crime.* New York: Rhinehart, 1952.

Friedman, Milton. "Price, Income and Monetary Changes in Three Wartime Periods." *American Economic Review* (May 1952): 612–25.

Friedman, Milton, and Anna J. Schwartz. *A Monetary History of the United States, 1867–1960.* Princeton: Princeton Univ. Press, 1963. Chapter 10, pp. 546–85.

Galbraith, John Kenneth. *A Life in Our Times.* Boston: Houghton Mifflin, 1981.

———. *A Theory of Price Control.* Cambridge: Harvard Univ. Press, 1952.

Gemery, Henry A., and Jan S. Hogendorn. "The Microeconomic Bases of Short Run Learning Curves: Destroyer Production in World War II." In Mills and Rockoff.

Glenn, Norval D. "Changes in the American Occupational Structure and Occupational Gains of Negroes during the 1940's." *Social Forces* 41 (1962): 188–95.

Gordon, David L. and Royden Dangerfield. *The Hidden Weapon: The Story of Economic Warfare.* New York: Harper, 1947.

Higgs, Robert. *Crisis and Leviathan: Critical Issues in the Emergence of the Mixed Economy.* New York: Oxford Univ. Press, 1986.

———. "Private Profit, Public Risk: Institutional Antecedents of the Modern Military Procurement System in the Rearmament Program of 1940–1941." In Mills and Rockoff.

Janeway, Eliot. *The Struggle for Survival: A Chronicle of Economic Mobilization in World War II.* New Haven: Yale Univ. Press, 1951.

Kuznets, Simon. "National Product War and Prewar." New York: National Bureau of Economic Research, Occasional Paper 17, 1944.

Lane, Frederick C. *Ships for Victory: A History of Shipbuilding Under the U.S. Maritime Commission in World War II.* Baltimore: The Johns Hopkins Press, 1951.

Lingeman, Richard R. *Don't You Know There's A War On? The American Home Front, 1941–1945.* New York: Putnam, 1970.

Maines, Rachel. "Twenty-nine Thirty-seconds or Fight: Goal Conflict and Reinforcement in the U.S. Cotton Policy, 1933–1946." In Mills and Rockoff.

Mills, Geofrey T. and Hugh Rockoff. *Sinews of War: Essays on the Economic History of World War II.* Ames, Iowa: Iowa State Univ. Press, forthcoming.

Millward, Alan S. *War, Economy and Society, 1939–1945.* Berkeley: Univ. of California Press, 1977.

Nelson, Donald M. *Arsenal of Democracy: The Story of American War Production.* New York: Harcourt Brace, 1946.

Novick, D., M. Anshen, and W. C. Truppner. *Wartime Production Controls.* New York: Columbia Univ. Press, 1949.

Polenberg, Richard. *War and Society: The United States 1941–1945.* Philadelphia: J. B. Lippincott, 1972.

Rockoff, Hugh. *Drastic Measures: A History of Wage and Price Controls in the United States.* New York: Cambridge Univ. Press, 1984.

———. "Indirect Price Increases and Real Wages during World War II." *Explorations in Economic History* 15 (Oct. 1978): 407–20.

———. "The Response of the Giant Corporations to Wage and Price Controls in World War II." *Journal of Economic History* 41 (1981): 123–28.

Rupp, Leila J. *Mobilizing Women for War: German and American Propaganda, 1939–1945.* Princeton: Princeton Univ. Press, 1978.

U.S. Bureau of the Budget, War Records Section. *The United States at War: The Development and Administration of the War Program by the Federal Government.* Washington, D.C.: GPO, 1946.

Vatter, Harold G. *The U.S. Economy in World War II.* New York: Columbia Univ. Press, 1985.

Wilcox, Walter W. *The Farmer in the Second World War.* Ames: Iowa State College Press, 1947.

CHAPTER 26

Monetary and Fiscal Policy Since the Second World War

GUARANTEEING ECONOMIC STABILITY

From the founding of the first Bank of the United States in 1791 to the establishment of the Federal Reserve in 1913, there were attempts to mitigate the effects of business fluctuations by manipulating the money supply. But during the first two decades of the Federal Reserve System's history, the money managers had no clear concept of a monetary policy aimed at broad stabilization objectives. The failure of the System to prevent the Great Depression and, worse, its seeming inability to bring about a revival disillusioned economists and laymen alike. People began to wonder if they had been wise to attribute so much importance to money as a causal and controlling factor in economic fluctuations.

Meanwhile, in 1936, a rather remarkable book appeared, *The General Theory of Employment, Interest, and Money*, written by John Maynard Keynes, an eminent English economist. He argued that one of the key factors driving the economy is investment and that there might be times when there is not enough investment demand to use up all the savings in the economy. When this occurred production would slow and unemployment would rise. To counter this, he, and especially his U.S. disciples such as Paul Samuelson and Alvin Hansen, recommended increased spending and reduced taxes. *Deficit spending* and the more general term *fiscal policy* became academically acceptable and the huge deficits that arose and the fall in unemployment seemed, during the Second World War, to validate Keynes' theory.

In the immediate aftermath of the war the apprehension that the Depression might return gave way to optimism when it did not materialize. Academic economists were particularly optimistic because of the growing belief that Keynes had proved that a modern industrial economy could be kept on an even keel with fiscal policy.

The mood of optimism was ultimately strengthened by the handling of the *first* postwar recession in 1948–49. Industrial production dropped 10 percent and the GNP fell 4 percent. The Truman administration moved quickly, however, to award military contracts in "distressed areas," and although unemployment rose above 5 percent of the workforce for several months, revival came so quickly that public clamor for action never became very loud.

Indeed, the macroeconomic problems of the postwar period turned out to be very different from any the nation had experienced previously. Depression-level unemployment rates were never approached, even in the most severe postwar recessions. Instead, inflation became the primary problem. Looking closely at Figures 26-1 and 26-2, we can see that inflation tended to fall and unemployment rise in each recession. But the trouble was that inflation did not fall as much in each recession as it had risen in

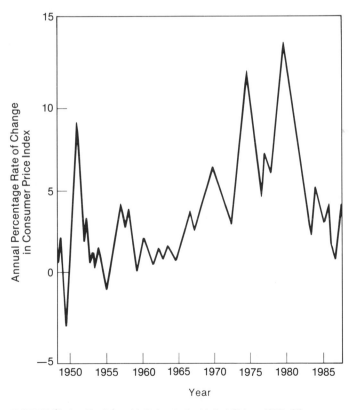

FIGURE 26-1   The Rate of Inflation in the United States, 1950–87.

Source: U.S. Department of Labor.

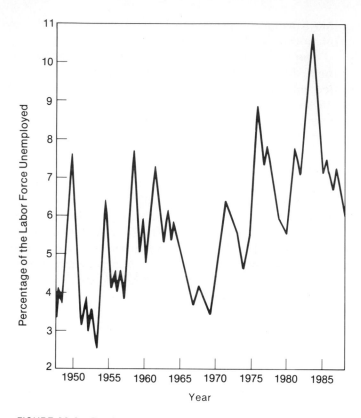

FIGURE 26-2   The Civilian Unemployment Rate, 1950–1987.

Source: U.S. Department of Labor.

the previous expansion, so that the core or base rate of inflation moved ever upward. Similarly, the unemployment rate did not fall as much in each expansion as it rose in each recession. The core or, as some called it, the natural rate of unemployment increased steadily. By the late 1970s "stag-flation" seemed to be as troubling an economic problem as depression had been to an earlier generation. To see how we reached this state of affairs it is necessary to examine the evolution of postwar monetary and fiscal policy.

THE KOREAN WAR

On June 25, 1950, North Korean forces crossed the 38th parallel and attacked South Korea. President Truman responded quickly by authorizing the use of U.S. forces to repel the attack. Less than five years after the end of the Second World War, the United States found itself at war once again.

Consumers responded by attempting to stock up on items that had been in short supply during the war years—sugar, consumer durables, and so on. The surge of consumer demand and the anticipation of a wartime economy led to an acceleration of inflation, clearly visible as the first spike in Figure 26-1. This time, as opposed to the Second World War years, policymakers responded swiftly with a strong anti-inflation program. The lesson drawn from the experience of the Second World War was that half measures do not work.

First, taxes were raised. The Revenue Act of 1950 providing for both higher personal and corporate tax rates was enacted in September 1950. The Revenue Act of 1951, although less comprehensive than the Truman administration wanted, provided for further increases in individual and corporate taxes.

Second, price and wage controls were adopted. A debate quickly developed between those within the administration who favored a gradual approach to controlling prices and those who favored an immediate across-the-board freeze. This time the advocates of a freeze quickly won their point: An across-the-board freeze was announced in late January 1951. Michael V. DiSalle, the director of the Office of Price Stabilization, and a major advocate of a freeze, explained his position by reference to an old maxim. Controlling prices was like "bobbing a cat's tail"—it was better to do it all at once close to the body, otherwise the result would be a mad cat and a sore tail.

But the management of the U.S. economy during the Korean War differed the most from that during the Second World War was in monetary policy. During World War II, as we noted in Chapter 25, the Fed followed a policy of pegging interest rates, even though this forced the Fed to purchase more federal debt than it wanted, thus expanding the stock of money. Pegging was continued in the early postwar years at the request of the Treasury despite growing resentment of this constraint by the Fed. The outbreak of the Korean War, and the growing threat of inflation, brought the conflict into the open. After discussions conducted at the urging of President Truman, the Fed and the Treasury announced that they had reached an agreement on March 4, 1951.

Because the joint statement issued by the two agencies said that they had reached "full accord," this agreement came to be known as the *Treasury-Federal Reserve Accord*. This was essentially a victory for the Fed, although it agreed to certain restrictions desired by the Treasury. Henceforth, the Fed would be free to limit its purchase of government debt and the resulting increase in the stock of money, even if the result was higher interest rates. There were predictions that financial markets would be sent into shock by the emergence of a less predictable interest rate structure. But as it turned out, financial markets adapted quickly to the new regime. The Accord permitted the Fed to follow a noninflationary monetary policy during the war; for the entire period of the war, money per unit of real GNP actually fell slightly.

The anti-inflation program adopted during the Korean War worked well. Consumer prices rose at an annual rate of only 2.1 percent from the price freeze in January 1951 to the termination of controls in February 1953. When controls were terminated many prices were under their ceilings, and there was no post-control price explosion. Consumer prices rose at an annual rate of only 2.6 percent from the termination of controls until the postwar price peak.

The lesson here is that price controls were effective because they were merely a part of the government's response to the fears of runaway inflation produced by the outbreak of the war. While they were being used the Fed was following a monetary policy aimed at bringing inflation under control, a policy reinforced with strong efforts to maintain the integrity of the federal budget. As we shall see, controls were used again in the 1970s. But at that time monetary and fiscal policy were set at cross purposes with the price policy, and controls were not successful.

UNEMPLOYMENT AND INFLATION

During 1953, the key indicators of economic well-being took an unfavorable turn. Industrial production, the GNP, construction contracts, and manufacturers' new orders dropped and unemployment jumped in the last quarter of the year. Because these changes did not occur all at once their impact on income earners was not severe. But as the boom of the early 1950s faded, a pessimism that had not shown itself in 1949 pervaded the country. The magnitude of the drop was approximately the same as the first post-Second World War downturn. In about nine months, industrial production fell 10 percent, the GNP declined 4 percent, and manufacturing employment dropped 10 percent. There was much talk of another "inventory recession" like the one in 1949, but it was clear that entrepreneurs had good reason for reducing inventories. This *second* postwar recession was widely forcast by Keynesian economists. National-defense spending and therefore total government spending declined $11 billion between the second quarter of 1953 and the second quarter of 1954. In short, the federal government caused the recession; since there was a $10 billion drop in gross investment—mostly in inventories—the gross product would have declined more than $21 billion if there had not been offsetting expenditures. Fortunately, state and local governments spent more during the year, exports exceeded imports, and personal consumption expenditures increased; the total offset amounted to a little over $7 billion.

This was far from a serious decline. Compared to the full-blown depressions of former years, the 1953–54 recession seemed small indeed. Nevertheless, it aroused great concern. Unemployment in several areas of manufacturing exceeded 10 percent of the local workforce, and many families exhausted their unemployment insurance benefits before any clear signs of improvement were visible. The fact that the economy leveled off for several months during the summer and fall of 1954 was far from comforting to those who knew that output could not stand still if net additions to the workforce of about 750,000 people a year were to be absorbed.

The administration, reassured by the Council of Economic Advisers, took no drastic steps to combat the recession by fiscal means. A moderate cash deficit, partly the result of a reduction in federal income-tax rates effective January 1, 1954, had a stimulating effect. A Federal Reserve policy of "active ease" was adopted before most informed people were aware that the business indicators had taken a turn for the worse.

It was apparent that there were strong sustaining forces in the economy. A continuing rapid increase in population and a substantial rate of household formation created a demand for consumer goods. To such long-term natural supports were added the *automatic stabilizers*. Unemployment insurance payments, a reduction in the total tax bill as the incomes of individuals and corporations declined, the price supports for agriculture, and even some increase in Social Security payments all acted to cushion the decline in aggregate spending.

After a four-year respite from inflationary pressures, prices began a steady rise in mid-1955 that continued until early 1957; the increase amounted to about 8.5 percent during this brief period. Inflation became the pressing domestic problem of the day. The Fed responded with a restrictive monetary policy that continued until well past the point of economic downturn in the late summer of 1957, not reversing itself until November. A recession of substantial proportions followed—the *third* and deepest of the postwar period thus far. By the spring of 1958, the gap between output and capacity had reached $40 billion, and unemployment at 7.5 percent of the civilian labor force was frightening. The remarkable resilience of the U.S. economy was once again evidenced by a rebound that began in April 1958. But the recovery through 1959 was disappointing, and when the indicators took another adverse turn at the end of the year, the frustration of policymakers was evident.

On average, however, the 1950s were good years: Business cycles were modest in amplitude and duration. Persistently high levels of unemployment or inflation did not occur, at least by the standard of subsequent periods, and the economy continued to make strong advances in productivity and national output. Nevertheless, policymakers remained sensitive to the threats of inflation and unemployment.

At this time economists began to change their thinking about the relationship between inflation and unemployment. Previously they had considered them opposites: prices would rise after the economy reached full employment. Now they began to think that for a variety of reasons (monopoly power in labor markets, lags in the adjustment process, and so on) continuing inflation could be consistent with fairly high levels of unemployment. In 1958, A. W. Phillips published a path-breaking paper in which he showed that in Great Britain there was an inverse relationship between wage increases (later, economists substituted prices) and unemployment; he showed that only very high levels of unemployment were consistent with perfectly stable wages.

The policy implication of the "Phillips Curve," as it came to be known, was that a government could choose the combination of inflation and unemployment it wanted from the possible combinations on the curve. A conservative administration might choose a relatively high rate of unemployment and low level of inflation. A liberal administration could choose to move the economy (by using monetary and fiscal policy) to a lower level of unemployment, but only at the cost of higher inflation.

THE KENNEDY-JOHNSON YEARS

The economy was clearly an issue in the election of 1960. Democrat John F. Kennedy promised to get the economy moving, placing more emphasis on full employment and economic growth and (presumably) less on price stability. Although the *fourth* postwar recession in 1959–60 was mild and short, it was an important factor in Kennedy's narrow 100,000-vote victory over Vice President Nixon.

The economy began its resurgence in February 1961, but at a rate that disappointed the Kennedy team.[1] In *The Economic Reports of the President* in 1962 and 1963, written by the Council of Economic Advisers under the guidance of Chairman Walter Heller, plans were formed for an experimental tax cut in 1964. After Kennedy's shocking assassination in November 1963, the politically astute Lyndon B. Johnson assumed the presidency and promptly guided the tax-cut legislation through Congress and into law.

This was a historic tax cut. The federal budget was then in deficit; orthodox economic theory called for tax increases to balance the budget. But President Kennedy's advisers believed in the "New Economics" of John Maynard Keynes.[2] They argued that as long as the economy was operating at less than full employment (the rate of unemployment was then about 5.5 percent) a tax cut was justified because it would leave more income in the hands of the public, creating more demand for goods and services. As they pointed out, a budget that was in deficit under current conditions might turn out to be balanced or in surplus at full employment because taxes tend to rise, and certain categories of spending fall, as the economy approaches full employment.

---

[1] Peaks and troughs in the business cycle are dated by the National Bureau of Economic Research, a private research group, that initiated much research on the business cycle. The precise date is usually a matter of judgment.
[2] It was "new" in the sense that Keynesian ideas were at last influencing major policymakers.

Three presidents and a president to be—Kennedy, Johnson, Truman, and Eisenhower—at the 1962 preburial services for the Speaker of the House, Sam Rayburn.

In an often-quoted passage from the *General Theory* Keynes wrote the following:

> The ideas of economists and political philosophers, both when they are right and when they are wrong, are more powerful than is commonly understood. Indeed the world is ruled by little else. Practical men, who believe themselves to be quite exempt from any intellectual influences, are usually the slaves of some defunct economist. Madmen in authority, who hear voices in the air, are distilling their frenzy from some academic scribbler of a few years back. I am sure that the power of vested interest is vastly exaggerated compared with the gradual encroachment of ideas.[3]

Less than 30 years after the publication of the *General Theory*, Keynes's ideas were having a profound effect on U.S. fiscal policies.

The Kennedy tax cut was widely acclaimed as a great success. Unemployment fell from 5 percent of the labor force in 1964 to 4.4 percent in 1965 to 3.7 percent in 1966. But the Vietnam War buildup that followed

---

[3]The passage is quoted, it should not surprise us, mostly by economists. *The General Theory of Unemployment, Interest, and Money* (New York: Harcourt Brace, 1936; first Harbinger ed., 1964) p. 383.

closely upon the tax cut had not been part of the calculations when Kennedy's advisers had first planned a cut. The change in economic conditions encouraged Walter Heller and other creators of the tax cut to urge President Johnson to raise taxes. But this advice was not taken. Inflationary pressures began to build, and, as Figure 26-1 shows, the rate of inflation turned upward late in 1965.

For a time the Kennedy administration relied on "Wage-Price Guideposts" to control inflation. If labor received wage increases in proportion to increases in labor productivity then prices and labor's share of income could remain stable.[4] So the Council of Economic Advisers recommended that wage increases be kept within the limits set by productivity increases. In an early test, President Kennedy publicly chastised the steel industry when prices were raised more than the guideposts allowed, threatening a transfer of federal purchases to companies that remained within the guideposts and other sanctions. Eventually the steel industry backed down. But the government could not, of course, treat every price increase that violated the guideposts as a major crisis. When inflation accelerated in 1965 the guideposts fell into disuse.

It was not until the last quarter of 1969 that there was more than a brief pause in the rate of expansion of the economy. Indeed, the expansion from February 1961 to November 1969 was, to that time, the longest sustained rise in the postwar period. The *fifth* postwar recession, in 1969–70, was brief, with the major indicators showing a trough in the fourth quarter of 1970.

THE NIXON ADMINISTRATION AND WAGE AND PRICE CONTROLS

In 1971 the rate of inflation was around 4 percent per year and the rate of unemployment around 6 percent. Although inflation was down from the pre-recession peak, and probably coming down further, the public was bitter about what seemed a very heavy price for a small reduction in inflation. In addition, the United States now had some reason to be concerned about its international balance of payments. In the second half of the 1960s the United States began, year after year, to spend more on importing goods and services than it was earning on exports. As a result, foreign central banks were accumulating large amounts of dollars they were not happy about holding. In a few cases they had converted large amounts of dollars into gold. But it was clear that all could not do so since dollars held abroad

---

[4]An example will make the point clear. There are 10 students in a class each paying $100 tuition. The professor's wage is $500, 50 percent of total income ($500 ÷ $1,000). Now suppose that class size is increased to 15 (labor productivity has gone up 50 percent!). Even with the same tuition of $100 the teacher's salary can be raised to $750. The share of wages in total income is still 50 percent ($750 ÷ $1,500).

by foreign central banks far exceeded U.S. gold holdings. One solution was to devalue the dollar (make one dollar exchange for fewer units of foreign currency than before), and so make U.S. exports more attractive and imports less attractive. But the administration was reluctant to take this path because it would add to inflation (imports would cost more), and because it would mean a loss of prestige for the United States. The upcoming presidential election in 1972 added to the administration's anxieties.

So on August 15, 1971, the administration simultaneously "closed the gold window" and imposed a system of wage and price controls. Closing the gold window meant simply refusing to exchange dollars for gold. The international exchange value of the dollar was now to be determined in the marketplace, like the price of wheat or automobiles. A brief attempt to reestablish fixed rates was the Smithsonian agreement reached in December of 1971. It called for fixed exchange rates with the price of gold raised to $38 dollars (an 8 percent devaluation of the dollar). But the growing world-wide inflation made it difficult to stick to fixed exchange rates, and one country after another began to float its currency against the dollar. The resulting system is frequently described as a "dirty float." Private supplies and demands are the main determinants of exchange rates. But central banks often intervene, buying or selling currencies when the outcome of market forces is not to their liking.

The price controls imposed in 1971 were aimed, of course, at convincing U.S. citizens that something was being done about inflation. But controls also tied in nicely with what was happening to the dollar in international markets. The story was that the balance-of-payments problem was caused primarily by the inflation in the United States because inflation made imports more attractive and exports less attractive. Price controls would buy time while the United States put its house in order. When this was done (presumably sometime after the election), controls could be lifted and a fixed rate of exchange with other currencies based on a fixed price of gold could be restored.

Price controls went through a series of phases. The first three months, known as Phase I, was a price freeze. Because prohibiting all price increases would not work for a long period of time and would lead to shortages, evasions, and rationing, a system with greater flexibility had to be introduced. In Phase II prices were set by the Price Commission and wages by the Pay Board. These bureaus were given considerable latitude in terms of their ability to permit or deny increases, so shortages in individual markets could be addressed. In general the Price Commission aimed at a formula for the economy as a whole reminiscent of the Kennedy guideposts—prices could rise by the amount that the Pay Board permitted wages to rise, less the increase in productivity. But unlike the guideposts, the rules were enforced by the government.

Inflation was relatively low during 1972. On a year-to-year basis the rate of inflation was only 3.3 percent, lower than it had been since 1967 and lower than it would be again until 1983. Price controls, naturally, got much of the credit, although some economists believe that inflation would have slowed in any case. The time seemed right to begin dismantling controls before they became a permanent part of the economy. In Phase III, which began in January 1973, the rules were eased somewhat, and interpretation and administration of the rules were placed in the hands of the businesses themselves. Inflation accelerated from 3.3 percent in 1972 to 6.2 percent in 1973. Worse still, the volatile food index increased at an astonishing 14.5 percent.

The program of price controls came in for considerable criticism. Conservatives complained that inflation was up because the repressed inflation of Phases I and II could no longer be kept in check. Liberals complained that the Nixon administration had deliberately undermined the program because it was working all too well.

In response to the critics, and to the acceleration of inflation, a second freeze was imposed in June 1973, although ceiling prices had been imposed on meats at the end of March. A shortage of meat resulted; grocery meat counters in many cases were literally empty. The shortage was aggravated by the announcement of a date when controls would be lifted. Meat producers held their animals off the market in the almost certain knowledge that they would get a higher price later.

With meat shortages, distortions in other sectors, evasions, and rising prices, the control program was in a sorry state. Phase IV replaced Freeze II in August 1973. (It was really Phase V, but by that time no one was counting). During this phase prices were decontrolled sector by sector. The price controllers tried to prompt producers in sectors that were being decontrolled into promising not to raise their prices too much after controls were lifted. But such promises were mostly face-saving exercises for the controllers.

What was the overall effect on prices of the control program? In 1974 consumer prices rocketed upward at a 12.2 percent annual rate. Some observers have seen this as the release of inflationary pressures built up under controls. But others doubt that there was that much repressed inflation around after Phase III, and look to other factors—such as supply-side shocks in oil and food and the lagged response to previous increases in the stock of money—to explain the acceleration of inflation. Numerous econometric studies analyzed the episode (see the bibliography for references) with varying results. Most studies agree that controls were successful in repressing inflation for a time but differ on how much and for how long.

If the calm created by Freeze I and Phase II had been used to impose restrictive monetary and fiscal policies, the economy might have emerged from this experiment with controls, as it did from the Korean War controls, with stable prices. This, however, was not to be. The stock of money during peacetime rose at the unprecedented rate of 13.5 percent from December of 1970 to December of 1971 and at 13.0 percent from December of 1971 to December of 1972.[5] The inflation of 1974 was to some extent the result of these increments to the stock of money working through the economy. Fiscal policy was also not helpful. Deficits of $23 billion and $23.4 billion were run up in 1971 and 1972. In only one previous year in the postwar period had the deficit been larger, and typically they had been far smaller.

It is not clear why monetary and fiscal policy were so expansionary in these years, but it is possible that to some extent the controls themselves contributed to the easy money policy. By creating the false impression that inflation was under control (and creating a new set of people to blame if it accelerated), the existence of the control system encouraged the Fed to concentrate on reducing unemployment. In any case, it is clear that an opportunity to return to a stable price level, bought at considerable expense, was lost.

Most economists are opposed to the use of controls. Nevertheless, because of their political popularity and bureaucratic support, the advocacy of price and wage controls frequently resurfaced in the 1970s, as testified by President Jimmy Carter's 1978 plan for voluntary wage and price controls.

THE GROWING MENACE OF INFLATION

Although inflation moderated a bit during the recession of 1974–75, it accelerated again in 1976–80. In 1979 and 1980 inflation reached double-digit levels, causing widespread fear of economic disaster. Creditors who had not foreseen rising prices lost, and debtors gained. But even many people who gained or kept pace with inflation were nevertheless haunted by the fear that if they stumbled and failed to negotiate an adequate wage increase, inflation would quickly and seriously reduce their standard of living.

One of the most troubling aspects of the inflation in 1976–80 was the rise in interest rates. As Figure 26-3 shows, interest rates moved irregularly upward after 1965, falling in recessions, but then more than making up the lost ground during the subsequent expansion. During the remarkably volatile year of 1980, the prime rate (the rate charged by banks to their lowest-risk customers on short-term unsecured loans) tickled 20 percent in April, fell to 11 percent by midsummer, and reached the all-time record high of 21 percent by Christmas. High interest rates, both on bank loans and government borrowings, were maintained throughout 1981 and continued into early 1982.

Inflation was clearly an important factor in the rise of interest rates. Economists have long maintained that in a rational world an inflation

---

[5]There are various definitions of money depending on which financial assets are included. The figures here are for M2.

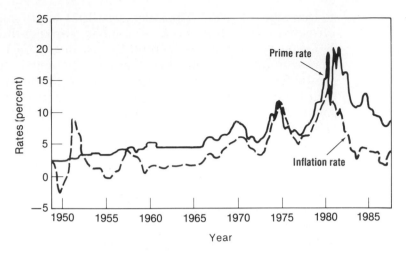

FIGURE 26-3 Prime Rate of Interest vs. Inflation Rate, 1950–87. The prime rate is the interest rate charged by banks to their best customers. The inflation rate is the percentage change in the consumer price index. The difference between the two is the real rate of interest. Note the increase in the real rate in the 1980s.

premium should be incorporated in the rate of interest. If a lender and a borrower could agree on a rate of 10 percent in a year when no price increases were expected, then they should set a rate of 15 percent if prices were expected to rise 5 percent. In the second case, inflation would wipe out 5 percent of the value of the principal and interest and leave the lender and borrower in the same real position as the first case. This idea is frequently known as the Fisher effect, named after Irving Fisher, the American economist who first studied the relationship between interest rates and inflation.

Historically, the relationship between inflation and interest rates has not always been as exact as this example might suggest. Interest rates have sometimes remained fairly stable despite short bursts of inflation. But as inflation persisted year after year, credit markets gradually learned to pay close attention to inflation signals, and the relationship between inflation and the rate of interest grew closer and closer. Economists were to some extent the teachers in this learning process. So even as economists tried to estimate the relationship between inflation and the rate of interest, the doctrines they professed were altering that relationship. (Note in Figure 26-3 how closely inflation and the prime rate coincided in the 1970s.) It would have been better for their professional reputations as prognosticators, perhaps, if they had not explained so clearly why interest rates should be increased during inflations.

Looking back, we can see that there were four major bursts of inflation—in 1965–66, 1967–69, 1973–75, and 1976–80—each with increasing duration and magnitude. Either in anticipation of or in response to these four bursts

Unemployment was of little public concern throughout the 1960s but had become a significant social problem by the 1970s, as these applicants for public-service jobs in Chicago in 1975 vividly attest.

of inflation, the Fed took strong measures to counter the inflationary forces. In 1966, 1969, 1970, and 1974, the Fed substantially lowered monetary growth and accompanied these moves with strong pronouncements (seconded by the White House) that a firm commitment had been made to stem the tide of inflation. On each occasion, anti-inflationary policies were abandoned within a year. In each case, both an underestimate of the length of time required to halt the inflation and the political pressures that rapidly built up when the economy showed signs of slowing down combined to produce a reversal in policy. Though strong but temporary measures slowed the inflation for a short time, the reversals produced new price surges and a growing conviction that inflation would not stop because the government lacked the will to stop it.

Such policies contributed to the long-run emergence of higher unemployment and higher inflation. In the 1960s, as we noted, economists had believed that there was a stable Phillips Curve: unemployment could be permanently lowered at the cost of permanently higher inflation. Now they began to see that the Phillips Curve represented only a temporary trade-off. Once workers and employers began to adjust to the new higher rate of inflation, unemployment would begin moving back to its "natural rate." A number of economists contributed to the new view of the relationship between inflation and unemployment; perhaps most influential was Milton Friedman. His address to the American Economic Association in 1967, "The Role of Monetary Policy," explained that increasing money growth reduced unemployment for a time because prices would initially rise faster than wages, and real wages would fall. But once workers caught on, they would demand wage increases in line with price increases and unemployment would return once again to its "natural rate."[6] The policy implications of this analysis were clear. Governments should not try to reduce unemployment to the lowest possible rate through monetary and fiscal policy because that would lead to ever higher rates of inflation. Better would be a stable monetary and fiscal framework. But, as Keynes noted in the passage previously quoted, new ideas are usually not implemented immediately, rather they gradually encroach upon policymakers.

THE CARTER YEARS

The brief trial of tight monetary policy under President Ford in 1974–75 contributed to a sharp recession that pushed unemployment upward and helped Jimmy Carter win the 1976 election. Inflation slowed temporarily, and by the fall of 1976 the rate of inflation had fallen below 5 percent.

---

[6]Liberal economists preferred the term *non-accelerating inflation rate of unemployment* (NAIRU) because it did not suggest that there was nothing to be done to improve on this rate of unemployment. (This is an example of the sort of humor that appeals to economists: the Nehru suit was fashionable at this time.)

When Carter took office his administration had an excellent opportunity to stamp out the long-building inflationary forces. But the Carter team missed the opportunity. Instead it went about the business of stimulating the economy. Political pressure for increases in Social Security benefits, veteran's benefits, farm subsidies, civil service pensions, grants to states, welfare programs, and other spending advances met favor with the Carter administration and with Congress. Meanwhile, and in contrast to the official rhetoric of the Fed, the stock of money advanced sharply. From 1975 to 1976 the stock of money increased at an annual rate of 13.7 percent, and from 1976 to 1977 it increased at 10.6 percent. By the fall of 1978, inflation was advancing at a rate twice that of two years earlier. But unemployment had fallen at a disappointing rate over the same period from 8.5 percent to 6.0 percent. Greater monetary ease could not be risked.

With the polls repeatedly showing that inflation was "enemy number one," Carter was compelled to act. He named Robert Strauss as his "anti-inflation chief."[7] As a gifted lawyer and political strategist, Strauss' influence on the Carter team was large; he headed and guided the reelection campaign for the President in 1980. But as an expert on inflation, his credentials were few. In a speech at the Columbia Business School Annual Dinner on April 26, 1978, he embarrassed the Carter administration with a speech, "Inflation: The Cost We Cannot Bear," that blamed most of the inflation on the private sector and the American people. In addition, his remarks suggested the highlights of Carter's new policies that were introduced a few months later, on October 24, 1978. Emphasizing that the costs of inaction were high, Strauss listed three options: "a mandatory controls policy, a cooperative approach, and a do-nothing stance." Rejecting the third, and noting the first was inappropriate in the absence of a national emergency, he asked "each American to insure that he make some contribution to lowering inflation rates this year." No mention was made of monetary policy.

Alfred Kahn, the Chairman of the Civil Aeronautics Board, who had spearheaded the deregulation of the airlines, soon replaced Strauss. But the change in chiefs came too late to fundamentally alter policy. By the time Kahn took over, Carter's anti-inflation program was comprised of (1) a commitment to *lower the increase* in government spending, (2) to reduce the federal deficit, (3) to increase the labor productivity and efficiency overall, and (4) to introduce "voluntary guidelines" for wage and price increases. Within a year it was clear that the program was an act of futility. The voluntary controls proved particularly unsettling and were a bone of contention by labor and business alike. While some large corporations and unions were ignored, smaller, less politically potent groups were forced by the President's Council on Wage and Price Controls (often with help from the Internal Revenue Service) to conform to the "advised constraints." In effect, the voluntary controls became *mandatory controls selectively applied*. Meanwhile, inflation continued to rise. By late 1978, inflation was rising at a

---

[7] Given ambassador status, Mr. Strauss' official title was Special Counselor on Inflation.

double-digit annual rate, and throughout 1979 it was rising at a rate above 12 percent.

An atmosphere of confusion prevailed as key members of the Carter team made conflicting public statements. In mid-1979, Charles Schultz, Chairman of the Council of Economic Advisers said he expected the administration's program to take hold later in the year, moderating inflation generally, and in particular, the rate of increase for food.[8] A month earlier, upon hearing that prices had risen 1.1 percent in one month, Alfred Kahn said, "the government can do some things, but not a helluva lot, for the most part it rests with the consumer." Unlike Nixon, who could justifiably claim that OPEC's (Organization of Petroleum Exporting Countries) price increases in oil and other external shocks were important forces behind inflation during the years between 1973 and 1976, the Carter team could find no one to share the blame other than the nation's private sector.[9]

Indeed the rationale for the wage and price guidelines was precisely for that purpose and politically it served to shift the blame for inflation from government mismanagement to the private sector. Throughout these years the news media helped to promote this misplaced emphasis. Routinely, monthly inflation data were reported in a form that attributed price rises to particular sectors or industries. For example, reporters would say that this month most of the inflation was *caused* by the rise in the price of housing (or food, or energy) or whatever rose the most that month. But such advances were the *result* of inflation; they did not cause it.

By late 1978, the United States and much of the rest of the world was engulfed in an economic and political crisis of growing proportions. The polls repeatedly showed that the majority of Americans lacked confidence in the nation's major institutions. A dramatic and influential illustration of voter outrage over high taxes and perceived government waste was the 1978 landslide passage of Proposition 13 in California.[10] Other states quickly followed suit and several passed legislation limiting the growth of either state government expenditures and/or taxes. Perhaps the most startling development was the rising call for a Constitutional Convention to require the federal government to balance its budget. By 1980, 31 out of the 34 states required had called for such a convention and, in March 1982, President Reagan announced his support for such a measure. Clearly, fiscal policy and deficit spending were no longer viewed with the favor that had prevailed in the pre-Vietnam War era. The *cumulative* effects of government's post-1965 commitment to inflation is shown in Figure 26-4 for the

---

[8] Washington (UPI) May 26, 1979.
[9] Although the large shift in wealth caused by OPEC is beyond dispute, its impact on inflation is less clear. For instance, West Germany and Switzerland were far more vulnerable to the real shocks produced by OPEC and failing agricultural crops than was the United States. Yet they managed, by a determined effort to reduce their monetary growth, to lower their inflations, 1973–76, to the vanishing point.
[10] The basic feature of the bill was to reduce property taxes sharply in the state, and thereby limit spending.

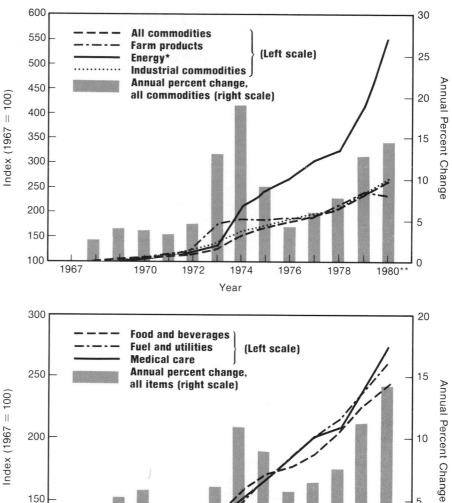

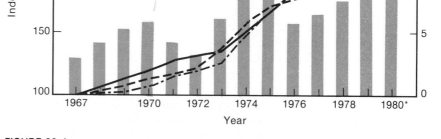

FIGURE 26-4

Producer Price Indexes, 1967–80 (1967 = 100). (Upper figure)

* Fuel, power, and related products.

**Annual rate for five months ending May. For 1980, percent change, May 1979–80.

Consumer Price Indexes, 1967–80 (1967 = 100). (Lower figure)

*Annual rate for five months ending May. For 1980, percent change May 1979–80.

Source: Chart prepared by the U.S. Bureau of the Census.

major sectors of the economy. Similar to the form of most news media's inflationary reports of the day, it is tempting to single out those sectors revealing the most rapid rise in prices. But clearly, *the general rise of prices* did not stem from any single sector. *All sectors*, albeit with variation, responded to the underlying inflationary forces. As during the Great Depression, many policies were initiated or enlarged in the 1970s to provide relief for needy individuals and families. These were largely redistributive to help correct for the disruptions caused by inflation. For instance, as food prices rose, food stamps were distributed more liberally—thus adding to demand and the rise of prices in that sector. As hospital and medical treatment costs soared, government attempted to assume the medical costs of the needy, who in turn, because of lower personal costs for treatment, increased their demand for services. This increased the costs of medical services and added to inflation in the medical sector. Many communities, such as Berkeley and Santa Monica, California, passed rent controls, which hastened the rate of conversion of apartments to condominiums as owners scrambled to avoid the controls. Though helping some people, attacks on the symptoms of inflation often made conditions worse for the average American.

As interest rates rose with inflation, many people found themselves unable to afford housing. Indeed, the pervasive speculation in housing in the second half of the 1970s, while enriching many, provided a haunting signal to the young. Each generation in the post-Second World War period had grown to expect that they would live a life of greater material comfort than had the preceding generation. Now this view no longer held, and many feared a bleak future for their children. As the young increasingly found housing difficult to obtain, the old were becoming increasingly concerned over the plight of the Social Security system: payment increases linked to inflation threatened to bankrupt the system.

The clash of political forces over these and other issues intensified as inflation accelerated. Effective and satisfactory resolutions became more difficult as distrust and a sense of injustice mounted. Ironically, the decline in public confidence revealed in the polls would not have surprised John Maynard Keynes. In his 1919 book, *Economic Consequences of the Peace*, he eloquently stated:

> Lenin is said to have declared that the best way to destroy the Capitalist System was to debauch the currency. By a continuing process of inflation, governments can confiscate, secretly and unobserved, an important part of the wealth of their citizens. By this method they not only confiscate, but they confiscate *arbitrarily*; and, while the process impoverishes many, it actually enriches some. The sight of this arbitrary rearrangement of riches strikes not only at security, but at confidence in the equity of the existing distribution of wealth. Those to whom the system brings windfalls, beyond their deserts and even beyond their expectations or desires, become "profiteers," who are the object of the hatred of the bourgeoisie, whom the inflation has impoverished, not less than of the proletariat. As the inflation proceeds and the real value of the currency

fluctuates wildly from month to month, all permanent relations between debt-ors and creditors, which form the ultimate foundation of capitalism, become so utterly disordered as to be almost meaningless; and the process of wealth-getting degenerates into a gamble and a lottery.

Lenin was certainly right. There is no subtler, no surer means of over-turning the existing basis of society than to debauch the currency. The process engages all the hidden forces of economic law on the side of destruction, and does it in a manner which not one man in a million is able to diagnose.[11]

THE FED, OCTOBER 6, 1979

Recognizing that Carter's policies were not working and that the American people were becoming increasingly cynical about the prospects of reining-in inflation, the Fed finally took dramatic steps. On October 6, 1979, the Federal Reserve Board announced a fundamental shift in policy. Hence-forth, interest rates were going to assume less importance in their decision making. More attention was to be paid to the monetary aggregates (differ-ent measures of the money stock) and new techniques were introduced to control the growth of the money stock.

This shift appeared to be a triumph for the doctrines of Milton Friedman and other monetarists. For several decades they had been making four principal points based on their reading of monetary history. (1) Inflation was primarily a monetary phenomenon: "Too much money chasing too few goods." Therefore, to reduce inflation the Fed had to reduce the growth of the stock of money. (2) Money affected the economy with a long and variable lag. Therefore, the best policy was the simplest: gradually reduce the rate of growth of the stock of money to a low rate and then hold it. Attempts to fine-tune the economy might end up making matters worse. (3) The trade-off between inflation and unemployment was only temporary. Again, the conclusion was don't try to fine-tune the economy. (4) Interest rates are a misleading guide to monetary policy despite the man-in-the-street's convic-tion that the Fed simply sets interest rates at whatever level it chooses. During the Great Depression low interest rates had given the misleading signal that money was easy. Now, high interest rates were giving the mis-leading signal that money was tight.

A related but distinct line of thought concerning "rational expectations" held that the costs of disinflation, unemployment, and reduced output were largely the result of mistaken expectations. If workers continued to demand wage increases based on expectations of inflation and those expectations

---

[11]John Maynard Keynes, *The Economic Consequences of the Peace* (New York: Harcourt, Brace, 1920), pp. 235–36.

were disappointed, they would end up pricing themselves out of the market. The policy implication of this line of thought was also clear. Even an abrupt change in monetary policy would cause little damage, *if* people truly believed that the Fed would hold true to its new policy. Expectations would change rapidly and no one would be priced out of the market.

Once more policymakers were turning to academic economists for ideas about how to manage the economy. Of course, policymakers could not be forced to carry out the experiment in the way that monetarists would have liked. Monetarists complained that rather than smoothly and slowly reducing the growth rate of the stock of money, the fluctuations in the growth rate were becoming greater than ever. As in the Kennedy-Johnson years, policymakers could pay lip service to ideas and adopt the part of the program that suited them, while ignoring the advice they did not want to hear. In this case, moreover, adopting a new set of doctrines had the advantage that if the policy didn't work, or the costs of disinflation were high, the monetarists could be blamed.

Under the leadership of Paul Volcker, chairman of the Federal Reserve Board, the growth rate of the stock of money was curtailed and inflation dropped dramatically. Inflation had fallen from 13.3 to 8.9 percent between 1980 and 1981 and rates were below 6.0 percent through the first half of 1982. Seizing the opportunity to eradicate inflation, Volcker tenaciously held to his policy throughout 1981 and early 1982. He did so despite an increase in unemployment from 5.8 percent in 1979 to 9.5 percent in 1982 (the highest rate since the Great Depression[12]) and despite official predictions of federal deficits in the early years of Reagan's presidency that would also be record setting. The political pressure to change course and relax the tight money policy were intense, but the Fed held to its course. In 1982 inflation was 3.9 percent. The cost of disinflation, however, was high despite the predictions of some economists that once the commitment of the Fed to stable prices was taken seriously the real adjustments would be small. Of course, on this occasion there was little reason based on past experience to take the Fed seriously.

Beginning in 1982 the economy began the longest peacetime expansion on record. Unemployment gradually declined and inflation remained at tolerable levels through the remainder of the Reagan presidency. After two terms Ronald Reagan left the presidency in 1989 as one of, if not the most, popular presidents of the postwar period. Much of that popularity rested on the contrast between economic conditions as he found them and as he left them.

How much of that record was due to monetary policy is difficult to say. One of the mysteries of the period is that the economy seemed able to absorb

---

[12] The frequent repetition of this fact in the media misled many people into thinking that the unemployment rate was almost as high as it had been in the Great Depression. This, of course, was not the case. See Chapter 23.

Paul Volcker, former chairman of the powerful Federal Reserve Board, was one of the principal leaders advocating tight money to reduce double-digit inflation in the late 1970s and early 1980s.

a considerable amount of new money without experiencing a return to high rates of inflation. From December of 1980 to December of 1986 the stock of money grew at an annual rate of 9.0 percent per year. Some observers saw this as natural as long as the economy was emerging from the deep trough of the early 1980s. Others suggested that deregulation of the banking system, and particularly the payment of interest on bank deposits, had independently increased the demand for money.

In any case, with money growing rapidly, frequently in excess of the targets proclaimed by the Fed, and little evidence of unacceptably high rates of inflation, the Fed gradually abandoned its emphasis on monetary growth and began to pay attention once more to interest rates, and (something new) the international value of the dollar.

REAGANOMICS

The landslide victory by Ronald Reagan in the 1980 election, and the dramatic shift in power in Congress—and particularly in the Senate—to the Republicans provided both a mandate for change and the political coalition to realize it. As soon as the Reagan administration was formed, it moved swiftly to implement Reagan's economic campaign promises. These centered on a large tax cut achieved by lowering marginal tax rates especially for very high incomes, elimination of the federal deficit, a reduction in the role of the federal government both in terms of spending and regulation, and a buildup of the armed forces.

Once again a new school of economic thought was influential in altering the course of economic policy. *Supply-side* economists such as Arthur Laffer argued that economic growth was being inhibited by high tax rates. Lowering rates would give people more incentive to work, invest, and innovate. Lowering rates would even produce more tax revenue by expanding the tax base, thus helping to balance the budget. The relationship between tax rates and tax revenues became known as the Laffer Curve: over some range, raising rates would increase revenues, but at some point further increases would lead to large reductions in work effort and increases in tax evasion; then total tax revenue would fall. Laffer and other supply-side economists believed that the economy had already entered this range. But while most economists agreed that high tax rates tended in some degree to discourage productive effort, many disputed that the effects of cutting rates would be as large as the supply-siders thought. In the campaign for the Republican nomination, George Bush, then Reagan's rival, spoke for many when he denounced the idea of balancing the budget through tax cuts as Voodoo economics, a term that gained wide currency among critics of supply-side economics.

After the election, Congress moved swiftly to reduce income and other taxes by 25 percent over a three-year period. But it should not surprise us that reductions in spending were much harder to achieve. As David Stockman, who was in charge of planning the Reagan spending cuts, tells us in his memoir, even the most commonsense cuts were strongly resisted by an "iron triangle": the direct beneficiaries of government spending in the private sector, the government bureaucrats who administered the program, and the Congressmen who were particularly beholden to the beneficiaries.

Tax cuts, the early recession, failure to make proposed spending cuts, and continued increases in the military budget produced deficits in the federal budget unprecedented in peacetime, although the exact amount to be attributed to each factor is in dispute. Figure 26-5 shows the deficit during four presidencies. It reveals both the long-term nature of the problem—the deficit has been growing for over two decades now—and the acceleration of growth in the deficit under President Reagan.

What were the consequences of such deficits? Neither Keynesian economists who count on deficits to produce increased demand nor supply-side economists who count on tax reductions to spur work effort were surprised by the long economic expansion that followed the recession of the early 1980s. On the other hand, some economists predicted that large federal deficits would lead to skyrocketing real interest rates (the market rate less inflation) because deficits meant that a much augmented demand for credit

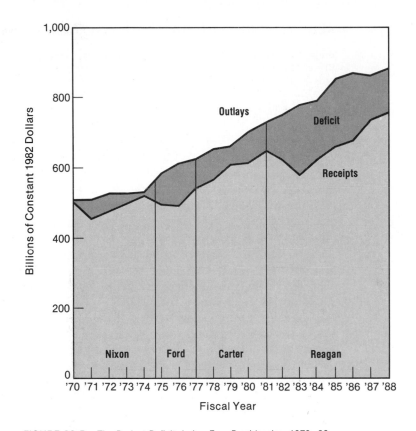

FIGURE 26-5   The Budget Deficit during Four Presidencies, 1970–88.

Source: U.S. Department of Commerce.

would face the same supply. But while real interest rates were high in the 1980s, the supply of credit proved more elastic than had been anticipated. Foreign lenders rushed into the U.S. market by purchasing government bonds, private securities, real estate, and other assets. Real interest rates were held down, and the dollar remained strong (worth a large number of units of foreign currency) despite a growing gap between exports and imports.

It was widely believed that there was a close relationship between the "twin deficits." If the federal deficit could be closed, real interest rates would fall, and the dollar would decline relative to other currencies, spurring exports and inhibiting imports. Thus the trade deficit would disappear. This was the consensus view of the economic scene when George Bush took the oath of office as president of the United States in January 1989. It remained to be seen whether substantial progress could be made on curing the budget deficit, and whether, if the budget deficit were reduced, the international economy would work as the theory predicted.

SELECTED REFERENCES AND SUGGESTED READINGS

Blinder, Alan S. *Economic Policy and the Great Stagflation.* New York: Academic Press, 1979.

Brimmer, Andrew F. "The Political Economy of Money: Evolution and Impact of Monetarism in the Federal Reserve System." *American Economic Review*, Papers and Proceedings 62 (May 1972): 344–52.

Brunner, Karl, and Allan H. Meltzer, eds. *The Economics of Price and Wage Controls.* Amsterdam: North-Holland, 1976.

Burns, Arthur. *Reflections of an Economic Policymaker.* Washington D.C.: American Enterprise Institute, 1978.

Cagan, Phillip. "Changes in the Recession Behavior of Wholesale Prices in the 1920s and Post-World War II." *Explorations in Economic Research* 2 (1975): 54–104.

David, Paul A., and Peter Solar. "A Bicentenary Contribution to the History of the Cost of Living in America." *Research in Economic History* 2 (1977): 1–80.

Eckstein, Otto. *The Great Recession.* Amsterdam: North-Holland, 1978.

Eisner, Robert. "Fiscal and Monetary Policy Reconsidered." *American Economic Review* 59 (1969): 897–905.

Feldstein, Martin S. "Social Security, Induced Retirement and Aggregate Capital Formation." *Journal of Political Economy* 82 (Sept.-Oct. 1974): 905–26.

Friedman, Benjamin M. "Postwar Changes in the American Financial Markets." In *The American Economy in Transition*, ed. Martin Feldstein. Chicago: Univ. of Chicago Press, 1980.

Friedman, Milton. "The Demand for Money: Some Theoretical and Empirical Results." *Journal of Political Economy* 67 (Aug. 1959): 327–51.

———. "The Role of Monetary Policy." *American Economic Review* 58 (March 1968): 1–17.

Friedman, Milton, and Anna J. Schwartz. *A Monetary History of the United States, 1867–1960.* Princeton: Princeton Univ. Press, 1963.

Gordon, Robert J. "Alternative Responses to External Supply Shocks." *Brookings Papers on Economic Activity* 6 (1975): 183–206.

———. "Postwar Macroeconomics: The Evolution of Events and Ideas." In *The American Economy in Transition*, ed. Martin Feldstein. Chicago: Univ. of Chicago Press, 1980.

———. "Understanding Inflation in the 1980s." *Brookings Papers on Economic Activity* 16 (no. 1, 1985): 263–99.

Heller, Walter W. *New Dimensions of Political Economy.* New York: W. W. Norton, 1966.

Holmans, A. E. *United States Fiscal Policy.* Oxford: Oxford Univ. Press, 1961.

Jorgenson, Dale W. "The Role of Energy in the U.S. Economy." *National Tax Journal* 31 (Sept. 1978): 209–20.

Lanzillotti, Robert F., Mary T. Hamilton, and Blaine R. Roberts. *Phase II in Review: The Price Commission Experience.* Washington D.C.: The Brookings Institution, 1975.

Lucas, Robert E., Jr. "Some International Evidence on Output Inflation Trade-offs." *American Economic Review* 63 (1973): 326–34.

———. "Econometric Policy Evaluation: A Critique." In *The Phillips Curve and Labor Markets*," ed. K. Brunner and A. H. Meltzer. Carnegie-Rochester Conference Series on Public Policy, vol. 1. Amsterdam: North Holland, 1976.

———. "Understanding Business Cycles." In *Stabilization of the Domestic and International Economy*, ed. Karl Brunner and Allan Meltzer. Amsterdam: North Holland, Carnegie-Rochester Conference Series, vol. 5, 1977.

Nordhaus, William D. "The Political Business Cycle." *Review of Economic Studies* 42 (April 1975) 169–90.

Okun, Arthur M. "Measuring the Impact of the 1964 Tax Reduction." In *Perspectives on Economic Growth*, ed. Walter W. Heller. New York: Random House, 1968.

Phelps, Edmund S. "Phillips Curves, Expectations of Inflation and Optimal Unemployment Policy Over Time. *Economica* 34 (1967): 254–81.

Phillips, A. W. "The Relation between Unemployment and the Rate of Change of Money Wage Rates in the United Kingdom, 1861–1957." *Economica* 25 (Nov. 1958): 283–99.

Phillips, Cabell. *The Truman Presidency*. New York: Macmillan, 1969.

Poole, William. "Federal Reserve Operating Procedures: A Survey and Evaluation of the Historical Record Since October 1979." *Journal of Money, Credit, and Banking* 14 (Nov. 1982, Part 2): 575–96.

Roberts, Paul Craig. *The Supply-Side Revolution*. Cambridge: Harvard Univ. Press, 1984.

Sachs, Jeffrey. "The Changing Cyclical Behavior of Wages and Prices, 1890–1976." *American Economic Review* 70 (1980): 78–90.

Sarget, Thomas, and Neil Wallace. "Rational Expectations and the Theory of Economic Policy." *Journal of Monetary Economics* 2 (April 1976): 241–54.

Schultz, George P., and Kenneth W. Dam. *Economic Policy beyond the Headlines*. New York: W. W. Norton, 1977.

Stein, Herbert. *The Fiscal Revolution in America*. Chicago: Univ. of Chicago Press, 1969.

———. *Presidential Economics*. New York: Simon & Schuster, 1984.

Sundquist, James L. *Politics and Policy: The Eisenhower, Kennedy and Johnson Years*. Washington, D.C. The Brookings Institution, 1968.

Tobin, James. *The New Economics One Decade Older*. Princeton: Princeton Univ. Press, 1974.

CHAPTER 27

Manufacturing, Marketing, and Industrial Productivity

To many, industrial growth is both the wellspring of American progress and a major threat to economic justice. By nearly any measurement we choose to take, manufacturing has been and continues to be a major force in the modern U.S. economy. Despite a decline in manufacturing *employment* from 35 percent of all nonfarm wage and salary employment in 1947 to under 20 percent by 1985, manufacturing is still a crucial provider of jobs. In 1985 manufacturing accounted for 21.7 percent of GNP, and together with mining and construction accounted for 29.9 percent.

MANUFACTURING GROWTH PATTERNS

According to a number of studies on growth patterns of industries and sectors,[1] and contrary to popular belief, an industry does not usually reach a peak and then level off; once it ceases to grow, it normally begins to decline. Moreover, all individual industries exhibit an acceleration phase, followed by a retardation in their growth rates. More specifically, when it is first introduced, a product normally goes through a brief period of slow growth while it is gaining acceptance. If it gains acceptance (and many products do not), output increases for a time at an accelerating rate. But as

---

[1] See in particular, Arthur F. Burns, *Production Trends in the United States Since 1870* (New York: National Bureau of Economic Research, 1934); Simon Kuznets, *Secular Movements in Production and Prices* (Boston: Houghton Mifflin, 1930); and J. Paradiso and Francis L. Hirt, "Growth Trends in the Economy," *Survey of Current Business* (Jan. 1953), pp. 5–10.

years pass, the growth rate tends to decline, although retardation in expansion may be interrupted by sharp upward thrusts in demand resulting from such causes as an outbreak of war, stoppage of foreign supplies of the product, or an increase in consumer income.

At first it may appear that such a proposition is just a mathematical truism—that an initial increase in production at a rate of, say, 100 percent per annum obviously cannot be maintained forever. It is more informative however, to note that declines in the growth rates of particular industries are concomitants of rapid growth in total production. The continual introduction of new goods and services restricts the demand for older ones, and the faster the introduction of new commodities, the greater the restrictive influence on older ones.[2] Interindustry and interproduct competition may have effects on a particular line of production, ranging from diversion of demand to the outright undoing of an established industry. For example, the rapid acceptance of frozen foods adversely affected the output of canned foods. Television hurt the motion picture industry badly, changed radio production altogether, raised problems in the spectator sports industry, and affected book sales and the custom of restaurant dining. But television, in turn, has been affected by the growth of cable television and video cassettes. Nor is this all. Besides the increase in the number and variety of commodities, the methods of producing a given commodity may also multiply over time. Steel-reinforced aluminum cable, which is both stronger and lighter than an electrically equivalent copper cable, has captured the high-voltage transmission-line business and is rapidly winning in the so-called secondary distribution field.

Finally, there is persistent competition between old and new industries for the factors of production as well as for customer favor. Indeed, the very existence of an economic system implies a bidding among entrepreneurs for the use of scarce resources. Technological advances reduce the restrictions imposed by a scarcity of resources, but as we have just observed, the stimulation that one industry receives from technical developments is likely to lead to retardation in competing industries.

The Rise and Fall of Industries

Data collected by the Department of Commerce on 160 industries in the 1940s and early 1950s reveals more specific changes and classifications. Against the average annual growth rate of 5 percent for these industries, three classes may be distinguished: (1) rapid-growth industries with a rate of 7.5 percent or more, (2) moderate-growth industries, 0 to 7.5 percent, and (3) declining industries.

More than 60 products fell in the rapid-growth category, including producer and consumer goods, both durable and nondurable, as well as

---

[2] Burns, p. xvi.

services. Only about one-third of these rapidly growing items were new products; the remainder had long been on the market. Antibiotics exhibited the highest average growth rate—a phenomenal 118 percent per year. Output of television sets was almost as great; home freezers and clothes dryers followed. But among the fast-growing industries, growth rates varied considerably toward the end of the period. Since 1948, for example, frozen foods and phosphoric acid exceeded their 1940–51 average rate of growth, whereas tractors, locomotives, and rayon and acetate showed a definite tendency to slow down. Such abrupt changes remind us that we must always be careful about inferring a *future* rate of growth from any average of past growth rates.

The intermediate group, as might be expected, was comprised predominantly of older industries. The greater part of American industrial output lies in this category. Items such as shipping containers, glass containers, and truck and bus tires were at the top of the list, with increases above 5 percent but below 7.5 percent. Goods such as electric lamps, canned fruits and vegetables, lubricating oil, salt, and electric fans showed output increases approximately identical to that of the gross national product. Staple foods such as sugar and wheat flour and standard goods such as wool carpets and rugs, radios, and cigars had barely measurable annual rates of increase.

Out of the 160 industries studied, 17 showed a declining trend in output. Changes in consumer tastes accounted for some of these declines, as in the cases of pipe and chewing tobacco, and lamb and mutton. Average annual rates of decline in the production of men's suits and overcoats were accounted for partly by changes in taste and partly by the entry into military service of a large proportion of young males during the period. For the most part, however, the retrogressing industries had fallen victim to the competition of substitute or alternative products. Radiators, convectors, and mechanical stokers were rapidly displaced as better heating systems became popular. Butter experienced an average annual decline in output of around 4 percent since 1940, not because margarine was better but because it was so much cheaper. And so it was for windmill pumps, soap, steam locomotives, and wood shingles.

It is instructive to observe how growth patterns shift with the selection of a different time span. During the period 1948–60, fast-growth products changed remarkably.[3] Of the more than 70 items in this group, 10 percent showed uninterrupted growth at a rate of over 15 percent per year. Outstanding examples included polyethylene and transistors. Some fast-growth products accelerated their rate of growth in the last six years of the period; some slowed their rate of growth, while others that averaged more than a

---

[3] For the average annual rates of growth of 304 products during 1948–60, see Francis L. Hirt, "New Light on Patterns of Output Growth," *Survey of Current Business* (Sept. 1961), pp. 14–15.

7.5 percent rate of increase for the whole period reached a leveling stage or actually declined.

Rapidly growing industries are important to development because they give impetus to the economy. One type of output that provides the economy with an undercurrent of great strength is the manufacture of household durables. For a while after its introduction, a new durable shows slowly increasing sales. Shortly, if it is to gain acceptance at all, the durable makes rapid gains—gains so great that they can sometimes affect incomes and employment in the entire economy. Before the First World War, automobiles and washing machines gave the economy a boost. Electric refrigerators and radios got their start early in the 1920s and were a positive force through the 1930s. After the Second World War, automatic washing machines, television sets, home freezers, and, more recently, room air conditioners, dehumidifiers, clothes dryers, electric typewriters, and personal computers made their mark. As the 1960s progressed, textile mill consumption of glass fibers soared, and knit cloth regained favor in many uses. Central air conditioning and electric heating systems, including heat pumps, vied with color television sets for a rapidly increasing share of household outlays. In the 1970s recreational and avocational expenditures on new designs of old products rose spectacularly, as families turned to cameras, stereos, boats, campers, and other leisure-time vehicles and activities.

Today, as in the past, American manufacturers endlessly strive to develop new products; in 1984 alone U.S. industry spent more than $71 billion on research and development. But despite this effort, roughly five out of every six items introduced into supermarket channels each year fail to sell. Consequently, business emphasis has shifted away from technological efforts to make old products perform better and toward meeting the basic market demands of the consumer. Market testing alone can cost vast sums and market-tested products can fail even when they are backed by massive advertising campaigns on national television.

On rare occasions, a totally new product is introduced. But Polaroid cameras, personal computers, Xerox copiers, and video games are not commonplace. Products like Gillette's Trac-II razor, Eastman Kodak's cartridge-loaded Instamatic camera, and General Foods Corporation's Maxim coffee have enjoyed rapid and continuing success largely because they are much more convenient to use than old forms of the same product. Yet more often than not, such attempts fail. The example of Ford Motor Corporation's Edsel is legendary. No less prestigious a firm than duPont lost $100 million on Corfam, simply because people would not accept artificial leather shoes despite their porosity and low-care requirements. General Foods dropped an estimated $15 million on a cereal containing freeze-dried strawberries because children rejected the berries as "mushy and soggy."[4] There are

---

[4]"New Products: The Push Is on Marketing," *Business Week* (March 4, 1972), pp. 72–77.

those, of course, who argue that the rejection process is wasteful of resources and that it raises the costs of accepted products. The alternative is a system in which political commissars make choices for people; yet the Soviet Union, China and other centralized economies are now trying to introduce reforms modeled on the capitalist system.

MARKETING AND THE CONSUMER

The development of markets remains crucial to the success of manufacturing activities. In 1985, the wholesale-retail sector generated 16.9 percent of GNP, which was almost 80 percent of the income generated by the manufacturing sector. Employment in wholesale-retail trade was actually greater than in manufacturing, almost 20 percent greater.

Manufacturers in the late nineteenth century, as we noted before, began to disregard the wholesaler and to sell directly to retail outlets. The "general merchandise" wholesaler, with a warehouse of heterogeneous goods in many product lines, had declined rapidly before the First World War and was no longer to be a significant figure in the marketing process. As of 1920, however, the full-service, full-line wholesale house that furnished goods to retailers in one particular line, such as hardware, groceries, or drugs, over great regions and even nationally, was still in a commanding position. But this position was maintained primarily in industries where production remained small-scale. Perhaps the major trend in wholesaling over the past 45 to 50 years has been the lessening relative importance of these great houses and the increasing relative importance of the specialty wholesaler, or "short-line" distributor. To a significant extent this has been due to shifting markets. The specialty firm, which confines its selling activity to a portion of the products within a single line of merchandise, has fitted into the changing scene by providing expert knowledge from which small retailers can benefit.

We must not conclude that the decline in importance of the traditional wholesale house meant a reduction in the total flow of goods through wholesale channels. There has simply been a change in the way goods move from manufacturers (or from farm and mine) to the retailer. During the 1920s, there was a substantial change in the wholesale *structure* as the wholesalers lost ground to manufacturers' sales branches, agents and brokers, assemblers and rural buyers, bulk tank stations, and chain-store warehouses, in that order. Since 1929, the relative position of the different types of establishments has remained so nearly identical that for our purposes we need not trace the developmental changes. The total volume of wholesale trade has fluctuated with changes in business activity, moving spectacularly neither upward nor downward.

Wholesale houses have continued since 1929 to handle about two-fifths of the wholesale business as measured in net sales. This group is still the most important performer of wholesale functions, but within it the old order has disappeared from most product lines. A few of the traditional names remain. But inroads have consistently been made into the full-line wholesaler's territory—to some extent by the limited-function companies (drop shippers, cash-and-carry wholesalers, and wagon distributors), but largely by the specialty firms that serve small geographic areas. The specialty wholesalers handle an assortment of items within one product line (coffee, tea, and condiments instead of "groceries"; cutlery instead of "hardware"). They can furnish fresh or new goods rapidly and they know their particular field of merchandising thoroughly.

The nature of wholesaling has been affected by the great structural shifts in retailing. It has been the growth in the size of the retail firm that has brought about the present-day orientation of the marketing process toward the manufacturer–retailer axis.

Large-scale Retailing

Department stores were well established by 1900 and were popularly accepted in the first decade of the century. Between 1910 and 1920, the mail-order companies began to make great gains. By 1919, the chain stores showed signs of being a potent marketing form, and in the 1920s they became a major force in retailing. How have these types of stores fared since?

It is all too easy to think of the department store as a fading institution, but we must not yet count "the big store" out as a merchandising forum. During the 1920s and 1930s, department stores maintained a constant proportion of retail sales, indicating that they were just about holding their own in the economy. The Second World War with its supply shortages restored some of the advantages of shopping under one roof, and department-store business increased to about 10 percent of retail sales—a gain of perhaps two percentage points. Since 1947, department stores, although not without a struggle, have moved slowly back to this position, and in 1982 once again accounted for 10 percent of retail sales. Increasing traffic congestion in the downtown areas of cities, the rise of suburban shopping centers, and the expansion of variety chains and mail-order companies into broader fields have been the chief factors working against the independent department store. Yet many large stores have shown unexpected resilience. Ownership groups have bought control of stores in many cities, thereby bringing the advantages of tremendous buying power to many of the stores that have continued to operate under their well-known old names. More recently, alert managements have followed the suburban trend by establishing branches, some of them rivaling the central-city store in volume. To fight the discount houses, with their emphasis on plain décor and a minimum of service, department stores have either met discount-house prices in their old locations or opened new and less pretentious outlets for the purpose of discounting. A final irony of this competition has been the opening of glossy, new central-city stores by the discounters; like every other major retailing form before them, they have finally succumbed to the compulsion to become respectable.

Mail-order houses have fared better in recent years than might have been expected but only because they have changed their business methods to suit the times. Since 1929, the mail-order business has been fairly constant at roughly 1 percent of all retail sales. A number of companies specializing in a single line or a few items have sprung up. The application of new advertising techniques to catalog illustrations and the opening of "catalog stores" in small towns have helped the older houses maintain their sales volume. Two-earner families with high incomes and little time to shop have turned to catalogs, offsetting the decline of the traditional catalog user, the farm family. The two great mail-order firms, moreover, have completely changed their sales methods to fit the times. In 1925, Montgomery Ward established its first retail store in Marysville, Kansas, and Sears, Roebuck quickly tried the same experiment. At the end of a decade and a half, these retail stores numbered in the hundreds, and more than one-half of the "mail order" business was conducted over a counter. At the end of the Second World War, Sears boldly expanded by building great department stores in readily accessible sections of major cities. Montgomery Ward, because it was timorous in carrying out its expansion program, lost ground to such an extent that in 1950 its sales were less than one-half of the sales of its major competitor. During the ensuing decade, Sears became the fifth largest employer in the United States, with a dollar volume of retailing of more than $4 billion a year—a retail sales figure exceeded only by A&P. In 1971, Sears was still the fifth largest employer in the country, and its sales of $10 billion were nearly twice the sales of A&P and Safeway, which were second and third on the retailer list, respectively. In the late 1970s Sears' position deteriorated as competition from discounters and small retailers based in malls increased. But in the 1980s management reforms paved the way for a rebound. By 1987 Sears was the fourteenth largest company in the country.

Mention of the great grocery chains reminds us that the past 45 years have witnessed a widespread acceptance of the chain principle of merchandising. Between 1919 and 1929, chain sales rose from an estimated 4 percent of retail sales to slightly less than 25 percent—a proportion that has not varied much since in both good times or bad. Since 1929, however, the number of retail units in chain organizations has declined, possibly by as much as one-third, as the trend has been toward fewer stores and greater volume. There has also been some shift in the use of the chain form in various lines of business. The opening of department stores by Sears, Roebuck and Montgomery Ward has been reflected statistically in a definite spread of chains to the department-store, drygoods, and general-merchandise fields. Chain-store growth has been especially marked in drugs, shoes, women's ready-to-wear, and jewelry, whereas only moderate gains have been made in variety merchandise, food, and automobile accessories and equip-

In 1925 Sears, Roebuck opened its first retail store while continuing its mail-order business.

ment. At the same time, a high degree of concentration has developed within chain-store groups; as the six largest concerns in each field have attained a preponderance of chain sales in the general merchandise (department store), variety, grocery, and drug lines.

Chains have unquestionably found a place in U.S. economic life from which they will not soon be dislodged. In an effort to obtain some of the advantages of the chains, independent retailers have achieved some success in establishing informal buying pools and voluntary chains. But the historical trend toward distributor integration was slowed greatly, if not actually halted, by the fair trade laws of the 1930s, which attacked chains as anti- or "unfairly" competitive.

In concentrating on the spectacular growth in *absolute* volume of the big merchandisers, we should not forget that their *relative* strength has not changed much since before the Great Depression. Limited-line stores, widely varying in size and under independent ownership, have continued to conduct more than one-half of the retail business in the United States. Independents have located in the suburban shopping centers and malls that have sprung up so conspicuously since the Second World War. Although the chains were pioneers in the development of the supermarket, independents have competed successfully as supermarkets in the grocery business. Independents have also been successful in metropolitan-area stores selling higher-priced goods such as clothing, appliances, and even automobiles. In an age in which deference is paid to the specialist, specialists in the retail field have been able to hold their own, because they—like the large-scale retailers—can successfully differentiate their product.

Product Differentiation

Product differentiation may be achieved by adjusting the conditions of the sale of the product or by varying the quality or appearance of the product itself. Independent retailers have traditionally operated neighborhood stores to reap the rewards of a good location, and they are still able to do so in suburban shopping centers and malls, which contain parking space for thousands of automobiles. Retailers may be equally successful in differentiating their establishment in other ways. They can carry the goods of nationally known manufacturers or "private" lines and appeal to customers who prefer a certain personal quality when dealing with merchants.

The successful differentiation of a product sold in the nationwide market typically requires large advertising outlays. Consumers must be persuaded that there is a good reason to buy one brand of cigarettes, cornflakes, or washing machines rather than another. Advertising is profitable to the firm if it convinces buyers that one brand of any item is clearly preferable to another. As early as 1910 the annual volume of advertising expenditure reached $1 billion. By 1920, this figure was almost $3 billion; by 1929, the estimated outlay had passed $3.4 billion. Advertising declined greatly during the 1930s to an annual average of perhaps $1.7 billion, only to rise rapidly in the 1940s and early 1950s to nearly $8 billion in 1953. A decade later, advertising outlays passed the $12 billion mark and by 1985 advertising expenditures exceeded $94 billion, exceeding expenditures by industry on research and development.

Economists have long debated whether advertising, and the product differences it promotes, are socially productive. Wouldn't we all be better off, some have asked, if some of the money being spent to convince us to buy one brand of automobile rather than another were spent instead on developing safer and more efficient automobiles? In the 1920s and early 1930s, economist Edward Hastings Chamberlin brought this issue to the fore with his theory of monopolistic competition.[5] But despite the continued rise in advertising, and the continuation of research, no consensus has been reached. Perhaps it is fair to say that today economists have a better appreciation of the large number of cases in which advertising is informative and of the potential costs of limiting advertising, even if they are not completely reconciled to it.

Paradoxically, the successful differentiation of products by the largest firms in oligopolistic industries and the development of shopping malls help to account for the unexpected strength of the small outlet in its continuing competitive struggle with large retailers. Since the products that the retailer sells have been differentiated by costly national advertising, independent retailers need only inform the public of their existence and depend on their location and the tone of their establishment to bring them a profitable volume of trade.

MECHANIZATION AND AUTOMATION

Because the applications of science in the modern era have been so varied among industries, it is impossible to review technological advance in great detail, so a brief summary must suffice. Power-driven devices that performed feats of amazing dexterity on the one hand and of great strength on the other were introduced at a high rate during the 1920s and again during and after the Second World War. But two other forces have recently brought about important changes in technology: (1) recent applications of the discoveries of science to industrial processes and (2) the development of unified systems of automatic control. So great has been the impact of the scientist, who can now actually engineer living organisms, and so fundamental have been the developments of control mechanisms that beginning in the early 1960s, commentators spoke of a "new technology" and a "second Industrial Revolution." Decades later after the computer revolution reached proportions no one could have imagined in the 1960s, social scientists are still debating the consequences of these changes.

It should be emphasized that mechanization is many-sided. Sometimes gains in mechanization result from the introduction of a completely new machine; sometimes they result from making old machines larger or faster. Not infrequently, the introduction of mechanical innovations will be combined with the removal of discontinuities in processing, and sometimes

---

[5] Edward H. Chamberlin, *Theory of Monopolistic Competition* (Cambridge: Harvard Univ. Press, 1933).

mechanization will take place because the materials being prepared have changed. Sometimes, as in the case of the mechanization of coal mining, new and powerful devices are used to help workers perform essentially the same old jobs.

In the primary metal industries, almost unbelievable advances have been made in the handling of materials. The strip mining of coal, which furnishes so much of the energy needed for metals processing, has recently accounted for about 60 percent of total output. The mechanical mining of ores and the mechanical charging of furnaces are almost universal. The continuous rolling of sheet metal, introduced in the steel industry in 1926, is now commonplace. More and more primary metals industries have achieved uninterrupted production in huge integrated plants. In the case of steel, this means that molten iron can be converted into steel beams, sheets, and plates without the great losses of heat that were usual until 1920. And throughout the process, heavy handling is done by all kinds of mechanical conveyors, from forklift trucks to giant cranes.

These changes are spectacular. But improvements in mechanization have been taking place for nearly two centuries. The question that entrepreneurs as well as economists are now asking is this: has there been any fundamental shift in the nature of innovation and, consequently, in its social impact? During the 1920s and 1930s, as the mechanization of industry continued, we heard much about the problem of "technological unemployment." Even in 1962, President Kennedy remarked that the "major domestic challenge of the sixties is to maintain full employment at a time when automation is replacing men." With postwar unemployment only a minor problem until recently, few knowledgeable economists or labor leaders were disposed to blame automation. Indeed, the vocal demands of workers to be relieved of unpleasant, routine jobs made it clear that automation was often viewed as a boon instead of a burden. Moreover, such fears can be dispelled by recalling that automatic machines usually have been successfully introduced and operated without mass unemployment resulting.

The cost savings that result from technological innovations are passed along to consumers (if competitive pressures are strong) in the form of lower prices. This means that the consumers have more money to purchase more of the good whose price has fallen or more of any other good or service that they want. So, for the economy as a whole, technological progress need not lead, and has not led, to unemployment. However, unemployment may rise in the industry being mechanized. And workers whose skills once brought a high premium may find themselves competing with unskilled workers for jobs. It is little comfort to them to know that the aggregate unemployment rate has remained unchanged.

Automation is more than simply the speed-up of production lines. The "revolutionary" feature of automation centers on the issue of control and automatic adjustment, through computerized decision making. Modern oil refineries and chemical plants approach the extreme of automation and more and more products that lend themselves to continuous-process manufacture and assembly-line techniques are being brought under complete automatic control. Since the system is based on the "feedback" principle, the control mechanism operates on a basis of *actual* performance instead of *expected* performance. If a part is turned out incorrectly, a sensory device tells the control mechanism, which either allows further time for machining or rejects the part. All feedback devices are tied together in a closed-loop system, so that the assembly or manufacture of a product or of multiple products can be performed without the intervention of a human hand. To repeat, the essence of automation is the giving of orders by computer to a self-correcting mechanism.

This revolutionary approach to manufacturing has required the redesign of products and machines—and even of entire processes. Redesign implies large additions to cost, but the computers that perform the logical tasks of

Robot welders at work on an automated assembly line.

control, although once inordinately expensive, have rapidly become less and less costly. As the new technology has become more familiar, broad principles of design have evolved, and something approaching quantity production of the control devices that have considerably similar parts has been achieved. Furthermore, flexibility of both materials-handling mechanisms and machine tools has been attained, so that a given automatic line can be shifted from the production of one product to another. Perhaps the ultimate achievement of automation is the large-scale application of robotics. The innovative use of robots that can not only perform routine production-line chores but can also sense their environment and make responses like the neurophysiological responses of human beings are currently being introduced in a wide range of manufacturing processes.

POSTWAR PRODUCTIVITY TRENDS

A review of the advances in production techniques suggests that aggregate productivity must have risen rapidly in the postwar period. To an extent this is borne out by the data in Table 27-1 which shows the rate of growth of labor productivity for three subperiods of 1948–86. The table is read this way. From the fourth quarter of 1948 to the third quarter of 1973 farm output per hour of work, to take one example, increased on average by 5.1 percent per year. If farmers were producing 100 units of output per hour in a given year, then the next year, typically, they would be able to produce 105.1 units due to improved plant strains, better fertilizers, better equipment, and so on. But, as the table shows, the growth of productivity slowed dramatically after 1973. Since the ability of the economy to generate a rising standard of living depends on its ability to generate productivity increases, this slowdown has become a major concern of economists and policymakers.

Why did productivity slow down in this fashion? A number of factors seem to have been at work. Michael Darby has argued that changes in the structure of the labor force can account for much of the slowdown.[6] For one thing, many young and therefore inexperienced workers were entering the labor force for the first time in the 1970s. Another factor that has been cited is the sharp increase in oil prices. Industries and agricultural producers who had relied on cheap abundant oil suddenly were forced to adjust to much higher prices. Large investments were required to replace older equipment with more energy-efficient equipment even if that equipment led to the same output per labor hour. The growth of capital per unit of labor input also slowed in the 1970s. To some extent this may have been the result of the rising inflation that disrupted financial markets and discouraged saving. The highly variable rate of inflation in the 1970s may have

---

[6]Michael R. Darby, "The U.S. Productivity Slowdown: A Case of Statistical Myopia," *American Economic Review* 74 (June 1984): 301–22.

TABLE 27-1 Labor Productivity Growth Rates by Sector, 1948–86 (average annual percentage change)

Period	Sector		
	Farm	Manufacturing	Other
1948 IV to 1973 IV	5.1	2.7	2.1
1973 IV to 1981 III	4.3	1.5	0.1
1981 III to 1986 III	1.3	3.8	0.1

Source: *Economic Report of the President, 1987* (Washington, D.C.: GPO, 1987), p. 46.

distorted the signals provided by the market system and prevented the reallocation of resources to their most efficient uses. How can workers or investors know in an inflationary environment whether their real income has fallen because they are in a declining sector or because their nominal income has temporarily lagged behind prices in general? Some blame probably also attaches to the high cost of complying with new government regulations stemming from legislation passed in the 1960s. A lack of savings has also been blamed. Perhaps if we could add to our stock of plant and equipment faster, we could offset many of the negative factors. This issue will be discussed further in Chapter 31.

But when all is said and done, most economists who have studied this issue agree that there still remains a residual that cannot be explained by the factors we have enumerated. It remains something of a mystery. Our common sense tells us that the computer revolution should have spurred a great advance in productivity, yet in both the United States and much of the rest of the industrial world productivity growth slowed. There is some recent evidence (see the last line of Table 27-1) that the slowdown has ended especially in manufacturing. But it is too early to tell whether this is just a reaction to the economic expansion of the 1980s or the beginning of a new trend.

CONCENTRATION IN INDUSTRY

It is understandable that observers of the Great Depression era became concerned about the "decline of competition." First, as shown in Figure 27-1, the decade of the 1920s brought a wave of business consolidation that was comparable at least in some respects to the merger movement of 1897–1904.[7] Second, a startlingly large proportion of corporate wealth was

---

[7]The comparisons are only very approximate for these periods because of data limitations preventing the measure of mergers by value for the years 1920 through 1948. Nevertheless, the 1920s wave is distinct.

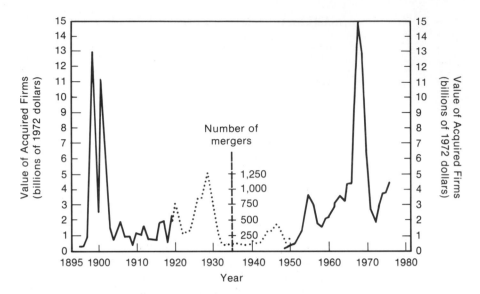

FIGURE 27-1   Volume of manufacturing and mining firm mergers and acquisitions, by value, 1895–1919 and 1948–77, and by number of mergers 1920–48.

Source: Based on data from F. M. Sherer, *Industrial Market Structure and Economic Performance*, 2d ed. (Chicago: Rand McNally, 1980), Fig. 4.5.

concentrated in the hands of a few firms. In 1933, well over 50 percent of all corporate wealth outside the financial field was controlled by 200 firms. Third, new and subtle ways of reducing price competition seemed to be gaining popularity and even overt government sanction. Among these, the most effective was to organize all the producers in a field into manufacturers' institutes or trade associations. Finally, and most importantly, it was apparent during the depression that prices were stickier and output declines were more severe in those industries where a few firms were dominant.

There was a noticeable difference in the character of the mergers of the 1920s compared with the great wave of mergers near the turn of the century when they typically produced a high degree of control of the industry's output, usually in excess of 50 percent.[8] Indeed, one of the major objectives of such combinations was a high degree of market control, although pure monopolies rarely resulted. In the post-First World War years, the mergers continued to be predominantly horizontal, as shown in Table 27-2, but most of the merged firms secured much smaller percentages of an industry's output, because mergers usually took place among companies that were smaller than the dominant company in the industry. In the meantime, the dominant firm, which had frequently held a partial monopolistic position,

---

[8] George J. Stigler, "Monopoly and Oligopoly by Merger," *American Economic Review* 40 (May 1950): 23–33.

TABLE 27-2   Percentage Distribution of Mergers by Type in Manufacturing and Mining
              Companies, 1926–77

TYPE OF MERGER	1926–30	1940–47	1948–55	1956–63	1964–72	1973–77
Horizontal	75.9	62.0	36.8	19.2	12.4	15.1
Vertical	4.8	17.0	12.8	22.2	7.8	5.8
Conglomerate	19.3	21.0	50.4	58.6	79.8	78.1
Total	100.0	100.0	100.0	100.0	100.0	100.0

Source: U.S. Congress, Senate, Committee on the Judiciary, Subcommittee on Antitrust and Monopoly, *Economic Concentration*, Hearings pursuant to S. Res. 40, Part 8A (Federal Trade Commission, *Economic Report on Corporate Mergers*) (Washington, D.C.: GPO, 1969), p. 637; Federal Trade Commission, *Statistical Report on Mergers and Acquisitions* (various issues).

gradually came to control a smaller share of the industry's production. The steel industry best exemplified this trend. United States Steel's share of ingot capacity dropped as Bethlehem and Republic sharply increased their shares through mergers. The shift from partial monopoly markets to oligopolies was also notable in cement, cans, petroleum, agricultural instruments, and glass.[9]

Some industries that had approached the competitive norm, in that they had been composed of large numbers of firms, became oligopolies during the third merger movement. Dairy products and packaged foods were the outstanding examples of this kind of rapid change in market structure, but liquors and beverages, paper and printing, machinery and machine tools, and even motion pictures were all eventually produced in markets characterized by "few" sellers. In short, the third wave of mergers led primarily to oligopolistic market structures.

Modern Mergers

The great wave of post-Second World War mergers has taken a new form. In the past, merger strategy, if not for gains of monopoly power, at least normally followed the logical extension of product lines either to create new demands for existing products or to make new uses of materials developed for existing products. As shown in Table 27-2, the more recent merger type is the conglomerate that combines unrelated commodities and business activities. These are frequently financially motivated, often for tax-avoidance purposes. Their fundamental purpose is to maximize the value of the common stock of a firm acquiring companies felt to be underpriced in the market. A characteristic of the conglomerate is its management organization. A small, elite headquarters staff attends to such general matters as financial planning, capital allocations, legal and accounting tasks, and operations research. Operating managers, motivated by handsome stock options, are usually given wide latitude in managing their subsidiaries.

[9]Stigler, p. 31.

Thus, Ling-Temco-Voight, one of the first and most successful companies of its type, began in 1958 as a small firm called Ling Electronic, with annual sales of less than $7 million. During the next ten years, Ling acquired or merged with Temco Aircraft, Chance-Voight, Okonite, Wilson and Company, Wilson Sporting Goods Company, the Greatamerica Corporation, and some 24 other companies. Its revenues in 1968 were close to $3 billion. When LTV acquired the Jones and Laughlin Steel Company in 1969, the merger meant that two corporations in the list of the nation's 100 largest companies were combining to make LTV the fourteenth largest company in the United States.[10] Comparably spectacular results have been achieved by other conglomerates, such as Gulf and Western Industries, International Telephone and Telegraph, Litton Industries, Boise Cascade, and the "Automatic" Sprinkler Corporation. Although these and other conglomerates have been plagued with both financial and managerial difficulties from time to time, they characterize much of the glamour and excitement associated with fast-paced financial action.

In the late 1970s and early 1980s merger activity intensified. Table 27-3 shows that the number of merger and acquisition announcements increased by more than 30 percent between 1975 and 1985 and the value of merged firms rose, probably, by a large multiple although statistics are incomplete. New terms such as *junk bonds* and *leveraged buyouts*, and new personalities such as Michael Milken and T. Boone Pickens, came to dominate the financial pages of newspapers. In the typical case, the acquiring firm issued so-called junk bonds and offered some combination of these bonds and cash to the holders of the stock of the firm being acquired. Michael Milken of the investment banking firm of Drexall, Burnham, Lambert was instrumental in drawing attention to and utilizing junk bonds for takeovers. These are simply bonds that the market thinks are extremely risky and that therefore pay a high rate of interest to compensate the owner for the risk. It was Milken's contention that these bonds typically did not prove to be as risky in the long run as conventional wisdom would have it.

But how can acquiring firms afford to pay more for common stock than it currently sold for in the market? Ultimately, each leveraged buyout (leverage is the ratio of debt to equity) depends on a belief that the flow of income generated by the firm being acquired can be increased by an amount sufficient to cover the interest on the new debt and still leave an ample return to shareholders. The many ways of doing this include replacing incompetent management, exploiting underutilized holdings of natural resources, reducing "excessive" contributions to pension funds, and so on. But without the prospect of a higher corporate income, a leveraged buyout would not make sense. Critics of leveraged buyouts argue that the ratios of debt to

---

[10]Richard W. McLaren, then Assistant Attorney General for antitrust, obtained an injunction against LTV halting the final merger of the two companies. In 1971 LTV agreed to divest itself of Braniff Airlines and other assets as a condition of merger with Jones and Laughlin.

TABLE 27-3   Recent Merger Trends in the United States, 1975–87

Year	Total Net Mergers and Acquisitions	Total Value (in billions)[a]
1975	2,297	$ 11.8
1980	1,889	44.3
1981	2,395	82.6
1982	2,346	53.8
1983	2,533	73.1
1984	2,543	122.2
1985	3,001	179.8
1986	3,336	173.1
1987	2,032	163.7

[a]Refers to a subset of the total net mergers for which data was available.

Source: *Mergerstat Review 1987* (Chicago: W. T. Grimm & Co., 1988) p. 103. Copyright © 1988 by W. T. Grimm & Co. Reprinted with permission.

equity for many of the resulting firms have been dangerously high, and that these firms will be unable to meet their interest payments during the next recession. The result would be that these firms would fail and that the recession would be much worse than it need be. Defenders of leveraged buyouts, on the other hand, claim that buyouts have made the economy more efficient and more competitive in world markets. To find out who was right, we will have to wait until the next severe recession tests the structure of these firms.

Concentration and Competition

The largest companies in the manufacturing sector produce a substantial portion of total output, although the share of large firms in total output has not been rising as rapidly as the volume of merger activity might suggest. This is illustrated in Table 27-4.

TABLE 27-4   Shares of Total Value Added in Manufacturing Produced by the 50 and 200 Largest Companies

Year	50 Largest Companies	200 Largest Companies
1947	17	30
1954	23	37
1963	25	41
1972	25	43
1982	24	43

Source: U.S. Bureau of the Census, "Concentration Ratios in Manufacturing," *1982 Census of Manufacturers* (Washington, D.C.: GPO, 1983), Table 1.

But we are confronted with a paradox. By any measure we choose, the U.S. consumer's position has progressively improved over the past half-century. But how *can* an economy weighted down with oligopoly so readily make available to consumers such an abundance of the world's goods and services? Basically the answer to this question appears to rest on the fact that—especially since 1939—interindustry competition and, to a lesser extent, competition among products and processes *within* certain industries have caused the seller's power to wane. The demand for any particular firm's products today is not as stable and assured as it used to be, because the alternative (substitute) products of firms in *other* industries are becoming a greater part of the competition.[11] So, counting only market shares of top firms within a particular "industry" tells us very little. Instead, we must count *categories of uses* for the output of an industry and consider the products of other industries that directly compete within these categories. This is a more complicated process because it requires an understanding of many varied technologies as we will now show for the case of aluminum in its alternative uses.

The competition of aluminum with other metals in the category of electrical cable and conductors is a good illustration of interindustry competition. It is well known that aluminum and copper compete in this use, but it is not enough simply to observe this fact. The essence of the competition lies in the "bundle of properties" of each of the two metals. The two bundles have marked likenesses and differences.[12] Both copper and aluminum exhibit high electrical conductivity, but the specific gravity of aluminum is slightly less than one-third that of copper, so the mass conductivity of aluminum is twice that of copper. Thus, a steel-reinforced aluminum cable, both stronger and lighter than an electrically equivalent copper cable, can be used in longer spans with fewer supporting structures. On the basis of aluminum and copper prices prevalent in the last two decades, copper has lost the high-voltage transmission-line business. At the other extreme, copper with its higher electrical conductivity still has a decided advantage over aluminum where wire of fine sizes is used and space must be conserved. Between the two extremes, there is a vigorous, persistent competition on a pure cost basis—the costs of product design, investment in tools and dies, and so on. Large motor windings, power and feeder cable, and bus bars in central power stations are alternatively made from either material. In this use, firms in the copper industry and their copper and brass fabricating subsidiaries are direct rivals of the major aluminum companies.

---

[11] The question of interproduct and interindustry competition received considerable attention in the early 1950s. See David E. Lilienthal, *Big Business: A New Era* (New York: Harper & Row, 1952), pp. 47–94; Sumner H. Slichter, "The Growth of Competition," *Atlantic Monthly* (Nov. 1953), pp. 66–70; A. D. H. Kaplan, *Big Enterprise in the Competitive System* (Washington, D.C.: Brookings Institution, 1953); and Edward S. Mason, "The New Competition," *The Yale Review* (Autumn 1953), pp. 37–48.
[12] Kaplan, p. 19

Now consider another use. In the field of die castings, aluminum alloys have greatly supplanted zinc castings, which have long been dominant. In this field, there is also competition with the brasses and, more and more, with alloys of magnesium and the plastics. If we add sand and permanent-mold castings to this category, we must include almost any metal that can be melted—gray and malleable iron and cast steel being the chief additions to the competition, which is decided (once weight, strength, and finish have been considered) on a basis of costs, including those of dies and machining.

The rivalry between aluminum and the steels is keen in the manufacture of truck, van, and trailer bodies (where magnesium and plastics are also alternative materials) and in certain construction uses. In making truck bodies, the competition between aluminum and steel involves a balancing of manufacturing costs and costs in use; the higher cost of aluminum bodies is generally much more than offset by the greater average payloads, reduced license fees, and increased tire mileage that result from the lower weight of the product. In construction uses, the cost advantage may turn on savings in maintenance, as in the case of industrial windows.

As we proceed to examine the main uses of aluminum, the other metals appear and reappear; as unlikely a competitor as lead is an alternate material for at least two uses (collapsible tubes and cable coverings). The plastics also reappear; wood, rubber, fiberglass, and even conventional building facings like brick and stone enter the system of alternatives.

In sum, if we consider interindustry competition, the number of competing firms rapidly moves from "few" to "many," but two exceptions should be noted. First, even after interindustry competition has been taken into account, rivalry may be limited to a few firms. For one use—for instance, castings—the competition is with 100 or more producers of primary materials outside the aluminum industry, but for another use—such as conductors—the number of competitors may be reduced to four outside the industry. It appears, however, that as we cut across industry lines, the conditions of rivalry differ greatly from those of intraindustry competition. The managers of firms usually cannot have the technological or accounting knowledge that enables them to predict the reactions of other-industry rivals as well as they can predict those of rivals within the industry.

A further objection may be that after all such considerations, the aluminum industry is left with a hard oligopolistic core. Although there is an ever-growing list of alternative materials, aluminum is still economically necessary in the manufacture of structural parts for aircraft. Many of the alloys commonly employed in aircraft manufacture have a host of applications; but the high-strength alloy that is used for the skin of an airplane has few other uses, and there is no feasible alternative material for airplane skins. It is conceivable that the companies in the industry could collude, tacitly or explicitly, in discriminating against airplane manufacturing companies, especially in view of the fact that aluminum from the secondary (used) market is not suitable for aircraft. It seems unlikely that discrimi-

nation to maintain monopoly power in such a small market would be worthwhile, but this is a fact that has to be ascertained. To say the least, the
problem of monopoly in the aluminum industry has been narrowed to
manageable proportions.

Although we could trace similar examples in industry after industry and
arrive at similar conclusions, we still could not assert with complete assurance that interproduct and interindustry competition provided adequate
protection against monopolistic power. *The point is that simply counting the
number of producers within an industry is a poor way to evaluate the degree of
competition in a market.* After making allowances for interindustry and interproduct competition of both domestic and foreign firms, it is possible that
monopolistic elements remaining in some industries may still be large. Again
it is a question of the facts. For nearly a century, the steels have had no close
competition for a large number of applications in which weight, strength,
and durability are of primary importance; rails, heavy structural members,
pressure vessels, and heavy machinery are some examples. But the advance
of foreign competition has changed that. Furthermore, even today, the
marginal effect of competition on the steel industry is much smaller than
the effect on the competing industries.

Finally, competitive forces, such as the ones we have just examined, work
over long periods of time. It may require years for a change to be made
from one process to another or from one material to another. In assessing
the presence or absence of a competitive system, we cannot base our judgment on the existence of temporary abnormal profits, like those reported
in the news media. As the evidence in Table 27-5 convincingly shows, there
has been no trend toward greater profits in the post-Second World War
period. If anything, the trend has been slightly downward. The ageless
quest for monopoly power has not succeeded in terms of higher average
profits in modern times.

Antitrust Policy

Since 1937, the courts have rarely taken the view that interindustry competition is adequate to protect consumers. After Thurman W. Arnold became
head of the antitrust division of the Justice Department, a vigorous program of antitrust prosecution was instituted that continued after Arnold's
resignation. Between 1937 and 1948, more prosecutions were begun than
in the entire history of the Sherman Act before 1937, and the cases instituted were largely directed toward established oligopolies. Emphasis was
placed on dissolution, divorcement, and divestiture cases—that is, on the
actual breaking up of industrial concentration in the old "trust busting"
sense.[13] But although the government won most of its major cases, the

---

[13] Walter Adams, "The Aluminum Case: Legal Victory—Economic Defeat," *American Economic
Review* 41 (Dec. 1951): 915.

TABLE 27-5   Profit Rates of Manufacturing Corporations, 1950–85

Year	Ratio of Profits after Taxes to Shareholders' Equity	Profits after Taxes per Dollar of Sales (in cents)
1950	16.4%	8.5
1955	13.4	6.4
1960	9.8	5.2
1965	13.9	6.7
1970	9.9	4.8
1975	11.6	4.6
1980	13.9	4.8
1985	10.1	3.8

Note: The figures from 1950 to 1970 have been adjusted upward to reflect a change in computational methods introduced in 1973. Equity is derived from balance-sheet data; it does not reflect movements in stock prices.
Source: *Economic Report of the President, 1987* (Washington, D.C.: GPO, 1987), p. 347.

penalties imposed by the courts were mild—for the simple reason that drastic penalties would have resulted in units of uneconomic size.

The case against the Aluminum Company of America provides the best example of the perplexities that have confronted the courts in modern antitrust actions. In 1937, a complaint was instituted against ALCOA alleging that it monopolized the manufacture and sale of virgin aluminum and fabricated shapes. In 1942, the District Court found the defendant company not guilty, but in March 1945, this decision was reversed by the Circuit Court of Appeals, Judge Learned Hand, a famous jurist, giving the opinion.[14] Judge Hand ruled that ALCOA, which at the time made and fabricated over 90 percent of the virgin aluminum manufactured in the United States, was a monopoly. Turning away from the old dictum that "mere size is no offense," Judge Hand ruled that size, in the sense of market control, was the very essence of the offense. Even though the company had engaged in no immoral or predatory competitive practices, it was still in violation of the Sherman Act if, through normal business practice, it controlled most of the output of the industry. But having pronounced ALCOA a monopoly, the court refused to order dissolution of the company or divestiture of its assets. Instead, the court recommended that remedial measures be withheld until the effect on competition of the government disposal of war-surplus aluminum plants could be determined. Further attempts by the government to force ALCOA to divest itself of assets met with little success. In 1950, with Kaiser and Reynolds firmly established in the industry, the Court held that competition had still not been established in the aluminum industry; but the only relief granted was to require persons who held stock in

---

[14]On appeal to the Supreme Court, a quorum could not be obtained because some justices had been previously involved in the case. Consequently, the Circuit Court decision stood.

both ALCOA and ALTED, the Canadian subsidiary, to divest themselves of the stock of one corporation or the other.

In the case of *United States* v. *United Shoe Machinery Corporation*, the courts concluded that United's control of the shoe machinery market was indisputable but that the company's practices had been neither predatory nor discriminatory between different customers. Judge C. E. Wyzanski held that the United Shoe Machinery case fell "within the main thrust of the doctrine applied in the *Aluminum* and subsequent cases" and that United had violated the Sherman Act.[15] But he refused to dissolve the company and ordered three forms of relief that would do little to weaken United's monopoly.

By this time, the courts appeared to have brought the legal concern of monopoly into line by establishing the concept that size alone determines a company's power to affect prices by varying output. To be sure, in *United States* v. *Columbia Steel Company, et al.*, a 1948 case, the Supreme Court had flirted once again with the rule of reason in deciding that Columbia Steel, a subsidiary of United States Steel, had not violated the Sherman Act in purchasing the Consolidated Steel Corporation, the largest independent steel fabricator on the West Coast. In *United States* v. *Paramount Pictures, Inc., et al.*, another 1948 case, the Court ordered major motion picture producers to divest themselves of exhibitors on the ground that separating the functions of the production and the distribution of films did not produce higher production costs for the firms. And in the Cellophane Case (*United States* v. *E. I. duPont de Nemours and Company*, 1953), it seemed that the Supreme Court would move in the direction of considering interproduct competition in determining the extent of monopolistic power when the Court defined the relevant market to include all the wrap that competed with cellophane— from brown paper to polyethylene film. By the mid-1950s, the judiciary had apparently accepted the propositions that modern productive methods leave no economic alternative to concentration of production in a few large firms in most manufacturing industries and that breaking up large firms could well lead to inefficient production.

Yet in the field of antitrust, it seems that once the law appears reasonably certain, the Supreme Court changes direction and charts a new course. Just four years after the Cellophane decree, pursuant to an action brought against the same company, the Court reversed itself, narrowly defining the market for finishes and fabrics to include not the *entire* market but only the *automobile* market. Moreover, this second duPont case produced the startling realization that any large corporation that has achieved size through stock acquisitions since 1914—the year of passage of the Clayton Act—can be required to divest itself of those holdings, no matter what the cost to the firm or how complicated the proceedings. But it was in the landmark case of *Brown Shoe Company* v. *United States* in 1962 that the Supreme Court

---

[15] *United States* v. *United Shoe Machinery Corp.*, 110 F. Suppl. 295.

greatly strengthened the hand of the Justice Department in merger cases. The Brown Shoe Company and the G. R. Kinney Company were both engaged in the manufacture and retail marketing of shoes. Brown accounted for about 4 percent of the national output of shoes; Kinney, for about 1.5 percent. But the government argued that the relevant lines of commerce were not just "footwear" but rather men's, women's, and children's shoes. The Court also ruled that the "section of the country" within which the anticompetitive effect of a merger is to be judged could be every city with a population of 10,000 or more in which Brown or Kinney shoes were sold. Thus, in Dodge City, Kansas, the combined share of the market was over 57 percent for women's shoes and 49 percent for children's shoes—a dangerous horizontal concentration. Oddly, this was followed by the assertion that it was the intent of Congress when passing the Celler-Kefauver Amendments to the Celler-Kefauver Act in 1950 to stop "incipient" oligopoly on a national scale.

The same definition of markets was successfully attempted in other cases. Yet due to a lack of resources and the ambivalence of succeeding Attorneys General, little effort was made to arrest the tide of mergers that marked the 1960s. Another explanation for so little force on the part of the Justice Department was that, as we have noted, most recent mergers have been of the conglomerate type. Donald F. Turner, Assistant Attorney General for Antitrust in the Johnson administration, and a legal scholar with degrees in both economics and law, took the view that the Clayton Act could not be applied against conglomerate mergers unless the government could demonstrate that anticompetitive results occurred in a specific market. William H. Rehnquist, Turner's successor under Nixon, and later a Supreme Court justice, took the tougher stance that major conglomerate acquisitions (such as LTV's purchase of Jones and Laughlin) must be offset by the spinoff of an approximately equal amount of other assets. The consequence has been that attacks on "product extension," such as the one initiated by the Federal Trade Commission against Procter & Gamble's acquisition of the assets of the Chlorox Chemical Company, have been trivial. In this particular case, decided in 1967, Procter & Gamble (by no means a conglomerate) was required to divest itself of Chlorox on the grounds that P&G's tremendous marketing power would give the product a great advantage over the three major competing products and keep Procter & Gamble from entering the market as a separate competitor.

But in a series of decisions issued in 1974 the Supreme Court shifted toward a more skeptical view of alleged anticompetitive effects of mergers and acquisitions. In *U.S.* v. *Marine Bancorporation*, for example, the court was called upon to examine an acquisition of a bank in Spokane, Washington, by one in Seattle. The court decided that, since there was virtually no other route for the Seattle bank to follow if it wanted to enter the Spokane market, competition had not been hurt. Claims that the Seattle bank would then control a larger share of the state's banking assets were not relevant.

The biggest cases in recent years were those launched against International Business Machines and American Telephone and Telegraph Company. The IBM case (*U.S.* v. *International Business Machines Corp.*) was launched in 1969. After years of costly legal proceedings it was finally dropped by the government in 1982. Some observers have seen this as simply the result of the Reagan administration's pro-business attitude. But the computer industry had changed dramatically in the 1970s. While it was possible to view IBM as an impregnable monopolist in 1969, by 1982 it was faced in many markets by domestic and foreign competitors. The telephone case (*U.S.* v. *American Telegraph and Telephone Co.*) was launched in 1974. This case was also settled in 1982, but AT&T was forced to give up its operating companies, although it was permitted to enter new communication and data processing markets it had previously been barred from. Opinion is divided on whether the break-up of AT&T was in the public interest. Long distance rates have come down, but there have been some increases in local rates. Over the years AT&T had developed an outstanding record as a source of scientific and technological innovations. Ultimately, a judgment about the value of this case will depend on how well AT&T and its competitors perform in this area.

If, as suggested earlier, interindustry competition affords effective protection to consumers for most categories of goods, many economists feel that the Justice Department would be well advised to stop trying to add one or two more firms to industries that must always remain oligopolistic—and, for that matter, to stop worrying about the purchase of one company by another *when market structure does not change after the acquisition*. Instead, the Department might concentrate on detecting products for which there are few alternative suppliers, within or without the "industry," and bring actions in these relatively few cases. Such a course would enable the Justice Department to root out genuine instances of monopoly, negotiate downward price adjustments, and avoid much useless and costly litigation.[16]

SELECTED REFERENCES AND SUGGESTED READINGS

Asch, Peter, and Rosalind S. Seneca. *Government and the Marketplace*, 2nd ed. Chicago: Dryden Press, 1989.

Baumol, William J., John C. Panzar, and Robert D. Willig. *Contestable Markets and the Theory of Industry Structure*. New York: Harcourt Brace Jovanovich, 1982.

Bork, Robert H. *The Antitrust Paradox*. New York: Basic Books, 1978.

Caves, Richard B. "The Structure Of Industry." In *The American Economy in Transition*, ed. Martin Feldstein. Chicago: Univ. of Chicago Press, for the NBER, 1980.

Darby, Michael R. "The U.S. Productivity Slowdown: A Case of Statistical Myopia." *American Economic Review* 74 (June 1984): 301–22.

---

[16]See Peter Asch and Rosalind S. Seneca, *Government and the Marketplace* (Chicago: Dryden Press, 1989), pp. 262–71, for a balanced discussion of the pros and cons of various antitrust policies.

Denison, Edward F. *Accounting for Slower Economic Growth: The United States in the 1970s*. Washington: The Brookings Institution, 1979.

———. *Accounting for United States Economic Growth, 1929–1969*. Washington D.C.: The Brookings Institution, 1974.

Didrichsen, Jon. "The Development of Diversified and Conglomerate Firms in the United States, 1920–1970." *Business History Review* 36 (Summer 1972): 202–19.

Elzinga, Kenneth G. "The Goals of Antitrust: Other Than Competition and Efficiency, What Else Counts?" *University of Pennsylvania Law Review* 125 (1977): 1191–213.

Fisher, Franklin. *Folded, Spindled, and Mutilated*. Boston: M.I.T. Press, 1983.

Galbraith, John Kenneth. *The New Industrial State*. Boston: Houghton Mifflin, 1967.

Harberger, Arnold C. "Monopoly and Resource Allocation." *American Economic Review* 44 (May 1954): 77–87.

Magaziner, Ira C., and Robert Reich. *Minding America's Business: The Decline and Rise of the American Economy*. New York: Harcourt Brace Jovanovich, 1982.

Manne, Henry G. "Mergers and the Market for Corporate Control." *Journal of Political Economy* 73 (April 1965): 110–20.

Mansfield, Edwin. "Technology and Productivity in the United States." In *The American Economy in Transition*, ed. Martin Feldstein. Chicago: Univ. of Chicago Press, for the NBER, 1980.

Mueller, Willard F., and Larry G. Hamm. "Trends In Industrial Market Concentration 1947 to 1970." *Review of Economics and Statistics* 56 (Nov. 1974): 511–20.

Posner, Richard A. "A Statistical Study of Antitrust Enforcement." *Journal of Law and Economics* 13 (Oct. 1970): 365–419.

———. *Antitrust Law*. Chicago: Univ. of Chicago Press, 1976.

Scherer, Frederic M. *Industrial Market Structure and Economic Performance*, 2nd ed. Chicago: Rand McNally, 1980.

Steiner, Peter O. *Mergers: Motives, Effects, Policies*. Ann Arbor, Mich.: Univ. of Michigan Press, 1975.

Stigler, George J. The Economic Effects of Antitrust Laws." *Journal of Law and Economics* 9 (Oct. 1966): 225–58.

Stonebraker, Robert J. "Turnover and Mobility among the 100 Largest Firms: An Update." *American Economic Review* 69 (Dec. 1979): 968–73.

Temin, Peter. *The Fall of the Bell System*. New York: Cambridge Univ. Press, 1988.

Tiffany, Paul A. "The Roots of Decline: Business-Government Relations in the American Steel Industry, 1945–1960." The *Journal of Economic History* 44 (June 1984): 407–19.

Williamson, Oliver S. "Economies as an Antitrust Defense Revisited." *University of Pennsylvania Law Review* 125 (April 1977): 699–736.

CHAPTER 28

The Growth of Government

INCREASED GOVERNMENT SPENDING

Perhaps the most profound change in the U.S. economy in the postwar period was the growth in the size and role of government at all levels, but especially at the federal level. Let us begin by looking at a very simple measure of the size of government, total spending by government relative to the size of the economy (GNP). This measure is shown in Table 28-1. The table tells what appears to be a simple story. Inexorably, decade after decade, government spending has grown relative to the size of the economy. This is the most commonly used measure of the size of government. But although it appears straightforward the story contains many ambiguities.

Government spending includes not only purchases of goods and services (paper clips, tanks, dams; the salaries of members of Congress, Supreme Court justices and army privates; and so on), but also "transfer payments" (welfare expenditures, subsidies for state and local governments, and so on). Transfer payments, at least in the first instance, do not actually use up GNP. People on welfare can buy more goods and services, but people who pay taxes buy less. Indeed, since most of us receive subsidies and pay taxes, there is really no upper limit to the ratio of government spending to GNP; it could easily exceed 100 percent. In any one year the government could tax and transfer the same dollar many times over.

But that is not the end of the story. Each time the government imposes a tax, it affects incentives to work and invest, and that in turn affects GNP. People who receive as much in government subsidies as they pay in taxes nevertheless have an incentive to reduce their taxes. If they do so by working less hard or by investing their capital in less productive uses, the total product of the economy will be reduced. Most economists would agree with this analysis of the *direction* of the effects of tax and transfer policies. But one

590

TABLE 28-1 Government Spending Relative to GNP, 1949–85 (percentage of GNP)

Year	Federal	State and Local	Total
1949	16.1%	7.8%	23.0%
1959	18.5	9.5	26.6
1969	19.8	12.4	30.1
1979	20.8	13.1	30.6
1985	24.6	12.9	35.1

Note: Federal expenditures include grants to state and local governments. These are deducted before computing total government expenditures to prevent double counting.

Source: *Economic Report of the President, 1987* (Washington D.C.: GPO, 1987), pp. 256, 335.

of the major economic controversies of the postwar period has concerned the *magnitude* of these disincentive effects.

Let us exclude transfer payments from our discussion and consider simply the government's purchases of goods and services relative to GNP. These figures are shown in Table 28-2 and tell a different story. There was a marked upward trend in the shares of government in the first postwar decade, but then a levelling off and an actual decline occurred at the federal level. On the basis of these figures alone, we could argue that the federal government was relatively smaller in recent years than in the 1950s. Transfer payments, particularly at the federal level, were clearly the dynamic element in the growth of public spending in the postwar period.

To set the growth of transfer payments in perspective, consider Table 28-3, which shows the major categories of federal government spending in total dollar amounts and the growth rates from 1949 to 1985. It is not hard to pick out the big winners in the budget process—income security (Social Security, federal employee retirement and disability insurance, housing assistance, food and nutrition assistance, and so on), which grew at 12.4 percent per year; education, which grew at 14.4 percent per year; and health (Medicare, health care services, health research, and so on), which grew at an astounding 17.2 percent per year. The rapid growth in these

TABLE 28-2 Government Purchases Relative to GNP, 1949–85 (percentage of GNP)

Year	Federal	State and Local	Total
1949	8.1%	6.9%	15.0%
1959	11.0	8.7	19.7
1969	10.4	11.1	21.5
1979	7.1	11.6	18.7
1985	8.9	11.5	20.4

Source: *Economic Report of the President, 1987* (Washington D.C.: GPO, 1987), pp. 244–45.

TABLE 28-3   Federal Government Spending by Major Category, 1949–85 (in billions)

Category of Spending	1949	1959	1969	1979	1985	Growth[a] Rate 1949–85
Total Outlays	$40.6	$92.1	$184.5	$503.5	$946.3	8.75%
National Defense	13.1	46.6	81.2	116.3	252.7	8.22
Veteran's Benefits	6.6	5.4	7.6	19.9	26.4	3.85
International Affairs	6.1	3.3	3.8	7.5	16.2	2.70
Income Security[b]	3.6	17.2	37.7	170.5	316.8	12.44
Agriculture	2.5	5.4	6.2	11.2	25.6	6.41
Education	.2	.9	6.5	30.2	29.3	14.39
Health[c]	.2	.7	11.6	47.0	99.3	17.24
Commerce and Transport	1.5	4.5	7.9	22.2	30.0	8.36
Interest	5.4	7.1	15.8	42.6	129.4	8.82
All other	1.4	1.2	6.1	36.1	20.6	7.51

[a]The average annual percentage increase
[b]Includes Social Security
[c]Includes Medicare

Source: (1949–69) *Historical Statistics of the United States, Colonial Times to 1970* (Washington, D.C.: 1986), series Y472, Y473, Y474, Y475, Y476, Y477, Y478, Y479, Y480, Y485; (1979–85), *Statistical Abstract of the United States: 1987* (Washington, D.C.: GPO, 1986), pp. 293–94.

categories has been the result of new programs designed (partly) to protect and expand the choices of less well-off people.

Let's take a closer look at the history of these rapidly growing areas of the federal budget. Annual data for national defense, health, education, and income security as shares of federal spending are plotted in Figure 28-1. As we can see these areas followed somewhat different patterns. Military spending as a share of total federal spending increased primarily in three major buildups. The first was associated with the Korean War in the early 1950s, the second with the Vietnam War in the late 1960s, the third with the Reagan administration's buildup in the 1980s. Spending on health and education, however, accelerated in the period of liberal activism in the mid-1960s. As late as 1959 spending in each of these categories was less than $1 billion.[1] Health, which includes Medicare, took another leap forward in the 1970s and 1980s, as eligibility for various benefits expanded. Finally, although there were some fluctuations, expenditures for income security grew steadily throughout the period, accelerating (as did health spending) in the 1970s as eligibility for benefits expanded. To see why individual categories and the budget as a whole grew during the postwar period we need to see how the political philosophies of the occupants of the White House were translated into budget realities.

---

[1]Although as the late Senator Everett Dirksen of Illinois is credited with saying, "A billion here, a billion there, and pretty soon you are talking about real money."

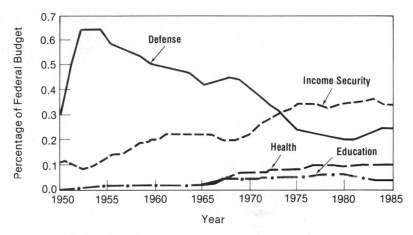

FIGURE 28-1   The Changing Structure of the Federal Budget

Source: *Statistical Abstract of the United States*, various years.

PRESIDENTIAL POLITICS, 1945–1969

During the first three postwar decades, a period of unprecedented prosperity, liberal Democrats pressed hard for an expansion of New Deal reforms. Fighting a rear-guard action against them, conservatives tried to delay the advance of the welfare state when they could, and retreated to new positions when they could not. The first postwar president, Harry S Truman, a Democrat, favored a major expansion of the New Deal. His program, which he called the Fair Deal, called for a wide range of economic legislation including repeal of the Taft-Hartley Act, increased Social Security benefits, a higher minimum wage, federal subsidies for housing, compulsory federal health insurance, and authority to build industrial plants to overcome "shortages." Some parts of his program, those that were extensions and modifications of existing programs, were enacted; Social Security benefits were extended and the minimum wage was raised. But new programs were blocked by a congressional coalition of Republicans and southern Democrats. Special interest groups played an important role in lobbying Congress to oppose legislation they thought was contrary to their interests. The American Medical Association, for example, lobbied vigorously against Truman's health insurance proposals, which they denounced as the forerunner of "socialized medicine."

The philosophy of Republican President Dwight D. Eisenhower's administration was generally opposed to new initiatives in the economic sphere. The administration's motto, "Less government in business and more business in government," summed up its basic attitude. But existing programs around which a consensus had formed continued to be expanded. Social Security benefits were increased and extended to more workers, the

minimum wage was raised from $.75 to $1.00 per hour, and more money
was provided for housing.

The breakthrough in welfare legislation occurred during the presidencies of John F. Kennedy and Lyndon B. Johnson. Kennedy termed his
legislative program the New Frontier. It was similar to Truman's Fair Deal;
but in many ways it did not go as far. Kennedy's narrow victory over Vice
President Richard Nixon in 1960 hardly seemed like a mandate for radical
change. The program called for federal medical insurance for the elderly,
aid to education, more federal money for housing and "urban renewal,"
and increased Social Security benefits. As in previous administrations, existing programs were expanded. Social Security benefits were increased, the
minimum wage was raised from $1.00 to $1.25 (over a four-year period)
and was made applicable to more workers, and more money was made
available for federal housing projects.

Also new initiatives were enacted. Concern over poverty in Appalachia
and other depressed areas led to the Area Redevelopment Act that provided
low-cost loans for businesses in these areas and money for training workers.
Other legislation provided for aid to medical education, college construction projects, and relief for areas adversely affected by federal projects. But
Kennedy's proposals for medical care for the aged and federal aid for public
schools were defeated.

Events, however, were moving rapidly. The civil-rights movement accelerated, drawing attention to the plight of blacks and other disadvantaged
groups. On college campuses students were drawn to the liberal faith in
government. For a time, it seemed that Joseph Schumpeter's prediction
that capitalism would be undermined by the children of the bourgeoisie
who would lose faith in the system that had created the basis for their own
high standard of living had at last begun to come true.[2] When Lyndon
Johnson took office in 1963 after the assassination of President Kennedy,
the prospects for enacting economic legislation were very different than
when Kennedy entered office. Lyndon Johnson proclaimed his intention
of fighting an undeclared "War on Poverty." The result was the Economic
Opportunity Act of 1964. It established training camps in rural and urban
areas, provided grants for farmers and small businesses and for communities to help them fund their own antipoverty programs. In 1964 President
Johnson was elected by a large majority, and this mandate, and his own
long experience in Washington, helped him in pushing for the programs
which he now referred to as the basis for the "Great Society."

A wide range of important legislation followed. Indeed, there had been
nothing like it since the New Deal, and in some respects it was even more
radical. A medical care program for those aged 65 or over was at last added
to Social Security. A billion dollars was voted for Appalachia to improve
land and highways and to provide health centers. The Department of

[2]Joseph Schumpeter, *Capitalism, Socialism, and Democracy* (London: Allen and Unwin, 1943).

Housing and Urban Development was created and its head was made a cabinet-level secretary. The Housing Act was passed which provided, among other things, for federal rent subsidies for the poor, a new departure in welfare legislation. The minimum wage, a familiar part of liberal democratic programs, was raised and extended to cover farm laborers, workers in small retail shops, and hospital workers. The Mass Transportation Act, which provided money to improve rail transportation, was passed, and the Department of Transportation, the twelfth cabinet-level department, was created. And the list of reforms could be extended.

These were exciting times. To liberals it seemed that at last the promise of the New Deal would be realized. A rapidly growing economy (managed according to Keynesian full-employment policies) would provide plenty of resources to solve the persistent problems of poverty and inequality of opportunity. But conservatives worried about costs and the resulting turmoil in the social order. Already by 1966 there were signs that the "Little New Deal" was losing momentum. Congress was willing to vote only $1 billion for Johnson's Model Cities program. But new welfare and regulatory legislation would continue to be passed for the remainder of the decade and into the early 1970s.

PRESIDENTIAL POLITICS, 1969–1990

Although few observers realized it at the time, subsequent administrations, although making efforts to expand government in certain areas, would never return to the optimistic "social engineering" of the 1960s. During the second administration of Richard Nixon, and under Republican Gerald Ford and Democrat Jimmy Carter, new federal initiatives would be few and far between. The underlying reason was the widespread disillusionment with government produced by the long and futile war in Vietnam and the deterioration in the performance of the economy. Productivity growth slowed, inflation accelerated, and unemployment remained at high levels. The belief that the economy could easily generate a large surplus with which the government could do good works now appeared naive.

In previous years the election of Democrat Jimmy Carter would have signalled a new round of social legislation of the New Deal type. But the Carter administration, while supporting traditional democratic programs in certain areas, emphasized economy and efficiency in government and surprisingly, deregulation of certain areas of the economy. The administration argued that some regulations were no longer necessary or that the original intent of the legislation had been subverted by the very groups that the legislation was intended to control.

It had long been recognized in academic circles that regulatory agencies were often "captured" by the very industries they were supposed to regulate. The history of many industries could be summarized in this way: the public would be aroused by the revelation of an abuse in a certain industry, and a regulatory agency would be created, staffed initially by people representing the public interest. But after the initial crisis passed only the regulated industry itself would maintain an interest in who was appointed to the agency and what decisions it rendered. The result, naturally enough, would be that in the long run people who were sympathetic to the regulated industry would be appointed to the regulatory agency, and rulings would be made in the interest of the industry rather than of the general public. Partly as a result of such ideas, Carter supported decontrol of natural gas prices; deregulation of the airlines, trucking, and railroad industries; and deregulation of the financial services industry, including the elimination of deposit ceilings on interest rates in 1980.

Alfred E. Kahn, whom Carter chose to deregulate the airlines, was both symbolic of the new era and a major player in it.[3] By upbringing and sentiment Kahn was a liberal Democrat. But he believed that the general interest would best be served if regulators stressed competition and marginal cost pricing rather than traditional forms of regulation. Marginal cost pricing said, to take a simple example, that airline seats should be priced at the cost of actually carrying one more passenger rather than at a high average cost. At a time when many airline seats were unfilled, Kahn's emphasis on marginal cost pricing was not totally unwelcomed by the industry.

But it was Republican Ronald Reagan, first elected in 1980, who attempted to alter the basic ideological thrust of government in the postwar period. Reagan put it simply in his inaugural address, "Government is not the solution to our problem; government is the problem." His policy, often referred to as "Reaganomics" had several elements. One was the reduction in taxes, which we have already discussed in relation to postwar monetary and fiscal policy. An important element in the tax cuts was the reduction of marginal rates (the rates applied to additional income). The Reagan administration claimed that such cuts were necessary to create incentives to work and invest. Its critics complained that such cuts were a giveaway for the rich.

The Reagan administration wanted to radically alter budget priorities, and to a degree it succeeded. Simply put, the Reagan administration wanted to increase defense expenditures and reduce civilian expenditures. On the military side it had little trouble. Between 1980 and 1983 national defense expenditures rose from $134 billion to $210 billion. But spending cuts on the civilian side, although some were made, were harder to get through Congress. Between 1980 and 1983 all spending other than national defense increased from $457 billion to $598 billion. Prices were rising over the same

---

[3] See Thomas K. McCraw, *Prophets of Regulation* (Cambridge: Harvard Univ. Press, 1984), Chapter 7, for an absorbing account of Kahn's role in the regulatory revolution. In the same volume, McCraw's accounts of earlier regulators, Charles Francis Adams, Louis D. Brandeis, and James M. Landis, are also well worth reading.

History was provided a rare occurrence when three former presidents joined President Reagan at the White House on October 13, 1981—Ford, Carter, and Nixon.

period (the rise in civilian expenditures was 27 percent, while the rise in the GNP deflator was 19 percent) and certain areas of the civilian budget were hit hard (the budget category of "education, training, employment and social services" fell from $32 billion to $27 billion). But on the whole, it was extremely difficult to make cuts, particularly after Reagan's initial "honeymoon" with Congress ended. Reagan's budget director, David Stockman, was in charge of proposing the cuts to be made and selling them to Congress. His book *The Triumph of Politics* describes in case after case how difficult it was to cut programs, even if they had little justification, once the affected interests and their allies in Congress and the government bureaucracy were alerted for battle.[4] In the end, the conservative Reagan administration was unable to turn back the tide of government spending and regulation.

----

[4]David Stockman, *The Triumph of Politics: How the Reagan Revolution Failed* (New York: Harper & Row, 1986).

THE UNDERLYING ECONOMICS OF GOVERNMENT GROWTH

We have discussed the growth of government in the postwar period as the outcome of an ongoing battle between liberal and conservative political philosophies. Liberal historian Arthur Schlesinger, Jr., has described this as an alternation in the dominant philosophy between "public purpose" and "private interest." It leads, in the long run, to the growth of government because programs initiated by liberal administrations are seldom eliminated by the conservatives who follow. In his view, the appropriate image is that of government as a spiral that widens during periods of liberal dominance, but never contracts.[5] Conservative economists Milton Friedman and Rose D. Friedman have described the same phenomenon, but in less favorable language. In their view the ability of liberal programs to resist conservative attempts to eliminate them is due to the "tyranny of the status quo." An "iron triangle" of bureaucrats, beneficiaries in the private sector, and politicians protects programs even when it has been shown that they are clearly detrimental to the general interest. Measured across all voters the gain from eliminating a program may be large. But for each voter individually, the gain may be too small to make fighting for it worthwhile.[6]

Below the changing tides of politics, a number of economists have detected deeper currents that determine the size of government. One factor may simply be the increase of real per capita income. Governmental programs that help the disadvantaged, protect the environment, and so on, may be luxury goods—we buy proportionately more of them when our income rises. To the extent that voting patterns reflect views about long-run incomes, the belief that productivity growth has slowed might produce a substantial decrease in the demand for such expenditures. Other long-run trends may also increase the demand for government. Population growth and urbanization, for example, may have increased the demand for programs to preserve the environment or provide mass transportation.[7]

Economists Allan Meltzer and Scott Richard have attempted to devise a rational theory of transfer payments. In their model, people vote for programs that redistribute income in their favor but also take into account the disincentive affects of higher taxes. The poor do not automatically vote for "soak the rich" taxes because they think that such taxes would make the whole economy less productive and that they would end up with less in the

[5] Arthur Schlesinger, Jr., *The Cycles of American History* (Boston: Houghton Mifflin, 1986) Chapter 2.

[6] Milton Friedman and Rose Friedman, *Tyranny of the Status Quo* (San Diego: Harcourt Brace Jovanovich, 1983) pp. 41–51.

[7] See Solomon Fabricant, *The Trend in Government Activity in the United States since 1900*, (New York: National Bureau of Economic Research, 1952), for an early statement of this view of the growth of government.

end than before.[8] Economist Sam Peltzman has developed a related theory based on international comparisons. He argues that, paradoxically, a more equal distribution of income (even when generated by the market) accelerates the growth of government because it increases the political strength of the group that favors further redistribution through the government.[9] It is too early to say whether theories such as these will be able to account for the expansion of government which until recently was the dominant trend in most industrial countries.

THE NEW REGULATION

During the nineteenth century, and with a few exceptions until the Second World War, federal regulation was designed to deal with specific problems in specific industries. The Interstate Commerce Commission, for example, was concerned mostly with regulation of prices charged by railroads, trucking companies, and water carriers, while the Federal Reserve System regulated the banks, and so on. But in the postwar period that emphasis changed. Regulatory agencies were set up with broad powers to interfere with decision making in a wide range of industries and in relation to a broad array of problems. For example, in 1970 Congress set up the Occupational Health and Safety Administration (OSHA) to set standards for working conditions throughout the workplace. This agency's penchant for issuing irritating (to business) regulations was one of Ronald Reagan's main examples that "government is the problem."

One of the most dramatic developments of the postwar period was the passage of major pieces of legislation designed to protect the consumer from the purchase of dangerous or otherwise unsatisfactory goods and services. Consumer protection is by no means unique to this period. But as Table 28-5 makes clear the rate of passage of such legislation has accelerated in the postwar period. Why this should have been so is not entirely clear.

Some pieces of legislation can be traced to particularly dreadful events. One of the earliest examples dating back to 1852 was the Steamboat Inspection Service that was established due to boiler explosions that slaughtered crews and passengers alike—many explosions were caused by races between steamboats on the Mississippi River. The Food, Drug and Cosmetic Act of 1938 followed the Elixir Sulfanilamide tragedy. In this case, the particular

---

[8] Allan H. Meltzer and Scott F. Richard, "Why Government Grows (and Grows) in a Democracy," *Public Interest* 52 (Summer 1978): 111–18; "A Rational Theory of the Size of Government," *Journal of Political Economy* 89 (Oct. 1981): 914–27; "Tests of a Rational Theory of the Size of Government," *Public Choice* 41 (1983): 403–18.
[9] Sam Peltzman, "The Growth of Government," *Journal of Law and Economics* 23 (Oct. 1980): 220–85.

TABLE 28-5   Major Consumer Safety Laws of the United States

Year	Law	Main Provisions
1906	Food and Drug Act	Prohibits misbranding and adulteration of foods and drugs. Requires listing of medicine ingredients on product labels.
1906	Meat Inspection Act	Provides for federal inspection of slaughtering, packaging, and canning plants that ship meat interstate.
1938	Food, Drug, and Cosmetic Act	Defines as "adulterated" any food or drug that contains a substance unsafe for human use. Requires application for introduction of new drugs supported by tests of safety.
1938	Wheeler-Lea Amendment to Federal Trade Commission Act (1914)	Extends prohibitions of FTC Act to "unfair or deceptive acts or practices."
1953	Flammable Fabrics Act	Prohibits manufacture, import, or sale of products so "flammable as to be dangerous when worn by individuals."
1958	Food Additives Amendment to Food, Drug, and Cosmetic Act (1938)	Prohibits use of food additives shown to cause cancer in man or animals.
1960	Hazardous Substances Labeling Act	Requires labeling of hazardous household substances.
1962	Kefauver-Harris Amendments to Food, Drug, and Cosmetic Act (1938)	Requires additional tests of both safety and efficacy for new drugs.
1965	Cigarette Labeling and Advertising Act	Requires use of health warnings on cigarette packages and in advertising.
1966	Fair Packaging and Labeling Act	Requires listing of product contents and manufacturer.
1966	Child Protection Act (Amendment to Hazardous Substances Labeling Act of 1960)	Prohibits sales of hazardous toys and other items used by children.
1966	National Traffic and Motor Vehicle Safety Act	Provides for establishment of safety standards for vehicles and parts, and for vehicle recalls.
1967	Amendments to the Flammable Fabrics Act (1953)	Extends federal authority to establish safety standards for fabrics, including "household" products.
1970	Public Health Cigarette Smoking Act	Prohibits broadcast advertising of cigarettes.
1970	Poison Prevention Packaging Act	Provides for "child-resistant" packaging of hazardous substances.
1972	Consumer Product Safety Act	Establishes the Consumer Product Safety Commission, with authority to set safety standards for consumer products and to ban products that present undue risk.
1977	Saccharin Study and Labeling Act	Requires use of health warnings on products containing saccharin; postpones saccharin ban.

form in which this drug was sold proved to be toxic and left about 100 dead, many of them children. But the producer was held under existing law to be guilty of no more than mislabelling his product.

The Kefauver-Harris Amendments of 1962 to the Food, Drug and Cosmetic Act followed in the wake of the thalidomide tragedy. It was found in Europe that thalidomide produced severe birth defects when it was given to pregnant women. This tragedy was avoided in the United States. But it appeared to legislators that tragedy had been avoided mainly due to the resolute behavior of one public official, Dr. Ann Kelsy of the Food and Drug Administration. She had resisted enormous pressure to license the drug. Legislators felt that without additional legal safeguards future situations might merge in which an absence of such a resolute regulator would lead to tragedy. The Flammable Fabrics Act of 1953 is still another example. This act also followed in the wake of a number of tragic accidents. The industry, it should be noted, did not resist this legislation. By being able to show that their fabrics met federal safety standards, manufacturers hoped to increase demand. And the legislation provided a basis for a defense in legal suits.

But such events are not the whole story. The passage of legislation for consumer protection also seems to have been related to the swings in public opinion between liberal and conservative that can be seen in a wide range of other legislation. Notice in Table 28-5 that eight major pieces of consumer protection legislation were passed in 1965–72 including the Fair Packaging and Labelling Act, the National Traffic and Motor Vehicle Safety Act, and the Consumer Product Safety Act. This burst of legislative activity was not related, for the most part, to individual tragedies, but rather to the general lack of faith in the market. In recent years, as we noted, the liberal faith in the ability of government to improve on the outcome of market forces has been on the defensive. The Reagan administration opposed such extensions of federal authority, and there have been no major pieces of consumer protection legislation in recent years.

Weighing the costs and benefits of such legislation is a difficult task, and economists are still far from a consensus on even individual regulations, let alone the whole trend. The benefits of regulation are relatively easy to see: The consumer is protected from consuming a dangerous food, using a dangerous drug, or driving a dangerous car. But costs are also incurred because regulation may well raise production costs, limit competition, and stifle innovation. It has been contended, for example, that regulation of the drug industry has limited the number of new drugs being brought to market.[10]

In this chapter we have had space to discuss the trends in the role of government only in the broadest terms. In the next chapter we shall examine the postwar relationship between government and three sectors that have been a major concern throughout our discussion: agriculture, the environment, and transportation.

SELECTED REFERENCES AND SUGGESTED READINGS

Aaron, Henry J. *Politics and the Professors: The Great Society in Perspective.* Washington, D.C.: Brookings Institution, 1978.

---

[10]See Peter Asch, *Consumer Safety Regulation* (New York: Oxford Univ. Press, 1988), Chapter 7, for a fair-minded review of the literature on this question.

Asch, Peter. *Consumer Safety Legislation: Putting a Price on Life and Limb.* New York: Oxford University Press, 1988.

Bennett, James T., and Manuel H. Johnson. *The Political Economy of Federal Government Growth, 1959–1978.* College Station, Texas: Center for Education and Research in Free Enterprise, 1980.

Bernstein, Barton J. and Alan I. Matusow. *The Truman Administration: A Documentary Record.* New York: Harper & Row, 1968.

Borcherding, Thomas E. "The Sources of Growth of Public Expenditures in the United States, 1902–1970." In *Budgets and Bureaucrats: The Sources of Government Growth,* ed. Thomas E. Borcherding. Durham N.C.: Duke Univ. Press, 1977.

Break, George F. "Issues in Measuring the level of Government Activity." *American Economic Review* 72 (May 1982): 288–95.

Buchanan, James M. *Public Finance in Democratic Process: Fiscal Institutions and Individual Choice.* Chapel Hill: Univ. of North Carolina Press, 1967.

Fabricant, Solomon. *The Trend of Government Activity in the United States since 1900.* New York: National Bureau of Economic Research, 1952.

Friedman, Milton, and Rose D. Friedman. *Tyranny of the Status Quo.* San Diego: Harcourt Brace Jovanovich, 1983.

Galbraith, John K. *The Affluent Society.* Boston: Houghton Mifflin, 1969.

Glasner, David. *Politics, Prices, and Petroleum: The Political Economy of Energy.* Cambridge, MA: Ballinger, 1985.

Heller, Walter. *New Dimensions of Political Economy.* Cambridge: Harvard Univ. Press, 1969.

Higgs, Robert. *Crisis and Leviathan: Critical Episodes in the Growth of American Government.* New York: Oxford Univ. Press, 1987.

Hughes, Jonathan, R.T. *The Governmental Habit.* New York: Basic Books, 1977.

Larkey, Patrick D., Chandler Stolp, and Mark Winer. "Theorizing about the Growth of Government: A Research Assessment." *Journal of Public Policy* 1 (May 1981): 157–220.

Lilley, William, III, and James C. Miller III. "The New 'Social Regulation.' " *The Public Interest* 47 (1977): 49–61.

McCraw, Thomas K. *Prophets of Regulation.* Cambridge: Harvard Univ. Press, 1984.

Meltzer, Allan H., and Scott F. Richard. "A Rational Theory of the Size of Government." *Journal of Political Economy* 89 (Oct. 1981): 914–27.

———. "Tests of a Rational Theory of the Size of Government." *Public Choice* 41 (1983): 403–18.

———. "Why Government Grows (and Grows) in a Democracy." *Public Interest* 52 (Summer 1978): 111–118.

Niskanen, William A. *Bureaucracy and Representative Government.* Chicago: Aldine-Atherton, 1971.

Peltzman, Sam. "The Growth of Government." *Journal of Law and Economics* 23 (Oct. 1980): 220–85.

Roberts, Paul Craig. *The Supply-Side Revolution: An Insider's Account of Policymaking in Washington.* Cambridge: Harvard Univ. Press, 1984.

Schlesinger, Arthur M., Jr. *The Cycles of American History.* Boston: Houghton Mifflin, 1986.

Schumpeter, Joseph. *Capitalism, Socialism, and Democracy.* London: Allen and Unwin, 1943.

Stockman, David A. *The Triumph of Politics: How the Reagan Revolution Failed.* New York: Harper & Row, 1986.

Stone, Alan. *Economic Regulation and the Public Interest: The Federal Trade Commission in Theory and Practice.* Ithaca, NY: Cornell Univ. Press, 1977.

Vatter, Harold G. *The U.S. Economy in the 1950s.* New York: W. W. Norton, 1963.

Wildavsky, Aaron. *The Politics of the Budgetary Process.* Boston: Little, Brown, 1964.

C H A P T E R 29

Government and the Economy: Agriculture, the Environment, and Transportation

At one time agriculture might have been the model of the economist's concept of perfect competition. Agriculture was characterized by numerous competitors, each too small to significantly influence total supply, acting as price-takers. In the nineteenth century, American farmers operating in this kind of market vastly expanded the land under cultivation, adopted a wide range of technological improvements, and generated an unprecedented increase in total output. In many ways the system worked well, although life for the farmer, subject as he was to the vagaries of world markets, was often bitter. This characterization is, admittedly, overly simple. The nineteenth-century politicians who had wrestled with questions like land policy, Indian policy, usury laws, and so on, all policies of great interest to farmers, would have been surprised to hear that the federal government had nothing to do with farmers. Nevertheless, in the nineteenth century and well into the twentieth, market forces were the primary determinant of farm prices and farm income. By the end of the Second World War, the situation was very different. The farmer, the cynic would say, had become a ward of the state. Life on farms, especially for the poor, was still far from easy. But prices and output were now determined as much by politicians in Washington as by world supplies and demands for agricultural products.

The Postwar Surplus Problems

Farm prices and income began a downward trend in July 1948. With the high support prices required by the Agricultural Acts of 1948 and 1949, price declines meant increases in loans and accumulation of inventories, for

603

which the Commodity Credit Corporation (CCC) was prepared. In June 1948, Congress had given the CCC a borrowing authorization of $4.75 billion and permanent status. During the fiscal years 1949 and 1950, price-support loans and inventories climbed to a total "investment" of over $3.5 billion. Corn stocks owned by the CCC or pledged to it as collateral were greater than they had been at any previous time. Wheat inventories were about the same as those held in the previous peak year of 1942. Although cotton holdings did not approach the massive inventories of 1939–41, they were not far from those of 1942, another high year.

To understand why CCC inventories increased so markedly in years of mild recession, it is helpful to review postwar farm legislation. A presidential declaration that the war was officially over, made in December 1946, signaled the termination of rigid wartime supports at the end of 1948. Although it had been amended several times, the basic farm law was still the old Agricultural Adjustment Act of 1938, which was generally felt to be in need of revision. Consequently, extensive discussion of the whole farm problem went on during 1947 and the first half of 1948. Farm leaders, government experts, and university professors testified before the House Agricultural Committee. The result was the Agricultural Act of 1948—passed in haste in the last days of the congressional session—which maintained price-support levels through 1949 at the magical 90 percent of parity for a wide range of commodities.

The contribution of the midwestern farm states to the Democratic victory of 1948 led to a lengthy reconsideration of the policy laid down by the Republican-controlled Eightieth Congress in the 1948 act. It seemed for a while that a novel and imaginative method of subsidizing agriculture might be implemented. In the spring of 1949, Secretary of Agriculture C. F. Brannan announced the plan of compensatory payments to which the press and public quickly attached his name, although its central ideas had been developing for many years in academic writings. The Brannan plan would have allowed the prices of certain perishable commodities to seek their own level in the marketplace, the difference between the market price and a "modernized" parity price to be paid to the farmer (up to a certain maximum number of "units") with a check from the Treasury. The advantages of the Brannan plan were substantial. Surpluses would be eliminated, saving storage costs. And the public, the poor in particular, would be able to buy food cheaply. After months of heated argument, during which the National Grange and the American Farm Bureau Federation aligned themselves against such an unconcealed payment of subsidies, the House of Representatives refused to give the Brannan plan a trial run on even three commodities. Opponents of the Brannan plan won the day by castigating such a straightforward subsidy as "socialism."

In the fall of the year, the Agricultural Act of 1949 was passed. The law distinguished among three groups of commodities: (1) the six "basics"—

wheat, corn, cotton, tobacco, rice, and peanuts; (2) five "designated non-basic" commodities—wool and mohair, tung nuts, honey, Irish potatoes, and milk and milk products; and (3) "other nonbasic" commodities—the rest of some 170 U.S. commodities. The Secretary of Agriculture was required to support the basic commodities, provided they were under production controls of marketing quotas, but a rigid support of 90 percent of parity was permanently mandatory only in the case of tobacco. After 1952, the other basic commodities were to be supported at between 75 and 90 percent of parity, the level of support depending on the supply of each commodity. The 1949 act, like the 1948 law before it, provided a new parity formula. The "modernized" method of computing parity prices took into consideration prices received and prices paid during the most recent ten-year period instead of the relationships prevailing during the golden 1910–14 period. However, parity prices computed under the new formula could not drop more than 5 percent per year below what they would have been under the old formula, and until the end of 1954, the parity price for any basic commodity could not be lower than it was under the old method of computation. The 1949 legislation also made use of methods devised in the preceding 17 years to restrict the supply of farm products. However, a decision was made in favor of *flexible* price supports and against the wartime *rigid* supports, tobacco being the one exception. And the new method of computing parity prices had the merit of basing the program (after 1954, at least) on a current experience that was no longer of another age and time.

Neither flexible supports nor the new parity formula became effective as planned. After the start of the Korean War, Congress amended the law to make 90 percent support of the basics mandatory, and the old method of computing parity prices remained more favorable to farmers than the new one. The war once again enabled the CCC to reduce embarrassingly high inventories and loans, and total "investment" fell to $2 billion in mid-1951. The crops of 1952 and 1953, however, required an inordinate amount of support, and by August 1954 CCC loans and inventories amounted to nearly $7 billion. Twice during 1954 it was necessary to increase CCC authority to borrow for support operations—the last change bringing total authority to $10 billion.

After procrastinating for more than a year, the Eighty-Third Congress at last came up with its version of a farm program in the Agricultural Act of 1954. The inner circle of Department of Agriculture officials strove valiantly to find a fresh approach to the problem of price maintenance, but in the end advocated making the major provisions of the 1949 act effective. Secretary of Agriculture Ezra Taft Benson was especially insistent on the restoration of flexible supports, which were finally set for five of the six basic commodities at 82.5 to 90 percent of parity. The 1954 act again postponed changing to the modernized parity price formula for basic commodities; the notion that the 1910–14 period represented parity ("fairity") was too deeply ingrained to die easily. In an attempt to "insulate" the massive stocks of the CCC from the market, Congress authorized that $2.5 billion of CCC stocks be set aside for donation or sale for enumerated worthy causes.

But feed grain and wheat carry-overs continued to swell, and other surpluses, although not as alarming, showed no signs of lessening. The Soil Bank Act of 1956 was devised to reduce supplies of the six basic commodities by achieving a 10–17 percent reduction in plowland through payments to farmers who "voluntarily" shifted land out of production into the "soil bank." The diversion payments were based on the old formula of *multiplying* a base unit rate ($1.20 for wheat, $0.90 for corn, and so on, in the beginning) *by* normal yield per acre *by* the numbers of acres withdrawn. The plan was disguised as a conservation program to avoid the appearance of controlling farm decisions. The results were unexpected, but easy to understand in retrospect. Farmers placed their least productive land in the soil bank and cultivated the remainder more intensively. Carry-overs went right on mounting, reaching astronomical heights in 1961 after nine consecutive years of increase.

The Kennedy Years to the Present

The Kennedy Administration had no choice but to be hardboiled. Secretary of Agriculture Orville Freeman devised no new techniques. He simply made an honest approach to the problem by dropping any pretense of maintaining freedom and controls at the same time. The Emergency Feed Grain Bill of 1961 encouraged drastic reductions in acreages devoted to corn and grain sorghums by offering $1.20 a bushel in diversion payments to farmers who reduced their acreage by 20 percent. Even higher payments were offered for the diversion of an additional 20 percent of feed-crop acreage. On the whole, the plan worked in 1962 because the reduction was large enough to offset attempts by farmers to minimize its effects. For the first time in a decade, feed grain carry-over actually dropped, and in 1962, a continuing reduction was predicted. This modest success encouraged the administration to attack massive surpluses of wheat with a similar, but incredibly expensive, plan. Wealthy farmers and their organization, the Farm Bureau Federation, although at first opposed, quickly saw the error of their ways and joined wholeheartedly in forging the Food and Agriculture Act of 1965. A monstrous giveaway, this act cost the American taxpayer $5–$6 billion a year to make rich farmers richer while allowing a little to trickle down to poor farmers.

It is curious that farmers, particularly in the Midwest, who are predominantly Republican, have gained their assistance largely from Democratic farm programs. And just as surely as a Republican administration attains power with the help of the farm vote, the new Secretary of Agriculture will recommend a farm bill guaranteed to disenchant all but the wealthiest agricultural operators. For example, consider Secretary of Agriculture Clifford M. Hardin's Agricultural Act of 1970 passed and signed by President Nixon in November 1970. Basically, the law suspended marketing quotas and acreage allotments for wheat, feed grains, and cotton, requiring farmers to "set aside" or divert from production a certain amount of acres previously devoted to *any* kind of crop. Great corporate operations were thereby given the right to grow as much of any *one* crop as they wished, provided they took sufficient *total* acres out of production. The 1970 Act *did* provide a $55,000 limit on the direct subsidy of any one crop, but a single grower could obtain the maximum subsidies for each of three crops.

A 1971 corn crop of more than 5 billion bushels, bringing corn prices down to less than $0.90 a bushel at local elevators, suggested that disaster might be in the offing. The appointment of Purdue University Dean Earl Butz as Secretary of Agriculture to succeed the discredited Hardin did not reassure many farmers; Butz was obviously committed to agribusiness and the promotion of corporate farming. Secretary Butz tried to demonstrate the administration's good faith by keeping farm prices free of the constraints of the price controls being put in place, but farmers remained wary.

As consumers and taxpayers became more vocal in the 1970s, Congress found it more difficult to respond unilaterally to farm interests. The Democrat-dominated Congress and President Carter made a heroic effort to balance these three opposing interests by passing the Food and Agriculture Act of 1977. This monument of complication set support prices within specified ranges on wheat, feed grains, cotton, dairy products, sugar, peanuts, and other commodities. In the winter of 1978, however, protesting farmers obtained higher support prices through the Emergency Act of 1978. As in the past, farmers could obtain Commodity Credit Corporation loans to keep their crops off the market, and acreage controls were imposed by requiring farmers receiving payments to set aside at least 20 percent of their land for "soil conservation uses."[1]

Reagan's Farm Bill passed in late 1981 exceeded $22.6 billion in expenditures with more than $10 billion of it being allocated for the food-stamp program, and price supports were continued on peanuts, sugar, wheat, feed grains, rice, soybeans, cotton, and wool, although these supports were reduced from their higher levels during the Carter years. As expected, both Democrat and Republican farm interests claimed that the cutbacks were dictated by the administration, leaving no effective protection for farmers facing severely depressed incomes.

---

[1]For more details, see D. Gale Johnson, "The Food and Agriculture Act of 1977: Implications for Farmers and Taxpayers," in *Contemporary Economic Problems,* ed.William Fellner, (Washington, D C.: American Enterprise Institute, 1978) pp. 167–210.

The Political Economy of Agricultural Subsidies

Clearly, government agricultural policy has been based on an attempt to redistribute income to farmers. In doing so, food production has been curtailed, higher prices have been imposed, and taxes have been elevated. It is now routine procedure for farmers and their lobbyists to ask for and receive help from government. But even this help has produced unexpected results for the farmers themselves.

Unquestionably, farm programs have helped operators who were well down in the income scale, but it is just as clearly true that the lion's share of assistance has gone to those who were already at the top of the heap. The biggest direct subsidies have gone to the biggest producers; when acreage restrictions were put into effect, those who were in a position to reduce acreage the most received the largest checks. As the government has supported commodity prices, those with the most bushels or bales to sell have received the chief benefits. Studies indicate that inequality of incomes in agriculture is greater today than it was three decades ago. There has been some recent improvement for the bottom half of the farm population, but only due to the relief afforded by some farmers quitting the business.

Outmigration, however, should not be viewed as simply a sign of failure in U.S. farm policy. In a technologically progressive society resources must be continually reallocated. As our knowledge and intelligence grow, fewer and fewer resources must be devoted to obtaining the necessities of life and more and more resources may be devoted to obtaining conveniences and luxuries. This has been true throughout the entire economic history of the United States. In 1790, nearly 90 percent of the work force was employed in agriculture; in 1960, the figure was less than 10 percent. At its peak in 1916, the farm population was 32.5 million; in 1954 it stood at 19 million, and in 1961 it was under 15 million, or 8.1 percent of the population. In 1985, the farm population stood at fewer than 5.4 million, or about 2.2 percent of the total population, and farm employment of 3.1 million was 3.7 percent of the work force. Favorable as the exodus has been, there are still far too many people in agriculture, especially in the South. It is likely that 2 percent of the work force or even less could produce all the farm products that the United States and a large part of the rest of the world could use at profitable prices.

Farmers, represented by their organizations and by the farm block in Congress, continue to support federal legislation similar to the programs discussed here. Today's farmers know perfectly well that acreage restrictions are of little avail over a period of years because they encourage more intensive cultivation of the remaining acreage. Farmers also know that price-support operations lead to tremendous stockpiles of commodities, which can be liquidated without lowering agricultural prices only in wartime or by dumping abroad. Responsible farm leaders are aware, too, that unfavorable press stories in conjunction with the accumulation of huge government-owned stocks of commodities excite public hostility to farm programs.

Yet a combination of acreage restrictions and CCC-type price supports has the unquestioned political advantage of masking the amount and extent of the subsidy to agriculture. Department of Agriculture outlays on the subsidy program, great as they are, do not include the higher prices paid by consumers for food and fiber as a consequence of support operations. Moreover, tying price and income maintenance to conservation dilutes the element of subsidy in the public mind. Finally, because the subsidy is provided by a market mechanism, it seems respectable, whereas subsidy checks paid at the end of the growing season to make up for the amount of income deemed necessary seem too obvious to be tolerated. For these reasons, farmers generally support proven methods of government subsidy. Within agriculture, the only serious differences arising in recent years have been concerned with the question of rigorous versus mild controls over output. The American Farm Bureau Federation, which speaks for the more affluent farmers, wants lower support prices and greater freedom to plant, because Farm Bureau membership makes huge profits on large volume. Supporting sharp restrictions on acreage combined with astronomical support prices are the organizations of small farmers, chiefly the National Farmers Union, the National Farmers Organization, and the National Grange.

Many agricultural economists who are definitely sympathetic to agriculture feel that policies established over the last four decades may, in the long run, prevent a satisfactory solution to the farm problem. There has long been an objection to the ideal of "parity," partly on the ground that no group in society is entitled, by right, to a fixed portion of the real national income. But there is a stronger argument. Successful attempts to maintain prices of farm commodities in the same *relative* position over time may keep consumers from obtaining the supplies that they want most. Parity prices tend to keep agricultural resources employed in the production of products that people have wanted in the past. If some agricultural prices are not allowed to fall *relative* to others, the pattern of cultivation will remain too rigid, and the result will be chronic "surpluses" of some crops.

Although economists look with disfavor on present types of agricultural subsidies, many agree that *some* kind of a federal farm program may be necessary because the transition from rural to urban life is exceedingly difficult. Many poor farmers remain on the land simply because they have no other skills with which to make a living. For others the pain of giving up a cherished way of life is too much. So a case can be made for slowing the rate at which family farms disappear and for subsidizing the training of the displaced rural poor for urban pursuits. But no one familiar with the facts can advocate the artificial support of prices to aid the wealthy when a plan of compensatory payments would maintain incomes of poor farmers satisfactorily. In addition to the $7.7 billion cost of subsidy programs as of

1985, we must also add higher consumer prices.[2] Unfortunately for consumers, they are less effectively represented in Congress than are farmers.

THE ENVIRONMENT

Another deep American concern today is the environment. In many ways, current environmentalists are very similar to conservationists of an earlier day. The central issue to both is how to best use our natural resources—broadly defined—on a long-term basis. Conservation and preservation (or repair) of the environment refers to some "proper" allocation of resource uses over time. Therefore, the aim of a true conservation or environmental program ought to be to preserve the future productivity of a soil area, a stand of timber, or a mineral deposit or to protect a natural beauty spot or the quality of life in urban areas. Moreover, to conserve a natural resource or location for future use it is usually necessary to make a current expenditure of capital and labor, rather than simply to withdraw what is to be preserved from use.[3]

Some public expenditures of capital and labor, rationalized on the grounds that they are made in the interests of conservation or the environment, actually amount to nothing more than outlays to increase *present* production. These outlays could be made now or 100 years from now and produce no deterioration in our natural resources. Thus, irrigation and drainage projects do not ordinarily prevent diminution of future production. A piece of Arizona desert land can be irrigated at any time in the future and the resultant increase in production will be just as great as it would if the improvement were made now. *Reclamation is not the same thing as conservation.*

The conflict between development and preserving nature erupts because some values can be protected only through social action. If an expenditure is to be made for the purpose of increasing the income stream from a given resource, a complete calculation of benefits versus costs may require a consideration of "costs" (for example, natural beauty) for which no private entrepreneur would voluntarily pay anything. For instance, a developer may ruin the water quality of a lake in an attempt to build homes and maximize profit unless government coercion forces him to bear the costs or clean up the waste discharge. This is the economist's concept of external costs, and it finds its most frequent application in relation to environmental problems.

---

[2]For recent history of farm policy, see Willard W. Cochrane, *American Farm Policy,* 1976. (Minneapolis: University of Minnesota Press, 1976).
[3]For a more technical exposition of such matters, see Earl O. Heady, "Soil-Conservation Programs," *Journal of Political Economy,* 59:1 (February 1951), p. 48.

Conservation and the careful nurturing of fields have also increased farm productivity—and unintentionally exacerbated the farm problem in the process.

Conservation in Twentieth-Century Perspective

The conservation movement in the twentieth century began auspiciously with Theodore Roosevelt's policy to involve the federal government in the control and acquisition of natural resources. By the mid-1920s, however, this policy had suffered from mismanagement and the Teapot Dome scandal. From this bleak period there was an upward surge in the movement under the administrations of Franklin D. Roosevelt. Old methods were carried out with renewed vigor, and two innovations marked a new approach. First, the government took steps to conserve the soil owned by *private* individuals. Second, it insisted that a meaningful program of conservation required the simultaneous protection of many resources within an entire region.

Along lines of traditional policy, perhaps the most important step was the withdrawal from entry of the remaining public domain—nearly 175 million acres—until the land could be classified as to its best use. A small portion of the public domain was later made available for private entry, but most of it was organized into grazing districts under the Taylor Grazing Act of 1934. Before the passage of the Act, stockmen let their animals feed on the great public ranges without restraint. Under the new system, permits were issued that limited the number of grazing animals to the amount that a given range could accommodate without depleting the forage. By 1950, there were 59 grazing districts that included 145 million acres, and in addition, grazing leases were issued on scattered public-domain lands and on Indian reservations. A generation after passage of the original act, controversy still smolders over the proper disposition of these lands. Among westerners, there is substantial opinion that the federal government should oversee only those areas that are suitable for recreation, national forests, wildlife refuges, and reclamation and power projects and sell remainders of the public domain to the highest bidders; but on the East and West coasts there is resistance to the sale of any part of the public domain.

During the Depression, the government made great expenditures on conservation. Late in 1933, Harold Ickes could remark, with truth, that the Civilian Conservation Corps had accomplished more reforestation in six months than all the federal agencies had in the preceding 15 years. More importantly, funds were obtained to expand the national forests by purchasing poorly kept private forest lands, located for the most part in the Southeast. By 1950, national forest acreage had risen to 180 million, and the government controlled some 200 million acres of additional forested land in Indian reservations, wildlife refuges, national parks, and other public holdings.

About 116 million acres, or one-quarter of the U.S. total, was publicly owned commercial forest land divided between federal agencies, which managed 89 million acres, and state and local agencies, which controlled 27 million acres. The very best timber owned by the federal government was located in the West, far from markets and in inaccessible areas, so that investments in roads would be necessary before it could be used. But much of the noncommercial forest land owned by the government was to become merchantable—far sooner than it would have in private hands.

Old-line conservation efforts included some incidental preservation of the soil. Not until New Deal days, however, were serious efforts made to systematically conserve agricultural land. These efforts began with the establishment of the Soil Erosion Service in 1933 in the Department of the Interior. In 1935, the Soil Conservation Service became an agency of the Department of Agriculture. Originally, contracts were made with individual farmers; the Service furnished technical assistance and some materials, and the farmers furnished labor and the remaining materials. Early in 1937, President Roosevelt wrote the governors of the states requesting that their legislatures pass acts enabling landowners and occupiers to form soil-conservation districts. By 1954, about 2,500 soil-conservation districts, including 80 percent of all U.S. farms, had been organized.

Any discussion of new concepts of conservation must contain some mention of what may constitute the ultimate solution to the whole problem—the inclusion of water control and of major valleys in programs of great scope. Some advocates argue that nothing less can produce permanently successful conservation. The evidence is not conclusive, although the Tennessee Valley Authority (TVA)—one outstanding example—has unquestionably done a remarkable job of upgrading an entire region.

There will certainly be enough cropland to spare for another quarter-century, although prudence suggests the maintenance of a soil area sufficient to meet possible explosive demands as the twenty-first century nears. If we have limited funds to spend on conservation, they must be used to conserve, not simply to raise short-run productivity. Expenditures for irrigation, drainage, better crop rotation on level land, and the like, cannot be justifiably included in a conservation program unless these practices do indeed save the soil. And there is a further point to be considered. Soils in different geographical areas vary greatly in quality. With limited funds, it is more advantageous from society's point of view to give priority to the conservation of the better soils. This sounds like hard doctrine, and it is. Conservation policy tends to neglect such realistic considerations, partly because the execution of such a policy is fraught with political difficulties; it is easy to point out that the farmer who owns poor land needs assistance more than the farmer who owns good land.

Technical advances have made possible the reclamation of arid land that was once considered certain waste. Only water is needed to transform most desert into croplands. Pumps driven by 65,000 horsepower motors have been installed at the Grand Coulee Dam to lift water 280 feet from the Columbia River into the Coulee, from which it can then be diverted to irrigate vast areas. By means of complex systems of dams, reservoirs, pumps and tunnels, water from northern California has been diverted to southern California. The Bureau of Reclamation estimates that eventually 50 million acres west of the Rockies can be converted to fertile land. Such developments lead us to ask whether the whole problem of soil conservation should not be closely related to reclamation (that is, soil-development) programs. Would it be possible to increase future output to a greater degree by investing a given amount in, say, irrigation than by investing the same amount in the prevention of soil erosion? The answer to this question is that to be on the *safe* side society should decide to preserve rather than to develop. If soil erodes away, it is gone forever. A compromise would assure a "stand-by" production capacity. Marginal land in quantity could be withdrawn from production and seeded down, to be returned to use only if great domestic or world population growth one day made such a step necessary. For a time such considerations appeared to be mundane, if not trivial, compared with the new threats to the environment.

During the 1960s the public awakened to the belief that the environment had become polluted with numerous dangerous by-products of industry. Making the environment whole again, many argued, was more important than continued rapid economic growth. Public attention shifted from problem to problem depending on the events of the day. Rachel Carson's book *Silent Spring* heightened concern about the danger of indiscriminate uses of pesticides, and in 1969 the Department of Agriculture banned the use of DDT. A major oil spill off the coast of beautiful Santa Barbara, California, in 1969 raised concerns about the danger of off-shore oil drilling. And related fears were raised about the environmental impact of the proposed Alaska Pipeline. The recent oil-spill in Alaska produced by the *Exxon Valdez* reinforced such fears. Responding to these and other environmental concerns, Congress passed the Clean Air Act and Water Quality Improvement Act in 1970 and established the Environmental Protection Agency and the Occupational Health and Safety Administration.

But coming on the heels of the new environmentalism was the "energy crisis" and increasing fear that the U.S. economy was stagnating. Proposed solutions to the energy crisis often seemed in conflict with programs to improve the environment. Beginning in 1973 the Organization of Petroleum Exporting Countries (OPEC), which at that time controlled a dominant share of the world market, began to flex its muscles. The price of a barrel of crude oil quadrupled between 1973 and 1975. Particularly disruptive was the oil embargo (the refusal of primarily the Arab producers to sell to supporters of Israel) that followed the Arab-Israeli war in 1973. The result was long lines at gas pumps, rationing by waiting time rather than price.

This experience touched off a fundamental debate on how to meet the "energy crisis." Should it be through government—rationing, subsidies for the poor, and federal expenditures for new sources of energy—or through the price mechanism? Advocates of the price system held that higher prices would produce the most efficient results. Higher prices would reduce demand (by making smaller, more fuel-efficient cars more attractive, for example) and increase supplies. A bureaucratic response was tried. A federal energy administration was established in 1974, and a cabinet-level Department of Energy followed in 1977. Spending on a wide range of federal energy projects was increased. But in the end much of the painful adjustment was the response to higher prices. Americans cut their energy consumption by buying smaller cars (many of them from foreign producers), insulating their homes, and investing in more fuel-efficient productive processes. On the supply side, higher prices led to a rapid increase in production in countries outside of OPEC, undermining its monopoly power. The price system worked much as many of its advocates had suggested it would, although not perhaps as quickly and painlessly as some had expected.

The Reagan administration tended to resolve conflicts between environmentalists and the energy-producing industry in favor of the latter. But America's concern with the environment has been a long one, and it seems likely that policies designed to protect the environment will continue to get a sympathetic hearing. There is, after all, a mocking irony in the fact that the major federal statute designed to rectify environmental abuses—the

National Environmental Policy Act of 1969—consists largely of amendments to the Clean Air Act of 1894 and the Refuse Act of 1899. For three-quarters of a century, despite laws to the contrary, American business had paid little attention to the social costs of disposing of wastes. Now efforts are being made to address those costs. Unfortunately, the fact is that energy problems are intensified by environmental concerns. For instance, to obtain cleaner air in urban places, we impose smog controls, ban low-grade fuels, and take similar actions. This raises the costs of energy and more rapidly depletes vital energy sources. It is a matter of choices. The Bush administration, in its early days, has made it clear that it intends to increase the priority given to environmental concerns. But what this will mean when hard choices must be confronted remains to be seen.

THE TRANSPORTATION INFRASTRUCTURE

Unlike agriculture, the provision of transportation services has always been subject to considerable government involvement. Transportation frequently appears to be a natural monopoly. We need a road between Centerville and Middletown, but only one. Regulation through competition is not feasible, so throughout our history government has been involved with many aspects of transportation—the building of roads, harbor improvements, and lighthouses, and in the nineteenth century the regulation of shipping rates. Nevertheless, the scale and scope of government involvement in transportation increased dramatically in the postwar period.

The Highways

The cry for federal assistance to develop the nation's highways began almost from the first automobile show held in the Old Madison Square Garden in New York in 1900. The American Automobile Club, formed in 1902, joined with the American Road Builder's Association, and the American Association of State Highway Officials to lobby for an integrated interstate highway system.[4] But it was really the farmers who pressed hardest to get out of the mud. Despite the Federal Aid Road Act of 1916 and the Federal Highway Act of 1921, federal outlays, and state and local outlays too, remained sporadic. As a consequence, the traveler of the 1920s often found a smooth strip of concrete ending suddenly in a sea of mud or terminating at a stream that lacked a ferry or a bridge. Within the states, the most densely populated areas naturally tended to receive the "primary" road designations and consequently the good roads. In the great agricultural midlands, highways remained in unbelievably poor condition as late as the early 1930s. In Kansas, for example, long after the cities of Kansas City, Topeka, and Wichita

---

[4]F. L. Paxon, "The Highway Movement, 1916–1935," *American Historical Review* 51 (1946): 236–53.

were connected by a concrete slab, travelers along the old Pike's Peak Ocean-to-Ocean Highway, designated U.S. Highway 36, were frequently stranded hubcap deep in mud. The dirt roads of Kansas were connected to Nebraska's major highways, then topped with a magnificent layer of gravel and the county and township roads had not been noticeably improved for 50 years. Under such conditions, a trip of only a few miles could not be undertaken until favorable weather was certain.

One major outcome of the Depression was the impetus given road programs by the relief and recovery agencies. Roads received large shares of public expenditures undertaken to stimulate the economy. Before 1932, federal funds had not amounted to as much as 10 percent of total revenues for highways. In 1932, they rose to 30 percent and climbed to over 40 percent the next year. Federal participation, as a percentage of expenditures, did not drop to pre-Depression levels until the beginning of the Second World War, when federal dollars were directed to sterner activities. Meanwhile, the concept of federal aid had expanded, and after 1933, "secondary" roads—that is, roads other than the primary 7 percent—were included in the assistance programs, and money was authorized to improve portions of highways that ran through cities and to eliminate grade crossings.

During the war years, proper highway maintenance was not possible, and some major routes deteriorated rapidly. In anticipation of the rebuilding program, Congress passed the Federal-Aid Highway Act of 1944, making $1.5 billion available for expenditure in the three fiscal years following the end of the war. The law provided for the designation of an interstate highway system of not over 40,000 miles; this system was to receive the largest single portion of the appropriated funds. Secondary and feeder routes, including farm-to-market roads, received specific appropriations. Recognizing the seriousness of the growing congestion in urban areas, the law set aside monies for use exclusively on those segments of the basic interstate system lying within the limits of cities of 5,000 or more.

Within a decade after the end of the Second World War, it became apparent that the narrow, two-lane highways that constituted most of the U.S. highway network could no longer meet the nation's transportation needs. Spurred by the "highway lobby," Congress authorized the Interstate and Defense Highway System in 1956.[5] Designed to provide some 41,000 miles of limited-access, multilane mileage connecting the principal centers of the United States, the project was scheduled for completion in 13 years and was estimated to cost $27 billion. Fifteen years later, 42,500 miles had been completed at a cost of $43 billion, and 10,500 additional miles were completed by 1977. The interstate system was financed on the familiar grant-

---

[5]The highway lobby includes the American Association of State Highway Officials, the American Automobile Association, American Trucking Association, Automobile Manufacturers Association, American Road Builders Association, and many other organizations, which spend millions each year to influence highway legislation.

Superhighways such as these compete with houses for room to grow. Complex highway systems have revolutionized the inventory policies of some companies by making truck transportation rapid and dependable.

29 GOVERNMENT AND THE ECONOMY

in-aid basis; the federal government contributed 90 percent of the money and the states provided 10 percent. Additional excise taxes on petroleum products, tires, and trucks were to be placed in a highway trust fund to finance the new system on a pay-as-you-go basis, grumblingly called a "paid-before-you-go" basis by critics. Into this trust fund poured an increasing stream of earmarked user taxes, which has amounted to more than $14 billion in 1985.

Airways and Airports

Before 1920, the airplane had practically no economic significance. For more than a decade after the first flight of a heavier-than-air craft in 1903, the new machines were the playthings of eccentric sports enthusiasts and scientists. The First World War gave impetus to the development of airplane engines and structures, but major improvements lay in the future. In 1918, a military airplane was used for a commercial purpose when the Post Office Department and the War Department jointly sponsored an airmail route between Washington and New York. The project was soon dropped, but in the early 1920s the Post Office Department established airmail service between major cities. In 1925, when it appeared that airmail was practical, Congress ordered that all contracts be let to privately owned airlines. The Air Commerce Act of 1926 marked the first federal attempt to promote civil aviation. Funds were provided for a civil airways system as well as for improvements in navigation facilities. Meanwhile, sensational long-distance flights, financed by the rich, caught the public imagination and furnished evidence of the great future of commercial aviation.

The U.S. government was expected to assist this infant industry. Its first direct contribution, aside from subsidies granted through airmail payments, was the establishment of marked routes, equipped at first with beacon lights and then with radio markers and radio-range beacons. With the growth of the private airline companies, route mileage rose from less than 2,000 miles in 1926 to 22,000 miles in 1935, when plans to modernize and improve the airways were drawn up in the interest of airline safety. In 1949, there were 57,000 miles of federally owned air routes operating in the United States and its territories; by 1960, this figure had soared to 220,000. The system, made up largely of "VHF" airways and "superskyways" above the 17,000-foot level, was equipped with navigational aids, instrumental approach systems, air-route traffic-control centers, an extensive weather-reporting service, and traffic control towers at major airports. From 1925 to 1961, government expenditures on the construction, maintenance, and operation of airways amounted to approximately $3 billion and many times that amount was spent in the following decades without recovering any funds from the users of the system.

Long after the beginning of commercial aviation in 1926, the federal government assumed no responsibility for airport construction except for the provision of emergency landing fields. Until 1933, airports were built as private business ventures or as projects of municipalities. Municipal financial troubles accompanying the Depression made investment in such long-range projects difficult, and the federal government then began to participate in these ventures as a part of the relief program. Between 1933 and 1940, the federal government contributed just over 70 percent of the funds for airport construction, and municipalities furnished most of the rest. Because the main object of government expenditure was unemployment relief, no comprehensive plan of location and design was followed, and much of the construction was wasted. In 1940, Congress provided for a systematic extension of airport facilities, but the war intervened before it could go into effect. During the war years, practically all activity occurred at the federal level, and military objectives were the primary factor in all decisions.

The 1946 Federal Airport Act attempted to provide consistent long-range planning in airport construction. Of the available funds, 75 percent were to be apportioned among the states based on population and area; the remainder was to constitute a discretionary fund. Federal participation in small airports was limited to 50 percent of construction costs, discounting land acquisition; in large airports, federal participation might be more than

Fast domestic and foreign air travel has made airports more dependent on long runways and nearby residents painfully aware of the screech of jet engines. Drastically shortened travel time has greatly increased the productivity of business and professional people and has changed the character of many service trades as well.

50 percent. In 1958 the Eisenhower Administration tried to prevent the act's extension beyond June 30, 1959. However, Congress did not concur in the view that the government should "begin an orderly withdrawal from the airport grant program" and continued to grant federal aid, but federal spending was reduced. In 1969, several airports were so congested at peak traffic hours that controllers staged slowdowns, and the Federal Aviation Administration imposed air-traffic quotas on the nation's five busiest airports. With administration urging, Congress passed the Airport and Airway Development Act of 1970, which established an "Airport and Airway Trust Fund" to be fed by user tax revenues. By 1985, that fund was generating some $3.6 billion for airports and airways.

As late as 1940, most airports did not earn sufficient revenues to meet operating expenses, let alone capital costs. However, with the great increase in air passenger traffic in wartime and postwar years, users paid a much greater share of airport expenses, and almost all major air terminals, if properly managed, began to cover their maintenance and operating costs; a few actually covered *all* their costs, including rental payments, landing fees, aviation fuel sales, and restaurant and other concessions. Airports in small cities often failed to meet their operating expenses. Yet a national system of air transport required federal planning of minimum facilities, and the government got something else for its subsidy—free use of the airports by military aircraft and space for air traffic control and weather observers.

FEDERAL REGULATION OF TRANSPORTATION

The Railroads

Federal regulation of the transportation industries began with the railroads and acquired a complexity there that is not found in water, air, or highway transportation. Before 1920, the chief emphasis was on protecting the public from discriminatory railroad rates. After 1920, the competition of trucks and automobiles brought a complete turnabout in the objectives of government control; since then, the railroads—not the public—have obtained the protection of the regulatory authority.

The railroads were nationalized midway through the First World War. Then in 1920, when the return of the railroads to their owners was imminent, major financial problems appeared. The government had to be reimbursed for improvements to the railroads made during government seizure, funds had to be raised for modernization, and money had to be found to bring together scattered employees and equipment.

The Transportation Act of 1920 was a heroic effort to solve both the transitional and long-run problems. The act guaranteed that for six months after the return of the railroads to private operation, railroad owners would receive a net income equal to that of the best six-month period under federal control. The carriers were permitted to fund the debt owed for government improvements at 6 percent interest. For loans with maturities up to 15 years, $300 million was provided, and financial help was extended to short lines that had been especially hurt by wartime losses of traffic volume. It was felt that if the railroads were given this much assistance during the transitional period, permanent policy decisions regarding rates and the consolidation of companies into systems could be made to produce a sound, healthy industry.

Section 15a of the act outlined a rule of rate-making for the Interstate Commerce Commission (ICC). The ICC was instructed to set rates that would enable the railroads, as a whole or in certain groups, to earn "under honest, efficient and economical management a fair return upon the aggregate value of the railway property." The rule, we stress, applied to the railroads as a whole or in groups, not to individual carriers. But some roads were high-cost carriers, and others were low-cost carriers. A rate that would yield a handsome profit to one road might net a loss to another. What was the solution? The answer was given in the "recapture clause," which required that one-half of the earnings of any railroad in excess of a fair return should be paid to the ICC. These earnings were to be placed in a contingent fund from which loans could be made to weak lines for capital expenditures or to refund maturing obligations. The other half of the excess was placed in a reserve fund from which interest, dividends, and rentals could be paid in bad years.

Another provision of the act reversed policy toward pooling agreements—devices for splitting either traffic or profits among colluding companies. Long considered a monopolistic practice, pooling was henceforth not regarded as restrictive of competition if it was in the "public interest" and was carried out under ICC regulation. Legalization of the practice reflected congressional feeling that highway competition would effectively protect the consumer from monopolistic restrictions of the railroads. Thus, policies once condemned by the muckrakers as outrageous violations of public responsibility now became sanctioned by law. In this sense the ICC was finally captured.

The guide to rate-making, the recapture clause, and permissive pooling were more than transitional measures, but they were not considered final solutions. The ICC was also granted the authority to consolidate roads into systems and to control the rate of investment and disinvestment. Great hopes were placed in consolidation. The ICC was instructed to devise a plan whereby each individual line would be assigned to a system, and each system would be set up so that a uniform rate scale would yield approximately the same return on the fair value of the property. The ICC was then to publish a final plan and assist in proposed consolidations. Any two companies could combine properties, provided that the merger was in accordance with the master plan and was agreeable to the stockholders and to the ICC.

The grandiose consolidation scheme was supported by provisions giving the ICC numerous controls over the railroads. For example, after 1920 no railroad line could cease operation without the permission of the ICC, and it could require the construction of new lines where traffic justified extensions. Because of competition from buses and private automobiles, the railroads' passenger business began to decline in the 1920s. In only one year was the "fair-return" standard of 5.5 percent on the "fair value" of properties actually reached by the railroads as a whole. With the onset of depression in 1929, the financial position of all the companies deteriorated rapidly. By 1931, railroad managements were demanding rate increases, just when shippers could least afford them and when competing agencies were striving desperately to take away business. The ICC could offer only a little relief. With 60 percent of their total capitalization in bonds, on which interest was payable regardless of earnings, the railroads were in a critical position. Many were saved from outright collapse only by loans from the Reconstruction Finance Corporation. Deficits in 1932 and the failure to recover in the first half of the next year led to the Emergency Transportation Act of 1933.

The Emergency Act contained two parts. One was designed to relieve the railroads of immediate financial pressure; the other made important

The railroad still accounts for more intercity freight traffic than any other mode of transportation. One of the few postwar technological innovations in railroading—the "piggyback" of long-distance truck cargoes—is shown here.

amendments to the Interstate Commerce Act. The emergency provisions tried to promote cooperation among the lines, elimination of "wasteful competitive practices," and financial reorganizations to reduce fixed charges. But in the years of severe strain not even temporary relief was secured by these means. Changes in the Interstate Commerce Act marked the passing of two cherished notions. The 1920 rule of rate-making was abandoned. Instead of fixing rates on the old "fair-return" standard, the ICC was directed to consider the carriers' need for sufficient revenues to provide an adequate transportation service. Further, the highly controversial "recapture" clause was repealed. Railroads with high earnings had continuously resisted efforts to take away their excesses over a "fair-return" standard, and weak roads that needed loans from recaptured funds could not meet the stringent mortgage requirements. No one argued to retain this foolish law.

The 1933 act tenaciously clung to the idea of consolidation, even though by then it had lost its universal appeal. The combination of strong and weak roads to form large rail systems was resisted, for obvious reasons, by the stockholders of the money-making lines. Labor feared such consolidations because they would mean a reduction in jobs. Shippers believed consolidations would result in higher rates. Yet those who dealt with the problem of the financial deterioration of the railroads could cling only to this one hope.

The severity and length of the depression in railroading was bewildering. Ton-miles of freight and passenger-miles fell even more than in competing transportation modes. What was worse, recovery in the railroad industry lagged far behind the rest of the economy. In 1938, roads controlling one-third of total mileage were in receivership, and only the threat of war in Europe created enough business to keep many lines from bankruptcy. The chief source of difficulty was the Depression, of course, but the failure of the railroads to respond to the general improvement in the economy in the mid-1930s must be blamed on other causes. Competition from the trucking industry and the private automobile, as well as from pipelines and water carriers, produced devastating effects. Coal, the principal commodity carried by the railroads, was losing ground to other energy sources, and shipments of building materials—also an important source of railroad revenue—did not recover to pre-Depression levels.

The railroads were buoyed up by the Second World War. To the credit of the industry, it must be said that the handling of traffic was as admirable as it had been sorry during the First World War. Facilities for handling traffic were about the same. Cars and locomotives were fewer in number, but their capacities were greater; railroad mileage was less in 1941 than it was in 1916, but there were more sidings and more double track. The roads were helped by the fact that traffic did not all flow to one coast, by much more commodious port facilities, and by the efficient use of equipment through the car-service division of the American Association of Railroads. An incentive to cooperative effort was the fearsome specter of immediate and probably permanent nationalization of the railroads in the event of a breakdown comparable to that during the First World War. Finally, the Office of Defense Transportation, headed by Joseph B. Eastman, did a masterful job of coordinating the entire effort. The expeditious handling of a volume of rail traffic almost twice that of the First World War stood as a first-class achievement.

Yet only a little while after the war, it became apparent that the railroads were still in serious trouble. From carrying two-thirds of all intercity freight traffic in 1946, the roads slid to little more than two-fifths in 1961; in the meantime, rail passenger traffic dropped from just under 20 percent to less than 3 percent of all passenger-miles. In 1961, the industry earned a minuscule 1.9 percent on its total investment of $27 billion, and railroad employment on Class I lines was only 664,000, less than one-third of the total employed in 1921.

The railroad industry's difficulties were readily attributable to a relative, even absolute, decline in the demand for railroad services. But what caused this catastrophic drop in demand? In part, it resulted from a continuing erosion of the bulk-commodity traffic. Much of the coal business, for example, disappeared as the transmission of electricity over long-distance, high-voltage lines made it possible to burn coal at a mine site or at a generating station along the Ohio River. The St. Lawrence Seaway diverted enormous tonnages of grain from the eastern trunk lines to waterways, and iron ore can now be shipped from foreign countries to salt water's edge instead of traveling cross-country and adding to domestic ton-miles. Water transport by river and canal has chewed away at the carriage of bulk goods at one extreme, and motor carriers have skimmed much of the traffic cream by moving high-tariff items swiftly across an ever-improving highway network. It was not just *how much* the trucks hauled but *what* they hauled that mattered.

The growing competitive problems of the railways were recognized by legislators. By stating a new rule of rate-making in the Transportation Act of 1958, Congress encouraged the ICC to stimulate weakened business with rates that would bring lost business back. Section 15a was amended by the following paragraph:

> In a proceeding involving competition between carriers of different modes of transportation subject to this Act, the Commission, in determining whether a rate is lower than a reasonable minimum rate, shall consider the facts and circumstances attending the movement of the traffic by the carrier or carriers to which the rate is applicable. Rates of a carrier shall not be held up to a particular level to protect the traffic of any other mode of transportation, giving due consideration to the objectives of the national transportation policy declared in this Act.

Although written in the language of bureaucratese, this passage is fairly clear. The ICC can allow the railroads or other carriers to compete by lowering prices, but it does not have to.

In the 1970s and 1980s the railways held their own, perhaps even made something of a comeback. Higher fuel prices made motor carriers and airlines somewhat less effective competitors than they had been. The formation of the National Railroad Passenger Corporation (Amtrak) in 1970 nationalized passenger transport and left the private lines with the more profitable freight business. Railroads will continue to play a major role in this sector. But their long-run position will depend on relative price changes, relative demands for the bulk commodities that railroads like to carry, and technological improvements that are hard to forecast.

Motor Carriers

Improved highways, better trucks, and the large pneumatic tire were responsible for the commercial success of a new form of transportation— the truck line. It was not hard to get into the trucking business. A few hundred dollars would make the down payment on a truck, and one truck was the only piece of equipment many of the early operators owned. When the Depression came, many unemployed truck drivers purchased a truck on credit and started an intercity truck "line." In this way, they bought themselves a job that would last as long as they could pay out-of-pocket expenses like gas and oil and meet the equipment payments. These shoe-string operators did not keep books or take out insurance, and few worried about covering all their costs. Thousands of them hauled freight, and the mushrooming industry soon began to suffer all the pangs of over supply, at least temporarily.

There were those who argued that truck lines ought to compete freely among themselves and that competition should be carried further to permit all of the various transportation modes to strive in any way to take business away from rivals. But there were many sources of opposition to such a policy. The large, well-established operators in the trucking industry felt their profits being reduced by the undercutting of a mass of small-scale carriers. The market, as they put it, was "chaotic" and needed the quick restoration of order.[6] Some New Dealers even proposed that all of the competing transportation industries should be welded into rational systems, and that each type of carrier should perform the service for which it was best suited.

But the idea of forming great regional transportational systems comprised of all different types of carriers was abandoned in favor of a plan of interindustry competition. Each new transportation industry was nevertheless to be regulated in Washington as it approached maturity. The Motor Carriers Act of 1935 was the first major attempt to bring an industry other than the railroads under almost total regulation. This act became Part II

---

[6]To this day, the first argument for regulation advanced by large trucking interests has been that a regulatory authority prevents "chaos," meaning that the big companies are thereby spared certain of the less pleasant manifestations of a competitive industry.

of the Interstate Commerce Act. The law exempted certain types of motor carriers, such as vehicles used to carry agricultural products, and subjected trucks and buses owned and operated by firms that were not in the transport business to only minor supervision.

The Motor Carriers Act directed the ICC to license carriers and set rates. In general, rates were to be "just and reasonable" and nondiscriminatory, but the rule of rate-making, like the one applying to the railroads, allowed the ICC to exercise wide discretion. The ICC *might* fix both maximum and minimum rates for common carriers; for contract carriers, only minimum rates might be prescribed, and no undue advantage over any common carriers was to be granted. Other provisions were included to assure *total* regulation of interstate motor carriers, like that of the railroads. Records and accounts were to be kept and reports made as prescribed. Securities issues of large lines were placed under the scrutiny of the ICC, and all of the provisions governing intercorporate relationships of the railroads—the control of consolidations, pooling, and the like—applied to motor carriers as well.

For a while after 1935, it appeared that the hand of the regulatory authority would weigh as heavily on the trucking industry as it had on the railroads. But after a desperate time during the Second World War due to tire and gasoline rationing, the motor-carrier industry expanded tremendously, and the greatest growth was that of private trucks rather than common carriers. The Interstate Highway System, by adding speed and flexibility and thereby permitting refinements of scheduling, encouraged the expansion of private trucking, because from this point inventories could be largely carried in transit. Yet the relatively slower growth of the common motor carrier meant that in the 1960s and 1970s only one-third of all truck traffic was regulated. By keeping new competitors out of the business and setting rates that protected the least-efficient common carriers, the ICC encouraged shippers to maintain their own transportation facilities. Even though private carriers were fully loaded in both directions little more than 7 percent of the time, it is apparently cheaper for companies to own their own fleets than to hire specialists who are granted monopoly rates by the ICC.[7]

The Airlines

During the 1930s, people were still thrilling to the new speed records that were being set by aviators. As multiengined aircraft provided safer and more economical flights, people began to travel by air. The early airlines did not fail to take advantage of the adventuresome appeal of their service. They were clever enough to capitalize on the luxury and glamour of air

---

[7]Though few would disagree that the ICC has been a failure, there is considerable disagreement as to why it has failed. For one assessment, see Ari and Olive Hoogenboom, *A History of the ICC* (New York: W.W. Norton, 1976).

travel. Hostesses were also registered nurses, meals were served on a complimentary basis, and attention was lavished on the traveler. Such treatment eased the qualms of passengers who reflected on the unenviable safety records of airlines in the early years of commercial air transportation.

Regulation of the growing air transportation industry had long been under consideration by the government. By the mid-1930s, three administrative agencies were rivals for regulatory authority: the Department of Commerce, the ICC, and the Post Office Department, the last by virtue of its power to fix rates and subsidies for airmail. In 1937, legislation was proposed that would have placed commercial air transportation, along with the railroads and the motor carriers, under the jurisdiction of the ICC. This legislation was not enacted, partly because President Roosevelt, himself an aviation enthusiast, wanted a separate commission to be created that had promotional as well as regulatory powers.

The Civil Aeronautics Act of 1938, which created the Civil Aeronautics Authority, established the first real economic regulation of commercial air transport. Two years later the Authority was reorganized. At this time, Congress established within the Authority (then an agency in the Department of Commerce) the Civil Aeronautics Administration (CAA) and the Civil Aeronautics Board (CAB). The CAA was to handle all matters pertaining to the airways system, enforcement of safety rules laid down by the CAB, and promotion of airline traffic. The CAB was to be in charge of economic regulation and the determination and issuance of all rules relating to safety.

From its inception, the Civil Aeronautics Board exercised authority over the airlines similar to the authority exercised by the ICC over land carriers. The CAB issued certificates of public convenience and necessity to domestic carriers and permits to lines operating between the United States and foreign countries. It set minimum and maximum tariffs. Control over intercompany relationships has been complete and final. Provisions of the law have permitted a tighter regulation than that exercised over any other kind of transportation facility. Moreover, the CAB was directed to do everything in its power to further the progress of commercial aviation. This provision has resulted in a rate-making policy that until recently protected the airlines from continuing losses and in a paternalism that has neglected the welfare of competing transportation industries altogether.

For more than a decade, the CAB assured the airlines of profitable operations by means of an airmail subsidy. The Civil Aeronautics Act directed the CAB, in fixing rates, to consider "the need of each such carrier for compensation for the transportation of mail sufficient to ensure the performance of such service and, together with all other revenue of the air carrier under honest, economical, and efficient management, to maintain and continue the development of air transportation to the extent and of the character and quality required for the commerce of the United States, the Postal Service, and the United States." The Board interpreted the "need" of the airlines in a sense most favorable to them. Any company that was not run dishonestly or inefficiently could obtain sufficient airmail payments to make up any operating losses and provide stockholders with a "fair" return on their investment. Under this system, of course, there was no way to be sure what portion of payments was a proper reimbursement for carrying the mail and what portion was pure subsidy. Congress had said, in effect, that the airlines could operate on a cost-plus basis.

Due to the growing complexity of air traffic, the Federal Aviation Act of 1958 established a Federal Aviation Agency (FAA) to exercise control over the physical facilities of civil aviation, including the safety regulatory functions of the Civil Aeronautics Board. The agency's administrator, who reported directly to the President, coordinated the requirements of national defense and commercial aviation and in effect had complete charge of the aviation system. The Transportation Act of 1966, which established the Department of Transportation, kept the acronym FAA while redesignating the agency the Federal Aviation Administration. Although air-traffic control is the agency's most time-consuming function, it also conducts an aggressive program of research and development on air safety, maintains training and mechanical facilities, and works in cooperation with the International Civil Aviation Organization (ICAO) to achieve uniformity of standards, practices, and safety rules throughout the world.

The CAB maintained high air fares to keep total returns up, and freely awarded new operating rights on trunk routes. In 1967–68, the CAB allowed American, TWA, and United to increase the number of daily nonstop flights between New York and Chicago from 102 to 135. Introducing larger planes, the carriers increased average aircraft capacity by 4.4 seats at the same time. Although air traffic rose 10 percent, total capacity increased so much that the average load factor (percentage of seats occupied) dropped from 59 to 47. As load factors and profits dropped, the three companies appealed to the CAB for fare increases, which the obliging agency granted.[8] Because of episodes like this, new laws in the 1970s deregulated the airlines and eliminated the CAB. As a result, many fares on heavily used routes were reduced, and many smaller cities were dropped from routes.

Domestic Water Carriers

Although water traffic continued to fall in relative importance, it remained important on the Great Lakes, the Ohio River, and on the coastal lanes in the early twentieth century. Proponents of inland water use, along with the Army Corps of Engineers to abet them, were repeatedly successful in per-

---

[8]That CAB-approved rates were often on the high side is evidenced by the California experience of the 1960s and 1970s where state-regulated fares were 40 percent below those elsewhere in the United States and despite phenomenally high traffic between Los Angeles and San Francisco.

suading Congress for funds for harbors, and rivers, especially with the impetus of the Great Depression.

Like all other transportation systems, domestic water carriers also eventually fell under federal regulation. During the 1930s, there was agitation for unified government control over inland water carriers, although the reasons for regulation were less compelling than in the cases of the motor carriers and the airlines. By 1938, common carriers in the intercoastal, coastal, and Great Lakes trade were required under Maritime Commission

Despite new modes of travel, the canal remains charmingly inexpensive, particularly to bulk-cargo shippers. Here, an oil tanker clears a lock in the Erie Canal near Waterford, New York, with its usual few inches to spare.

authority to fix rates, but contract carriers were excluded from regulation. The ICC had jurisdiction over the common ship carriers owned by the railroads. The railroads complained that their water lines were much more restricted than those under Maritime Commission control, and lobbied steadily for the inclusion of all lines in a comprehensive regulatory act. Sentiment among transportation experts and members of Congress was generally also favorable toward unifying legislation. The Transportation Act of 1940 transferred jurisdiction over all water carriers engaged in interstate commerce from the Maritime Commission to the ICC. Control provisions with regard to water carriers were similar to those previously applied to railroads and motor carriers, and these provisions became Part III of the Interstate Commerce Act. However, so many exemptions were granted (all private carriers were exempt for example) that there was little left to regulate; and not more than 10 percent of inland-waterway traffic was under ICC jurisdiction in the 1970s.

The Merchant Marine

Consistent with the laissez-faire philosophy of the decade, the Merchant Marine Act of 1920 was designed to remove the federal government from the foreign shipping business. Government-owned vessels were to be sold at low prices to shipping companies, which were to receive tax advantages and construction loans on favorable terms. But even though these ships moved into private hands, the merchant marine continued to dwindle. An act of 1928, which attempted to bolster the merchant marine by increasing indirect subsidies, especially through mail payments, was of no avail. Tonnage in the foreign trade dropped from 11 million in 1920 to 7 million in 1929; a decade later, tonnage was down to about 3.3 million. By 1935, only one-third of U.S. exports and imports, and a negligible portion of the remainder of world trade, was carried by American ships. Although in the late 1930s, the American merchant fleet was still second only to that of Britain in tonnage, it was slow and old; within another few years, it would have been almost entirely obsolete.

For reasons of national defense, in 1936 Congress reversed the long-standing policy of not granting direct subsidies to carriers in the foreign service. The Merchant Marine Act established a new government bureau, the United States Maritime Commission, which was authorized to grant "construction differential" and "operating differential" subsidies. The purpose of the act was to help American shipbuilders and ship operators compete so that the American merchant fleet would carry a substantial part of U.S. foreign commerce. On application by a qualified concern, the commission would undertake construction of a vessel in an American shipyard, at the same time contracting to sell it to the applicant for a price equal to the cost of building the vessel abroad. The difference between the actual cost and the estimated foreign cost was the amount of the "construction differential" subsidy, which was supposed to be no more than 50 percent of the cost of construction in an American shipyard. If, however, certain features especially useful for national defense were incorporated in the ship, the government would absorb their costs.[9]

The principle of the operational subsidy was the same; the Commission would make up the difference between the cost of operation under U.S. ownership and the cost of operation under a foreign flag. A recapture clause in the contracts enabled the government to claim half of any profits in excess of 10 percent per year over a ten-year period.

The assistance rendered to the shipping industry between 1936 and 1941 did not produce a merchant fleet large enough to transport troops and supplies to the fighting fronts in the Second World War. The Liberty ships and Victory ships of the war years were built on government account, so the construction and operating programs under the Maritime Commission were interrupted. After Pearl Harbor, shipyards that had been acres of weeds, rotting timbers, and rusting iron were refurbished, and new shipyards sprang up on inland waterways, in back channels, and on the Great Lakes. For the first time in the history of shipbuilding, component parts were fabricated at inland points and assembled on the coasts.

Since the Second World War, the merchant marine has enjoyed indirect benefits that are of greater monetary value than the amounts it has received for construction and operational differential subsidies. In the Merchant Ship Sales Act of 1946, Congress provided for the sale of hundreds of high-quality ships on terms especially favorable to American-flag operators. Several hundred first-rate dry-cargo vessels were sold for as low as one-third their prewar cost. Other indirect benefits have included the charter of government-owned vessels under favorable terms, assured loans at low interest rates for ship-construction programs, and the guarantee to U.S. operators of half the business shipped under the European Recovery Program and the military-aid program. Direct subsidy payments have been resumed under the Federal Maritime Commission—an independent agency that performs the standard regulatory functions of determining the rates, services, and practices of seagoing vessels that serve as common carriers and that actually executes the subsidy contracts with shipping companies.

In the intensely competitive world of international ocean shipping, the United States lost its leadership more than a century ago, largely because foreign-built and foreign-operated ships produced a service at lower cost per ton-mile than American-built and -operated ships did. Beginning in the mid-1960s, there were signs of a possible revival of American leadership in this field. The innovation was the container ship, with its containers loaded six deep in the holds and three deep above deck. Specially designed

---

[9]Through this device, the liner *United States,* which cost an estimated $70 million, was made available to the United States Lines for only $28 million. The great liner was retired in 1969 because it could not cover costs despite the receipt of both construction and operating subsidies.

vessels, such as the Lancer and the SL-7, with top speeds of 24–33 knots, had tremendous competitive advantages, but the primary U.S. advantage was the drastic reduction in labor costs that resulted from container loading. The United States did not gain a monopoly in container shipping, which constitutes 60 percent of the shipping on the North Atlantic run, but a few such companies as Sea Land Service, Incorporated, and United States Lines, Incorporated, at least compete for business outside the constraints of the primitive labor relations that nearly destroyed the American shipping industry.

Government and Transportation Today

Despite President Kennedy's plea in 1962 for greater reliance on "unsubsidized privately owned facilities, operating under the incentives of private profit and the checks of competition," the federal government continues to play a major role in the financing of transportation. Table 29-1 summarizes federal expenditures for transportation by function for 1970–85. In 1985 $25.8 billion, 2.7 percent of the federal budget, was spent on transportation. The first Reagan administration did succeed in reducing the growth rate of transportation expenditures, and, due to the continuing inflation, was even able to cut them somewhat in real terms. But given the long history of federal spending in this area, and given the relentless pursuit of these funds by powerful special interests, it would be premature to predict that a new era has arrived.

We tend to be more optimistic, however, about the trend toward deregulation of the transport sector. As many advocates of deregulation have noted, the growth of private transportation, while leaving a few pockets of monopoly, has removed much of the need for conventional regulation; the greatest measure of consumer and customer protection now lies in the power of individuals to move themselves and their goods by *private* vehicles

TABLE 29-1   Federal Expenditures for Transportation, 1970–85 (in billions)

	1970	1975	1980	1985
Expenditures in current dollars				
Ground	$4.7	$ 7.0	$15.3	$17.6
Air	1.4	2.4	3.7	4.9
Water	.9	1.4	2.2	3.2
Other	.03	.07	.1	.1
Total	7.0	10.9	21.3	25.8
Total expenditures in 1970 dollars[a]	7.0	7.7	10.5	9.7
Percent of total federal expenditures	3.6	3.3	3.6	2.7

[a]Adjusted using the GNP deflator.

Source: *Statistical Abstract of the United States, 1987* (Washington, D.C.: GPO, 1986), pp. 417 and 578.

over public highways, waterways, and air routes. Government can exercise its most effective control and influence through public expenditures on public transportation.

SELECTED REFERENCES AND SUGGESTED READINGS

Armstrong, Ellis L., ed. *History of Public Works of the United States, 1776–1976.* Chicago: American Public Works Association, 1976.

Bain, Joe S. *Environmental Decay.* Boston: Little, Brown, 1973.

Baker, Gladys, and Wayne Rasmussen. *The Department of Agriculture.* New York: Praeger, 1972.

Barger, Harold. *The Transportation Industries, 1889–1946: A Study of Output, Employment, and Productivity.* New York: National Bureau of Economic Research, 1951.

Benedict, Murray R. *Farm Policies of the United States, 1790–1950.* New York: Twentieth Century Fund, 1953.

Caves, Richard. *Air Transport and Its Regulators.* Cambridge: Harvard Univ. Press, 1962.

Cochrane, Willard W. *American Farm Policy.* Minneapolis: Univ. of Minnesota Press, 1976.

Cochrane, Willard W., and Mary E. Ryan. *American Farm Policy, 1948–1973.* Minneapolis: Univ. of Minnesota Press, 1976.

Droze, Walmon H. *High Dams and Slack Waters: T.V.A. Rebuilds a River.* Baton Rouge: Louisiana State Univ. Press, 1965.

Hoogenboom, Ari, and Olive Hoogenboom. *A History of the ICC.* New York: W.W. Norton, 1976.

Howe, Charles W., et al. *Inland Waterway Transportation.* Washington D.C.: Resources for the Future, 1969.

Johnson, D. Gale. "The Food and Agriculture Act of 1977: Implications for Farmers and Taxpayers." In *Contemporary Economic Problems,* ed. William Fellner. Washington, D.C.: American Enterprise Institute, 1978, pp. 167–210.

Lawrence, Samuel A. *United States Merchant Shipping Policies and Politics.* Washington, D.C.: Brookings Institution, 1966.

Mathiessen, Peter. *Sal Si Puedes: Cesar Chavez and the New American Revolution.* New York: Random House, 1969.

Merck, Frederick. *History of the Westward Movement.* New York: Knopf, 1978.

Meyer, John R., et al. *The Economics of Competition in the Transportation Industries.* Cambridge: Harvard Univ. Press, 1959.

O'Loughlin, Carleen. *Economics of Sea Transport.* London: Pergamon Press, 1967.

Paxon, F. L. "The Highway Movement, 1916–1935." *American Historical Review* 51 (1946): 236–53.

President's National Commission on Rural Poverty. *The People Left Behind.* Washington D.C.: GPO, 1967.

Rasmussen, Wayne D., ed. *Agriculture in the United States,* vol. 4. New York: Random House, 1975.

Ruttan, Vernon W., et al. *Agricultural Policy in an Affluent Society.* New York: W.W. Norton, 1969.

Schlebecker, John T. *Whereby We Thrive, A History of American Farming, 1607–1972.* Ames: Iowa State Univ. Press, 1975.

Seneca, Joseph J., and Michael K. Taussig. *Environmental Economics,* 3rd ed. Englewood Cliffs, N.J.: Prentice-Hall, 1984.

Stover, John F. *The Life and Decline of the American Railroad.* New York: Oxford Univ. Press, 1970.

White, Lawrence J. *The Automobile Industry Since 1945.* Cambridge: Harvard Univ. Press, 1971.

C H A P T E R　　30

Labor's Progress since 1945

HOURS AND WAGES

To assess the important gains of labor in modern times, we begin with the issue of hours and wages. To recall, during the First World War the 48-hour workweek was accepted and standardized in many manufacturing industries, and by 1920 some agreements granted a half-holiday on Saturday. Not until 1930, however, was a 48-hour week standard for most occupations. Pressures to "share the work" helped to shorten the standard workweek during the 1930s. The Fair Labor Standards Act of 1938, covering industries engaged in interstate commerce, set a maximum standard workweek of 40 hours and authorized "time and a half" rates for overtime work. In 1940, half a day's work on Saturday was still not uncommon, but the end of the Second World War saw its virtual disappearance. There was an expansion of weekend and evening work in retailing and services, but by 1950, the 40-hour week was standard in manufacturing. In some industries and in offices many workers were becoming accustomed to a 35-hour week. Continued advances in the postwar period lowered the average workweek for all workers by nearly 10 percent, even though no change occurred in manufacturing.

As well as more leisure time, nearly all workers had higher incomes by mid-century. As illustrated in Figure 30-1, the average weekly income of wage earners in manufacturing increased more than nine-fold over the years 1929–77, while consumer prices were more than tripling during the same period. Taking into account the rising cost of living, *real* weekly earnings in manufactures advanced more than 160 percent during these years.[1]

Of particular interest are the movements of real earnings over shorter periods. During the Great Depression money wages fell moderately with earnings dropping somewhat more because of less hours worked per week.

---

[1]This more than doubling in the 50-year period does not include the increase in "fringe benefits" such as paid vacations and company pension plans, which were also important gains.

634

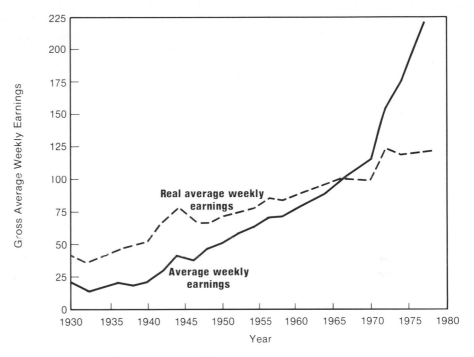

FIGURE 30-1   Indexes of Weekly Earnings in Manufacturing (1967 = 100).

Sources: *Historical Statistics of the United States, Colonial Times to 1970* (Washington D.C.: GPO, 1975), series D804, E135 and (for 1971–1977 data) *Economic Report of the President, 1987* (Washington D.C.: GPO, 1987), pp. 293, 307.

Because of sharp price reductions, however, average *real* earnings fell only slightly. These figures do not reflect the great burden imposed on unemployed workers who had no earnings at all, but precisely for that reason it is surprising that real earnings per employed worker did not fall by more. We would expect, in other words, that a fall in the demand for labor would produce a decline in the real wage rate, and that a new equilibrium would be reached with supply equal to demand. Instead, real wages remained fairly high, and there was a large gap between the supply and demand for labor in the 1930s.

Various explanations have been offered for this phenomenon. John Maynard Keynes, for example, argued that unions refused to agree to nominal wage cuts because they had no way of knowing that such cuts would help push the real wage toward equilibrium.[2] Others have argued that unemployed workers followed a strategy of lowering their reservation wage (the

---

[2]On Keynes's ideas see Axel Leijonhufvud, *On Keynesian Economics and the Economics of Keynes* (New York: Oxford Univ. Press, 1968), pp. 331–53.

wage at which they would agree to work) slowly. In any case, the problem of downward wage rigidity was a part of the unemployment problem in the Depression and subsequent recessions.

In the immediate postwar period, 1945–48, money earnings in manufacturing advanced by 25 percent, and yet the inflation of these years was so great that real earnings actually fell.[3] Not until 1949 did real earnings begin to advance steadily.

The data in Figure 30-2 provides a more detailed look at recent years. Real earnings are the average hourly earnings of production workers or nonsupervisory workers divided by the consumer price index. Real compensation includes fringe benefits such as pensions and health insurance. A break seems to have occurred in 1972 when real earnings levelled off and then declined. Partly this was a statistical phenomenon. If we take employer contributions to pensions and health plans into account (the upper line) then we see growth continuing after 1972, but at a reduced rate. This slowdown—linked, as it was, with a productivity slowdown and a decline in international competitiveness—was a cause of much concern, and we will analyze it further in Chapter 31.

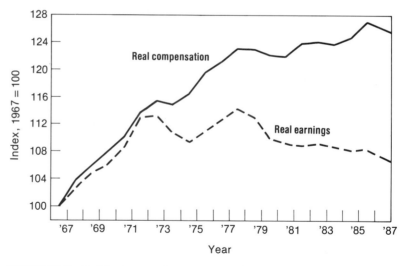

FIGURE 30-2   Real Earnings and Compensation, 1967–87.

Source: *Economic Report of the President, 1988* (Washington, D.C.: GPO, 1988), p. 70.

---

[3]The price statistics, however, probably failed to fully incorporate the improvements in the quality and availability of goods and services that occurred as the economy converted to a peacetime basis, and so overstate the inflation.

THE RISE OF THE SERVICE SECTOR

The most important change in the demand for labor since the Second World War was the growth of the white-collar sector, that diverse grouping that includes retail trade, finance, education, medicine, entertainment, and so on. Table 30-1 shows the expansion of this sector in quantitative terms. As we can see, the major declining sectors were agriculture, mining, and construction. Their combined share of GNP fell from 19.5 percent in 1949 to 10.7 percent in 1985. The major expanding sectors were finance and services; their share rose from 21.7 percent of GNP in 1949 to 29.6 percent in 1985. Certain sectors in Table 30-1 may surprise us. Manufacturing has not been a declining sector in the postwar period. Overall the manufacturing sector was able to hold on to or even increase its share of GNP. Certain subsectors of manufacturing in the older industrial regions, of course, have declined in the postwar period. But other sectors such as computers and certain regions such as the South and West have prospered. More rapid productivity growth, however, meant that the share of manufacturing in employment (as opposed to GNP) declined. Perhaps the most surprising trend is in the government's share, which has fallen from 14.8 percent in 1949 to 11.1 percent in 1985. But remember that this figure is based on the goods and services produced by the government. Transfer payments such as Social Security do not enter into this measure of the relative size of government. When these are included, an upward trend in the role of government emerges.

Most new jobs were created in the expanding sectors. These jobs were white-collar jobs in which education and experience were more important to success than physical strength. This was one cause of the rapid assimilation of female workers into the labor force that we will explore in the next section. To a large extent the pattern of rising and falling sectors was a matter of demand. As real incomes rose, the demand for certain products

TABLE 30-1   The Changing Pattern of Economic Activity, 1949–85 (percent of GNP)

Sector	1949	1959	1969	1979	1985
Agriculture	5.5%	4.0%	2.7%	2.4%	2.6%
Mining	5.9	5.8	5.3	4.1	3.6
Construction	8.1	9.8	7.6	5.4	4.5
Manufacturing	20.4	20.7	22.1	21.8	21.7
Transportation	8.2	7.6	8.3	9.2	9.0
Wholesale and retail trade	15.0	14.8	14.9	16.0	16.9
Finance	10.1	12.0	13.0	14.4	14.6
Services	11.6	11.3	11.9	13.5	15.0
Government	14.8	14.3	14.0	11.8	11.1
Rest of the world and residual	.4	-.3	.2	1.4	.9

Source: *Economic Report of the President, 1987* (Washington, D.C.: GPO, 1987), p. 257.

such as consumer durables increased slowly, while demand for others such as medical care or insurance increased rapidly. But other trends played a role in the growth of the financial and service sectors. The expansion of educational opportunities lowered the relative wages of highly skilled workers, increasing output in sectors that rely on these services. Inflation and deregulation encouraged firms in the financial sector to offer an array of new products.

Sometimes people question whether the white-collar sectors are truly productive. There is an ancient prejudice against people who merely push papers around in favor of those who produce something physical like wheat or automobiles. Even Adam Smith distinguished between productive labor (used to produce goods) and unproductive labor (used to produce services). And recent proposals to "reindustrialize" America derive part of their influence from this prejudice. But clearly these sectors do contribute to our economic welfare. Extra life insurance, for example, may contribute as much to the purchaser's sense of well-being as an extra automobile. It is true that mistakes are made; on occasion capital may be invested in a business producing a service that could have been more profitably invested in manufacturing. But on the whole the reason why finance and services have expanded more rapidly in the postwar period is that we valued their output more than the product of other sectors.

Productivity growth in the expanding sectors has been comparatively slow, and this has contributed to the slowdown in the growth of real wages. However, this does not mean that the economy would grow faster if we invested more in other sectors. Expansion of some sectors has favorable external effects on others. For example, productivity growth in education may be relatively slow, but the expansion of the education sector contributes to the manufacturing sector by supplying new techniques and better-educated workers.

The growth of the financial and service sectors has also contributed to economic stability. A decrease in demand often leads quickly to unemployment in the manufacturing sector. But in the white-collar sectors employers are often willing to continue to employ workers even though they do not make a positive contribution to current profits. Oftentimes, for example, an employee will have specialized knowledge or long-term relationships with customers that make the employee hard to replace. So the rise of the service and financial sectors has tended to lessen the impact of recessions on employment in the postwar period.

THE CHANGING ROLE OF WOMEN IN THE LABOR FORCE

The most dramatic trend in the supply of labor after the war was the increase in the proportion of women in the paid labor force. Table 30-2 shows the key ratios at decade-long intervals. Since the war the proportion of women

TABLE 30-2   Labor Force Participation of Men and Women, 1949–86 (workers as a percentage of the noninstitutional population)

Year	Total	Male	Female
1949	58.9%	86.4%	33.1%
1959	59.3	83.7	37.1
1969	60.1	79.8	42.7
1979	63.7	77.8	50.9
1986	65.3	76.3	55.3

Source: *Economic Report of the President, 1987* (Washington, D.C.: GPO, 1987), p. 284.

in the labor force has increased steadily. The proportion of men in the labor force has declined, but less rapidly; so overall the proportion of Americans who are working or seeking work in the paid labor force has risen steadily and is now at an all-time peak.

The explanation for this trend is complex. Demographic factors have played an important role. The average number of children in a family declined from three or four at the beginning of the century to one or two in the 1980s. Over the same period the average life expectancy of women increased. Together these trends meant that women had many more years to pursue a career after the burdens of rearing a family moderated. The increased rate of divorce also encouraged women to invest in a career outside the home. We should not forget, however, that the interaction of these trends was complicated. For example, the rising participation rate of women in the paid labor force encouraged women to choose divorce who would have been unable to afford it in earlier periods; causation, in other words, ran from the divorce rate to the labor-force participation rate of women, and back again from the participation rate to the divorce rate.

Other trends were also important. For much of this period, real wages were rising, which, other things being equal, would tend to draw women into the paid work force. We have already mentioned another important development. The rapidly growing sectors, finances and services, put a premium on education (and educational opportunities for women were expanding rapidly), rather than on physical strength, the area in which male workers typically had a comparative advantage. Some historians would assign some weight to the growing availability and technological sophistication of consumer durables. Labor-saving devices such as electric washing machines and refrigerators, low maintenance fabrics, telephone answering machines, and so on reduced the labor input in home maintenance.

The new feminist movement also helped to break down discrimination against women workers through moral suasion and political action. Until the 1960s the postwar period had seen little activity that would predict the feminist movement to come. A key event was President Kennedy's appointment of a Presidential Commission on the Status of Women in 1961 with the venerable Eleanor Roosevelt as its honorary chairwoman. Partly as a result of the recommendations of the Commission, Congress passed the Equal Pay Act in 1963, which called for equal pay for equal work. Title VII of the Civil Rights Act passed in the following year, barred discrimination in hiring, promoting, or firing workers on the basis of race, color, religion, national origin, or sex and set up the Equal Employment Opportunity Commission to help enforce the law. Some lawsuits under the 1964 Act have been for substantial amounts. In 1973 AT&T settled out of court a complaint concerning equal pay for $45 million. In 1965 the President created the Office of Federal Contract Compliance Program to require affirmative action plans from employers doing business with the federal government. Affirmative action is more than a color-blind, sex-neutral labor policy; it requires positive efforts to find workers traditionally discriminated against. In 1966 the National Organization for Women was founded partly to pressure the government into vigorous use of its new antidiscriminatory legislation.

The 1970s witnessed further successes for the feminist movement. Title IX of the Educational Amendments Act of 1972 extended the Civil Rights Act to educational institutions. One consequence of Title IX was to increase the participation of women in high school and college sports. But in the late 1970s and in the 1980s the new feminist movement seemed to lose momentum and was unable to win major legislative victories.

The Gender Gap

Despite federal legislation, a considerable gap remained between the earnings of men and women in a variety of occupations. Table 30-3, which is taken from a paper by Claudia Goldin, one of the leading experts in the field, shows the gender gap in six broad occupational classifications in 1890, 1930, and 1970. It is surprising that the persistence of the gender gap and its tendency in every class of occupations except "professional" increased between 1930 and 1970. The factor that seems to have produced much of the increase in the relative earnings of women between 1890 and 1930 was

TABLE 30-3   The Gender Gap: Ratios of Female to Male Earnings

Occupation	1890	1930	1970
Professional	.263	.385	.710
Clerical	.487	.706	.686
Sales	.595	.607	.438
Manual	.535	.575	.557
Service	.530	.598	.558
Farm	.530	.598	.589

Source: Claudia D. Goldin, "The Gender Gap in Historical Perspective," in *Quality and Quantity,* ed. Peter Kilby (Middletown, CT: Wesleyan Univ. Press, 1987), p. 151.

the decline in the premiums for physical strength and education. The premium for physical strength was a victim of the development of muscle-saving technology. The premium for education was a victim of the vast increase in the availability of schooling. Typically men invest more (or have more invested in them by their parents) in the form of education and skill development. So the decline in this premium also tended to put men and women on more of an equal footing in the job market.

What has kept the gender gap from closing is the increase in the participation rate of women. Increasing participation means that the average years of experience of women in the labor force remains relatively low because so many have just entered the labor force. Moreover, since discrimination often blocks women from entering or advancing in certain fields, women entering the labor force have crowded into areas open to them and prevented wages in those areas from rising as fast as in the rest of the economy. In the future, as the labor-force participation rate of women stabilizes and the entire array of jobs created by the economy are opened to women, the gender gap should decline.

MINORITIES

The attempt to bring African-Americans, Hispanic-Americans, and other minority workers into the economic mainstream met with important but limited success in the postwar period. Table 30-4 shows the ratios of black to white, and Spanish-origin to white median-family incomes at five-year intervals from 1950 to 1985. Over the whole period we see a slight increase in the black-white ratio. Black women in particular now earn on a par with white women. Labor economists have not been able to untangle all of the

TABLE 30-4   Black to White and Spanish-Origin to White Median-Family Income Ratios, 1950–85

Year	Black	Spanish Origin[b]
1950	.54[a]	—
1955	.55[a]	—
1960	.55[a]	—
1965	.55[a]	—
1970	.61	—
1975	.62	.67
1980	.58	.67
1985	.58	.65

[a]Includes other races.
[b]Data not available for 1950–70.

Source: *Statistical Abstract of the United States: 1987* (Washington, D.C.: GPO, 1986), p. 436.

factors influencing the trends in the relative earnings of blacks, and especially the relatively strong gains of black women.[4] But it is clear that overcoming traditional discriminatory barriers has been an important part of the story.

The fight for civil rights was a continuous one in the postwar period. In 1947 one of the most famous events occurred, Jackie Robinson broke the color barrier in professional baseball. This was important not only for black athletes who would earn their living in professional sports in the postwar period, but also for the effect it would have on white stereotypes about black abilities. In 1954 the Supreme Court ruled in *Brown* v. *Board of Education of Topeka* that segregated schools were unconstitutional. This decision would have far-reaching consequences for American education. Although many school districts then claimed that they were providing a separate-but-equal education for blacks (a formula laid down by the Supreme Court in *Plessy* v. *Fergusson* in 1896), this was not the case. As documented by Robert Margo in important recent research, black schools were systematically underfunded, and blacks entered the labor force with a severe handicap.[5] *Brown* v. *Board of Education* did not bring about change overnight. Many school districts dragged their feet, and not until the late 1960s when courts began to order busing to achieve racial integration was significant progress made in many areas. Other visible signs of discrimination, such as segregated transportation, were also crumbling as a result of the civil rights movement. The culmination of that movement was the march on Washington in August 1963 at which the young leader of the civil-rights movement, Dr. Martin Luther King, Jr., gave his unforgettable "I Have a Dream" speech. Less than a year later, although one filled with momentous events including the assassination of President Kennedy, the Civil Rights Act was passed, which among other things, as we noted, made it illegal to discriminate in employment.

Between 1965 and 1975 as Table 30-4 shows, there was an increase in the ratio of nonwhite to white median-family incomes and some of this gain, although it is hard to say exactly how much, was due to the breakdown of discriminatory barriers in industries targeted by civil-rights activists and federal authorities. In some industries the changes were dramatic. In southern textiles, for example, whole sectors of the industry that had excluded blacks for generations except in the most menial jobs, now began hiring blacks in significant numbers.

---

[4]In particular, equality of earnings does not mean that there is no discrimination against black women. Greater attachment to the labor force, or other factors, may offset discrimination in pay, promotion, and hiring.

[5]Robert Margo, "Race Differences in Public School Expenditures," *Social Science History* 6 (Winter 1982): pp. 9–33; and "Educational Achievements in Segregated Schools," *American Economic Review* 76 (Sept. 1986): 794–801.

As Gavin Wright explains in his thoughtful book, *Old South, New South*, at this time southern political and business leaders were trying to attract new businesses to the South; they soon realized that a quick resolution of civil rights turmoil was necessary if they were to continue to compete successfully for outside capital. In 1970 the president of Allis-Chalmers Corporation visited Jackson, Mississippi, and expressed doubts about locating a plant there because of the violent ongoing confrontation between black students at Jackson State University and local police. As a result, the deadlock over school integration, then seven years old, was broken and Allis-Chalmers announced plant construction plans.[6] In the late 1970s, however, the ratio of nonwhite to white median-family incomes levelled off, as shown in Table 30-4, and in the 1980s it declined as the nation's attention turned to inflation, the foreign trade deficit, and related problems.

THE NEW IMMIGRATION

There was little change in the immigration laws from the establishment of the quota system in the 1920s until 1965. Perhaps the major exception to this generalization was a program under which Mexican agricultural workers (the Braceros) could work temporarily in the United States. This program was begun during the war (although it is doubtful that it served much of a military purpose) and ended in 1964, a casualty of the wave of liberal legislation in the 1960s.[7]

But in the 1960s a new immigration system was instituted. President Kennedy, in particular, was strongly opposed to a system that he felt reflected racial and ethnic prejudice. The new law eliminated quotas based on the ethnic composition of the population. Instead, a complex system of priorities was established that gave very high priority to uniting families. A limit was placed on the total number of immigrants, but that limit did not include spouses, minor children, or parents of U.S. citizens. In 1980 a separate program for admitting political refugees was created. As a result of these changes the number of immigrants increased, many coming from "new" areas—Latin America, Central America, Asia, and the Caribbean.

Table 30-5 shows annual immigration to the United States at five-year intervals from 1950 to 1985. The acceleration of the rate of immigration after the change in the law in 1965 is obvious from the table; the rate increased from 1.5 per thousand in 1965 to 2.4 in 1985.

---

[6]Gavin Wright, *Old South, New South* (New York: Basic Books, 1986), pp. 266–67.
[7]Lee J. Alston and Joseph P. Ferrie, "The Bracero Program and Farm Labor Legislation in World War II," in *Sinews of War: Essays on the Economic History of World War II*, ed. Geofrey T. Mills and Hugh Rockoff (Ames: Iowa State Univ. Press, forthcoming).

TABLE 30-5   Immigration, 1950–85

Year	Total (in thousands)	Rate (per 1,000 of U.S. population)
1950	249	1.6
1955	238	1.4
1960	265	1.5
1965	297	1.5
1970	373	1.8
1975	386	1.8
1980	531	2.3
1985	570	2.4

Source: (1950–60), *Historical Statistics of the United States, Colonial Times to 1970,* (Washington, D.C.: GPO, 1975), series A29, C89; (1965–85), *Statistical Abstract of the United States: 1987* (Washington, D.C.: GPO, 1986), p. 11.

Immigrants have tended to concentrate in large cities in six states: New York, California, Florida, Texas, New Jersey, and Illinois. The effects of immigration are controversial, and labor economists are far from having reached a consensus on what those effects are. For the immigrants themselves, migration to the United States is often a major economic boon. And immigrants tend on average to do well after arriving here. According to Barry Chiswick, after a decade or two the typical male immigrant earns more than a native-born worker with comparable education and experience.[8] The countries from which the United States receives its immigrants also experience a variety of effects. In recent years considerable concern has been expressed about the "brain drain," the tendency of engineers, scientists, physicians, and similar personnel in developing countries to migrate to the United States.

Many native Americans benefit from immigration: those who own firms that employ immigrants (remember that many people own firms indirectly through retirement funds); those who possess special skills that become more valuable when unskilled labor is widely available; those who consume the products and services that immigrants help produce; those who provide the services consumed by immigrants; and, of course, those who own property in neighborhoods in which immigrants settle. On the other hand, those who compete directly with immigrants may face lower real wages and fewer job opportunities. This has been a problem in particular for unskilled workers in urban areas. But it is hard to say whether these effects have been large or small. Some labor economists have stressed the substitutability between immigrants and native workers which implies lower wages.[9] But others have

[8]Barry R. Chiswick, "The Effect of Americanization on the Earnings of Foreign-born Men," *Journal of Political Economy* 86 (Oct. 1978): 897–921.
[9]Jean Baldwin Grossman, "The Substitutability of Natives and Immigrants in Production," *Review of Economic Statistics,* 64 (1982): 596–603; Vernon M. Briggs, "The Imperative of Immi-

found evidence of complementarity.[10] A sophisticated recent study found evidence of both effects, depending on the group being considered, but stressed that these effects have been small.[11]

Perhaps even more controversial than legal immigration has been the large, although extremely difficult to measure, volume of illegal immigration particularly from Mexico and Latin America. Pressure to do something about illegal immigration led in 1986 to the Immigration Reform and Control Act (Simpson-Rodino bill), which put tough new controls on illegal immigration while at the same time creating an amnesty program for illegal immigrants who had put down roots in this country. Even by 1990 it is still too early to see what the effects of this legislation will be on the volume of illegal immigration and on labor markets.

ORGANIZED LABOR AFTER THE WAR

Membership in labor unions increased sharply during the Depression and the Second World War. The percentage of the nonagricultural unionized labor force rose from 14.7 percent to 20.4 percent between 1933 and 1938, and from 22.5 percent in 1940 to 31.6 percent in 1950, stabilizing in the 1950s. At its peak in 1953, nearly one-third of the nonagricultural labor force was enrolled in labor unions. Since that time, however, there has been a decline that has become precipitate since 1970. This can be seen in Table 30-6, which shows the percentage of the unionized labor force. By 1988 the percentage of the nonagricultural labor force enrolled in unions had fallen back to the level of the early 1930s.

There have been several reasons for the deterioration in the strength of organized labor. We have already discussed one important factor: the rise of the service sector, where employee groups are usually small and have proved more difficult to organize. Moreover, within the goods-producing sector there has been a steady shift from blue-collar to white-collar employment that has slowed the pace of union growth because white-collar workers are less prone to organize. The shift of manufacturing to the South and West, areas traditionally hostile to the labor movement, has also tended to undermine union power. Foreign industrial competition has also undermined organized labor, by making workers in traditional bastions of union

gration Reform," in *Essays on Legal and Illegal Immigration* ed. S. Pozo (Washington D.C.: W. E. Upjohn Institute, 1986), pp. 43–71.

[10]George J. Borjas, "The Substitutability of Black, Hispanic and White Labor," *Economic Inquiry* 21 (1983): 93–106.

[11]Francisco L. Rivera-Batiz and Selig L. Sechzer, "Substitution and Complementarity Between Immigrant and Native Labor in the United States," in *U.S. Immigration Patterns and Policy Reform in the 1980s*, ed. Ira Gang, Francisco L. Rivera-Batiz, and Selig L. Sechzer (forthcoming).

Mass labor meetings like this one are becoming less and less typical of American labor strategy.

strength, such as automobile and steel manufacturing, fearful of layoffs. And foreign-owned plants have been hard to organize because of the unions' lack of control over other operations of the firm and the different traditions of labor relations.

In addition to these economic trends, changes in the legal environment have worked against the unions. Because of opportunities for legislation established by the Taft-Hartley Act, numerous states passed "right-to-work" laws. In 1982, right-to-work laws were on the books in 19 states, many of them in the South, including North Carolina, Florida, and Texas.[12] By making it illegal to enforce the union-shop provisions of an agreement

---

[12]Leo Troy and Neil Sheflin, *U.S. Union Sourcebook,* (West Orange, NJ: Industrial Relations Data and Information Services, 1985), p. 7–9.

TABLE 30-6   Union Membership, 1950–83

Year	Total (in thousands)	Percent of Civilian Nonagricultural Labor Force	Percent of Total Civilian Labor Force
1950	14,294	31.6%	23.0%
1955	16,127	31.8	24.8
1960	15,516	28.6	22.3
1965	18,269	30.1	24.5
1970	20,990	29.6	25.4
1975	22,211	28.9	23.7
1980	20,823	23.0	19.5
1985	19,126	19.6	16.6
1988p	18,150	17.1	14.9

p = preliminary
Source: Leo Troy and Neil Sheflin, *U.S. Union Sourcebook* 1990, second edition, (West Orange, NJ: Industrial Relations Data and Information Services, forthcoming).

within the state concerned, "right-to-work" legislation kept efforts to unionize in a continuous state of reorganization and were a source of friction among union and nonunion workers.

As the decade of the 1950s closed, labor's public relations continued to suffer. The Labor-Management Reporting and Disclosure Act of 1959 (the Landrum-Griffin Act) tightened restrictions on secondary boycotting and organized picketing, required detailed reports on all financial transactions between unions and their officers and members, and provided for secret-ballot elections of union officers, whose terms of office were restricted. Few could object to the provision preventing felons from being union officers for five years after conviction, nor could there be serious reservations about the new rules restricting the freewheeling use of union funds. But the effect of the new law, and the congressional hearings that led up to it, was to focus attention on the minority of corrupt or radical union officials and so undermine the confidence of the public in the union movement.

Intra-labor squabbles have also undermined the movement. At the peak of union strength in 1955 the American Federation of Labor (AFL) and the Congress of Industrial Organizations (CIO) merged, with George Meany becoming the first president. The radical dream of uniting all workers in one big union seemed near at hand, but harmony could not be maintained. Labor unity suffered a particularly severe blow in 1968 when the United Automobile Workers (UAW) under their dynamic leader Walter Reuther left the AFL-CIO in a dispute over politics. Many of the organizational gains, moreover, were being made by independent unions such as the Teamsters, who had been ousted from the AFL-CIO. Thus, critics who blame mainstream union leadership for part of the decline in labor's influence may have a valid point.

Can organized labor regain some of its former influence? The economic trends we have been examining in connection with the union movement seem likely to continue. Perhaps, however, it is best to remember that unionism in the United States has traditionally grown in unexpected jumps that were never predicted by the experts.

SELECTED REFERENCES AND SUGGESTED READINGS

Briggs, Vernon M., Jr. *Immigration Policy and the American Labor Force.* Baltimore: Johns Hopkins Press, 1984.

Chiswick, Barry R. "The Effect of Americanization on the Earnings of Foreign-born Men." *Journal of Political Economy* 86 (Oct. 1978): 897–921.

Cobb, James C. *The Selling of the South: The Southern Crusade for Industrial Development 1936–1980.* Baton Rouge: Louisiana State Univ. Press, 1982.

Cogan, John. "The Decline in Black Teenage Employment: 1950–1970." *American Economic Review* 72 (1982): 621–38.

Freeman, Richard B. "Unionism Comes to the Public Sector." *Journal of Economic Literature* 24 (March 1986): 41–86.

Freeman, Richard B., and James L. Medoff. *What do Unions Do?* New York: Basic Books, 1984.

Goldin, Claudia. "The Changing Economic Role of Women: A Quantitative Approach." *Journal of Interdisciplinary History* 13 (Spring 1983): 707–733.

———. "The Female Labor Force and Economic Growth in the United States, 1890–1980." In *Long Term Trends in the American Economy,* ed. Stanley L. Engerman and Robert Gallman (Chicago: Univ. of Chicago Press, 1986).

———. "The Gender Gap in Historical Perspective." In *Quantity and Quidity: Essays in U.S. Economic History,* ed. Peter Kilby. Middletown, CT: Wesleyan Univ. Press, 1987.

Jacoway, Elizabeth, and David R. Colburn. *Southern Businessmen and Desegregation.* Bagon Rouge: Louisiana State Univ. Press, 1982.

Lloyd, Cynthia B., and Beth T. Niemi. *The Economics of Sex Differentials.* New York: Columbia Univ. Press, 1979.

Mandle, Jay. *The Roots of Black Poverty.* Durham, NC: Duke Univ. Press, 1978.

———. "Race Differences in Public School Expenditures: Disenfranchisement and School Finance in Louisiana, 1890–1910." *Social Science History* 6 (Winter 1982): 9–33.

Margo, Robert. "Educational Achievement in Segregated Schools: The Effects of Separate But Equal." *American Economic Review* 76 (Sept. 1986): 794–801.

———. "Race Differences in Public School Expenditures: Disenfranchisement and School Finance in Louisiana, 1890–1910." *Social Science History* 6 (Winter 1982): 9–33.

Marshall, F. Ray. *Labor in the South.* Cambridge: Harvard Univ. Press, 1967.

Masters, Stanley M. *Black-White Income Differentials.* New York: Academic Press, 1973.

Newman, Robert J. *Growth in the American South: Changing Regional Employment and Wage Patterns in the 1960s and 1970s.* New York: New York Univ. Press, 1984.

Musoke, Moses S., and Alan L. Olmstead. "The Rise of the Cotton Industry in California: A Comparative Perspective." *Journal of Economic History* 42 (1982): 385–412.

O'Neill, June. "Trend in the Male-Female Wage Gap in the United States." *Journal of Labor Economics* 3 (Jan. 1984): S91–S116.

Piore, Michael J. *Birds of Passage.* Cambridge, Eng.: Cambridge Univ. Press, 1979.

Rees, Albert. *The Economics of Trade Unions,* rev. ed. Chicago: Univ. of Chicago Press, 1977.

Street, James H. *The New Revolution in the Cotton Economy.* Chapel Hill: Univ. of North Carolina Press, 1957.

Weinstein, Bernard, and Robert E. Firestone. *Regional Growth and Decline in the United States.* New York: Praeger, 1978.

Wilson, William Julius. *The Declining Significance of Race,* 2nd ed. Chicago: Univ. of Chicago Press, 1980.

Wright, Gavin. *Old South, New South: Revolutions in the Southern Economy Since the Civil War.* New York: Basic Books, 1986.

CHAPTER 31

Has the United States Passed Its Peak?

As the United States entered its third century as a nation, there was much to celebrate. The 200 years since the birth of the nation were mostly years of progress, both social and economic. Though not equally shared among its people, America's tremendous wealth and power were both envied and scorned by people throughout the world.

Although the festivities of the 1976 Bicentennial added historical perspective to the nation's accomplishments and to the richness of the lives of Americans, most generations judge their conditions strictly within the context of their own immediate past. From the short perspective of the 1970s, the Bicentennial provided welcomed relief to many. The nation was in the depth of its sixth post-Second World War recession, and inflation had persisted at high levels for nearly a decade. But there were more than economic events negatively impacting on the nation. The loss of the Vietnam War and its attendant human suffering, both at home and on the battlefields, damaged America's spirit, pride, and trust. The apparent erosion of American influence in world affairs was reinforced by Iran's holding 57 Americans hostage throughout the last 444 days of President Carter's administration. Added to these events were perceptions of failure to meet many domestic social objectives set out in the 1960s. Growing concern over environmental decay and the political trauma of Watergate and presidential disgrace dimmed the brightness of the nation's postwar achievements.

It is now clear that much of the economic strength and many of the achievements of the pre-1965 period have not been maintained since then. The economic expansion that began in President Reagan's first term, as welcome as it was, only seemed to underscore the nation's long-run problems because many of the difficulties that emerged in the 1970s were reduced rather than eliminated. This development raises some tough questions. Were these failures due to unusual "shocks" to the economy unlikely to be repeated, or were they the beginning of an ominous new trend? If it is a trend, is there anything the government can do about it? Or is the government the problem rather than the solution, as the Reagan administration maintained? Putting the developments of these years in historical perspective will help us toward some tentative conclusions.

REAL INCOME

We judge the performance of our economy, first of all, by its ability to generate a rising level of real income for the American people. Table 31-1 shows one source of concern in vivid detail. Median family income is computed by listing the incomes of families in order from high income to low and then finding the one in the absolute middle. It's a better measure of income than a simple average because the average can be distorted by what happens to the relatively small number of families of great wealth and income. A family is defined here as two or more related individuals living in one household. For each quinquennium (a beautiful word meaning a five-year period) prior to 1970 real family income rose by substantial amounts. After 1970 growth virtually ceased, however.

The numbers in Table 31-1 are merely cold statistics. But the nearly 85 percent increase in real median family income between 1950 and 1970 represented a tremendous improvement in U.S. living standards. Civilian per capita consumption of preferred foods like beef, veal, chicken, turkey, ice cream, and processed fruits and vegetables nearly doubled in the postwar period, while much less pork, lard, potatoes, cornmeal, and corn flour were being consumed, although these trends also reflect changes in tastes

TABLE 31-1   Real Median Family Income, 1950–85

Year	Median Gross Family Income (in 1985 dollars)	Annual Growth Rate (percent)
1950	$14,832	—
1955	17,749	3.59%
1960	20,414	2.80
1965	23,720	3.00
1970	27,336	2.84
1975	27,421	.06
1980	27,446	.02
1985	27,735	.21

Source: *Statistical Abstract of the United States, 1987* (Washington, D.C.: GPO, 1986), pp. 436.

as well as incomes. However, the share of consumer spending used for food *fell* from 31 percent in 1941 to 15 percent in 1986. And that spent on clothing also fell, from 12 to 5 percent. In contrast, the share of total consumer spending used to buy or rent a home advanced slightly from 17 to 18 percent, that for transportation rose from 10 to 21 percent, and modest increases also occurred for spending on recreation, and various personal services.

Overall, after 1945 Americans spent more on their homes and house-related items. They used more electricity, more telephones, and heated their homes by gas and oil rather than by coal and wood. Indeed, nearly every American house is now wired for electricity, and more than 90 percent of them are equipped with electric refrigerators, electric washers, and television sets. Perhaps more important, private baths or showers and private flush toilets are available today in more than three out of four American homes. After the war, Americans bought less recreational admissions tickets, but more toys, TVs, sporting equipment, and recreational items and spent more on that great source of freedom, the automobile. Today more than three-fourths of all families own at least one automobile, and one-sixth own two or more. The number of weeks of vacation had doubled in the postwar period to more than 80 million weeks a year by 1960. Those who did not spend leisure time in travel could add to real income by engaging in do-it-yourself projects about the home or could read, play musical instruments, listen to phonograph records or cassettes sold in astronomical numbers, ride recreation vehicles from boats to airplanes, or simply restore vitality by loafing on a patio or in air-conditioned comfort.

On average the level of material well-being changed in form and improved rather dramatically. The basic necessities of life—food, shelter, and clothing—demanded smaller proportions of the family budget, and all groups, poor and rich, shared in these economic advances, although not equally.

After the early 1970s, growth of median real family income slowed to a crawl as shown in Table 31-1. The figures do show that people were about as well off after 1970 as they were before, but the direction of change was crucial. Throughout most of U.S. history with the possible exception of the Great Depression, and especially in the first part of the postwar period, Americans assumed that each succeeding generation would be better off than the one before. Now they were not sure. Their children might be no better off, and possibly worse off than they were.

Before accepting these statistics at face value, we should note that they are influenced by a variety of social and economic trends beyond the capacity of the economy to generate higher incomes. The divorce rate, for example, is influential. If a husband and wife are divorced and, say, the husband lives separately, then what was once a household with a median income could become a household with a reduced income (containing the mother and children) with the husband now recorded as an unrelated individual.

The aging of the population would also have an effect depending on the incomes of older households. The rise of two-earner households, in certain cases but not all, tended to raise median family income.[1]

Some insight into these issues can be gleaned from an examination of Table 31-2. As we can see, the only group that made substantial gains between 1970 and 1984 were females living separately. They were able to take the most advantage of the new job opportunities being opened to women. All of the family structures (both husband and wife present, male head of household only, and so on) experienced income stagnation during this period.

The fear of a stagnant or even declining economy, moreover, radically altered public perceptions of the trade-offs involved in public policy decisions. A decision to provide more for disadvantaged minorities or for environmental protection is easiest to make when the additional resources come out of an expanding economy. Such a decision is very difficult when providing more resources for some purposes means providing less for others. The economy, to use the term made popular by Lester Thurow, had apparently become a zero-sum game.

THE DISTRIBUTION OF INCOME

Turning now to the larger issue of the distribution of income generally, we see from Table 31-3 that there were notable changes toward greater equality during the years of the Great Depression and again during and just after the Second World War. Individuals with the highest incomes (the top 5 percent of the population) had their share drop from 30 percent to just under 20 percent between 1929 and 1962, while the poorest fifth of the population gained from 3.5 percent to 4.6 percent of total income in the same period.[2] It is important to note that the relative gains to the poorest fifth came in two bursts—in the early 1930s and again in the early 1940s. The gains to the second and third poorest segments grew more steadily between 1929 and 1947, and the only segments to gain in the postwar period up to 1962 were the middle and second richest fifth. Overall, the shift toward greater income equality, as revealed in Table 31-3, came primarily before 1947, and although alterations occurred after 1947, these were minor and there was no significant change overall. While the middle and second richest fifth gained slightly between 1947 and 1962, the richest and two poorest fifths had their shares modestly reduced.

---

[1] In college campus faculties, the young DINCs (double income no children) were often the envy of older colleagues trying to make ends meet on one academic salary.
[2] Note that these are for families and unrelated family units combined and that Census Income is essentially the measure used. For greater detail see Edward C. Budd, *Inequality and Poverty*, (New York: W. W. Norton, 1967).

TABLE 31-2 Median Incomes of Families and Unrelated Individuals, 1960–84 (in 1984 dollars)

Family Structure	1960	1965	1970	1975	1980	1984
Families						
Married-couple families	$20,599	$24,131	$28,130	$28,692	$29,170	29,612
Wife in paid labor force	24,201	28,420	32,838	33,266	33,882	34,668
Wife not in paid labor force	19,360	22,077	24,888	24,610	23,915	23,582
Male householder, no wife present. . . .	17,046	21,448	24,107	25,079	22,083	23,325
Female householder, no husband present . . .	10,410	11,637	13,624	13,208	13,120	12,803
Unrelated individuals						
Male	8,698	10,515	12,144	12,761	13,789	13,566
Female.	4,830	7,463	6,642	7,677	8,405	9,501

Source: *Statistical Abstract of the United States, 1987* (Washington, D.C.: GPO, 1986), p. 439.

TABLE 31-3 Prewar and Postwar Income Distributions (as percentage of share)

Year	Lowest Fifth	Second Fifth	Middle Fifth	Fourth Fifth	Highest Fifth	Top 5%
1929	3.5	9.0	13.8	19.3	54.4	30.0
1935–36	4.1	9.2	14.1	20.9	51.7	26.5
1941	4.1	9.5	15.3	22.3	48.8	24.0
1947	5.0	11.0	16.0	22.0	46.0	20.9
1962	4.6	10.9	16.3	22.7	45.5	19.6

Source: Edward C. Budd, *Inequality and Poverty* (New York: W. W. Norton, 1967), Table 1, p. XIII.

To extend the analysis forward, we turn to Table 31-4, which shows the distributions of income for families and unrelated individuals combined for many of the post-World War II years.[3] As the table reveals, the distribution of income among all income units has changed very little in the postwar period. Whereas we observed earlier that the *level* of income increased throughout much of the period, we find here that the *distribution* of income apparently has remained nearly constant since the Second World War. Can we conclude then that all have shared fairly equally in the economic gains of the postwar expansion? Table 31-4 certainly suggests that the gains to the poor paralleled those of the rich, but more detailed analysis adds perspective and caution to this conclusion.

[3] Although similar, because the income concepts used in Table 31-4 are not identical to those in Table 31-3, the measured distributions are not perfectly comparable.

TABLE 31-4   The Distribution of Income, Families and Unrelated individuals Combined, 1947–77 (as percentage of share)

Year	Lowest Fifth	Second Fifth	Middle Fifth	Fourth Fifth	Highest Fifth	Top 5%
1947	3.5	10.6	16.8	23.6	45.5	18.7
1952	3.5	10.9	17.3	24.1	44.3	18.4
1957	3.4	10.9	18.0	24.7	42.9	16.5
1962	3.4	10.4	17.5	24.8	43.9	16.8
1967	3.6	10.6	17.5	24.8	43.4	16.5
1972	3.7	10.0	16.9	24.7	44.8	17.4
1977	3.8	9.7	16.5	24.9	45.2	17.3

Source: U.S. Bureau of the Census, *Current Population Reports,* series P-60 (Washington, D.C.: GPO) no. 118, Table 13.

Further insight is gained by comparing Tables 31-5 and 31-6, which allows us to separate the trends in the distribution of incomes among families and among unrelated individuals. For families (Table 31-5) we observe some modest increase in equality up to 1957, but little or no change after 1957. The upper fifth (and upper 5 percent) lost ground in 1947–57, with the second, middle, and fourth fifths gaining during that ten-year period. The poorest fifth did gain rather sharply between 1961 and 1966—with their share rising from under 5.0 percent to 5.5 percent—as a host of public assistance policies were introduced and expanded at that time. But overall, there is little change in income distribution for families in the post-1957 years.

The story is different and somewhat more complex with unrelated individuals (Table 31-6). There is little alteration in the distribution of income after the spurt toward greater equality between 1947 and 1952. Then, in the 1960s, there is another marked advance toward greater equality. The gains to the poorest two segments beginning in the early 1960s are consistent with the observed gains over the same time for the poorest fifth of families. Again it appears to have come at the expense of the upper fifth (and upper 5 percent). Beginning in 1960 the shares of the richest segments exhibit a noticeable decline.

Although the two time periods for growing equality differ among the distributions of families and unrelated individuals, how can their combination (Table 31-4) with *each* showing some gains toward equality (Tables 31-5 and 31-6) reveal *no* trend toward greater equality overall? This statistical puzzle is solved by knowing two facts: (1) During the period there was a decrease in the proportion of the population that was families, and (2) there was a widening gap between the incomes of families and incomes of unrelated individuals between 1947 and 1957 and a narrowing of that gap between 1967 and 1977. These along with the different periods of growing equality for the two separate populations all combine—like conflicting forces

TABLE 31-5   The Distribution of Income Among Families, 1947–77 (as percentage share)

Year	Lowest Fifth	Second Fifth	Middle Fifth	Fourth Fifth	Highest Fifth	Top 5%
1947	5.0	11.9	17.0	23.1	43.0	17.5
1952	4.9	12.3	17.4	23.4	41.9	17.4
1957	5.1	12.7	18.1	23.8	40.4	15.6
1962	5.0	12.1	17.6	24.0	41.3	15.7
1967	5.5	12.4	17.9	23.9	40.4	15.2
1972	5.4	11.9	17.5	23.9	41.4	15.9
1977	5.2	11.6	17.5	24.2	41.5	15.7

Source: See Table 31-4.

TABLE 31-6   The Distribution of Income Among Unrelated Individuals, 1947–77 (as percentage share)

Year	Lowest Fifth	Second Fifth	Middle Fifth	Fourth Fifth	Highest Fifth	Top 5%
1947	2.0	6.2	12.7	22.5	56.6	29.3
1952	2.6	7.7	14.7	25.4	49.7	20.2
1957	2.6	7.3	13.7	25.4	50.9	19.7
1962	2.6	7.5	12.8	24.4	52.7	20.8
1967	3.0	7.5	13.5	24.5	51.5	21.1
1972	3.3	8.2	13.8	23.9	50.9	21.4
1977	4.1	9.0	14.7	24.0	48.2	19.6

Source: See Table 31-4.

neutralizing each other—to render very little trend overall, even though both component distributions show trends toward greater equality.

Unfortunately, there are additional complications that demand careful consideration. First, we turn to the issue of income measures and improve on the census measure of income by adding in and determining the effect of changes in personal taxes and transfers in kind on the distribution of income. In any one year the impact of personal taxes on the measured distribution of income is to reduce the degree of inequality. Clearly the progressive federal income tax favors those in lower tax brackets and, although the payroll tax is regressive relative to earnings, it is much less regressive relative to income because the poor receive large shares of their income from nontaxable transfers. However, a careful study of the period from 1950 to 1970 shows that while taxes modestly equalized the distribution of income in any given year, they had no effect on the *trend* over time.[4] This

---

[4]Morgan Reynolds and Eugene Smolensky, *Public expenditures, Taxes, and the Distribution of Income: The U.S., 1950, 1960, 1970*, (New York: Academic Press, 1977), or their article, "The Fading Effect of Government on Inequality," *Challenge* (July/August, 1978), pp. 32–37.

is because the regressive payroll tax has been growing relative to the income tax and the progressivity of the income tax has been declining throughout most of the postwar period. Again, these offsetting forces have neutralized their individual effects to leave the *trend* in measured income distribution unchanged.

The inclusion of transfers in kind, however, alters the distribution of income, both in a single year and in its trend over time. Transfers in kind, which include educational transfers, food stamps, public housing, medical services (Medicare and Medicaid) and others have grown much faster than incomes in the postwar period and, of course, have favored the poor relative to other groups. In 1978, the impact of transfers in kind on the shares to the lowest and highest fifths was to alter them by approximately 2 percentage points each. This adjustment is imprecise because we cannot treat a dollar-value of services received as identical to a dollar received in cash. For instance, a dollar subsidy for education may not be worth a dollar in cash to the recipient. Nevertheless, a variety of alternative, reasonable assumptions suggests that transfers in kind raised the share of the poorest fifth in 1978 from between 5 and 6 percent to between 7 and 8 percent of total income. Similarly, when transfers in kind are included, the richest fifth had its share reduced from slightly more than 41 percent to just over 39 percent.[5] Since transfers in kind were very small in the early postwar years, we may conclude that their impact on the trend for the bottom and top income fifths between the late 1940s and the early 1980s was similar in magnitude.

These and other changes in the distribution of income, (after taxes, and including transfers in kind) strongly indicate that *the gains* of the postwar period *were* indeed *widely shared.* Although a shifting age distribution, with relatively more old and young in the population today compared with 1947, and an increasing incidence of female-headed households tended to advance the trend toward more measured inequality, they were offset by government actions. Certainly, there were no deteriorations in the economic well-being of major individual groups. The rapid growth of cash transfers (the principal weapon of President Johnson's war on poverty), the rapid growth of transfers in kind in the 1970s, and the introduction of other recent programs producing affirmative action and equal opportunity assured gains for low-income groups. Overall, the evidence suggests only modest change in the distribution of income, with slight gains going to the lower fifth while the top fifth's share was modestly reduced.

---

[5] For more details, see Blinder "The Level and Distribution of Economic Well-being," in *The American Economy*, ed. Martin Feldstein (Chicago: Univ. of Chicago Press, 1980), p. 455; and Edgar K. Browning and William R. Johnson, "Taxes, Transfers, and Income Inequality," in *Regulatory Change in an Atmosphere of Crisis: Current Implications of the Roosevelt Years*, ed. Gary M. Walton (New York: Academic Press, 1979).

POVERTY

Perhaps even more important to us as a nation than the relative distribution of income is the number of people living below the "poverty line." This is the number of people who have less income than the amount needed, according to the government, to maintain a decent standard of living. Of course, over time the definition of the minimum amount of income needed to rise above the poverty line changes. We are a much richer society than we were in 1900, and consequently most of us today would define a higher minimum than would have been proposed in those days. The arbitrariness of the definition of poverty in turn sets the stage for politically motivated attempts to manipulate the official poverty line. People who would like to see more money spent on the poor (including government bureaucrats who administer poverty programs) favor adjustments that raise the poverty line. People who would like to see less government spending generally push for a lower definition. Nevertheless, most of us have at least a vague notion of poverty, and so the government's official statistics are of some interest.

During the 1960s, the number of families with incomes below the poverty line decreased sharply, as revealed in Figure 31-1. In the late 1960s, less than 25 million Americans were classified as living in poverty. But after leveling off in the 1970s, the number of people living in poverty, both in absolute numbers and relative to the population, rose substantially. There were a number of causes (including a change in the definition) although it is difficult to determine the relative importance of various factors. The

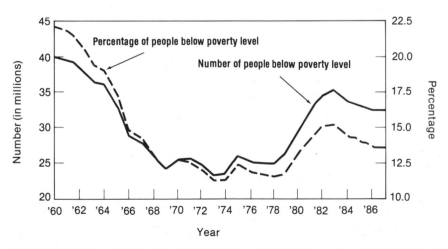

FIGURE 31-1   Persons Living Below the Poverty Line, 1960–87. The number of individuals classified as poor fell steadily from 1960 through 1969, remained stable to 1978, and then increased rapidly until it leveled off after 1983.

Source: *Economic Report of the President, 1988* (Washington, D.C.: GPO, 1988), p. 282.

severe recession of the early 1980s was undoubtedly the most important. And the Reagan administration's attempts to check public spending in this area have been criticized. In any case, the failure to maintain the gains of the 1960s has been seen as another sign of a faltering economy.

The stresses and tensions of low-income households have been increasingly mitigated by the intervention of government. It has become an accepted role of government to modify the impact of competitive forces. This intervention, as we know, spans the whole of economic life, but nowhere has it been as remarkable as it has in its direct outlays for public welfare. In 1890, total social-welfare expenditures were an estimated $318 million, or 2.4 percent of GNP. By 1913, the figure was $1 billion, or 2.8 percent of GNP; by 1929, it had risen to $4.3 billion, or 4.1 percent of GNP.[6] The common impression that the "welfare state" began in the 1930s is borne out by the data. Social-welfare programs in 1935 required a $6.7 billion outlay—9.8 percent of that year's GNP and slightly more than one-half of government expenditures at all levels for all purposes in 1935. Although such expenditures declined both absolutely and relatively during the Second World War, they rose steadily after the war—amounting to $58 billion, or approximately 11.5 percent of GNP, in 1961. In the ensuing decade, federal welfare expenditures soared to $198.3 billion and state welfare funds rose to $133 billion, which together represented 19.6 percent of the 1976 GNP. Public outlays for social-welfare spending in 1971 at all levels of government represented 51 percent of total government spending for all purposes, compared with the 38 percent recorded in both 1950 and 1960. Measured in constant prices, social-welfare expenditures rose slightly more than 80 percent between 1965 and 1971 and continued to climb throughout the 1970s.

A large number of articulate welfare supporters advocate much greater public expenditures than are presently undertaken. On the other hand, an equally vocal group insists that growing welfare expenditures undermine the social progress by destroying incentives to work and invest. The uncontested fact is that nearly 27 percent of GNP was annually appropriated for public and private expenditures on health, education, and welfare in the late 1970s and early 1980s.[7]

Our perception of poverty is undoubtedly highly personal and subjective. What determines a poor person's wants and a rich person's needs? Many perceived to be adequately fed, sheltered, and clothed may still be

---

[6]These data are taken from Series N 1–29, "Social Welfare Expenditures Under Civilian Public Programs: 1890–1956," *Historical Statistics of the United States, Colonial Times to 1957,* pp. 189, 193. Included in the category of social-welfare expenditures are all social-insurance programs, public aid, health and medical programs, vocational rehabilitation, institutional care, school lunch programs, child welfare, public housing, and education. A definition of welfare programs that includes education may seem too broad, but the use of this concept is dictated by the need for a generally accepted and continuous time series.

[7]Wilbur J. Cohen, "Economic Well-being and Income Distribution," in *The American Economy in Transition,* ed. Martin Feldstein (Chicago: Univ. of Chicago Press, 1980) p. 489.

seen as poor, but not as problematically poor. Equally important is our perception of opportunity—the opportunity to move out of poverty. Clearly, poverty is of less concern if it is not viewed as a permanent condition. Indeed, the prospects of advance may generate more happiness for the aspiring poor than minimally contented individuals in the middle class.

ECONOMIC WELL-BEING AND PERSONAL HAPPINESS

None of the measures of income we have been discussing, of course, is perfectly correlated with personal happiness. One of the difficulties is what economists know as the "index number problem." We compute real income by dividing money income by a weighted average of prices. But the weights are based on amounts consumed in some base period. This works fine for some commodity that was consumed in about the same relative amounts throughout the period of comparison. But what happens when consumption of one commodity declines because it is replaced by something new and better? In that case, the use of the price index based on the old weights tends to understate the increase in real income. Although the government agencies that compute price indices are well aware of the problem, they can

Happiness from the perspective of a second grader.

Source: Devon Walton, 2nd Grade, Flatirons Elementary School.

seldom fully take into account the constant flux of the marketplace. In practical terms, this means that the electronic revolution of the past several decades is only partially taken into account in computing the statistics. Pocket calculators, personal computers, VCR's, electronic chess partners, compact disks, video games, and so on have all added to our well-being, but are only imperfectly reflected in our measures of price trends and real income, victims of the "index number problem."

Yet our problems in measuring material standards of living pale when compared with trying to determine whether people are happier today than they were several decades ago, a question that cannot be answered even with the help of other social scientists and humanists. So much depends on our perspective. Past productivity, for example, has increased so fast that the average American worker produces nearly ten times as much per hour of work as our great-great-grandparents did in 1860. And work is clearly less burdensome than it has ever been. One worker with power-driven mechanical equipment can do as much work in a 40-hour week as three of our ancestors could do in the 70 hour week common a hundred years ago. Leisure time has at least doubled since 1910, as American workers in the past half-century or so have taken about two-thirds of national productivity gains in the form of goods and services and about one-third in the form of increased leisure.

Health

While life in America was becoming less arduous in the postwar period, it was also spent in better physical health and was certainly longer. When the United States became a going concern in 1789, the life expectancy of a white baby at birth was a little more than 30 years. By 1900, a white male child could be expected to live 48.2 years; for blacks the level was lower, but the rate of progress was also very high. As shown in Table 31-7, much

TABLE 31-7   Changes in Life Expectancy at Birth, 1940–85 (in years)

Year	ALL RACES			BLACK AND OTHER RACES		
	Total	Male	Female	Total	Male	Female
1940	62.9	60.8	65.2	53.1	51.5	54.9
1950	68.2	65.6	71.1	60.8	59.1	62.9
1955	69.6	66.7	72.8	63.7	61.4	66.1
1960	69.7	66.6	73.1	63.6	61.1	66.3
1965	70.2	66.8	73.7	64.1	61.1	67.4
1970	70.8	67.1	74.7	65.3	61.3	69.4
1975	72.6	68.8	76.6	68.0	63.7	72.4
1980	73.7	70.0	77.4	69.5	65.3	73.6
1985	74.7	71.2	78.2	71.2	67.2	75.2

Source: *Statistical Abstract of the United States, 1987* (Washington, D.C.: GPO, 1986), p. 69

progress has occurred since 1940. In 1940 all males on average had a life expectancy at birth of almost 61; this increased until 1955, then held steady before increasing again in the 1970s to 71 by 1985. Females fared even better, as shown in Table 31-7, and they gained life expectancy of 13 years over the period. Blacks and other races still had shorter life expectancies in 1985 than did whites, but they had made even larger gains. As Table 31-7 shows, for males the increase in life expectancy at birth was almost 16 years between 1940 and 1985; for females it was, remarkably enough, over 20 years.

Infant mortality is another sensitive indicator of well-being. Table 31-8 shows infant mortality rates from 1940 to 1983. The decline in these rates, particularly in the neonatal rate, has been dramatic, at least until 1980. Similar gains have been made in the postwar period in reducing the death rates from numerous diseases. Some examples are shown in Table 31-9. Rapid increases in medical technology and improved living standards have

TABLE 31-8   Infant Mortality, 1940–83 (per 1,000 live births)

Year	Neonatal[a]	Postneonatal[b]	Total Infant Mortality
1940	28.8	18.2	47.0
1945	24.3	14.0	38.3
1950	20.5	8.7	29.2
1960	18.7	7.3	26.0
1965	17.7	7.0	24.7
1970	15.1	4.9	20.0
1975	11.6	4.5	16.1
1980	8.5	4.1	12.6
1983	7.3	3.9	11.2

[a]Birth to 28 days
[b]28 days to one year.

Source: *Historical Statistics of the United States* (Washington, D.C.: GPO, 1975), series B139, B142; and *Statistical Abstract of the United States, 1987* (Washington, D.C.: GPO, 1986), p. 74

TABLE 31-9   Deaths from Selected Illness and Diseases, 1940–83 (per 100,000)

Disease	1940	1970	1983
Tuberculosis	45.9	2.6	.8
Cirrhosis of the liver	8.6	15.5	11.7
Influenza and pneumonia	70.3	30.9	23.9
Diabetes	26.6	18.9	15.5
Malignancies	120.3	162.8	189.3
Major cardiovascular diseases	485.7	496.0	419.2

Source: *Historical Statistics of the United States* (Washington, D.C.: GPO, 1975), series B149, B157, B158, B159, B160, B162; *Statistical Abstract of the United States, 1987* (Washington, D.C.: GPO, 1986), p. 75

been crucial in producing these improvements. However, as we might expect with an aging population, heart attacks and cancer remain principal causes of death.

Also important in the decline of the infant mortality rate and various adult diseases has been the extension of hospital, surgical, and medical expense coverage. As late as 1940 only 10 million Americans, or about 7 percent of the population, had any kind of hospital insurance (that is, any kind of prepayment of hospital costs that one day must be met by nearly everyone). In 1970 more than 150 million persons, or more than 75 percent of the population had such protection, nearly that many were protected against surgical expense, and perhaps 50 million were protected against the hazards of major medical costs. Moreover, federal old-age, survivors', and disability insurance benefits exceeded $25 billion a year by 1970. And if the number of doctors per 100,000 of population had remained constant for more than a decade, physicians were plainly more efficient (if less personal) in treating patients than they had ever been in the history of medical science.

But, as revealed in Table 31-8 or by some of the entries in Table 31-9, we have seemingly reached a plateau in the 1980s, a plateau that leaves us worse off in some categories (the infant mortality rate, for example) than the populations of some other industrialized nations. Is this due to government policies? Or is it due to adverse social trends? The widespread use of drugs such as crack, for example, is thought to have influenced the infant mortality rate.

Other social indicators of well-being also reveal "deterioration" in the 1970s. As shown in Table 31-10, births to unmarried women, the divorce rate, the suicide rate, and the murder rate—all rose in the early 1970s and 1980s. In some cases we could argue that part of the trend represented an

TABLE 31-10   Changes in Selected Social Indicators

Year	(1) Births to Unmarried Women[a]	(2) Divorce Rate[b]	(3) Suicide Rate[c]	(4) Murder Rate[d]
1950	3.9	2.6	11.4	—
1955	4.5	2.3	10.2	5.5[e]
1960	5.3	2.2	10.6	5
1965	7.7	2.5	11.1	5
1970	10.7	3.5	11.6	8
1975	14.2	4.8	12.6	8.8[f]
1980	18.4	5.2	11.9	10.2
1985	21.0	4.9	12.1[g]	7.9

[a]A percentage of all births.   [d]Per 100,000 population.   [g]1983
[b]Per 1,000 population.   [e]1957
[c]Per 100,000 population.   [f]1976

Sources: Column 1 *Historical Statistics of the United States* (Washington, D.C.: GPO, 1975), series B1, B28; *Statistical Abstract of the United States, 1987* (Washington, D.C.: GPO, 1986), p. 61. Column 2 *Historical Statistics*, series B216; *Statistical Abstract*, p. 80. Column 3 *Historical Statistics*, series B166; *Statistical Abstract*, pp. 8, 75, 80. Column 4 *Historical Statistics*, series H954; *Statistical Abstract*, p. 155.

increase in well-being. People may be happier divorcing rather than remaining married merely because of strong social pressures to do so. But in general, the adverse movements in these trends were another reflection of the malaise that engulfed the nation during the second part of the postwar period.

AN AGING POPULATION

One of the major worries intensified by the decline in real family income growth was how the nation was going to take care of an increasingly elderly population. As Table 31-11 shows, the percentage of individuals over 65 years of age increased steadily. This trend created severe strains for the Social Security system, and doubts about its future. In 1980, 11.3 percent of the population was 65 and older, and projections indicate a rise of the age group eligible for Social Security to 12.7 percent in the year 2000 and 19.4 percent in 2030. Whereas in 1980 there were 3.3 covered workers per beneficiary, by 2030 it was projected there would only be 2.0 workers per recipient. Because of the expansion of coverage and benefits, the indexing of benefits to increase automatically with inflation, and this aging trend, the employee-employer tax rate was raised from 2.0 percent in 1935 to 12.26 percent in 1980. The maximum tax payment rose by a factor of 47, from $60 to $2,808. The number of beneficiaries was 220,000 in 1941 and they were supported by 35 million paying workers. In 1980 there were 115 million workers paying into the system to support 36 million beneficiaries.[8] The sharp fall in the ratio of workers to beneficiaries, from over 100 to 1 in 1941, to 3 to 1 today, has required higher and higher rates. Because this trend will continue, rates must either rise, or benefits must be curtailed. The outcome, although economic, demands a political solution.[9]

The Social Security system came perilously close to bankruptcy. On April 1, 1982, the Social Security system's trustees reported that "Social Security will be unable to pay retirees' and survivors' benefits on time starting in July 1983 unless Congress takes corrective action." Congressman Claude Pepper, a Democrat from Florida, leading spokesman for the aging, and chairman of the House Select Committee on Aging, said the trustees' report "confirms my belief that the poor performance of the economy is robbing

---

[8] Initially, the Social Security system was partially an insurance system, one built on the principle of an actuarially sound reserve that would allow payment to potential claims from those who had paid into the system. It was also partially a pay-as-you-go system. Taxes were collected beginning in 1937, but no benefits were paid until 1942, in order to accumulate a reserve. The political temptation to increase benefits became too great, however, and soon the system converted entirely to a pay-as-you-go system, with beneficiaries being supported entirely by those paying in.

[9] For more on this nagging problem see Carolyn L. Weaver, *Understanding the Sources and Dimensions of Crisis in Social Security* (Washington, D.C.: Fiscal Policy Council, 1981).

TABLE 31-11   The Elderly Population, 1960–85

Age Group	1960	1970	1980	1985
Persons 65 and over (in millions)	16.7	20.1	25.7	28.5
Percent of total population	9.2%	9.8%	11.3%	11.9%
Persons 65 and over per 100 persons aged 18–64	17	17	19	19

Source: *Statistical Abstract of the United States, 1987* (Washington, D.C.: GPO, 1986), p. 34.

the Social Security trust funds." But it was no temporary matter and no April Fools' joke. For the seventieth straight year the combined old age and disability trust fund paid out more than they took in and soon they would be depleted. Legislation based on recommendations of a presidential commission headed by Alan Greenspan rescued the system; today there is a substantial surplus. But the basic problem of an aging population remains. Without continued economic growth it is hard to see how today's workers can expect to receive the current level of benefits when they retire.

THEORIES OF DECLINE

Thus, as we have seen, there is strong evidence then that sometime, perhaps in the late 1960s or early 1970s, the United States entered a period of deteriorating economic performance. Measures such as real family income, labor productivity, and even measures of physical or social health show evidence of a slowdown in progress or an absolute decline. Comparisons with other economies—such as those of Germany, Japan, and other Asian-rim nations that seemed to do a better job of coping with the economic problems of the 1970s—heightened concern about the long-run health of the economy. Not all observers, however, see this period as the beginning of the end. There is a strong current of opinion, for example, that an advanced nation like the United States will naturally grow at a slower rate than a latecomer still in the process of industrialization. So at least the slowdown of the U.S. economy relative to those of other nations should not seem so alarming.

One of the earliest formulations of this view is in Walt Rostow's book *Stages of Economic Growth.*[10] Rostow argues that all countries tend to go through the same series of stages. Growth is fastest in what Rostow calls the

---

[10]W. W. Rostow, *The Stages of Economic Growth* (Cambridge: Cambridge Univ. Press, 1960 and 1971).

"take-off" stage—when rapid economic growth began—and the "drive to maturity" stage—when economic growth becomes the top priority—and slower in the following stage, "the era of high mass consumption"—when other values surface. If certain countries are growing faster than the United States (today we would point to the Asian-rim countries, not the European countries Rostow had in mind), it is because they have only lately entered the "drive to maturity." Later they would slow down when they joined the United States in the "era of high mass consumption." Rostow's theory has been strongly criticized, and important alternatives have been offered. One of the best known of the latter is Alexander Gershenkron's argument that the nature and rate of industrialization depend on the type of society into which the process of industrialization is introduced.[11]

Although Rostow's theory and Gershenkron's have often been criticized, a key element of both, the notion of a catch-up by latecomers to the industrialization process and the related tendency of output per capita in different nations to converge, has received wider acceptance. Moses Abramovitz argues that the catch-up process has been at work, but that for a long time the United States remained far ahead of other nations because of special circumstances. For one, new technologies in the nineteenth century tended to conserve labor and require capital and natural resources, a demand pattern that matched U.S. resource endowments. The First World War, a major setback for many countries other than the United States, also worked to prolong the U.S. lead.[12]

We can take some comfort in such ideas that interpret our current problems as partly the natural consequence of economic maturity. But there are many other experts who warn that without major structural changes, the economy of the United States will spiral downward. The dominant concern has been with the supply of savings in the 1970s and 1980s.

SAVINGS, THE GOVERNMENT DEFICIT, AND FOREIGN TRADE

Policymakers in the 1970s and 1980s became concerned (some would say obsessed) with the problem of a decline in the funds available for investment—the funds to build new plants and equipment. The reason for the concern is illustrated in Figure 31-2. The willingness of the United States to build its capital stock lagged far behind that of other industrial nations throughout the entire decade. These and other factors contributed to a deteriorating competitive position for U.S. products in both world and

---

[11] Alexander Gershenkron, *Economic Backwardness in Historical Perspective* (New York: Praeger, 1962).
[12] Moses Abramovitz, "Catching Up, Forging Ahead, and Falling Behind," *Journal of Economic History* 46 (1986): 397–98.

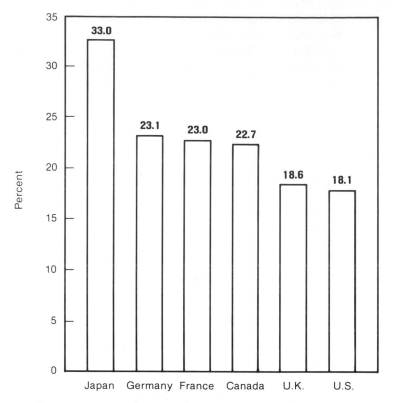

FIGURE 31-2   Gross Fixed Capital Formation as a Percent of GNP, 1970–79 Average. (*Note:*) The United
               States trailed other major industrialized competitors in gross fixed capital formation as a
               percent of GNP. This chart compares the records of six major industrialized countries
               during the 1970 to 1979 period. The United States at 18.1 percent lagged behind Japan
               at 33.0 percent, Germany at 23.1 percent, France at 23.0 percent, Canada at 22.7 percent
               and the United Kingdom at 18.6 percent.

Source: U.S. Department of the Treasury, Office of the Secretary, "Background Charts and Graphs," in *The President's Tax Policy*
(Washington, D.C.: GPO, February 18, 1981), n.p.

domestic markets. As investment shares fell, the rate of growth of productivity and output also slowed.

It naturally followed from this observation that low investment was the
cause of the slowdown in productivity growth. As we noted in Chapter 27
labor productivity grew at 2.8 percent per year from the fourth quarter of
1948 to the fourth quarter of 1973, but at only .7 percent per year from
the fourth quarter of 1973 to the fourth quarter of 1981. More machinery
would mean higher productivity. Productivity, moreover, came to be seen
as the key to economic and, perhaps, social revival. It was this concern with
the savings gap between the United States and its foreign competitors that
focused the attention of many economists on the deficit in the federal bud-

get and the excess of imports over exports of goods and services because the three are closely tied together.

It is an identity that savings must equal the sum of money spent on domestic investment, the government deficit, and net foreign investment. Table 31-12 puts it slightly differently. Column 1 of the table shows the funds available from savings to purchase securities or otherwise invest in the economy. Add to that any funds made available from a government surplus, or subtract the funds used to purchase new government debt when the economy runs a deficit (column 2), subtract any funds used to invest in foreign countries (column 3), and the result is gross private investment in the United States (column 4). As we can see, the gross savings ratio did not show a distinct trend during this period. But the same cannot be said of gross private investment. First, the decline in governmental surpluses and then the rising deficit caused an alarming drop in the gross investment rate after 1965. In 1975, for example, the gross investment rate was down to 13.6 percent.

The 1980s witnessed something of a turnaround, but the reason was surprising. For most of the postwar period the United States had been investing abroad. Now the United States was running a current account deficit and foreigners were investing in the United States. This partial turnaround did mean that Americans would now be experiencing the higher labor productivity growth normally associated with an expanding stock of capital. But considerable future profits would have to be sent abroad: the United States would be forced to export more than it imported. To do so in a highly competitive world market would not be easy.

What could be done about the "twin deficits" and the dangers they create? The basic tool would be the federal budget. And many economists,

TABLE 31-12   Savings and Investment in the United States, 1950–85 (percent of GNP)

Year	(1) Gross Private Savings	+	(2) Government Surplus	–	(3) Net Foreign Investment	=	(4) Gross Private Investment
1950	15.4%		2.8%		–.6%		18.8%
1955	16.1		.8		.1		16.8
1960	15.7		.6		.6		15.7
1965	17.4		.1		.9		16.6
1970	16.2		–1.0		.5		14.7
1975	19.0		–4.1		1.4		13.6
1980	17.5		–1.3		.5		15.8
1985	17.2		–3.4		–2.9		16.7

Source: *Economic Report of the President, 1987* (Washington, D.C.: GPO, 1987), pp. 244 and 276.

although not all, recommend some combination of higher taxes or spending cuts to close the budget deficit. Taxes, moreover, could be raised on consumption expenditures and lowered on savings to stimulate further capital formation. Critics of the latter policy note that it would tend to fall more heavily on the poor than on the rich, since the rich typically spend a smaller fraction of their income on consumption. Spending cuts that would be politically acceptable are hard to imagine. Some economists have suggested "means testing" federal transfer expenditures, for example, further reducing the net amount of Social Security benefits received by wealthy but elderly individuals. Others have called for a scaling back of defense spending. Furthermore, historian Paul Kennedy has likened the difficulties of the United States to those of other great powers of the past that brought about their own economic decline by making excessive foreign commitments.[13]

No one can be sure that even if the budget deficit is closed, through some combination of policies, it will solve the nation's savings and trade problems. Economic reactions are often hard to predict. For example, many economists have contended that closing the budget deficit will reduce interest rates in the United States and make U.S. assets less attractive to foreigners thus producing a decline in foreign investment, a decline in the value of the dollar, and a rise in U.S. exports and a fall in imports. But whether any of this sequence will occur, and certainly the extent, are hotly debated by economists.

Another group of experts see the budget deficit as more of a symptom of the destructive tendencies of our political and economic institutions rather than the cause of it. Our failure to make any progress on reducing the federal deficit can be viewed simply as another example of the ability of special interests to block policies that are clearly in the public interest. Japan is often held up as an example of a country where a system worth emulating exists. Labor relations in the United States have traditionally been built on conflict rather than cooperation. If U.S. firms would begin to emulate the Japanese system where a great effort is made to incorporate the ideas of the worker into the production process, perhaps faster productivity growth could be achieved. We do not have space here to develop these or related ideas in detail. Our point is simply that in recent decades economists and other experts have been offering a wide range of potential medicines to cure the nation's ills. Unfortunately, unlike physicians who can rely on controlled testing to determine which medicines work and which do not, economists have only the ambiguous natural experiments of history from which to draw their conclusions.

---

[13] Paul Kennedy, *The Rise and Fall of the Great Powers: Economic Change and Military Conflict from 1500 to 2000* (New York: Random House, 1987).

Through a Glass Darkly

Is the bottle half-full or half-empty; how well-off are we? The answer, of course, is "it depends." It depends on our physical and mental health, on matters of the spirit, on friendship, and on how much we have compared with others. It depends on our sense of security and confidence, both individually and collectively. It depends on our perception of fairness, on our prospects for the future, on a great number of things.

Will the future see a renewal of productivity growth, real income growth, and improving health and welfare? Or are our current problems the sign of the end of the American era? Will the future see other nations replace the United States as the world's financial and industrial leader? Are we doomed to a future of declining income and economic uncertainty? No one can answer these questions with any confidence. But if our history teaches us anything, it is that this period of economic travail is not unique. American economic history is indeed a record of economic success. But it is also a record of financial crises, bitter labor relations, severe inflations, and prolonged depressions—all of which we have surmounted with our economic and political freedoms intact.

SELECTED REFERENCES AND SUGGESTED READINGS

Abramovitz, Moses. "Catching Up, Forging Ahead, and Falling Behind." *Journal of Economic History* 46 (1986): 385–406.

Blinder, Alan S. "The Level and Distribution of Economic Well-being." In *The American Economy in Transition,* ed. Martin Feldstein. Chicago: Univ. of Chicago Press, 1980, Chapter 6.

Browing, Edgar K., and William R. Johnson. "Taxes, Transfers, and Income Equality." In *Regulatory Change in an Atmosphere of Crisis: Current Implications of the Roosevelt Years,* ed. Gary Walton. New York: Academic Press, 1979.

Budd, Edward C. *Inequality and Poverty.* New York: W. W. Norton, 1967.

Cherlin, Andrew J. *Marriage, Divorce, Remarriage.* Cambridge: Harvard Univ. Press, 1981.

Clark, Colin. *The Conditions of Economic Progress,* 3rd ed. New York: St. Martin's Press, 1981.

Cohen, Wilbur J. "Economic Well-being and Income Distribution." In *The American Economy in Transition,* ed. Martin Feldstein. Chicago: Univ. of Chicago Press, 1980.

Cooper, Richard N. "Dealing with the Trade Deficit in a Floating Rate System." *Brookings Papers on Economic Activity* (1986): 195–207.

Easterlin, Richard A., *Birth and Fortune.* New York: Basic Books, 1980.

———. "Does Economic Growth Improve the Human Lot? Some Empirical Evidence." In *Essays in Honor of Moses Abramovitz,* ed. Paul David and Melvin Reder. New York: Academic Press, 1974.

Gershenkron, Alexander. *Economic Backwardness in Historical Perspective.* New York: Praeger, 1962.

Joyce, Theodore, Hope Corman, and Michael Grossman. "A Cost-Effectiveness Analysis of Strategies to Reduce Infant Mortality." *Medical Care* 26 (April 1988): 348–60.

Kennedy, Paul. *The Rise and Fall of the Great Powers: Economic Change and Military Conflict from 1500 to 2000.* New York: Random House, 1987.

Lebergott, Stanley. *The American Economy: Income, Wealth and Want.* Princeton: Princeton Univ. Press, 1976.

Levy, Frank. *Dollars and Dreams: The Changing American Income Distribution.* New York: W. W. Norton, 1988.

Madison, Angus. *Phases of Capitalist Development.* New York: Oxford Univ. Press, 1982.

Murray, Charles. *In Pursuit of Happiness and Good Government.* New York: Simon and Shuster, 1988.

Murray, Charles A. *Losing Ground: American Social Policy, 1950–1980*. New York: Basic Books, 1984.

Pechman, Joseph. *Who Pays the Taxes, 1966–1985*. Washington, D.C. Brookings Institution, 1985.

Reich, Robert. *The New American Frontier*. New York: New York Times Publishers, 1983.

Reynolds, Morgan, and Eugene Smolensky. *Public Expenditures, Taxes and the Distribution of Income: The U.S. 1950, 1960, 1970*. New York: Academic Press, 1977.

———. "The Fading Effect of Government on Inequality." *Challenge* 21 (July/Aug. 1978): 32–37.

Rostow, W. W. *The Stages of Economic Growth*. Cambridge: Cambridge University Press, 1960 and 1971.

———. *The World Economy: History & Prospect*. Austin: Univ. of Texas Press, 1978.

Ruggles, Patricia, and Michael O'Higgins. "The Distribution of Public Expenditure Among Households in the United States." *Review of Income and Wealth* 27 (June 1981): 137–63.

Sundquist, James L. *Politics and Policy, The Eisenhower, Kennedy, and Johnson Years*. Washington, D.C.: Brookings Institution, 1968.

Thurow, Lester. *The Zero-Sum Game*. New York: Basic Books, 1980.

———. *The Zero-Sum Solution*. New York: Simon & Shuster, 1985.

Weaver, Carolyn L. *Understanding the Sources and Dimensions of Crisis in Social Security*. Washington, D.C.: Fiscal Policy Council, 1981.

Weitzman, Martin. *The Share Economy*. Cambridge: Harvard Univ. Press, 1986.

Index